Mark J. Stellfox

STRATEGIES
IN PROSE

STRATEGIES
IN PROSE

WILFRED A. FERRELL
NICHOLAS A. SALERNO
ARIZONA STATE UNIVERSITY

HOLT, RINEHART AND WINSTON, INC.
New York • Chicago • San Francisco • Atlanta • Dallas

PREFACE

Strategies in Prose is a collection of prose selections designed for use in the freshman composition course. In editing this collection we followed our commitment to recognized principles and practices that justify the reader as a text for the composition course. These derive from the long-established fact that people best learn to write by writing. But the writing experience serves this purpose only when the writer has something to say and has a reason for saying it. The student in the freshman composition course may discover the substance for his writing by reading and discussing those writings that lie within the range of his interests and experiences, that engage his intellectual capabilities, and that cause him to make a response. And by analyzing and studying *how* the authors present their ideas, he may develop a sense for stylistics and rhetorical strategy.

The selections in *Strategies in Prose* reflect the range of interest and experience of freshman composition students. It further reflects what we believe should be the province of their awareness and concerns.

To obtain a desirable range of subjects and viewpoints we chose eighty-two selections and have organized them into six sections: the individual, modern social problems, science, language, education, and popular culture. Our purpose in each section is to offer a variety of writings about the general area, as well as a number of different styles and rhetorical methods.

As a special feature in each of the six sections we have included a selection by a controversial writer or a chapter from a controversial book. Immediately following each of these we have a *pro* review and a *con* review of the book from which the selection was taken. The reviews lend another dimension to the variety of viewpoints in the sections, as well as giving the student an opportunity to analyze critical writing and to examine several forms of the review, a type of essay he may be required to produce many times during his college years.

To provide still another level of diversity in each section we have included at least one short story. Related to their section by subject or theme, these may be used for an individual study and analysis or for comparison and contrast with the other rhetorical types in this section.

The authors of the selections are, for the most part, all recognized authorities, either as writers or as experts in their field of specialization. We give a brief biographical sketch of the author on the first page of each selection and indicate when and where the selection originally appeared. Several authors have selections in two different sections. Our purpose here is to give the student an opportunity to see how a writer may adjust his style and rhetorical approach to serve different subjects, purposes, and audiences. In addition to the obvious reasons for selecting known writers, we chose them to emphasize the importance of authority in the prose voice. Our purpose is to help the student recognize that a basic requirement for effective prose is the authority of a voice that has something to say and a compelling reason for saying it. We want to stress the student's need to prepare before he writes, not necessarily so that he may speak as an expert, but to give genuine thought to his subject before he attempts to write about it.

Although most of our selections come from twentieth-century writers, we do include a few from writers of earlier periods. Most of these latter selections have gained acceptance as classics of their type. Their place in the collection is to demonstrate how many of the issues and ideas of today were the concern of writers in earlier times. They also provide a means for the student to compare and contrast the styles and rhetorical methods of different periods.

The study questions at the end of each selection are intended to help the student read the selection critically and to assist him in analyzing the writer's method and techniques. The questions are not intended to be exhaustive for these purposes, but suggest ways the student may start his study and analysis.

In the table of contents we have indicated the rhetorical type of each selection. These labels are not to be considered exclusive, since any given essay may incorporate forms of several different rhetorical methods and modes. Our designations are intended to serve as a ready reference for those who wish to examine a particular rhetorical type.

We gratefully acknowledge the many recommendations and suggestions our colleagues generously gave us for this reader. To the freshmen who have populated our composition classes over the years we are especially grateful. The experience we gained from working with them helped prepare us for our tasks as editors of this book.

W.A.F.
N.A.S.

TEMPE, ARIZONA

JANUARY 1968

CONTENTS

2 MODERN SOCIAL PROBLEMS

STRATEGIES
IN PROSE

SECTION 1 | THE INDIVIDUAL

"This Above All"

A BOLD AND

Benjamin Franklin   **ARDUOUS PROJECT**

Benjamin Franklin (1706–1790) was born in Boston, Massachusetts. Perhaps the best representative of the American Enlightenment, he has been called the founder of America's first circulating library, first colonial hospital, and first learned society. He studied earthquakes, the Gulf Stream, and electricity and lightning, becoming famous as a scientist with the publication of *Experiments and Observations on Electricity* (1751–1753). His political career was equally distinguished—clerk to the Pennsylvania assembly; member of the Second Continental Congress, the committee which drafted the Declaration of Independence, and the Constitutional Convention; and ambassador to France. Jefferson, who followed Franklin as ambassador to France, said: "No one can replace him, Sir; I am only his successor." Franklin's *Poor Richard's Almanack* and his *Autobiography* have earned him a place in American literary history.

It was about this time I conceived the bold and arduous project of arriving at moral perfection. I wished to live without committing any fault at any time; I would conquer all that either natural inclination, custom, or company might lead me into. As I knew, or thought I knew, what was right and wrong, I did not see why I might not always do the one and avoid the other. But I soon found I had undertaken a task of more difficulty than I had imagined. While my care was employed in guarding against one fault, I was often surprised by another; habit took the advantage of inattention; inclination was sometimes too strong for reason. I concluded, at length, that the mere speculative conviction that it was our interest to be completely virtuous was not sufficient to prevent our slipping; and that the contrary habits must be broken, and good ones acquired and established, before we can have any dependence on a

First published 1868.

steady, uniform rectitude of conduct. For this purpose I therefore contrived the following method.

In the various enumerations of the moral virtues I had met with in my reading, I found the catalogue more or less numerous, as different writers included more or fewer ideas under the same name. Temperance, for example, was by some confined to eating and drinking, while by others it was extended to mean the moderating every other pleasure, appetite, inclination, or passion, bodily or mental, even to our avarice and ambition. I proposed to myself, for the sake of clearness, to use rather more names, with fewer ideas annexed to each, than a few names with more ideas; and I included under thirteen names of virtues all that at that time occurred to me as necessary or desirable, and annexed to each a short precept, which fully expressed the extent I gave to its meaning.

These names of virtues, with their precepts, were:

1. TEMPERANCE

Eat not to dullness; drink not to elevation.

2. SILENCE

Speak not but what may benefit others or yourself; avoid trifling conversation.

3. ORDER

Let all your things have their places; let each part of your business have its time.

4. RESOLUTION

Resolve to perform what you ought; perform without fail what you resolve.

5. FRUGALITY

Make no expense but to do good to others or yourself; i.e., waste nothing.

6. INDUSTRY

Lose no time; be always employed in something useful; cut off all unnecessary actions.

7. SINCERITY

Use no hurtful deceit; think innocently and justly; and, if you speak, speak accordingly.

8. JUSTICE

Wrong none by doing injuries, or omitting the benefits that are your duty.

9. MODERATION

Avoid extremes; forbear resenting injuries so much as you think they deserve.

10. CLEANLINESS

Tolerate no uncleanliness in body, clothes, or habitation.

11. TRANQUILLITY

Be not disturbed at trifles, or at accidents common or unavoidable.

12. CHASTITY

13. HUMILITY

Imitate Jesus and Socrates.

My intention being to acquire the *habitude* of all these virtues, I judged it would be well not to distract my attention by attempting the whole at once, but to fix it on one of them at a time; and, when I should be master of that, then to proceed to another, and so on, till I should have gone through the thirteen; and as the previous acquisition of some might facilitate the acquisition of certain others, I arranged them with that view, as they stand above. Temperance first, as it tends to procure that coolness and clearness of head, which is so necessary where constant vigilance was to be kept up, and guard maintained against the unremitting attraction of ancient habits and the force of perpetual temptations. This being acquired and established, Silence would be more easy; and my desire being to gain knowledge at the same time that I improved in virtue, and considering that in conversation it was obtained rather by the use of the ears than of the tongue, and therefore wishing to break a habit I was getting into of prattling, punning, and joking, which only made me acceptable to trifling company, I gave Silence the second place. This and the next, Order, I expected would allow me more time for attending to my project and my studies. Resolution, once become habitual, would keep me firm in my endeavors to obtain all the subsequent virtues; Frugality and Industry, freeing me from my remaining debt and producing affluence and independence, would make more easy the practice of Sincerity and Justice, etc., etc. Conceiving then, that, agreeably to the advice of Pythagoras in his Golden Verses, daily examination would be necessary, I contrived the following method for conducting that examination.

I made a little book, in which I allotted a page for each of the virtues. I ruled each page with red ink, so as to have seven columns, one for each day of the week, marking each column with a letter for the day. I crossed these columns with thirteen red lines, marking the beginning of each line with the first letter of one of the virtues, on which line, and in its proper column, I might mark, by a little black spot, every fault I found upon examination to have been committed respecting that virtue upon that day.

I determined to give a week's strict attention to each of the virtues successively. Thus, in the first week, my great guard was to avoid even the least offense against Temperance, leaving the other virtues to their ordinary chance, only marking every evening the faults of the day. Thus, if in the first week I could keep my first line, marked T, clear of spots, I supposed the habit of that virtue so much strengthened, and its opposite weakened, that I might venture extending my attention to include the next, and for the following week keep both lines clear of spots. Proceeding thus to the last, I could go through a course complete in thirteen weeks, and four courses in a year. And like him who, having a garden to weed, does not attempt to eradicate all the bad herbs at once, which would exceed his reach and his strength, but works on one of the beds at a time, and, having accomplished the first, proceeds to a second, so I should have, I hoped, the encouraging pleasure of seeing on my pages the progress I made in virtue, by clearing successively my lines of their spots, till in the end, by a number of courses, I should be happy in viewing a clean book, after a thirteen weeks' daily examination.

Forms of the Pages

TEMPERANCE						
EAT NOT TO DULLNESS; DRINK NOT TO ELEVATION.						
	S.	M.	T.	W.	T.	F.	S.
T.							
S.	✿	✿		✿		✿	
O.	✿ ✿	✿	✿		✿	✿	✿
R.			✿			✿	
F.		✿			✿		
I.			✿				
S.							
J.							
M.							
C.							
T.							
C.							
H.							

The precept of Order requiring that *every part of my business should have its allotted time,* one page in my little book contained the following scheme of employment for the twenty-four hours of a natural day.

I entered upon the execution of this plan for self-examination, and continued it with occasional intermissions for some time. I was surprised

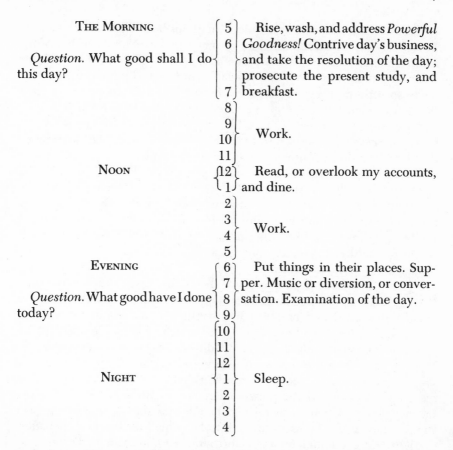

THE MORNING	5	Rise, wash, and address *Powerful*
	6	*Goodness!* Contrive day's business,
Question. What good shall I do		and take the resolution of the day;
this day?		prosecute the present study, and
	7	breakfast.
	8	
	9	
	10	Work.
	11	
NOON	12	Read, or overlook my accounts,
	1	and dine.
	2	
	3	
	4	Work.
	5	
EVENING	6	Put things in their places. Sup-
	7	per. Music or diversion, or conver-
Question. What good have I done	8	sation. Examination of the day.
today?	9	
	10	
	11	
	12	
NIGHT	1	Sleep.
	2	
	3	
	4	

to find myself so much fuller of faults than I had imagined; but I had the satisfaction of seeing them diminish. To avoid the trouble of renewing now and then my little book, which, by scraping out the marks on the paper of old faults to make room for new ones in a new course, became full of holes, I transferred my tables and precepts to the ivory leaves of a memorandum book, on which the lines were drawn with red ink, that made a durable stain, and on those lines I marked my faults with a black lead pencil, which marks I could easily wipe out with a wet sponge. After a while I went through one course only in a year, and afterward only one in several years, till at length I omitted them entirely, being employed in voyages and business abroad, with a multiplicity of affairs that interfered; but I always carried my little book with me.

My scheme of Order gave me the most trouble; and I found that, though it might be practicable where a man's business was such as to leave him the disposition of his time, that of a journeyman printer, for instance, it was not possible to be exactly observed by a master, who must mix with the world, and often receive people of business at their own hours. Order, too, with regard to places for things, papers, etc., I found extremely difficult to acquire. I had not been early accustomed to it, and having an exceeding good memory, I was not so sensible of the inconvenience attending want of method. This article, therefore, cost me so much painful attention, and my faults in it vexed me so much, and I made so little progress in amendment, and had such frequent relapses, that I was almost ready to give up the attempt, and content myself with a faulty character in that respect, like the man who, in buying an ax of a smith, my neighbor, desired to have the whole of its surface as bright as the edge. The smith consented to grind it bright for him if he would turn the wheel; he turned, while the smith pressed the broad face of the ax hard and heavily on the stone, which made the turning of it very fatiguing. The man came every now and then from the wheel to see how the work went on, and at length would take his ax as it was, without further grinding. "No," said the smith, "turn on, turn on; we shall have it bright by and by; as yet, it is only speckled." "Yes," says the man, *"but I think I like a speckled ax best."*

And I believe this may have been the case with many, who, having, for want of some such means as I employed, found the difficulty of obtaining good and breaking bad habits in other points of vice and virtue, have given up the struggle, and concluded that *"a speckled ax was best"*; for something that pretended to be reason was every now and then suggesting to me that such extreme nicety as I exacted of myself might be a kind of foppery in morals, which, if it were known, would make me ridiculous; that a perfect character might be attended with the inconvenience of being envied and hated; and that a benevolent man should allow a few faults in himself, to keep his friends in countenance.

In truth, I found myself incorrigible with respect to Order; and now I am grown old, and my memory bad, I feel very sensibly the want of it. But, on the whole, though I never arrived at the perfection I had been so ambitious of obtaining, but fell far short of it, yet I was, by the endeavor, a better and a happier man than I otherwise should have been if I had not attempted it; as those who aim at perfect writing by imitating the engraved copies, though they never reach the wished-for excellence of those copies, their hand is mended by the endeavor.

It may be well my posterity should be informed that to this little artifice, with the blessing of God, their ancestor owed the constant felicity of his life, down to his seventy-ninth year, in which this is written. What reverses may attend the remainder is in the hand of Providence; but, if they arrive, the reflection on past happiness enjoyed ought to help his bearing them with more resignation. To Temperance he ascribes his long-continued health, and what is still left to him of a good constitution; to Industry and Frugality, the early easiness of his circumstances and acquisition of his fortune, with all that knowledge that enabled him to be a useful citizen, and obtained for him some degree of reputation among the learned; to Sincerity and Justice, the confidence of his country, and the honorable employs it conferred upon him; and to the joint influence of the whole mass of the virtues, even in the imperfect state he was able to acquire them, all that evenness of temper, and that cheerfulness in conversation, which makes his company still sought for, and agreeable even to his younger acquaintance. I hope, therefore, that some of my descendants may follow the example and reap the benefit.

It will be remarked that, though my scheme was not wholly without religion, there was in it no mark of any of the distinguishing tenets of any particular sect. I had purposely avoided them; for, being fully persuaded of the utility and excellency of my method, and that it might be serviceable to people in all religions, and intending some time or other to publish it, I would not have anything in it that should prejudice anyone, of any sect, against it. I purposed writing a little comment on each virtue, in which I would have shown the advantages of possessing it, and the mischiefs attending its opposite vice; and I should have called my book *The Art of Virtue,* because it would have shown the means and manner of obtaining virtue, which would have distinguished it from mere exhortation to be good, that does not instruct and indicate the means, but it like the apostle's man of verbal charity, who, without showing to the naked and hungry how or where they might get clothes or victuals, only exhorted them to be fed and clothed.—James 2:15, 16.

But it so happened that my intention of writing and publishing this comment was never fulfilled. I did, indeed, from time to time, put down short hints of the sentiments, reasonings, etc., to be made use of in it, some of which I have still by me; but the necessary close attention to private business in the earlier part of my life, and public business since, have occasioned my postponing it; for, it being connected in my mind with *a great and extensive project* that required the whole man to execute, and which an unforseen succession of employs prevented my attending to, it has hitherto remained unfinished.

In this piece it was my design to explain and enforce this doctrine, that vicious actions are not hurtful because they are forbidden, but forbidden because they are hurtful, the nature of man alone considered; that it was, therefore, everyone's interest to be virtuous who wished to be happy even in this world; and I should, from this circumstance (there being always in the world a number of rich merchants, nobility, states, and princes, who have need of honest instruments for the management of their affairs, and such being so rare), have endeavored to convince young persons that no qualities were so likely to make a poor man's fortune as those of probity and integrity.

My list of virtues contained at first but twelve; but a Quaker friend having kindly informed me that I was generally thought proud; that my pride showed itself frequently in conversation; that I was not content with being in the right when discussing any point, but was overbearing and rather insolent, of which he convinced me by mentioning several instances; I determined endeavoring to cure myself, if I could, of this vice or folly among the rest, and I added Humility to my list.

I cannot boast of much success in acquiring the *reality* of this virtue, but I had a good deal with regard to the *appearance* of it. I made it a rule to forbear all direct contradiction to the sentiments of others, and all positive assertion of my own. I even forbade myself, agreeably to the old law of our Junto, the use of every word or expression in the language that imported a fixed opinion, such as *certainly, undoubtedly,* etc., and I adopted, instead of them, *I conceive, I apprehend,* or *I imagine* a thing to be so or so; or it *so appears to me at present.* When another asserted something that I thought an error, I denied myself the pleasure of contradicting him abruptly, and of showing immediately some absurdity in his proposition; and in answering I began by observing that in certain cases or circumstances his opinion would be right, but in the present case there *appeared* or *seemed* to me some difference, etc. I soon found the advantage of this change in my manner; the conversations I engaged in went on more pleasantly. The modest way in which I proposed my opinions procured them a readier reception and less contradiction; I had less mortification when I was found to be in the wrong, and I more easily prevailed with others to give up their mistakes and join with me when I happened to be in the right.

And this mode, which I at first put on with some violence to natural inclination, became at length so easy and so habitual to me that perhaps for these fifty years past no one has ever heard a dogmatical expression escape me. And to this habit (after my character of integrity) I think it principally owing that I had early so much weight with my fellow citizens when I proposed new institutions, or alterations in the old, and so much influence in public councils when I became a member; for I was but a bad speaker, never eloquent, subject to much hesitation in my choice of words, hardly correct in language, and yet I generally carried my points.

In reality, there is, perhaps, no one of our natural passions so hard to subdue as *pride.* Disguise it, struggle with it, beat it down, stifle it, mortify it as much as one pleases, it is still alive, and will every now and then peep out and show itself; you will see it, perhaps, often in this history; for, even if I could conceive that I had completely overcome it, I should probably be proud of my humility.

STUDY QUESTIONS

1.   Can Franklin's project of arriving at moral perfection justifiably be called "a kind of foppery in morals"?

2. Franklin's description of how he set up the pages in his little book will
    be meaningful only if the reader can reconstruct the format of those
    pages. Write a simpler set of directions which will result in the same
    format.
3. Why was it difficult for Franklin to acquire Virtue # 3?
4. Why are Franklin's similes about weeding a garden and the man with a
    new ax so effective?
5. Define *artifice* as Franklin uses it in the sentence: "It may be well my
    posterity. . . ." What more general meaning is attached to the word
    today?
6. Why did Franklin deliberately avoid mentioning religion in his project?

THE DYNAMO
Henry Adams   AND THE VIRGIN

Henry Adams (1838–1918) was born in Quincy, Massachusetts,
the son of Charles Francis Adams, the grandson of John Quincy
Adams, and the great-grandson of John Adams. He was educated
at Harvard and the University of Berlin, and his experiences in
Europe while his father was minister to England during the Civil
War, profoundly influenced him. Adams edited the writings of
Albert Gallatin (1879) and wrote a nine-volume history of the
United States under Jefferson and Madison (1889–1891). He
also published two novels—*Democracy* (1880) and *Esther*
(1884); *The Memoirs of Marau Taaroa, Last Queen of Tahiti*
(1893); *Mont-Saint-Michel and Chartres* (1904), which he called
"a study of thirteenth-century unity"; and his autobiography
(1907), which he called "a study of twentieth-century multiplicity."

Until the Great Exposition of 1900 closed its doors in November,
Adams haunted it, aching to absorb knowledge, and helpless to find it.
He would have liked to know how much of it could have been grasped
by the best-informed man in the world. While he was thus meditating
chaos, Langley came by, and showed it to him. At Langley's behest, the
Exhibition dropped its superfluous rags and stripped itself to the skin,
for Langley knew what to study, and why, and how; while Adams might
as well have stood outside in the night, staring at the Milky Way. Yet
Langley said nothing new, and taught nothing that one might not have

"The Dynamo and The Virgin" from *The Education of Henry Adams*. Reprinted by
permission of the publisher, Houghton Mifflin Company.

learned from Lord Bacon, three hundred years before; but though one should have known the "Advancement of Science" as well as one knew the "Comedy of Errors," the literary knowledge counted for nothing until some teacher should show how to apply it. Bacon took a vast deal of trouble in teaching King James I and his subjects, American or other, towards the year 1620, that true science was the development or economy of forces; yet an elderly American in 1900 knew neither the formula nor the forces; or even so much as to say to himself that his historical business in the Exposition concerned only the economies or developments of force since 1893, when he began the study at Chicago.

Nothing in education is so astonishing as the amount of ignorance it accumulates in the form of inert facts. Adams had looked at most of the accumulations of art in the storehouses called Art Museums; yet he did not know how to look at the art exhibits of 1900. He had studied Karl Marx and his doctrines of history with profound attention, yet he could not apply them at Paris. Langley, with the ease of a great master of experiment, threw out of the field every exhibit that did not reveal a new application of force, and naturally threw out, to begin with, almost the whole art exhibit. Equally, he ignored almost the whole industrial exhibit. He led his pupil directly to the forces. His chief interest was in new motors to make his airship feasible, and he taught Adams the astonishing complexities of the new Daimler motor, and of the automobile, which, since 1893, had become a nightmare at a hundred kilometres an hour, almost as destructive as the electric tram which was only ten years older; and threatening to become as terrible as the locomotive steam-engine itself, which was almost exactly Adams's own age.

Then he showed his scholar the great hall of dynamos, and explained how little he knew about electricity or force of any kind, even of his own special sun, which spouted heat in inconceivable volume, but which, as far as he knew, might spout less or more, at any time, for all the certainty he felt in it. To him, the dynamo itself was but an ingenious channel for conveying somewhere the heat latent in a few tons of poor coal hidden in a dirty engine-house carefully kept out of sight; but to Adams the dynamo became a symbol of infinity. As he grew accustomed to the great gallery of machines, he began to feel the forty-foot dynamos as a moral force, much as the early Christians felt the Cross. The planet itself seemed less impressive, in its old-fashioned, deliberate, annual or daily revolution, than this huge wheel, revolving within arm's-length at some vertiginous speed, and barely murmuring—scarcely humming an audible warning to stand a hair's-breadth further for respect of power—while it would not wake the baby lying close against its frame. Before the end, one began to pray to it; inherited instinct taught the natural expression of man before silent and infinite force. Among the thousand symbols of ultimate energy, the dynamo was not so human as some, but it was the most expressive.

Yet the dynamo, next to the steam-engine, was the most familiar of exhibits. For Adams's objects its value lay chiefly in its occult mechanism. Between the dynamo in the gallery of machines and the engine-house outside, the break of continuity amounted to abysmal fracture for a historian's objects. No more relation could he discover between the steam and the electric current than between the Cross and the cathedral. The forces were interchangeable if not reversible, but he could see only an absolute *fiat* in electricity as in faith. Langley could not help him. Indeed, Langley seemed to be worried by the same trouble, for he constantly repeated that the new forces were anarchical, and especially that he was not responsible for the new rays, that were little short of parricidal in their wicked spirit towards science. His own rays, with which he had doubled the solar spectrum, were altogether harmless and beneficent; but Radium denied its God—or, what was to Langley the same thing, denied the truths of his Science. The force was wholly new.

A historian who asked only to learn enough to be as futile as Langley or Kelvin, made rapid progress under this teaching, and mixed himself up in the tangle of ideas until he achieved a sort of Paradise of ignorance vastly consoling to his fatigued senses. He wrapped himself in vibrations and rays which were new, and he would have hugged Marconi and Branly had he met them, as he hugged the dynamo; while he lost his arithmetic in trying to figure out the equation between the discoveries and the economies of force. The economies, like the discoveries, were absolute, supersensual, occult; incapable of expression in horse-power. What mathematical equivalent could he suggest as the value of a Branly coherer? Frozen air, or the electric furnace, had some scale of measurement, no doubt, if somebody could invent a thermometer adequate to the purpose; but X-rays had played no part whatever in man's consciousness, and the atom itself had figured only as a fiction of thought. In these seven years man had translated himself into a new universe which had no common scale of measurement with the old. He had entered a supersensual world, in which he could measure nothing except by chance collisions of movements imperceptible to his senses, perhaps even imperceptible to his instruments, but perceptible to each other, and so to some known ray at the end of the scale. Langley seemed prepared for anything, even for an indeterminable number of universes interfused—physics stark mad in metaphysics.

Historians undertake to arrange sequences,—called stories, or histories—assuming in silence a relation of cause and effect. These assumptions, hidden in the depths of dusty libraries, have been astounding, but commonly unconscious and childlike; so much so, that if any captious critic were to drag them to light, historians would probably reply, with one voice, that they had never supposed themselves required to know what they were talking about. Adams, for one, had toiled in vain to find out what he meant. He had even published a dozen volumes of American history for no other purpose than to satisfy himself whether, by the severest process of stating, with the least possible comment, such facts as seemed sure, in such order as seemed rigorously consequent, he could fix for a familiar moment a necessary sequence of human movement. The result had satisfied him as little as at Harvard College. Where he saw sequence, other men saw something quite different, and no one saw the same unit of measure. He cared little about his experiments and less about his statesmen, who seemed to him quite as ignorant as himself and, as a rule, no more honest; but he insisted on a relation of sequence, and if he could not reach it by one method, he would try as many methods as science knew. Satisfied that the sequence of men led to nothing and that the sequence of their society could lead no further, while the mere sequence of time was artificial, and the sequence of thought was chaos, he turned at last to the sequence of force; and thus it happened that, after ten years' pursuit, he found himself lying in the Gallery of Machines at the Great Exposition of 1900, his historical neck broken by the sudden irruption of forces totally new.

Since no one else showed much concern, an elderly person without other cares had no need to betray alarm. The year 1900 was not the first to upset schoolmasters. Copernicus and Galileo had broken many professorial necks about 1600; Columbus had stood the world on its head towards 1500; but the nearest approach to the revolution of 1900 was that of 310, when Constantine set up the Cross. The rays that Langley disowned, as well as those which he fathered, were occult, supersensual, irrational; they were a revelation of mysterious energy like that of the Cross; they were what, in terms of mediaeval science, were called immediate modes of the divine substance.

The historian was thus reduced to his last resources. Clearly if he was bound to reduce all these forces to a common value, this common value could have no measure but that of their attraction on his own mind. He must treat them as they had been felt; as convertible, reversible, interchangeable attractions on thought. He made up his mind to venture it; he would risk translating rays into faith. Such a reversible process would vastly amuse a chemist, but the chemist could not deny that he, or some of his fellow physicists, could feel the force of both. When Adams was a boy in Boston, the best chemist in the place had probably never heard of Venus except by way of scandal, or of the Virgin except as idolatry; neither had he heard of dynamos or automobiles or radium; yet his mind was ready to feel the force of all, though the rays were unborn and the women were dead.

Here opened another totally new education, which promised to be by far the most hazardous of all. The knife-edge along which he must crawl, like Sir Lancelot in the twelfth century, divided two kingdoms of force which had nothing in common but attraction. They were as different as a magnet is from gravitation, supposing one knew what a magnet was, or gravitation, or love. The force of the Virgin was still felt at Lourdes, and seemed to be as potent as X-rays; but in America neither Venus nor Virgin ever had value as force—at most as sentiment. No American had ever been truly afraid of either.

This problem in dynamics gravely perplexed an American historian. The Woman had once been supreme; in France she still seemed potent, not merely as a sentiment, but as a force. Why was she unknown in America? For evidently America was ashamed of her, and she was ashamed of herself, otherwise they would not have strewn fig-leaves so profusely all over her. When she was a true force, she was ignorant of fig-leaves, but the monthly-magazine-made American female had not a feature that would have been recognized by Adam. The trait was notorious, and often humorous, but any one brought up among Puritans knew that sex was sin. In any previous age, sex was strength. Neither art nor beauty was needed. Every one, even among Puritans, knew that neither Diana of the Ephesians nor any of the Oriental goddesses was worshipped for her beauty. She was goddess because of her force; she was the animated dynamo; she was reproduction—the greatest and most mysterious of all energies; all she needed was to be fecund. Singularly enough, not one of Adams's many schools of education had ever drawn his attention to the opening lines of Lucretius, though they were perhaps the finest in all Latin literature, where the poet invoked Venus exactly as Dante invoked the Virgin:—

"Quae quoniam rerum naturam *sola* gubernas." [1]

The Venus of Epicurean philosophy survived in the Virgin of the Schools:—

"Donna, sei tanto grande, e tanto vali,
Che qual vuol grazia, e a te non ricorre,
Sua disianza vuol volar senz' ali." [2]

All this was to American thought as though it had never existed. The true American knew something of the facts, but nothing of the feelings; he read the letter, but he never felt the law. Before this historical chasm, a mind like that of Adams felt itself helpless; he turned from the Virgin

---

[1] "Since Thou then art the sole mistress of the nature of things."
[2] "Thou art so great, O Lady, and hast such force,
That he who would have grace but seeks it not from Thee,
Would join that his longing fly without wings."

to the Dynamo as though he were a Branly coherer. On one side, at the Louvre and at Chartres, as he knew by the record of work actually done and still before his eyes, was the highest energy ever known to man, the creator of four-fifths of his noblest art, exercising vastly more attraction over the human mind than all the steam-engines and dynamos ever dreamed of; and yet this energy was unknown to the American mind. An American Virgin would never dare command; an American Venus would never dare exist.

The question, which to any plain American of the nineteenth century seemed as remote as it did to Adams, drew him almost violently to study, once it was posed; and on this point Langleys were as useless as though they were Herbert Spencers or dynamos. The idea survived only as art. There one turned as naturally as though the artist were himself a woman. Adams began to ponder, asking himself whether he knew of any American artist who had ever insisted on the power of sex, as every classic had always done; but he could think only of Walt Whitman; Bret Harte, as far as the magazines would let him venture; and one or two painters, for the flesh-tones. All the rest had used sex for sentiment, never for force; to them, Eve was a tender flower, and Herodias an unfeminine horror. American art, like the American language and American education, was as far as possible sexless. Society regarded this victory over sex as its greatest triumph, and the historian readily admitted it, since the moral issue, for the moment, did not concern one who was studying the relations of unmoral force. He cared nothing for the sex of the dynamo until he could measure its energy.

Vaguely seeking a clue, he wandered through the art exhibit, and, in his stroll, stopped almost every day before St. Gaudens's General Sherman, which had been given the central post of honor. St. Gaudens himself was in Paris, putting on the work his usual interminable last touches, and listening to the usual contradictory suggestions of brother sculptors. Of all the American artists who gave to American art whatever life it breathed in the seventies, St. Gaudens was perhaps the most sympathetic, but certainly the most inarticulate. General Grant or Don Cameron had scarcely less instinct of rhetoric than he. All the others—the Hunts, Richardson, John La Farge, Stanford White—were exuberant; only St. Gaudens could never discuss or dilate on an emotion, or suggest artistic arguments for giving to his work the forms that he felt. He never laid down the law, or affected the despot, or became brutalized like Whistler by the brutalities of his world. He required no incense; he was no egoist; his simplicity of thought was excessive; he could not imitate, or give any form but his own to the creations of his hand. No one felt more strongly than he the strength of other men, but the idea that they could affect him never stirred an image in his mind.

This summer his health was poor and his spirits were low. For such a temper, Adams was not the best companion, since his own gaiety was not *folle;* but he risked going now and then to the studio on Mont Parnasse to draw him out for a stroll in the Bois de Boulogne, or dinner as pleased his moods, and in return St. Gaudens sometimes let Adams go about in his company.

Once St. Gaudens took him down to Amiens, with a party of Frenchmen, to see the cathedral. Not until they found themselves actually studying the sculpture of the western portal, did it dawn on Adams's mind that, for his purposes, St. Gaudens on that spot had more interest to him than the cathedral itself. Great men before great monuments express great truths, provided they are not taken too solemnly. Adams never tired of quoting the supreme phrase of his idol Gibbon, before the Gothic cathedrals: "I darted a contemptuous look on the stately monuments of superstition." Even in the footnotes of his history, Gibbon had never inserted a bit of humor more human than this, and one would have paid largely for a photograph of the fat little historian, on the background of Notre Dame of Amiens, trying to persuade his readers—perhaps himself—that he was darting a contemptuous look on the stately monument, for which he felt in fact the respect which every man of his vast study and active mind always feels before objects worthy of it; but besides the humor, one felt also the relation. Gibbon ignored the Virgin, because in 1789 religious monuments were out of fashion. In 1900 his remark sounded fresh and simple as the green fields to ears that had heard a hundred years of other remarks, mostly no more fresh and certainly less simple. Without malice, one might find it more instructive than a whole lecture of Ruskin. One sees what one brings, and at that moment Gibbon brought the French Revolution. Ruskin brought reaction against the Revolution. St. Gaudens had passed beyond all. He liked the stately monuments much more than he liked Gibbon or Ruskin; he loved their dignity; their unity; their scale; their lines; their lights and shadows; their decorative sculpture; but he was even less conscious than they of the force that created it all—the Virgin, the Woman—by whose genius "the stately monuments of superstition" were built, through which she was expressed. He would have seen more meaning in Isis with the cow's horns, at Edfoo, who expressed the same thought. The art remained, but the energy was lost even upon the artist.

Yet in mind and person St. Gaudens was a survival of the 1500s; he bore the stamp of the Renaissance, and should have carried an image of the Virgin round his neck, or stuck in his hat, like Louis XI. In mere time he was a lost soul that had strayed by chance into the twentieth century, and forgotten where it came from. He writhed and cursed at his ignorance, much as Adams did at his own, but in the opposite sense. St. Gaudens was a child of Benvenuto Cellini, smothered in an American cradle. Adams was a quintessence of Boston, devoured by curiosity to think like Benvenuto. St. Gaudens's art was starved from birth, and Adams's instinct was blighted from babyhood. Each had but half of a nature, and when they came together before the Virgin of Amiens they ought both to have felt in her the force that made them one; but it was not so. To Adams she became more than ever a channel of force; to St. Gaudens she remained as before a channel of taste.

For a symbol of power, St. Gaudens instinctively preferred the horse, as was plain in his horse and Victory of the Sherman monument. Doubtless Sherman also felt it so. The attitude was so American that, for at least forty years, Adams had never realized that any other could be in sound taste. How many years had he taken to admit a notion of what Michael Angelo and Rubens were driving at? He could not say; but he knew that only since 1895 had he begun to feel the Virgin or Venus as force, and not everywhere even so. At Chartres—perhaps at Lourdes— possibly at Cnidos if one could still find there the divinely naked Aphrodite of Praxiteles—but otherwise one must look for force to the goddesses of Indian mythology. The idea dies out long ago in the German and English stock. St. Gaudens at Amiens was hardly less sensitive to the force of the female energy than Matthew Arnold at the Grande Chartreuse. Neither of them felt goddesses as power—only as reflected emotion, human expression, beauty, purity, taste, scarcely even as sympathy. They felt a railway train as power; yet they, and all other artists, constantly complained that the power embodied in a railway train could never be embodied in art. All the steam in the world could not, like the Virgin, build Chartres.

Yet in mechanics, whatever the mechanicians might think, both energies acted as interchangeable forces on man, and by action on man all known force may be measured. Indeed, few men of science measured force in any other way. After once admitting that a straight line was the shortest distance between two points, no serious mathematician cared to deny anything that suited his convenience, and rejected no symbol, unproved or unproveable, that helped him to accomplish work. The symbol was force, as a compass-needle or a triangle was force, as the mechanist might prove by losing it, and nothing could be gained by ignoring their value. Symbol or energy, the Virgin had acted as the greatest force the Western world ever felt, and had drawn man's activities to herself more strongly than any other power, natural or supernatural, had ever done; the historian's business was to follow the track of the energy; to find where it came from and where it went to; its complex source and shifting channels; its values, equivalents, conversions. It could scarcely be more complex than radium; it could hardly be deflected, diverted, polarized, absorbed more perplexingly than other radiant matter. Adams knew nothing about any of them, but as a mathematical problem of influence on human progress, though all were occult, all reacted on his mind, and he rather inclined to think the Virgin easiest to handle.

The pursuit turned out to be long and tortuous, leading at last into the vast forests of scholastic science. From Zeno to Descartes, hand in hand with Thomas Aquinas, Montaigne, and Pascal, one stumbled as stupidly as though one were still a German student of 1860. Only with the instinct of despair could one force one's self into this old thicket of ignorance after having been repulsed at a score of entrances more promising and more popular. Thus far, no path had led anywhere, unless perhaps to an exceedingly modest living. Forty-five years of study had proved to be quite futile for the pursuit of power; one controlled no more force in 1900 than in 1850, although the amount of force controlled by society had enormously increased. The secret of education still hid itself somewhere behind ignorance, and one fumbled over it as feebly as ever. In such labyrinths, the staff is a force almost more necessary than the legs; the pen becomes a sort of blind-man's dog, to keep him from falling into the gutters. The pen works for itself, and acts like a hand, modelling the plastic material over and over again to the form that suits it best. The form is never arbitrary, but is a sort of growth like crystallization, as any artist knows too well; for often the pencil or pen runs into side-paths and shapelessness, loses its relations, stops or is bogged. Then it has to return on its trail, and recover, if it can, its line of force. The result of a year's work depends more on what is struck out than on what is left in; on the sequence of the main lines of thought, than on their play or variety. Compelled once more to lean heavily on this support, Adams covered more thousands of pages with figures as formal as though they were algebra, laboriously striking out, altering, burning, experimenting, until the year had expired, the Exposition had long been closed, and winter drawing to its end, before he sailed from Cherbourg, on January 19, 1901, for home.

STUDY QUESTIONS

1. Why would a man who wished to study new applications of force "naturally" throw out the study of art exhibits?
2. Why does the awed spectator begin to pray to the dynamo?
3. In what way could the new forces be termed *anarchical*? What connection is there between Langley's worries about new forces and Adams's description of man's new "supersensual world"?
4. What similarities does Adams find in the revolutions of 310 and 1900?
5. Are there any contemporary writers who insist upon the *power* of sex?
6. Explain why Adams felt that the mere sequence of time was artificial and the sequence of thought chaos. What modern thinkers have echoed the same idea?

THE LORD
H. G. Wells   OF THE DYNAMOS

H. G. Wells (1866–1946) was born in Bromley, England, and was
an apprentice draper before going to the University of London.
Greatly influenced by Thomas Henry Huxley, he first wrote articles and then books on science. Among his numerous books are
science-fiction classics—*The Time Machine* (1895), *The Invisible
Man* (1897), and *The War of the Worlds* (1898); and novels of
contemporary life—*Kipps* (1905), *Tono-Bungay* (1909), *The History
of Mr. Polly* (1910), and *Mr. Britling Sees It Through* (1916). An
original member of the Fabian Society, his interest in social problems found a vent in *A Modern Utopia* (1905) and *The Shape of
Things To Come* (1933). His *Outline of History* (1920) has been
widely criticized.

The chief attendant of the three dynamos that buzzed and rattled
at Camberwell, and kept the electric railway going, came out of York-
shire, and his name was James Holroyd. He was a practical electrician,
but fond of whiskey, a heavy red-haired brute with irregular teeth. He
doubted the existence of the deity, but accepted Carnot's cycle, and he
had read Shakespeare and found him weak in chemistry. His helper
came out of the mysterious East, and his name was Azuma-zi. But
Holroyd called him Pooh-bah. Holroyd liked a nigger help because he
would stand kicking—a habit with Holroyd—and did not pry into the
machinery and try to learn the ways of it. Certain odd possibilities of the
negro mind brought into abrupt contact with the crown of our civilisation Holroyd never full realised, though just at the end he got some
inkling of them.

To define Azuma-zi was beyond ethnology. He was, perhaps, more
negroid than anything else, though his hair was curly rather than frizzy,
and his nose had a bridge. Moreover, his skin was brown rather than
black, and the whites of his eyes were yellow. His broad cheek-bones
and narrow chin gave his face something of the viperine V. His head,
too, was broad behind, and low and narrow at the forehead, as if his

From *Short Stories of H. G. Wells* (1929) by H. G. Wells. Reprinted by permission
of Collins-Knowlton-Wing, Inc. Copyright © 1963 by Frank Wells and George
Philip Wells.

brain had been twisted round in the reverse way to a European's. He was short of stature and still shorter of English. In conversation he made numerous odd noises of no known marketable value, and his infrequent words were carved and wrought into heraldic grotesqueness. Holroyd tried to elucidate his religious beliefs, and—especially after whiskey—lectured to him against superstition and missionaries. Azuma-zi, however, shirked the discussion of his gods, even though he was kicked for it.

Azuma-zi had come, clad in white but insufficient raiment, out of the stoke-hole of the *Lord Clive,* from the Straits Settlements, and beyond, into London. He had heard even in his youth of the greatness and riches of London, where all the women are white and fair, and even the beggars in the streets are white; and he had arrived, with newly earned gold coins in his pocket, to worship at the shrine of civilisation. The day of his landing was a dismal one; the sky was dun, and a wind-worried drizzle filtered down to the greasy streets, but he plunged boldly into the delights of Shadwell, and was presently cast up, shattered in health, civilised in costume, penniless, and, except in matters of the direst necessity, practically a dumb animal, to toil for James Holroyd and to be bullied by him in the dynamo shed at Camberwell. And to James Holroyd bullying was a labour of love.

There were three dynamos with their engines at Camberwell. The two that have been there since the beginning are small machines; the larger one was new. The smaller machines made a reasonable noise; their straps hummed over the drums, every now and then the brushes buzzed and fizzled, and the air churned steadily, whoo! whoo! whoo! between their poles. One was loose in its foundations and kept the shed vibrating. But the big dynamo drowned these little noises altogether with the sustained drone of its iron core, which somehow set part of the ironwork humming. The place made the visitor's head reel with the throb, throb, throb of the engines, the rotation of the big wheels, the spinning ball-valves, the occasional spittings of the steam, and over all the deep, unceasing, surging note of the big dynamo. This last noise was from an engineering point of view a defect; but Azuma-zi accounted it unto the monster for mightiness and pride.

If it were possible we would have the noises of that shed always about the reader as he reads, we would tell all our story to such an accompaniment. It was a steady stream of din, from which the ear picked out first one thread and then another; there was the intermittent snorting, panting, and seething of the steam-engines, the suck and thud of their pistons, the dull beat on the air as the spokes of the great driving-wheels came round, a note the leather straps made as they ran tighter and looser, and a fretful tumult from the dynamos; and, over all, sometimes inaudible, as the ear tired of it, and then creeping back upon the senses again, was this trombone note of the big machine. The floor never felt steady and quiet beneath one's feet, but quivered and jarred. It was a confusing, unsteady place, and enough to send anyone's thoughts jerking into odd zigzags. And for three months, while the big strike of the engineers was in progress, Holroyd, who was a blackleg, and Azuma-zi, who was a mere black, were never out of the stir and eddy of it, but slept and fed in the little wooden shanty between the shed and the gates.

Holroyd delivered a theological lecture on the text of his big machine soon after Azuma-zi came. He had to shout to be heard in the din. "Look at that," said Holroyd; "where's your 'eathen idol to match 'im?" And Azuma-zi looked. For a moment Holroyd was inaudible, and then Azuma-zi heard: "Kill a hundred men. Twelve per cent on the ordinary shares," said Holroyd, "and that's something like a Gord!"

Holroyd was proud of his big dynamo, and expatiated upon its size and power to Azuma-zi until heaven knows what odd currents of thought that, and the incessant whirling and shindy, set up within the curly, black cranium. He would explain in the most graphic manner the dozen or so ways in which a man might be killed by it, and once he gave Azuma-zi a shock as a sample of its quality. After that, in the breathing-times of his labour—it was heavy labour, being not only his own but most of Holroyd's—Azuma-zi would sit and watch the big machine. Now and then the brushes would sparkle and spit blue flashes, at which Holroyd would swear, but all the rest was as smooth and rhythmic as breathing. The band ran shouting over the shaft, and ever behind one as one watched was the complacent thud of the piston. So it lived all day in this big airy shed, with him and Holroyd to wait upon it; not prisoned up and slaving to drive a ship as the other engines he knew—mere captive devils of the British Solomon—had been, but a machine enthroned. Those two smaller dynamos, Azuma-zi by force of contrast despised; the large one he privately christened the Lord of the Dynamos. They were fretful and irregular, but the big dynamo was steady. How great it was! How serene and easy in its working! Greater and calmer even than the Buddhas he had seen at Rangoon, and yet not motionless, but living! The great black coils spun, spun, spun, the rings ran round under the brushes, and the deep note of its coil steadied the whole. It affected Azuma-zi queerly.

Azuma-zi was not fond of labour. He would sit about and watch the Lord of the Dynamos while Holroyd went away to persuade the yard porter to get whiskey, although his proper place was not in the dynamo shed but behind the engines, and, moreover, if Holroyd caught him skulking he got hit for it with a rod of stout copper wire. He would go and stand close to the colossus and look up at the great leather band running overhead. There was a black patch on the band that came round, and it pleased him somehow among all the clatter to watch this return again and again. Odd thoughts spun with the whirl of it. Scientific people tell us that savages give souls to rocks and trees—and a machine is a thousand times more alive than a rock or a tree. And Azuma-zi was practically a savage still; the veneer of civilisation lay no deeper than his slop suit, his bruises and the coal grime on his face and hands. His father before him had worshipped a meteoric stone; kindred blood, it may be, had splashed the broad wheels of Juggernaut.

He took every opportunity Holroyd gave him of touching and handling the great dynamo that was fascinating him. He polished and cleaned it until the metal parts were blinding in the sun. He felt a mysterious sense of service in doing this. He would go up to it and touch its spinning coils gently. The gods he had worshipped were all far away. The people in London hid their gods.

At last his dim feelings grew more distinct, and took shape in thoughts and acts. When he came into the roaring shed one morning he salaamed to the Lord of the Dynamos; and then, when Holroyd was away, he went and whispered to the thundering machine that he was its servant, and prayed it to have pity on him and save him from Holroyd. As he did so a rare gleam of light came in through the open archway of the throbbing machine-shed, and the Lord of the Dynamos, as he whirled and roared, was radiant with pale gold. Then Azuma-zi knew that his service was acceptable to his Lord. After that he did not feel so lonely as he had done, and he had indeed been very much alone in London. And even when his work time was over, which was rare, he loitered about the shed.

Then, the next time Holroyd maltreated him, Azuma-zi went presently to the Lord of the Dynamos and whispered, "Thou seest, O my Lord!" and the angry whirr of the machinery seemed to answer him. Thereafter it appeared to him that whenever Holroyd came into the shed a different note came into the sounds of the great dynamo. "My Lord bides his time," said Azuma-zi to himself. "The iniquity of the fool is not yet ripe." And he waited and watched for the day of reckoning. One day there was evidence of short circuiting, and Holroyd, making an unwary examination—it was in the afternoon—got a rather severe shock. Azuma-zi from behind the engine saw him jump off and curse at the peccant coil.

"He is warned," said Azuma-zi to himself. "Surely my Lord is very patient."

Holroyd had at first initiated his "nigger" into such elementary conceptions of the dynamo's working as would enable him to take temporary charge of the shed in his absence. But when he noticed the manner in which Azuma-zi hung about the monster, he became suspicious. He dimly perceived his assistant was "up to something," and connecting him with the anointing of the coils with oil that had rotted the varnish in one place, he issued an edict, shouted above the confusion of the machinery, "Don't 'ee go nigh that big dynamo any more, Pooh-bah, or a'll take thy skin off!" Besides, if it pleased Azuma-zi to be near the big machine, it was plain sense and decency to keep him away from it.

Azuma-zi obeyed at the time, but later he was caught bowing before the Lord of the Dynamos. At which Holroyd twisted his arm and kicked him as he turned to go away. As Azuma-zi presently stood behind the engine and glared at the back of the hated Holroyd, the noises of the machinery took a new rhythm, and sounded like four words in his native tongue.

It is hard to say exactly what madness is. I fancy Azuma-zi was mad. The incessant din and whirl of the dynamo shed may have churned up his little store of knowledge and big store of superstitious fancy, at last, into something akin to frenzy. At any rate, when the idea of making Holroyd a sacrifice to the Dynamo Fetich was thus suggested to him, it filled him with a strange tumult of exultant emotion.

That night the two men and their black shadows were alone in the shed together. The shed was lit with one big arc light that winked and flickered purple. The shadows lay black behind the dynamos, the ball governors of the engines whirled from light to darkness, and their pistons beat loud and steady. The world outside seen through the open end of the shed seemed incredibly dim and remote. It seemed absolutely silent, too, since the riot of the machinery drowned every external sound. Far away was the black fence of the yard with grey, shadowy houses behind, and above was the deep blue sky and the pale little stars. Azuma-zi suddenly walked across the centre of the shed above which the leather bands were running, and went into the shadow by the big dynamo. Holroyd heard a click, and the spin of the armature changed.

"What are you dewin' with that switch?" he bawled in surprise. "Ha'n't I told you—"

Then he saw the set expression of Azuma-zi's eyes as the Asiatic came out of the shadow towards him.

In another moment the two men were grappling fiercely in front of the great dynamo.

"You coffee-headed fool!" gasped Holroyd, with a brown hand at his throat. "Keep off those contact rings." In another moment he was tripped and reeling back upon the Lord of the Dynamos. He instinctively loosened his grip upon his antagonist to save himself from the machine.

The messenger, sent in furious haste from the station to find out what had happened in the dynamo shed, met Azuma-zi at the porter's lodge by the gate. Azuma-zi tried to explain something, but the messenger could make nothing of the black's incoherent English, and hurried on to the shed. The machines were all noisily at work, and nothing seemed to be disarranged. There was, however, a queer smell of singed hair. Then he saw an odd-looking, crumpled mass clinging to the front of the big dynamo, and, approaching, recognised the distorted remains of Holroyd.

The man stared and hesitated a moment. Then he saw the face and shut his eyes convulsively. He turned on his heel before he opened them, so that he should not see Holroyd again, and went out of the shed to get advice and help.

When Azuma-zi saw Holroyd die in the grip of the Great Dynamo he had been a little scared about the consequences of his act. Yet he felt strangely elated and knew that the favour of the Lord Dynamo was upon him. His plan was already settled when he met the man coming from the station, and the scientific manager who speedily arrived on the scene jumped at the obvious conclusion of suicide. This expert scarcely noticed Azuma-zi except to ask a few questions. Did he see Holroyd kill himself? Azuma-zi explained he had been out of sight at the engine furnace until he heard a difference in the noise from the dynamo. It was not a difficult examination, being untinctured by suspicion.

The distorted remains of Holroyd, which the electrician removed from the machine, were hastily covered by the porter with a coffee-stained tablecloth. Somebody, by a happy inspiration, fetched a medical man. The expert was chiefly anxious to get the machine at work again, for seven or eight trains had stopped midway in the stuffy tunnels of the electric railway. Azuma-zi, answering or misunderstanding the questions of the people who had by authority or impudence come into the shed, was presently sent back to the stoke-hole by the scientific manager. Of course a crowd collected outside the gates of the yard,—a crowd, for no known reason, always hovers for a day or two near the scene of a sudden death in London; two or three reporters percolated somehow into the engine-shed, and one even got to Azuma-zi; but the scientific expert cleared them out again, being himself an amateur journalist.

Presently the body was carried away, and public interest departed with it. Azuma-zi remained very quietly at his furnace, seeing over and over again in the coals a figure that wriggled violently and became still. An hour after the murder, to any one coming into the shed it would have looked exactly as if nothing remarkable had ever happened there. Peeping presently from his engine-room the black saw the Lord Dynamo spin and whirl beside his little brothers, the driving wheels were beating round, and the steam in the pistons went thud, thud, exactly as it had been earlier in the evening. After all, from the mechanical point of view, it had been a most insignificant incident—the mere temporary deflection of a current. But now the slender form and slender shadow of the scientific manager replaced the sturdy outline of Holroyd travelling up and down the lane of light upon the vibrating floor under the straps between the engines and the dynamos.

"Have I not served my Lord?" said Azuma-zi, inaudibly, from his shadow, and the note of the great dynamo rang out full and clear. As he looked at the big, whirling mechanism the strange fascination of it that had been a little in abeyance since Holroyd's death resumed its sway.

Never had Azuma-zi seen a man killed so swiftly and pitilessly. The big, humming machine had slain its victim without wavering for a second from its steady beating. It was indeed a mighty god.

The unconscious scientific manager stood with his back to him, scribbling on a piece of paper. His shadow lay at the foot of the monster.

"Was the Lord Dynamo still hungry? His servant was ready."

Azuma-zi made a stealthy step forward, then stopped. The scientific manager suddenly stopped writing, and walked down the shed to the end-most of the dynamos, and began to examine the brushes.

Azuma-zi hesitated, and then slipped across noiselessly into the shadow by the switch. There he waited. Presently the manager's footsteps could be heard returning. He stopped in his old position, unconscious of the stoker crouching ten feet away from him. Then the big dynamo suddenly fizzled, and in another moment Azuma-zi had sprung out of the darkness upon him.

First, the scientific manager was gripped round the body and swung towards the big dynamo, then, kicking with his knee and forcing his antagonist's head down with his hands, he loosened the grip on his waist and swung round away from the machine. Then the black grasped him again, putting a curly head against his chest, and they swayed and panted as it seemed for an age or so. Then the scientific manager was impelled to catch a back ear in his teeth and bite furiously. The black yelled hideously.

They rolled over on the floor, and the black, who had apparently slipped from the vise of the teeth or parted with some ear—the scientific manager wondered which at the time—tried to throttle him. The scientific manager was making some ineffectual efforts to claw something with his hands and to kick, when the welcome sound of quick footsteps sounded on the floor. The next moment Azuma-zi had left him and darted towards the big dynamo. There was a splutter amid the roar.

The officer of the company, who had entered, stood staring as Azuma-zi caught the naked terminals in his hands, gave one horrible convulsion, and then hung motionless from the machine, his face violently distorted.

"I'm jolly glad you came in when you did," said the scientific manager, still sitting on the floor.

He looked at the still quivering figure. "It is not a nice death to die, apparently—but it is quick."

The official was still staring at the body. He was a man of slow apprehension.

There was a pause.

The scientific manager got up on his feet rather awkwardly. He ran his fingers along his collar thoughtfully, and moved his head to and fro several times.

"Poor Holroyd! I see now." Then almost mechanically he went towards the switch in the shadow and turned the current into the railway circuit again. As he did so the singed body loosened its grip upon the machine and fell forward on its face. The cone of the dynamo roared out loud and clear, and the armature beat the air.

So ended prematurely the Worship of the Dynamo Deity, perhaps the most shortlived of all religions. Yet withal it could boast a Martyrdom and a Human Sacrifice.

STUDY QUESTIONS

1. Although there are three or four characters who fulfill an obvious function in Wells's story, the narrator himself is a character. Why?
2. At what point in "The Lord of the Dynamos" does Wells begin to prepare the reader for the conflict that will end in Holroyd's death?
3. How is Azuma-zi's new god superior to the gods he formerly worshipped? How does Holroyd add to Azuma-zi's idolization of the dynamo? What is meant by *Fetich?*❧ ❧
4. Is there any evidence from which to conclude that Azuma-zi was mad?
5. What does the reaction of the "civilized" men to Holroyd's death contribute to the over-all effect of the story?

STRAIGHT MEN

Joseph Wood Krutch **IN A CROOKED WORLD**

Joseph Wood Krutch (1893–   ) was born in Knoxville, Tennessee. He received his B.A. (1915) from the University of Tennessee and his M.A. (1916) and Ph.D. (1932) from Columbia University. He has taught English, journalism, and drama at Co-

Reprinted from *The American Scholar,* Volume 29, Number 3, Summer 1960. Copyright © 1960 by the United Chapters of Phi Beta Kappa. By permission of the publishers and the author.

Some years ago a distinguished playwright told me how he had taken his East Side mother-in-law to see Maurice Evans in *Richard III.* The old lady—whose experience with both literature and the theatre was extremely limited—listened intently in silence for half an hour, then waved a derisive thumb in the direction of the mellifluously complaining Richard and announced firmly: "I don't sympathize."

Now this was, of course, a fine tribute to the purely dramatic skill of Shakespeare. He had provoked the reaction he aimed at without any direct indication of what his own attitude was. I remember the anecdote at the moment for a simple reason. "I don't sympathize" vigorously sums up my own response to certain modern Richards, namely those who enlarge with too much self-pity upon their "alienation" from modern society, modern man and, indeed, from the universe as a whole. On the one hand I find myself ready to agree with a good deal of their criticism; on the other I am irritated by their chronic reaction to the things we both abhor.

To take the most obvious and least significant case, consider the beatniks. I dislike—almost if not quite as much as they do—the dominant middle-class and organization-man concept of the Good Life. Although we can't all be philosophers, scholars, artists or monks, I agree that too many moderns aspire to nothing more than the "status symbols" that money can buy, and far too few to what George N. Shuster recently defined as the ultimate aim of education: "sharing the life of the scholar, poet and saint." But to respond to this situation by taking a shot of heroin and driving a car at ninety miles an hour seems unlikely either to improve society or, what is more relevant, lead to a Good Life.

Sympathetic interpreters of the beatniks have described them as "taking a revenge on society." For example, the hero of a recent novel is described by a reviewer thus: "Seeing too well in a world dazed by the bomb, Renaud undertakes an alcoholic strike against humanity." But the phrase "an alcoholic strike," like "a revenge on society," seems to me merely comic. It suggests the popular saying about "biting off your nose to spite your face," that being precisely what some intellectuals (including many somewhat above the beatnik level) are doing—as though turning into a dope addict does not hurt oneself even more than it hurts anyone else. It seems only slightly less obvious that the more respectable intellectuals who devote themselves exclusively to exploring and exploiting their "alienation" are doing much the same thing. Surely it is more productive of personal happiness and even "more useful to society" to be a candle throwing its beams into a naughty world than a beatnik crying "revenge, revenge" from the gutter. We hear a great deal about the responsibility of society toward the individual. The individual also has a responsibility toward society. And if things are as bad as the alienated say, the only way one can discharge that responsibility is by being an honorable man.

I presume that this thesis hardly needs elaboration and is not likely to be contested outside beatnik circles. But a considerable number of the most talented novelists, poets, painters and composers of the present day reveal, even if they do not proclaim, their alienation; and it seems to me that their most frequent response is only less grotesque, not more fruitful, than that of the beatniks. Even granted, as most of them proclaim in some version of Yeats's often quoted words that "Things fall apart; the center cannot hold," is there still nothing for a wise man to do except take heroin with the beatniks or, as is usual among the alienated squares, elaborate in more and more complicated phrases their dark convictions?

To this question the hearty do-gooder will of course reply: "Why obviously the thing to do is to work for social improvement. Join the party of your choice and the church of your choice; be sure to register for all elections and attend the meetings of your local P.T.A." Without entering into any question concerning the ultimate effectiveness of such a method of employing one's time, it must be admitted that your alienated artist or philosopher is no more likely than a beatnik to undertake it. Let us suppose, therefore, that he has, like Thoreau, both "signed off" from the church and wished that he could as easily sign off from society as a whole. Of course he will be thoroughly disapproved of almost everywhere outside the circle of the completely alienated; but he might, like a few others besides Thoreau, find in this determination to stand alone the possibility of making for himself a private world from which he was *not* alienated, instead of devoting himself exclusively to the task of saying just how alienated he is. He could even find a few justifications formulated in the past for doing just what he has done.

I seem to remember somewhere in Plato the opinion that when times are thoroughly bad a wise man will merely stand by the wall. Similarly, it would appear from the *Meditations* of Marcus Aurelius that although the Emperor was no less aware than Yeats of a world in which "things fall apart," he spent relatively little time in either elaborating or bemoaning the lack of wisdom or virtue in society. He determined instead to cultivate them in himself. Then there is even a wholehearted defense of the mere slacker, which is quoted by Montaigne from one Theodorus who held that "It is not just that a wise man should risk his life for the good of his country and imperil wisdom for fools."

As I see it, the question is not so much whether the alienated would do better to imitate Marcus Aurelius rather than Baudelaire and Apollinaire, for it is a larger and, so many will think, an outrageous question. Is it possible that present-day civilization would be in some important respects better than it is if more people had thought less about how to improve society and more about how to improve themselves?

No doubt the medieval monk was too exclusively concerned with his private salvation. But we have gone to the other extreme and are so obsessed with the idea of society as a whole that it no longer seems quite respectable to seek even intellectual or spiritual self-improvement. I am not saying that we are, in actual fact, excessively unselfish. But the cant of the time requires that we should always be asking of any proposed good, "Can everybody have it?" or "Is it an answer to the general problem?" With astonishing regularity I get letters from people who comment on something I have written with a "Well that's the answer so far as you are concerned; I guess it could be the answer so far as I am concerned. But only the privileged, or the lucky, or the well educated, or the intelligent, or the whatnot, can do what you and I can. So what is the answer for society as a whole?"

No doubt it would be fine if we could find a universal formula for salvation. I would welcome a convincing one if I ever heard it. But I never have, and I see no reason why, this being true, the individual should not save himself so long as he is not doing so at somebody else's expense. After all, society is composed of individuals. It cannot be "saved" except insofar as the individuals who compose it are.

I am not preaching universal indifference to society and social action as the highest wisdom. I am saying simply that if and when one individual feels (as so many articulate people do seem to feel) that the world is hopeless, then it is wiser to see what one can do about oneself than to give up all hope of that also. "I came into this world," said Thoreau, "not primarily to make it better but to live in it be it good or bad." If you insist, you may soften that a little by substituting "exclusively" for "primarily," but the meaning will still point in the same direction. Or as the same argument was recently discussed in that excellent "little magazine" called *Manas:* "If an artist can find nothing but bad brushes to paint with, he will not dissipate all his energies leading a revolution against bad brushes—but will develop techniques which make it possible for him to paint with bad brushes. He may even discover things that bad brushes do better than good brushes. It is one thing to fight the good fight for good brushes, and another to start to paint."

During the thirties, when most intellectuals moved leftward, quite a number of those who confessed (at least to their friends) that they had embraced communism were nevertheless engaged in writing movies for Hollywood or advertisements for Madison Avenue, while at the same time professing to regard both the movies and advertising as poisonous exhalations from a deliquescent society. Often (and I report from my own experience) they justified themselves by saying that there was no use trying to be anything but rotten in a rotten society. Comes the revolution and we will all be decent. Meanwhile, since we live in an evil society, we submit to it without any bourgeois nonsense about merely personal decency.

Such an attitude is only a logical extreme of the one taken by those who may not completely renounce either personal integrity or personal happiness, but insist upon our duty to think primarily in terms of what can be done for "society," and who sink into despair if we do not know an answer. I will even go so far as to suggest the possibility that society may be in a bad way partly because we have laid so much stress on public education—to take one example—and so little upon self-education. (Perhaps it also has something to do with the fact that I have met "educators" who were not and made no effort to be educated themselves.)

"Philanthropy," so Thoreau wrote, "is almost the only virtue which is sufficiently appreciated by mankind. . . . The kind uncles and aunts of the race are more esteemed than its true spiritual fathers and mothers. I once heard a reverend lecturer on England, a man of learning and intelligence, after enumerating her scientific, literary and political worthies, Shakespeare, Bacon, Cromwell, Milton, Newton and others, speak next of her Christian heroes, whom, as if his profession required it of him, he elevated to a place far above all the rest, as the greatest of the great. They were Penn, Howard and Mrs. Fry. Everyone must feel the falsehood and cant of this. The last were not England's best men and women; only, perhaps, her best philanthropists." This is a tough-minded opinion. It is stated with characteristic exaggeration. But at least there is something to be said for those who do their best even though they do not see at the moment just what practical good it is going to do "for the common man."

After all the medieval monk did perform a service. Neither the God he served nor the learning he preserved counted for much in the world from which he had retired. But he did exemplify in himself virtues that might otherwise have ceased to exist entirely, and he did preserve learning that without him would have been lost.

What it all comes down to in practice is simply this: if you despair of the world, don't despair of yourself. And it is because so many of the alienated critics of our society with whose criticisms I agree seem unable to do anything of the sort that I find myself alienated from them also.

Thirty years ago when I published a book much more pessimistic than I could possibly write now, I received a good many letters that might have been boiled down to a sentence in one of them: "If these are your convictions why don't you go hang yourself?" The answer was, and has continued to be through all such changes of opinion as I have undergone, that there is a private world of thought and endeavor which society has never been able to take away from me.

Perhaps the most curious and shocking result of the exclusive stress upon social rather than upon private ethics is the disappearance of the concept of honor as distinct from that of morality. One of the differences between the two is simply that honor is relevant to the individual only. True, society may be more affected than some social scientists seem to think by the prevalence or scarcity of honor in the code of the individuals who make it up. But the man of honor always asks first whether or not an action would dishonor him personally, and he is not influenced by an argument that his dishonorable act would have no bad (perhaps even some good) effect upon society and is therefore "moral" even if dishonorable.

The world would not now be as profoundly shocked as it was a generation ago by the phrase "a scrap of paper." We are used to having promises so treated. But the Junkers were merely a little ahead of us in their willingness to believe that since the triumph of Germany would promote the advent of the superman, there was nothing immoral in a broken oath.

Many college students, so the pollsters tell us, see nothing wrong about cheating on examinations. "Everybody does it and it doesn't really *hurt* anyone."

In such statements it is easy to see a reasonable application of the two leading principles of ethics-without-absolutes-and-without-honor, which is sometimes called "socialized morality." These two leading principles are: (1) What everybody does must be permissible since the *mores* determine morality; and (2) "Wrong" can mean only "socially harmful."

If you believe all this and also that the only difference between, let us say, an honest man and a thief is the difference between a man who has been "conditioned" to act honestly and one who has not, then there isn't much basis for argument with the student opinion.

When some scandal breaks in government or journalism or business or broadcasting, the usual reaction of even that part of the public which is shocked by it is to say that it could not have happened if there had been adequate laws supervising this or that activity. But, usually, is it not equally true that it could not have happened if a whole group of men, often including the supposed guardians of public morality, had not been devoid of any sense of the meaning and importance of individual integrity? May one not go further and ask whether any amount of "social consciousness" and government control can make decent a society composed of people who have no conception of personal dignity and honor? It was a favorite and no doubt sound argument among early twentieth-century reformers that "playing the game" as the gentleman was supposed to play it was not enough. But has the time not come to add that it is, nevertheless, indispensable?

If the relevance of all this to the first part of the present discussion is not obvious, please allow me to dot the *i*'s. To those who believe that society is corrupt beyond redemption I propose the ancient but neglected concept of personal integrity, virtue and honor accompanied, if they feel it necessary, with the contempt and scorn recently advocated in a telling article in the [*American*] *Scholar* itself.

Those who hold that "social morality" is the only kind worth considering tend to assume that the end justifies the means. If a broken promise or a cynical invasion of a private right promotes "the greatest good of the greatest number" then it is an act of "higher morality." That seems to me a curiously inverted, soft-hearted and soft-headed Machiavellianism. The man of honor is reluctant to use dishonorable means no matter what ends seem to justify them. And he seems to me to be a safer member of society.

STUDY QUESTIONS

1. Explain George N. Shuster's definition of the ultimate aim of education. Is this indeed the ultimate aim of education?
2. What responsibility *does* society have toward the individual? The individual toward society?
3. What reasons can you posit for the almost overwhelming discussion of *alienation* in modern literature?
4. In recent years, what groups have been notably and noticeably alienated from society? The beats? The angry young men? The hippies? Hell's angels? How does the behavior of these groups reveal their alienation?
5. Krutch feels that we are in a bad way partly because we have laid too much emphasis on public education and too little on self-education. How has public education contributed to the alienation of contemporary youth?

THE ANATOMY
Time   **OF ANGST**

The automatic elevator stops with a jolt. The doors slide open, but instead of the accustomed exit, the passenger faces only a blank wall. His fingers stab at buttons: nothing happens. Finally, he presses the alarm signal, and a starter's gruff voice inquires from below: "What's the matter?" The passenger explains that he wants to get off on the 25th floor. "There is no 25th floor in this building," comes the voice over the loudspeaker. The passenger explains that, nonsense, he has worked here for years. He gives his name. "Never heard of you," says the loudspeaker. "Easy," the passenger tells himself. "They are just trying to frighten me."

But time passes and nothing changes. In that endless moment, the variously pleading and angry exchanges over the loudspeaker are the passenger's only communication with the outside world. Finally, even that ceases; the man below says that he cannot waste any more time. "Wait! Please!" cries the passenger in panic—"Keep on talking to me!" But the loudspeaker clicks into silence. Hours, days or ages go by. The passenger cowers in a corner of his steel box, staring at the shining metal grille through which the voice once spoke. The grille must be worshiped; perhaps the voice will be heard again.

This is not a story by Franz Kafka or by one of his contemporary imitators. It is a recent dream remembered in precise detail by a successful New Yorker (one wife, three children, fair income, no analyst) who works with every outward appearance of contentment in one of Manhattan's new, midtown office buildings. Whatever Freudian or other analysis might make of it, the dream could serve as a perfect allegory for an era that is almost universally regarded as the Age of Anxiety. It speaks of big city towers in which life is lived in compartments and cubicles. It speaks of the century's increasingly complex machines that no one man can control. It speaks of the swift ascents and descents not only in a competitive business existence but in an ever-fluid society. It speaks of man's dreaded loss of identity, of a desperate need to make contact with his fellow man, with the world and with whatever may be beyond the world. Above all, it speaks of God grown silent.

Stage Whines. Anxiety seems to be the dominant fact—and is threatening to become the dominant cliché—of modern life. It shouts in the headlines, laughs nervously at cocktail parties, nags from advertisements, speaks suavely in the board room, whines from the stage, clatters from the Wall Street ticker, jokes with fake youthfulness on the golf course and whispers in privacy each day before the shaving mirror and the dressing table. Not merely the black statistics of murder, suicide, alcoholism and divorce betray anxiety (or that special form of anxiety which is guilt), but almost any innocent, everyday act: the limp or overhearty handshake, the second pack of cigarettes or the third martini, the forgotten appointment, the stammer in mid-sentence, the wasted hour before the TV set, the spanked child, the new car unpaid for.

Although he died in 1855, the great Danish existentialist Sören Kierkegaard described the effects of anxiety in terms that are strikingly apt today. He spoke of his "cowardly age," in which "one does everything possible by way of diversions and the Janizary music of loud-voiced enterprises to keep lonely thoughts away." Yet all the noise is in vain: "No Grand Inquisitor has in readiness such terrible tortures as has anxiety, and no spy knows how to attack more artfully the man he suspects, choosing the instant when he is weakest, nor knows how to lay traps where he will be caught and ensnared, and no sharp-witted judge knows how to interrogate, to examine the accused, as anxiety does, which never lets him escape, neither by diversion nor by noise, neither at work nor at play, neither by day nor by night."

War or Peace. When a fact is as universal as love, death or anxiety, it becomes difficult to measure and classify. Man would not be human were he not anxious. Is his anxiety today really greater than ever before—different from Job's? Or is modern man simply a victim of distorted historical vision that always sees the present as bigger and worse than the past?

There is general agreement among psychiatrists, theologians, sociologists and even poets that in this era, anxiety is indeed different both in quantity and quality.

Other eras were turbulent, insecure and complex—the great migrations after the fall of the Roman Empire; the age of discovery; Copernicus and Galileo's tinkering with the universe, removing the earth and man from its center; the industrial revolution. But in a sense, the 20th century U.S. is the culmination of all these upheavals—itself the product of a gigantic migration, itself both champion and victim of the industrial revolution, itself faced with the necessity not only of accepting a new universe but of exploring it.

The American today is told without pause that the world is up to him—war or peace, prosperity or famine, the welfare or literacy of the last, remotest Congolese, Tibetan or Laotian. And he is facing his demanding destiny in a state of psychological and religious confusion.

For centuries of Christian civilization (and not Christian alone), man assumed that anxiety and guilt were part of his nature and that as a finite and fallen being, he had plenty to be guilty about. The only remedies were grace and faith. When the age of reason repealed the Fall, man was thrust back onto himself and, for a time, reason seemed to be an adequate substitute for the certainties of faith. Spinoza could write confidently: "Fear arises from a weakness of mind and therefore does not appertain to the use of reason." But it was soon clear that reason alone could not answer all man's questions, could not provide what he desperately needs: order and purpose in the universe. And so man invented substitute deities—History, the State, Environment. But in the end all these only led back to the nearly unbearable message that man is alone in a meaningless cosmos, subject only to the blind forces of evolution and responsible only to himself. As Kirilov puts it in Dostoevsky's *The Possessed:* "If there is no God, then I am god."

The discovery of the unconscious depths of man's mind by Schopenhauer, Freud and others seemed to offer an escape; here was a dark, mysterious realm, irrational as man knew himself to be irrational, to which he might shift responsibility for his acts. But this worked only partly; ultimately even the cult of the unconscious (psychoanalysis) directed man back to himself and his own resources. Many rejoice that man has been freed from the fear of demons, not realizing that it may be worse to have to fear himself. Many similarly rejoice that, to some extent, he has been freed from the fear of hell-fire, not realizing that he has instead been condemned to the fear of nothingness—what Paul Tillich calls the fear of "nonbeing."

Widespread awareness of all this has itself contributed to the change. Psychologists report that 30 years ago the U.S. was in an "age of covert anxiety." It is now in an age of "overt anxiety." People tend to believe that it is wrong and "sick" to feel anxious or guilty; they are beset by guilt about guilt, by anxiety about anxiety.

Bound and Free. Psychiatrists and theologians know, of course, that a certain amount of guilt and anxiety is inevitable and necessary in man. They are like pain: "bad" because they are discomforting, but in normal quantities necessary for survival because they warn of danger and because they make a human being responsible to others. The rare individual who feels neither guilt nor anxiety is a monster—a psychopath with no conscience. What psychologists call *Urangst*, or original anxiety, the anxiety that is inevitably part of any human being, is well described by Theologian Reinhold Niebuhr, who believes that it springs from

man's dual character: on the one hand, man is involved in the contin-
gencies of nature, like the animals; on the other, he has freedom and
understanding of his position. "In short, man, being both bound and
free, both limited and limitless, is anxious."

This basic, or existential, anxiety (which Niebuhr sees as the pre-
condition of sin) is no more disturbing, in normal quantities, than is
rational fear of danger. In contrast, neurotic anxiety is irrational fear, a
response to a danger that is unknown, internal, intangible or unreal.
Anxiety is fear in search of a cause. Authorities differ on the relationship
of guilt to anxiety, but Dr. John Donnelly of Hartford's Institute of
Living offers what is for laymen the most sense-making distinction: guilt
is apprehension over some transgression in the past, whether actually
committed or merely contemplated, whereas anxiety involves only the
possible and the future. Because the German equivalent, *die Angst,*
carries a stronger connotation of dread, many psychiatrists prefer this
term to the English word. Of itself, anxiety is not a neurosis, but it is an
essential ingredient in almost all neuroses, most major mental and psychosomatic illnesses. Its victims fall into three broad categories:

1. The whole men and women, who have such minor emotional
disturbances as fear about the war or a compulsion to twist and untwist
paper clips (symbolically twisting the boss's neck). Their aggressiveness,
perfectionism or shyness are not exaggerated.

2. The walking wounded, who can usually control their anxiety
and its symptoms well enough to function as breadwinners or housewives, but periodically break down and wind up, in a severe anxiety
state, in a psychiatrist's office or, briefly, in a mental hospital.

3. The ambulance cases, who spend months or years or drag out
their lives in mental hospitals, or (in some cases still not recognized
often enough) land in the emergency rooms of general hospitals with
psychosomatic illnesses often mistaken for heart attacks, asthma or pregnancy complications.

All the neurotic symptoms, major or minor, originate in the same
way: they are defenses against anxiety. The most common are the phobias in which—to cover up anxiety and guilt too painful to be acknowledged—people develop an irrational aversion to some act or object seemingly unconnected with their anxiety. Phobias seem to occur in dazzling
profusion: Blakiston's *New Gould Medical Dictionary* lists 217 of them.
More prevalent but less generally recognized as cover-ups for anxiety
are compulsive forms of behavior and addictions to alcohol and narcotics.

Little Hans. How does a man become anxious to the point of
phobia or compulsion? After decades of debate psychologists and psychiatrists are at last substantially agreed that anxiety arises from feelings

of helplessness.[1] According to the best modern thinking, Freud never fully understood the essential nature of anxiety. His first theory, propounded in 1894, was that repressed libido (sexual energy) becomes anxiety, which later reappears as free-floating anxiety or a symptom (phobia of compulsion) that is equivalent to it. This, as critics pointed out, was a theory of mechanism and not an explanation of causes. So he tried again, and decided in 1923 that a totally different process was involved: anxiety was the cause of repression.

Freud's classic example was of little Hans, aged five, who was panic-stricken at the idea of having to go out in the street. Why? Freud explained that little Hans had strong Oedipal feelings toward his mother; therefore he had hostility toward his father and therefore anxiety. He repressed the anxiety and converted it into hippophobia—he was afraid to go out because he was afraid of being castrated by the bite of a horse. To Freud the horse represented little Hans's father. This elaborate hypothesis neatly fitted Freud's preoccupation with castration fears, which Psychoanalyst Rollo May now interprets as the fear of losing mother's love and, hence, self-esteem.

Otto Rank (1884–1939), disciple of Freud, who later split with him, made a cult of birth trauma. To him life was a process of individuation, which meant a series of separations—birth, weaning, going to school, heading a household. To Rank, anxiety was the apprehension involved in these separations. Alfred Adler, apostle of inferiority feelings, never formulated a full-blown theory of anxiety, but showed more insight than his Vienna rivals in seeing the uses that the neurotic makes of anxiety. If it blocks his activity, it permits him to retreat to a previous state of security, to evade decisions and responsibility—and, therefore, dangers. Also, as happens in many families, it can be forged into a weapon for dominating others, who would rather yeild to unreasonable demands than be made to feel guilty.

Power Drive. Anxiety won belated recognition as a social phenomenon in the U.S. from Karen Horney, Erich Fromm and Harry Stack Sullivan. To Fromm, the Freudian frustration of sex energy becomes anxiety only when it involves some value or way of life that the individual holds vital to his security—for instance, the prestige of having a pretty wife. Horney believed that Freud put the cart before the horse; anxiety, she held, came before the instinctual drives—the instincts developed into drives only under the whiplash of anxiety. To Sullivan, devotee of the "power motive," which drives man to pursue security, anxiety arose from the infant's apprehension of disapproval. And Sullivan had one signifi-

---

[1]Anxiety is not the same as depression. While anxiety is helplessness, depression is hopelessness. But helplessness unendurably prolonged leads inevitably to hopelessness. So anxiety and depression are seen together as often as not, in many classes of mental patients.

cant insight: experiences that create anxiety not only limit the victim's activities, but also actually set limits to his awareness and hence to his learning ability.

University of Illinois' Psychologist O. Hobart Mowrer agrees with Freud on the mechanism of anxiety's creation. But Mowrer differs on basic cause. To him the conflicts that cause anxiety are not so much animal and sexual as human and ethical. They involve the repression of moral strivings. Mowrer notes that anxiety arises when the person feared is also loved. Similarly, Psychoanalyst May sees anxiety in his patients not only when sexual or aggressive urges are revealed but also when the need or desire for constructive new powers is exposed. Thus, it is from the repression of *agape*, love of one's fellow men, as well as from the repression of *eros*, or sexual love, that anxiety springs.

As the earth-moving machines have bulldozed the landscape, so have the technologists bulldozed the manscape. Human nature, says Dr. May, has been made the object of control measures, just like any other part of nature. "Keeping busy" for its own sake has become a neurotic anxiety. While it may allay superficial anxiety, Dr. May holds that it exacerbates the deeper and more pervasive existential anxiety, about being and nonbeing. A do-it-yourselfer in a basement workshop may be too busy watching the guard on his bench saw to worry about traditional causes of anxiety, but at heart he eventually begins to wonder what is the meaning of life for him. That existential question, says May, is now the prevailing cause of the anxiety states that send patients to psychoanalysts. They are dealing less with "*Sexschmerz*" than with *Weltschmerz*.

Orthodoxy of Change. In the U.S. today, causes for such *Weltschmerz* are easy to find. Psychologists know that all change is threat and that all threat produces anxiety. The U.S., more than any other society in history, believes in change. Conservative in many ways, the U.S. has never been conservative in the sense of trying to preserve things the way they were yesterday. Its very orthodoxy is based on the idea of change: the most orthodox tenet in the American creed is that the individual can accomplish anything if he tries hard enough. It may be one of the glories of a free society, but it also carries great potential danger and may well be the greatest single cause of anxiety on the American scene. From the noble notion that man is free to do anything that he can do, the U.S. somehow subtly proceeds to the notion that he *must* do anything he can and, finally, that there is nothing he cannot do.

This leads to a kind of compulsory freedom that encourages people not only to ignore their limitations but to defy them: the dominant myth is that the old can grow young, the indecisive can become leaders of men, the housewives can become glamour girls, the glamour girls can become actresses, the slow-witted can become intellectuals.

Almost every boy in the U.S. has dinned into him the idea that he must excel his father—a guaranteed producer of anxiety, by Freudian theory, if the boy has grown up idolizing his father as a paragon of power and virtues. The process is severest in the sons of outstandingly successful men: their anxiety neuroses are as notorious as the traditional case of the preacher's son becoming a drunkard. A career girl is shredded by the need to excel father or mother or both, and for her the problem may be complicated by Oedipal feelings toward mother.

Many people feel guilty simply about not being talented enough or intelligent enough or well-informed enough. If anybody can be anything he wishes, no wonder the businessman is made to feel guilty—he has neither ear nor taste for modern music (but somehow, the artist never seems to feel guilty about not understanding business). No wonder, too, that the adman thinks he ought to be able to write a novel or to know all about the atom. In an absurd misapplication of the ideal of equality, one man's opinions become as valid as another's. Thus, every man competes not only in his own job or his own social setting; he also somehow feels he must compete with the TV newscaster and the editorial writer (not very difficult), with the physics professor and the philosopher (very difficult indeed).

Why Grow Old?   Every girl is tight-corseted with the propaganda that she must have a slim, svelte figure, no matter what her natural body build or bone structure. She may react to this either by trimming down mercilessly and suffering near starvation; or she may surrender to the neurotic pleasures of overeating—all the time rationalizing that the trouble is in her glands (which it almost never is). Another deliberate anxiety builder is the slogan, "Why grow old?" It introduces a prescription containing a teaspoonful of wisdom, such as the values of exercise and a balanced diet, diluted in an ocean of nonsense about wrinkle erasers and pep medicines. Actually, the less anxiety is associated with the inevitable aging process, the better are people's chances of growing old gracefully and with a sense of fulfillment.

The phenomenon of change in the U.S. contributes to anxiety in another way: no one "knows his place," and even if he does and likes it, there are no easy ways of announcing the fact to others. The worker can indeed still become boss, the immigrant a settled American. But how do they show their newly acquired place in life? No aristocratic titles, no rigid distinctions of dress are available; man's achievements can be signaled only by the fascinating game of displaying "status symbols." Hence the endless American preoccupation with what is "in" and what is "out"—clothes, addresses, speech, schools, cars. The phenomenon (well understood by U.S. novelists, most notably John O'Hara) tends to force Americans into infinite patterns of snobbery and reverse snobbery. The first step after success is to display wealth; the second step is to learn that flashy display is wrong; the third step is to learn that, if one is really "secure," one can afford even to be flashy. This interminable dialectic of snobbery can produce genuine anxiety, as is shown by the innumerable cases of people who frantically seek to hide their families, change their names, tailor their accents—and wind up losing their identities.

This particular form of social anxiety is the most potent of the "hidden persuaders" used by admen. Vance (*The Status Seekers*) Packard, while superficial in much of his work, is correct in pointing out that a key element in selling is to present a product so that it promises to satisfy some need for security or power.

Abstract and Atonal.   Two of the forces that might be counted on to reduce anxiety in U.S. life—the artists and the social scientists—are contributing to it. In abstract painting and atonal music, the modern artist has largely destroyed recognizable reality, creating a world in which he is master because it is incomprehensible to others: he is alone, but at least he is boss. In literature and drama, he has just moved through a long period of writing psychiatric case histories, and is now experimenting with improvised works that seek to destroy the barrier between audience and artist. His traditional role is to assume the burdens of guilt and anxiety freely, transforming them in his own soul into works of art that can offer the audience catharsis or clarity. This is the function for which the artist is applauded, adored—and paid. More and more today, he rejects that function and insists on dragging his audiences into his own neurosis, shifting the burden of guilt and anxiety on to them.

The social scientists have helped make the U.S. the most self-analytic civilization ever known. Rome was not conscious of the "fall of the Roman Empire"; the Crusaders scarcely analyzed the infectious new ideas they brought back from the East; the romantics wrote new kinds of poetry, but did not turn out essays on the alarming death wishes in those poems. Americans cannot make a move without having it declared a trend, viewed critically in innumerable books deploring *The Lonely Crowd, The Status Seekers, The Organization Man.* The exhortations offered to the U.S. public are always contradictory. No sooner had Americans learned that they must not be rugged individualists but must practice "adjustment," than they were told that they were all turning into conformists. No sooner had they learned that children must be raised progressively and permissively than they were told that children desperately want discipline. No sooner had they accepted the fact that women deserved and needed equal rights than they were informed that women had become too much like men.

Anxious Intellectuals.   This kind of ever-contradictory ferment gives the U.S. an exciting intellectual life, but it also makes anxious intellectuals. The intellectuals, in turn, carry their anxiety to the rest of the country through the immensely fast popularization of new ideas. U.S. intellectuals are forever complaining that no one pays attention to their opinions. This is patently untrue: very likely, they complain merely to cover their own guilt at not being as certain about things as they secretly feel they should be—in short, at not being leaders.

This points to what may be the ultimate cause of anxiety in the U.S.: pragmatism. It not only—legitimately—questions every truth, but it also questions whether the concept of truth itself has any meaning. When mixed with logical positivism, it leads to the notion that philosophy, the search for truth beyond mere language or mathematical symbols, is impossible. Few things could produce more anxiety in people who either believe in, or want to believe in, a moral order.

High Places and Dirt. Fantastic and confused though symptoms of anxiety can be, there is often a kind of logic, even a dramatic beauty or poetic justice, about them. They seek to compensate for what is lacking. Thus, according to the Jungian school, the unconscious tries to correct or heal disorganization of the ego—or of society—by doggedly creating images of value, order and meaning. This process can produce fanatics, prophets and saints; it did produce, according to the analytic view of history, Torquemada, Calvin, Knox and Jonathan Edwards. No one can say what prophets or fanatics the U.S. may produce to combat its Age of Anxiety, but its people are certain to react—possibly in futile and less spectacular ways—to the disorder and the threats of their environment.

Logically enough, considering the environment, the phobias most often found in U.S. metropolitan areas have to do with high places, airplanes and dirt. Fear of heights is not a serious matter if it involves only skyscrapers: an occasional high-steel worker or window-washer has to change his job because of this. But many people, as they grow older, become neurotically cautious, get to the stage where they cannot even go near a window above the ground floor. In such severe cases, the anxiety usually extends far beyond this symptom and pervades the whole personality. Airplanes evoke a comparable phobia. In practical terms, such case histories seem relatively simple:

A traveling salesman may be economically crippled and have to change jobs if his company orders him to leave the rails and take to the air. Viewed more philosophically, such cases may suggest a protest against man's high-flying pride.

Dread of dirt (mysophobia) goes hand in overwashed hand with the cleanliness compulsion. The victim must carry out his cleansing routine even though he knows it is unreasonable. Otherwise, he finds himself the prisoner of intolerable anxiety. The cleanliness compulsion commonly arises from conflict involving a strict and perfectionist parent. The victim begins by being simply overneat and fussy about cleanliness.

Then he gets into conflict with all the people around him who do not comply with his compulsive standards. His compulsion may drive him to excessive washing of his body, of clothes, and even doorknobs. (One legendary American tycoon would not shake hands or touch a doorknob unless he had on white cotton gloves.) He gets to the point where he actually washes the skin off his hands and has to go into a hospital.

Most in the Middle. Research in recent years has shown some fairly clear patterns about where anxiety develops. It is greatest where change is swiftest. Children are not very susceptible to it; their problems of adjustment are normal for their age (adolescents show confusing symptoms). Anxiety is most apparent in the 20-to-40 age group. These youngish adults may not suffer from it more than their elders, but they talk more about it. In any case, they are the most active and mobile members of society, constantly making decisions, changing jobs or moving to new locations. From 40 to 70, anxiety is usually better controlled or concealed. Above 70, it breaks out again, now that modern medicine has so greatly prolonged the lives of so many people who are financially and socially insecure, who feel unwanted, useless and rejected.

By social stratification, reports Cornell University's Dr. Lawrence Hinkle, there is least anxiety at the top and bottom, and most in between. An upsurge of anxiety has begun, and more is predicted, among Negroes, for whom possiblities of social and economic advancement, to a degree undreamed of at war's end, are now developing. Puerto Rican and Mexican immigrants will have their innings with anxiety later; opportunities for mobility and morbidity go together.

Wherever there is opportunity, there is anxiety: it is just as severe in the ivied halls of research institutions as it is in the garment district—or in some Government offices. And it is far more severe than it used to be on farms. Big business, on the other hand, is not, as often described, a single pail of anxiously writhing worms. Some giant corporations have become "settled societies" of their own, in which the rungs of the promotion ladder are neatly numbered and everybody knows when he may have his chance to step up. But in advertising, communications and entertainment, anxiety is extensive and vociferously proclaimed; half the name actors on Broadway and in Hollywood have been analyzed, and the others should never be allowed off the couch.

Priests and Prisoners. It is among writers and other editorial workers that Raymond B. Cattell and Ivan H. Sheier of the University of Illinois have found the highest anxiety ratings, based on complex personality tests. That they come just ahead of the Navy's underwater demolition teams (frogmen) is probably due more to their higher verbal abilities than to on-the-job hazards. Air pilots in training have, naturally, more anxiety than business executives; priests have less—but this may be a reflection of their having found a certainty of faith and of a rigid routine that conceals if it does not catharize anxiety. Convicts have far less than average. This reflects both routine and the high prison population of conscienceless psychopaths. Least anxious of all, on the Cattell-Sheier scale, are university administrators.

Cattell and Sheier give the U.S. a lower anxiety rating than Britain. Explaining this apparent surprise, they suggest that what passes for anxiety in the U.S. is really the stress of effort in a land of ambition, competition and challenge. More convincingly, they note that anxiety is higher in situations where the individual feels unable to save himself. The anxiety of waiting for D-day is worse than the fear of walking through a field of land mines. This principle may help explain the attitude of many U.S. scientists and liberal intellectuals toward The Bomb. The possibility of civilization's total destruction is usually cited as one of the great factors contributing to anxiety in the U.S. But there is a strong suggestion that The Bomb is merely a handy device, welcomed almost with relief, for the release of anxiety and guilt that have little to do with the subject as such. For many Bomb worriers, it seems to be a true phobia, a kind of secular substitute for the Last Judgment, and a truly effective nuclear ban would undoubtedly deprive them of a highly comforting sense of doom.

Drugs for the Mind. What can psychiatry do to combat anxiety and the various mental illnesses it feeds? The Joint Commission on Mental Illness and Health, set up by Congress in 1955, last week issued an ambitious prescription in a report asking for $3 billion to be spent annually by 1971 (three times the present amount) and for other sweeping reforms to make better psychiatric service more generally available. It also called for a study to find out what is "the public's image of the psychiatrist," suggesting that there is guilt and anxiety within the profession itself.

As for treatment of patients, sedatives ranging in potency from aspirin to barbiturates and narcotics have no effect on the underlying emotional state; all they can do is relieve the symptoms temporarily. Only since 1954 have there been tranquilizing drugs specifically designed and directed toward relieving signs of anxiety. For depression, psychiatrists are now prescribing the psychic energizers, of which half a dozen, such as Marplan and Niamid, have won fairly general acceptance. But talking it out in psychotherapy is generally recognized as the only measure that offers the possibility of a true cure. There is still controversy as to the value of different types of treatment, especially between the advocates of the analytic schools and the psychiatrists who favor shorter, more "directive" therapy. There is some question as to whether guilt feelings should be relieved in all cases. Dr. May reports that diluting a patient's guilt feelings allays superficial anxiety but sometimes obscures the "genuine if confused insights of the patient into himself."

Order Out of Chaos. Beyond curing the obviously sick, psychologists and psychiatrists evidently must make an effort to teach people not so much to eliminate guilt and anxiety as to understand them and live with them constructively. That is the point made by Hans Hofmann, associate professor of theology at Harvard Divinity School, in a new book called *Religion and Mental Health* (Harper). Writes Hofmann:

"Our time is one of ferment and potential rebirth. This is so precisely because it is a time full of chaos . . . It was only natural that Sigmund Freud should at the beginning of his career have thought of the irrational aspects of the human personality as chaotic and potentially dangerous powers . . . It did not occur to him that chaos in itself may represent a very positive and fertile current of life. For the people of the Old Testament, especially in the creation story, the question was not: 'Why is there chaos?' but rather: 'Why is there order?' For them, order was the outgrowth of daily living . . . The unique function of man, in their view, is to live in close, creative touch with chaos, and thereby experience the birth of order . . . Surprisingly enough, modern psychotherapists share this ancient knowledge."

A GLOSSARY OF PHOBIAS

	Fear of:
achluophobia	darkness
aichmophobia	pointed objects
ailurophobia	cats
anthophobia	flowers
astrophobia	stars
ballistophobia	missiles
barophobia	gravity
cherophobia	gaiety
chionophobia	snow
chronophobia	time
climacophobia	staircases
dextrophobia	objects on the right side of the body
erythrophobia	red
gephyrophobia	crossing bridges
graphophobia	writing
hypengyophobia	responsibility

kathisophobia	sitting down
levophobia	objects on the left side of the body
linonophobia	string
ophidiophobia	snakes
pantophobia	everything
phobophobia	being afraid
phonophobia	one's own voice
photophobia	light
phronemophobia	thinking
scopophobia	being seen
siderodromo-	
phobia	railroad traveling
sitophobia	eating
stasibasiphobia	walking or standing
thalassophobia	the ocean
vermiphobia	infestation with worms

STUDY QUESTIONS

1. Does *Time* magazine's analysis of *angst* vindicate Henry Adams's fears of the anarchical new forces?
2. Why did men feel insecure when Copernicus and Galileo tinkered with the universe?
3. According to *Time,* why do psychiatrists and theologians feel that a certain amount of guilt and anxiety is *inevitable* and *necessary* in man?
4. When does *existential anxiety* become *neurotic anxiety?*
5. Why do we find it so hard to accept such Freudian analyses as that of little Hans?
6. How has the artist contributed to the anxiety of contemporary man?

Nathaniel Hawthorne   YOUNG GOODMAN BROWN

Nathaniel Hawthorne (1804–1864) was born in Salem, Massachusetts. Among his ancestors was the Judge Hathorne who presided over the Salem witch trials. He graduated from Bowdoin College, where his classmates included Henry Wadsworth Longfellow and Franklin Pierce. His first novel, *Fanshawe,* was pub-

First published 1835.

lished in 1828. This was followed by *Twice-Told Tales* (1837),
Mosses from an Old Manse (1846), *The Scarlet Letter* (1850),
The House of Seven Gables (1851), *The Blithedale Romance* and
A Wonder Book (1852), *Tanglewood Tales* (1853), and *The
Marble Faun* (1860). Hawthorne served as surveyor at the Boston
Custom House and, after the publication of *The Life of Franklin
Pierce* (1852), was named consul to Liverpool.

Young Goodman Brown came forth at sunset into the street at
Salem village; but put his head back, after crossing the threshold, to
exchange a parting kiss with his young wife. And Faith, as the wife was
aptly named, thrust her own pretty head into the street, letting the wind
play with the pink ribbons of her cap while she called to Goodman
Brown.

"Dearest heart," whispered she, softly and rather sadly, when her
lips were close to his ear, "prithee put off your journey until sunrise and
sleep in your own bed tonight. A lone woman is troubled with such
dreams and such thoughts that she's afeard of herself sometimes. Pray
tarry with me this night, dear husband, of all nights in the year."

"My love and my Faith," replied young Goodman Brown, "of all
nights in the year, this one night must I tarry away from thee. My
journey, as thou callest it, forth and back again, must needs be done
'twixt now and sunrise. What, my sweet, pretty wife, dost thou doubt me
already, and we but three months married?"

"Then God bless you!" said Faith, with the pink ribbons; "and may
you find all well when you come back."

"Amen!" cried Goodman Brown. "Say thy prayers, dear Faith, and
go to bed at dusk, and no harm will come to thee."

So they parted; and the young man pursued his way until, being
about to turn the corner by the meeting-house, he looked back and saw
the head of Faith still peeping after him with a melancholy air, in spite
of her pink ribbons.

"Poor little Faith!" thought he, for his heart smote him. "What a
wretch am I to leave her on such an errand! She talks of dreams, too.
Methought as she spoke there was trouble in her face, as if a dream had
warned her what work is to be done tonight. But no, no; 't would kill her
to think it. Well, she's a blessed angel on earth; and after this one night
I'll cling to her skirts and follow her to heaven."

With this excellent resolve for the future, Goodman Brown felt
himself justified in making more haste on his present evil purpose. He
had taken a dreary road, darkened by all the gloomiest trees of the
forest, which barely stood aside to let the narrow path creep through,
and closed immediately behind. It was all as lonely as could be; and
there is this peculiarity in such a solitude, that the traveller knows not
who may be concealed by the innumerable trunks and the thick boughs

overhead; so that with lonely footsteps he may yet be passing through an unseen multitude.

"There may be a devilish Indian behind every tree," said Goodman Brown to himself; and he glanced fearfully behind him as he added, "What if the devil himself should be at my very elbow!"

His head being turned back, he passed a crook of the road, and, looking forward again, beheld the figure of a man, in grave and decent attire, seated at the foot of an old tree. He arose at Goodman Brown's approach and walked onward side by side with him.

"You are late, Goodman Brown," said he. "The clock of the Old South was striking as I came through Boston, and that is full fifteen minutes agone."

"Faith kept me back a while," replied the young man, with a tremor in his voice, caused by the sudden appearance of his companion, though not wholly unexpected.

It was now deep dusk in the forest, and deepest in that part of it where these two were journeying. As nearly as could be discerned, the second traveller was about fifty years old, apparently in the same rank of life as Goodman Brown, and bearing a considerable resemblance to him, though perhaps more in expression than features. Still they might have been taken for father and son. And yet, though the elder person was as simply clad as the younger, and as simple in manner too, he had an indescribable air of one who knew the world, and who would not have felt abashed at the governor's dinner table or in King William's court, were it possible that his affairs should call him thither. But the only thing about him that could be fixed upon as remarkable was his staff, which bore the likeness of a great black snake, so curiously wrought that it might almost be seen to twist and wriggle itself like a living serpent. This, of course, must have been an ocular deception, assisted by the uncertain light.

"Come, Goodman Brown," cried his fellow-traveller, "this is a dull pace for the beginning of a journey. Take my staff, if you are so soon weary."

"Friend," said the other, exchanging his slow pace for a full stop, "having kept covenant by meeting thee here, it is my purpose now to return whence I came. I have scruples touching the matter thou wot'st of."

"Sayest thou so?" replied he of the serpent, smiling apart. "Let us walk on, nevertheless, reasoning as we go; and if I convince thee not thou shalt turn back. We are but a little way in the forest yet."

"Too far! too far!" exclaimed the goodman, unconsciously resuming his walk. "My father never went into the woods on such an errand, nor his father before him. We have been a race of honest men and good Christians since the days of the martyrs; and shall I be the first of the name of Brown that ever took his path and kept—"

"Such company, thou wouldst say," observed the elder person, interpreting his pause. "Well said, Goodman Brown! I have been as well acquainted with your family as with ever a one among the Puritans; and that's no trifle to say. I helped your grandfather, the constable, when he lashed the Quaker woman so smartly through the streets of Salem; and it was I that brought your father a pitch-pine knot, kindled at my own hearth, to set fire to an Indian village, in King Philip's war. They were my good friends, both; and many a pleasant walk have we had along this path, and returned merrily after midnight. I would fain be friends with you for their sake."

"If it be as thou sayest," replied Goodman Brown, "I marvel they never spoke of these matters; or, verily, I marvel not, seeing that the least rumor of the sort would have driven them from New England. We are a people of prayer, and good works to boot, and abide no such wickedness."

"Wickedness or not," said the traveller with the twisted staff, "I have a very general acquaintance here in New England. The deacons of many a church have drunk the communion wine with me; the selectmen of divers towns make me their chairman; and a majority of the Great and General Court are firm supporters of my interest. The governor and I, too—But these are state secrets."

"Can this be so?" cried Goodman Brown, with a stare of amazement at his undisturbed companion. "Howbeit, I have nothing to do with the governor and council; they have their own ways, and are no rule for a simple husbandman like me. But, were I to go on with thee, how should I meet the eye of that good old man, our minister, at Salem village? Oh, his voice would make me tremble both Sabbath day and lecture day."

Thus far the elder traveller had listened with due gravity; but now burst into a fit of irrepressible mirth, shaking himself so violently that his snake-like staff actually seemed to wriggle in sympathy.

"Ha! ha! ha!" shouted he again and again; then composing himself, "Well, go on, Goodman Brown, go on; but, prithee, don't kill me with laughing."

"Well, then, to end the matter at once," said Goodman Brown, considerably nettled, "there is my wife, Faith. It would break her dear little heart; and I'd rather break my own."

"Nay, if that be the case," answered the other, "e'en go thy ways, Goodman Brown. I would not for twenty old women like the one hobbling before us that Faith should come to any harm."

As he spoke he pointed his staff at a female figure on the path, in whom Goodman Brown recognized a very pious and exemplary dame, who had taught him his catechism in youth, and was still his moral and spiritual adviser, jointly with the minister and Deacon Gookin.

"A marvel, truly, that Goody Cloyse should be so far in the wilderness at nightfall," said he. "But with your leave, friend, I shall take a cut through the woods until we have left this Christian woman behind. Being a stranger to you, she might ask whom I was consorting with and whither I was going."

"Be it so," said his fellow-traveller. "Betake you to the woods, and let me keep the path."

Accordingly the young man turned aside, but took care to watch his companion, who advanced softly along the road until he had come within a staff's length of the old dame. She, meanwhile, was making the best of her way, with singular speed for so aged a woman, and mumbling some indistinct words—a prayer, doubtless—as she went. The traveller put forth his staff and touched her withered neck with what seemed the serpent's tail.

"The devil!" screamed the pious old lady.

"Then Goody Cloyse knows her old friend?" observed the traveller, confronting her and leaning on his writhing stick.

"Ah, forsooth, and is it your worship indeed?" cried the good dame. "Yea, truly is it, and in the very image of my old gossip, Goodman Brown, the grandfather of the silly fellow that now is. But—would your worship believe it?—my broomstick hath strangely disappeared, stolen, as I suspect, by that unhanged witch, Goody Cory, and that, too, when I was all anointed with the juice of smallage, and cinquefoil, and wolf's bane—"

"Mingled with fine wheat and the fat of a new-born babe," said the shape of old Goodman Brown.

"Ah, your worship knows the recipe," cried the old lady, cackling aloud. "So, as I was saying, being all ready for the meeting, and no horse to ride on, I made up my mind to foot it; for they tell me there is a nice young man to be taken into communion tonight. But now your good worship will lend me your arm, and we shall be there in a twinkling."

"That can hardly be," answered her friend. "I may not spare you my arm, Goody Cloyse; but here is my staff, if you will."

So saying, he threw it down at her feet, where, perhaps, it assumed life, being one of the rods which its owner had formerly lent to the Egyptian magi. Of this fact, however, Goodman Brown could not take cognizance. He had cast up his eyes in astonishment, and, looking down again, beheld neither Goody Cloyse nor the serpentine staff, but his fellow-traveller alone, who waited for him as calmly as if nothing had happened.

"That old woman taught me my catechism," said the young man; and there was a world of meaning in this simple comment.

They continued to walk onward, while the elder traveller exhorted his companion to make good speed and persevere in the path, discoursing so aptly that his arguments seemed rather to spring up in the bosom of his auditor than to be suggested by himself. As they went, he plucked a branch of maple to serve for a walking stick, and began to strip it of the twigs and little boughs, which were wet with evening dew. The moment his fingers touched them they became strangely withered and dried up as with a week's sunshine. Thus the pair proceeded, at a good free pace, until suddenly, in a gloomy hollow of the road, Goodman Brown sat himself down on the stump of a tree and refused to go any farther.

"Friend," said he, stubbornly, "my mind is made up. Not another step will I budge on this errand. What if a wretched old woman do choose to go to the devil when I thought she was going to heaven: is that any reason why I should quit my dear Faith and go after her?"

"You will think better of this by and by," said his acquintance, composedly. "Sit here and rest yourself a while; and when you feel like moving again, there is my staff to help you along."

Without more words, he threw his companion the maple stick, and was as speedily out of sight as if he had vanished into the deepening gloom. The young man sat a few moments by the roadside, applauding himself greatly, and thinking with how clear a conscience he should meet the minister in his morning walk, nor shrink from the eye of good old Deacon Gookin. And what calm sleep would be his that very night, which was to have been spent so wickedly, but so purely and sweetly now, in the arms of Faith! Amidst these pleasant and praiseworthy meditations, Goodman Brown heard the tramp of horses along the road, and deemed it advisable to conceal himself within the verge of the forest, conscious of the guilty purpose that had brought him thither, though now so happily turned from it.

On came the hoof tramps and the voices of the riders, two grave old voices, conversing soberly as they drew near. These mingled sounds appeared to pass along the road, within a few yards of the young man's hiding-place; but, owing doubtless to the depth of the gloom at that particular spot, neither the travellers nor their steeds were visible. Though their figures brushed the small boughs by the wayside, it could not be seen that they intercepted, even for a moment, the faint gleam from the strip of bright sky athwart which they must have passed. Goodman Brown alternately crouched and stood on tiptoe, pulling aside the branches and thrusting forth his head as far as he durst without discerning so much as a shadow. It vexed him the more, because he could have sworn, were such a thing possible, that he recognized the voices of the minister and Deacon Gookin, jogging along quietly, as they were wont to do, when bound to some ordination or ecclesiastical council. While yet within hearing, one of the riders stopped to pluck a switch.

"Of the two, reverend sir," said the voice like the deacon's, "I had rather miss an ordination dinner than tonight's meeting. They tell me that some of our community are to be here from Falmouth and beyond, and others from Connecticut and Rhode Island, besides several of the Indian powwows, who, after their fashion, know almost as much deviltry as the best of us. Moreover, there is a goodly young woman to be taken into communion."

"Mighty well, Deacon Gookin!" replied the solemn old tones of the minister. "Spur up, or we shall be late. Nothing can be done, you know, until I get on the ground."

The hoofs clattered again; and the voices, talking so strangely in the empty air, passed on through the forest, where no church had ever been gathered or solitary Christian prayed. Whither, then, could these holy men be journeying so deep into the heathen wilderness? Young Goodman Brown caught hold of a tree for support, being ready to sink down on the ground, faint and overburdened with the heavy sickness of his heart. He looked up to the sky, doubting whether there really was a heaven above him. Yet there was the blue arch, and the stars brightening in it.

"With heaven above and Faith below, I will yet stand firm against the devil!" cried Goodman Brown.

While he still gazed upward into the deep arch of the firmament and had lifted his hands to pray, a cloud, though no wind was stirring, hurried across the zenith and hid the brightening stars. The blue sky was still visible, except directly overhead, where this black mass of cloud was sweeping swiftly northward. Aloft in the air, as if from the depths of the cloud, came a confused and doubtful sound of voices. Once the listener fancied that he could distinguish the accents of towns-people of his own, men and women, both pious and ungodly, many of whom he had met at the communion table, and had seen others rioting at the tavern. The next moment, so indistinct were the sounds, he doubted whether he had heard aught but the murmur of the old forest, whispering without a wind. Then came a stronger swell of those familiar tones, heard daily in the sunshine at Salem village, but never until now from a cloud of night. There was one voice of a young woman, uttering lamentations, yet with an uncertain sorrow, and entreating for some favor, which, perhaps, it would grieve her to obtain; and all the unseen multitude, both saints and sinners, seemed to encourage her onward.

"Faith!" shouted Goodman Brown, in a voice of agony and desperation; and the echoes of the forest mocked him, crying, "Faith! Faith!" as if bewildered wretches were seeking her all through the wilderness.

The cry of grief, rage, and terror was yet piercing the night, when the unhappy husband held his breath for a response. There was a scream, drowned immediately in a louder murmur of voices, fading into far-off laughter, as the dark cloud swept away, leaving the clear and

silent sky above Goodman Brown. But something fluttered lightly down
through the air and caught on the branch of a tree. The young man
seized it, and beheld a pink ribbon.

"My Faith is gone!" cried he, after one stupefied moment. "There
is no good on earth; and sin is but a name. Come, devil; for to thee is
this world given."

And, maddened with despair, so that he laughed loud and long,
did Goodman Brown grasp his staff and set forth again, at such a rate
that he seemed to fly along the forest path rather than to walk or run.
The road grew wilder and drearier and more faintly traced, and vanished at length, leaving him in the heart of the dark wilderness, still
rushing onward with the instinct that guides mortal man to evil. The
whole forest was peopled with frightful sounds—the creaking of the trees,
the howling of wild beasts, and the yell of Indians; while sometimes the
wind tolled like a distant church bell, and sometimes gave a broad roar
around the traveller, as if all Nature were laughing him to scorn. But he
was himself the chief horror of the scene, and shrank not from its other
horrors.

"Ha! ha! ha!" roared Goodman Brown when the wind laughed at
him. "Let us hear which will laugh loudest. Think not to frighten me
with your deviltry. Come witch, come wizard, come Indian powwow,
come devil himself, and here comes Goodman Brown. You may as well
fear him as he fear you."

In truth, all through the haunted forest there could be nothing
more frightful than the figure of Goodman Brown. On he flew among the
black pines, brandishing his staff with frenzied gestures, now giving vent
to an inspiration of horrid blasphemy, and now shouting forth such
laughter as set all the echoes of the forest laughing like demons around
him. The fiend in his own shape is less hideous than when he rages in
the breast of man. Thus sped the demoniac on his course, until, quivering among the trees, he saw a red light before him, as when the felled
trunks and branches of a clearing have been set on fire, and throw up
their lurid blaze against the sky, at the hour of midnight. He paused, in
a lull of the tempest that had driven him onward, and heard the swell of
what seemed a hymn, rolling solemnly from a distance with the weight
of many voices. He knew the tune; it was a familiar one in the choir of
the village meeting-house. The verse died heavily away, and was
lengthened by a chorus, not of human voices, but of all the sounds of the
benighted wilderness pealing in awful harmony together. Goodman
Brown cried out, and his cry was lost to his own ear by its unison with
the cry of the desert.

In the interval of silence he stole forward until the light glared full
upon his eyes. At one extremity of an open space, hemmed in by the
dark wall of the forest, arose a rock, bearing some rude, natural resem-

blance either to an altar or a pulpit, and surrounded by four blazing pines, their tops aflame, their stems untouched, like candles at an evening meeting. The mass of foliage that had overgrown the summit of the rock was all on fire, blazing high into the night and fitfully illuminating the whole field. Each pendent twig and leafy festoon was in a blaze. As the red light arose and fell, a numerous congregation alternately shone forth, then disappeared in shadow, and again grew, as it were, out of the darkness, peopling the heart of the solitary woods at once.

"A grave and dark-clad company," quoth Goodman Brown.

In truth they were such. Among them, quivering to and fro between gloom and splendor, appeared faces that would be seen next day at the council board of the province, and others which, Sabbath after Sabbath, looked devoutly heavenward, and benignantly over the crowded pews, from the holiest pulpits in the land. Some affirm that the lady of the governor was there. At least there were high dames well known to her, and wives of honored husbands, and widows, a great multitude, and ancient maidens, all of excellent repute, and fair young girls, who trembled lest their mothers should espy them. Either the sudden gleams of light flashing over the obscure field bedazzled Goodman Brown, or he recognized a score of the church members of Salem village famous for their especial sanctity. Good old Deacon Gookin had arrived, and waited at the skirts of that venerable saint, his revered pastor. But, irreverently consorting with these grave, reputable, and pious people, these elders of the church, these chaste dames and dewy virgins, there were men of dissolute lives and women of spotted fame, wretches given over to all mean and filthy vice, and suspected even of horrid crimes. It was strange to see that the good shrank not from the wicked, nor were the sinners abashed by the saints. Scattered also among their pale-faced enemies were the Indian priests, or powwows, who had often scared their native forest with more hideous incantations than any known to English witchcraft.

"But where is Faith?" thought Goodman Brown; and, as hope came into his heart, he trembled.

Another verse of the hymn arose, a slow and mournful strain, such as the pious love, but joined to words which expressed all that our nature can conceive of sin, and darkly hinted at far more. Unfathomable to mere mortals is the lore of fiends. Verse after verse was sung; and still the chorus of the desert swelled between like the deepest tone of a mighty organ; and with the final peal of that dreadful anthem there came a sound, as if the roaring wind, the rushing streams, the howling beasts, and every other voice of the unconcerted wilderness were mingling and according with the voice of guilty man in homage to the prince of all. The four blazing pines threw up a loftier flame, and obscurely discovered shapes and visages of horror on the smoke wreaths above the impious assembly. At the same moment the fire on the rock shot redly forth and formed a glowing arch above its base, where now appeared a figure. With reverence be it spoken, the figure bore no slight similitude, both in garb and manner, to some grave divine of the New England churches.

"Bring forth the converts!" cried a voice that echoed through the field and rolled into the forest.

At the word, Goodman Brown stepped forth from the shadow of the trees and approached the congregation, with whom he felt a loathful brotherhood by the sympathy of all that was wicked in his heart. He could have well-nigh sworn that the shape of his own dead father beckoned him to advance, looking downward from a smoke wreath, while a woman, with dim features of despair, threw out her hand to warn him back. Was it his mother? But he had no power to retreat one step, nor to resist, even in thought, when the minister and good old Deacon Gookin seized his arms and led him to the blazing rock. Thither came also the slender form of a veiled female, led between Goody Cloyse, that pious teacher of the catechism, and Martha Carrier, who had received the devil's promise to be queen of hell. A rampant hag was she. And there stood the proselytes beneath the canopy of fire.

"Welcome, my children," said the dark figure, "to the communion of your race. Ye have found thus young your nature and your destiny. My children, look behind you!"

They turned; and flashing forth, as it were, in à sheet of flame, the fiend worshippers were seen; the smile of welcome gleamed darkly on every visage.

"There," resumed the sable form, "are all whom ye have reverenced from youth. Ye deemed them holier than yourselves, and shrank from your own sin, contrasting it with their lives of righteousness and prayerful aspirations heavenward. Yet here are they all in my worshipping assembly. This night it shall be granted you to know their secret deeds: how hoary-bearded elders of the church have whispered wanton words to the young maids of their households; how many a woman, eager for widows' weeds, has given her husband a drink at bedtime and let him sleep his last sleep in her bosom; how beardless youths have made haste to inherit their fathers' wealth; and how fair damsels—blush not, sweet ones—have dug little graves in the garden, and bidden me, the sole guest to an infant's funeral. By the sympathy of your human hearts for sin ye shall scent out all the places—whether in church, bedchamber, street, field, or forest—where crime has been committed, and shall exult to behold the whole earth one stain of guilt, one mighty blood spot. Far more than this. It shall be yours to penetrate, in every bosom, the deep mystery of sin, the fountain of all wicked arts, and which inexhaustibly supplies more evil impulses than human power—than my power at its utmost—can make manifest in deeds. And now, my children, look upon each other."

They did so; and, by the blaze of the hell-kindled torches, the wretched man beheld his Faith, and the wife her husband, trembling before that unhallowed altar.

"Lo, there ye stand, my children," said the figure, in a deep and solemn tone, almost sad with its despairing awfulness, as if his once angelic nature could yet mourn for our miserable race. "Depending upon one another's hearts, ye had still hoped that virtue were not all a dream. Now are ye undeceived. Evil is the nature of mankind. Evil must be your only happiness. Welcome again, my children, to the communion of your race."

"Welcome," repeated the fiend worshippers, in one cry of despair and triumph.

And there they stood, the only pair, as it seemed, who were yet hesitating on the verge of wickedness in this dark world. A basin was hollowed, naturally, in the rock. Did it contain water, reddened by the lurid light? or was it blood? or, perchance, a liquid flame? Herein did the shape of evil dip his hand and prepare to lay the mark of baptism upon their foreheads, that they might be partakers of the mystery of sin, more conscious of the secret guilt of others, both in deed and thought, than they could now be of their own. The husband cast one look at his pale wife, and Faith at him. What polluted wretches would the next glance show them to each other, shuddering alike at what they disclosed and what they saw!

"Faith! Faith!" cried the husband, "look up to heaven, and resist the wicked one."

Whether Faith obeyed he knew not. Hardly had he spoken when he found himself amid calm night and solitude, listening to a roar of the wind which died heavily away through the forest. He staggered against the rock, and felt it chill and damp; while a hanging twig, that had been all on fire, besprinkled his cheek with the coldest dew.

The next morning young Goodman Brown came slowly into the street of Salem village, staring around him like a bewildered man. The good old minister was taking a walk along the graveyard to get an appetite for breakfast and meditate his sermon, and bestowed a blessing, as he passed, on Goodman Brown. He shrank from the venerable saint as if to avoid an anathema. Old Deacon Gookin was at domestic worship, and the holy words of his prayer were heard through the open window. "What God doth the wizard pray to?" quoth Goodman Brown. Goody Cloyse, that excellent old Christian, stood in the early sunshine at her own lattice, catechizing a little girl who had brought her a pint of morning's milk. Goodman Brown snatched away the child as from the grasp of the fiend himself. Turning the corner by the meeting-house, he spied the head of Faith, with the pink ribbons, gazing anxiously forth, and bursting into such joy at sight of him that she skipped along the street and almost kissed her husband before the whole village. But Goodman Brown looked sternly and sadly into her face, and passed on without a greeting.

Had Goodman Brown fallen asleep in the forest and only dreamed a wild dream of a witch-meeting?

Be it so if you will; but, alas! it was a dream of evil omen for young Goodman Brown. A stern, a sad, a darkly meditative, a distrustful, if not a desperate man did he become from the night of that fearful dream. On the Sabbath day, when the congregation were singing a holy psalm, he could not listen because an anthem of sin rushed loudly upon his ear and drowned all the blessed strain. When the minister spoke from the pulpit with power and fervid eloquence, and, with his hand on the open Bible, of the sacred truths of our religion, and of saint-like lives and triumphant deaths, and of future bliss or misery unutterable, then did Goodman Brown turn pale, dreading lest the roof should thunder down upon the gray blasphemer and his hearers. Often, waking suddenly at midnight, he shrank from the bosom of Faith; and at morning or eventide, when the family knelt down at prayer, he scowled and muttered to himself, and gazed sternly at his wife, and turned away. And when he had lived long, and was borne to his grave a hoary corpse, followed by Faith, an aged woman, and children and grandchildren, a goodly procession, besides neighbors not a few, they carved no hopeful verse upon his tombstone, for his dying hour was gloom.

STUDY QUESTIONS

1. What is an allegory? A parable? Is "Young Goodman Brown" either allegory or parable?
2. Why does Hawthorne repeatedly focus attention on Faith's pink ribbons?
3. What is the significance of Young Goodman Brown's "excellent resolve for the future"?
4. Does Young Goodman Brown see the minister and Deacon Gookin?
5. Why does the narrator call Young Goodman Brown the "chief horror of the scene"?
6. Cite instances in "Young Goodman Brown" when reality and appearance are called into question.

HAWTHORNE'S
"YOUNG GOODMAN BROWN":
AN ATTACK ON PURITANIC
Thomas E. Connolly **CALVINISM**

Thomas E. Connolly (1918–   ) was born in New York. He received an S.B. (1939) from Fordham University and an A.M. (1947) and a Ph.D. (1951) from the University of Chicago. He has taught at the University of Idaho and Creighton University, and is currently at the State University of Buffalo, New York. In addition to his contributions to scholarly journals, he has published three books about James Joyce.

It is surprising, in a way, to discover how few of the many critics who have discussed "Young Goodman Brown" agree on any aspect of the work except that it is an excellent short story. D. M. McKeithan says that its theme is "sin and its blighting effects." [1] Richard H. Fogle observes, "Hawthorne the artist refuses to limit himself to a single and doctrinaire conclusion, proceeding instead by indirection," [2] implying, presumably, that it is inartistic to say something which can be clearly understood by the readers. Gordon and Tate assert, "Hawthorne is dealing with his favorite theme: the unhappiness which the human heart suffers as a result of its innate depravity." [3] Austin Warren says, "His point is the devastating effect of moral scepticism." [4] Almost all critics agree, however, that Young Goodman Brown lost his faith. Their conclusions are based, perhaps, upon the statement, "My Faith is gone!" made by Brown when he recognizes his wife's voice and ribbon. I should like to examine the story once more to show that Young Goodman Brown did

Reprinted from *American Literature*, XXVIII (1956), by permission of the Duke University Press and Thomas E. Connolly.

[1] D. M. McKeithan, "Hawthorne's 'Young Goodman Brown': An Interpretation," *Modern Language Notes*, LXVII (February, 1952), 94.
[2] Richard H. Fogle, "Ambiguity and Clarity in Hawthorne's 'Young Goodman Brown,' " *New England Quarterly*, XVIII (December, 1945), 453.
[3] Caroline Gordon and Allen Tate (eds.), *The House of Fiction* (New York, 1950), p. 38.
[4] Austin Warren, *Nathaniel Hawthorne* (New York, 1934), p. 362.

not lose his faith at all. In fact, not only did he retain his faith, but during his horrible experience he actually discovered the full and frightening significance of his faith.

Mrs. Leavis comes closest to the truth in her discussion of this story in the *Sewanee Review* in which she says: "Hawthorne has imaginatively recreated for the reader that Calvinist sense of sin, that theory which did in actuality shape the early social and spiritual history of New England." [5] But Mrs. Leavis seems to miss the critical implications of the story, for she goes on to say: "But in Hawthorne, by a wonderful feat of transmutation, it has no religious significance, it is a psychological state that is explored. Young Goodman Brown's Faith is not faith in Christ but faith in human beings, and losing it he is doomed to isolation forever." [6] Those who persist in reading this story as a study of the effects of sin on Brown come roughly to this conclusion: "Goodman Brown became evil as a result of sin and thought he saw evil *where none existed.*" [7] Hawthorne's message is far more depressing and horrifying than this. The story is obviously an individual tragedy, and those who treat it as such are right, of course; but, far beyond the personal plane, it has universal implications.

Young Goodman Brown, as a staunch Calvinist, is seen at the beginning of this allegory to be quite confident that he is going to heaven. The errand on which he is going is presented mysteriously and is usually interpreted to be a deliberate quest of sin. This may or may not be true; what is important is that he is going out to meet the devil by prearrangement. We are told by the narrator that his purpose in going is evil. When the devil meets him, he refers to the "beginning of a journey." Brown admits that he "kept covenant" by meeting the devil and hints at the evil purpose of the meeting.

Though his family has been Christian for generations, the point is made early in the story that Young Goodman Brown has been married to his Faith for only three months. Either the allegory breaks down at this point or the marriage to Faith must be looked upon as the moment of conversion to grace in which he became fairly sure of his election to heaven. That Goodman Brown is convinced he is of the elect is made clear at the beginning: ". . . and after this one night I'll cling to her skirts and follow her to heaven." In other words, at the start of his adventure, Young Goodman Brown is certain that his faith will help man get to heaven. It is in this concept that his disillusionment will come. The irony of this illusion is brought out when he explains to the devil the reason for his tardiness: "Faith kept me back awhile." That is what

[5] Q. D. Leavis, "Hawthorne as Poet," *Sewanee Review*, LIX (Spring 1951), 197–198.
[6] *Ibid.*
[7] McKeithan, *op. cit.*, p. 95. Italics mine.

he thinks! By the time he gets to the meeting place he finds that his Faith is already there. Goodman Brown's disillusionment in his belief begins quickly after meeting the devil. He has asserted proudly that his ancestors "have been a race of honest men and good Christians since the days of the martyrs," and the devil turns his own words on him smartly:

> Well said, Goodman Brown! I have been as well acquainted with your family as with ever a one among the Puritans; and that's no trifle to say. I helped your grandfather, the constable, when he lashed the Quaker woman so smartly through the streets of Salem; and it was I that brought your father a pitch-pine knot, kindled at my own hearth, to set fire to an Indian village, in King Philip's war. They were my good friends, both; and many a pleasant walk have we had along this path, and returned merrily after midnight. I would fain be friends with you for their sake.

Goodman Brown manages to shrug off this identification of his parental and grandparental Puritanism with the devil, but the reader should not overlook the sharp tone of criticism in Hawthorne's presentation of this speech.

When the devil presents his next argument, Brown is a little more shaken. The devil has shown him that Goody Cloyse is of his company and Brown responds: "What if a wretched old woman do choose to go to the devil when I thought she was going to heaven: is that any reason why I should quit my dear Faith and go after her?" He still believes at this point that his faith will lead him to heaven. The devil's reply, "You will think better of this by and by," is enigmatic when taken by itself, but a little earlier the narrator had made a comment which throws a great deal of light on this remark by the devil. When he recognized Goody Cloyse, Brown said, "That old woman taught me my catechism," and the narrator added, "and there was a world of meaning in this simple comment." The reader at this point should be fairly well aware of Hawthorne's criticism of Calvinism. The only way there can be a "world of meaning" in Brown's statement is that her catechism teaches the way to the devil and not the way to heaven.

From this point on Brown is rapidly convinced that his original conception about his faith is wrong. Deacon Gookin and the "good old minister," in league with Satan, finally lead the way to his recognition that this faith is diabolic rather than divine. Hawthorne points up this fact by a bit of allegorical symbolism. Immediately after he recognizes the voices of the deacon and the minister, we are told by the narrator that "Young Goodman Brown caught hold of a tree for support, being ready to sink down on the ground, faint and overburdened with the heavy sickness of his heart. He looked up to the sky, doubting whether there really was a heaven above him. Yet there was a blue arch, and the stars brightened in it." Here the doubt has begun to gnaw, but the stars are symbols of the faint hope which he is still able to cherish, and he is able to say: "With heaven above and Faith below, I will yet stand firm against the devil." But immediately a symbolic cloud hides the symbolic stars: "While he still gazed upward into the deep arch of the firmament and had lifted his hands to pray, a cloud, though no wind was stirring, hurried across the zenith and hid the brightening stars." And it is out of this black cloud of doubt that the voice of his faith reaches him and the pink ribbon of his Faith falls.[8] It might be worthwhile to discuss Faith's pink ribbons here, for Hawthorne certainly took great pains to call them to our attention. The ribbons seem to be symbolic of his initial illusion about the true significance of his faith, his belief that his faith will lead him to heaven. The pink ribbons on a Puritan lady's cap, signs of youth, joy, and happiness, are actually entirely out of keeping with the severity of the rest of her dress which, if not somber black, is at least gray. When the ribbon falls from his cloud of doubt, Goodman Brown cries in agony, "My Faith is gone!" and it is gone in the sense that it now means not what it once meant. He is quick to apply the logical, ultimate conclusion of Goody Cloyse's catechizing: "Come, devil; for to thee is this world given."

Lest the reader miss the ultimate implication of the doctrine of predestination, Hawthorne has the devil preach a sermon at his communion service: "Welcome, my children . . . to the communion of your race. Ye have found thus young your nature and your destiny." Calvinism teaches that man is innately depraved and that he can do nothing to merit salvation. He is saved only by the whim of God who selects some, through no deserts of their own, for heaven while the great mass of mankind is destined for hell. The devil concludes his sermon: "Evil is the nature of mankind. Evil must be your only happiness. Welcome again, my children, to the communion of your race." It is not at all insignificant that the word *race* is used several times in this passage, for it was used earlier by Goodman Brown when he said, "We have been a race of honest men and good Christians. . . ." After this sermon by the devil, Young Goodman Brown makes one last effort to retain the illusion that faith will lead him to heaven; he calls out: "Faith! Faith! . . . look up to heaven, and resist the wicked one." But we are fairly sure that he is unsuccessful, for we are immediately told: "Whether Faith obeyed he knew not."

Young Goodman Brown did not lose his faith (we are even told that his Faith survived him); he learned its full and terrible significance.

---

[8] F. O. Matthiessen made entirely too much of the wrong thing of this ribbon. Had Young Goodman Brown returned to Salem Village clutching the ribbon, there might be some point in what Matthiessen says (*American Renaissance*, New York, 1941, pp. 282–284). As it is, the ribbon presents no more of a problem than do the burning trees turned suddenly cold again.

This story is Hawthorne's criticism of the teachings of Puritanic-Calvinism. His implication is that the doctrine of the elect and damned is not a faith which carries man heavenward on its skirts, as Brown once believed, but, instead, condemns him to hell—bad and good alike indiscriminately—and for all intents and purposes so few escape as to make one man's chance of salvation almost disappear. It is this awakening to the full meaning of his faith which causes Young Goodman Brown to look upon his minister as a blasphemer when he teaches "the sacred truths of our religion, and of saint-like lives and triumphant deaths, and of future bliss or misery unutterable," for he has learned that according to the truths of his faith there is probably nothing but "misery unutterable" in store for him and all his congregation; it is this awakening which causes him to turn away from prayer; it is this awakening which makes appropriate the fact that "they carved no hopeful verse upon his tombstone."

Though much is made of the influence of Puritanism on the writings of Hawthorne, he must also be seen to be a critic of the teachings of Puritanism. Between the position of Vernon L. Parrington,[9] who saw Hawthorne as retaining "much of the older Calvinistic view of life and human destiny," and that of Régis Michaud,[10] who saw him as "an antipuritan and prophet heralding the Freudian gospel," lies the truth about Hawthorne.

STUDY QUESTIONS

1.   Connolly quotes Richard H. Fogle and then interprets Fogle's statement. Is Connolly's interpretation of Fogle a just one?

2.   What is the thesis of Connolly's essay? Is this purpose stated explicitly or implicitly?

3.   Connolly feels that the narrator's comment on Young Goodman Brown's remark about Goody Cloyse reveals Hawthorne's criticism of Calvinism. Can you interpret Brown's remark in another way? The narrator's comment?

4.   What does Connolly think Faith's ribbons symbolize?

5.   Does Connolly's last paragraph suggest that his purpose was twofold: to interpret Hawthorne's short story for the reader, and to interpret Hawthorne *himself* for the reader?

---

[9] *Main Currents in American Thought* (New York, 1927), II, 443.
[10] "How Nathaniel Hawthorne Exorcised Hester Prynne," *The American Novel Today* (Boston, 1928), pp. 25–46.

HAWTHORNE'S CHOICE:
THE VEIL OR
Robert W. Cochran **THE JAUNDICED EYE**

Robert W. Cochran (1926–   ) was born in Williamsport, Penn-
sylvania. He received his A.B. (1948) from Indiana University,
and his M.A. (1949) and Ph.D. (1957) from the University of
Michigan. He is currently Associate Professor of English at the
University of Vermont. Cochran contributes regularly to *College
English*.

In his stories "Young Goodman Brown" and "The Minister's Black
Veil," Hawthorne presents the opposite extremes of reaction to mankind
within a single alternative view of man's nature. Both young Goodman
Brown and the Reverend Mr. Hooper view men as sinners. Yet Brown
ends his life in darkness, disillusionment, and despair; whereas Mr.
Hooper achieves a steady acceptance of life through relative enlightenment, a total recognition of sin and sorrow, and a firm belief in a
traditional afterlife.

Such an interpretation of "The Minister's Black Veil" is at sharp
variance with the consensus view that Hooper, like Brown, lives out his
days and enters the grave the victim of a dark obsession. In his admir-
ably balanced reading of "The Minister's Black Veil," R. H. Fogle interprets the tale as mirroring the ambiguity of life in a parallel ambiguity of
meaning.[1] But the veil can be more definitely identified, without the
oversimplification of which Mr. Hooper's parishioners are guilty and
without arriving at what Fogle terms "a single dogmatic conclusion."

The Reverend Mr. Hooper is regularly said to indulge in a special
form of self-pity, masochistic at base: Hooper is characterized by Fogle
as having an "infatuated love of mystification." The best that may be

Robert W. Cochran, "Hawthorne's Choice: The Veil or The Jaundiced Eye,"
College English, XXIII (1962). Reprinted with the permission of the National
Council of Teachers of English and Robert W. Cochran.

[1] R. H. Fogle, " 'An Ambiguity of Sin or Sorrow,' " *The New England
Quarterly*, 21 (September 1948), 342–349.

said of Hooper, in keeping with the generally accepted interpretation of his actions, is to be found in a question Fogle raises:

> . . . is it possible that we can go further afield and determine that the message of the veil *is* representative and universal: that the failure to recognize it is simply the last and most chilling proof of man's imprisonment within himself?

Considering the implications of his question with respect to Hawthorne's problem of achieving artistic unity, Fogle concludes:

> . . . in order to present forcibly the tragic isolation of one man, Hawthorne is obliged to consider society as a solid group arrayed against his hero, ignoring for the time being the fact that this hero is Everyman.

But, to pursue the direction of Fogle's question yet a step further, Hawthorne's hero is not Everyman: Hooper's experience is not typical, for that which he glimpses is the outer limit of earthly wisdom. The vision he gains is granted to few, though the perception is of a truth which is at the very heart of the nature of all mortal existence.

Ironically, from this new point of view Rev. Hooper achieves a far more penetrating equivalent of that "steady view of life, the *aurea mediocritas*" which Fogle assigns only to Hooper's sweetheart, Elizabeth, and which Fogle believes to be Hawthorne's conception of the "highest good."

II

By considering the two stories and their protagonists together, it is possible to reject not only Fogle's interpretation of "The Minister's Black Veil," but Thomas E. Connolly's interpretation of "Young Goodman Brown" as well. "Young Goodman Brown" is not, as Connolly says it is, a specific attack on Puritanic Calvinism.[2] In Hawthorne's tales and romances, the Puritan New England setting in time and place is illustrative, not restrictive. The diametrically opposed perspectives on man to which the main characters of these two stories come represent a universal difference in approach to the reading of the human condition.

Just as surely as Aylmer, Dr. Rappaccini, or Ethan Brand, Young Goodman Brown is guilty of the Unpardonable Sin of Pride. In fact, Young Goodman Brown's mistake is essentially the same as that which Hawthorne laments in Aylmer, in the concluding sentence of "The Birthmark." In his impatience with human imperfection, Brown loses his Faith in mankind; the milk of human kindness dries up within him. Connolly's argument that "Young Goodman Brown did not lose his faith

---

[2] Thomas E. Connolly, "Hawthorne's 'Young Goodman Brown': An Attack on Puritanic Calvinism," *American Literature*, 28 (November 1956), 370–375.

(we are even told that his Faith survived him)" is certainly based on a too strictly theological interpretation. Hawthorne explicitly states that Faith survives Brown to symbolize the very general religious belief that Faith is always available to the man capable of embracing her. This belief in the availability of Faith to the human heart which remains open to invite her in is familiar to any reader who knows conventional Christianity: invitations to Christ to "enter in" are central to traditional Christian worship.

That Hawthorne uses the term "Goodman" in Brown's name to indicate that Brown is a member of the race which includes Goody Cloyse, Deacon Gookin, and his own father and grandfather is generally recognized (one could go much farther in citing evidence from the story suggesting a breadth of applicability, to include all strata and all generations of Salem society and, by extension, of all human society). But the deeper irony—that Brown is but a youth—is curiously overlooked. That Brown is young suggests that his journey into the forest is not simply premeditated and prearranged, but that it is inevitable. Brown's is therefore a typical human journey—out of innocence and into experience. To borrow from William Blake, Brown is pictured in this story at the moment when he leaves the realm of pink ribbons and the gentle lamb to enter into the disquieting and mysterious realm where the tiger burns bright in the forests of the night.

To this extent, Young Goodman Brown is representative of all mankind; we all have a rendezvous with the Devil. Only the form which the Prince of Darkness takes varies in individual cases. Brown's journey is inevitable, but the results of his journey are not. That Brown is young is significant; that he is called "Goodman" is ironic but primarily tragic, in the sense that it helps the reader to identify with Brown not only the other characters in the story, but himself as well. But that Brown is "but three months married" to Faith is especially meaningful. Brown is representative of all who are innocent and undeveloped. Had he been wed to his Faith longer, had he put his Faith and himself to the test by degrees, he might have won through in his struggle with despair. But he did not because he could not. If the reader condemns Brown, he, like Brown, has become self-righteous. Or, if the reader believes, conversely, that Young Goodman Brown is representative of all mankind and that there is no escape from despair once evil is encountered, he, like Brown, delivers himself into the hands of the Devil, in the terms of the story.

III

The Reverend Mr. Hooper does not make Brown's mistake. He does not view his fellow creatures with a jaundiced eye. Father Hooper sees the same truth about human nature that Young Goodman Brown sees, but he does not fall prey to Evil by obsessively viewing man as hopelessly sinful and disqualified from Salvation.

Unlike Goodman Brown, Father Hooper profits from his vision: he becomes more understanding of human frailty than he was before he learned his lesson and donned the veil. This increased compassion and pity is the product of Mr. Hooper's sharpened awareness that the black veil figuratively covers all faces, including even the Earth's face. Thus Hooper's isolation is different from other men's only in degree—in intensity—and not in kind.

Hawthorne called "The Minister's Black Veil" a "parable," and one purpose of a parable is to clarify. The parable of the veil clarifies not simply by mirroring the ambiguity of life in a parallel ambiguity of meaning which Fogle has so ably demonstrated, but also by identifying the source of life's ambiguity. In the story, the veil is frequently identified as an emblem of mortality, of human imperfection. It is therefore comparable to the small hand on Georgiana's cheek in "The Birthmark"; for it is similarly a mark visited by Nature on all human beings, although seldom in so concrete a form.

After he has put on the veil, Father Hooper becomes a man apart, in that for him the secret of sin lies in its mysterious depths and not in a sense of particular shame or guilt. He is awed by Sin, rather than fearful of any single manifestation or consequence of sin. One important result of his vision of the truth about the human condition is of course his heightened sense of isolation. Even Elizabeth, the woman he truly loves, is cut off from him. But no two humans can be completely wed, as Hooper is made to realize very sharply when he sees his own reflection in a mirror, just after he has officiated at the wedding ceremony. His spiritual chill upon glimpsing the outside of the veil, presumably coupled with a keen sense that no earthly marriage can be the wedding of two isolated spirits—the perfect union which romantic young couples dimly hope for—indicates the price Reverend Hooper must pay for his vision.

Still, that vision even as it isolates and chills also provides Reverend Hooper with the ultimate in earthly wisdom; for, having recognized the fearful truth of human isolation, Hooper does not withdraw from the human race. The reality of man's innate depravity blinds Goodman Brown to man's innate goodness. Hooper, on the other hand, sees man's mixed nature precisely because he faces at every moment that same reality embodied in the veil.

As Fogle observes, "In one respect, however, the veil makes Mr. Hooper a more efficient clergyman, for 'it enabled him to sympathize with all dark affections.'" From the moment of his vision of the truth, Mr. Hooper becomes a more effective instrument of God, if indeed he does not become the very voice of God:

Mr. Hooper had the reputation of a good preacher, but not an energetic one: he strove to win his people heavenward by mild, persuasive influences, rather than to drive them thither by the thunders of the Word. The sermon which he now delivered was marked by the same characteristics of style and manner as the general series of his pulpit oratory. But there was something, either in the sentiment of the discourse itself, or in the imagination of the auditors, which made it greatly the most powerful effort that they had ever heard from their pastor's lips. It was tinged, rather more darkly than usual, with the gentle gloom of Mr. Hooper's temperament.

The subject had reference to secret sin, and those sad mysteries which we hide from our nearest and dearest, and would fain conceal from our own consciousness, even forgetting that the Omniscient can detect them. A subtle power was breathed into his words. Each member of the congregation, the most innocent girl, and the man of hardened breast, felt as if the preacher had crept upon them, behind his awful veil, and discovered their hoarded iniquity of deed or thought. Many spread their clasped hands on their bosoms. There was nothing terrible in what Mr. Hooper said, at least, no violence; and yet, with every tremor of his melancholy voice, the hearers quaked. An unsought pathos came hand in hand with awe. So sensible were the audience of some unwonted attribute in their minister, that they longed for a breath of wind to blow aside the veil, almost believing that a stranger's visage would be discovered, though the form, gesture, and voice were those of Mr. Hooper.

Furthermore, from this point in the story forward, those who will not—indeed, cannot bring themselves to—admit their sins, even to themselves, shun Hooper's presence or defensively "throw themselves in his way." But those who recognize their own sins call for the one minister who has "qualified" himself by previous words and actions, and Mr. Hooper does not fail them. At the same time that the veil isolates Father Hooper from meaningful human relationships, then, it increases his communicative power as a minister. Paradoxically, Mr. Hooper is not so isolated or so misunderstood as the villagers' oversimplified interpretations of why he wears the veil would lead us to suppose.

The Reverend Mr. Hooper has been permitted to cross over beyond the veil of mystery to achieve the ultimate in human knowledge. By reason of his intellect and his years of dedication to God and devotion to duty, he has been vouchsafed a unique comprehension of what mortality means. The danger to Hooper, as any careful reader of Hawthorne will know, is that, being only in part spirit and in part frail flesh, he may exult in his superior knowledge and fall victim to the sin of Pride. That he does not become self-righteous or contemptuous in his dealings with his fellows is, of course, painstakingly established by Hawthorne.

The veil, then, serves two large functions: First, it captures the imagination of men, not merely during Mr. Hooper's lifetime, but also after his physical death:

Still veiled, they laid him in his coffin, and a veiled corpse they bore him
to the grave. The grass of many years has sprung up and withered on
that grave, the burial stone is moss-grown, and good Mr. Hooper's face is
dust; but awful is still the thought that it mouldered beneath the Black
Veil!

And equally important, the veil is a constant reminder to Hooper of his
fellowship with man and of his obligation to God. Hooper's sorrow is his
steady and painful awareness that all men are sinners and that all men,
himself most particularly, are isolated in this life. Hooper's reward is his
conviction that " '. . . .hereafter there shall be no veil over my face,
no darkness between our souls! It is but a mortal veil—it is not for
eternity!' " For all the horror he feels whenever he sees his reflection in
a mirror or a fountain, Mr. Hooper's sad smiles and his "gentle, but
unconquerable obstinacy" whenever he is begged to remove the veil
show the minister to be a man of comparative serenity and of great
steadfastness. Hooper's refusal to remove the veil demonstrates that he
is wed to it in this life. The veil represents harsh reality, and Hooper
understands that so long as he exists in the mortal condition, his spirit is
bound to the veil.

Thus, "The Minister's Black Veil" is central to Hawthorne's view
of life: in life there is little cause for joy and much cause for gloom; yet
wisdom lies not in submitting to despair but in developing a quiet,
hopeful patience—in the promise of a traditional Christian afterlife.

How different in effect is Mr. Hooper's comprehension that all men
are sinners from Young Goodman Brown's destructive discovery. After
his physical death, Mr. Hooper achieves even earthly immortality, in
that he inspires feelings of awe in those who survive him. It is not too
much to suggest that in contrast Young Goodman Brown, on whose
tombstone "no hopeful verse" was carved, lies in an absolutely desolate
grave, like Hooper's untended in fact, but unlike Hooper's in that it is
not kept green in memory.

Unquestionably, Hawthorne himself felt the pull toward Young
Goodman Brown's view of man. His publication of "The Minister's Black
Veil" and other parables of life may be interpreted as Hawthorne's
public displaying of a black veil over his own face. Hawthorne's works
are, therefore, both a measure of his own need for a reminder that he
was a member of the human race and a signal of his success in avoiding
the Unpardonable Sin.

STUDY QUESTIONS

1.   What does Cochran mean when he says that Hawthorne's Puritan New
     England setting is "illustrative, not restrictive"?

2.   Why does Cochran feel that Young Goodman Brown's youth is signifi-
     cant?

3.   Does Cochran's discussion of "The Minister's Black Veil" lend credence
      to his interpretation of "Young Goodman Brown"?
4.   According to Cochran, what is Hawthorne's view of life?
5.   In what way do Cochran and Connolly reach similar conclusions in their
      interpretation of the story?

HOW YOUNG GOODMAN
BROWN BECAME OLD
Thomas E. Connolly   **BADMAN BROWN**

Mr. Cochran's thought-provoking essay on Hawthorne's two short
stories, "Hawthorne's Choice: Veil or Jaundiced Eye" (*CE*, February
1962), prompted me to review my own thoughts on "Young Goodman
Brown" (*AL*, November 1956). Unfortunately, I was not moved to renounce my position, but, like a hardened sinner confirmed in my sin, I
reject the new way to light and cling to the old habits. Mr. Cochran
unconsciously contributed to the hardening of my heart by a few com-
ments. First, he referred to my theological interpretation as being "too
theological." This is very much like saying, "His artistic interpretation is
too artistic"; or "His political interpretation is too political." Second, the
placement of the adverb *explicitly* in this sentence in his article confirmed me in my Calvinistic awareness of sin in this world: "Hawthorne
explicitly states that Faith survives Brown to symbolize the very general
religious belief that Faith is always available to the man capable of
embracing her." The casual reader might feel from this sentence that it
was Hawthorne who had made that symbolic interpretation. I went back
to the short story and could find Hawthorne saying nothing of the kind.

Third, Mr. Cochran emphasizes that the protagonist Brown is
young. I answer that he is young at the beginning of the story but old at
the end.

I went back, as I say, and reconsidered my theological interpretation of the story and decided to cling to it, but, as a concession to Mr.
Cochran, I decided to broaden the base of it and to parallel the theological (spiritual) with a sexual (naturalistic) interpretation. With all this
concentration on sin, I asked myself, just what sin did Young Goodman

Thomas E. Connolly, "How Young Goodman Brown Became Old Badman Brown,"
College English, XXIV (1962). Reprinted by permission of the National Council of
Teachers of English and Thomas E. Connolly.

Brown contemplate (not, I suggest, commit)? The only sin that begs for recognition is that of sexual infidelity. But the sting in the newly married Young Goodman Brown's temptation to have one last fling is that he realizes (from Faith's warning to him as he marches off to his tryst in the forest) that marital infidelity is a game at which two can play. The first note is struck by Faith as she begs her husband, ". . . prithee, put off your journey until sunrise and sleep in your own bed tonight. . . ." His reply is significant: "What, my sweet, pretty wife, dost thou doubt me already, and we but three months married?" Faith immediately responds with a grim warning: "Then God bless you! and may you find all well when you come back."

As he goes off to the tryst, Brown's conscience gives him a slight marital and theological twinge: "Well, she's a blessed angel on earth; and after this one night I'll cling to her skirts and follow her to heaven." The disillusionment comes as he realizes that, while he is on his way to his sin, his wife may very well be on her way to hers: "Moreover, there is a goodly young woman to be taken into communion."

Finally, turning back from what he thought would be a theologically (he is of the Elect and therefore not vulnerable) and maritally (he is married to a blessed angel) safe last fling, Young Goodman Brown is shocked to discover that his faith-Faith is not what he thought it-her to be (a doctrine that smugly places him in the Elect whatever he does, or a wife that is beyond the temptations of the flesh) and spends his life alternating from attraction to and revulsion from faith-Faith: often, awakening at midnight, he shrank from the bosom of Faith," and "Children and grandchildren, a goodly procession," followed him to his grave.

Robert W. Cochran   REPLY

First, any theological interpretation which is strictly theological, restrictively theological is "too" theological. I am not immediately suspicious of art or artistic interpretation; but with politics as with theology, I consider any unreconstructed political position "too political."

Second, the statement is explicit, the symbolism implicit.

Third, Mr. Connolly's casual reader might suppose from one of Mr. Connolly's sentences that Hawthorne refers to Brown as "old" and not as "young," as "Badman" and not as "Goodman" toward the end of the

Robert W. Cochran, "Reply," *College English*, XXIV (1962). Reprinted by permission of the National Council of Teachers of English and Robert W. Cochran.

story. On the contrary, Hawthorne writes "young Goodman Brown" and "Goodman Brown" even in his final paragraph.

Fourth, I caution Mr. Connolly not to harden in his "broadened" interpretation, based as it is on an attempt to identify the sin which Young Goodman Brown contemplated. I remind Mr. Connolly of Edgar Allan Poe's similarly oversimplified interpretation of why Reverend Hooper donned the black veil.

In conclusion, I feel that Brown's belief that his Faith was "a blessed angel on earth" is not only hopelessly naive, but hopelessly demanding. The wife Faith cannot be angelic, for she is "on earth." But Brown makes impossible demands on his wife and on all the other townspeople as well. Thus he remains young and foolish to his death. A "good man" he has never been; and an intimate, meaningful relationship in his "own bed" and in "the bosom of Faith," he has never had, his "goodly procession" of children and grandchildren notwithstanding. (The purpose of reference to succeeding as well as preceding generations is to place Brown in the human continuum.)

STUDY QUESTIONS

1. How does Connolly answer Cochran's criticism that his interpretation of "Young Goodman Brown" is "too theological"?
2. Is Connolly's point about the adverb *explicitly* well taken?
3. Does Connolly's decision "to broaden the base" of his argument make that argument more convincing?
4. Comment on the difference of opinion between Connolly and Cochran on the words *young* and *Goodman.*
5. How significant is Cochran's seemingly parenthetical last sentence?

AN ARGUMENT
AGAINST ABOLISHING
Jonathan Swift **CHRISTIANITY**

Jonathan Swift (1667–1745) is one of England's greatest prose writers. He was born in Dublin, Ireland, and was educated there at Trinity College. The fact that he took orders in the Church of England did not prevent him from becoming one of the Tory propagandists. However, Queen Anne disapproved of *A Tale of a*

First published 1711.

Tub (1704), and Swift was given the deanery of St. Patrick's, Dublin, instead of the English preferment he wanted. Among his now-classic works are *The Battle of the Books* (1704), *Gulliver's Travels* (1726), *A Modest Proposal* (1729), and *The Journal to Stella* (1766).

I am very sensible what a weakness and presumption it is, to reason against the general humor and disposition of the world. I remember it was with great justice, and a due regard to the freedom both of the public and the press, forbidden upon severe penalties to write or discourse, or lay wagers against the Union, even before it was confirmed by parliament; because that was looked upon as a design, to oppose the current of the people, which, besides the folly of it, is a manifest breach of the fundamental law that makes this majority of opinion the voice of God. In like manner, and for the very same reasons, it may perhaps be neither safe nor prudent to argue against the abolishing of Christianity, at a juncture when all parties appear so unanimously determined upon the point, as we cannot but allow from their actions, their discourses, and their writings. However, I know not how, whether from the affectation of singularity, or the perverseness of human nature, but so it unhappily falls out, that I cannot be entirely of this opinion. Nay, although I were sure an order were issued for my immediate prosecution by the Attorney General, I should still confess that in the present posture of our affairs at home or abroad, I do not yet see the absolute necessity of extirpating the Christian religion from among us.

This perhaps may appear too great a paradox even for our wise and paradoxical age to endure; therefore I shall handle it with all tenderness, and with the utmost deference to that great and profound majority which is of another sentiment.

And yet the curious may please to observe, how much the genius of a nation is liable to alter in half an age. I have heard it affirmed for certain by some very old people, that the contrary opinion was even in their memories as much in vogue as the other is now; and, that a project for the abolishing of Christianity would then have appeared as singular, and been thought as absurd, as it would be at this time to write or discourse in its defense.

Therefore I freely own that all appearances are against me. The system of the Gospel, after the fate of other systems, is generally antiquated and exploded; and the mass or body of the common people, among whom it seems to have had its latest credit, are now grown as much ashamed of it as their betters; opinions, like fashions, always descending from those of quality to the middle sort, and thence to the vulgar, where at length they are dropped and vanish.

But here I would not be mistaken, and must therefore be so bold as to borrow a distinction from the writers on the other side, when they make a difference between nominal and real Trinitarians. I hope no reader imagines me so weak to stand up in the defense of *real* Christianity, such as used in primitive times (if we may believe the authors of those ages) to have an influence upon men's belief and actions. To offer at the restoring of that would indeed be a wild project; it would be to dig up foundations; to destroy at one blow *all* the wit, and *half* the learning of the kingdom; to break the entire frame and constitution of things; to ruin trade, extinguish arts and sciences with the professors of them; in short, to turn our courts, exchanges, and shops into deserts; and would be full as absurd as the proposal of Horace, where he advises the Romans all in a body to leave their city, and seek a new seat in some remote part of the world, by way of cure for the corruption of their manners.

Therefore I think this caution was in itself altogether unnecessary (which I have inserted only to prevent all possibility of caviling), since every candid reader will easily understand my discourse to be intended only in defense of *nominal* Christianity; the other having been for some time wholly laid aside by general consent, as utterly inconsistent with our present schemes of wealth and power.

But why we should therefore cast off the name and title of Christians, although the general opinion and resolution be so violent for it, I confess I cannot (with submission) apprehend the consequence necessary. However, since the undertakers propose such wonderful advantages to the nation by this project, and advance many plausible objections against the system of Christianity, I shall briefly consider the strength of both, fairly allow them their greatest weight, and offer such answers as I think most reasonable. After which I will beg leave to show what inconveniences may possibly happen by such an innovation, in the present posture of our affairs.

First, One great advantage proposed by the abolishing of Christianity is, that it would very much enlarge and establish liberty of conscience, that great bulwark of our nation, and of the Protestant religion, which is still too much limited by priestcraft, notwithstanding all the good intentions of the legislature, as we have lately found by a severe instance. For it is confidently reported, that two young gentlemen of real hopes, bright wit, and profound judgment, who upon a thorough examination of causes and effects, and by the mere force of natural abilities, without the least tincture of learning, having made a discovery, that there was no God, and generously communicating their thoughts for the good of the public, were some time ago, by an unparalleled severity, and upon I know not what *obsolete* law, broke *only* for *blasphemy*. And as it hath been wisely observed, if persecution once begins, no man alive knows how far it may reach, or where it will end.

In answer to all which, with deference to wiser judgments, I think this rather shows the necessity of a *nominal* religion among us. Great wits love to be free with the highest objects; and if they cannot be allowed a *God* to revile or renounce, they will *speak evil of dignities*, abuse the government, and reflect upon the ministry; which I am sure few will deny to be of much more pernicious consequence, according to the saying of Tiberius, *Deorum offensa diis curae*.

As to the particular fact related, I think it is not fair to argue from one instance, perhaps another cannot be produced; yet (to the comfort of all those who may be apprehensive of persecution) blasphemy we know is freely spoken a million of times in every coffeehouse and tavern, or wherever else *good company* meet. It must be allowed indeed, that to break an *English freeborn* officer only for blasphemy, was, to speak the gentlest of such an action, a very high strain of absolute power. Little can be said in excuse for the general; perhaps he was afraid it might give offense to the allies, among whom, for aught I know, it may be the custom of the country to believe a God. But if he argued, as some have done, upon a mistaken principle, that an officer who is guilty of speaking blasphemy, may some time or other proceed so far as to raise a mutiny, the consequence is by no means to be admitted; for, surely the commander of an *English* army is likely to be but ill obeyed, whose soldiers fear and reverence him as little as they do a deity.

It is further objected against the Gospel system that it obliges men to the belief of things too difficult for freethinkers, and such who have shaken off the prejudices that usually cling to a confined education. To which I answer, that men should be cautious how they raise objections which reflect upon the wisdom of the nation. Is not everybody freely allowed to believe whatever he pleases, and to publish his belief to the world whenever he thinks fit, especially if it serves to strengthen the party which is in the right? Would any indifferent foreigner, who should read the trumpery lately written by Asgil, Tindal, Toland, Coward, and forty more, imagine the Gospel to be our rule of faith, and confirmed by parliaments? Does any man either believe, or say he believes, or desire to have it thought that he says he believes one syllable of the matter? And is any man worse received upon that score, or does he find his want of *nominal* faith a disadvantage to him in the pursuit of any civil or military employment? What if there be an old dormant statute or two against him, are they not now obsolete, to a degree, that Empson and Dudley themselves if they were now alive, would find it impossible to put them in execution?

It is likewise urged, that there are, by computation, in this kingdom, above ten thousand parsons, whose revenues added to those of my lords the bishops, would suffice to maintain at least two hundred young gentlemen of wit and pleasure, and freethinking, enemies to priestcraft, narrow principles, pedantry, and prejudices; who might be an ornament to the court and town. And then, again, so great a number of able (bodied) divines might be a recruit to our fleet and armies. This indeed appears to be a consideration of some weight. But then, on the other side, several things deserve to be considered likewise: As, first, whether it may not be thought necessary that in certain tracts of country, like what we call parishes, there should be *one* man at least of abilities to read and write. Then it seems a wrong computation, that the revenues of the Church throughout this island would be large enough to maintain two hundred young gentlemen, or even half that number, after the present refined way of living; that is, to allow each of them such a rent, as in the modern form of speech, would make them *easy*. But still there is in this project a greater mischief behind; and we ought to beware of the woman's folly, who killed the hen that every morning laid her a golden egg. For, pray what would become of the race of men in the next age, if we had nothing to trust to beside the scrofulous, consumptive productions, furnished by our men of wit and pleasure, when, having squandered away their vigor, health, and estates, they are forced by some disagreeable marriage to piece up their broken fortunes and entail rottenness and politeness on their posterity? Now, here are ten thousand persons reduced by the wise regulations of Henry the Eighth, to the necessity of a low diet, and moderate exercise, who are the only great restorers of our breed, without which the nation would in an age or two become but one great hospital.

Another advantage proposed by the abolishing of Christianity, is the clear gain of one day in seven, which is now entirely lost, and consequently the kingdom one-seventh less considerable in trade, business, and pleasure; beside the loss to the public of so many stately structures now in the hands of the clergy, which might be converted into theaters, exchanges, market houses, common dormitories, and other public edifices.

I hope I shall be forgiven a hard word, if I call this a perfect cavil. I readily own there has been an old custom time out of mind, for people to assemble in the churches every Sunday, and that shops are still frequently shut, in order as it is conceived, to preserve the memory of that ancient practice; but how this can prove a hindrance to business or pleasure, is hard to imagine. What if the men of pleasure are forced one day in the week, to game at home instead of the chocolate house? Are not the taverns and coffeehouses open? Can there be a more convenient season for taking a dose of physic? Are fewer claps got upon Sundays than other days? Is not that the chief day for traders to sum up the accounts of the week, and for lawyers to prepare their briefs? But I would fain know how it can be pretended that the churches are misapplied? Where are more appointments and rendezvous of gallantry?

Where more care to appear in the foremost box with greater advantage of dress? Where more meetings for business? Where more bargains driven of all sorts? And where so many conveniences or incitements to sleep?

There is one advantage greater than any of the foregoing, proposed by the abolishing of Christianity: that it will utterly extinguish parties among us, by removing those factious distinctions of High and Low Church, of Whig and Tory, Presbyterian and Church of England, which are now so many grievous clogs upon public proceedings, and dispose men to prefer the gratifying themselves, or depressing their adversaries, before the most important interest of the state.

I confess, if it were certain that so great an advantage would redound to the nation by this expedient, I would submit and be silent. But will any man say, that if the words *whoring, drinking, cheating, lying, stealing,* were by act of parliament ejected out of the English tongue and dictionaries, we should all awake next morning chaste and temperate, honest and just, and lovers of truth? Is this a fair consequence? Or, if the physicians would forbid us to pronounce the words *pox, gout, rheumatism,* and *stone,* would that expedient serve like so many talismans to destroy the diseases themselves? Are party and faction rooted in men's hearts no deeper than phrases borrowed from religion, or founded upon no firmer principles? And is our language so poor that we cannot find other terms to express them? Are envy, pride, avarice, and ambition such ill nomenclators, that they cannot furnish appellations for their owners? Will not *heydukes* and *mamalukes, mandarins* and *potshaws,* or any other words formed at pleasure, serve to distinguish those who are in the ministry from others who *would be in it if they could?* What, for instance, is easier than to vary the form of speech, and instead of the word *Church,* make it a question in politics, whether the *Monument* be in danger? Because religion was nearest at hand to furnish a few convenient phrases, is our invention so barren, we can find no others? Suppose, for argument sake, that the Tories favored Margarita, the Whigs Mrs. Tofts, and the Trimmers Valentini, would not *Margaritians, Toftians,* and *Valentinians* be very tolerable marks of distinction? The *Prasini* and *Veneti,* two most virulent factions in Italy, began (if I remember right) by a distinction of colors in ribbons, which we might do, with as good a grace, about the dignity of the *Blue* and the *Green;* and would serve as properly to divide the court, the parliament, and the kingdom between them, as any terms of art whatsoever, borrowed from religion. Therefore, I think there is little force in this objection against Christianity, or prospect of so great an advantage as is proposed in the abolishing of it.

It is again objected, as a very absurd, ridiculous custom, that a set of men should be suffered, much less employed and hired, to bawl one day in seven against the lawfulness of those methods most in use toward the pursuit of greatness, riches, and pleasure, which are the constant practice of all men alive on the other six. But this objection is, I think, a little unworthy so refined an age as ours. Let us argue this matter calmly. I appeal to the breast of any polite freethinker, whether in the pursuit of gratifying a predominant passion, he hath not always felt a wonderful incitement, by reflecting it was a thing forbidden; and therefore we see, in order to cultivate this taste, the wisdom of the nation hath taken special care, that the ladies should be furnished with prohibited silks, and the men with prohibited wine. And indeed it were to be wished, that some other prohibitions were promoted, in order to improve the pleasures of the town; which, for want of such expedients, begin already, as I am told, to flag and grow languid, giving way daily to cruel inroads from the spleen.

It is likewise proposed as a great advantage to the public, that if we once discard the system of the Gospel, all religion will of course be banished forever; and consequently, along with it, those grievous prejudices of education, which under the names of virtue, conscience, honor, justice, and the like, are so apt to disturb the peace of human minds; and the notions whereof are so hard to be eradicated by right reason or freethinking, sometimes during the whole course of our lives.

Here first, I observe how difficult it is to get rid of a phrase, which the world is once grown fond of, although the occasion that first produced it, be entirely taken away. For several years past, if a man had but an ill-favored nose, the deep thinkers of the age would some way or other contrive to impute the cause to the prejudice of his education. From this fountain are said to be derived all our foolish notions of justice, piety, love of our country; all our opinions of God, or a future state, Heaven, hell, and the like. And there might formerly perhaps have been some pretense for this charge. But so effectual care has been taken to remove those prejudices, by an entire change in the methods of education, that (with honor I mention it to our polite innovators) the young gentlemen who are now on the scene, seem to have not the least tincture left of those infusions, or string of those weeds; and, by consequence, the reason for abolishing *nominal* Christianity upon that pretext, is wholly ceased.

For the rest, it may perhaps admit a controversy, whether the banishing all notions of religion whatsoever, would be convenient for the vulgar. Not that I am in the least of opinion with those who hold religion to have been the invention of politicians, to keep the lower part of the world in awe by the fear of invisible powers; unless mankind were then very different from what it is now. For I look upon the mass or body of our people here in England, to be as freethinkers, that is to say, as staunch unbelievers, as any of the highest rank. But I conceive some

scattered notions about a superior power to be of singular use for the
common people, as furnishing excellent materials to keep children quiet
when they grow peevish and providing topics of amusement in a tedious
winter night.

Lastly, it is proposed as a singular advantage, that the abolishing
of Christianity will very much contribute to the uniting of Protestants,
by enlarging the terms of communion so as to take in all sorts of
dissenters, who are now shut out of the pale upon account of a few
ceremonies which all sides confess to be things indifferent: That this
alone will effectually answer the great ends of a scheme for comprehension, by opening a large noble gate, at which all bodies may enter;
whereas the chaffering with dissenters, and dodging about this or the
other ceremony, is but like opening a few wickets, and leaving them ajar,
by which no more than one can get in at a time, and that, not without
stooping, and sidling, and squeezing his body.

To all this I answer; that there is one darling inclination of mankind, which usually affects to be a retainer to religion, though she be
neither its parent, its godmother, or its friend; I mean the spirit of
opposition, that lived long before Christianity, and can easily subsist
without it. Let us, for instance, examine wherein the opposition of
sectaries among us consists, we shall find Christianity to have no share
in it at all. Does the Gospel anywhere prescribe a starched, squeezed
countenance, a stiff, formal gait, a singularity of manners and habit, or
any affected modes of speech different from the reasonable part of
mankind? Yet, if Christianity did not lend its name to stand in the gap,
and to employ or divert these humors, they must of necessity be spent in
contraventions to the laws of the land, and disturbance of the public
peace. There is a portion of enthusiasm assigned to every nation, which,
if it hath not proper objects to work on, will burst out, and set all in a
flame. If the quiet of a state can be bought by only flinging men a few
ceremonies to devour, it is a purchase no wise man would refuse. Let the
mastiffs amuse themselves about a sheepskin stuffed with hay, provided
it will keep them from worrying the flock. The institution of convents
abroad, seems in one point a strain of great wisdom, there being few
irregularities in human passions, which may not have recourse to vent
themselves in some of those orders, which are so many retreats for the
speculative, the melancholy, the proud, the silent, the politic, and the
morose, to spend themselves, and evaporate the noxious particles; for
each of whom we in this island are forced to provide a several sect of
religion, to keep them quiet: And whenever Christianity shall be abolished, the legislature must find some other expedient to employ and
entertain them. For what imports it how large a gate you open, if there
will be always left a number who place a pride and a merit in refusing to
enter?

Having thus considered the most important objections against Christianity, and the chief advantages proposed by the abolishing thereof, I shall now with equal deference and submission to wiser judgments as before, proceed to mention a few inconveniences that may happen, if the Gospel should be repealed; which perhaps the projectors may not have sufficiently considered.

And first, I am very sensible how much the gentlemen of wit and pleasure are apt to murmur, and be shocked at the sight of so many draggled-tail parsons, who happen to fall in their way, and offend their eyes; but at the same time, these wise reformers do not consider what an advantage and felicity it is, for great wits to be always provided with objects of scorn and contempt, in order to exercise and improve their talents, and divert their spleen from falling on each other or on themselves; especially when all this may be done without the least imaginable *danger to their persons.*

And to urge another argument of a parallel nature: If Christianity were once abolished, how would the freethinkers, the strong reasoners, and the men of profound learning, be able to find another subject so calculated in all points whereon to display their abilities? What wonderful productions of wit should we be deprived of, from those whose genius by continual practice hath been wholly turned upon raillery and invectives against religion, and would therefore never be able to shine or distinguish themselves upon any other subject! We are daily complaining of the great decline of wit among us, and would we take away the greatest, perhaps the only topic we have left? Who would ever have suspected Asgil for a wit, or Toland for a philosopher, if the inexhaustible stock of Christianity had not been at hand to provide them with materials? What other subject, through all art or nature, could have produced Tindal for a profound author, or furnished him with readers? It is the wise choice of the subject that alone adorns and distinguishes the writer. For, had a hundred such pens as these been employed on the side of religion, they would have immediately sunk into silence and oblivion.

Nor do I think it wholly groundless, or my fears altogether imaginary, that the abolishing of Christianity may perhaps bring the Church into danger, or at least put the senate to the trouble of another securing vote. I desire I may not be mistaken; I am far from presuming to affirm or think that the Church is in danger at present, or as things now stand; but we know not how soon it may be so when the Christian religion is repealed. As plausible as this project seems, there may a dangerous design lurk under it. Nothing can be more notorious, than that the atheists, deists, Socinians, anti-Trinitarians, and other subdivisions of free-thinkers, are persons of little zeal for the present ecclesiastical establishment: Their declared opinion is for repealing the Sacramental

Test; they are very indifferent with regard to ceremonies; nor do they hold the *jus divinum* of Episcopacy. Therefore this may be intended as one politic step toward altering the constitution of the Church established, and setting up Presbytery in the stead, which I leave to be further considered by those at the helm.

In the last place, I think nothing can be more plain, than that by this expedient, we shall run into the evil we chiefly pretend to avoid; and that the abolishment of the Christian religion will be the readiest course we can take to introduce popery. And I am the more inclined to this opinion, because we know it has been the constant practice of the Jesuits to send over emissaries, with instructions to personate themselves members of the several prevailing sects among us. So it is recorded, that they have at sundry times appeared in the guise of Presbyterians, Anabaptists, Independents, and Quakers, according as any of these were most in credit; so, since the fashion hath been taken up of exploding religion, the popish missionaries have not been wanting to mix with the freethinkers; among whom, Toland the great oracle of the anti-Christians is an Irish priest, the son of an Irish priest; and the most learned and ingenious author of a book called *The Rights of the Christian Church* was in a proper juncture reconciled to the Romish faith, whose true son, as appears by a hundred passages in his treatise, he still continues. Perhaps I could add some others to the number; but the fact is beyond dispute, and the reasoning they proceed by is right; for, supposing Christianity to be extinguished, the people will never be at ease until they find out some other method of worship; which will as infallibly produce supersitition, as this will end in popery.

And therefore, if notwithstanding all I have said, it shall still be thought necessary to have a bill brought in for repealing Christianity, I would humbly offer an amendment; that instead of the word *Christianity*, may be put *Religion* in general; which I conceive will much better answer all the good ends proposed by the projectors of it. For, as long as we leave in being a God and his providence, with all the necessary consequences which curious and inquisitive men will be apt to draw from such premises, we do not strike at the root of the evil, although we should ever so effectually annihilate the present scheme of the Gospel. For, of what use is freedom of thought, if it will not produce freedom of action, which is the sole end, how remote soever in appearance, of all objections against Christianity? And therefore, the freethinkers consider it as a sort of edifice, wherein all the parts have such a mutual dependence on each other, that if you happen to pull out one single nail, the whole fabric must fall to the ground. This was happily expressed by him who had heard of a text brought for proof of the Trinity, which in an ancient manuscript was differently read; he thereupon immediately took the hint, and by a sudden deduction of a long sorites, most logically concluded: "Why, if it be as you say, I may safely whore and drink on, and defy the parson." From which, and many the like instances easy to be produced, I think nothing can be more manifest, than that the quarrel is not against any particular points of hard digestion in the Christian system, but against religion in general; which, by laying restraints on human nature, is supposed the great enemy to the freedom of thought and action.

Upon the whole, if it shall still be thought for the benefit of Church and state, that Christianity be abolished; I conceive however, it may be more convenient to defer the execution to a time of peace, and not venture in this conjuncture to disoblige our allies, who, as it falls out, are all Christians, and many of them, by the prejudices of their education, so bigoted, as to place a sort of pride in the appellation. If upon being rejected by them, we are to trust to an alliance with the Turk, we shall find ourselves much deceived: For, as he is too remote, and generally engaged in war with the Persian emperor, so his people would be more scandalized at our infidelity, than our Christian neighbors. Because the Turks are not only strict observers of religious worship, but, what is worse, believe a God; which is more than is required of us, even while we preserve the name of Christians.

To conclude: Whatever some may think of the great advantages to trade by this favorite scheme, I do very much apprehend, that in six months' time after the act is passed for the extirpation of the Gospel, the Bank and East India stock may fall, at least, one *per cent*. And, since that is fifty times more than ever the wisdom of our age thought fit to venture for the *preservation* of Christianity, there is no reason we should be at so great a loss, merely for the sake of *destroying* it.

STUDY QUESTIONS

1. By what means does Swift try to convince his readers of his obvious sincerity?
2. What distinction does he make between *real* Christianity and *nominal* Christianity?
3. How does Swift turn to his advantage the argument that the Gospels oblige men to believe things too difficult for freethinkers?
4. What use does Swift make of the seemingly incontrovertible evidence of statistics?
5. How does he appeal to the economic interests of his audience? What is his concluding and most important argument against abolishing Christianity?

FOR TWO CENTS

Harry Golden   **PLAIN**

Harry Golden (1902–   ) was born in New York City. He
attended The City College of New York from 1919 to 1922, and
was named Doctor of Letters by Belmont Abbey College in 1962.
He lives in Charlottesville, North Carolina, where he has edited
the *Carolina Israelite* since 1942. His books include *Only in
America* (1958), *For 2¢ Plain* (1959), *Enjoy! Enjoy!* and *Carl
Sandburg* (1961), *You're Entitle* (1962), *Forgotten Pioneer*
(1963), *Mr. Kennedy and the Negro* (1964), and *So What Else Is
New?* and *A Little Girl Is Dead* (1965).

The rabbinical students in Europe and in America had a regular
schedule of "eating days." Mondays he ate with family A; Tuesdays with
B; and so forth. On the Lower East Side this system still lingered to
some extent, but it usually involved a young boy who had immigrated
without a family. His fellow-townsmen set up his seven eating days.
Usually this was a very religious boy who would not take a chance to eat
"out" or could not yet afford to buy his meals. Some of the hosts on these
eating days used the fellow to check up on the melamed (Hebrew
teacher). The melamed came at half past three and taught the children
for a half-hour—for a twenty-five-cent fee. Learning the prayers was
entirely by rote. There was no explanation or translation of the Hebrew
into English or Yiddish. Once in a while the mother would ask the
eating-days fellow to come a half-hour earlier. The boy came with his
usual appetite, but soon learned the reason for the early appointment.
The mother wanted him to test the children to see if the melamed was
doing all right. The boy always gave the melamed a clean bill of health.
     Sometimes the eating-days boy ate too much and in poor house-
holds this was quite a problem. But in most homes the mother saw to it
that he kept packing it away, and in addition always had something
wrapped up for him to take back to his room—for later. Many households
had these strangers at their tables, but only the very religious boys
remained, those who expected to continue their religious studies.
     The others were soon gone. America was too great and too won-

derful; there were too many things to see and do, and even a hot dog at a pushcart was an adventure, to say nothing of the wonderful Max's Busy Bee.

The streets were crowded with vendors with all sorts of delightful and exotic tidbits and nasherei (delicacies).

Across the border (the Bowery) was the Italian hot-dog man. The hot plate (a coal fire) was mounted on his pushcart, and behind the stove was a barrel of lemonade to which he added chunks of ice every few hours. The hot dog, roll, mustard, and relish was three cents; the drink, two cents; and it was all a memorable experience.

A few years ago I saw a fellow with a similar cart near the Battery on Lower Broadway and I made a mad dash for him. The whole operation was now fifteen cents, but it wasn't anywhere near as wonderful as it was when I was twelve years old.

In the late fall and winter came the fellow with the haiseh arbus (hot chick-peas). He started to make his rounds a few minutes before noon as the children were leaving the schools for lunch. You sat in the classroom and everything was quiet and dignified, and all of a sudden you heard those loud blasts—"Haiseh arbus," "Haiseh, haiseh" (hot, hot)—and you knew it was time to go. Sometimes he was a little early and the teacher had to close the window. The price was one penny for a portion which the man served in a rolled-up piece of newspaper, like the English working people buy their fish and chips. There were also fellows with roasted sweet potatoes; two cents each, and three cents for an extra large one. These people used a galvanized tin contraption on wheels which looked exactly like a bedroom dresser with three drawers. In the bottom drawer were the potatoes he was roasting, while in the upper drawers were the two different sizes ready to serve. On the bottom of everything, of course, was the coal-burning fire. He had a small bag of coal attached to the front of the stove and every once in a while he shook up the fire.

My uncle Berger once operated one of those sweet-potato push-carts with the stove on the bottom, and years later he always said that he began life in America as an engineer. He boasted of this after he had made a million dollars operating the Hotel Normandie on Broadway and 38th Street during World War I.

An interesting fellow was the peddler with a red fez, a "Turk," who sold an exotic sweet drink. He carried a huge bronze water container strapped to his back. This beautiful container had a long curved spout which came over his left shoulder. Attached to his belt, in front, was a small pail of warm water to rinse his two glasses. The drink was one penny. You held the glass, and he leaned toward you as the liquid came forth.

Nuts were very popular. There were pushcarts loaded down with "polly seeds." I have forgotten the authentic name for this nut but the East Side literally bathed in the stuff. "Polly seed" because it was the favorite food of parrots—"Polly want a cracker?"

Indian nuts, little round brown nuts. The father of one of the kids on the block sold Indian nuts, of all things. On his pushcart he had a huge glass bowl the size of an army soup vat, and it was filled with Indian nuts. I had daydreams of taking my shoes off and jumping up and down in that vat of Indian nuts, like the French girls make champagne.

This was the era when people walked a great deal. Shoeshine parlors were all over the place. On Sunday mornings you went out to get a shine and did not mind waiting in line for it either. "We are going for a walk next Saturday night." Sounds silly today, but it was an event, and make no mistake. And on every corner there were pushcarts selling fruit in season. Apples, pears, peaches, and above all, grapes. A common sight was a boy and girl eating grapes. The boy held the stem aloft as each of them pulled at the bunch and walked along the street. The grapes were sold by weight per bunch; the other fruits were sold individually, of course. And "in season" there was the man or the woman with "hot corn." I did not hear the term "corn-on-the-cob" till quite a few years later. We knew it only as "hot corn." The vendor had boiled the ears at home and usually carried the large vat to a convenient street corner, or he put the vat on a baby carriage and wheeled it around the neighborhood. A lot of women were in this hot-corn business. The hot corn was a nickel, and there was plenty of bargaining. "Throw it back, give me that one, the one over there." We kids waited around until the lady was all sold out, except the ones which had been thrown back, and often we paid no more than a penny. There are two moments when it is best to buy from a peddler, a "first" and the "close-out."

Confections of all sorts were sold, many of them famous in the Orient and eastern Europe. Fellows sold candy known as "rah-hott," which sounds Turkish or Arabic. It was beautiful to look at and there were two or three different tastes with each bite. Halvah, of course, was the real big seller, and the memory of this has lingered to this day. No delicatessen store today is without halvah, although I shall not do them the injustice of comparing the East Side halvah and the stuff they sell today. But at least you are getting a whiff of it, which is worth anything you pay. I had a Gentile friend here who had been courting a widow for years without any success and I gave him a box of chocolate-covered halvah to take to her, and the next time I saw the guy he was dancing in the streets of Charlotte. We used to eat it between slices of rye bread, "a halvah sonavich," and it was out of this world. There was another candy called "buckser" (St. John's bread), imported from Palestine. It had a long, hard, curved shell and inside a very black seed with an interesting taste which is hard to describe.

There were pushcarts loaded down with barrels of dill pickles and pickled tomatoes, which we called "sour tomatoes." Working people, men and women on the way home from the needle factories, stopped off to buy a sour tomato as a sort of appetizer for their evening meal, or perhaps to take the edge off the appetite. These tidbits sold for two and three cents each, and you served yourself. You put your hand into the vinegar barrel and pulled one out. Years later a relative of mine asked me to accompany him to a lawyer's office to "talk for him." I met him on the old East Side and we decided to walk out of the district and into Lower Broadway.

Suddenly I noticed that he was no longer at my side. I looked back and there he was biting into one sour tomato and holding a fresh one in the other hand, all ready to go. I had become a fancy guy by then and he was afraid he would embarrass me, but my mouth was watering, Broadway and all.

And then there were the permanent vendors—the soda-water stands. On nearly every corner a soda-water stand. These were the size and shape of the average newsstand you see in most of the big cities today. There was a soda fountain behind a narrow counter, and a rack for factory-made American candy, which was becoming increasingly popular, especially the Hershey bar. The fellow also sold cigarettes. No woman was ever seen smoking a cigarette in those days. The brands were Mecca, Hassan, Helmar, Sweet Caporal (which are still sold), Egyptian Deities, Moguls, Schinasi, Fifth Avenue, and Afternoons.

My father smoked Afternoons. Half the cigarette was a hard mouthpiece, or what the advertising boys today call a filter. I bought many a box of Afternoons and they were seven cents for ten cigarettes. I also bought whiskey. There was no inhibition about it and no sense of guilt. We had no drunks down there, and a kid could buy a bottle of whiskey for his father the same as he could buy a loaf of bread. I read the label many times on the way home, "Pennsylvania Rye Whiskey; we guarantee that this whiskey has been aged in the wood twenty years before bottling; signed, Park and Tilford." Cost, $1.80 for an imperial quart. No fancy "fifth-shmifth" business.

The fellow with the stand had a small marble counter on which he served his drinks and made change for candy and cigarettes. Along the counter were jars of preserves—cherry, raspberry, mulberry—for his mixed drinks. He also had a machine to make malted milks. How the immigrants took to the malted milk!

Like the other folks, my mother pronounced it "ah molta." But, of course, the big seller was seltzer (carbonated water), either plain or with syrup. A small glass of seltzer cost a penny—"Give me a small plain." That meant no syrup. And for the large glass you said, "Give me for two cents plain." For an extra penny he ladled out a spoonful of one of his syrups and mixed it with the seltzer. Here, too, there was plenty of bargaining. A fellow said, "Give me for two cents plain," and as the man was filling the glass with seltzer the customer said, casuallike, "Put a little on the top." This meant syrup, of course, and yet it did not mean the extra penny. You did not say, "Give me a raspberry soda." It was all in the way you said it, nonchalantly and in a sort of deprecating tone, "Put a little on the top." It meant that you were saving the fellow the trouble of even stirring the glass. Well, the man had already filled the glass with seltzer and what could he do with it unless you paid for it? So he "put a little on the top" but not the next time if he could help it. Often he would take the two cents first and give you a glass of plain. "I know my customers," he'd say. The man who had the stand on our corner was an elderly gent, "Benny," and once when I was playing around his counter, one of his jars fell down and the syrup got all over me. Every time I came near Benny's stand after that he took extra precautions; "Go way hard luck," he always said to me. Benny wore a coat he had brought from Europe and it reached down to his ankles. He would take a handful of that coat, feel it a while, and tell you whether it was going to rain the next day. People came from blocks around to get a weather forecast from Benny and his coat. He rarely missed.

And so you can hardly blame the young boy, the eating-days boy, when he quit the table of those home-cooked meals and went down into this world of pleasures and joys.

STUDY QUESTIONS

1. There is, of course, no question of the Jewish family's desire to help an eating-day fellow. But what advantage did they take of him?
2. Which is the thesis sentence of Golden's essay?
3. Golden uses parentheses rather freely. Explain why he uses them when he does.
4. In the discussion of street vendors, are there any vendors who do not logically belong in this essay by virtue of the wares they peddle? What is the organizing principle for the two paragraphs on page 85 beginning, "And then there were the permanent vendors—the soda-water stands." and "My father smoked Afternoons."? Do these paragraphs have topic sentences?
5. How does the audience for which Golden wrote, and the medium in which this essay appeared explain the tone and style of "For two cents plain"?

Charles Lamb DREAM-CHILDREN

Charles Lamb (1775–1834) was born in London and attended
Christ's Hospital School. He began his public career as a clerk in
the South Sea House, and worked a total of thirty-three years for
The East India Company. Unlike the other major Romantics
(Wordsworth, Coleridge, and Keats were his close friends), he
preferred the city to the country, did not admire Shelley, and
remained quietly conservative. Walter Pater compared Lamb's life
to "an old Greek tragedy": Lamb's sister, Mary, stabbed their
mother to death and remained in Lamb's care for those periods
when she was released from the insane asylum to which she was
committed. Lamb published *Rosamund Gray*, a novel, in 1798
and *John Woodvil*, a play, in 1802; however, his fame rests on
Essays of Elia (1823), *More Essays of Elia* (1833), his dramatic
criticism, and his *Tales from Shakespeare* (1807), of which his sister
was coauthor.

Children love to listen to stories about their elders when *they* were
children; to stretch their imagination to the conception of a traditionary
great-uncle, or grandame whom they never saw. It was in this spirit that
my little ones crept about me the other evening to hear about their great-
grandmother Field who lived in a great house in Norfolk (a hundred
times bigger than that in which they and papa lived) which had been
the scene—so at least it was generally believed in that part of the country
—of the tragic incidents which they had lately become familiar with from
the ballad of *The Children in the Wood.* Certain it is that the whole
story of the children and their cruel uncle was to be seen fairly carved
out in wood upon the chimney-piece of the great hall, the whole story
down to the Robin Redbreasts, till a foolish rich person pulled it down
to set up a marble one of modern invention in its stead, with no story
upon it. Here Alice put out one of her dear mother's looks, too tender to
be called upbraiding. Then I went on to say how religious and how good
their great-grandmother Field was, how beloved and respected by every
body, though she was not indeed the mistress of this great house, but
had only the charge of it (and yet in some respects she might be said to
be the mistress of it too) committed to her by the owner, who preferred
living in a newer and more fashionable mansion which he had pur-
chased somewhere in the adjoining county; but still she lived in it in a

First published 1822.

manner as if it had been her own, and kept up the dignity of the great house in a sort while she lived, which afterwards came to decay, and was nearly pulled down, and all its old ornaments stripped and carried away to the owner's other house, where they were set up, and looked as awkward as if some one were to carry away the old tombs they had seen lately at the Abbey, and stick them up in Lady C.'s tawdry gilt drawing-room. Here John smiled, as much as to say, "that would be foolish indeed." And then I told how, when she came to die, her funeral was attended by a concourse of all the poor, and some of the gentry too, of the neighborhood for many miles round, to show their respect for her memory, because she had been such a good and religious woman; so good indeed that she knew all the Psaltery, by heart, ay, and a great part of the Testament besides. Here little Alice spread her hands. Then I told what a tall, upright, graceful person their great-grandmother Field once was; and how in her youth she was esteemed the best dancer—here Alice's little right foot played an involuntary movement, till, upon my looking grave, it desisted—the best dancer, I was saying, in the county, till a cruel disease, called a cancer, came, and bowed her down with pain; but it could never bend her good spirits, or make them stoop, but they were still upright, because she was so good and religious. Then I told how she was used to sleep by herself in a lone chamber of the great lone house; and how she believed that an apparition of two infants was to be seen at midnight gliding up and down the great staircase near where she slept, but she said "those innocents would do her no harm"; and how frightened I used to be, though in those days I had my maid to sleep with me, because I was never half so good or religious as she—and yet I never saw the infants. Here John expanded all his eye-brows and tried to look courageous. Then I told how good she was to all her grand-children, having us to the great-house in the holydays, where I in particular used to spend many hours by myself, in gazing upon the old busts of the Twelve Cæsars, that had been Emperors of Rome, till the old marble heads would seem to live again, or I to be turned into marble with them; how I never could be tired with roaming about that huge mansion, with its vast empty rooms, with their worn-out hangings, fluttering tapestry, and carved oaken panels, with the gilding almost rubbed out—sometimes in the spacious old-fashioned gardens, which I had almost to myself, unless when now and then a solitary gardening man would cross me—and how the nectarines and peaches hung upon the walls, without my ever offering to pluck them, because they were forbidden fruit, unless now and then,—and because I had more pleasure in strolling about among the old melancholy-looking yew trees, or the firs, and picking up the red berries, and the fir apples, which were good for nothing but to look at—or in lying about upon the fresh grass, with all the fine garden smells around me—or basking in the orangery, till I could almost fancy myself ripening too along with the oranges and the limes in that grateful warmth—or in watching the dace that darted to and fro in the fishpond, at the bottom of the garden, with here and there a great sulky pike hanging midway down the water in silent state, as if it mocked at their impertinent friskings,—I had more pleasure in these busy-idle diversions than in all the sweet flavors of peaches, nectarines, oranges, and such like common baits of children. Here John slyly deposited back upon the plate a bunch of grapes, which, not unobserved by Alice, he had meditated dividing with her, and both seemed willing to relinquish them for the present as irrelevant. Then in somewhat a more heightened tone, I told how, though their great-grandmother Field loved all her grand-children, yet in an especial manner she might be said to love their uncle, John L——, because he was so handsome and spirited a youth, and a king to the rest of us; and, instead of moping about in solitary corners, like some of us, he would mount the most mettlesome horse he could get, when but an imp no bigger than themselves, and make it carry him half over the county in a morning, and join the hunters when there were any out—and yet he loved the old great house and gardens too, but had too much spirit to be always pent up within their boundaries—and how their uncle grew up to man's estate as brave as he was handsome, to the admiration of every body, but of their great-grandmother Field especially; and how he used to carry me upon his back when I was a lame-footed boy—for he was a good bit older than me—many a mile when I could not walk for pain;—and how in after life he became lame-footed too, and I did not always (I fear) make allowances enough for him when he was impatient, and in pain, nor remember sufficiently how considerate he had been to me when I was lame-footed; and how when he died, though he had not been dead an hour, it seemed as if he had died a great while ago, such a distance there is betwixt life and death; and how I bore his death as I thought pretty well at first, but afterwards it haunted and haunted me; and though I did not cry or take it to heart as some do, and as I think he would have done if I had died, yet I missed him all day long, and knew not till then how much I had loved him. I missed his kindness, and I missed his crossness, and wished him to be alive again, to be quarrelling with him (for we quarrelled sometimes) rather than not have him again, and was as uneasy without him, as he their poor uncle must have been when the doctor took off his limb. Here the children fell a-crying, and asked if their little mourning which they had on was not for uncle John, and they looked up, and prayed me not to go on about their uncle, but to tell them some stories about their pretty dead mother. Then I told how for seven long years, in hope sometimes, sometimes in despair, yet persisting ever, I courted the fair Alice W—n; and, as much as children could understand, I explained to them what coyness, and difficulty, and denial meant in maidens—when suddenly, turning to Alice, the soul of the first Alice looked out at her eyes with such a reality of re-presentment, that I became in doubt which of them stood there before me, or whose that bright hair was; and while I stood gazing, both the children gradually grew fainter to my view, receding, and still receding till nothing at last but two mournful features were seen in the uttermost distance, which, without speech, strangely impressed upon me the effects of speech: "We are not of Alice, nor of thee, nor are we children at all. The children of Alice called Bartrum father. We are nothing; less than nothing, and dreams. We are only what might have been, and must wait upon the tedious shores of Lethe millions of ages before we have existence, and a name"———and immediately awaking, I found myself quietly seated in my bachelor arm-chair, where I had fallen asleep, with the faithful Bridget unchanged by my side—but John L. (or James Elia) was gone forever.

STUDY QUESTIONS

1. Why are certain sentences in Lamb's essay so long; that is, "Then I went on to say. . . ."
2. What devices does Lamb use to make individuals of the children?
3. Which characters in "Dream-Children" seem to have been based on actual persons in Lamb's life?
4. At what point does Lamb realize that his little ones are only dream children?
5. Lamb's friends customarily described him as "gentle-hearted." Does this essay demonstrate the justice of the description?

A BUNCH
Osbert Sitwell OF SNOWDROPS

Osbert Sitwell (1892–   ) was born in London. Educated at Eton, he is notoriously and charmingly famous for his barbed wit and felicitous style. His works include *Who Killed Cock Robin?* (1921), *Dumb Animal and Other Stories* (1930), *Collected Poems and Satires* (1931), *Sing High! Sing Low!* (1944), a five-volume autobiography (1945–1950), *Death of A God* (1949),

Collected Short Stories (1953), *Fee Fi Fo Fum* (1959), *Tales My Father Taught Me* (1962), and *Pound Wise* (1963). With his brother Sacheverell and his sister Edith, he published *Trio* in 1938.

For those who are no longer children, Christmas, whether they enjoy it or not, must inevitably be a brief season of nostalgia—and this is all the more to be savoured in a foreign land whose habits at this season greatly resemble those one knew at home. (*Foreign* is a word inapt to describe how an Englishman feels in the States or, I hope, how an American feels in England.) In Italy, on the other hand, Christmas is very different from ours: there are the old, indigenous customs, many of them pagan in origin, others touchingly and tenderly Christian and medieval, as when the *Pifferi* come from the mountains to blow their bagpipes in front of the lighted images of the Virgin throughout the length of Italy. But the American Christmas so greatly resembles our own—or let me qualify that by saying the English Christmas of thirty years ago—that it is bound to bring back memories. In an age of catastrophe and dissolution, these memories, albeit they may in themselves be happy, are bound to give life to old regrets.

One Christmas, then, I passed at Boston—and, as might be expected, the occasion itself was happy. To one fresh from the splendours and exaggerative beauties of New York, which I so greatly love, Boston seems as English in its architecture, in the houses on Beacon Hill, and the shell-like spires of its churches, as does its climate at Christmas. The actual eve of Christmas I spent in the house of my two dearest friends in Boston, and in the atmosphere of pervading hospitality and affection which they evoked—and under the influence, I may add, of the delectable society and excellent claret they provided—all feelings of sadness were quickly forgotten, and I enjoyed every moment of the evening, the company of the people in the room, the crowds outside, the lighted candles in the windows, the carols. . . . Only in the darkness of the night, when I woke up, a sudden scent of snowdrops assailed me—are snowdrops also an American flower?—and it seemed to me suddenly that I had come a long and tiring way from the point at which I started. I was now, I believed—but how could one ever be sure?—a celebrated writer, I was certainly delivering lectures in a great and distant land, at fifty-six years of age. In a way it sounded comforting. By today's standards, fifty-six is no great age: but the people I knew as a child were dead, the world in which they lived was dead, and even though I had not liked all of them or it, it was borne in on me how quickly life could change its surface.

As I lay there in the darkness, the Christmas Days I had spent in my childhood loomed up at me like beads on a chain, or snowdrops gathered in a bunch. . . . The first I remember was spent under the hospitable roof of Ganton, the country-house of the Legards in York-shire, and a name known to all lovers of memoirs because of its frequent occurrence in the pages of the Comtesse de Boigne's reminiscences. Sir Charles Legard, portly and affable in the manner of the Prince of Wales (for we are still in Queen Victoria's reign), wearing a bowler hat and a dark suit, and Lady Legard, my godmother, tight-waisted, charitable, dressed in lilac and white, are drawn for ever in my memory against a back-ground of snow.

There was a famous frost that winter, and they were forced to walk delicately when they went out, as if walking on ropes—and I remember that the cold had obliged the rabbits to nibble every morsel of stick or leaf left above snow level. The memory is sweet, tender and bitter as the smell of the bunches of early snowdrops from Renishaw, which reached us when we returned to our house at Scarborough; and which remain for me ever associated with the festival.

The first snow must have gone at Renishaw, or the flowers would not have come out. It was early for them. As they lay there, before my nurse took them from their damp box, I well remember my rapture at seeing those delicate, green-veined, frosty flowers, gothic in shape and edged with green, and with a particularly evasive and enticing scent; indeed, invented for what reason except to please human beings, be-cause assuredly no insects are present at that season to be attracted?

After that first festival to be recalled, when I was three or four, came a Christmas spent in London. At that stage of infancy, the fact of mortality was still beyond my understanding, and I remember wonder-ing what my father meant as, looking at a letter received from his father-in-law, Lord Londesborough, he remarked to my mother: "As they've been invited, the children had better spend Christmas in London, with your father and mother. They're growing old, and may not be here much longer."

What, I wondered, did he mean, and where would old people like that go to, at their age? (About their destination, perhaps, a doubt still lingers in my mind.) However, I entered enthusiastically into the idea of spending Christmas in London. It meant, I knew, that we should be taken on the night of Boxing Day to the opening of the Christmas pantomime at Drury Lane—an occasion for which all children longed—and see the great Dan Leno as the Widow Twankey in *Aladdin*.

The atmosphere of London at Christmas proved overwhelming: the moment we reached the station, after a journey of five unheated hours, it came at us. The station was a cavern of iron, with a glass roof, crammed with the fog and smoke of eons: from its menacing, dark shelter, full of shouts and bustle, we stepped into a four-wheeler, bitterly cold and smelling of oats, beer and fog in equal proportions. Even the hoarse voice of the red-nosed cabman carried out, as it were, the same stupendous epitome of the season.

We drove to Grosvenor Square, where was the family mansion, and in it an exotic air of warmth, excitement and Christmas delights and surprises; which prevailed, too, in the day-time in the near-by streets, in the bouquets of sweet-scented flowers in the windows, in the toy-shops, crowded with ingenious mechanical treasures, and the fruit-shops, now full of southern fruits, such as tangerines, Elvas plums, starred with coloured paper, dates and raisins.

The size of London, in its thick muffling canopy of white or yellow fog, was immense, imposing: a fog lit by flares and torches, and through its often impenetrable texture would sound perpetually the cheerful, faintly contaminated Cockney vowels, as the shoppers at stalls and small stores called, one to another, and spoke of the weather, and of Christmas.

Yet, in spite of that urban experience of it, Christmas remains for me essentially a rural feast. Only a few Christmases did we spend at Renishaw—and these were overshadowed by my father's disapproval of the whole occasion, and by his fear of "getting the children into extravagant habits by giving them presents." (He hated to give presents to people who expected them, or when they expected them, and I still recall, with tremors of discomfort, the Christmas I spent with him in Venice some decades after, and how, when the amiable Italian waiter remarked to him: "Good morning, Sir George, and a happy Christmas!," he replied in a tone of disillusioned comprehension: "I know!")

My mother certainly made up for our lack of amusements as much as she could: yet Christmas at home remained a rather barren festival. But when I was about eight, my grandfather died and we began to spend Christmas every year in the house of his son. And it was this series of ten or so Christmases, spent under the roof of my uncle and aunt Londesborough at Blankney, that have subsequently conditioned and defined my ideas of Christmas, its horrors and pleasures.

It was perhaps not a typical Christmas, being more international and exotic, and scarcely Christian, except for brief desultory, purely formal appearances in church. No, pleasure, comfort, warmth, sport were the objectives, and these were obtained.

The large house was always full of relatives of every age, from second childhood down to first: some were in bathchairs, others in perambulators, some remembered King George IV and the great Duke of Wellington, some remembered nothing, from having left off remembering, others had not yet begun to remember. There would often be foreign connections present as well as English.

As for the children, we were tied to compulsory pleasure, as later, at school, to compulsory games. We took part certainly in the feasting of our elders. We watched them hunting, shooting and engaged in other diverse and repulsive sports, such as clubbing rabbits on the head, but we were, on the other hand, made to perform a French play, under the tuition of a whole platoon of governesses. This would be given before villagers who understood no word of French, and were there by a kind of corvée.

But, above all, Christmas was henceforth to be associated for me with my giant and genial uncle and his two passions, for music and mechanics. In the passages he had accumulated some twelve or fourteen mechanical organs; cases with glass fronts that revealed trumpets and drums that, when set in motion, could be seen indulging in an orgy of self-blowing and self-beating. This elementary, if expensive, form of juke-box greatly pleased the children, even if it acerbated the nerves of our elders, who did not like their favourite selections from Verdi—for such they usually were—played in this fashion.

But now the music is stilled, the machines are obsolete; the fashionable beauties and the plain, poor relations are equally unfashionable, for they are dead, even most of those who were young children fifty years ago—and the dead are always unfashionable.

As I look back, I see the vast tents of the rooms, lighted during the day's dark as well as the night's, shining out for miles over untrodden fields of snow that ended beyond our vision in the white-fringed sea; rooms that were filled with the contemporary symbols of luxury, palm trees of exceptional stature, poinsettias that seemed to bear as flowers stars cut out of red flannel; a fragrance of wood-smoke, and jonquils and freesias, hung in the air. . . . But, framing all these and bringing them back to me, is the more rustic smell of snowdrops, edged with a few prickly green leaves, their stalks tied roughly, inexpertly, with thin, damp string, lying in a damp cardboard box that has just been opened.

STUDY QUESTIONS

1. How and why does Sitwell qualify his statement that the American Christmas resembles the English Christmas?
2. What adjectives does Sitwell use to describe the scent of the snowdrops? Do they seem appropriate as descriptions of the scent of a flower? Why does he feel the scent was *invented?*
3. Explain Sitwell's phrase, "the . . . stupendous epitome of the season."
4. Sitwell speaks of the horrors and pleasures of his idea of Christmas. What horrors does he recall?
5. In what sense are "the dead . . . always unfashionable"?

THE REVOLVER
Graham Greene   **IN THE CORNER CUPBOARD**

Graham Greene (1904–   ) was born in Berkhamstead, England, and educated at Balliol College, Oxford. He holds an honorary Litt. D. from Cambridge University. Although a well-known
playwright, essayist, and short-story writer, he is most famous for
his novels and "entertainments." These include *Babbling April*
(1925), *It's a Battlefield* (1934), *A Gun for Sale* (1926), *Brighton
Rock* (1938), *The Power and the Glory* (1940), *The Ministry of
Fear* (1943), *The Heart of the Matter* (1948), *The Third Man*
(1950), *The End of the Affair* (1951), *Twenty-one Stories* (1954),
The Quiet American (1955), *Our Man in Havana* (1958), *A
Burnt-out Case* (1961), and *The Comedians* (1966). His latest
volume of short stories was published in 1967.

I can remember very clearly the afternoon I found the revolver in
the brown deal corner cupboard in the bedroom which I shared with my
elder brother. It was the early autumn of 1922. I was seventeen and
terribly bored and in love with my sister's governess—one of those miserable, hopeless, romantic loves of adolescence that set in many minds the
idea that love and despair are inextricable and that successful love
hardly deserves the name. At that age one may fall irrevocably in love
with failure, and success of any kind loses half its savour before it is
experienced. Such a love is surrendered once and for all to the singer at
the pavement's edge, the bankrupt, the old school friend who wants to
touch you for a dollar. Perhaps in many so conditioned it is the love for
God that mainly survives, because in his eyes they can imagine themselves
remaining always drab, seedy, unsuccessful, and therefore worthy of
notice.

The revolver was a small genteel object with six chambers like a
tiny egg stand, and there was a cardboard box of bullets. It has only
recently occurred to me that they may have been blanks; I always
assumed them to be live ammunition, and I never mentioned the discovery to my brother because I had realized the moment I saw the
revolver the use I intended to make of it. (I don't to this day know why

he possessed it; certainly he had no licence, and he was only three years older than myself. A large family is as departmental as a Ministry.)

My brother was away—probably climbing in the Lake District—and until he returned the revolver was to all intents mine. I knew what to do with it because I had been reading a book (the name Ossendowski comes to mind as the possible author) describing how the White Russian officers, condemned to inaction in South Russia at the tail-end of the counter-revolutionary war, used to invent hazards with which to escape boredom. One man would slip a charge into a revolver and turn the chambers at random, and his companion would put the revolver to his head and pull the trigger. The chance, of course, was six to one in favour of life.

How easily one forgets emotions. If I were dealing now with an imaginary character, I would feel it necessary for verisimilitude to make him hesitate, put the revolver back into the cupboard, return to it again after an interval, reluctantly and fearfully, when the burden of boredom became too great. But in fact I think there was no hesitation at all, for the next I can remember is crossing Berkhamstead Common, gashed here and there between the gorse bushes with the stray trenches of the first Great War, towards the Ashridge beeches. Perhaps before I had made the discovery, boredom had already reached an intolerable depth.

I think the boredom was far deeper than the love. It had always been a feature of childhood: it would set in on the second day of the school holidays. The first day was all happiness, and, after the horrible confinement and publicity of school, seemed to consist of light, space and silence. But a prison conditions its inhabitants. I never wanted to return to it (and finally expressed my rebellion by the simple act of running away), but yet I was so conditioned that freedom bored me unutterably.

The psycho-analysis that followed my act of rebellion had fixed the boredom as hypo fixes the image on the negative. I emerged from those delightful months in London spent at my analyst's house—perhaps the happiest months of my life—correctly orientated, able to take a proper extrovert interest in my fellows (the jargon rises to the lips), but wrung dry. For years, it seems to me, I could take no aesthetic interest in any visual thing at all: staring at a sight that others assured me was beautiful, I would feel nothing. I was fixed in my boredom. (Writing this I come on a remark of Rilke: "Psycho-analysis is too fundamental a help for me, it helps you once and for all, it clears you up, and to find myself finally cleared up one day might be even more helpless than this chaos.")

Now with the revolver in my pocket I was beginning to emerge. I had stumbled on the perfect cure. I was going to escape in one way or another, and because escape was inseparably connected with the Common in my mind, it was there that I went.

The wilderness of gorse, old trenches, abandoned butts was the unchanging backcloth of most of the adventures of childhood. It was to the Common I had decamped for my act of rebellion some years before, with the intention, expressed in a letter left after breakfast on the heavy black sideboard, that there I would stay, day and night, until either I had starved or my parents had given in; when I pictured war it was always in terms of this Common, and myself leading a guerilla campaign in the ragged waste, for no one, I was persuaded, knew its paths so intimately (how humiliating that in my own domestic campaign I was ambushed by my elder sister after a few hours).

Beyond the Common lay a wide grass ride known for some reason as Cold Harbour to which I would occasionally with some fear take a horse, and beyond this again stretched Ashridge Park, the smooth olive skin of beech trees and the thick last year's quagmire of leaves, dark like old pennies. Deliberately I chose my ground, I believe without any real fear—perhaps because I was uncertain myself whether I was play-acting; perhaps because so many acts which my elders would have regarded as neurotic, but which I still consider to have been under the circumstances highly reasonable, lay in the background of this more dangerous venture.

There had been, for example, perhaps five or six years before, the disappointing morning in the dark room by the linen cupboard on the eve of term when I had patiently drunk a quantity of hypo under the impression that it was poisonous: on another occasion the blue glass bottle of hay fever lotion which as it contained a small quantity of cocaine had probably been good for my mood: the bunch of deadly nightshade that I had eaten with only a slight narcotic effect: the twenty aspirins I had taken before swimming in the empty out-of-term school baths (I can still remember the curious sensation of swimming through wool): these acts may have removed all sense of strangeness as I slipped a bullet into a chamber and, holding the revolver behind my back, spun the chambers round.

Had I romantic thoughts about the governess? Undoubtedly I must have had, but I think that at the most they simply eased the medicine down. Boredom, aridity, those were the main emotions. Unhappy love has, I suppose, sometimes driven boys to suicide, but this was not suicide, whatever a coroner's jury might have said of it: it was a gamble with six chances to one against an inquest. The romantic flavour —the autumn scene, the small heavy compact shape lying in the fingers— that perhaps was a tribute to adolescent love, but the discovery that it was possible to enjoy again the visible world by risking its total loss was one I was bound to make sooner or later.

I put the muzzle of the revolver in my right ear and pulled the trigger. There was a minute click, and looking down at the chamber I could see that the charge had moved into place. I was out by one. I remember an extraordinary sense of jubilation. It was as if a light had been turned on. My heart was knocking in its cage, and I felt that life contained an infinite number of possibilities. It was like a young man's first successful experience of sex—as if in that Ashridge glade one had passed a test of manhood. I went home and put the revolver back in the corner cupboard.

The odd thing about this experience was that it was repeated several times. At fairly long intervals I found myself craving for the drug. I took the revolver with me when I went up to Oxford and I would walk out from Headington towards Elsfield down what is now a wide arterial road, smooth and shiny like the walls of a public lavatory. Then it was a sodden unfrequented country lane. The revolver would be whipped behind my back, the chambers twisted, the muzzle quickly and surreptitiously inserted beneath the black and ugly winter tree, the trigger pulled.

Slowly the effect of the drug wore off—I lost the sense of jubilation, I began to gain from the experience only the crude kick of excitement. It was like the difference between love and lust. And as the quality of the experience deteriorated so my sense of responsibility grew and worried me. I wrote a very bad piece of free verse (free because it was easier in that way to express my meaning without literary equivocation) describing how, in order to give a fictitious sense of danger, I would "press the trigger of a revolver I already know to be empty." This piece of verse I would leave permanently on my desk, so that if I lost my gamble, there would be incontrovertible evidence of an accident, and my parents, I thought, would be less troubled than by an apparent suicide—or than by the rather bizarre truth.

But it was back at Berkhamstead that I paid a permanent farewell to the drug. As I took my fifth dose it occurred to me that I wasn't even excited: I was beginning to pull the trigger about as casually as I might take an aspirin tablet. I decided to give the revolver—which was six-chambered—a sixth and last chance. Twirling the chambers round, I put the muzzle to my ear for the last time and heard the familiar empty click as the chambers revolved. I was through with the drug, and walking back over the Common, down the new road by the ruined castle, past the private entrance to the gritty old railway station—reserved for the use of Lord Brownlow—my mind was already busy on other plans. One campaign was over, but the war against boredom had got to go on.

I put the revolver back in the corner cupboard, and going downstairs I lied gently and convincingly to my parents that a friend had invited me to join him in Paris.

1. If Greene's essay were based on an imaginary character instead of himself, what concessions would he make for the sake of verisimilitude?
2. Why did Greene run away from school?
3. Was Greene deliberately attempting suicide? Had he attempted suicide earlier?
4. How did the governess contribute to Greene's state of mind? Was she the main reason for it?
5. Why did Greene eventually stop playing his dangerous, solitary game?
6. What is the point of the lie he tells his parents?

George Orwell   A HANGING

George Orwell (1903–1950) was the pen name of Eric Blair, who was born in Bengal, India. He graduated from Eton College, served with the Indian Imperial Police in Burma from 1922 to 1927, and then returned to England to begin his career as a writer. His works include *Burmese Days* (1934), *Homage to Catalonia* (1936), *Dickens, Dali and Others* (1946), and *Shooting an Elephant* (1950). However, his fame is primarily the result of *Animal Farm* (1946), and *1984* (1949), the former a classic novel of social protest, and the latter one of the most famous modern satires.

It was in Burma, a sodden morning of the rains. A sickly light, like yellow tinfoil, was slanting over the high walls into the jail yard. We were waiting outside the condemned cells, a row of sheds fronted with double bars, like small animal cages. Each cell measured about ten feet by ten and was quite bare within except for a plank bed and a pot for drinking water. In some of them brown, silent men were squatting at the inner bars, with their blankets draped round them. These were the condemned men, due to be hanged within the next week or two.

One prisoner had been brought out of his cell. He was a Hindu, a puny wisp of a man, with a shaven head and vague liquid eyes. He had a thick, sprouting moustache, absurdly too big for his body, rather like the

From *Shooting An Elephant and Other Essays* by George Orwell, copyright 1945, 1946, 1949, 1950 by Sonia Brownell Orwell. Reprinted by permission of Harcourt, Brace & World, Inc.

moustache of a comic man on the films. Six tall Indian warders were guarding him and getting him ready for the gallows. Two of them stood by with rifles and fixed bayonets, while the others handcuffed him, passed a chain through his handcuffs and fixed it to their belts, and lashed his arms tight to his sides. They crowded very close about him, with their hands always on him in a careful, caressing grip, as though all the while feeling him to make sure he was there. It was like men handling a fish which is still alive and may jump back into the water. But he stood quite unresisting, yielding his arms limply to the ropes, as though he hardly noticed what was happening.

Eight o'clock struck and a bugle call, desolately thin in the wet air, floated from the distant barracks. The superintendent of the jail, who was standing apart from the rest of us, moodily prodding the gravel with his stick, raised his head at the sound. He was an army doctor, with a grey toothbrush moustache and a gruff voice. "For God's sake hurry up, Francis," he said irritably. "The man ought to have been dead by this time. Aren't you ready yet?"

Francis, the head jailer, a fat Dravidian in a white drill suit and gold spectacles, waved his black hand. "Yes sir, yes sir," he bubbled. "All iss satisfactorily prepared. The hangman iss waiting. We shall proceed."

"Well, quick march, then. The prisoners can't get their breakfast till this job's over."

We set out for the gallows. Two warders marched on either side of the prisoner, with their rifles at the slope; two others marched close against him, gripping him by arm and shoulder, as though at once pushing and supporting him. The rest of us, magistrates and the like, followed behind. Suddenly, when we had gone ten yards, the procession stopped short without any order or warning. A dreadful thing had happened—a dog, come goodness knows whence, had appeared in the yard. It came bounding among us with a loud volley of barks and leapt round us wagging its whole body, wild with glee at finding so many human beings together. It was a large woolly dog, half Airedale, half pariah. For a moment it pranced round us, and then, before anyone could stop it, it had made a dash for the prisoner, and jumping up tried to lick his face. Everybody stood aghast, too taken aback even to grab the dog.

"Who let that bloody brute in here?" said the superintendent angrily. "Catch it, someone!"

A warder detached from the escort, charged clumsily after the dog, but it danced and gambolled just out of his reach, taking everything as part of the game. A young Eurasian jailer picked up a handful of gravel and tried to stone the dog away, but it dodged the stones and came after us again. Its yaps echoed from the jail walls. The prisoner, in the grasp of the two warders, looked on incuriously, as though this was another formality of the hanging. It was several minutes before someone managed to catch the dog. Then we put my handkerchief through its collar and moved off once more, with the dog still straining and whimpering.

It was about forty yards to the gallows. I watched the bare brown back of the prisoner marching in front of me. He walked clumsily with his bound arms, but quite steadily, with that bobbing gait of the Indian who never straightens his knees. At each step his muscles slid neatly into place, the lock of hair on his scalp danced up and down, his feet printed themselves on the wet gravel. And once, in spite of the men who gripped him by each shoulder, he stepped lightly aside to avoid a puddle on the path.

It is curious, but till that moment I had never realized what it means to destroy a healthy, conscious man. When I saw the prisoner step aside to avoid the puddle I saw the mystery, the unspeakable wrongness, of cutting a life short when it is in full tide. This man was not dying, he was alive just as we are alive. All the organs of his body were working—bowels digesting food, skin renewing itself, nails growing, tissues forming—all toiling away in solemn foolery. His nails would still be growing when he stood on the drop, when he was falling through the air with a tenth-of-a-second to live. His eyes saw the yellow gravel and the grey walls, and his brain still remembered, foresaw, reasoned—even about puddles. He and we were a party of men walking together, seeing, hearing, feeling, understanding the same world; and in two minutes, with a sudden snap, one of us would be gone—one mind less, one world less.

The gallows stood in a small yard, separate from the main grounds of the prison, and overgrown with tall prickly weeds. It was a brick erection like three sides of a shed, with planking on top, and above that two beams and a crossbar with the rope dangling. The hangman, a grey-haired convict in the white uniform of the prison, was waiting beside his machine. He greeted us with a servile crouch as we entered. At a word from Francis the two warders, gripping the prisoner more closely than ever, half led, half pushed him to the gallows and helped him clumsily up the ladder. Then the hangman climbed up and fixed the rope round the prisoner's neck.

We stood waiting, five yards away. The warders had formed in a rough circle round the gallows. And then, when the noose was fixed, the prisoner began crying out to his god. It was a high, reiterated cry of "Ram! Ram! Ram! Ram!" not urgent and fearful like a prayer or cry for help, but steady, rhythmical, almost like the tolling of a bell. The dog answered the sound with a whine. The hangman, still standing on the gallows, produced a small cotton bag like a flour bag and drew it down over the prisoner's face. But the sound, muffled by the cloth, still persisted, over and over again: "Ram! Ram! Ram! Ram! Ram!"

The hangman climbed down and stood ready, holding the lever.

Minutes seemed to pass. The steady, muffled crying from the prisoner went on and on, "Ram! Ram! Ram!" never faltering for an instant. The superintendent, his head on his chest, was slowly poking the ground with his stick; perhaps he was counting the cries, allowing the prisoner a fixed number—fifty, perhaps, or a hundred. Everyone had changed colour. The Indians had gone grey like bad coffee, and one or two of the bayonets were wavering. We looked at the lashed, hooded man on the drop, and listened to his cries—each cry another second of life; the same thought was in all our minds: oh, kill him quickly, get it over, stop that abominable noise!

Suddenly the superintendent made up his mind. Throwing up his head he made a swift motion with his stick. "Chalo!" he shouted almost fiercely.

There was a clanking noise, and then dead silence. The prisoner had vanished, and the rope was twisting on itself. I let go of the dog, and it galloped immediately to the back of the gallows; but when it got there it stopped short, barked, and then retreated into a corner of the yard, where it stood among the weeds, looking timorously out at us. We went round the gallows to inspect the prisoner's body. He was dangling with his toes pointed straight downwards, very slowly revolving, as dead as a stone.

The superintendent reached out with his stick and poked the bare brown body; it oscillated slightly. "*He's* all right," said the superintendent. He backed out from under the gallows, and blew out a deep breath. The moody look had gone out of his face quite suddenly. He glanced at his wrist-watch. "Eight minutes past eight. Well, that's all for this morning, thank God."

The warders unfixed bayonets and marched away. The dog, sobered and conscious of having misbehaved itself, slipped after them. We walked out of the gallows yard, past the condemned cells with their waiting prisoners, into the big central yard of the prison. The convicts, under the command of warders armed with lathis, were already receiving their breakfast. They squatted in long rows, each man holding a tin pannikin, while two warders with buckets marched round ladling out rice; it seemed quite a homely, jolly scene, after the hanging. An enormous relief had come upon us now that the job was done. One felt an impulse to sing, to break into a run, to snigger. All at once everyone began chattering gaily.

The Eurasian boy walking beside me nodded towards the way we had come, with a knowing smile: "Do you know, sir, our friend (he meant the dead man) when he heard his appeal had been dismissed, he pissed on the floor of his cell. From fright. Kindly take one of my cigarettes, sir. Do you not admire my new silver case, sir? From the boxwallah, two rupees eight annas. Classy European style."

Several people laughed—at what, nobody seemed certain.

Francis was walking by the superintendent, talking garrulously: "Well, sir, all hass passed off with the utmost satisfactoriness. It was all finished—flick! like that. It iss not always so—oah, no! I have known cases where the doctor wass obliged to go beneath the gallows and pull the prissoner's legs to ensure decease. Most disagreeable!"

"Wriggling about, eh? That's bad," said the superintendent.

"Ach, sir, it iss worse when they become refractory! One man, I recall, clung to the bars of hiss cage when we went to take him out. You will scarcely credit, sir, that it took six warders to dislodge him, three pulling at each leg. We reasoned with him, 'My dear fellow,' we said, 'think of all the pain and trouble you are causing to us!' But no, he would not listen! Ach, he wass very troublesome!"

I found that I was laughing quite loudly. Everyone was laughing. Even the superintendent grinned in a tolerant way. "You'd better all come out and have a drink," he said quite genially. "I've got a bottle of whisky in the car. We could do with it."

We went through the big double gates of the prison into the road. "Pulling at his legs!" exclaimed a Burmese magistrate suddenly, and burst into a loud chuckling. We all began laughing again. At that moment Francis' anecdote seemed extraordinarily funny. We all had a drink together, native and European alike, quite amicably. The dead man was a hundred yards away.

STUDY QUESTIONS

1. Why is the superintendent irritated by the delay in the hanging?
2. How does the incident with the dog contribute to the effectiveness of "A Hanging"?
3. Why does the prisoner's stepping aside to avoid a puddle bring Orwell to a full realization of the scene before him?
4. Why do the men feel an impulse to sing after the hanging?
5. Explain why Orwell ends his essay with, "The dead man was a hundred yards away."

Reynolds Price   LIFE FOR LIFE

Reynolds Price (1933–   ) was born in Macon, North Carolina. He received his B.A. from Duke University in 1955, then attended Merton College, Oxford, as a Rhodes Scholar. His novel, A

Reprinted by permission of Esquire Magazine. © 1966 by Esquire, Inc.

Long and Happy Life, published in 1962, was an immediate critical success. Equally admired are its sequel, *A Generous Man* (1966), and a book of short stories, *The Names and Faces of Heroes* (1963).

Sifting the debris of my mother's death—Death Mother of Trash (old bankbooks, canceled checks)—my numb hands find an emblem of her life, a stack of records (brittle 78's) which I have not played through in twenty years, island planted by her in her death, pleasant garbage to relieve my chore. I rock back on numb haunches, smile, suck breath (hot July breath), then lift the records to a cooler room, unlid the old Victrola, throw its switch. Like every other thing here now she's dead, it leaps to duty; eager, accurate spins. I pile on half the stack, fall heavily into my father's chair still dark with his hair oil, he dead ten years, surrender to the waiting random order—hoot of Emmy Destinn as Mignon, Lucrezia Bori's lean *Vedrai, carino;* then suddenly as bombs within the room, the Forties: Spike Jones's *Chloe,* crash of kitchens (through laughter, crash of Warsaw, London, Frankfurt); then Franklin Roosevelt, 1941, December Eighth, "I ask that the Congress declare. . . ." At thirteen on my own I sent for this, from N.B.C., a birthday gift for Father. Half-pained, half-peeved, I rise, reject it harshly. Still covered by one more, the next disc falls, clatter of changer, roar of needle, voice: "Good morning, Mrs. Jones. My name is Price. I've come to show. . . ."

My father's voice. Forgotten. Lost. Now around me in his room. Slow, calm—the only music he could make. Twenty-one years of daily hearing it; but ten years gone, I could no more have heard it in my head than Lincoln's voice; have often tried at night to dredge it back, send it looping through some favorite joke, some mimic, even to bear again its last few words (nonsense fierce as flail across my eyes, gargled from cancerous lungs through silver tube). But here again I have him and remember. A demonstration record made by him in 1940 when he had sold more toasters, fans, lamps, stoves than any other salesman in the state and as reward was asked to speak his pitch in lasting wax (*reward* when he was locked in blank torment—downing his thirst to drink, drown finally, and baffled to find ten simple dollar bills to meet this month's new howling creditor).

I down my own new need to stop him. I grant him the rest of his respite, reward.

". . . Mrs. Jones, do you know that many children" (*chirren,* he says) "will suffer poor eyes in years to come just because of the light they study by?" (His *just* is *jest.*)

I had even lost that—the *jest* that littered his life, every speech of the thousands he for years unreeled on the stoops of strangers, incurious, ungrateful, merely and rightly bored, whole lives being daily laid at their feet, reeled out from twitching guts like garden hose, the past shames, present needs of grinning beggars. Postman, parents, lovers, mirrored selves.

"Now, Mrs. Jones, if you will say the word, I'll bring you on approval our new floor lamp. No obligation on your part at all. . . ."

I say the word she never can, a calm No, and end his endless bottled plea for hope. Next record plays, bald irony, black jest, Anderson sings *Komm Süsser Tod* of Bach.

So Father, sweet death I have given you, mere silence, rest; vowed not to force you through your pitch again. To seal the vow I look up to your picture on the wall. Deep walnut frame, deep window on your face. Nineteen Eighteen, you eighteen yourself, the worst of wars hung bleeding overhead (your brother Edward's lungs already gassed; your own Guard button in your left lapel, an eagle spread above a waiting world; you will be called weeks from now yourself but saved in port by the Armistice) and still your gaze though high is clear, undoubting; a surety that even now seems firm, not boyish foolishness, seems well-informed as though you saw sure detailed happy futures, a life like water (clear, needed, useful, permanent, free), spared all you will so soon acquire (drink, wife, sons, labor, thirty-six more years). I touch the glass above your silent mouth.

Dear boy (dear grey eyes, broad nose, curling lip) locked on your browning, cracking paper card, I offer you my life—look, it will serve. Cancel all plan of me, let me not be, so you may have free time, move always sure, accept with smooth hands what your eyes still see, elude brute ambush of your gurgling death.

STUDY QUESTIONS

1. Price begins his reminiscence as he sifts the debris of his mother's death, yet he writes primarily of his father. Why then mention his mother at all?
2. Why does he harshly reject the N.B.C. record? Is there a possible double meaning in *reject?*
3. Why does Price vow not to force his father through his sales pitch again? How does he give his father "sweet death"?
4. What is a *black jest?*
5. Relate the title of Price's essay to the last paragraph.

| # MODERN
SOCIAL
PROBLEMS

"Some Must Watch"

DOWN WITH
THE RAT RACE:
Lawrence Lipton **THE NEW POVERTY**

Lawrence Lipton (1898–   ), poet and novelist identified with
the beat generation, has published widely in such magazines as
The Atlantic Monthly, The Nation, Chicago Review, and the *Quarterly Review of Literature.* He has conducted a Jazz Canto Poets
and Musicians Workshop in Venice, California, an area that has become famous as the home of beat generation writers and artists.
His books include two novels, *Brother, the Laugh Is Bitter* (1942)
and *In Secret Battle* (1944); and three collections of poetry, *Pacifica:
Inferno Records, Jazz Canto: Volume,* and *Rainbow at Midnight*
(1955). The last book won a Book Club Selection for Poetry in 1955.
He is best known to the general public for *The Holy Barbarians*
(1959), the story of the beat generation.

Those who see the American businessman as the fount from
whence all blessings flow, enterpriser *par excellence,* organizer of Progress, job-maker, charity-giver, endower of churches and universities and
patron of the arts, who has given us the highest standard of living in the
world, have never been able to understand why the figure of the businessman has fared so badly at the hands of the intellectuals. As for the
businessmen themselves, the early industrialists were never worried
about their reputation with the intellectuals. Many of them were only
semiliterate, and while they were quick to retaliate against sticks and
stones, whether thrown by labor or by their competitors, they were
merely contemptuous of words. But the growth of advertising as a
formidable weapon opened the businessman's eyes to the possibility that
while he was watching out for sticks and stones, words might break his
bones.

It was not until after the Depression, the New Deal and World War II, though, that the public relations men and the advertising men were able to arouse the businessmen to active retaliation against the treatment he was receiving in novels, plays, radio and films, and even in the churches and classrooms. During the Depression he had to lick his wounds in bitter silence while he heard himself called a "malefactor of great wealth" by that "traitor to his class" Franklin D. Roosevelt. He had to suffer in silence while detractors were being entertained in the White House and providing verbal ammunition for a New Deal that looked to him like nothing more than a "hate business" conspiracy which his political spokesmen have since rephrased as "twenty years of treason." It is little wonder that his pent-up resentments should have taken the form of a vengeful "house cleaning" after the war, not only of political officeholders but of the New Deal's intellectual and literary friends as well.

Hand in hand with the loyalty oaths and investigations has gone a widespread propaganda campaign on the platform and in the press against all intellectuals, a campaign in which friendly highbrows are regarded as only a little less dangerous than unfriendly ones and potentially treasonous. The halfhearted and timorous "wooing back" of the egghead that began with the successful Soviet orbiting of Sputnik I is confined to scientists and technicians, and is concerned, characteristically, with *buying brains* rather than encouraging the intellectual to think straight and speak out plainly.

The word intellectual has never been altogether free from suspicion in the United States; calling a man a brain has been fightin' words for a hundred years. Intellectualism is, needless to say, equated with leftism, a proposition that has at least the merit of being half true, but not in the way *they* mean it. It is even equated with modernism in art—unless it can be turned into window displays, high fashion fabrics, liquor ads and clever television commercials.

But the businessman had a bad conscience long before he ever became a target of the intellectual. Profit, which is the basis of business, has been under a cloud for centuries, certainly since the time of the prophet Hosea and probably long before him. Among the Church Fathers there were not a few who echoed the words of the Hebrew prophets against malefactors of great wealth, well before "That Man" in the White House blasted them on the radio.

And when Dave Gelden speaks of writing poetry in the lavatory of the airplane plant on the boss' time and on the boss' toilet paper and says, "It wasn't stealing, I was just getting my own," he speaks out of an old and honored tradition. He speaks for the few who *can* reject the rewards that a business civilization offers those who are willing to help it sell its ideology.

Moneytheism is everywhere, in everything we see and read and hear. The child is indoctrinated with it from birth, not in the schools, which try to counter it with the humanities—as much as they dare—but in the large school of experience where most of our education is received. It is only after a long process of diseducation and re-education that one sees it clearly and sees it whole—the price-wage shell game, the speed-up treadmill, the Save!-Spend! contradictions dinned into our ears night and day, the heartbreaking brutalities of class-made law, lawyer-made law, judge-made law, money-made law, and the unspeakable vulgarities of hypocritical religion, the nerve-shattering Stop! and Go! Hurry! and Go Slow! Step Lively! and Relax! warnings flashing before our eyes and bombarding our ears without letup, making the soul a squirrel cage whirligig from the first stimulant in the morning till the last sedative at night. The rat race. A rat race that offers only two alternatives: to run with the hare or hunt with the hounds.

Disaffiliation: The Way of the Beat Generation

Disaffiliation is a voluntary self-alienation from the family cult, from Moneytheism and all its works and ways.

The disaffiliate has no blueprint for the future. He joins no political parties. He is free to make his own inner-directed decisions. If he fails to vote altogether, that, too, is a form of political action; half the eligible voters of the United States normally fail to do so. In his case it is a no-confidence vote.

The disaffiliate doesn't like the smell of burning human flesh, whether it come from the lynching tree, the witness chair or the electric chair.

Having read history from the bottom up as well as from the top down, he knows that culture moves both ways, interactively, and there are times—the present is one of them—when the cultural top is at the economic bottom.

He is not against industrialization. He is not against "things," material things as opposed to spiritual things.

Why, then, disaffiliation in an era when *Time-Life-Fortune* pages are documenting an American Way of Life that is filled with color-matched stainless steel kitchens, bigger and faster cars, electronic wonders, and a future of unlimited luxuries like television-telephones and rocket trips to the moon? Because it is all being corrupted by the cult of Moneytheism. In the eyes of a Nelson Algren it is all a "neon wilderness." In the eyes of a Henry Miller it is all an "air-conditioned nightmare." Because, as Kenneth Rexroth has put it, you can't fill the heads of young lovers with "buy me the new five-hundred-dollar deep-freeze and I'll love you" advertising propaganda without poisoning the very act of love itself; you can't hop up your young people with sadism in the movies and television and train them to commando tactics in the army camps, to say nothing of brutalizing them in wars, and then expect to "untense" them with Coca-Cola and Y.M.C.A. hymn sings. Because underneath Henry Luce's "permanent revolution"—the New Capitalism, the People's Capitalism and Prosperity Unlimited—lies the ugly fact of an economy geared to war production, a design, not for living, but for death.

If the disaffiliate is on the side of the accused instead of on the side of the accusers, it is because the accuser *has* his spokesmen, a host of them, well paid, with all the mass media at their command and all the laws and police on their side.

Where the choice is between two rival tyrannies, however pious their pretentions, the disaffiliate says, not a plague but a pity on both your houses.

The Art of Poverty

The New Poverty is the disaffiliate's answer to the New Prosperity.

It is important to make a living, but it is even more important to make a life.

Poverty. The very word is taboo in a society where success is equated with virtue and poverty is a sin. Yet it has an honorable ancestry. St. Francis of Assisi revered Poverty as his bride, with holy fervor and pious rapture.

The poverty of the disaffiliate is not to be confused with the poverty of indigence, intemperence, improvidence or failure. It is simply that the goods and services he has to offer are not valued at a high price in our society. As one beat generation writer said to the square who offered him an advertising job: "I'll scrub your floors and carry out your slops to make a living, but I will not lie for you, pimp for you, stool for you, or rat for you."

It is not the poverty of the ill-tempered and embittered, those who wooed the bitch goddess Success with panting breath and came away rebuffed.

It is an independent, voluntary poverty.

It is an art, and like all arts it has to be learned. It has its techniques, its tricks and short cuts, its know-how.

What is poverty for one may be extravagance for another. The writer must have his basic library, the composer his piano, the painter his canvases and tools, and everyone must have at least a few of the books he wants, if only in paperback editions, a few good recordings and some objects of art, if only in prints and cheap imitations.

It all depends on what the disaffiliate values most. Kenneth Rexroth, for instance, has a scholar's library that may be worth ten thousand
dollars—all of it shelved in packing cases set up one above the other to
serve as bookshelves—in a fifty dollar slum apartment. A composer I
know has a microfilm library of the world's best music that is matched
only by that of the Library of Congress and perhaps a few private
collections, and stints on food and clothing almost to the point of beg-
gary. Each must work out the logistics of the problem to fit his own case.

The writer as disaffiliate has a special problem of his own. He may
not have much control over the size of his income—a book may flop or it
may be a runaway best seller—but he does have some measure of control
over how much he spends. And how he spends it. And where he lives.
For, as Nelson Algren has expressed it, "Scarcely any way now remains of
reporting the American Century except from behind the tote-board.
From behind the TV commercials and the Hearst headlines, the car ads
and the subtitles, the editorials and the conventions. For it is only there
that the people of Dickens and Dostoevski may be found any more."

Behind the billboards lie the slums. Here one may hold his standard of living down to the level of a dedicated independent poverty with
some measure of ease and self-respect. It is a way of life that is obliga-
tory only on the truth-telling artist but it is a good way of life for him; it
helps him keep the long, lean view. He will go farther on less if he learns
how to travel light. In the slum he will learn that the health of a
civilization should be judged by the maxim laid down by one of humanity's greatest physicians: "Inasmuch as ye did it not unto one of these
least, ye did it not unto me." He will learn what Diane Lattimer (in
George Mandel's novel, *Flee the Angry Strangers*) meant when, at the
last, out of the depths of her agony and pain, she said: "Come, sit in the
Cosmopole. You don't need anything in this world; only poverty is
holy."

The Logistics of Poverty

The dedicated independent poverty is an art, but it is also a
science of survival. It has its strategies and logistics.

Those who choose manual labor soon find out that, so far as the
trades are concerned, breaking into the ranks of labor is neither easy nor
cheap. Joining the proletariat is like trying to join an exclusive club and
often quite as expensive, what with trade union initiation fees and
numerous qualifications and restrictions. For the most part the beat
generation disaffiliate is confined to the fringe jobs in the labor market,
like small house painting jobs if he is an artist trying to find part-time
work to pay for his colors and canvases and keep some canned goods in
the larder. Some painters in the Los Angeles area have occasionally

found cartooning jobs and sculpting on a part-time basis in the studios, particularly at the Walt Disney Studio. Ceramics has provided some income for artists, as well as costume jewelry designing, free lance or in the employ of some small businessman. Frame making can be a source of income. And some artists do not mind teaching a few hours a week at some art school or as private tutors.

In Venice West some have made it for a while as typewriter repairmen, postal employees and arts and crafts teachers—"occupational therapy"—in mental hospitals, or attendants in the mental wards, or psychology assistants giving Rorschach tests. In San Francisco they sometimes ship out with a crew for a few months and come home with a bank roll, or join a road construction gang in Canada or Alaska. Allen Ginsberg financed a trip to North Africa and Europe that way. The lumber camps of the Northwest sometimes serve the same purpose for a while. Some part-time jobs are to be found as laboratory technicians, X-ray technicians and the like, if one is willing to spend a few months preparing himself for the job.

In New York there are jobs that offer an opportunity to work in odd-hour shifts, much desired by the beat, as art gallery guards, deck hands on ferryboats, and for those who seek solitude and plenty of time to think, goof or write, the job of barge captain is the answer. Those who are polylingual or have traveled abroad can find part-of-the-year employment as travel guides, either self-employed if they have a little organizing ability or in the employ of travel agencies.

In Greenwich Village there are some who make it by doing hauling in small trucks, and some by delivering packages and messages. New Yorkers also find good pickings at the many openings and *premières* in art galleries and other places—to say nothing of pickups, but for this racket you have to own at least one good party suit, unless you can pass for a painter or an interesting "character." New York is also good for free-lance manuscript reading jobs for publishers and part-time jobs reading proof for publishers or printers. Musicians who are making the beat scene do copy work for composers and music publishers, or compile "fake books" containing melodies and chord symbols, with or without words, and peddle them to commercial musicians in a kind of under-the-counter deal, sometimes on the union hall floor and other hangouts for musicians in New York and Hollywood.

In Venice West and elsewhere there is always the possibility of an occasional hitch with the gas and electric company as a meter reader. There is clerking in bookstores and now there are a few jobs in espresso coffeehouses. For those who live near a university there is library work on an hourly basis. Landscape gardening is a year-round possibility for West Coast beatniks. Some of them have made it as counselors for juvenile delinquents, in the employ of the city or county. The job of shipping clerk is a popular one. When you have saved all the money you think you are going to need for a while, you quit and pass the word around to your friends to go there and apply. In this way a job is "kept in the family," just as the pads are kept in the family by being passed on from one tenant to the next, with the landlord often none the wiser—or richer.

Job opportunities are always more numerous for the girls, of course. They can always find work in dress shops and department stores, with the telephone company and the telephone answering services. As doctors' reception clerks and dental assistants. If they have had some dancing school they can find part-time jobs as dancing teachers in private schools and summer jobs in girls' camps. There are any number of office jobs a girl can fill. There is manuscript typing and other free-lance typing work. In Los Angeles some find jobs as script girls in the TV and movie studios. Comparison shopping and the *sub rosa* job of starting whispering campaigns in the subways for commercial products is strictly for the "angle-shooters" among the Village chicks in New York. Modeling is open to those who have the face and the figure for it. The job of B-girl in the taverns is very much sought after because it pays well and the hours are desirable, but rarely do the chicks of beatland double as call girls or do a week-end stint in the whorehouses. That is a monopoly of respectable working girls and housewives in need of extra money to support their families or expensive tastes in clothes and cars. It is no part of the beat scene.

The musically inclined among the girls seek jobs in record shops and with music and record publishers. The artistically talented among the chicks sometimes make it as dress designers, window dressers and interior decorators, but here they run into competition with the beat homosexuals. Homosexual writers and artists are the most hard put to it to find—and hold onto—employment of any kind.

If all else fails there are always the foundations, the Huntington Hartford Foundation near Venice West, where one can find food and shelter for three months (renewable for three months longer) if he is judged eligible and comes properly recommended, and, on the East Coast, Yaddo and the McDowell colony. Some have been the recipients of Guggenheim fellowships or other grants.

There are windfalls now and then. An industrial firm or a university will let it be known that it needs guinea pigs for some research test, like the sleep tests at the U. of C., or some other research problem. One beatnik I know made it for some months as a sweater. He sweated so many hours a day for a cosmetics firm testing a new product.

And there are the standard jobs for itinerants and occasional workers—cab driving, dish washing, bus boy work, filling station work, and, for the girls, jobs as car-hops in drive-in restaurants or waitresses.

In Venice West there are jobs for girls on the Pacific Ocean Park Amusement Pier. Some of the younger chicks who are still going to college—or can keep up a reasonable appearance of doing so—get money from home. If you are older and have children to support and no visible means of support, the county will come to your aid.

With all that, there are still many problems. Poverty is not easy to manage. It requires some planning and some conniving. The pressure is toward conformity, with regular working hours and consumer spending in ways and in quantities that will make the American Way of Life look good in the Labor Department reports and the Department of Commerce statistics. Buying a secondhand suit for five or ten dollars at a Windward Avenue uncalled-for clothing store or a three-dollar second-hand dress at an East Side rummage shop does nothing for the statisticians or the Chamber of Commerce.

Sponging, scrounging, borrowing and angle-shooting are too undependable as a regular source of income, and street begging takes too much time, as Henry Miller has shown, with inspired documentation, in *Tropic of Cancer*. Pushing pot is too hazardous and peddling heroin is a one-way ticket to the penitentiary, if not to the grave. Shoplifting is only a stopgap measure at best. It is an art that takes long practice to master if one is to make a living at it, and is better left to those who have a talent for it. One amateur I know found herself confronted one day with an ideological, if not a moral, problem. The supermarket where she sometimes shoplifted a quarter of a pound of butter—more as social protest when butter prices took a sudden jump than from any actual necessity—was being picketed by strikers. Out of sympathy with the striking union she went across the street to the little independent grocer and did her shoplifting there till the strike was over.

Inheritances sometimes provide a few valuables to be divided among the needy in true communal fashion. Somebody who has wigged out and been committed to a mental institution for a while, or been busted for pot for the third or fourth time and sent up for a long stretch, will leave behind a pad with household effects, furniture, clothes, books, phonograph records, pictures and hi-fi equipment. The accepted practice is that such stuff becomes community property. If a cat moves out of town he sometimes wills such things to his friends quite informally rather than try to tote them with him or go to the expense of having them shipped. When he comes back he will find any pad open to him, or can divide his guesting between several of his choosing. It is the traditional hospitality of the poor, one of the few traditions of the square that the beat honor scrupulously.

"Why don't more of them simply marry rich women?" I heard a square ask one evening at a party in one of the Venice West pads. Chuck Bennison took it upon himself to answer.

"It's a full-time job," he said.

STUDY QUESTIONS

1. According to Lipton, who are the disaffiliated? What do they have in common with the "new aristocrats" described by Goodman in "The New Aristocrats," (see p. 455)?

2. Lipton claims that the way the disaffiliated practice poverty, it is an art. In what ways is it an art?

3. How does the concept of work held by the disaffiliated compare with the concept of work described in Goodman's "Jobs"?

4. Note the number of slang words and expressions in this selection. Are they appropriate to the presentation and subject?

5. From what you know about the hippies, do they correspond with the disaffiliates? If not, what are the differences?

AN EVENING WITH
BODGIES AND WIDGIES
Malcolm Muggeridge **IN MELBOURNE**

Malcolm Muggeridge (1903–   ) is a British writer whose incisive criticisms of the contemporary scene have earned him a reputation in America as well as in his own country. He received his A.B. from Selwyn College, Cambridge. He has served on the editorial staff of the *Manchester Guardian*, the *Calcutta Statesman*, and the *Evening Standard*. From 1953 to 1957 he was editor of *Punch*, the famous British magazine. He has contributed to many magazines, both in America and in England. His books include *Autumnal Face* (1931), *Winter in Moscow* (1933), *The Earnest Atheist* (1936), *In a Valley of This Restless Wind* (1938), *Affairs of the Heart* (1949), *Tread Softly For You Tread on My Jokes* (1966), and *London à la Mode* (1966)

The faces of the bodgies and their female equivalents, widgies, were pinched and, for their years, sadly dilapidated—bad teeth, debauched eyes peering out uneasily from youthful features, sideburns (after their hero, Elvis Presley), and with it all an air of remote, unexpected innocence tinged with melancholy.

They described their police convictions and undetected misdemeanors with quiet pride—breaking and entering, larceny, carnal knowledge. They might have been going over cricket scores. It was difficult to remember that what they were talking about so vaingloriously were serious crimes. They were showing off and might well have been exaggerating, or even lying. It was not, however, what they had done or pretended to have done which was significant, but their attitude of mind.

Their clothing is lurid and basically American—long jackets almost to their knees, jeans or narrow trousers, brightly colored socks. They work, earning between ten and fourteen pounds a week, of which they spend more than half on clothes and pleasures. As for school—they stayed the minimum permissible time.

"I expect I fell in with the wrong set," one of them said. They, too, follow the prevailing fashion, and put forward environmental explanations of personal misbehavior. There is quite a bit of whining mixed up with their boasting. Their parents scarcely seemed to play any part in their lives. They are prematurely adult—sleep with girls, drink, stay up late, come and go as they please.

We went on to a dance hall packed tight with rocking and rolling bodgies and widgies. A picture of Presley dominated the proceedings. I mentioned that I had read in the newspapers of how, when he reported for military service and his hair had to be cut, the suggestion was made that the precious snippets might be sold or distributed. This did not go down well. In bodgie ears it seemed a bit blasphemous, I felt.

The insistent Negro rhythm got going, and as the dancing worked up to its frenzied climax famous characters were pointed out—this one helped organize the pajama party the other night, this one was just out after a stretch for robbery with violence, and so on. They were the big shots. There was no one present over nineteen, and most were fifteen or sixteen—a motley, runtish, spiritually undernourished sort of gathering, lubricated by soft drinks and animated by an American-transmitted jungle beat. The tang of adolescent sex was in the air, or rather of carnal knowledge—perhaps of carnal ignorance, perhaps just hysteria. Who knows?

Waifs of a materialist society, I reflected, proletarian outsiders, surrealists of the gutter. They exist everywhere in more or less the same form. I have seen those long jackets and padded shoulders and ferret faces in Tottenham Court Road, Third Avenue, Montparnasse, the Kurfuerstandamn. It is a world-wide phenomenon, existing, if the Soviet Press is to be believed, equally on the other side of the Iron Curtain, where there are no pictures of Elvis Presley, no jukeboxes, no erotic literature on easy sale.

These adolescents choose to stand apart, with their own fantasies, their own ways and language, preying upon the society from which they have deliberately excluded themselves. They cannot be accounted for by saying that they come from bad homes and have been neglected by their parents. Many of them have come from good homes and responsible parents. The social-science copybook maxims are not applicable. Nor are the psychiatrist's case-book maxims.

In a sense, the bodgies are over rather than under privileged. They are in full enjoyment of the material benefits which, it is constantly being contended, make for a full and serene life. Though Australian, they pursue happiness in the American style, and have the means so to do. If they are famished, it is spiritually; if they are deprived, the deprivation is within themselves rather than in their material circumstances.

It is no good asking them to become Boy Scouts. They will Be Prepared all right, but with a bicycle chain. Boys' clubs are unlikely to be of much use to them because they are not boys, but adolescents who have come to look old and wizened without growing up. The eroticism to which they, along with the rest of us, are continuously subjected cannot be held accountable for them. This drenches one and all. They cannot be said to be products of horror comics. Rather, they *are* horror comics, written and produced with musical accompaniments and décor, by Mid-Twentieth Century Inc.

What, then, can be done about them? The police think physical chastisement is the answer, and resent not being allowed to administer it except with great discretion. Physical chastisement would no doubt serve to keep the bodgies off the streets, but it is improbable that it would eliminate them. Nor for that matter would moral homilies, and cheerful old sports, whether clerical collared or not, being hearty and cheerful over a pipe.

The bodgies and widgies, in all their different variants all over the world, must be considered as products of the fear and rootlessness and bewilderment which is noticeably present everywhere today. They are not criminals in the ordinary sense. Crime implies a motive, and they have none. They are not just larrikins or hooligans who, unlike the bodgies, hunted in exclusively male packs, and were addicted to violence rather than viciousness. These starvelings in their colored clothes, with their drooping cigarettes, their furtive glances and quick movements, are emanations of an urban way of life which is probably more empty and aimless than any hitherto known.

Thomas Mann says in one of his books that, in a disintegrating civilization, there are only two possible reactions—that of the saint and that of the gangster. The bodgies have chosen the latter.

1.   In describing the bodgies and widgies Muggeridge conveys his personal
      feelings about them. What are these feelings, and what particular words
      and expressions convey them?
2.   What evidence in words and expressions used in this essay do you find
      that suggests the essay was written by somebody other than an Ameri-
      can?
3.   Muggeridge asks what can be done about the bodgies and widgies. What
      is his answer?
4.   According to Muggeridge, what are the sources of the values and atti-
      tudes of the bodgies and widgies?
5.   Do they correspond to any group in this country?

Paul Goodman   JOBS

Paul Goodman (1911–   ) was born in New York City. He
received his B.A. from The City College of New York and his
Ph.D. from the University of Chicago. An expert in city planning
and the many problems inherent in urban growth, he has lectured
at M.I.T., the University of Pennsylvania, Western Reserve University, Columbia University, and the University of California. He
has taught at the University of Chicago, New York University, and
Black Mountain University. He is currently a practicing psychotherapist affiliated with the New York Institute for Gestalt Therapy. A regular contributor to journals and magazines, Mr. Goodman has also written a number of books. His early works include
Stop Light (1942), a volume of poetry; and two novels, *The
Grand Piano* (1942) and *State of Nature* (1945). He is coauthor
with his brother of *Communitas* (1947), a work on city planning,
and is author of *Gestalt Therapy* (1951). His recent books are
Structure of Literature (1954) and *Growing Up Absurd* (1960).
The latter has proved to be extremely popular, with recent sales
exceeding 1000 copies a week.

1.

It's hard to grow up when there isn't enough man's work. There is
"nearly full employment" (with highly significant exceptions), but there
get to be fewer jobs that are necessary or unquestionably useful; that

require energy and draw on some of one's best capacities; and that can be done keeping one's honor and dignity. In explaining the widespread troubles of adolescents and young men, this simple objective factor is not much mentioned. Let us here insist on it.

By "man's work" I mean a very simple idea, so simple that it is clearer to ingenuous boys than to most adults. To produce necessary food and shelter is man's work. During most of economic history most men have done this drudging work, secure that it was justified and worthy of a man to do it, though often feeling that the social conditions under which they did it were *not* worthy of a man, thinking, "It's better to die than to live so hard"—but they worked on. When the environment is forbidding, as in the Swiss Alps or the Aran Islands, we regard such work with poetic awe. In emergencies it is heroic, as when the bakers of Paris maintained the supply of bread during the French Revolution, or the milkman did not miss a day's delivery when the bombs recently tore up London.

At present there is little such subsistence work. In *Communitas* my brother and I guess that one-tenth of our economy is devoted to it; it is more likely one-twentieth. Production of food is actively discouraged. Farmers are not wanted and the young men go elsewhere. (The farm population is now less than 15 per cent of the total population.) Building, on the contrary, is immensely needed. New York City needs 65,000 new units a year, and is getting, net, 16,000. One would think that ambitious boys would flock to this work. But here we find that building, too, is discouraged. In a great city, for the last twenty years hundreds of thousands have been ill housed, yet we do not see science, industry, and labor enthusiastically enlisted in finding the quick solution to a definite problem. The promoters are interested in long-term investments, the real estate men in speculation, the city planners in votes and graft. The building craftsmen cannily see to it that their own numbers remain few, their methods antiquated, and their rewards high. None of these people is much interested in providing shelter, and nobody is at all interested in providing new manly jobs.

Once we turn away from the absolutely necessary subsistence jobs, however, we find that an enormous proportion of our production is not even unquestionably useful. Everybody knows and also feels this, and there has recently been a flood of books about our surfeit of honey, our insolent chariots, the follies of exurban ranch houses, our hucksters and our synthetic demand. Many acute things are said about this useless production and advertising, but not much about the workmen producing it and their frame of mind; and nothing at all, so far as I have noticed, about the plight of a young fellow looking for a manly occupation. The eloquent critics of the American way of life have themselves been so seduced by it that they think only in terms of selling commodities and point out that the goods are valueless; but they fail to see that people are being wasted and their skills insulted. (To give an analogy, in the many gleeful onslaughts on the Popular Culture that have appeared in recent years, there has been little thought of the plight of the honest artist cut off from his audience and sometimes, in public arts such as theater and architecture, from his medium.)

What is strange about it? American society has tried so hard and so ably to defend the practice and theory of production for profit and not primarily for use that now it has succeeded in making its jobs and products profitable and useless.

2.

Consider a likely useful job. A youth who is alert and willing but not "verbally intelligent"—perhaps he has quit high school at the eleventh grade (the median), as soon as he legally could—chooses for auto mechanic. That's a good job, familiar to him, he often watched them as a kid. It's careful and dirty at the same time. In a small garage it's sociable; one can talk to the customers (girls). You please people in trouble by fixing their cars, and a man is proud to see rolling out on its own the car that limped in behind the tow truck. The pay is as good as the next fellow's, who is respected.

So our young man takes this first-rate job. But what when he then learns that the cars have a built-in obsolescence, that the manufacturers do not want them to be repaired or repairable? They have lobbied a law that requires them to provide spare parts for only five years (it used to be ten). Repairing the new cars is often a matter of cosmetics, not mechanics; and the repairs are pointlessly expensive—a tail fin might cost $150. The insurance rates therefore double and treble on old and new cars both. Gone are the days of keeping the jalopies in good shape, the artist-work of a proud mechanic. But everybody is paying for foolishness, for in fact the new models are only trivially superior; the whole thing is a sell.

It is hard for the young man now to maintain his feelings of justification, sociability, serviceability. It is not surprising if he quickly becomes cynical and time-serving, interested in a fast buck. And so, on the notorious *Reader's Digest* test, the investigators (coming in with a disconnected coil wire) found that 63 per cent of mechanics charged for repairs they didn't make, and lucky if they didn't also take out the new fuel pump and replace it with a used one (65 per cent of radio repair shops, but *only* 49 per cent of watch repairmen "lied, overcharged, or gave false diagnoses").

There is an hypothesis that an important predisposition to juvenile delinquency is the combination of low verbal intelligence with high manual intelligence, delinquency giving a way of self-expression where other avenues are blocked by lack of schooling. A lad so endowed might well apply himself to the useful trade of mechanic.

3.

Most manual jobs do not lend themselves so readily to knowing the facts and fraudulently taking advantage oneself. In factory jobs the workman is likely to be ignorant of what goes on, since he performs a small operation on a big machine that he does not understand. Even so, there is evidence that he has the same disbelief in the enterprise as a whole, with a resulting attitude of profound indifference.

Semiskilled factory operatives are the largest category of workmen. (I am leafing through the U.S. Department of Labor's *Occupational Outlook Handbook*, 1957.) Big companies have tried the devices of applied anthropology to enhance the loyalty of these men to the firm, but apparently the effort is hopeless, for it is found that a thumping majority of the men don't care about the job or the firm; they couldn't care less and you can't make them care more. But this is *not* because of wages, hours, or working conditions, or management. On the contrary, tests that show the men's indifference to the company show also their (unaware) admiration for the way the company has designed and manages the plant; it is their very model of style, efficiency, and correct behavior. (Robert Dubin, for the U.S. Public Health Service.) Maybe if the men understood more, they would admire less. The union and the grievance committee take care of wages, hours, and conditions; these are the things the workmen themselves fought for and won. (Something was missing in that victory, and we have inherited the failure as well as the success.) The conclusion must be that workmen are indifferent to the job because of its intrinsic nature: it does not enlist worth-while capacities; it is not "interesting"; it is not his, he is not "in" on it; the product is not really useful. And indeed, research directly on the subject, by Frederick Herzberg on Motivation to Work, shows that it is defects in the intrinsic aspects of the job that make workmen "unhappy." A survey of the literature (in Herzberg's *Job Attitudes*) shows that Interest is second in importance only to Security, whereas Wages, Conditions, Socializing, Hours, Ease, and Benefits are far less important. But foremen, significantly enough, think that the most important thing to the workman is his wages. The investigators do not seem to inquire about the usefulness of the job—as if a primary purpose of *working* at a job were not that it is good *for* something! My guess is that a large factor in "Security" is the resigned reaction to not being able to take into account whether the work of one's hands is useful for anything; for in a normal life situation, if what we do is useful, we feel secure about being needed. The other largest factor in "Security" is, I think, the sense of being needed for one's unique contribution, and this is measured in these tests by the primary importance the workers assign to being "in" on things and to "work done being appreciated."

Limited as they are, what a remarkable insight such studies give us, that men want to do valuable work and work that is somehow theirs! But they are thwarted.

Is not this the "waste of our human resources"?

The case is that by the "sole-prerogative" clause in union contracts the employer has the sole right to determine what is to be produced, how it is to be produced, what plants are to be built and where, what kinds of machinery are to be installed, when workers are to be hired and laid off, and how production operations are to be rationalized. (Frank Marquart.) There is *none* of this that is inevitable in running a machine economy; but *if* these are the circumstances, it is not surprising that the factory operatives' actual code has absolutely nothing to do with useful service or increasing production, but is notoriously devoted to "interpersonal relations"; (1) don't turn out too much work; (2) don't turn out too little work; (3) don't squeal on a fellow worker; (4) don't act like a big-shot. This is how to belong.

4.

Let us go on to the Occupational Outlook of those who are verbally bright. Among this group, simply because they cannot help asking more general questions—e.g., about utility—the problem of finding man's work is harder, and their disillusion is more poignant.

> He explained to her why it was hard to find a satisfactory job of work to do. He had liked working with the power drill, testing the rocky envelope of the shore, but then the employers asked him to take a great oath of loyalty.
>
> "What!" cried Rosalind. "Do you have scruples about telling a convenient fib?"
>
> "No, I don't. But I felt uneasy about the sanity of the director asking me to swear to opinions on such complicated questions when my job was digging with a power drill. I can't work with a man who might suddenly have a wild fit."
>
> . . . "Why don't you get a job driving one of the big trucks along here?"
>
> "I don't like what's in the boxes," said Horatio sadly. "It could just as well drop in the river—and I'd make mistakes and drop it there."
>
> "Is it bad stuff?"

> "*No, just useless. It takes the heart out of me to work at something useless and I begin to make mistakes. I don't mind putting profits in somebody's pocket—but the job also has to be useful for something.*"
>
> . . . "*Why don't you go to the woods and be a lumberjack?*"
>
> "*No! they chop down the trees just to print off* The New York Times!"
> *(The Empire City,* III, i, 3.)

The more intelligent worker's "indifference" is likely to appear more nakedly as profound resignation, and his cynicism may sharpen to outright racketeering.

"Teaching," says the *Handbook,* "is the largest of the professions." So suppose our now verbally bright young man chooses for teacher, in the high school system or, by exception, in the elementary schools if he understands that the elementary grades are the vitally important ones and require the most ability to teach well (and of course they have less prestige). Teaching is necessary and useful work; it is real and creative, for it directly confronts an important subject matter, the children themselves; it is obviously self-justifying; and it is ennobled by the arts and sciences. Those who practice teaching do not for the most part succumb to cynicism or indifference—the children are too immediate and real for the teachers to become callous—but, most of the school systems being what they are, can teachers fail to come to suffer first despair and then deep resignation? Resignation occurs psychologically as follows: frustrated in essential action, they nevertheless cannot quit in anger, because the task is necessary; so the anger turns inward and is felt as resignation. (Naturally, the resigned teacher may then put on a happy face and keep very busy.)

For the job is carried on under impossible conditions of overcrowding and saving public money. *Not* that there is not enough social wealth, but first things are not put first. Also, the school system has spurious aims. It soon becomes clear that the underlying aims are to relieve the home and keep the kids quiet; or, suddenly, the aim is to produce physicists. Timid supervisors, bigoted clerics, and ignorant school boards forbid real teaching. The emotional release and sexual expression of the children are taboo. A commercially debauched popular culture makes learning disesteemed. The academic curriculum is mangled by the demands of reactionaries, liberals, and demented warriors. Progressive methods are emasculated. Attention to each case is out of the question, and all the children—the bright, the average, and the dull—are systematically retarded one way or another, while the teacher's hands are tied. Naturally the pay is low—for the work is hard, useful, and of public concern, all three of which qualities tend to bring lower pay. It is alleged that the low pay is why there is a shortage of teachers and why the best do not choose the profession. My guess is that the best avoid it because of the certainty of miseducating. Nor are the best *wanted* by the system, for they are not safe. Bertrand Russell was rejected by New York's City College and would not have been accepted in a New York grade school.

5.

Next, what happens to the verbally bright who have no zeal for a serviceable profession and who have no particular scientific or artistic bent? For the most part they make up the tribes of salesmanship, entertainment, business management, promotion, and advertising. Here of course there is no question of utility or honor to begin with, so an ingenuous boy will not look here for a manly career. Nevertheless, though we can pass by the sufferings of these well-paid callings, much publicized by their own writers, they are important to our theme because of the model they present to the growing boy.

Consider the men and women in TV advertisements, demonstrating the product and singing the jingle. They are clowns and mannequins, in grimace, speech, and action. And again, what I want to call attention to in this advertising is not the economic problem of synthetic demand, and not the cultural problem of Popular Culture, but the human problem that these are human beings working as clowns; that the writers and designers of it are human beings thinking like idiots; and the broadcasters and underwriters know and abet what goes on—

> *Juicily glubbily*
> Blubber *is dubbily*
> *delicious and nutritious*
> *—eat it, Kitty, it's good.*

Alternately, they are liars, confidence men, smooth talkers, obsequious, insolent, etc., etc.

The popular-cultural content of the advertisements is somewhat neutralized by *Mad* magazine, the bible of the twelve-year-olds who can read. But far more influential and hard to counteract is the *fact* that the workmen and the patrons of this enterprise are human beings. (Highly approved, too.) They are not good models for a boy looking for a manly job that is useful and necessary, requiring human energy and capacity, and that can be done with honor and dignity. They are a good sign that not many such jobs will be available.

The popular estimation is rather different. Consider the following: "As one possible aid, I suggested to the Senate subcommittee that they alert celebrities and leaders in the fields of sports, movies, theater and television to the help they can offer by getting close to these [delinquent] kids. By giving them positive 'heroes' they know and can talk to, instead of the misguided image of trouble-making buddies, they could aid greatly in guiding these normal aspirations for fame and status into wholesome progressive channels." (Jackie Robinson, who was formerly on the Connecticut Parole Board.) Or again: when a mass cross-section of Oklahoma high school juniors and seniors was asked which living person they would like to be, the boys named Pat Boone, Ricky Nelson, and President Eisenhower; the girls chose Debbie Reynolds, Elizabeth Taylor, and Natalie Wood.

The rigged Quiz shows, which created a scandal in 1959, were a remarkably pure distillate of our American cookery. We start with the brute facts that (a) in our abundant expanding economy it is necessary to give money away to increase spending, production, and profits; and (b) that this money must not be used for useful public goods in taxes, but must be plowed back as "business expenses," even though there is a shameful shortage of schools, housing, etc. Yet when the TV people at first tried simply to give the money away for nothing (for having heard of George Washington), there was a great Calvinistic outcry that this was demoralizing (we may gamble on the horses only to improve the breed). So they hit on the notion of a real contest with prizes. But then, of course, they could not resist making the show itself profitable, and competitive in the (also rigged) ratings with other shows, so the experts in the entertainment-commodity manufactured phony contests. And to cap the climax of fraudulence, the hero of the phony contests proceeded to persuade himself, so he says, that his behavior was educational!

The behavior of the networks was correspondingly typical. These business organizations claim the loyalty of their employees, but at the first breath of trouble they were ruthless and disloyal to their employees. (Even McCarthy was loyal to his gang.) They want to maximize profits and yet be absolutely safe from any risk. Consider their claim that they knew nothing about the fraud. But if they watched the shows that they were broadcasting, they could not *possibly*, as professionals, not have known the facts, for there was obvious type-casting, acting, plot, etc. If they are not professionals, they are incompetent. But if they don't watch what they broadcast, then they are utterly irresponsible and on what grounds do they have the franchises to the channels? We may offer them the choice: that they are liars or incompetent or irresponsible.

The later direction of the investigation seems to me more important, the inquiry into the bribed disk-jockeying; for this deals directly with our crucial economic problem of synthesized demand, made taste, debauching the public and preventing the emergence and formation of natural taste. In such circumstances there cannot possibly be an American culture; we are doomed to nausea and barbarism. And *then* these baboons have the effrontery to declare that they give the people what the people demand and that they are not responsible for the level of the movies, the music, the plays, the books!

Finally, in leafing through the *Occupational Outlook Handbook*, we notice that the armed forces employ a large number. Here our young man can become involved in a world-wide demented enterprise, with personnel and activities corresponding.

6.

Thus, on the simple criteria of unquestioned utility, employing human capacities, and honor, there are not enough worthy jobs in our economy for average boys and adolescents to grow up toward. There are of course thousands of jobs that are worthy and self-justifying, and thousands that can be made so by stubborn integrity, especially if one can work as an independent. Extraordinary intelligence or special talent, also, can often carve out a place for itself—conversely, their usual corruption and waste are all the more sickening. But by and large our economic society is *not* geared for the cultivation of its young or the attainment of important goals that they can work toward.

This is evident from the usual kind of vocational guidance, which consists of measuring the boy and finding some place in the economy where he can be fitted; chopping him down to make him fit; or neglecting him if they can't find his slot. Personnel directors do not much try to scrutinize the economy in order to find some activity that is a real opportunity for the boy, and then to create an opportunity if they can't find one. To do this would be an horrendous task; I am not sure it could be done if we wanted to do it. But the question is whether anything less makes sense if we mean to speak seriously about the troubles of the young men.

Surely by now, however, many readers are objecting that this entire argument is pointless because people in *fact* don't think of their jobs in this way at all. *Nobody* asks if a job is useful or honorable (within the limits of business ethics). A man gets a job that pays well, or well enough, that has prestige, and good conditions, or at least tolerable conditions. I agree with these objections as to the fact. (I hope we are wrong.) But *the question is what it means to grow up into such a fact as: "During my productive years I will spend eight hours a day doing what is no good."*

7.

Yet, economically and vocationally, a very large population of the young people are in a plight more drastic than anything so far mentioned. In our society as it is, there are not enough worthy jobs. But if our society, being as it is, were run more efficiently and soberly, for a majority there would soon not be any jobs at all. There is at present nearly full employment and there may be for some years, yet a vast number of young people are rationally unemployable, useless. This paradox is essential to explain their present temper.

Our society, which is not geared to the cultivation of its young, *is* geared to a profitable expanding production, a so-called high standard of living of mediocre value, and the maintenance of nearly full employment. Politically, the chief of these is full employment. In a crisis, when profitable production is temporarily curtailed, government spending increases and jobs are manufactured. In "normalcy"—a condition of slow boom—the easy credit, installment buying, and artificially induced demand for useless goods create jobs for all and good profits for some.

Now, back in the Thirties, when the New Deal attempted by hook or crook to put people back to work and give them money to revive the shattered economy, there was an outcry of moral indignation from the conservatives that many of the jobs were "boondoggling," useless made-work. It was insisted, and rightly, that such work was demoralizing to the workers themselves. It is a question of a word, but a candid critic might certainly say that many of the jobs in our present "normal" production are useless made-work. The tail fins and built-in obsolescence might be called boondoggling. The $64,000 Question and the busy hum of Madison Avenue might certainly be called boondoggling. Certain tax-dodge Foundations are boondoggling. What of business lunches and expense accounts? fringe benefits? the comic categories of occupation in the building trades? the extra stagehands and musicians of the theater crafts? These jolly devices to put money back to work no doubt have a demoralizing effect on somebody or other (certainly on me, they make me green with envy), but where is the moral indignation from Top Management?

Suppose we would cut out the boondoggling and gear our society to a more sensible abundance, with efficient production of quality goods, distribution in a natural market, counterinflation and sober credit. At once the work week would be cut to, say, twenty hours instead of forty. (Important People have already mentioned the figure thirty.) Or alternately, half the labor force would be unemployed. Suppose too—and how can we not suppose it?—that the automatic machines are used generally, rather than just to get rid of badly organized unskilled labor. The unemployment will be still more drastic.

(To give the most striking example: in steel, the annual increase in productivity is 4 per cent, the plants work at 50 per cent of capacity, and the companies can break even and stop producing at *less than 30 per cent* of capacity.) These are the conditions that forced the steel strike, as desperate self-protection. (Estes Kefauver, quoting Gardiner Means and Fred Gardner.)

Everybody knows this, nobody wants to talk about it much, for we don't know how to cope with it. The effect is that we are living a kind of lie. Long ago, labor leaders used to fight for the shorter work week, but now they don't, because they're pretty sure they don't want it. Indeed, when hours are reduced, the tendency is to get a second, part-time, job and raise the standard of living, *because* the job is meaningless and one must have something; but the standard of living is pretty meaningless, too. Nor is this strange atmosphere a new thing. For at least a generation the maximum sensible use of our productivity could have thrown a vast population out of work, or relieved everybody of a lot of useless work, depending on how you take it. (Consider with how little cutback of useful civilian production the economy produced the war goods and maintained an Army, economically unemployed.) The plain truth is that at present very many of us are useless, not needed, rationally unemployable. It is in this paradoxical atmosphere that young persons grow up. It looks busy and expansive, but it is rationally at a stalemate.

8.

These considerations apply to all ages and classes; but it is of course among poor youth (and the aged) that they show up first and worst. They are the most unemployable. For a long time our society has not been geared to the cultivation of the young. In our country 42 per cent have graduated from high school (predicted census, 1960); less than 8 per cent have graduated from college. The high school trend for at least the near future is not much different: there will be a high proportion of drop-outs before the twelfth grade; but *markedly more* of the rest will go on to college; that is, the stratification will harden. Now the schooling in neither the high schools nor the colleges is much good—if it were better more kids would stick to it; yet at present, if we made a list we should find that a large proportion of the dwindling number of unquestionably useful or self-justifying jobs, in the humane professions and the arts and sciences, require education; and in the future, there is no doubt that the more educated will have the jobs, in running an efficient, highly technical economy and an administrative society placing a premium on verbal skills.

(Between 1947 and 1957, professional and technical workers increased 61 per cent, clerical workers 23 per cent, but factory operatives only 4½ per cent and laborers 4 per cent.—Census.)

For the uneducated there will be no jobs at all. This is humanly most unfortunate, for presumably those who have learned something in schools, and have the knack of surviving the boredom of those schools, could also make something of idleness; whereas the uneducated are useless at leisure too. It takes application, a fine sense of value, and a powerful community-spirit for a people to have serious leisure, and this has not been the genius of the Americans.

From this point of view we can sympathetically understand the pathos of our American school policy, which otherwise seems so inexplicable; at great expense compelling kids to go to school who do not want to and who will not profit by it. There are of course unpedagogic motives, like relieving the home, controlling delinquency, and keeping kids from competing for jobs. But there is also this desperately earnest pedagogic motive, of preparing the kids to take *some* part in a democratic society that does not need them. Otherwise, what will become of them, if they don't know anything?

Compulsory public education spread universally during the nineteenth century to provide the reading, writing, and arithmetic necessary to build a modern industrial economy. With the overmaturity of the economy, the teachers are struggling to preserve the elementary system when the economy no longer requires it and is stingy about paying for it. The demand is for scientists and technicians, the 15 per cent of the "academically talented." "For a vast majority [in the high schools]," says Dr. Conant in *The Child, the Parent, and the State*, "the vocational courses are the vital core of the program. They represent something related directly to the ambitions of the boys and girls." But somehow, far more than half of these quit. How is that?

9.

Let us sum up again. The majority of young people are faced with the following alternative: Either society is a benevolently frivolous racket in which they'll manage to boondoggle, though less profitably than the more privileged; or society is serious (and they hope still benevolent enough to support them), but they are useless and hopelessly out. Such thoughts do not encourage productive life. Naturally young people are more sanguine and look for man's work, but few find it. Some settle for a "good job"; most settle for a lousy job; a few, but an increasing number, don't settle.

I often ask, "What do you want to work at? If you have the chance. When you get out of school, college, the service, etc."

Some answer right off and tell their definite plans and projects, highly approved by Papa. I'm pleased for them, but it's a bit boring, because they are such squares.

Quite a few will, with prompting, come out with astounding stereotyped, conceited fantasies, such as becoming a movie actor when they are "discovered"—"like Marlon Brando, but in my own way."

Very rarely somebody will, maybe defiantly and defensively, maybe diffidently but proudly, make you know that he knows very well what he is going to do; it is something great; and he is indeed already doing it, which is the real test.

The usual answer, perhaps the normal answer, is "I don't know," meaning, "I'm looking; I haven't found the right thing; it's discouraging but not hopeless."

But the terrible answer is, "Nothing." The young man doesn't want to do anything.

—I remember talking to half a dozen young fellows at Van Wagner's Beach outside of Hamilton, Ontario; and all of them had this one thing to say: "Nothing." They didn't believe that what to work at was the kind of thing one *wanted.* They rather expected that two or three of them would work for the electric company in town, but they couldn't care less. I turned away from the conversation abruptly because of the uncontrollable burning tears in my eyes and constriction in my chest. Not feeling sorry for them, but tears of frank dismay for the waste of our humanity (they were nice kids). And it is out of that incident that many years later I am writing this book.

STUDY QUESTIONS

1. Compare Goodman's concept of work with that held by the disaffiliates described in the Lipton selection, "Down with the Rat Race: The New Poverty."

2. In what ways does Goodman support his generalizations and conclusions? What kind of evidence does he use?

3. What effect does Goodman achieve with the concluding two paragraphs?

4. According to Goodman, what are useless jobs? Can you think of any that fit his definition?

5. From what you know about job opportunities, do you agree with Goodman that there are not enough worthy jobs today?

Dan Jacobson CRAZY YOUNG ALLIES

Dan Jacobson (1929–   ) was born in Johannesburg, South Africa. He received his B.A. from the University of Witwater-

Reprinted from *The Spectator* (March 24, 1961), by permission of the publishers.

strand and attended Stanford University on a fellowship in creative writing. He lives in London, England. He contributes reviews, critical studies, and fiction to the leading magazines and
journals. His works of fiction include: *The Trap* (1955), *A Dance
in the Sun* (1956), *The Price of Diamonds* (1958), *Evidence of
Love* (1960), and *No Further West* (1961).

Our cities stink; our politicians lie; our military men send hydro-
gen bombs flying round and round the world; our teachers resign to get
better-paid jobs. Garage mechanics cheat us; policemen bully us; movie
stars inflame us; advertisers deprave us. . . . But why go on? Anybody
can draw up his own list; and many people seem to spend their time
doing practically nothing else. And the scanning of every list deepens
our conviction that the mess is so *big* that none of us can ever hope to do
anything about it.

But here's an American, Mr. Paul Goodman, who feels that it isn't
too late to try; and who offers us, as his contribution to the cleansing
campaign, a book about the problems of "Youth in the Organised Society," *Growing Up Absurd.* Mr. Goodman's book has, one gathers, caused
something of a stir in American intellectual circles, and comes here with
the approval of Mr. Norman Podhoretz, the editor of the influential New
York monthly *Commentary,* and of Professor J. K. Galbraith, who needs,
as they say, no introduction. On this side of the Atlantic an older
generation of radicals, represented somewhat dismayingly by Mr. A. S.
Neill and Sir Herbert Read, have added their applause. I wish I could
say that I felt impelled to join in.

I would have liked to be enthusiastic about the book for many
reasons, the first being simply that one is prepared to welcome any book
which is directed explicitly against our prevailing social apathy and
cynicism. But there are more specific reasons why we should be willing
to give Mr. Goodman our attention. Though he is writing only of conditions in the United States, many of his remarks have a direct relevance
to conditions in this country. Mr. Goodman is earnest; he is indignant;
and he is willing to take a chance, even in the strategy of his book. He
does not discuss how best we can get our youth to "adjust" to our
society; rather, he asks us quite bluntly why they *should* adjust to it, the
society being as corrupt and effete as he believes it to be.

Most of the book is given over to illustrating the proposition that
"our abundant society is at present simply deficient in many of the most
elementary objective opportunities and worth-while goals that could
make growing up possible." The author begins by discussing the meaninglessness of the jobs that are open to young people today, whether
they work with their hands in a local garage or with their heads in some
bureaucratic corporation. He then discusses the class-structure of the
United States, and points out that while poverty among the unskilled

workers continues to exist, the affluence of the other sectors of the economy makes it more difficult than ever to be "decently poor." This is perhaps the most telling chapter in the book. Successive chapters analyse the experiences of those young people who do try to "adjust" to the society; and of those who try to opt out of the society, and attempt to construct meaningful communities among themselves. Juvenile delinquents and the Beat Generation come in for particularly close examination under the last heading. Finally, Mr. Goodman puts forward his positive aims or suggestions; he believes that the ills he has diagnosed are "by no means inherent in modern technological conditions, nor in the American Constitution as such."

> But they have followed from the betrayal and neglect of the old radical-liberal program and other changes proposed to keep up with the advancing technology, the growth of population, and the revolution in morals. Important reforms did not occur when they were ripe, and we have inherited the consequences: a wilderness of unfinished situations, unequal developments and inconsistent standards, as well as new business. And now, sometimes the remedy must be stoically to go back and carry *through* the old programs (as we are having to do with racial integration). . . . And sometimes, finally, we have to invent really new devices—e.g., how to make the industrial technology humanly important for its workmen, how to use leisure nobly, or even how, in a rich society, to be decently poor if one so chooses.

In view of the way I have written about it so far, I must emphasise that *Growing Up Absurd* is not intended to be a theoretical work of social criticism. On the contrary: it is presented as a direct report on the author's own experience and that of others—felt, pondered over, and understood. And it is precisely for this reason that it does not seem to me frivolous or "literary" to say that *Growing Up Absurd* fails because it is so very badly written. (I am not talking here of minor ineptitudes and inelegances of expression, though these can be counted in their scores.) Mr. Goodman tries hard to be earthy, slangy, brisk, and intimate with the experience he is concerned to describe; but over almost everything in the book there hangs a fog of remoteness and abstraction, which conceals and smothers whatever life is supposed to be beneath it. Even in the quotation given above it seems to me that there are too many useless abstractions; and I did not choose it to enforce this point. I could do much better elsewhere. For instance, in a single paragraph Mr. Goodman can present us with "pragmatism, instrumentalism, and technologism . . . academic culture, caste morals and formal religion, unsocial greed . . . abundant production, social harmony, practical virtues and more honest perception and feeling . . . efficient abundant poduction, social harmony and one popular culture . . . an abstract and inhuman physical environment, a useless economy, a caste system, a dangerous conformity, a trivial and sensational leisure."

Are you still with me? The truth is, of course, that no rigorous theoretical essay could possibly support such bumpy, lumpy, repetitive catalogues. How much less, then, can a book whose purpose it is, in the first place, to give us the very quality of modern life as people have inwardly experienced it, and secondly to remind us of the values of— well, to draw a deep breath and to quote Mr. Goodman once again— "utility, quality, rational productivity, personal freedom, independent enterprise, human scale, manly vocation, or genuine culture." *Growing Up Absurd* is altogether more depressing, and depressing in more ways, than the author intended it to be.

For even where Mr. Goodman does see cause for hope, and tries to give us the grounds of his hope, as in his discussion of the Beat Generation, his matter remains curiously thin and unconvincing. In fairness, it must be said that the chapter devoted to the Beat Generation is one of the better in the book. Mr. Goodman is quick to penetrate Beat pretensions; but he does so without malice or self-satisfaction. And he comes to the conclusion that the Beats have managed to achieve "a simpler fraternity, animality and sexuality than we have had, at least in America, in a long, long time." Now whatever one may think, in the abstract, of this particular trio of abstractions, one would like to believe that Mr. Goodman is telling some kind of truth here. But he offers us so little evidence for his assertion, one just does not know how to take it. Indeed, the actual evidence all seems to go the other way. He describes Beat language, which, from his account of it, is stiflingly narrow and restricted. He describes Beat art, which he calls "a personal cultivation, not much different from finger-painting." He describes Beat "self-transcendence" (through drugs, Zen, or whatever), and says that

> an awkward consequence of heightening experience when one is inexperienced, of self-transcendence when one has not much world to lose, is that afterwards one cannot be sure that one was somewhere or had newly experienced anything.

Yet when it comes to talking about the positive values that Mr. Goodman perceives in Beat life, to the proffered sexuality, for example, we have, lamely, "My impression is that . . . Beat sexuality is in general pretty good . . . if inhibition is relaxed and there is courage to seek for experience, there ought to be good natural satisfaction." This is not really very persuasive or informative. And a similar lack of persuasive force characterises the author's descriptions of Beat fraternity. In this connection, Mr. Goodman tells one anecdote which is worth transcribing—it is quite the liveliest passage in the book.

> An incident at a party for Patchen. Patchen is a poet of the "previous" generation of long-proven integrity . . . but has achieved no public acclaim, no money, no easy publication. Now at this party, one of

the best "Beat" writers, a genuine young artist, came demanding that the
older poet give some recognition to the tribe of Beat poets . . . Patchen
asked for the names. The Beat poet reeled off twenty, and Patchen
unerringly pointed out the two who were worth while. This threw the
younger poet into a passion . . . So he insulted the older man. Patchen
rose to his height, called him a punk, and left. The young man was
crushed, burst into tears (he was drunk) and also left. At this, a young
woman who often accompanied him, came up to me and clutched me by
the knees, pleading with me to help him grow up, for nobody, she said,
paid him any attention.

In discussing the juvenile delinquents, Mr. Goodman has some
acute, compassionate things to say: he points out, for example, that one
of the compulsive motives for delinquency is the need to be caught and
punished. However, once again Mr. Goodman is driven to assert that
some vague, undefined, superior virtue is inherent in "the fatalistic self-
destruction of the kids," though the evidence he offers for this assertion
is even more tenuous than that offered on behalf of the virtues of Beat
living. In fact, his definition of the virtue he has in mind, and his
evidence for it, consist of nothing more than an obscure and unsatisfactory account of the works of Jean Genet.

Mr. Goodman is not afraid to condemn almost entirely the "successful doings" of his society; but he is, it is quite clear, afraid to
condemn in the same wholesale way those whom he believes to be in
rebellion against that society. Reading this book one cannot help feeling that the author is looking around desperately for some kind of community with which he can identify himself; and though the Beats and
the delinquents appear weak and cramped to him, he nevertheless clings
to them—for if "these crazy young allies," as he calls them, are not on his
side, who is? But surely anybody who is really disturbed about the mess
we are in, and who wants to do something about it, should be prepared
to accept his own isolation with more stoicism. The critic of society must
certainly try to find friends, colleagues and an audience; he must try to
work through existing institutions or to establish new ones. But the
search for allies is not his business.

In its tone of irritation and disgust with American life, Mr. Goodman's book is characteristic of much of the writing we have had from
America over the last few years. Some of the disgust—more perhaps than
was commonly admitted—undoubtedly arose from the fact that for almost
a decade the administration of the country was in the hands of people
who did not merely ignore intellect, but made every effort to show that
they held it in positive disesteem. President Kennedy is making an
effort of a very different kind. Even before his election the notoriously
intransigent Norman Mailer had hailed him as "Superman come to the
Supermart," and since the election Robert Lowell has commented, with
simple relief, "At last the Goths have left the White House." It seems

that we may expect the American intellectuals to begin speaking a little more cheerfully, now that they have a friend in high places. A friend, not an ally.

STUDY QUESTIONS

1. In this review of Goodman's *Growing Up Absurd,* Jacobson criticizes the book as badly written. What evidence does he cite to support this criticism?
2. Jacobson does, however, find parts of the book to praise. What does he find of value in the chapter on the beat generation?
3. What distinction does Jacobson make between *ally* and *friend?*
4. Does Jacobson pass judgment on Goodman as a person, as well as a writer?
5. Describe the general structure of this review. How effective is the opening paragraph in gaining the reader's interest?

ASSAULT
Saul Maloff ON THE POINTLESS LIFE

Saul Maloff (1924–   ) was born in New York City and attended The City College of New York, Amherst College, and the University of Iowa. He has taught at a number of colleges, including Bennington College, Vermont. He is a contributor of fiction, reviews, and literary criticism to the leading magazines and journals.

To those who regard statistics as the very emblem of reality, for whom scientific rigor is the index and guarantor of truth, it must seem that the free-lance social critic is a nuisance let loose among men who have serious work to do. To the academic questionnaire-sociologists, idolatrous of quantity and measurement, the unaffiliated free-lance critic will not have really *useful* things to say, and can be interesting only as a gifted amateur may be interesting—interesting but not *valuable.*

Partly because a view something like this prevails in academic sociology, there has developed in recent years an opposition under-

Reprinted by permission of *The New Republic,* © 1960, Harrison-Blaine of New Jersey, Inc.

ground operating on two fronts: what has been called "Kitsch" sociology, which is at best muckraking and at worst merely sensational; and an important tendency (alive mostly in some highbrow periodicals) which attempts not merely to describe the structure but to define the quality of American life and level against it a serious and thoroughgoing moral and aesthetic criticism. Paul Goodman's *Growing Up Absurd* is in the second of these categories. It is all prose, lively, eccentric, colloquial prose, twisted to his own odd shape, fanciful, scattered, digressive as the best talk often is; full of feeling, raging, lyrical, caustic, scathing, roaring mad; imaginative, even reckless, fertile of ideas and crazy salvationist schemes which make remarkable good sense. There is nothing objective here: it is all intensely personal.

In a way, the title is misleading, creating, as it does, the impression that the book is about the process of growing up, which it is not. Goodman is interested not in the process itself but in its end, in what the boy has around him to grow up *to*. Sartre speaks somewhere of an absurd world as one without ends of meaning and value; and it is in this sense that young people—juvenile delinquents and junior executives, poor and rich, hipsters and squares—grow up absurd. To describe the depredations and empty wastes of that absurdity, to convey the look and the feel of it, and to reckon its appalling cost, is the burden of the book.

Goodman has the artist's eye for the right detail, the revealing instance, the surprising and illuminating juxtaposition; a reliance upon lived and felt experience; and a passionate heart. After the abstractness, the deadness, of so much of academic sociology, it is exhilarating to find a critic who begins and ends with people, who keeps the human person at the center of his vision so that we see not the "dynamics of society," but the figure itself. That is his method, to walk through the landscape and point, to show the ends toward which we compel people to grow up.

The argument moves from what Goodman calls "missed revolutions" (processes begun and then either distorted from their objectives toward some end which is alien to the original purpose or simply abandoned, blocked) to our present predicament; missed revolutions which add up to a legacy of betrayal, to a society which is (to use his word) a racket—eclectic, phony, sensational, trivial, boring; one in which there is little useful work and therefore little genuine leisure—in a period which he sees as one of "transition, uprootedness, inhuman scale, technical abstractness, affectlessness, and conformity." It is a massive indictment, and it commands assent; if young people—by no means only the beat young or the delinquent—respond to their world and ours by becoming cynical, indifferent, disaffected, this book is the most persuasive account I know of why they do.

This is not simply another example of the criticism of "mass culture" in a "mass society" (which is the form serious criticism took in the long interval during which there was hardly any criticism at all in this country); Goodman shares certain of its premises but ranges far beyond them, is more radical. His theme is that *"Growth, like any ongoing function, requires adequate objects in the environment* to meet the needs and capacities of the growing child, boy, youth, and young man, until he can better choose and make his own environment. It is not a 'psychological' question of poor influence and bad attitudes, but an objective question of real opportunities for worthwhile experience." He does not so much attack as dismiss the "psychology" of "adjustment" by facing it with what seems to him the crucial and dismantling question: adjustment to what? The "to what" is the substance of the book: ". . . Our abundant society is at present simply deficient in many of the most elementary objective opportunities and worthwhile goals that could make growing up possible. It is lacking in enough man's work. It is lacking in honest public speech, and people are not taken seriously. It is lacking in the opportunity to be useful. It thwarts aptitude and creates stupidity. It corrupts ingenuous patriotism. It corrupts the fine arts. It shackles science. It dampens animal ardor. It discourages the religious convictions of Justification and Vocation and it dims the sense that there is a Creation. It has no Honor. It has no Community."

If one sees less to hope for from alienated youth than does Goodman, indeed if one sees Goodman's hope as desperation, well, that's no great matter. He is, in the year 1960, unashamedly utopian, storming for excellence. If his terribly exacting demands do not receive the most urgent attention we can summon, it will be because we are staring fixedly at nothing much, because we cannot respond to demands.

But if Goodman brings to the work of social and cultural criticism the gifts of an artist to splendid effect, he comes to the art of the short story (in his book *Our Visit to Niagara*) too often as an analytic critic, and with disappointing results. The matter of the stories rises directly out of the preoccupations of *Growing Up Absurd*, is often a quasi-fictional treatment of them; but where it is marvelously appropriate in one, it is obtrusive and disconcerting in the other—insistently explicit, didactic, essayistic. Read in conjunction with *Growing Up Absurd*, the stories are disturbingly familiar, repetitive, yield no new light. But the book is a mixed lot. When he succeeds (as he does in some of the "American Stories," for example in the title story, and in "Bathers at Westover Pond"; and in some of the "Myths"), he succeeds brilliantly. At his best, he writes with exuberance, tremendous vitality and comes out somehow with a succession of startling imaginative achievements, of a kind that beautifully violates every known stricture of the well-made story. Unhappily, the level of his best fiction is not always achieved here.

STUDY QUESTIONS

1.   Compare this review with Jacobson's. Which of the two critics is more convincing? Why? Does being convincing in a review necessarily mean being accurate?
2.   How would you describe Maloff's attitude toward the subject of *Growing Up Absurd?* How does his attitude differ from Jacobson's?
3.   Compare the opening paragraph of this review with the opening paragraph of Jacobson's review. Which do you judge to be more effective? Why?
4.   In what ways does this review follow the general structure of Jacobson's?

DEMOGRAPHY:

Time **THE COMMAND GENERATION**

The U.S. has a ruling class. It is cloaked in a conspiracy of silence. It is a generation that dares not, or prefers not, to speak its name—middle age. Yet it is that one-fifth of the nation between the ages of 40 and 60 (42,800,000) who occupy the seats of power, foot the bills, and make the decisions that profoundly affect how the other four-fifths live. The halls of Congress ring with the medicares of the aged. Every anatomical twitch or psychedelic escapade of the teen-agers scares up worrywart headlines. Ironically, even the revolt of the teen-aged is subsidized by middle-agers. Those tiny secessionist principalities of the disdainful young that span the U.S. from the La Jolla, Calif., surfing set to the hobohemians of Greenwich Village could scarcely be sustained without the checkbooks of indulgent fathers.

In a perceptive commencement address delivered at N.Y.U. last month, Assistant Dean Milton R. Stern noted: "The young seem always to be in the public prints and on TV, but that doesn't mean that they control things. To the extent that young people wearing their hair longer or skirts shorter dominate the mass media, they are frequently being exploited for commercial reasons. Youth is used to sell—perfumes, cars, cigarettes, and everything else. Youth, indeed, learns to sell itself. What happens to the young people these days is the opposite of commercialized vice—it might be called commercialized innocence." The middle-agers attract little attention, inspire few learned treatises as to the state of their being—good, bad, or indifferent. Paradoxically, middle-agers are the invisible Indispensables.

Steps Steeper, Print Smaller. No one has had time to study middle age very much, since it is practically a modern invention, as well as a distinctly American one. Prehistoric man lived about 18 years. The life span of an ancient Greek or Roman averaged out to 33. When friends attempted to dissuade Cato the Younger from committing suicide at 48, he argued that he had already outlived most of his contemporaries. Even as recently as 1900, U.S. life expectancy was less than 50. Thanks to medical advances and high-protein diets, life has lengthened, and it has grown in the middle.

As to where the middle starts, medical theory is very sketchy, and any age grouping is arbitrary, more of a social and psychological norm than a physiological fact.

When does middle age begin?

"When all the policemen look young," says Leo Rosten, 58, creator of H°Y°M°A°N K°A°P°L°A°N. "And to me they're mere children."

"When the steps get steeper and the print gets smaller," says Whitney Young Jr., 45, executive director of the National Urban League.

"I'll let you know when I get there," snaps New York's Mayor Lindsay, 44.

In physical strength a man peaks at 21 and plateaus to the late 60s, the period when degenerative diseases stalk. The arduous training program of the astronauts, five of whom are over 40 (Walter Schirra, Alan Shepard, Donald Slayton, Scott Carpenter, Virgil Grissom), has proved that a man can double his normal physical competence at ages much beyond 21. Any middle-ager's physiological potential is probably as unique as his fingerprints. The hair may grow thinner, but the capacity for mental growth is unimpaired in middle age. It is obvious that a man or woman of 40 can understand *Moby Dick, The Waste Land* or *Ulysses* (which was published on James Joyce's 40th birthday) far better than the 18-year-old who is assigned it in freshman English.

Survivors at the Banquet. Over the past three decades, the concept of the middle years has vastly changed. In 1932, Walter B. Pitkin wrote *Life Begins at Forty* and it became an overnight inspirational bestseller, precisely because people thought life ended at 40 and there was nothing left to do but wait around for retirement and death. Perhaps no single figure stamped the modern view of middle age upon the era more forcefully than John F. Kennedy. He represented the generation, seasoned by World War II and tempered by 20th century adversity and affluence, that is now in command.

Senior members of the generation, now in their 50s, bear some added marks. "We were the Depression people," explains one. "In a way, we have the good-natured gaiety of survivors." Together they make up the generation of the middle years, of the flexible mind, the resilient spirit and the high heart. It has the assurance of having been tested and not found wanting. In its quenchless vitality, it drinks up the golden decades like nectar at the banquet table of life. It is invisible because it defies chronology. It measures age not by a date on a calendar but by a dance of the mind. Just prior to last week's marriage of Frank Sinatra, 50, to Mia Farrow, 21, Mia's mother Maureen O'Sullivan, 55, was asked how she felt about the 29-year age discrepancy. Said she: "It means nothing. I know people who are antiques at 35 and others who can watusi at 70."

Authentic and Beguilingly Lovely. It is this mercury of the spirit, this added luster of vitality that adorns the beauty within the beauty of Lauren Bacall. The theatergoers who have made her Broadway comedy *Cactus Flower* an S.R.O. hit since the night it opened seven months ago do not think of Bacall as a woman of 41, nor does she, nor does the amorous dentist-hero of the play, Barry Nelson, 44, whom she guilefully lures away from a mistress half her age.

What is fascinating about Bacall is not so much her kinetic sea-green eyes or her svelte-as-sin 129-lb. body, but the distillation of glamour into poise, inner amusement, and enriched femininity that no 20-year-old sex kitten has lived long enough to acquire. Playgoers can sense the discipline that shapes her performance, the reliable professionalism of the middle years, so that in her deft command of her craft as an actress-comedienne she is an authentic as well as beguilingly lovely symbol of the generation.

All Cliché, All True. The view from Lauren Bacall Bogart Robards' highceilinged fourth-floor apartment in the Dakota, Manhattan's imposing fortress of old-world luxury, is the dense green foliage of Central Park. For Betty Bacall, as her friends call her, the view from the 41st year is just as vernal. Little Sam, her four-year-old son by Jason Robards, trots into the room with his nurse for some hugs and kisses before being taken for a row on the park pond. As he pauses at the door, his mother says, "Throw me a kiss." Sam runs back into the room. "I wouldn't *throw* you a kiss," he murmurs, giving her a last affectionate smack.

At this moment, Betty Bacall is delighted with her life. "I've waited for this for 40,000 years," she says, meaning Broadway stardom. "It was my teen-age dream." Actually, it is her third career. Born in New York of a Russian-Polish medical-supplies salesman and his Rumanian wife, Betty Joan Perske, as she was then named, was an only child. The parents soon divorced and Betty, who has not seen her father since she was eight, was reared by her mother. She attended New York public schools, a Tarrytown, N.Y., boarding school called Highland Manor, and graduated from New York City's Julia Richman High School. She began modeling when she was twelve, "to make a little dough," and had graced the cover of *Harper's Bazaar* by the time she went to Hollywood at 18. In her very first film, *To Have and Have Not* (1945), she added a classic come-on line to U.S. cinema legend, and anyone who heard her utter it the first time around fully qualifies as middle-aged: "If you want anything, just whistle." Humphrey Bogart wanted her.

"If two people love each other," Hemingway once wrote, "there can be no happy end to it," meaning one must die before the other. "Being a widow is no picnic," says Betty Bacall, "you lose your place," a shattering experience that has befallen 1,900,000 women in the 40-to-60 age group. "I had to go on because of my children, and I had to because of my own sense of survival. Bogey's belief always was that if one mourns too long, one mourns for oneself rather than for the one who's gone. Life is for the living. It's all a cliché, but it's true."

A Time for Ultimatums. Luckier than most widows with two children (Stephen, now 17 and Leslie, 13) can hope to be, she met and married Jason Robards, a splendid actor and the most sensitive interpreter of O'Neill characters on the U.S. stage. A few years ago, while not yet middle-aged, she found herself drifting into the crisis of purposelessness that afflicts many women in their middle years: "I lost sight of myself as a woman, as an actress—even in my friendships I was neglectful. I knew I wasn't functioning well. I became rundown physically. When you have the responsibility of a husband and children, you also have a responsibility to yourself. If you neglect yourself, you actually are neglecting them. It's unfair to all."

So Betty Bacall issued a brisk ultimatum to herself: "Damn it, straighten up! Pull yourself together and *point* yourself in the right direction. MOVE!" The move was back to work: "It helped me enormously. There's always something about making a decision in your life. It takes a load off your back." At work she found herself possessed of one of the strengths peculiar to the middle years: "It is necessary for anyone to practice his craft to do it well and to improve. But also, in a strange way you have to live a certain amount of life, and even if you don't practice your craft you have lived, and when you go back you find you have learned something."

What has Bacall learned to value in her lifetime? "Character and a sense of humor are the two things that will carry you through." Her own wryly self-deflating humor ("It takes the sting out of things that hurt") neatly defines the dividing line between generations. The young laugh at the way things seem; the middle-aged laugh at the way things are.

What are her pleasures apart from husband, children, work and friends? "I'm an insane furniture and bibelot buyer. I love the ocean—it's one of the last free places on earth." Betty Bacall has also learned the ultimate wisdom of the middle years, to live in the here and now: "There are things in life that are pretty rotten. The part that's good you've got to enjoy while you have it."

Mold and Shape. Without the Bacall good looks but with the selfsame vitality, other members of the command generation are the helmsmen of U.S. society in government, politics, education, religion, science, business, industry and communications. From President Johnson, 57, and Vice President Humphrey, 55, through the entire Cabinet including Rusk, 57, and McNamara, 50, the top echelon of government is middle-aged. Including that anachronistic middle-ager, Bobby Kennedy, 40, the 100 U.S. Senators tally up an average age of 57, and the House of Representatives is seven years younger at a representative 50. Sixty-three percent of this country's Nobel prizewinners in the past ten years have been between 40 and 60. At 15 of the leading U.S. colleges and universities, the average presidential age is 55; of 900 executives in 300 top corporations, only a handful falls outside the 40–60 group.

Today's top-responsibility middle-ager might say with Shakespeare's Henry V at dawn of the Battle of Agincourt: "The day, my friends, and all things wait for me." Whether the hand holds the scalpel (Dr. Michael DeBakey, 57) or the baton (Leonard Bernstein, 48), it is watched by patient and public with rapt attention. Whether he is a Protestant evangelist (Billy Graham, 47) or a Catholic Archbishop (John Patrick Cody, 58, of Chicago, a U.S. cardinal-to-be), he lends spiritual guidance to attending multitudes. Whether he is a master of industry (Arjay Miller, 50, president of Ford) or a master of jurisprudence (Byron R. "Whizzer" White, 49, Supreme Court Justice), he determines the patterns of social change. Whether the opinion molder is at the University of Toronto (Marshall McLuhan, 55) or on Madison Avenue (David Ogilvy, 55), he shapes the thoughts and desires of a continent.

Positioning the Lever. It may seem axiomatic that the middle-aged are in control. It was not always so. John Paul Jones was in command of his own ship at 21, and Pitt the Younger was Prime Minister of England at 24. But complex technologies and lengthy professional studies have forced young men to play the waiting game. Also, they have lost what Lexicographer Bergen Evans notes was "the fastest path of advancement—dead men's shoes." In Europe and Asia, the old still hold sway. In the heart of Europe, De Gaulle is in full command at 75, and it is unlikely that Germany would defy ex-Chancellor Adenauer at 90.

Power, in a far less grandiose sense, is one of the daily pleasures of the middle-ager. Adept at his job, he has learned how to channel his energy, and can place Archimedes' lever in the exact spot that will shift the world a trifle closer to his heart's desire.

Delight and Risk. No man in the land gets a higher paycheck than the middle-ager. The average age for incomes of $10,000 to $15,000 is 47, for incomes of $15,000 and up, 51. This makes delayed pleasures possible. A man may have been sports-car minded for years, but when he climbs behind the wheel of a Mustang, his average age is 48. With no small children underfoot, husbands and wives discover the pleasures of each other's company, share convention trips, take that second honeymoon to Europe.

Change is a delight in the middle years. Columnist Art Buchwald, 40, pulled up stakes in Paris as the celebrity's celebrity, relocated himself in Washington, D.C., and mined it for satire. Astronaut John Glenn, 45, is a vice president of Royal Crown Cola. Sometimes the change is an allout risk. Maxwell Wihnyk, 54, was running a mildly profitable newspaper in Beaumont, Calif., five years ago, but there was no joy in it. With a wife and three dependent children, he decided to go to law school. Says he: "You can scare the hell out of yourself living off capital for three years; in fact, the only way to do it is not to think about it." Armed with a degree from the U.C.L.A. law school, he is now set up in a modest but personally satisfying law practice in Beaumont.

It is pretty quaint to recall that Franklin P. Adams said: "Middle age occurs when you are too young to take up golf and too old to rush up to the net." Today's middle-agers not only dot the greens, they vault the net. They sail, ski, water-ski, skin-dive and spelunk. They swim, walk and climb. They fish, hunt, camp and swarm all over the great outdoors from Big Sur to Cape Cod. They are a participating rather than a spectator generation.

Before 40, one adds and feeds to gorge the ego; after 40, one subtracts and simplifies to slim the soul. With the final image of one's existence even faintly in view, the self seems pettier and the words "service," "love of others," "compassion" not only creep into the middle-ager's vocabulary but add meaning to his life. In church work, social work, community fund drives, culture centers, middle-agers are always at the fore. Sol Linowitz, 52, chairman of the executive committee of Xerox Corp., defines his abiding purpose: "I want to leave the world a little better place than I found it."

Frustration Is Shirking. "When I was young, the whole world revolved around *my, my, my,*" says Columnist Ann Landers, 48. "Today, I don't think in terms of myself but rather how I can be part of something bigger and better." She echoes G. B. Shaw's creed: "Happiness, a paltry goal. The thing is to be used, spent, squandered in the splendor of one of life's consuming causes."

Sometimes a middle-ager finds that meaningful cause in adversity. Four years ago, Lynn Selwyn, now 40, was apathetic, morose, and her marriage was irreparably cracked up. One day, Jeanne Cagney, sister of Jimmy, said to her: "Frustration is the shirking of potentiality." Says

Lynn: "In that instant I knew I had to do something with my life, learn how to live without being dependent on someone else."

With two other women, she founded Everywoman's Village in Van Nuys, Calif. It consists of a grassless half-acre, six bungalows, and a staff of 15 teachers who give courses ranging from ballet, oil painting, psychology and foreign languages to exotica like yoga and flowered bead making. The classes are limited to 15, the atmosphere is totally informal and there are no grades. The school's aim is to be a link between the housewife and the university. "Most housewives are afraid to resume their education in a formal classroom," says Lynn, "because they feel threatened by the bright-eyed 19-year-olds. The Village is a stepping-stone, the first step for the woman trying to get out of the kitchen. We want to stimulate self-growth and human development."

Wisdom and Panic. As Aristotle once pointed out, there are no boy philosophers. One of the philosophical satisfactions of middle age is not being young. The sign of health for the middle-ager is that he prefers his own age; he has no desire to go back to 20 because he knows what 20 is in a way that 20 does not. It is a difference in perspective: youth's is flat, middle-age's is three-dimensional. It is the difference between ignorance and wisdom, impulse and judgment. The young think there is no tomorrow; middle age knows there is tomorrow and tomorrow and tomorrow. The young want to dynamite the treasure vaults of life; middle age has learned the combination. The young think they know; middle age knows that no one knows.

If the middle years can be wise and felicitous, they can also be foolish and frantic, fraught with nerve-frazzling doubts and despairs, somber with peril and melancholy. The middle-ager usually knows better than to stay up till 4 A.M., but he sometimes finds himself waking up at 4 or 5 A.M. in a swivet of inexplicable panic. He has reached the age of what T. S. Eliot called the hoo-ha's:

> *When you're alone in the middle of the night and you wake in a sweat*
> *and a hell of a fright*
> *When you're alone in the middle of the bed and you wake like someone*
> *hit you on the head*
> *You've had a cream of a nightmare dream and you've got the hoo-ha's*
> *coming to you.*°

Into the Televoid. Of course, there are His and Her hoo-ha's. The woman is faced with the fact and fear of a major physiological change, the menopause. The foremost cause among the middle-aged for first admissions to mental institutions is listed with the diagnosis "involutional psychosis," sometimes called "change-of-life melancholia." If her children are in their teens, the shadow of becoming an "empty nester" also falls across her spirit. She is becoming one of nature's unemploy-

---

° From "The Waste Land" by T. S. Eliot in *Collected Poems, 1909–1962*, New York: Harcourt, Brace & World, Inc., 1963.

ables, threatened both in her womanliness and in her family's need of her. "But what should a woman do after her children are grown?" asks Lynn Selwyn. "Should she shrivel up and die?"

This private womanly plight has become a vociferous public debate. Hold on to a job, coaches Betty Friedan (*The Feminine Mystique*). Come back for a refresher course, coaxes Radcliffe's Mary Bunting. Amid the pelted advice, there is a tendency to forget that many women are not equipped to do either. For them, the years of the hoo-ha's may consist of face lifts, hair tints, silicone shots, quack religions, quack diets, forever gazing, as Louis Auchincloss has put it, "over a sea of card tables" or blankly into the televoid.

The Gods Prove Intractable. When the hoo-ha's hit a man, he thumbs through his immediate worries: mortgages, unpaid bills, the children's education, the stab of a chest pain that could be a heart attack, the state of his marriage and job. But the free-floating anxiety that seeps into a man's bones at the onset of the middle years cannot be pinned to any one of these specific causes. Cyril Connolly calls 40 the age of saints and suicides. Eric Berne (*Games People Play*) calls it the time when people play "Balance Sheet."

What each is saying, in his different way, is that it is a climactic period of stocktaking, an often agonizing reappraisal of how one's achievements measure up against one's goals, and of the entire system of values one has lived by. What drastically confronts a middle-aged man at this moment is how the choices of the past have robbed him of choice in the present.

As a young man, he was a creature of infinite possibilities, and his dreams spangled the future like stars. In his 40s, he must live with one actuality—he is the fruit of his limitations. In his 30s, a man can still blame his luck and jolly himself along with the notion that, by unremitting work and determination, he will lick the gods and win the top prizes. The gods prove intractable, and in his 40s, a man is forced to acknowledge that he has done pretty much what he was capable of doing. More depressing, he knows that he will have to go on doing it with ever-brighter, ever-younger men nipping at his heels.

Fate's Straitjacket. Just how frustrated a middle-ager may feel in such a situation is amply documented in a book about the trials and torments of the middle years, called *The Middle-Aged Crisis* by Barbara Fried, which will be published in the spring of 1967. Mrs. Fried, 42, a psychology editor, interviewed countless middle-agers on their problems, and frequently encountered an unhappy sense of betrayal: "Sure I feel trapped. Why shouldn't I? Twenty-five years ago, a dopey 18-year-old college kid made up his mind that I was going to be a dentist. So now here I am, a dentist. I'm stuck. What I want to know is: who told that kid he could decide what I was going to do with the rest of my life?"

The trapped middle-ager wants to flee, like Gauguin to the South Seas, but erstwhile bankers of 45 who desert their Parisian families and become great painters are one of a kind. To blunt the pain of reality, he slips a whisky bottle into his desk and nips at it. (Alcoholism climbs a steep 50% in the 40–60 group over ages 30–39.) His medicine cabinet begins to look like a pharmaceutical display, and he retreats into hypochondria. Indeed, the sense of being straitjacketed by fate may contribute sizably to the cardiovascular and cardiopulmonary attacks that increasingly fell middle-agers.

Race Against Time.   The trapped middle-ager is introspective, resigned, and rebellious all at the same time. Modern literature and drama vividly depict his psychic desperation, from Bellow's *Herzog* to Miller's *After the Fall,* from Albee's *Virginia Woolf* to Osborne's *Inadmissible Evidence,* from the novels of John Marquand to the novels of John O'Hara. John Cheever, who writes of middle age with autumnal sadness, is its prose laureate. In *O Youth and Beauty!,* he tells of the ritual of Cash Bentley, a former track star turned 40 who, when the Saturday-night suburban party was guttering out between the empty gin bottles and the full ashtrays, would pile the furniture together in clumps and at a friend's revolver shot, go hurdling over it.

This is Cash Bentley's race against time, and he "ran it alone, but it was extraordinary to see this man of forty surmount so many obstacles so gracefully." At one party, he fails to clear a chest and slams to the floor, breaking his leg. He recovers, a morose and different man. Late one night at home, he is obsessed with running the race again. He hands the revolver to his wife, who is unfamiliar with it. With a hurried instruction about the safety catch, he is off. She shoots him dead in mid-air over the sofa.

Reverse Oedipal Tide.   Most middle-agers do not fight the clock as fatally as Cash Bentley, but many try to turn it back. Some middle-aged husbands decide that not time, but their wives, are sapping their lives. This is the age of the domestic tirade, à la *Virginia Woolf.* The wife feels neglected, the husband feels nagged, both feel thoroughly bored with each other. According to Dr. Masters and Psychologist Johnson in *Human Sexual Response,* there is a marked flagging of male potency in the 40s, but it is not so much physical as psychic impotence.

Psychoanalysts argue that both sexes enter a sort of second adolescence in the mid-40s, but the male has more sexual options. A kind of reverse Oedipal tide may run. Where he once craved his father's power, he may now covet his teen-ager son's potency. The sight of a young couple embracing in the park stabs him with a pang of envy. Meanwhile, he mercilessly scrutinizes every sag, bulge, and wrinkle that makes his wife unappetizing. In *The Revolt of the Middle-Aged Man,* Dr. Edmund Bergler records the rebel's plaint: "I want happiness, love, approval, admiration, sex, youth. All this is denied me in this stale marriage to an elderly, sickly, complaining, nagging wife. Let's get rid of her, start life all over again with another woman." Home-wrecking is an inside job.

The Cruelest Jest. The stage is set for the extramarital affair, frequently the office romance. The office romance thrives on contiguity, opportunity, and the fact that love feeds on shared experience. The man looks across the desk at this sweet young thing, and she stirs memories of playful erotic tenderness before he pulled on the heavy, encumbering armor of duty and responsibility. Whatever the wife is doing on her rounds, the husband and his secretary are doing something in common that draws them intensively closer, whether it is planning an ad layout or drafting a new skyscraper. Assuming the girl is about 20 years younger than the man, she is apt to find him not only more affluent, but considerably more interesting company than the boys in her own age group. It is worth remembering that it was on the set of *To Have and Have Not* that Bogey, married and 44, and Betty, single and 19, fell in love.

However, the extramarital affair does not lead straight to the divorce court. The median divorce age in the U.S. is 32. In the 40s and 50s, divorce is major surgery, and a man is reluctant to cut that much life out of his life. Besides, time sometimes taunts the older lover with the cruelest of jests. Having roused the ardor of a younger woman, he may find himself no match for her physical demands and end up more ruefully conscious of his age that when he set out to refute it.

Easing Ahead. The stresses and strains of the middle years may be considerably eased in the decade or two ahead. Dramatic changes are certain. Biologically, the systematic use of hormones may phase out woman's change-of-life crisis and make the menopausal trauma a thing of the past. If the point of view that inspired the 1965 federal anti-discriminatory legislation on the hiring of older men flourishes, middle-aged men will be rid of the fear they now legitimately have that being fired, or quitting a job after 40, means a long, scary interlude in limbo before getting rehired. Transitional schools like Lynn Selwyn's Every-woman's Village may help reorient women who see their grown children as their epitaph. The cultural explosion will give more middle-agers secondary interests in the arts, those exciting openers of the mind's eye that keep the human horizon from shriveling.

What might make middle age pleasantest of all is a reform that middle-agers could institute themselves. Middle-agers need prestige as well as power within U.S. society. They need to have their age role approved by those around them rather than feel defensive and self-conscious about it. What militates against this is the Youth Cult.

The Youth Cult is intimately related to the American denial of death. Europe has escaped it so far by retaining the tragic sense of life.

There it is recognized that each age has its unique joys and charms, and the entire span of life is valued as equally precious. In the U.S., the Youth Cult marches from trick to trick, the latest being a preparation called "Great Day," by which a man can rinse that grey right out of his hair.

It might be called Dorian Gray. It is true that Dorian Gray never grew old. His tragedy was that he never grew. Earthly immortality is a pathetic mirage. Time will not stop. In an attempt to stop it, one merely stunts one's self. The ultimate victims of the Youth Cult are the young, some of whom believe that turning 25 is the outer limit of human obsolescence. The Youth Cult misleads them into thinking that license is freedom, that untutored whims are tastes, and that ever-jittering motions are deeds. Since it is the specific problem and task of middle-agers to induct the promising young into the society of civilized men, it might be a boon to all generations to begin by debunking the stultifying Youth Cult.

Hallmark of Humor. In attempting to measure the ground between 50 and 20, Adlai Stevenson once put it this way to the students of Princeton: "What a man knows at 50 that he did not know at 20 boils down to something like this: the knowledge that he has acquired with age is not the knowledge of formulas, or forms of words, but of people, places, actions—a knowledge not gained by words but by touch, sight, sound, victories, failures, sleeplessness, devotion, love—the human experiences and emotions of this earth; and perhaps, too, a little faith and a little reverence for the things you cannot see."

Ask Lauren Bacall what she is going to do with the next 20 years and her mouth twists in a self-amused grimace: "Try to survive—for openers." The humor is symptomatic and the understatement characteristic. The generation that is in command has little taste for mock heroics and even less for overstatement. Its eyes are relatively clear, if at times somewhat troubled. Its productive record is vast and its potential still enormous. While at times it may seem hesitant and confused, it has pride in its competence, intelligence and tenacity, and staunch confidence in the future.

STUDY QUESTIONS

1. What means are used to attract and hold the reader's interest? In what ways is the presentation of this essay designed for the general reader?
2. For what purpose in the general structure of the essay is the material about Lauren Bacall threaded in and out of the essay?
3. What are some of the generalizations made about the "command generation"? How are these supported? With what type of evidence?
4. What is there in this essay that would appeal to a middle-aged reader? Is there anything that may not appeal to him?

5. Does the essay suggest that the middle years may be the most desirable years? Why, then, is youth used to "sell perfumes, cars, cigarettes, and everything else"?

UNNAMEABLE OBJECTS,
James Baldwin UNSPEAKABLE CRIMES

James Baldwin (1924–   ) has established a reputation as one of America's outstanding contemporary writers. Born and raised in Harlem, Baldwin received a Eugene F. Saxton Fellowship in 1945 that enabled him to devote his time to writing. He has written three novels: *Go Tell It on the Mountain* (1953), *Giovanni's Room* (1956), and *Another Country* (1962). His collections of essays are *Notes of a Native Son* (1955), *Nobody Knows My Name* (1960), and *The Fire Next Time* (1963). Active in civil rights activities, he has lectured in numerous colleges and universities. He is a member of the national advisory board of the Congress of Racial Equality. He has won Rosenthal, Guggenheim, and National Institute of Arts and Letters awards.

I have often wondered, and it is not a pleasant wonder, just what white Americans talk about with one another. I wonder this because they do not, after all, seem to find very much to say to *me*, and I concluded long ago that they found the color of my skin inhibitory. This color seems to operate as a most disagreeable mirror, and a great deal of one's energy is expended in reassuring white Americans that they do not see what *they* see. This is utterly futile, of course, since *they do* see what *they* see. And what they see is an appallingly oppressive and bloody history, known all over the world. What they see is a disastrous, continuing, present, condition which menaces them, and for which they bear an inescapable responsibility. But since, in the main, they appear to lack the energy to change this condition, they would rather not be reminded of it. Does this mean that, in their conversations with one another, they merely make reassuring sounds? It scarcely seems possible, and yet, on the other hand, it seems all too likely.

Whatever they bring to one another, it is certainly not *freedom from guilt*.

Reprinted from *The White Problem in America*. First published in *Ebony*, as "White Man's Guilt." With permission of the publishers and Robert Lantz, Literary Agent.

The guilt remains, more deeply rooted, more securely lodged, than the oldest of old trees; and it can be unutterably exhausting to deal with people who, with a really dazzling ingenuity, a tireless agility, are perpetually defending themselves against charges which one has not made.

One does not have to make them. The record is there for all to read. It resounds all over the world. It might as well be written in the sky.

One wishes that Americans, white Americans, would read, for their own sakes, this record, and stop defending themselves against it. Only then will they be enabled to change their lives. The fact that Americans, white Americans, have not yet been able to do this—to face their history, to change their lives—hideously menaces this country. Indeed, it menaces the entire world.

For history, as nearly no one seems to know, is not merely something to be read. And it does not refer merely, or even principally, to the past. On the contrary, the great force of history comes from the fact that we carry it within us, are unconsciously controlled by it in many ways, and history is literally *present* in all that we do. It could scarcely be otherwise, since it is to history that we owe our frames of reference, our identities, and our aspirations.

And it is with great pain and terror that one begins to realize this. In great pain and terror, one begins to assess the history which has placed one where one is, and formed one's point of view. In great pain and terror, because, thereafter, one enters into battle with that historical creation, oneself, and attempts to re-create oneself according to a principle more humane and more liberating; one begins the attempt to achieve a level of personal maturity and freedom which robs history of its tyrannical power, and also changes history.

But, obviously, I am speaking as an historical creation which has had bitterly to contest its history, to wrestle with it and finally accept it, in order to bring myself out of it. My point of view is certainly formed by my history, and it is probable that only a creature despised by history finds history a questionable matter. On the other hand, people who imagine that history flatters them (as it does, indeed, since they wrote it) are impaled on their history like a butterfly on a pin and become incapable of seeing or changing themselves or the world.

This is the place in which, it seems to me, most white Americans find themselves. They are dimly, or vividly, aware that the history they have fed themselves is mainly a lie, but they do not know how to release themselves from it, and they suffer enormously from the resulting personal incoherence. This incoherence is heard nowhere more plainly than in those stammering, terrified dialogues white Americans sometimes entertain with that black conscience, the black man in America.

The nature of this stammering can be reduced to a plea: Do not blame *me*. I was not there. I did not do it. My history has nothing to do with Europe or the slave trade. Anyway, it was *your* chiefs who sold *you* to *me*. I was not present on the middle passage. I am not responsible for the textile mills of Manchester, or the cotton fields of Mississippi. Besides, consider how the English, too, suffered in those mills and in those awful cities! I, also, despise the governors of Southern states and the sheriffs of Southern counties; and I also want your child to have a decent education and rise as high as his capabilities will permit. I have nothing against you, *nothing!* What have *you* got against *me? What do you want?*

But, on the same day, in another gathering, and in the most private chamber of his heart always, he, the white man, remains proud of that history for which he does not wish to pay, and from which, materially, he has profited so much. On that same day, in another gathering, and in the most private chamber of the black man's heart always, he finds himself facing the terrible roster of the lost: the dead, black junkie; the defeated, black father; the unutterably weary, black mother; the unutterably ruined black girl. And one begins to suspect an awful thing: that people believe that they *deserve* their history and that when they operate on this belief, they perish. But they can scarcely avoid believing that they deserve it—one's short time on this earth is very mysterious and very dark and hard. I have known many black men and women and black boys and girls, who really believed that it was better to be white than black, whose lives were ruined or ended by this belief; and I myself carried the seeds of this destruction within me for a long time.

Now, if I, as a black man, profoundly believe that I deserve my history and deserve to be treated as I am, then I must also, fatally, believe that white people deserve their history and deserve the power and the glory which their testimony and the evidence of my own senses assure me that they have. And if black people fall into this trap, the trap of believing that they deserve their fate, white people fall into the yet more stunning and intricate trap of believing that they deserve *their* fate, and their comparative safety; and that black people, therefore, need only do as white people have done to rise to where white people now are. But this simply cannot be said, not only for reasons of politeness or charity, but also because white people carry in them a carefully muffled fear that black people long to do to others what has been done to them. Moreover, the history of white people has led them to a fearful, baffling place where they have begun to lose touch with reality—to lose touch, that is, with themselves—and where they certainly are not happy. They do not know how this came about; they do not dare examine how this came about. On the one hand, they can scarcely dare to open a dialogue which must, if it is honest, become a personal confession—a cry for help and healing, which is really, I think, the basis of all dialogues—and, on the other hand, the black man can scarcely dare to open a dialogue which must, if it is honest, become a personal confession which, fatally, contains an accusation. And yet, if we cannot do this, each of us will perish in those traps in which we have been struggling for so long.

The American situation is very peculiar, and it may be without precedent in the world. No curtain under heaven is heavier than that curtain of guilt and lies behind which Americans hide: it may prove to be yet more deadly to the lives of human beings than that iron curtain of which we speak so much—and know so little. The American curtain is color. We have used this word, this concept, to justify unspeakable crimes, not only in the past, but in the present. One can measure very neatly the white American's distance from his conscience—from himself—by observing the distance between himself and black people. One has only to ask oneself who established this distance. Who is this distance designed to protect? And from what is this distance designed to protect him?

I have seen this very vividly, for example, in the eyes of Southern law enforcement officers barring, let us say, the door to the courthouse. There they stand, comrades all, invested with the authority of the community, with helmets, with sticks, with guns, with cattle prods. Facing them are unarmed black people—or, more precisely, they are faced by a group of unarmed people arbitrarily called black, whose color really ranges from the Russian steppes to the Golden Horn, to Zanzibar. In a moment, because he can resolve the situation in no other way, this sheriff, this deputy, this honored American citizen, must begin to club these people down. Some of these people may be related to him by blood; they are assuredly related to the black Mammy of his memory, and the black playmates of his childhood. And for a moment, therefore, he seems nearly to be pleading with the people facing him not to force him to commit yet another crime and not to make yet deeper that ocean of blood in which his conscience is drenched, in which his manhood is perishing. The people do not go away, of course; once a people arise, they never go away, a fact which should be included in the Marine handbook; and the club rises, the blood comes down, and our crimes and our bitterness and our anguish are compounded. Or, one sees it in the eyes of rookie cops in Harlem, who are really among the most terrified people in the world, and who must pretend to themselves that the black mother, the black junkie, the black father, the black child are of a different human species than themselves. They can only deal with their lives and their duties by hiding behind the color curtain. This curtain, indeed, eventually becomes their principal justification for the lives they lead.

But it is not only on this level that one sees the extent of our disaster. Not so very long ago, I found myself in Montgomery, with many, many thousands, marching to the Capitol. Much has been written about this march—for example, the Confederate flag was flying from the Capitol dome; the Federalized National Guard, assigned to protect the marchers, wore Confederate flags on their jackets; if the late Mrs. Viola Liuzzo was avoiding the patrols on that deadly stretch of road that night, she had far sharper eyesight than mine, for I did not see any. Well, there we were, marching to that mansion from which authority had fled. All along that road—I pray that my countrymen will hear me—old, black men and women, who have endured an unspeakable oppression for so long, waved and cheered and sang and wept. They could not march, but they had done something else: they had brought us to the place where we could march. How many of us, after all, were brought up on the white folks leavings, and how mighty a price those old men and women paid to bring those leavings home to us!

We reached the white section of town. There the businessmen stood, on balconies, jeering; there stood their maids, in back doors, silent, not daring to wave, but nodding. I watched a black, or rather, a beige-colored woman, standing in the street, watching us thoughtfully; she looked as though she probably held a clerical job in one of those buildings; proof, no doubt, to the jeering white businessmen that the South was making progress. This woman decided to join us, for when we reached the Capitol, I noticed that she was there. But, while we were still marching, through the white part of town, the watching, the waiting, the frightened part of town, we lifted our small American flags, and we faced those eyes—which could not face ours—and we sang. I was next to Harry Belafonte. From upstairs office windows, white American secretaries were leaning out of windows, jeering and mocking, and using the ancient Roman sentence of death: thumbs down. Then they saw Harry, who is my very dear friend and a beautiful cat, and who is also, in this most desperately schizophrenic of republics, a major, a reigning matinée idol. One does not need to be a student of Freud to understand what buried forces create a matinée idol, or what he represents to that public which batters down doors to watch him (one need only watch the rise and fall of American politicians. This is a sinister observation. And I mean it very seriously). The secretaries were legally white—it was on that basis that they lived their lives, from this principle that they took, collectively, their values; which is, as I have tried to indicate, an interesting spiritual condition. But they were also young. In that ghastly town, they were certainly lonely. They could only, after all, look forward to an alliance, by and by, with one of the jeering businessmen; their boyfriends could only look forward to becoming one of them. And they were also female, a word, which, in the context of the color curtain, has suffered the same fate as the word, "male": it has become practically obscene. When the girls saw Harry Belafonte, a collision occurred in them so visible as to be at once hilarious and unutterably sad. At one moment, the thumbs were down, they were barricaded within their skins, at the next moment, those downturned thumbs flew to their mouths, their fingers pointed, their faces changed, and exactly like bobbysoxers, they oohed, and aahed and moaned. God knows what was happening in the minds and hearts of those girls. Perhaps they would like to be free.

The white man's guilt, which he pretends is due to the fact that the world is a place of many colors, has nothing to do with color. If one attempts to reduce his dilemma to its essence, it really does not have much to do with his crimes, except in the sense that he has locked himself into a place where he is doomed to continue repeating them. The great, unadmitted crime is what he has done to himself. A man is a man, a woman is a woman, and a child is a child. To deny these facts is to open the doors on a chaos deeper and deadlier, and, within the space of a man's lifetime, more timeless, more eternal, than the medieval vision of Hell. And we have arrived at this unspeakable blasphemy in order to acquire things, in order to make money. We cannot endure the things we acquire—the only reason we continually acquire them, like junkies on a hundred dollar a day habit—and our money exists mainly on paper. God help us on that day when the population demands to know what is behind the paper. But, beyond all this, it is terrifying to consider the precise nature of the things we buy with the flesh we sell.

In Henry James' novel *The Ambassadors* published not long before World War I, and not long before his death, he recounts the story of a middle-aged New Englander, assigned by his middle-aged bride-to-be—a widow—the task of rescuing from the flesh-pots of Paris her only son. She wants him to come home to take over the direction of the family factory. In the event, it is the middle-aged New Englander—*The Ambassador*—who is seduced, not so much by Paris, as by a new and less utilitarian view of life. He counsels the young man to "live. Live all you can. It is a mistake not to." Which I translate as meaning "Trust life, and it will teach you, in joy and sorrow, all you need to know." Jazz musicians know this. Those old men and women who waved and sang and wept as we marched in Montgomery know this. White Americans, in the main, do not know this. They are still trapped in that factory to which, in Henry James' novel, the son returns. We never know what this factory produces, for James never tells us. He only conveys to us that the factory, at an unbelievable human expense, produces unnameable objects.

STUDY QUESTIONS

1. What is Baldwin's thesis, and how does he develop it?
2. In what way does his view of history relate to his thesis?
3. How does the "curtain of guilt" affect the white man?
4. Baldwin speaks with a prose voice of authority. In what ways does he establish and maintain this voice?
5. How does the concluding paragraph relate to the rest of the essay? What is Baldwin's strategy here?

WHAT WHITES CAN LEARN
Ebony # FROM NEGROES

Trouble don't last always, says an old Negro spiritual, but according to screaming newspaper headlines, convulsed TV commentators and a frayed-nerved public, Old Man Trouble has pitched his teepee square in the middle of the twentieth century and settled down for a record run.

The whole world is on edge. Nations are bickering with nations. Races are pitted against races. Everybody seems beset by fears, overwrought by frustrations. They are jittery about the war in Viet Nam that had no beginning and the war that has no ending in the Dominican Republic and the cold war that occasionally gets mighty warm. They are hearing noises that do not exist, seeing objects that are not there.

In times like these, white people seeking a panacea for their problems might well take a lesson from the Negro on how to live in a troubled world. The Negro is an expert. He has known nothing but trouble all of his life. His grievances are multiple for he has all of the white man's fears and doubts plus the additional burden of being black. Yet the Negro can still smile, for the progress that he has made up from slavery to his present status—short of first class citizenship though it is—is one of the most remarkable advancements in the history of mankind. In the process he has learned to turn his liabilities into assets, to adjust to that over which he has no control and to have faith in his ability to overcome all of the other obstacles between himself and full equality.

Reprinted from *The White Problem in America*. First published in *Ebony*, August 1965. With permission of the publishers.

The Philosophy of "If"

The way to tell a Negro from a white man when physical appearances failed, swore the old time armchair anthropologists, was to engage the suspect in conversation. Query him about his ambitions, his future plans, his next step. If he said he "hoped" to become a lawyer or a merchant, that he "wanted" to buy a car, spend his vacation in Canada, then that man was white. But if he prefaced his desire by the phrase: "If I live and nothing happens," he was colored. This homely philosophy with the built-in disaster clause allowed the Negro to take his setbacks and misfortunes in stride. It was this philosophy, born of heart-breaking experiences, which kept his insanity and suicide rates below those of his fair-skinned brothers. But today's Negro has added a positive dimension to a probable clause. If he lives, he will *make* something happen.

The white man stakes his all on a business venture or a political campaign. He will even put his life's savings in schemes that can pay off only with a hoped-for boom, and bet his last five dollars on a long-shot nag. If he loses he will have an opportunity to recoup and start all over again, but all too often, he is found below an open window or his last will and testament is contained in a brief note on the railing of a bridge.

The Negro, whose existence is riddled with reverses and disappointments, has learned not to put all of his eggs in one shopping bag or his complete trust in one man. He knows that if he fails, there is no second chance. For him there are no short cuts to success. Only through his own supreme efforts can he attain his cherished goal. When bad luck overtook him, he used to console himself with the adage that "everything happens for the best." Today, he does not wait for things to happen, and the best may not be good enough. Instead of taking his troubles to the window or the water, he is more likely to try them in the courts or dramatize them in the streets.

The Negro is particularly adept at making the best of a bad situation, not because of any inherent powers that he may have, but because he has had an abundance of practice and more bad situations than the white man. More put upon and less protected than any other ethnic group in our society except the Indian, he has been under the strain of racial tensions all of his life; has always been handicapped by patterns of prejudice and walls of discrimination. The Negro in America is kept so busy trying to live under the same flag as the Ku Klux Klan, the White Citizens Councils and other hate-Negro, hate-minority organizations, that he has little time to worry about communism in China or India's population explosion.

A nuclear bomb which he may never see is not nearly as imminent as an electric cattle prod he has felt. Wars in distant lands in which he too must fight, are not as personal as demonstrations in Chicago or boycotts in Birmingham. Although some white citizens would rather cloud the image of this country abroad than practice democracy here at home, the Negro remains loyal to America. He fights for it and he dies for it and he hopes fervently that it will soon be at peace, for he needs all his war-spent energies to earn his daily bread and a little butter. Now that his right to the ballot has been reaffirmed, he needs his war-spent strength to make things happen: to lead registration drives in the South and to discourage voter apathy in the North, to exercise his right to live where his money and desires dictate, to obtain better education for his children, to fit himself for a better job so that he can improve his standard of living. He knows that these things are now possible, but wishing alone will not make them so.

In the South and to some extent in the North, the Negro's very existence once depended upon his ability to get along with white people. The psychology of fear employed by race supremacists to frighten him into 100 years of submission is no longer applicable. His is the faith that overcomes, the courage that marches around bigots and laughs at the Klan. His is an example of faith and courage that other men might follow.

Trapped in a white-dominated world, the black man has learned to live with trouble. To yesterday's motto "don't get mad, get smart," he has added "do something!" If white men are to have peace of mind they must also stop getting mad and getting nervous and do something. For one thing, they must learn to live with men who are black and red and yellow and brown. They, too, must learn to become bedfellows with fear and frustration, to turn liabilities into assets, adjust to that which cannot be helped and change those things that are morally wrong.

To master the art of doing with and doing without is essential to all men. With very little of this world's goods the Negro has been able to an unbelievable degree to survive—even thrive—under oppressions, uncertainties and inconveniences. He has worn hand-me-down clothing, lived in second-class housing, worked at low-paying jobs. But those conditions were morally wrong and he found a way to change them. In doing so, he has transferred his disappointments into hopes and hopes into actions and actions into improvements which, if continued, will bring him the full equality and ultimate happiness all men seek.

If white people would profit by the Negro's ability to overcome, they can begin by cultivating his sense of humor. His public posture may be that of the angry young man, but his capacity to laugh at his troubles, even though he does so in the privacy of his race, is his means of releasing pent-up emotions. White people who would have peace of mind, must ease their guilty consciences. Like the Negro, they must put their trust in God and their shoulder to the wheel. Faith alone will not move mountains.

If the black man can make it by adding new dimensions to old adages, surely white men can follow his example. No people can have peace always nor can their prosperity continue unbroken. All of this country's citizens have worked hard and sacrificed much to make America the great nation that it is today. Surely those who by virtue of color have inherited the bulk of her many benefits can, like the Negro, learn to endure her limitations.

STUDY QUESTIONS

1. How does the author use comparison and contrast to develop his thesis?
2. What does the author mean by the philosophy of "if"?
3. According to the essay, how does the Negro's sense of humor serve him?
4. Do you regard the author's advice as practical? Is the white man prepared to follow such course of action as the author recommends?
5. Is the author's strategy to appeal to the reader's reason or his emotions?

ON FEAR: DEEP SOUTH
William Faulkner   **IN LABOR: MISSISSIPPI**

William Faulkner (1897–1962), winner of the Nobel Prize for Literature in 1950 and regarded as one of the leading novelists of this century, was born in New Albany, Mississippi. He attended the University of Mississippi, but did not graduate. During World War I he trained with the Royal Canadian Air Force, but the war ended before he went overseas. He is the author of more than twenty novels and several collections of short stories. His best-known works are *The Sound and the Fury* (1929), *Light in August* (1932), *Absalom, Absalom!* (1936), and *Go Down Moses* (1942).

Immediately after the Supreme Court decision abolishing segregation in schools, the talk began in Mississippi of ways and means to increase taxes to raise the standard of the Negro schools to match the white ones. I wrote the following letter to the open forum page of our most widely-read Memphis paper:

We Mississippians already know that our present schools are not good enough. Our young men and women themselves prove that to us every year by the fact that, when the best of them want the best of education which they are entitled to and competent for, not only in the humanities but in the professions and crafts—law and medicine and engineering—too, they must go out of the state to get it. And quite often, too often, they dont come back.

So our present schools are not even good enough for white people; our present State reservoir of education is not of high enough quality to assuage the thirst of even our white young men and women. In which case, how can it possibly assuage the thirst and need of the Negro, who obviously is thirstier, needs it worse, else the Federal Government would not have had to pass a law compelling Mississippi (among others of course) to make the best of our education available to him.

That is, our present schools are not even good enough for white people. So what do we do? make them good enough, improve them to the best possible? No. We beat the bushes, rake and scrape to raise additional taxes to establish another system at best only equal to that one which is already not good enough, which therefore wont be good enough for Negroes either; we will have two identical systems neither of which are good enough for anybody.

A few days after my letter was printed in the paper, I received by post the carbon copy of a letter addressed to the same forum page of the Memphis paper. It read as follows: "When Weeping Willie Faulkner splashes his tears about the inadequacy of Mississippi schools . . . we question his gumption in these respects" etc. From there it went on to cite certain facts of which all Southerners are justly proud: that the seed-stock of education in our land was preserved through the evil times following the Civil War when our land was a defeated and occupied country, by dedicated teachers who got little in return for their dedication. Then, after a brief sneer at the quality of my writing and the profit motive which was the obvious reason why I was a writer, he closed by saying: "I suggest that Weeping Willie dry his tears and work up a little thirst for knowledge about the basic economy of his state."

Later, after this letter was printed in the Memphis paper in its turn, I received from the writer of it a letter addressed to him by a correspondent in another small Mississippi town, consisting in general of a sneer at the Nobel Prize which was awarded me, and commending the Weeping Willie writer for his promptness in taking to task anyone traitorous enough to hold education more important than the color of the educatee's skin. Attached to it was the Weeping Willie writer's reply. It said in effect: "In my opinion Faulkner is the most capable commentator on Southern facts of life to date. . . . If we could insult him into acquiring an insight into the basic economy of our region, he could (sic) do us a hell of a lot of good in our fight against integration."

My answer was that I didn't believe that insult is a very sound method of teaching anybody anything, of persuading anyone to think or act as the insulter believes they should. I repeated that what we needed in Mississippi was the best possible schools, to make the best possible use of the men and women we produced, regardless of what color they were. And even if we could not have a school system which would do that, at least let us have one which would make no distinction among pupils except that of simple ability, since our principal and perhaps desperate need in America today was that all Americans at least should be on the side of America; that if all Americans were on the same side, we would not need to fear that other nations and ideologies would doubt us when we talked of human freedom.

But this is beside the point. The point is, what is behind this. The tragedy is not the impasse, but what is behind the impasse—the impasse of the two apparently irreconcilable facts which we are faced with in the South: the one being the decree of our national government that there be absolute equality in education among all citizens, the other being the white people in the South who say that white and Negro pupils shall never sit in the same classroom. Only apparently irreconcilable, because they must be reconciled since the only alternative to change is death. In fact, there are people in the South, Southerners born, who not only believe they can be reconciled but who love our land—not love white people specifically nor love Negroes specifically, but our land, our country: our climate and geography, the qualities in our people, white and Negro too, for honesty and fairness, the splendors in our traditions, the glories in our past—enough to try to reconcile them, even at the cost of displeasing both sides: the contempt of the Northern radicals who believe we dont do enough, the contumely and threats of our own Southern reactionaries who are convinced that anything we do is already too much.

The tragedy is, the reason behind the fact, the fear behind the fact that some of the white people in the South—people who otherwise are rational, cultured, gentle, generous and kindly—will—must—fight against every inch which the Negro gains in social betterment; the fear behind the desperation which could drive rational and successful men (my correspondent, the Weeping Willie one, is a banker, perhaps president of a—perhaps the—bank in another small Mississippi town like my own) to grasp at such straws for weapons as contumely and threat and insult to change the views or anyway the voice which dares to suggest that betterment of the Negro's condition does not necessarily presage the doom of the white race. Nor is the tragedy the fear so much as the tawdry quality of the fear—fear not of the Negro as an individual Negro nor even as a race, but as an economic class or stratum or factor, since what the Negro threatens is not the Southern white man's social system but the Southern white man's economic system—that economic system which the white man knows and dares not admit to himself is established on an obsolescence—the artificial inequality of man—and so is itself already obsolete and hence doomed. He knows that only three hundred years ago the Negro's naked grandfather was eating rotten elephant or hippo meat in an African rain-forest, yet in only three hundred years the Negro produced Dr. Ralph Bunche and George Washington Carver and Booker T. Washington. The white man knows that only ninety years ago not one percent of the Negro race could own a deed to land, let alone read that deed; yet in only ninety years, although his only contact with a county courthouse is the window through which he pays the taxes for which he has no representation, he can own his land and farm it with inferior stock and worn-out tools and gear—equipment which any white man would starve with—and raise children and feed and clothe them and send them to what schools are available and even now and then send them North where they can have equal scholastic opportunity, and end his life holding his head up because he owes no man, with even enough over to pay for his coffin and funeral. That's what the white man in the South is afraid of: that the Negro, who has done so much with no chance, might do so much more with an equal one that he might take the white man's economy away from him, the Negro now the banker or the merchant or the planter and the white man the share-cropper or the tenant. That's why the Negro can gain our country's highest decoration for valor beyond all call of duty for saving or defending or preserving white lives on foreign battle-fields yet the Southern white man dares not let that Negro's children learn their abc's in the same classroom with the children of the white lives he saved or defended.

Now the Supreme Court has defined exactly what it meant by what it said: that by "equality" it meant, simply, equality, without qualifying or conditional adjectives: not "separate but equal" nor "equally separate," but simply, equal; and now the Mississippi voices are talking of something which does not even exist anymore.

In the first half of the nineteenth century, before slavery was abolished by law in the United States, Thomas Jefferson and Abraham Lincoln both held that the Negro was not yet competent for equality.

That was more than ninety years ago now, and nobody can say whether their opinions would be different now or not.

But assume that they would not have changed their belief, and that that opinion is right. Assume that the Negro is still not competent for equality, which is something which neither he nor the white man knows until we try it.

But we do know that, with the support of the Federal Government, the Negro is going to gain the right to try and see if he is fit or not for equality. And if the Southern white man cannot trust him with something as mild as equality, what is the Southern white man going to do when he has power—the power of his own fifteen millions of unanimity backed by the Federal Government—when the only check on that power will be that Federal Government which is already the Negro's ally?

In 1849, Senator John C. Calhoun made his address in favor of secession if the Wilmot Proviso was ever adopted. On Oct. 12th of that year, Senator Jefferson Davis wrote a public letter to the South, saying: "The generation which avoids its responsibility on this subject sows the wind and leaves the whirlwind as a harvest to its children. Let us get together and build manufactures, enter upon industrial pursuits, and prepare for our own self-sustenance."

At that time the Constitution guaranteed the Negro as property along with all other property, and Senator Calhoun and Senator Davis had the then undisputed validity of States' Rights to back their position. Now the Constitution guarantees the Negro equal right to equality, and the states' rights which the Mississippi voices are talking about do not exist anymore. We—Mississippi—sold our states' rights back to the Federal Government when we accepted the first cotton price-support subsidy twenty years ago. Our economy is not agricultural any longer. Our economy is the Federal Government. We no longer farm in Mississippi cotton-fields. We farm now in Washington corridors and Congressional committee-rooms.

We—the South—didn't heed Senator Davis's words then. But we had better do it now. If we are to watch our native land wrecked and ruined twice in less than a hundred years over the Negro question, let us be sure this time that we know where we are going afterward.

There are many voices in Mississippi. There is that of one of our United States senators, who, although he is not speaking for the United States Senate and what he advocates does not quite match the oath he took when he entered into his high office several years ago, at least has made no attempt to hide his identity and his condition. And there is the voice of one of our circuit judges, who, although he is not now speaking from the Bench and what he advocates also stands a little awry to his oath that before the law all men are equal and the weak shall be succored and defended, makes no attempt either to conceal his identity and condition. And there are the voices of the ordinary citizens who, although they do not claim to speak specifically for the white Citizens' Councils and the NAACP, do not try to hide their sentiments and their convictions; not to mention those of the schoolmen—teachers and professors and pupils—though, since most Mississippi schools are State-owned or -supported, they dont always dare to sign their names to the open letters.

There are all the voices in fact, except one. That one voice which would adumbrate them all to silence, being the superior of all since it is the living articulation of the glory and the sovereignty of God and the hope and aspiration of man. The Church, which is the strongest unified force in our Southern life since all Southerners are not white and are not democrats, but all Southerners are religious and all religions serve the same single God, no matter by what name He is called. Where is that voice now, the only reference to which I have seen was in an open forum letter to our Memphis paper which said that to his (the writer's) knowledge, none of the people who begged leave to doubt that one segment of the human race was forever doomed to be inferior to all the other segments just because the Old Testament five thousand years ago said it was, were communicants of any church.

Where is that voice now, which should have propounded perhaps two but certainly one of these still-unanswered questions?

1. The Constitution of the U.S. says: Before the law, there shall be no artificial inequality—race, creed or money—among citizens of the United States.
2. Morality says: Do unto others as you would have others do unto you.
3. Christianity says: I am the only distinction among men since whosoever believeth in Me, shall never die.

Where is this voice now, in our time of trouble and indecision? Is it trying by its silence to tell us that it has no validity and wants none outside the sanctuary behind its symbolical spire?

If the facts as stated in the *Look* magazine account of the Till affair are correct, this remains: two adults, armed, in the dark, kidnap a fourteen-year-old boy and take him away to frighten him. Instead of which, the fourteen-year-old boy not only refuses to be frightened, but, unarmed, alone, in the dark, so frightens the two armed adults that they must destroy him.

What are we Mississippians afraid of ? Why do we have so low an opinion of ourselves that we are afraid of people who by all our standards are our inferiors?—economically: i.e., they have so much less than we have that they must work for us not on their terms but on ours; educationally: i.e., their schools are so much worse than ours that the Federal Government has to threaten to intervene to give them equal conditions; politically: i.e., they have no recourse in law for protection from nor restitution for injustice and violence.

Why do we have so low an opinion of our blood and traditions as to fear that, as soon as the Negro enters our house by the front door, he will propose marriage to our daughter and she will immediately accept him?

Our ancestors were not afraid like this—our grandfathers who fought at First and Second Manassas and Sharpsburg and Shiloh and Franklin and Chickamauga and Chancellorsville and the Wilderness; let alone those who survived that and had the additional and even greater courage and endurance to resist and survive Reconstruction, and so preserved to us something of our present heritage. Why are we, descendants of that blood and inheritors of that courage, afraid? What are we afraid of ? What has happened to us in only a hundred years?

For the sake of argument, let us agree that all white Southerners (all white Americans maybe) curse the day when the first Briton or Yankee sailed the first shipload of manacled Negroes across the Middle Passage and auctioned them into American slavery. Because that doesn't matter now. To live anywhere in the world today and be against equality because of race or color, is like living in Alaska and being against snow. We have already got snow. And as with the Alaskan, merely to live in armistice with it is not enough. Like the Alaskan, we had better use it.

Suddenly about five years ago and with no warning to myself, I adopted the habit of travel. Since then I have seen (a little of some, a little more of others) the Far and Middle East, North Africa, Europe and Scandinavia. The countries I saw were not communist (then) of course, but they were more: they were not even communist-inclined, where it seemed to me they should have been. And I wondered why. Then suddenly I said to myself with a kind of amazement: It's because of America. These people still believe in the American dream; they do not know yet that something happened to it. They believe in us and are willing to trust and follow us not because of our material power: Russia has that: but because of the idea of individual human freedom and liberty and equality on which our nation was founded, which our founding fathers postulated the word "America" to mean.

And, five years later, the countries which are still free of communism are still free simply because of that: that belief in individual liberty and equality and freedom which is the one idea powerful enough to stalemate the idea of communism. And we can thank our gods for that since we have no other weapon to fight communism with; in diplomacy we are children to communist diplomats, and production in a free country can always suffer because under monolithic government all production can go to the aggrandisement of the State. But then, we dont need anything more since that simple belief of man that he can be free is the strongest force on earth and all we need to do is use it.

Because it makes a glib and simple picture, we like to think of the world situation today as a precarious and explosive balance of two irreconcilable ideologies confronting each other: which precarious balance, once it totters, will drag the whole universe into the abyss along with it. That's not so. Only one of the opposed forces is an ideology. The other one is that simple fact of Man: that simple belief of individual man that he can and should and will be free. And if we who are still free want to continue so, all of us who are still free had better confederate and confederate fast with all others who still have a choice to be free—confederate not as black people nor white people nor blue or pink or green people, but as people who still are free, with all other people who are still free; confederate together and stick together too, if we want a world or even a part of a world in which individual man can be free, to continue to endure.

And we had better take in with us as many as we can get of the nonwhite peoples of the earth who are not completely free yet but who want and intend to be, before that other force which is opposed to individual freedom, befools and gets them. Time was when the nonwhite man was content to—anyway, did—accept his instinct for freedom as an unrealisable dream. But not anymore; the white man himself taught him different with that phase of his—the white man's—own culture which took the form of colonial expansion and exploitation based and morally condoned on the premise of inequality not because of individual incompetence but of mass race or color. As a result of which, in only ten years we have watched the nonwhite peoples expel, by bloody violence when necessary, the white man from all the portions of the Middle East and Asia which he once dominated, into which vacuum has already begun to move that other and inimical power which people who believe in freedom are at war with—that power which says to the nonwhite man: "We dont offer you freedom because there is no such thing as freedom; your white overlords whom you have just thrown out have already proved that to you. But we offer you equality, at least equality in slavedom; if you are to be slaves, at least you can be slaves to your own color and race and religion."

We, the western white man who does believe that there exists an individual freedom above and beyond this mere equality of slavedom, must teach the nonwhite peoples this while there is yet a little time left. We, America, who are the strongest national force opposing communism and monolithicism, must teach all other peoples, white and nonwhite, slave or (for a little while yet) still free. We, America, have the best opportunity to do this because we can begin here, at home; we will not need to send costly freedom task-forces into alien and inimical nonwhite places already convinced that there is no such thing as freedom and liberty and equality and peace for nonwhite people too, or we would practise it at home. Because our nonwhite minority is already on our side; we dont need to sell the Negro on America and freedom because he is already sold; even when ignorant from inferior or no education, even despite the record of his history of inequality, he still believes in our concepts of freedom and democracy.

That is what America has done for them in only three hundred years. Not done *to* them: done *for* them because to our shame we have made little effort so far to teach them to be Americans, let alone to use their capacities and capabilities to make us a stronger and more unified America;—the people who only three hundred years ago lived beside one of the largest bodies of inland water on earth and never thought of sail, who yearly had to move by whole villages and tribes from famine and pestilence and enemies without once thinking of wheel, yet in three hundred years have become skilled artisans and craftsmen capable of holding their own in a culture of technocracy; the people who only three hundred years ago were eating the carrion in the tropical jungles yet in only three hundred years have produced the Phi Beta Kappas and the Doctor Bunches and the Carvers and the Booker Washingtons and the poets and musicians; who have yet to produce a Fuchs or Rosenberg or Gold or Burgess or McLean or Hiss, and where for every Robeson there are a thousand white ones.

The Bunches and Washingtons and Carvers and the musicians and the poets who were not just good men and women but good teachers too, teaching him—the Negro—by precept and example what a lot of our white people have not learned yet: that to gain equality, one must deserve it, and to deserve equality, one must understand what it is: that there is no such thing as equality *per se*, but only equality *to:* equal right and opportunity to make the best one can of one's life within one's capacity and capability, without fear of injustice or oppression or violence. If we had given him this equality ninety or fifty or even ten years ago, there would have been no Supreme Court ruling about segregation in 1954.

But we didn't. We dared not; it is our southern white man's shame that in our present economy the Negro must not have economic equality; our double shame that we fear that giving him more social equality will jeopardise his present economic status; our triple shame that even then, to justify our stand, we must becloud the issue with the bugaboo of miscegenation; what a commentary that the one remaining place on earth where the white man can flee and have his uncorrupted blood protected and defended by law, is in Africa—Africa: the source and origin of the threat whose present presence in America will have driven the white man to flee it.

Soon now all of us—not just Southerners nor even just Americans, but all people who are still free and want to remain so—are going to have to make a choice, lest the next (and last) confrontation we face will be, not communists against anti-communists, but simply the remaining handful of white people against the massed myriads of all the people on earth who are not white. We will have to choose not between color nor race nor religion nor between East and West either, but simply between being slaves and being free. And we will have to choose completely and for good; the time is already past now when we can choose a little of each, a little of both. We can choose a state of slavedom, and if we are powerful enough to be among the top two or three or ten, we can have a certain amount of license—until someone more powerful rises and has us machine-gunned against a cellar wall. But we cannot choose freedom established on a hierarchy of degrees of freedom, on a caste system of equality like military rank. We must be free not because we claim freedom, but because we practise it; our freedom must be buttressed by a homogeny equally and unchallengeably free, no matter what color they are, so that all the other inimical forces everywhere—systems political or religious or racial or national—will not just respect us because we practise freedom, they will fear us because we do.

[*Harper's*, June 1956; the text printed here has been taken from Faulkner's revised typescript.]

STUDY QUESTIONS

1. Compare Faulkner's concept of the white man's fear with Baldwin's concept of the white man's guilt.
2. What line of reasoning does Faulkner follow in developing his thesis?
3. What are Faulkner's views on the position the church has taken on the civil rights issues?
4. On the basis of what Faulkner says in this essay, do you believe he would agree with the *Ebony* essay? Explain.
5. What appears to be Faulkner's attitude toward his subject? Note specific details that express his attitude.
6. Faulkner begins his essay with a personal anecdote. What is his strategy in this? Is it effective?

Jonathan Swift A MODEST PROPOSAL

Jonathan Swift (1667–1745) is one of England's greatest prose writers. He was born in Dublin, Ireland, and was educated there at Trinity College. The fact that he took orders in the Church of England did not prevent him from becoming one of the Tory

First published in 1729.

propagandists. However, Queen Anne disapproved of *A Tale of a Tub* (1704), and Swift was given the deanery of St. Patrick's, Dublin, instead of the English preferment he wanted. Among his now-classic works are *The Battle of the Books* (1704), *Gulliver's Travels* (1726), *A Modest Proposal* (1729), and *The Journal to Stella* (1766).

It is a melancholly Object to those, who walk through this great Town or travel in the Country, when they see the Streets, the Roads and Cabbin-doors crowded with Beggers of the Female Sex, followed by three, four, or six Children, all in Rags, and importuning every Passenger for an Alms. These Mothers instead of being able to work for their honest livelyhood, are forced to employ all their time in Stroling to beg Sustenance for their helpless Infants, who, as they grow up, either turn Thieves for want of Work, or leave their dear Native Country, to fight for the Pretender in Spain, or sell themselves to the Barbadoes.

I think it is agreed by all Parties, that this prodigious number of Children in the Arms, or on the Backs, or at the Heels of their Mothers, and frequently of their Fathers, is in the present deplorable state of the Kingdom, a very great additional grievance; and therefore whoever could find out a fair, cheap and easy method of making these Children sound and useful Members of the Common-wealth, would deserve so well of the publick, as to have his Statue set up for a Preserver of the Nation.

But my Intention is very far from being confined to provide only for the Children of professed Beggers, it is of a much greater Extent, and shall take in the whole Number of Infants at a certain Age, who are born of Parents in effect as little able to support them, as those who demand our Charity in the Streets.

As to my own part, having turned my Thoughts, for many Years, upon this important Subject, and maturely weighed the several Schemes of other Projectors, I have always found them grossly mistaken in their computation. It is true, a Child just dropt from its Dam, may be supported by her Milk, for a Solar Year with little other Nourishment, at most not above the Value of two Shillings, which the Mother may certainly get, or the Value in Scraps, by her lawful Occupation of Begging; and it is exactly at one Year Old that I propose to provide for them in such a manner, as, instead of being a Charge upon their Parents, or the Parish, or wanting Food and Raiment for the rest of their Lives, they shall, on the Contrary, contribute to the Feeding and partly to the Cloathing of many Thousands.

There is likewise another great Advantage in my Scheme, that it will prevent those voluntary Abortions, and that horrid practice of Women murdering their Bastard Children, alas! too frequent among us,

Sacrificing the poor innocent Babes, I doubt, more to avoid the Expense than the Shame, which would move Tears and Pity in the most Savage and inhuman breast.

The number of Souls in this Kingdom being usually reckoned one Million and a half, Of these I calculate there may be about two hundred thousand Couples whose Wives are Breeders; from which number I substract thirty Thousand Couples, who are able to maintain their own Children, although I apprehend there cannot be so many, under the present Distresses of the Kingdom; but this being granted, there will remain an hundred and seventy thousand Breeders. I again Substract fifty Thousand, for those Women who miscarry, or whose Children die by accident, or disease within the Year. There only remain an hundred and twenty thousand Children of poor Parents annually born: The question therefore is, How this number shall be reared, and provided for? which, as I have already said, under the present Situation of Affairs, is utterly impossible by all the Methods hitherto proposed; for we can neither employ them in Handicraft or Agriculture; we neither build Houses, (I mean in the Country) nor cultivate Land: They can very seldom pick up a Livelihood by Stealing till they arrive at six years Old; except where they are of towardly parts; although, I confess, they learn the Rudiments much earlier; during which time they can however be properly looked upon only as Probationers; as I have been informed by a principal Gentleman in the County of Cavan, who protested to me, that he never knew above one or two Instances under the Age of six, even in a part of the Kingdom so renowned for the quickest proficiency in that Art.

I am assured by our Merchants, that a Boy or a Girl before twelve years Old, is no saleable Commodity, and even when they come to this Age, they will not yield above three Pounds, or three Pounds and half a Crown at most, on the Exchange; which cannot turn to Account either to the Parents or Kingdom, the Charge of Nutriment and Rags having been at least four times that Value.

I shall now therefore humbly propose my own Thoughts, which I hope will not be liable to the least Objection.

I have been assured by a very knowing American of my acquaintance in London, that a young healthy Child well Nursed is at a year Old a most delicious nourishing and wholesome Food, whether Stewed, Roasted, Baked, or Boiled; and I make no doubt that it will equally serve in a Fricasie, or a Ragoust.

I do therefore humbly offer it to publick consideration, that of the Hundred and twenty thousand Children, already computed, twenty thousand may be reserved for Breed, whereof only one fourth part to be Males; which is more than we allow to Sheep, black Cattle, or Swine, and my Reason is, that these Children are seldom the Fruits of Marriage, a Circumstance not much regarded by our Savages, therefore, one Male will be sufficient to serve four Females. That the remaining Hundred thousand may at a year Old be offered in Sale to the Persons of Quality and Fortune, through the Kingdom, always advising the Mother to let them Suck plentifully in the last Month, so as to render them Plump, and Fat for a good Table. A Child will make two Dishes at an Entertainment for Friends, and when the Family dines alone, the fore or hind Quarter will make a reasonable Dish, and seasoned with a little Pepper or Salt will be very good Boiled on the fourth Day, especially in Winter.

I have reckoned upon a Medium, that a Child just born will weigh 12 pounds, and in a solar Year, if tolerably nursed, encreaseth to 28 Pounds.

I grant this food will be somewhat dear, and therefore very proper for Landlords, who, as they have already devoured most of the Parents seem to have the best Title to the Children.

Infant's flesh will be in Season throughout the Year, but more plentiful in March, and a little before and after; for we are told by a grave Author an eminent French Physician, that Fish being a prolifick Dyet, there are more Children born in Roman Catholick Countries about nine Months after Lent, than at any other Season; therefore reckoning a Year after Lent, the Markets will be more glutted than usual, because the Number of Popish Infants, is at least three to one in this Kingdom, and therefore it will have one other Collateral advantage, by lessening the Number of Papists among us.

I have already computed the Charge of nursing a Begger's Child (in which List I reckon all Cottagers, Labourers, and four fifths of the Farmers) to be about two Shillings per Annum, Rags included; and I believe no Gentleman would repine to give Ten Shillings for the Carcass of a good fat Child, which, as I have said will make four Dishes of excellent Nutritive Meat, when he hath only some particular Friend, or his own Family to dine with him. Thus the Squire will learn to be a good Landlord, and grow popular among his Tenants, the Mother will have Eight Shillings neat Profit, and be fit for Work till she produces another Child.

Those who are more thrifty (as I must confess the Times require) may flay the Carcass; the Skin of which, Artificially dressed, will make admirable Gloves for Ladies, and Summer Boots for fine Gentlemen.

As to our City of Dublin, Shambles may be appointed for this purpose, in the most convenient parts of it, and Butchers we may be assured will not be wanting; although I rather recommend buying the Children alive, and dressing them hot from the Knife, as we do roasting Pigs.

A very worthy Person, a true Lover of his Country, and whose

Virtues I highly esteem, was lately pleased, in discoursing on this matter, to offer a refinement upon my Scheme. He said, that many Gentlemen of this Kingdom, having of late destroyed their Deer, he conceived
that the Want of Venison might be well supply'd by the Bodies of young
Lads and Maidens, not exceeding fourteen Years of Age, nor under
twelve; so great a Number of both Sexes in every Country being now
ready to Starve, for want of Work and Service: And these to be disposed
of by their Parents if alive, or otherwise by their nearest Relations. But
with due deference to so excellent a Friend, and so deserving a Patriot, I
cannot be altogether in his Sentiments; for as to the Males, my American
acquaintance assured me from frequent Experience, that their Flesh was
generally Tough and Lean, like that of our Schoolboys, by continual
exercise, and their Taste disagreeable, and to fatten them would not
answer the Charge. Then as to the Females, it would, I think with
humble Submission, be a Loss to the Publick, because they soon would
become Breeders themselves: And besides it is not improbable that some
scrupulous People might be apt to Censure such a Practice, (although
indeed very unjustly) as a little bordering upon Cruelty, which, I confess, hath always been with me the strongest Objection against any
Project, how well soever intended.

But in order to justify my Friend, he confessed, that this expedient
was put into his Head by the famous Sallmanaazor, a Native of the
Island Formosa, who came from thence to London, above twenty Years
ago, and in Conversation told my Friend, that in his Country when any
young Person happened to be put to Death, the Executioner sold the
Carcass to Persons of Quality, as a prime Dainty, and that, in his Time,
the Body of a plump Girl of fifteen, who was crucified for an attempt to
poison the Emperor, was sold to his Imperial Majesty's prime Minister of
State, and other great Mandarins of the Court, in Joints from the Gibbet,
at four hundred Crowns. Neither indeed can I deny, that if the same Use
were made of several plump young Girls in this Town, who, without one
single Groat to their Fortunes, cannot stir abroad without a Chair, and
appear at a Play-house, and Assemblies in Foreign fineries, which they
never will pay for; the Kingdom would not be the worse.

Some Persons of a desponding Spirit are in great concern about
that vast Number of poor People, who are Aged, Diseased, or Maimed,
and I have been desired to imploy my Thoughts what Course may be
taken, to ease the Nation of so grievous an Incumbrance. But I am not in
the least Pain upon that matter, because it is very well known, that they
are every Day dying, and rotting, by cold and famine, and filth, and
vermin, as fast as can be reasonably expected. And as to the younger
Labourers, they are now in almost as hopeful a Condition. They cannot
get Work, and consequently pine away for want of Nourishment, to a
degree, that if at any Time they are accidentally hired to common

Labour, they have not Strength to perform it, and thus the Country and themselves are happily delivered from the Evils to come.

I have too long digressed, and therefore shall return to my Subject. I think the Advantages by the Proposal which I have made are obvious and many, as well as of the highest Importance.

For *First,* as I have already observed, it would greatly lessen the Number of Papists, with whom we are Yearly over-run, being the principal Breeders of the Nation, as well as our most dangerous Enemies, and who stay at home on purpose with a Design to deliver the Kingdom to the Pretender, hoping to take their Advantage by the Absence of so many good Protestants, who have chosen rather to leave their Country, than stay at home, and pay Tithes against their Conscience, to an Episcopal Curate.

Secondly, The poorer Tenants will have something valuable of their own which by Law may be made lyable to Distress, and help to pay their Landlord's Rent, their Corn and Cattle being already seized, and Money a Thing unknown.

Thirdly, Whereas the Maintenance of an hundred thousand Children, from two Years old, and upwards, cannot be computed at less than Ten Shillings a Piece per Annum, the Nation's Stock will be thereby increased fifty thousand Pounds per Annum, besides the Profit of a new Dish, introduced to the Tables of all Gentlemen of Fortune in the Kingdom, who have any Refinement in Taste, and the Money will circulate among our Selves, the Goods being entirely of our own Growth and Manufacture.

Fourthly, The constant Breeders besides the gain of eight Shillings Sterling per Annum, by the Sale of their Children, will be rid of the Charge of maintaining them after the first Year.

Fifthly, This Food would likewise bring great Custom to Taverns, where the Vintners will certainly be so prudent as to procure the best Receipts for dressing it to Perfection; and consequently have their Houses frequented by all the fine Gentlemen, who justly value themselves upon their Knowledge in good Eating; and a skilful Cook, who understands how to oblige his Guests, will contrive to make it as expensive as they please.

Sixthly, This would be a great Inducement to Marriage, which all wise Nations have either encouraged by Rewards, or enforced by Laws and Penalties. It would encrease the Care and Tenderness of Mothers towards their Children, when they were sure of a Settlement for Life, to the poor Babes, provided in some Sort by the Publick, to their annual Profit instead of Expence; we should soon see an honest Emulation among the married Women, which of them could bring the fattest Child to the Market. Men would become as fond of their Wives, during the Time of their Pregnancy, as they are now of their Mares in Foal, their Cows in

Calf, or Sows when they are ready to farrow, nor offer to beat or kick them (as is too frequent a Practice) for fear of a Miscarriage.

Many other Advantages might be enumerated. For Instance, the Addition of some thousand Carcasses in our Exportation of Barrel'd Beef: The Propagation of Swine's Flesh, and Improvement in the Art of making good Bacon, so much wanted among us by the great Destruction of Pigs, too frequent at our Tables, which are no way comparable in Taste, or Magnificence to a well grown, fat yearling Child, which roasted whole will make a considerable Figure at a Lord Mayor's Feast, or any other Publick Entertainment. But this, and many others, I omit, being studious of Brevity.

Supposing that one thousand Families in this City, would be constant Customers for Infant's Flesh, besides others who might have it at merry Meetings, particularly at Weddings and Christenings, I compute that Dublin would take off Annually about twenty thousand Carcasses, and the rest of the Kingdom (where probably they will be sold somewhat cheaper) the remaining eighty Thousand.

I can think of no one Objection, that will possibly be raised against this Proposal, unless it should be urged, that the Number of People will be thereby much lessened in the Kingdom. This I freely own, and 'twas indeed one principal Design in offering it to the World. I desire the Reader will observe, that I calculate my Remedy for this one individual Kingdom of Ireland, and for no Other that ever was, is, or, I think, ever can be upon Earth. Therefore let no man talk to me of other Expedients: Of taxing our Absentees at five Shillings a Pound: Of using neither Cloaths, nor Household Furniture, except what is of our own Growth and Manufacture: Of utterly rejecting the Materials and Instruments that promote Foreign Luxury: Of curing the Expensiveness of Pride, Vanity, Idleness, and Gaming in our Women: Of introducing a Vein of Parcimony, Prudence and Temperance: Of learning to love our Country, wherein we differ even from Laplanders, and the Inhabitants of Topinamboo: Of quitting our Animosities, and Factions, nor act any longer like the Jews, who were murdering one another at the very Moment their City was taken: Of being a little cautious not to sell our Country and Consciences for nothing: Of teaching Landlords to have at least one Degree of Mercy towards their Tenants. Lastly, Of putting a Spirit of Honesty, Industry, and Skill into our Shop-keepers, who, if a Resolution could now be taken to buy only our Native Goods, would immediately unite to cheat and exact upon us in the Price, the Measure, and the Goodness, nor could ever yet be brought to make one fair Proposal of just Dealing, though often and earnestly invited to it.

Therefore I repeat, let no Man talk to me of these and the like Expedients, till he hath at least some Glimpse of Hope, that there will ever be some hearty and sincere Attempt to put them in Practice.

But as to my self, having been wearied out for many Years with offering vain, idle, visionary Thoughts, and at length utterly despairing of Success, I fortunately fell upon this Proposal, which as it is wholly new, so it hath something Solid and Real, of no Expence and little Trouble, full in our own Power, and whereby we can incur no Danger in disobliging England. For this kind of Commodity will not bear Exportation, the Flesh being of too tender a Consistence, to admit a long Continuance in Salt, although perhaps I cou'd name a Country, which wou'd be glad to eat up our whole Nation without it.

After all, I am not so violently bent upon my own Opinion, as to reject any Offer, proposed by wise Men, which shall be found equally Innocent, Cheap, Easy, and Effectual. But before something of that Kind shall be advanced in Contradiction to my Scheme, and offering a better, I desire the Author or Authors, will be pleased maturely to consider two Points. *First,* As Things now stand, how they will be able to find Food and Raiment for a hundred Thousand useless Mouths and Backs. And *Secondly,* There being a round Million of Creatures in Human Figure, throughout this Kingdom, whose whole Subsistence put into a common Stock, would leave them in Debt two Millions of Pounds Sterling, adding those, who are Beggers by Profession, to the Bulk of Farmers, Cottagers and Labourers, with their Wives and Children, who are Beggers in Effect; I desire those Politicians, who dislike my Overture, and may perhaps be so bold to attempt an Answer, that they will first ask the Parents of these Mortals, Whether they would not at this Day think it a great Happiness to have been sold for Food at a Year Old, in the manner I prescribe, and thereby have avoided such a perpetual Scene of Misfortunes, as they have since gone through, by the Oppression of Landlords, the Impossibility of paying Rent without Money or Trade, the Want of common Sustenance, with neither House nor Cloaths to cover them from the Inclemencies of the Weather, and the most inevitable Prospect of intailing the like, or greater Miseries, upon their Breed for ever.

I profess in the Sincerity of my Heart, that I have not the least Personal Interest in endeavouring to promote this necessary Work, having no other Motive than the Publick Good of my Country, by advancing our Trade, providing for infants, relieving the Poor, and giving some Pleasure to the Rich. I have no Children, by which I can propose to get a single Penny; the youngest being nine Years Old, and my Wife past Child-bearing.

STUDY QUESTIONS

1. Before he reveals his proposal, Swift devotes the first part of his essay to describing the advantages of his proposal. What is his strategy in this?

2. At what point does the reader realize that Swift is not to be taken literally in his proposal?

3.   How does Swift give his proposal the appearance of authenticity?
4.   Swift follows a logical outline in presenting his proposal. What is the general framework of the outline?
5.   Swift makes a number of topical references and allusions that the reader will recognize only if he is familiar with the historical setting and context of the proposal. But why do you think he used "a very knowing American of my acquaintance" for one of his authorities?

Sir Julian Huxley   THE CROWDED WORLD

Sir Julian Huxley (1887–   ) is a British scientist and writer who has a distinguished reputation both in America and his own country. He has been a professor of zoology at King's College, University of London, and general director of UNESCO. He has been biology editor of the *Encyclopaedia Britannica,* and is the author of many scholarly articles and books. He was knighted for his many contributions and services to science.

Population has at last made the grade and emerged as a World Problem. Unfortunately, most of those who speak or write about the problem persist in thinking of it in terms of a race between human numbers and world resources, especially of food—a kind of competition between production and reproduction. The neo-Malthusians, supported by progressive opinion in the Western World and by leading figures in most Asian countries, produce volumes of alarming statistics about the world population explosion and the urgent need for birth-control, while the anti-Malthusians, supported by the two ideological blocs of Catholicism and Communism, produce equal volumes of hopeful statistics, or perhaps one should say of wishful estimates, purporting to show how the problem can be solved by science, by the exploitation of the Amazon or the Arctic, by better distribution, or even by shipping our surplus population to other planets.

Certainly, the statistics are important. The major fact emerging from them is that there really *is* a population explosion. During the millennia of man's early history, world population increased steadily but very slowly, so that by the end of the seventeenth century it had barely topped the half-billion mark. But then, as a result of the great explorations during and after the Renaissance, and still more of the rise of natural science and technology at the end of the seventeenth century, the process was stepped up, so that by the beginning of the present

Reprinted by permission of A. D. Peters & Co.

century world population stood at about 1½ billion, and its compound interest rate of increase had itself increased from under ½ of 1 per cent in 1650 to nearly 1 per cent (and we all know what big results can flow from even a small increase in compound interest rates).

But the real explosion is a twentieth-century phenomenon, due primarily to the spectacular developments in medicine and hygiene, which have drastically cut down death-rates without any corresponding reduction in birth-rates—death-control without birth-control. The compound interest rate of increase meanwhile crept, or rather leapt, up and up, from under 1 per cent in 1900 to 1½ per cent at mid-century, and nearly 1¾ per cent today; and it will certainly go on increasing for some decades more. This means that the *rate* of human doubling has itself been doubled within the past 80 years. World population has more than doubled since 1900 to reach about 2¾ billion today; and it will certainly reach well over 5½ billion, probably 6 billion, and possibly nearly 7 billion by the year 2000.

Coming down to details, Britons will be jolted by the fact that the net increase of world population amounts to about 150,000 every 24 hours, or the equivalent of a good-sized New Town every day—Hemel Hempstead yesterday, Harlow today, Crawley tomorrow, and so on through the weeks and months; while Americans will be startled out of any complacency they may have possessed by the fact that this is the equivalent of 10 baseball teams, complete with coach, every minute of every day and night. Such facts make the idea of interplanetary disposal of the earth's surplus population merely ridiculous.

It is also salutary to be reminded that the number of human beings alive in A.D. 1999—within the lifetime of many now living—will be about double that of those alive today; that some populations, like that of Barbados, are growing at a rate of over 3 per cent compound interest per annum, which means doubling in less than 20 years; that in an underdeveloped but already densely populated country like India, successful industrialization will be impossible unless the birth-rate is cut to about half within the next 30 or 40 years, for otherwise the capital and the trained man- and woman-power needed to give the country a stable industrial economy will be swallowed up in feeding, housing, educating, and servicing the excess population; that religious opposition to population-control is strongest and most effective in regions like Latin America, where population-increase is most rampant; that there is no provision for international study and research on population-control as there is on atomic energy, on the world's arid zones, on brain function, or on oceanography; that there is already an alarming (and increasing) shortage of available water-supplies, high-grade mineral resources, and educational facilities, even in industrially advanced countries like the U.S.A.; that the annual increase of Communist China's population is 13 million, more than the equivalent of a new Sweden and a new Denmark every year; or that the World Health Organization has twice been prevented by Roman Catholic pressure from even considering population-density as a factor in the world's health.

But in the broad view the most important thing about the population explosion is that it is making everyone—or rather everyone capable of serious thought—think seriously about the future of our human species on our human planet.

The Middle Ages were brought to an end by a major revolution in thought and belief, which stimulated the growth of science and the secularization of life at the expense of significance in art and religion, generated the industrial-technological revolution, with its stress on economics and quantitative production at the expense of significance in quality, human values and fulfilment, and culminated in what we are pleased to call the Atomic Age, with two World Wars behind it, the threat of annihilation before it, and an ideological split at its core.

Actually our modern age merits the adjective atomistic rather than atomic. Further, it will soon become very unmodern. For we are on the threshold of another major revolution, involving a new pattern of thought and a new approach to human destiny and its practical problems. It will usher in a new phase of human history, which I like to call the Evolutionary Age, because it envisages man as both product and agent of the evolutionary process on this planet.

The new approach is beginning to take effect in two rather distinct fields, of ecology and ideology, and is generating two parallel but linked currents of thought and action, that may be called the Ecological Revolution and the Humanist Revolution.

The population explosion is giving a powerful impetus to both these revolutionary currents. Ecology is the science of relational adjustment—the balanced relations of living organisms with their environment and with each other. It started botanically in a rather modest way as a study of plant communities in different habitats; went on to the fruitful idea of the ecological succession of different plant communities in a given habitat, leading up to an optimum climax community—mixed forest in the humid tropics, rich grassland on the prairies; was extended to take in animal communities, and so to the illuminating concepts of food-chains and adaptive niches; and finally, though rather grudgingly, was still further enlarged to include human as well as biological ecology.

The population explosion has brought us up against a number of tough ecological facts. Man is at last pressing hard on his spatial environment—there is little leeway left for his colonization of new areas of the world's surface. He is pressing hard on his resources, notably non-renewable but also renewable resources. As Professor Harrison Brown has so frighteningly made clear in his book, *The Challenge of Man's Future,* ever-increasing consumption by an ever-increasing number of human beings will lead in a very few generations to the exhaustion of all easily exploitable fossil fuels and high-grade mineral ores, to the taking up of all first-rate agricultural land, and so to the invasion of more and more second-rate marginal land for agriculture. In fact, we are well on our way to ruining our material habitat. But we are beginning to ruin our own spiritual and mental habitat also. Not content with destroying or squandering our resources of material things, we are beginning to destroy the resources of true enjoyment—spiritual, aesthetic, intellectual, emotional. We are spreading great masses of human habitation over the face of the land, neither cities nor suburbs nor towns nor villages, just a vast mass of urban sprawl or subtopia. And to escape from this, people are spilling out farther and farther into the wilder parts and so destroying them. And we are making our cities so big as to be monstrous, so big that they are becoming impossible to live in. Just as there is a maximum possible size for an efficient land animal—you can't have a land animal more than about twice as large as an elephant—so there is a maximum possible efficient size for a city. London, New York, and Tokyo have already got beyond that size.

In spite of all that science and technology can do, world food-production is not keeping up with world population, and the gap between the haves and the have-nots of this world is widening instead of being narrowed.

Meanwhile everywhere, though especially in the so-called Free Enterprise areas of the world, economic practice (and sometimes economic theory) is concerned not primarily with increased production, still less with a truly balanced economy, but with exploitation of resources in the interests of maximized and indiscriminate consumption, even if this involves present waste and future shortage.

Clearly this self-defeating, self-destroying process must be stopped. The population explosion has helped to take our economic blinkers off and has shown us the gross and increasing imbalance between the world's human population and its material resources. Unless we quickly set about achieving some sort of balance between reproduction and production, we shall be dooming our grandchildren and all their descendants, through thousands upon thousands of monotonous generations, to an extremely unpleasant and unsatisfactory existence, overworked and undernourished, overcrowded and unfulfilled.

To stop the process means planned conservation in place of reckless exploitation, regulation and control of human numbers, as well as of industrial and technological enterprise, in place of uninhibited expansion. And this means an ecological approach. Ecology will become the basic science of the new age, with physics and chemistry and technology as its hand-maidens, not its masters. The aim will be to achieve a balanced relation between man and nature, an equilibrium between human needs and world resources.

The Humanist Revolution, on the other hand, is destined to supersede the current pattern of ideas and beliefs about nature (including human nature) and man's place and role in it, with a new vision of reality more in harmony with man's present knowledge and circumstances. This new pattern of ideas can be called humanist, since it is focused on man as a product of natural evolution, not on the vast inanimate cosmos, nor on a God or gods, nor on some unchanging spiritual Absolute. For humanism in this sense, man's duty and destiny is to be the spearhead and creative agent of the overall evolutionary process on this planet.

The explosive growth of scientific and historical knowledge in the past hundred years, especially about biological and human evolution, coupled with the rise of rationalist criticism of established theologies and ancient philosophies, had cleared the ground for this revolution in thought and executed some of the necessary demolition work. But now the population explosion poses the world with the fundamental question of human destiny—*What are people for?* Surely people do not exist just to provide bomb-fodder for an atomic bonfire, or religion-fodder for rival churches, or cannon-fodder for rival nations, or disease-fodder for rival parasites, or labour-fodder for rival economic systems, or ideology-fodder for rival political systems, or even consumer-fodder for profit-making systems. It cannot be their aim just to eat, drink and be merry, and to hell with posterity. Nor merely to prepare for some rather shadowy after-life. It cannot be their destiny to exist in ever larger megalopolitan sprawls, cut off from contact with nature and from the sense of human community and condemned to increasing frustration, noise, mechanical routine, traffic congestion and endless commuting; nor to live out their undernourished lives in some squalid Asian or African village.

When we try to think in more general terms it is clear that the dominant aim of human destiny cannot be anything so banal as just maximum quantity, whether of human beings, machines, works of art, consumer goods, political power, or anything else. Man's dominant aim must be increase in quality—quality of human personality, of achievement, of works of art and craftsmanship, of inner experience, of quality of life and living in general.

"Fulfilment" is probably the embracing word: more fulfilment and less frustration for more human beings. We want more varied and fuller achievement in human societies, as against drabness and shrinkage. We want more variety as against monotony. We want more enjoyment and less suffering. We want more beauty and less ugliness. We want more adventure and disciplined freedom, as against routine and slavishness. We want more knowledge, more interest, more wonder, as against ignorance and apathy.

We want more sense of participation in something enduring and worth while, some embracing project, as against a competitive rat-race, whether with the Russians or our neighbours on the next street. In the most general terms, we want more transcendence of self in the fruitful development of personality: and we want more human dignity not only as against human degradation, but as against more self-imprisonment in the human ego or more escapism. But the inordinate growth of human numbers bars the way to any such desirable revolution, and produces increasing frustration instead of greater fulfilment.

There are many urgent special problems which the population explosion is raising—how to provide the increasing numbers of human beings with their basic quotas of food and shelter, raw materials and energy, health and education, with opportunities for adventure and meditation, for contact with nature and with art, for useful work and fruitful leisure; how to prevent frustration exploding into violence or subsiding into apathy; how to avoid unplanned chaos on the one hand and over-organized authoritarianism on the other.

Behind them all, the long-term general problem remains. Before the human species can settle down to any constructive planning of his future on earth (which, let us remember, is likely to be many times longer than his past, to be reckoned in hundreds of millions of years instead of the hundreds of thousands of his prehistory or the mere millennia of History), it must clear the world's decks for action. If man is not to become the planet's cancer instead of its partner and guide, the threatening plethora of the unborn must be for ever banished from the scene.

Above all we need a world population policy—not at some unspecified date in the future, but now. The time has now come to think seriously about population policy. We want every country to have a population policy, just as it has an economic policy or a foreign policy. We want the United Nations to have a population policy. We want all the international agencies of the U.N. to have a population policy.

When I say a population policy, I don't mean that anybody is going to tell every woman how many children she may have, any more than a country which has an economic policy will say how much money an individual businessman is allowed to make and exactly how he should do it. It means that you recognize population as a major problem of national life, that you have a general aim in regard to it, and that you try to devise methods for realizing this aim. And if you have an international population policy, again it doesn't mean dictating to backward countries, or anything of that sort; it means not depriving them of the right (which I should assert is a fundamental human right) to scientific information on birth-control, and it means help in regulating and controlling their increase and planning their families.

Its first aim must be to cut down the present excessive rate of increase to manageable proportions: once this is done we can think about planning for an optimum size of world population—which will almost certainly prove to be less than its present total. Meanwhile we, the people of all nations, through the U.N. and its Agencies, through our own national policies and institutions, and through private Foundations, can help those courageous countries which have already launched a population policy of their own, or want to do so, by freely giving advice and assistance and by promoting research on the largest scale.

When it comes to United Nations agencies, one of the great scandals of the present century is that owing to pressure, mainly from Roman Catholic countries, the World Health Organization has not been allowed even to consider the effects of population density on health. It is essential and urgent that this should be reversed.

There is great frustration in the minds of medical men all over the world, especially those interested in international affairs, who, at the cost of much devoted labour, have succeeded in giving people information on how to control or avoid disease. Malaria in Ceylon is a striking example. As a result of all this wonderful scientific effort and goodwill, population has exploded, and new diseases, new frustrations, new miseries are arising. Meanwhile medical men are not allowed to try to cope with these new troubles on an international scale—and indeed sometimes not even on a national scale. It is an astonishing and depressing fact that even in the advanced and civilized U.S.A. there are two States in which the giving of birth-control information on medical grounds even by non-Catholic doctors to non-Catholic patients, is illegal.

In conclusion I would simply like to go back to where I started and repeat that we must look at the whole question of population increase not merely as an immediate problem to be dealt with *ad hoc*. We must look at it in the light of the new vision of human destiny which human science and learning has revealed to us. We must look at it in the light of the glorious possibilities that are still latent in man, not merely in the light of the obvious fact that the world could be made a little better than it is. We must also look at it in the light of the appalling possibilities for evil and misery that still hang over the future of evolving man.

This vision of the possibilities of wonder and more fruitful fulfilment on the one hand as against frustration and increasing misery and regimentation on the other is the twentieth-century equivalent of the traditional Christian view of salvation as against damnation. I would indeed say that this new point of view that we are reaching, the vision of evolutionary humanism, is essentially a religious one, and that we can and should devote ourselves with truly religious devotion to the cause of ensuring greater fulfilment for the human race in its future destiny. And this involves a furious and concerted attack on the problem of population; for the control of population is, I am quite certain, a prerequisite for any radical improvement in the human lot.

We do indeed need a World Population Policy. We have learnt

how to control the forces of outer nature. If we fail to control the forces of our own reproduction, the human race will be sunk in a flood of struggling people, and we, its present representatives, will be conniving at its future disaster.

STUDY QUESTIONS

1. Huxley contends that the population problem is more than a "race between numbers and world resources." What does he regard to be the more important problem?
2. How does Huxley use comparison and contrast to develop his thesis?
3. He sees a relationship between the decrease of man's material resources and his resources of true enjoyment. What is this relationship?
4. He claims that the population explosion has caused man to ask, "What are people for?" What is Huxley's answer to this question? Would you say that most people agree?
5. Does Huxley appeal to our reason or to our emotions?
6. What is the effect of the repetitive sentence structure in the paragraph beginning " 'Fulfilment' is probably the embracing word"?

Arthur Schopenhauer   **ON NOISE**

Arthur Schopenhauer (1788–1860) was a German philosopher who became well known for his fine prose style and his pessimism. During his lifetime he had a large following who were attracted to his atheistic philosophy and his concept of blind will as the ultimate reality. His main work is *The World as Will and Idea* (1819), but his essays have been widely read, especially his bitter discussion "On Women."

Kant wrote a treatise on *The Vital Powers*. I should prefer to write a dirge for them. The superabundant display of vitality, which takes the form of knocking, hammering, and tumbling things about, has proved a daily torment to me all my life long. There are people, it is true—nay, a great many people—who smile at such things, because they are not sensitive to noise; but they are just the very people who are also not sensitive to argument, or thought, or poetry, or art, in a word, to any kind of intellectual influence. The reason of it is that the tissue of their

From *The Pessimist's Handbook*, by Arthur Schopenhauer translated by T. Bailey Saunders. By permission of George Allen & Unwin, Ltd., London.

brains is of a very rough and coarse quality. On the other hand, noise is a torture to intellectual people. In the biographies of almost all great writers, or wherever else their personal utterances are recorded, I find complaints about it; in the case of Kant, for instance, Goethe, Lichtenberg, Jean Paul; and if it should happen that any writer has omitted to express himself on the matter, it is only for want of an opportunity.

This aversion to noise I should explain as follows: If you cut up a large diamond into little bits, it will entirely lose the value it had as a whole; and an army divided up into small bodies of soldiers, loses all its strength. So a great intellect sinks to the level of an ordinary one, as soon as it is interrupted and disturbed, its attention distracted and drawn off from the matter in hand; for its superiority depends upon its power of concentration—of bringing all its strength to bear upon one theme, in the same way as a concave mirror collects into one point all the rays of light that strike upon it. Noisy interruption is a hindrance to this concentration. That is why distinguished minds have always shown such an extreme dislike to disturbance in any form, as something that breaks in upon and distracts their thoughts. Above all have they been averse to that violent interruption that comes from noise. Ordinary people are not much put out by anything of the sort. The most sensible and intelligent of all nations in Europe lays down the rule, *Never Interrupt!* as the eleventh commandment. Noise is the most impertinent of all forms of interruption. It is not only an interruption, but also a disruption of thought. Of course, where there is nothing to interrupt, noise will not be so particularly painful. Occasionally it happens that some slight but constant noise continues to bother and distract me for a time before I become distinctly conscious of it. All I feel is a steady increase in the labor of thinking—just as though I were trying to walk with a weight on my foot. At last I find out what it is.

Let me now, however, pass from genus to species. The most inexcusable and disgraceful of all noises is the cracking of whips—a truly infernal thing when it is done in the narrow resounding streets of a town. I denounce it as making a peaceful life impossible; it puts an end to all quiet thought. That this cracking of whips should be allowed at all seems to me to show in the clearest way how senseless and thoughtless is the nature of mankind. No one with anything like an idea in his head can avoid a feeling of actual pain at this sudden, sharp crack, which paralyzes the brain, rends the thread of reflection, and murders thought. Every time this noise is made, it must disturb a hundred people who are applying their minds to business of some sort, no matter how trivial it may be; while on the thinker its effect is woeful and disastrous, cutting his thoughts asunder, much as the executioner's axe severs the head from the body. No sound, be it ever so shrill, cuts so sharply into the brain as this cursed cracking of whips; you feel the sting of the lash right inside your head; and it affects the brain in the same way as touch affects a sensitive plant, and for the same length of time.

With all due respect for the most holy doctrine of utility, I really cannot see why a fellow who is taking away a wagon-load of gravel or dung should thereby obtain the right to kill in the bud the thoughts which may happen to be springing up in ten thousand heads—the number he will disturb one after another in half an hour's drive through the town. Hammering, the barking of dogs, and the crying of children are horrible to hear; but your only genuine assassin of thought is the crack of a whip; it exists for the purpose of destroying every pleasant moment of quiet thought that any one may now and then enjoy. If the driver had no other way of urging on his horse than by making this most abominable of all noises, it would be excusable; but quite the contrary is the case. This cursed cracking of whips is not only unnecessary, but even useless. Its aim is to produce an effect upon the intelligence of the horse; but through the constant abuse of it, the animal becomes habituated to the sound, which falls upon blunted feelings and produces no effect at all. The horse does not go any faster for it. You have a remarkable example of this in the ceaseless cracking of his whip on the part of a cab-driver, while he is proceeding at a slow pace on the lookout for a fare. If he were to give his horse the slightest touch with the whip, it would have much more effect. Supposing, however, that it were absolutely necessary to crack the whip in order to keep the horse constantly in mind of its presence, it would be enough to make the hundredth part of the noise. For it is a well-known fact that, in regard to sight and hearing, animals are sensitive to even the faintest indications; they are alive to things that we can scarcely perceive. The most surprising instances of this are furnished by trained dogs and canary birds.

It is obvious, therefore, that here we have to do with an act of pure wantonness; nay, with an impudent defiance offered to those members of the community who work with their heads by those who work with their hands. That such infamy should be tolerated in a town is a piece of barbarity and iniquity, all the more as it could easily be remedied by a police-notice to the effect that every lash shall have a knot at the end of it. There can be no harm in drawing the attention of the mob to the fact that the classes above them work with their heads, for any kind of headwork is mortal anguish to the man in the street. A fellow who rides through the narrow alleys of a populous town with unemployed post-horses or cart-horses, and keeps on cracking a whip several yards long with all his might, deserves there and then to stand down and receive five really good blows with a stick.

All the philanthropists in the world, and all the legislators, meeting to advocate and decree the total abolition of corporal punishment, will never persuade me to the contrary! There is something even more disgraceful than what I have just mentioned. Often enough you may see a carter walking along the street, quite alone, without any horses, and still cracking away incessantly; so accustomed has the wretch become to it in consequence of the unwarrantable toleration of this practice. A man's body and the needs of his body are now everywhere treated with a tender indulgence. Is the thinking mind then, to be the only thing that is never to obtain the slightest measure of consideration or protection, to say nothing of respect? Carters, porters, messengers—these are the beasts of burden amongst mankind; by all means let them be treated justly, fairly, indulgently, and with forethought; but they must not be permitted to stand in the way of the higher endeavors of humanity by wantonly making a noise. How many great and splendid thoughts, I should like to know, have been lost to the world by the crack of a whip? If I had the upper hand, I should soon produce in the heads of these people an indissoluble association of ideas between cracking a whip and getting a whipping.

Let us hope that the more intelligent and refined among the nations will make a beginning in this matter, and then that the Germans may take example by it and follow suit.[1] Meanwhile, I may quote what Thomas Hood says of them [2]: *For a musical nation, they are the most noisy I ever met with.* That they are so is due to the fact, not that they are more fond of making a noise than other people—they would deny it if you asked them—but that their senses are obtuse; consequently, when they hear a noise, it does not affect them much. It does not disturb them in reading or thinking, simply because they do not think; they only smoke, which is their substitute for thought. The general toleration of unnecessary noise—the slamming of doors, for instance, a very unmannerly and ill-bred thing—is direct evidence that the prevailing habit of mind is dullness and lack of thought. In Germany it seems as though care were taken that no one should ever think for mere noise—to mention one form of it, the way in which drumming goes on for no purpose at all.

Finally, as regards the literature of the subject treated of in this chapter, I have only one work to recommend, but it is a good one. I refer to a poetical epistle in *terzo rimo* by the famous painter Bronzino, entitled *De' Romori: a Messer Luca Martini*. It gives a detailed description of the torture to which people are put by the various noises of a small Italian town. Written in a tragicomic style, it is very amusing. The epistle may be found in *Opere burlesche del Berni, Aretino ed altri*, Vol. II., p. 258, apparently published in Utrecht in 1771.

---

[1] According to a notice issued by the Society for the Protection of Animals in Munich, the superfluous whipping and the cracking of whips were, in December, 1858, positively forbidden in Nuremberg.

[2] In *Up the Rhine*.

STUDY QUESTIONS

1.   Schopenhauer follows a fairly basic outline in this essay. Describe it, and note how he begins with something general (noise) and then narrows it down to something specific.

2.   Do you find any humor in this essay? If so, what is the source of the humor?

3.   Does Schopenhauer appear to be simply cranky, or does he convince you that he has a legitimate complaint? Explain.

4.   If Schopenhauer were living today, what noises would annoy him?

Robert Penn Warren   HER OWN PEOPLE

Robert Penn Warren (1905–   ), well-known novelist, poet, literary critic, and university professor, was born in Guthrie, Kentucky. He attended Vanderbilt University, the University of California, Yale University, and Oxford University where he was a Rhodes Scholar. He has received honorary degrees from a number of outstanding universities and colleges and has taught English at Southwestern at Memphis, Vanderbilt University, Louisiana State University, and the University of Minnesota. His many awards include the Pulitzer Prize for Fiction in 1947 and the Pulitzer Prize for Poetry in 1958. He is widely known among English teachers for his textbooks (with Cleanth Brooks) on poetry, fiction, and drama. Among his many publications are the novels *All the King's Men* (1946), *World Enough and Time* (1950), *Band of Angels* (1955), and *Flood* (1964). His interest in contemporary social problems is reflected in *Segregation* (1956) and *Who Speaks for the Negro* (1965).

Fishily, he stared at the high ceiling, where gray plaster, delicately ringed by marks of old damp, was still shadowy, although bright sunshine struck into the room between cracks in the drawn, blue curtains. Between the cracks in the curtain small waxy leaves were visible, brushing against the windowpane.

"Get up," the voice beside him said without much friendliness.

"I've got a slight head," he complained, still looking at the ceiling. A single fly, torpid, clung to the gray plaster directly above him, and he watched it.

"Last night you said it was the best corn we'd had."

"Did I say that?" He threw back the covers and let his feet drop to the floor, while he lay on his back, looking up. "I made a mistake then. And it's Sunday."

"If I'm doing the cooking from now on," the voice said, "you've got to help some."

"I'll help," he said and got up. He stood in the middle of the big room, surveyed the room once helplessly, and pulled off his pajama jacket. He was not very tall, but thick in the body. A purplish scar ran diagonally down the relaxed stomach, which pressed against the pajama string, and lost itself in the crisp black hairs. Meditatively he slipped his short forefinger along the scar. "My appendix is getting better. It doesn't look so much like bad blue carbon on yellow back-sheet any more."

"It's better"—there was a stir from the bed—"but you're getting a stomach. If you get a stomach, you've got to move out. There will be no stomachs in my house."

"It's because the muscles haven't knitted up yet," he said, and fingered the scar. "You haven't got any sympathy." He crossed to the dresser and studied himself in the mirror. "I can take it off right away," he said, patting it.

"Spading up the rest of the garden will take it off."

"I can't spade today. I'm paid to dish political dirt for the *Advocate*, not spade gardens. Spading is a luxury."

"You can spade an hour," she said.

"Look at my eyes," and he squinted closer to the mirror; "you can tell I've got a head."

"Spading will help your head."

He got a pair of corduroy trousers and a sweat shirt from the big walnut wardrobe in the corner, and put them on. For a minute he regarded the hump of bedclothes from which a few strands of blond hair strayed out on the pillow. "Aren't you getting up?" he said. "I want some breakfast."

"You start the fire in the stove."

Without haste he hunted for something about the room, standing in the middle of the floor to look all around, then on hands and knees peering under the bed. One hand touched the blue dress that lay on the floor by the bed and he picked it up. Under it the bedroom slippers lay. "You hid my slippers with your dress," he said, holding out the sky-blue dress, which dangled from his large hairy hand. "You ride me about not hanging my things up, and you go and throw your dress on the floor. On my slippers."

"Well," the voice said, "whose fault was it I threw it down last night?"

"Well," he said, and put on the slippers, and went out the door.

When he came back from the garden, grasping the new wet lettuce in his hands, she was ready to put slices of ham into a skillet on the stove. She wore a green gingham dress, her hair, yellowish in the sun from the kitchen windows, falling loose and uncombed over the crisp green cloth. Her bare feet were stuck into dirty buckskin oxfords, from which the untied laces trailed out. He leaned over the sink, washing the lettuce, leaf by leaf, then laying it on a towel. She stood beside him for an instant, too slender, almost skinny, and as tall as he was; then she turned to the stove with the bowl of eggs.

When it was ready they carried the food on platters into the dining room, where bright sun pouring from the open windows showed the full disorder. The split-bottom chairs were scattered about, one on its side. Dishes on the table held remnants of anchovy sandwiches, about which, without much interest, a fly buzzed. All sorts of glasses cluttered the sideboard, the mantelpiece, and the uneven stone hearth before the dead fireplace. "My God," she breathed, balancing the platter of ham, "my God, why do people have parties?" Then, with nervous, angular gestures, she set the platter down, swept off one end of the table, and laid two plates.

She ate hungrily, he slowly in dull, dutiful distaste. While she ate, she kept looking about her at the objects of the room, examining them with a resentful, curious glance. "We just can't have any more parties," she finally said.

"Suits me fine," he said.

"Not with all this mess next morning."

He looked about him with an air of discovery. "We might get some new friends. Some nice refined lady and gentlemen drinkers who wouldn't make a mess. I might run an ad in the *Advocate*."

"The friend I want this morning," she said, and glared at the old anchovy sandwiches, "is Viola. My God, why did she have to up and leave right now?"

"Once a nigger goes sour, it's all up. I told you that."

"I suppose you're right. And I'm worn out with all my lover's quarrels with her."

"She'll want to come back in a week," he said. Then, critically surveying the room, "And you'll take her back, all right."

"I told her if she went, it was the last time."

"We ought never brought her up here from Alabama," he said in gloom. "I told you at the time too." He got up from the table and crossed to the fireplace. From the mantel, among the clutter of glasses, he picked up a pipe, and lighted the half-burned tobacco in its bowl. Smoke from his short thick nostrils spun out in the sunlight.

Mournfully, she looked at him. "She was the cleanest nigger I ever saw," she said in some reproach. "She was so clean that when she was a little girl, she says she wouldn't sit on the ground with the other little niggers, she sat on a plate."

"She was fine in Alabama, but she's not worth a damn in Tennessee. She ought to go back to Alabama and sit on a plate."

"She *is* going home. She can't stay here with that old hussy of Jake's wife charging her nine dollars for a week's board and room while we went off, and it's the only place she can stay. Nine dollars, when we only pay her six! God, it makes me furious. I told the milk boy I was furious just so he'd tell Jake's wife."

"You needn't take it out on me," he said, regarding her outthrust nervous hands and her flushed cheeks. "You look like you were mad at me."

"I'm mad at that bitch," she said, suddenly more composed. "She's just trying to drive Viola off because she's jealous of that beautiful Jake of hers. She just doesn't like Viola. And she doesn't like me. You ought to hear the things Viola says she says about me."

Not answering, he turned to the open window. Beyond the rail fence of the yard, where strands of buckberry bushes exhibited the faintest tracery of green, the little valley fell sharply away. The lane went down the valley, bordered on one side by trees; the new flat leaves hung very still and bright. "The trouble is," he finally said, "that Viola is a white-folks' nigger."

"She's ashamed of her nigger blood, all right."

"She hasn't got too much nigger blood in her to be ashamed of. I bet she's cousin to a long line of drunken Alabama statesmen."

"She says niggers are dirty."

"Well," he said amiably, "aren't they?"

She rose abruptly from the table, glanced in despair at the articles on it and at his broad stubby back, then straightened herself. "I wish I had a dirty nigger here right now." She seized a plate in each hand and started for the kitchen. "Come on," she ordered, "you too."

He picked up two plates and followed her. Returning, he got two more, but paused as he passed the window. "Hey Annabelle," he called, "here comes Jake! He's got on his Sunday clothes, too."

"Let him come."

There was the sound of water running in the kitchen. He stood by the window, holding the plates, and looked down the valley. Below him the tall black-coated figure moved slowly up the lane, moving with unhurried dignity beside the new-leafed trees. He watched until the figure had passed out of vision from the window, then he went through the kitchen, where she bent over the steaming sink, and out the back.

Standing on the top of the back steps, he said, "Hello, Jake."

"Good morning, Mr. Allen," the Negro said, and approached the steps in his slow dignified pace. He stopped at the bottom of the steps, took off his black felt hat, and smiled gravely. "Kin I speak to Miz Allen?" he said.

"I'll see." He went inside.

"What does he want?" she demanded.

"He says he wants to talk to you."

"Bring him in the dining room."

He put his head out the kitchen door and called, "Jake, you come on in here."

The Negro man came in through the kitchen, bending his head at the door frame, treading very softly on the faded blue carpet on the dining room floor.

"Good morning, Jake," she said to him, and sank down in a chair at the table, laying her damp bony hands out on the cloth before her.

"Good morning, Miz Allen," he said.

She waited, looking at him. He stood carefully in the exact center of the open space between the table and sideboard, holding his hat decorously in his hand. He wore jean pants, pale blue from washings, and a black Prince Albert coat drooping from his high shoulders. A big gold watch chain hung across the black vest, which was too loose for him and not long enough. "Miz Allen," he said oratorically. Then he smiled, again gravely, but with no apology. "Miz Allen, I ain't accustomed to mess in no woman's affairs, but they's something I oughter tell you."

"All right, Jake," she said.

"Hit's this girl, Viola. She done said a lie about my wife and me. She done said to you we charged her nine dollars that week you and Mr. Allen went off and she ate down there with us."

"That's what she said," she agreed in some weariness. "And I gave her three dollars extra, I felt so sorry for her."

"That girl, Viola, she ain't said the truth. My wife never charged her no nine dollars," he said sadly. "We'se charged her seventy-five cents a week for that room, Miz Allen, that's ev'y God's penny. And when she eat there, my wife done said thirty cents a day, that oughter be enough." He stood patiently in the open space, his brown face, with the silky drooping mustache, decorous and unexpectant.

"So she lied to me," the girl at the table said after a little.

"Yassum," he said, "she lied. I dunno what else you might call hit."

"She wanted me to give her that three dollars, and I gave it to her."

"Yassum, she wanted that three dollars, I reckin." He hesitated, and cleared his throat. "Miz Allen." He shifted his hat to the other hand and continued, "I reckin I know what she wanted hit for."

"Yes?"

"She got herself a new coat. The other day she brought hit to the house and showed my wife hit. A gray coat what's got fur on hit, too."

"A new coat!" She got up from the table, jarring the dishes that remained there. "My Lord, a new coat. She didn't need a new coat. And she lied to me to get three dollars. After all the clothes I've given her this year. Jake, you've seen those clothes, haven't you?"

"I seed 'em," he said. "She brought 'em to the house."

"I gave her a coat too."

"Yassum, she didn't need no more clothes. She doan never go nowhere I knows of no way. She just comes in er-nights and gits herself all dressed up in them clothes you give her and combs her hair. She doan go nowhere, she just sets there in that room a time, then she gits in the bed."

"She hasn't got any friends, I know," she said.

"She doan ack like she wants no friends," Jake said.

The young white man, who leaned against the kitchen door, took the pipe from his mouth and wagged it at them. "The trouble," he said morosely, "is that we ought never brought her from Alabama away from her people."

The Negro pondered a moment, stroking his silky long mustache with a forefinger. "Maybe so," he admitted, "maybe she might do right well with her people. But she ain't my wife's and my kind of people. You ast anybody round here. We tries to do the fair and God-fearing thing towards ev'ybody, be he white or black. You ast anybody."

"I'm glad to know you all didn't charge her that nine dollars," she said.

"No, ma'm. And we never wanted her nohow. We owns our house and lot and I gits plenty work carpentering and bricklaying to git along. We ain't never wanted her. But I says to my wife, she's a girl a long way from home amongst strangers in a strange country. But we never wanted her." He intoned the words like a speech memorized, holding his black felt hat in his hands, looking straight out from his height over the head of the woman who stood before him. "She cain't stay no longer, lying like she done."

"She quit me last night, Jake. When some people were coming to a party, too," she said bitterly. "And I won't take her back this time either like I did before."

"She cain't stay at my house no more. I reckin she better go."

"I reckon so," she said.

He backed toward the kitchen door, sliding his flat heels soundlessly over the carpet, saying as he did so, "She better git back to her own people, wherever she come from." In the kitchen he paused and fumbled with his hat as if trying to remember just one more thing to say.

"Jake," the woman said, her face suddenly hard and pointed, "you tell Viola to come up here. Right away this morning."

"Yassum."

"Don't tell her what for, just send her up here."

"Yassum."

"All right, Jake."

He lingered in the kitchen a moment, still deliberating. Then he said, "Good morning, Miz Allen," and walked out the back way, shutting the porch door very gently behind him.

At the almost inaudible sound of the door closing she seemed to relax a little, sinking again into the chair by the table. "My God," she said, "the fool goes and spends all her money for a coat. When she's got a coat, and when I've been trying all winter to make her save."

"Niggers," he remarked with some unction, and stood straddle-legged in the space by the sideboard. "Niggers"—he paused to give the pipe a precautionary suck—"know how to live. Just like the good book says, 'Man does not live by bread alone.' Now Viola works all winter and you teach her to save money and when she gets it saved, she knows what to do with it."

"Oh, hush up, Bill." Distraught and unhappy, she sat at the table, working her bony fingers back and forth on the rough cloth.

"She got herself a new coat. Now that nigger's got a sense of values."

"She's got a sense of values all right. She got three dollars out of me."

"My little philanthropist," he said, and seized a dish of mangled crumby sandwiches and stamped toward the kitchen.

"Your little sucker," she said, and followed him.

He was sitting on the side porch off the dining room, leaning an elbow by the typewriter on the big unpainted table, when she came up the lane. When she passed just a little distance below him, her beanpole-thin, crooked legs working methodically over the rough ground, her body bent forward and her hands at her breast as if poked into an invisible muff, he pretended not to see, putting his face down toward the typewriter. His wife came out on the porch, a cigarette in her hand.

"There she is," she said.

"I saw her all right," he said. "She's got her new coat on."

"What'll I say to her?"

"Hell fire, you got her up here. I didn't."

"What'll I say?"

"Tell her she's a thief and a liar, and that you love her like a sister and want her to wash the dishes."

The old plowpoints hanging as weights for the gate chinked as the gate fell to. The Negro woman stood just inside the gate and regarded the porch with a gaze of meek question. "Come here, Viola," the woman on the porch said, and she came slowly.

She stopped at the foot of the steps, still mute and questioning, her hands still at her breast.

"Come up here, Viola."

She came up the steps. "Good morning, Miz Allen," she said, and her fingers absently brushed the gray fur on the open coat collar.

"You've got a new coat, Viola."

"Yassum," the Negro said, letting her hands drop with a delayed empty gesture.

"It's a pretty coat, Viola."

"I fancied hit," the Negro woman said. "I seed a girl one time outer my winder and she had on a gray dress and gray shoes and a gray coat and hat . . . all gray. . . ." She lifted her pale copperish face, and gazed at the woman from out yellowish eyes which, though depthless like an animal's, expressed a certain solicitude, a resignation. The woman met the gaze, put her cigarette to her lips, then puffed the smoke straight out into the air, with no pleasure. Suddenly she turned aside to the porch rail, leaning against it. "Viola," she said decisively, and hesitated. In a stiff-armed abrupt motion she flung the burning stub down to the yard, where it sent up a faint trail of smoke from the midst of new grass and the tattered winter-old spikes of sage. She swung round to face the Negro. "Viola, you said Jake's wife charged you nine dollars that week we went off."

"Yassum."

"That's what you said."

"Yassum, I did."

"Jake," the woman said, confronting the mild yellow eyes, "he's been up here and he said they didn't charge you nine dollars."

The face, the gazing yellow eyes, were unchanged and impassive.

"He said he charged you seventy-five cents a week for that room and thirty cents a day when you ate there. Is that right?"

"Yassum."

"You say 'yassum'!" A spasm of irritation swept over the woman's features, leaving them hurt and hard. "You lied to me. What made you lie?"

"That warn't no lie, Miz Allen."

"I don't know what else you'd call it. A lie's when you don't tell the truth." She fell into the patience of explanation, then pulled up sharply: "You lied."

"That warn't no lie, Miz Allen."

"Don't contradict me, Viola!"

The man at the table scraped the chair back, got up, bumping himself on the table, and went into the house.

"You lied," she continued, still hard, "because you wanted money out of me. Three dollars. You wanted to buy a coat. You stole three dollars."

The Negro woman began to move her head from side to side, not seekingly, but with an almost imperceptible motion, like a sick animal annoyed by flies. "I ain't never stole nothing," she said.

"You stole from me," the woman said, weakening a little, leaning against the porch rail. "After all I've done for you. After all the clothes I've given you. I gave you that dress you've got on, and it's a good dress."

"Yassum." She looked down at the green silk that hung in folds too big for her over the flat chest. "I kin give 'em back," she said.

"I don't want them back. I just want you to know I've been good to you and that you lied and stole, that's all the thankfulness you've got."

"I'se got thankfulness," she said.

The woman took the cigarette from the pocket of the green gingham and tried to light it, plunging its end into the shaking flame of the match, putting the match out. She removed the blackened cigarette from her lips and held it in her hand, which trembled a little. "I can't find my blue cook book, Viola," she said. "Now I want you to go in there and find it." Her voice was certain now.

The Negro moved across the porch and into the house, her bowed legs setting the feet down on the boards with a sort of painful accuracy, so that the heels twisted over at each step. The woman watched her go in, then lighted the cigarette and spewed the smoke out grayly before her face.

The Negro came back, holding the blue cook book out dangling as if her wrist were too weak to support it. "Here 'tis," she said. "Hit war just where I done left hit. Where it belong," she added, and her small features twitched into something near a tentative, deprecatory smile. Then the smile dissipated, and the features sank into their meekness.

The woman took the book. "Now, Viola, I want you to go away. You haven't treated me right. And you haven't treated right these Negroes round here who've tried to be nice to you, taking you in and inviting you to their parties and things." She looked off down the valley, speaking quickly and harshly. "You go away. You better go back to Alabama to your own people."

"Wellum," she said without any tone, and turned down the steps.

The woman came to the edge of the porch. "Go away," she said. "I don't ever want to see you again."

Slowly the Negro went down the uneven brick part toward the gate. At the gate she stopped, fingering the weather-gray palings. Then she looked round. "I wouldn't never say that 'bout you, Miz Allen," she said. "I wants to see you." She went out the gate and methodically down the hill.

The woman sat on the top step sucking her cigarette. Her husband came out the door. "Fire her," he said unsympathetically.

"I sent her away. But you—" she looked accusingly—"you would go off and leave me to do the dirty work. You always do."

"I couldn't bear to watch you in action," he said amicably. "I've got a very sensitive nature." He tapped the typewriter several times aimlessly. "What did you say?" he said.

"It was awful," she said. "I acted awful." She got up and moved to the open door. "I just behaved like some old self-righteous Methodist slut."

"You went to Sunday School, didn't you?"

She smoked her cigarette down to the dead end, jerked the paper loose from the flesh of her lip, and crushed the ash out against the door frame. "And I ended up," she said, "saying I never wanted to see her again."

He spaced the sheet in the typewriter for another paragraph, then leaned back. He said, "Well, you don't have to, you know."

Going down the hill, the heavy old car groaned and slithered in the gravel ruts, where water ran down from level to level, yellow and flecked by whitish foam. It was still raining, hard and straight down, for there was no wind in the valley. The new leaves on the trees by the lane hung limp and beaten under the steady impact.

"I come home," he said bitterly, "and you drag me out in this again."

"I suppose you think I love it."

When he had steered the car, clattering, over the loose planks of the bridge, beneath which the creek boiled hollowly against the stone supports, he said, "I'm fed up with those niggers."

"Well, Jake sent a boy up there through all this rain to say to come down, it was important."

"All right, all right," he said, "we're going, aren't we?"

They drew into the highway, where the asphalt was slick and black, glittering dully. The rain had let up a little. Down the highway two hundred yards, the house stood, bare and boxlike on its tall stone foundations, the roof sodden black beneath two oak trees that were not yet leafing. The man and the woman picked their way across the yard, which showed no grass, only flat packed earth where the water stood in little pools, giving forth no reflection.

He knocked on the door, and stepped aside so that his wife occupied the space before it. The tall Negro, wearing overalls now and in sock feet, opened it. "Good evening, Miz Allen," he said. "I'se much obliged to you for coming, and hit raining like this."

"What is it, Jake?"

"Hit's that girl, Viola," he said. He moved back, and they followed him inside. A Negro woman, black and angular in the face, rose from beside the stove in the center of the room, nodded stiffly and pushed a pair of steel-rimmed spectacles up on her forehead. "Hit's that girl," she said.

"What is it?" the woman said.

"She's done got in the bed and she won't git up. I done tole her she's gotta go, but she won't say nothing. She just lays there. Going on three days." She paused a moment, breathless and truculent, then spoke more moderately. "You kin see how it is."

"I'll talk to her."

The Negro woman stood with her hand on the knob of the door to another room. "You tell her, Miz Allen, she's gotta go."

The curtains at the window were almost drawn, only a little light coming in to mark the rocking chair where clothes and the gray coat were piled, the table by the wall, and the bed. She lay in the bed, on her back, with the sheet pulled up to her chin. When they entered, her eyes rolled to fix on them for a second, then slowly again looked at the ceiling.

"Viola," the woman said.

The woman on the bed said nothing, her face with no expression.

"Viola, you talk to me now." She went closer, putting her hand on the straight chair by the bed. On the chair a bucket of water stood, beside it a piece of cheese and an open box of crackers. "Do you hear me? Answer me!"

"I hears you."

"Now, Viola, you get up. You're making yourself sick." She shook the chair impatiently. "Cheese and crackers for three days."

The old Negro woman came closer, sticking her knotty black face out oracularly in the dim light. "You tell her she's gotta go," she said.

"You hear that, Viola? You're not treating these people right. You've got to go."

"I hears," the woman on the bed said, still looking at the ceiling.

"I'll buy you a ticket home. On the bus. But you've got to go."

"I'se got money," she said.

The white woman looked down at her for a minute, at the body under the tightly pulled sheet. "You can't stay here," she added.

"Yassum," the voice said from the bed.

"Now you get up from there and go right away. You hear me!"

"Yassum."

"Good-bye, Viola," she said; but there was no answer. She went into the other room, where the two men waited.

"Is she gonna go, Miz Allen?" the Negro man asked.

"I think so. She said she would, Jake."

"She ain't going neither," the Negro woman interrupted savagely. "She just says 'yassum.' You tell her she's gotta go. I ain't having nobody laying up in the bed in my house like that. You gotta tell—"

"You be quiet, Josie," the Negro man ordered.

"I've done what I can," the woman said. She took a bill from her purse and laid it on the table. "That's for her bus," she said, and went out on the porch, where her husband already was. She laid her hand on his arm. The Negro man followed them, carefully shutting the door after him. "Miz Allen," he said, hesitantly, but not in embarrassment, "my wife didn' mean nothin' talking like that. She's just worrit, and all. That girl layin' up there."

"It's all right, Jake."

They went down the steps and got into the car. It had stopped raining altogether now, and to the right of the highway the rays of the sun, now almost at setting, lay over the field of young wheat. They turned up the lane and over the plank bridge, beside the tree whose topmost leaves glistened in the level light. "It's right pitiful," she finally said, "thinking of her lying up there."

He slammed the gears into second for the grade.

"I'm fed up," he said.

"Then what the hell you think I am?" she said.

STUDY QUESTIONS

1. What effect does the author create by the use of descriptive details of the interior of the Allens' house?
2. How are descriptive details used to help characterize Bill and Annabelle Allen?
3. How would you describe the dominant tone of this story? What is the author's attitude toward the characters and the conflict?
4. Is there any indication that either Bill or Annabelle understand Viola?
5. What is the significance of the title of the story?
6. Why would Viola refuse to return to Alabama?

SECTION 3 | SCIENCE

"Brave New World"

INTRODUCING
Ashley Montagu **ANTHROPOLOGY**

Ashley Montagu (1905–   ) was born in England and became a United States citizen in 1940. An anthropologist and social biologist, he was educated at the Universities of London and Florence and received his Ph.D. from Columbia in 1937. He has taught at New York University, Rutgers—The State University, and the New School for Social Research. Since 1930 he has served as a legal expert on scientific problems related to race and, in 1949, helped draft the UNESCO statement on race. Among his books are *Coming into Being Among Australian Aborigines* (1937), *Man's Most Dangerous Myth: The Fallacy of Race* (1942), *The Natural Superiority of Women* (1953), *Life Before Birth* (1964), and *The Idea of Race* (1965).

Anthropology is the science of man. That's a pretty broad definition. Let's try to draw a line around it so that we can really grasp what the science is concerned with. The word "anthropology" is derived from two Greek words, the one *anthropos* meaning "man," and the other *logos* meaning "ordered knowledge." So anthropology is the ordered knowledge of man. The fact is that anything relating to man is grist to the anthropologist's mill. Anthropology is divided into two great divisions: (1) cultural anthropology, and (2) physical anthropology.

Cultural Anthropology

Cultural anthropology is concerned with the study of man's cultures. By "culture" the anthropologist understands what may be called the man-made part of the environment: the pots and pans, the laws and institutions, the art, religion, philosophy. Whatever a particular group of

Reprinted by permission of the publisher. *Man: His First Million Years* by Ashley Montagu. The World Publishing Company, 1957.

people living together as a functioning population have learned to do as human beings, their way of life, in short, is to be regarded as culture. The cultural anthropologist studies different cultures and compares them with one another in order to learn how it is that people come to do what they do in so many different ways, and also to learn, wherever possible, the relationships of one culture to another. He tries to find those common elements in all cultures which can be summarized in terms of generalizations or laws which are true of all cultures. Where there are differences, he tires to find the causes of these differences.

The cultural anthropologist is interested in all the forms that human social behavior assumes in organized societies. He cannot remain contented with the mere description of these forms, for he desires to understand how they have come into being, and so the cultural anthropologist must often be quite as good a psychologist as he is anything else. Fundamentally what he is really interested in is the nature of human nature. Today there is quite a flourishing school of anthropologists known as the personality-in-culture school. These cultural anthropologists, such as Margaret Mead, Clyde Kluckhohn, John Honigmann, Francis Hsu, and many others, are interested in tracing the relationship of the cultures in which human beings are socialized, that is, brought up, to the kind of personalities they develop.

Other cultural anthropologists are interested as specialists in studying such aspects of the cultures of different peoples as their legal institutions, social organization, religion, mythology, language, and their material culture such as their art, pottery, basketry, implements, and the like. Some cultural anthropologists take whole tribes for their special study and spend from many months to many years attempting to study every aspect of their culture.

Traditionally the cultural anthropologist has studied the so-called "primitive peoples" of this earth, and the major part of the anthropologist's attention still continues to be devoted to the cultures of such peoples, but in more recent years anthropologists have been turning their attention to the study of the technologically more advanced peoples of the earth. Today we have good anthropological studies not only of the Australian aborigines and the Congo pygmies, but also of the Japanese, the Chinese, the Germans, the Americans, the English, the Norwegians, and many others.

Formerly the study of modern societies was left to the sociologist (sociology = the study of society). Today the methods of the cultural anthropologist have greatly influenced those of the sociologist, but the difference between the two disciplines remains: the sociologist studies modern societies in great detail; the anthropologist brings to the study of modern societies a method which is at once wider and deeper than that of the sociologist.

Today there are specialists who are known as *applied* anthropologists. These are essentially cultural anthropologists who bring their special methods to bear principally upon the problems of industry. They go into a plant and study the relationships between the workers and their employers, between the worker and his work, and they advise on the methods of improving these relationships.

There are cultural anthropologists who work in hospitals in collaboration with psychiatrists. They study the relationships within the hospital between patient and doctor, administration and staff, and they conduct collaborative studies of whole districts in order to throw light upon the genesis of mental illness and its possible prevention.

The collaboration between anthropologists and psychiatrists in the study of the cultures of different societies has been very fruitful indeed, and holds much promise for the future.

Another branch of cultural anthropology is *archaeology* (often unkindly called the moldier part of anthropology). Archaeology is the science which studies cultures that no longer exist, basing its findings on the study of cultural products and subsistence remains recovered by excavation and similar means. If anthropologists are "the glamour boys" of the social sciences, archaeologists are "the glamour boys" of anthropology. All of which means that their specialty can be a very exciting one indeed, even though it generally entails a great deal of hard work, with far too much sand in one's hair, one's boots, and one's dried-out sandwiches. What the archaeologist is interested in doing is not merely to disinter an extinct culture, but to trace its relationships to other cultures. In this way archaeologists have been able to solve many problems which would otherwise have remained puzzling and to link up cultures which in their present form hardly seem related.

Anthropological archaeologists are to be distinguished from classical archaeologists; the latter are interested in the extinct cultures of classical antiquity, such as those of Greece, Rome, Crete, Persia, and Palestine.

Physical Anthropology

Just as the cultural anthropologist is interested in studying man as a cultural being, so the physical anthropologist is interested in the comparative study of man as a physical being. The physical anthropologist studies the origin and evolution of man's physical characters and the diversity of forms which those physical characters may take. He tries to discover the means by which the likenesses and the differences between groups of human beings have been produced. He tries to discover how man, in his various physical shapes, got to be the way he is now.

There are all sorts of specialists in physical anthropology. There are those who study man's origin and evolution; these are called paleo-anthropologists (paleo = old). They study the extinct remains of man and everything related to them. Then there are those who study the comparative anatomy of the primates, the classificatory group to which man in common with the apes and monkeys belongs. Here the primatologist, as he is called, is interested in discovering possible physical relationships between the large variety of types that constitute this group.

There are physical anthropologists who study growth and development. There are those who study physiology, and those who study the blood groups and blood types. There are those that study the so-called "races" of man, and there are a few who study all these subjects in the attempt to unify what they know into a consistent body of knowledge.

There are also applied physical anthropologists. These are largely concerned with the measurement of man, anatomically and physiologically, in order to determine, for example, standards for clothes, equipment in the armed forces, seats for railroad cars, hat sizes for men, shoe sizes for women, and the like.

There are also some constitutional physical anthropologists. These attempt to study the possible relationships between body-form and disease, body-form and personality, and even body-form and race.

Anthropology and Humanity

The anthropologist is first and foremost interested in human beings, no matter what the shape of their heads, the color of their skin, or the form of their noses. As a scientist he is interested in the facts about human beings, and as an anthropologist he knows that the facts are vastly more interesting than the fancies, the false beliefs, and the downright distortions of the facts, which some misguided persons seem always to have found it necessary to perpetrate. Humanity has a wonderfully interesting history, and it is the principal function of the anthropologist to reveal that history to the student as simply and as clearly as possible. This is what we shall now attempt to do in the following pages.

In concluding this introduction to anthropology I should like to quote the words of a great anthropologist, Thomas Henry Huxley (1825–95), writing in 1889 to a young man who later became a distinguished physical anthropologist at Cambridge University (Alfred Cort Haddon, 1855–1940). They are as true today as when they were written. Wrote Huxley: "I know of no department of natural science more likely to reward a man who goes into it thoroughly than anthropology. There is an immense deal to be done in the science pure and simple, and it is one of those branches of inquiry which brings one into contact with the great problems of humanity in every direction."

1. What are the main structural divisions of this essay? What part do definitions play in marking the points of division?
2. What does Montagu mean when he says: "Let's try to draw a line around it. . . ."?
3. How do you suppose a sociologist would react to Montagu's comment that anthropology has a method which is "wider and deeper" than that of sociology? Does Montagu provide any evidence for this statement?
4. Account for the departure from a baldly objective prose style in the paragraph about anthropological archeologists; that is, "All of which . . . sandwiches."
5. What does Montagu accomplish by quoting Thomas Henry Huxley in the last paragraph? Could this be considered a kind of name dropping?

John Ruskin OLIVE TREES

John Ruskin (1819–1900) was probably the most influential art critic and social critic of Victorian England. His astounding career began when he was twenty-three, with the publication of *Modern Painters,* ultimately a five-volume presentation of his aesthetic theories and an elaborate defense of J. M. W. Turner's painting. What Ruskin did for Turner, he did for the Pre-Raphaelite Brotherhood as well; through his influence, the Pre-Raphaelites achieved acceptance and fame. He later served as Slade Professor of Fine Arts at Oxford. Among his most famous works are *The Seven Lamps of Architecture* (1849), *The Stones of Venice* (1851–1853), *Unto This Last* (1860), *Fors Clavigera* (1871–1884), and his autobiographical *Praeterita* (1885–1889).

The reader is doubtless aware that the olive is one of the most characteristic and beautiful features of all Southern scenery. On the slopes of the northern Apennines, olives are the usual forest timber; the whole of the Val d'Arno is wooded with them, every one of its gardens is filled with them, and they grow in orchard-like ranks out of its fields of maize, or corn, or vine; so that it is physically impossible, in most parts of the neighbourhood of Florence, Pistoja, Lucca, or Pisa, to choose any

From "Conclusion" to *The Stones of Venice,* III. First published in three volumes, 1851–1853.

site of landscape which shall not owe its leading character to the foliage of these trees. What the elm and oak are to England, the olive is to Italy; nay, more than this, its presence is so constant, that, in the case of at least four-fifths of the drawings made by any artist in North Italy, he must have been somewhat impeded by branches of olive coming between him and the landscape. Its classical associations double its importance in Greece; and in the Holy Land the remembrances connected with it are of course more touching than can ever belong to any other tree of the field. Now, for many years back, at least one-third out of all the landscapes painted by English artists have been chosen from Italian scenery; sketches in Greece and in the Holy Land have become as common as sketches on Hampstead Heath; our galleries also are full of sacred subjects, in which, if any background be introduced at all, the foliage of the olive ought to have been a prominent feature.

And here I challenge the untravelled English reader to tell me what an olive-tree is like.

I know he cannot answer my challenge. He has no more idea of an olive-tree than if olives grew only in the fixed stars. Let him meditate a little on this one fact, and consider its strangeness, and what a wilful and constant closing of the eyes to the most important truths it indicates on the part of the modern artist. Observe, a want of perception, not of science. I do not want painters to tell me any scientific facts about olive-trees. But it had been well for them to have felt and seen the olive-tree; to have loved it for Christ's sake, partly also for the helmed Wisdom's sake which was to the heathen in some sort as that nobler Wisdom which stood at God's right hand, when He founded the earth and established the heavens. To have loved it, even to the hoary dimness of its delicate foliage, subdued and faint of hue, as if the ashes of the Gethsemane agony had been cast upon it for ever; and to have traced, line by line, the gnarled writhing of its intricate branches, and the pointed fretwork of its light and narrow leaves, inlaid on the blue field of the sky, and the small rosy-white stars of its spring blossoming, and the beads of sable fruit scattered by autumn along its topmost boughs—the right, in Israel, of the stranger, the fatherless, and the widow,—and, more than all, the softness of the mantle, silver grey, and tender like the down on a bird's breast, with which, far away, it veils the undulation of the mountains;—these it had been well for them to have seen and drawn, whatever they had left unstudied in the gallery.

And if the reader would know the reason why this has not been done (it is one instance only out of the myriads which might be given of sightlessness in modern art), and will ask the artists themselves, he will be informed of another of the marvellous contradictions and inconsistencies in the base Renaissance art; for it will be answered him, that it is not right, nor according to law, to draw trees so that one should be known from another, but that trees ought to be generalized into a universal idea of a tree: that is to say, that the very school which carries its science in the representation of man down to the dissection of the most minute muscle, refuses so much science to the drawing of a tree as shall distinguish one species from another; and also, while it attends to logic, and rhetoric, and perspective, and atmosphere, and every other circumstance which is trivial, verbal, external, or accidental, in what it either says or sees, it will *not* attend to what is essential and substantial,—being intensely solicitous, for instance, if it draws two trees, one behind the other, that the farthest off shall be as much smaller as mathematics show that it should be, but totally unsolicitous to show, what to the spectator is a far more important matter, whether it is an apple or an orange-tree. . . .

Now the main characteristics of an olive-tree are these. It has sharp and slender leaves of a greyish green, nearly grey on the under surface, and resembling, but somewhat smaller than, those of our common willow. Its fruit, when ripe, is black and lustrous; but of course so small, that, unless in great quantity, it is not conspicuous upon the tree. Its trunk and branches are peculiarly fantastic in their twisting, showing their fibres at every turn; and the trunk is often hollow, and even rent into many divisions like separate stems, but the extremities are exquisitely graceful, especially in the setting on of the leaves; and the notable and characteristic effect of the tree in the distance is of a rounded and soft mass or ball of downy foliage.

Supposing a modern artist to address himself to the rendering of this tree with his best skill: he will probably draw accurately the twisting of the branches, but yet this will hardly distinguish the tree from an oak: he will also render the colour and intricacy of the foliage, but this will only confuse the idea of an oak with that of a willow. The fruit, and the peculiar grace of the leaves at the extremities, and the fibrous structure of the stems, will all be too minute to be rendered consistently with his artistical feeling of breadth, or with the amount of labour which he considers it dexterous and legitimate to bestow upon the work: but, above all, the rounded and monotonous form of the head of the tree will be at variance with his ideas of "composition"; he will assuredly disguise or break it, and the main points of the olive-tree will all at last remain untold.

STUDY QUESTIONS

1. With what three Mediterranean countries does Ruskin associate the olive tree? Historically, what significance has the olive tree had in each of these countries?

2. Who is "the helmed Wisdom" of the third paragraph?
3. Is Ruskin's description of the olive tree a wholly objective one? Which words are particularly subjective?
4. Ruskin says that he does *not* want a painter to tell him any scientific facts about olive trees. What *does* he want a painter to tell him? Why have painters failed to do so?
5. This description of the olive tree is part of a much longer work. From the tone of this selection, decide what Ruskin's purpose was in writing the longer work.

Aldous Huxley THE OLIVE TREE

Aldous Huxley (1894–1963), English novelist and essayist, was the grandson of Thomas Henry Huxley, the grandnephew of Matthew Arnold, and the brother of Sir Julian Huxley. He attended Eton and Balliol College, Oxford, and was given a D. Litt. by the University of California in 1959. His books include *Limbo* (1920), *Chrome Yellow* (1921), *Antic Hay* (1923), *Point Counter Point* (1928), *Eyeless in Gaza* (1936), and *Literature and Science* (1963). Huxley's *Brave New World* (1932), *Brave New World Revisited* (1958), and *Island* (1961) are classics of utopian literature.

The Tree of Life; the Bodhi Tree; Yggdrasil and the Burning Bush:

Populus Alcidae gratissima, vitis Iaccho,
formosae myrtus Veneri, sua laurea Phoebo. . . .

Everywhere and, before the world was finally laicized, at all times, trees have been worshiped. It is not to be wondered at. The tree is an intrinsically "numinous" being. Solidified, a great fountain of life rises in the trunk, spreads in the branches, scatters in a spray of leaves and flowers and fruits. With a slow, silent ferocity the roots go burrowing down into the earth. Tender, yet irresistible, life battles with the unliving stones and has the mastery. Half hidden in the darkness, half displayed in the air of heaven, the tree stands there, magnificent, a manifest god. Even today we feel its majesty and beauty—feel in certain circumstances its rather fearful quality of otherness, strangeness, hostility.

Trees in the mass can be almost terrible. There are devils in the great pine-woods of the North, in the swarming equatorial jungle. Alone in a forest one sometimes becomes aware of the silence—the thick, clotted, living silence of the trees; one realizes one's isolation in the midst of a vast concourse of alien presences. Herne the Hunter was something more than the ghost of a Windsor gamekeeper. He was probably a survival of Jupiter Cernunnus; a lineal descendant of the Cretan Zeus; a wood god who in some of his aspects was frightening and even malignant.

> He blasts the tree, and takes the cattle,
> And makes milch-kine yield blood, and shakes a chain
> In a most hideous and dreadful manner.

Even in a royal forest and only twenty miles from London, the serried trees can inspire terror. Alone or in small groups, trees are benignly numinous. The alienness of the forest is so much attenuated in the park or the orchard that it changes its emotional sign and from oppressively sinister becomes delightful. Tamed and isolated, those leaping fountains of non-human life bring only refreshment to spirits parched by the dusty commerce of the world. Poetry is full of groves and shrubberies. One thinks of Milton, landscape-gardening in Eden, of Pope, at Twickenham. One remembers Coleridge's sycamore and Marvell's green thought in a green shade. Chaucer's love of trees was so great that he had to compile a whole catalogue in order to express it.

> But, Lorde, so I was glad and wel begoon!
> For over al, where I myn eyen caste,
> Weren trees, claad with levys that ay shal laste,
> Eche in his kynde, with colors fressh and grene
> As emerawde, that joy was for to sene.
> The bylder oke, and eke the hardy asshe,
> The peler (pillar) elme, the cofre unto careyne,
> The box pipe tree, holme to whippes lasshe,
> The saylynge firre, the cipresse deth to pleyne,
> The sheter (shooter) ewe, the aspe for shaftes pleyne,
> The olyve of pes, and eke the drunken vyne
> The victor palme, the laurere, to, devyne.

I like them all, but especially the olive. For what it symbolizes, first of all—peace with its leaves and joy with its golden oil. True, the crown of olive was originally worn by Roman conquerors at ovation; the peace it proclaimed was the peace of victory, the peace which is too often only the tranquillity of exhaustion or complete annihilation. Rome and its customs have passed, and we remember of the olive only the fact that it stood for peace, not the circumstances in which it did so.

Incertainties now crown themselves assur'd,
And peace proclaims olives of endless age.

We are a long way from the imperator riding in triumph through the streets of Rome.

The association of olive leaves with peace is like the association of the number seven with good luck, or the color green with hope. It is an arbitrary and, so to say, metaphysical association. That is why it has survived in the popular imagination down to the present day. Even in countries where the olive tree does not grow, men understand what is meant by "the olive branch" and can recognize, in a political cartoon, its pointed leaves. The association of olive oil with joy has a pragmatic reason. Applied externally, oil was supposed to have medicinal properties. In the ancient world those who could afford it were in the habit of oiling themselves at every opportunity. A shiny and well lubricated face was thought to be beautiful; it was also a sign of prosperity. To the ancient Mediterranean peoples the association of oil with joy seemed inevitable and obvious. Our habits are not those of the Romans, Greeks and Hebrews. What to them was "natural" is today hardly even imaginable. Patterns of behavior change, and ideas which are associated in virtue of the pattern existing at a given moment of history will cease to be associated when that pattern exists no more. But ideas which are associated arbitrarily, in virtue of some principle, or some absence of principle, unconnected with current behavior patterns, will remain associated through changing circumstances. One must be something of an archeologist to remember the old and once thoroughly reasonable association between olive oil and joy; the equally old, but quite unreasonable and arbitrary association between olive leaves and peace has survived intact into the machine age.

It is surprising, I often think, that our Protestant bibliolaters should have paid so little attention to the oil which played such an important part in the daily lives of the ancient Hebrews. All that was greasy possessed for the Jews a profound religious, social and sensuous significance. Oil was used for anointing kings, priests and sacred edifices. On festal days men's cheeks and noses fairly shone with it; a matt-surfaced face was a sign of mourning. Then there were the animal fats. Fat meat was always a particularly welcome sacrifice. Unlike the modern child, Jehovah reveled in mutton fat. His worshipers shared this taste. "Eat ye that which is good," advises Isaiah, "and let your soul delight itself in fatness." As for the prosperously wicked, "they have more than their heart can wish" and the proof of it is that "their eyes stand out with fatness." The world of the Old Testament, it is evident, was one where fats were scarce and correspondingly esteemed. One of our chief sources of edible fat, the pig, was taboo to the Israelites. Butter and lard depend on a supply of grass long enough for cows to get their tongues round. But the pastures of Palestine are thin, short and precarious. Cows there had no milk to spare, and oxen were too valuable as draught animals to be used for suet. Only the sheep and the olive remained as sources of that physiologically necessary and therefore delicious fatness in which the Hebrew soul took such delight. How intense that delight was is proved by the way in which the Psalmist describes his religious experiences. "Because thy lovingkindness is better than life, my lips shall praise thee. . . . My soul shall be satisfied as with marrow and fatness; and my mouth shall praise thee with joyful lips." In this age of Danish bacon and unlimited margarine it would never occur to a religious writer to liken the mystical ecstasy to a good guzzle at the Savoy. If he wanted to describe it in terms of a sensuous experience, he would probably choose a sexual metaphor. Square meals are now too common to be ranked as epoch-making treats.

The "olyve of pes" is, then, a symbol and I love it for what it stands for. I love it also for what it is in itself, aesthetically; for what it is in relation to the Mediterranean landscape in which it beautifully plays its part.

The English are Germans who have partially "gone Latin." But for William the Conqueror and the Angevins we should be just another nation of Teutons, speaking some uninteresting dialect of Dutch or Danish. The Normans gave us the English language, that beautifully compounded mixture of French and Saxon; and the English language molded the English mind. By Latin out of German: such is our pedigree. We are essentially mongrels: that is the whole point of us. To be mongrels is our mission. If we would fulfill this mission adequately we must take pains to cultivate our mongrelism. Our Saxon and Celtic flesh requires to be constantly rewedded to the Latin spirit. For the most part the English have always realized this truth and acted upon it. From the time of Chaucer onwards almost all our writers have turned, by a kind of infallible instinct, like swallows, toward the South—toward the phantoms of Greece and Rome, toward the living realities of France and Italy. On the rare occasions when, losing their orientation, they have turned eastward and northward, the results have been deplorable. The works of Carlyle are there, an awful warning, to remind us of what happens when the English forget that their duty is to be mongrels and go whoring, within the bounds of consanguinity, after German gods.

The olive tree is an emblem of the Latinity toward which our migrant's instinct commands us perpetually to turn. As well as for peace and for joy, it stands for all that makes us specifically English rather than Teutonic; for those Mediterranean influences without which Chaucer and Shakespeare could never have become what they learned from France and Italy, from Rome and Greece, to be—the most essentially native of our poets. The olive tree is, so to speak, the complement of the oak; and the bright hard-edged landscapes in which it figures are the necessary correctives of those gauzy and indeterminate lovelinesses of the English scene. Under a polished sky the olives state their aesthetic case without the qualifications of mist, of shifting lights, of atmospheric perspective, which give to English landscapes their subtle and melancholy beauty. A perfect beauty in its way; but, as of all good things, one can have too much of it. The British Constitution is a most admirable invention; but it is good to come back occasionally to fixed first principles and the firm outline of syllogistic argument.

With clarity and definition is associated a certain physical spareness. Most of the great deciduous trees of England give one the impression, at any rate in summer, of being rather obese. In Scandinavian mythology Embla, the elm, was the first woman. Those who have lived much with old elm trees—and I spent a good part of my boyhood under their ponderous shade—will agree that the Scandinavians were men of insight. There is in effect something blowsily female about those vast trees that brood with all their bulging masses of foliage above the meadows of the home counties. In winter they are giant skeletons; and for a moment in the early spring a cloud of transparent emerald vapor floats in the air; but by June they have settled down to an enormous middle age.

By comparison the olive tree seems an athlete in training. It sits lightly on the earth and its foliage is never completely opaque. There is always air between the thin grey and silver leaves of the olive, always the flash of light within its shadows. By the end of summer the foliage of our northern trees is a great clot of dark unmitigated green. In the olive the lump is always leavened.

The landscape of the equator is, as the traveler discovers to his no small surprise, singularly like the landscape of the more luxuriant parts of southern England. He finds the same thick woods and, where man has cleared them, the same park-like expanses of luscious greenery. The whole is illumined by the same cloudy sky, alternately bright and dark, and wetted by precisely those showers of hot water which render yet more oppressive the sultriness of July days in the Thames valley or in Devonshire. The equator is England in summer, but raised, so to speak, to a higher power. Falmouth cubed equals Singapore. Between the equatorial and the temperate zone lies a belt of drought; even Provence is half a desert. The equator is dank, the tropics and the subtropics are predominantly dry. The Sahara and Arabia, the wastes of India and Central Asia and North America are a girdle round the earth of sand and naked rock. The Mediterranean lies on the fringes of this desert belt and the olive is its tree—the tree of a region of sun-lit clarity separating the damps of the equator from the damps of the North. It is the symbol of a classicism enclosed between two romanticisms.

"And where," Sir George Beaumont inquired of Constable, "where do you put your brown tree?" The reply was disquieting: the eccentric fellow didn't put it anywhere. There are no brown trees in Constable's landscapes. Breaking the tradition of more than a century, he boldly insisted on painting his trees bright green. Sir George, who had been brought up to think of English landscape in terms of raw Sienna and ochre, was bewildered. So was Chantrey. His criticism of Constable's style took a practical form. When "Hadleigh Castle" was sent to the Academy he took a pot of bitumen and glazed the whole foreground with a coat of rich brown. Constable had to spend several hours patiently scratching it off again. To paint a bright green tree and make a successful picture of it requires genius of no uncommon order. Nature is embarrassingly brilliant and variegated; only the greatest colorists know how to deal with such a shining profusion. Doubtful of their powers, the more cautious prefer to transpose reality into another and simpler key. The key of brown, for example. The England of the eighteenth-century painters is chronically autumnal.

At all seasons of the year the olive achieves that sober neutrality of tone which the deciduous trees of the North put on only in autumn and winter. "Where do you put your gray tree?" If you are painting in Provence, or Tuscany, you put it everywhere. At every season of the year the landscape is full of gray trees. The olive is essentially a painter's tree. It does not need to be transposed into another key, and it can be rendered completely in terms of pigment that are as old as the art of painting.

Large expanses of the Mediterranean scene are by Nature herself conceived and executed in the earth colors. Your gray tree and its background of bare bone-like hills, red-brown earth and the all but black cypresses and pines are within the range of the most ascetic palette. Derain can render Provence with half a dozen tubes of color. How instructive to compare his olives with those of Renoir! White, black, *terra verde*—Derain's rendering of the gray tree is complete. But it is not the only complete rendering. Renoir was a man with a passion for bright gay colors. To this passion he added an extraordinary virtuosity in combining them. It was not in his nature to be content with a black, white and earth-green olive. His gray trees have shadows of cadmium green, and where they look toward the sun, are suffused with a glow of pink. Now, no olive has ever shown a trace of any color warmer than the faint ochre of withering leaves and summer dusts. Nevertheless these pink trees, which in Renoir's paintings of Cagnes recall the exuberant girls of his latest, rosiest manner, are somehow quite startlingly like the cold gray olives which they apparently misrepresent. The rendering, so different from Derain's, is equally complete and satisfying.

If I could paint and had the necessary time, I should devote myself for a few years to making pictures only of olive trees. What a wealth of variations upon a single theme! Above Pietrasanta, for example, the first slopes of the Apuan Alps rise steeply from the plain in a series of terraces built up, step after step, by generations of patient cultivators. The risers of this great staircase are retaining walls of unmortared limestone; the treads, of grass. And on every terrace grow the olives. They are ancient trees; their boles are gnarled, their branches strangely elbowed. Between the sharp narrow leaves one sees the sky; and beneath them in the thin softly tempered light there are sheep grazing. Far off, on a level with the eye, lies the sea. There is one picture, one series of pictures.

But olives will grow on the plain as well as on the hillside. Between Seville and Cordoba the rolling country is covered with what is almost a forest of olive trees. It is a woodland scene. Elsewhere they are planted more sparsely. I think, for example, of that plain at the foot of the Maures in Provence. In spring, beside the road from Toulon to Fréjus, the ploughed earth is a rich Pozzuoli red. Above it hang the olives, gray, with soft black shadows and their highest leaves flashing white against the sky; and, between the olives, peach trees in blossom—burning bushes of shell-pink flame in violent and irreconcilable conflict with the red earth. A problem, there, for the most accomplished painter.

In sunlight Renoir saw a flash of madder breaking out of the gray foliage. Under a clouded sky, with rain impending, the olives glitter with an equal but very different intensity. There is no warmth in them now; the leaves shine white, as though illumined from within by a kind of lunar radiance. The soft black of the shadows is deepened to the extreme of night. In every tree there is simultaneously moonlight and darkness. Under the approaching storm the olives take on another kind of being; they become more conspicuous in the landscape, more significant. Of what? Significant of what? But to that question, when we ask it, nature always stubbornly refuses to return a clear reply. At the sight of those mysterious lunar trees, at once so dark and so brilliant beneath the clouds, we ask, as Zechariah asked of the angel: "What are these two olive trees upon the right side of the candlestick and upon the left side thereof? What be these two olive branches which through the two golden pipes empty the golden oil out of themselves? And he answered me and said, Knowest thou not what these be? And I said, No, my lord. Then said he, These are the two anointed ones, that stand by the Lord of the whole earth." And that, I imagine, is about as explicit and comprehensible an answer as our Wordsworthian questionings are ever likely to receive.

Provence is a painter's paradise, and its tree, the olive, the painter's own tree. But there are disquieting signs of change. During the last few years there has been a steady destruction of olive orchards. Magnificent old trees are being cut, their wood sold for firing and the land they occupied planted with vines. Fifty years from now, it may be, the olive tree will almost have disappeared from southern France, and the Provence will wear another aspect. It may be, I repeat; it is not certain. Nothing is certain nowadays except change. Even the majestic stability of agriculture has been shaken by the progress of technology. Thirty years ago, for example, the farmers of the Rhône valley grew rich on silkworms. Then came the invention of viscose. The caterpillars tried to compete with the machines and failed. The female form is now swathed in wood-pulp, and between Lyons and Avignon the mulberry tree and its attendant worm are all but extinct. Vines were next planted. But North Africa was also planting vines. In a year of plenty *vin ordinaire* fetches about a penny a quart. The vines have been rooted up again, and today the prosperity of the Rhône valley depends on peach trees. A few years from now, no doubt, the Germans will be making synthetic peaches out of sawdust or coal tar. And then—what?

The enemy of the olive tree is the peanut. *Arachis hypogaea* grows like a weed all over the tropics and its seeds are fifty per cent pure oil. The olive is slow-growing, capricious in its yield, requires much pruning, and the fruit must be hand picked. Peanut oil is half the price of olive oil. The Italians, who wish to keep their olive trees, have almost forbidden the use of peanut oil. The French, on the other hand, are the greatest importers of peanuts in Europe. Most of the oil they make is re-exported; but enough remains in France to imperil the olives of Provence. Will they go the way of the mulberry trees? Or will some new invention come rushing up in the nick of time with a reprieve? It seems that, suitably treated, olive oil makes an excellent lubricant, capable of standing up to high temperatures. Thirty years from now, mineral lubricants will be growing scarce. Along with the castor-oil plant, the olive tree may come again triumphantly into its own. Perhaps. Or perhaps not. The future of Provençal landscape is in the hands of the chemists. It is in their power to preserve it as it is, or to alter it out of all recognition.

It would not be the first time in the course of its history that the landscape of Provence has changed its face. The Provence that we know—terraced vineyard and olive orchard alternating with pine-woods and those deserts of limestone and prickly bushes which are locally called garrigues—is profoundly unlike the Provence of Roman and medieval times. It was a land, then, of great forests. The hills were covered with a splendid growth of ilex trees and Aleppo pines. The surviving Forêt du Dom allows us to guess what these woods—the last outposts toward the south of the forests of the temperate zone—were like. Today the garrigues, those end products of a long degeneration, have taken their place. The story of Provençal vegetation is a decline and fall, that begins with the ilex wood and ends with the garrigue.

The process of destruction is a familiar one. The trees were cut for firewood and shipbuilding. (The naval arsenal at Toulon devoured the forest for miles around.) The glass industry ate its way from the plain into the mountains, carrying with it irreparable destruction. Meanwhile, the farmers and the shepherds were busy, cutting into the woods in search of more land for the plough, burning them in order to have more pasture for their beasts. The young trees sprouted again—only to be eaten by the sheep and goats. In the end they gave up the struggle and what had been forest turned at last to a blasted heath. The long process of degradation ends in the garrigue. And even this blasted heath is not quite the end. Beyond the true garrigue, with its cistus, its broom, its prickly dwarf oak, there lies a series of false garrigues, vegetably speaking worse than the true. On purpose or by accident, somebody sets fire to the scrub. In the following spring the new shoots are eaten down to the ground. A coarse grass—baouco in Provençal—is all that manages to spring up. The shepherd is happy; his beasts can feed, as they could not do on the garrigue. But the sheep and goats are ravenous. The new pasture is soon overgrazed. The baouco is torn up by the roots and disappears, giving place to ferocious blue thistles and the poisonous asphodel. With the asphodel the process is complete. Degradation can go no further. The asphodel is sheep-proof and even, thanks to its deeply planted tubers, fire-proof. And it allows very little else to grow in its neighborhood. If protected long enough from fire and animals, the garrigue will gradually build itself up again into a forest. But a desert of asphodels obstinately remains itself.

Efforts are now being made to reafforest the blasted heaths of Provence. In an age of cigarette-smoking tourists the task is difficult and the interruptions by fire frequent and disheartening. One can hardly doubt, however, of the ultimate success of the undertaking. The chemists may spare the olive trees; and yet the face of Provence may still be changed. For the proper background to the olive trees is the thinly fledged limestone of the hills—pinkish and white and pale blue in the distance, like Cézanne's Mont Sainte Victoire. Reafforested, these hills will be almost black with ilex and pine. Half the painter's paradise will have gone, if the desert is brought back to life. With the cutting of the olive trees the other half will follow.

STUDY QUESTIONS

1. Huxley makes some of the same symbolic associations with the olive tree that Ruskin makes. What additional symbolic associations does he make?
2. After discussing the olive as a symbol, Huxley suggests that he will discuss it "for what it is in itself, aesthetically. . . ." However, he then proceeds to the discussion of the olive as "the symbol of a classicism enclosed between two romanticisms." Explain what he means.
3. How do Ruskin's and Huxley's descriptions of the olive differ?
4. Can we draw any logical conclusions about the future of the olive oil industry from the history of the silkworm?
5. Huxley's essay begins as a kind of suggestive description of the olive tree; it ends as the eloquent plea of a conservationist. Is Huxley's conclusion rational or emotional?

John James Audubon THE WILD TURKEY

John James Audubon (1780?–1851) was born in New Orleans and educated in France. In 1803 he inherited the Audubon estate near Philadelphia, where he performed the first bird-banding experiments in America. From 1808–1820 he lived in Henderson, Kentucky, continuing his ornithological studies. A curious combination of scientist and artist, Audubon went to Great Britain in 1826 to find a publisher for his drawings of birds. *The Birds of America* was published between 1827 and 1838; *Ornithological Biographies,* the accompanying text, followed between 1831 and 1839. The Audubon Society, dedicated to the preservation and study of wildlife in America, was named for him.

The great size and beauty of the Wild Turkey, its value as a delicate and highly prized article of food, and the circumstance of its being the origin of the domestic race now generally dispersed over both continents, render it one of the most interesting of the birds indigenous to the United States of America.

The unsettled parts of the States of Ohio, Kentucky, Illinois, and Indiana, an immense extent of country to the north-west of these districts, upon the Mississippi and Missouri, and the vast regions drained by these rivers from their confluence to Louisiana, including the wooded

From *Ornithological Biography,* 1831.

parts of Arkansas, Tennessee, and Alabama, are the most abundantly supplied with this magnificent bird. It is less plentiful in Georgia and the Carolinas, becomes still scarcer in Virginia and Pennsylvania, and is now very rarely seen to the eastward of the last mentioned States. In the course of my rambles through Long Island, the State of New York, and the country around the Lakes, I did not meet with a single individual, although I was informed that some exist in those parts. Turkeys are still to be found along the whole line of the Alleghany Mountains, where they have become so wary as to be approached only with extreme difficulty. While, in the Great Pine Forest, in 1829, I found a single feather that had been dropped from the tail of a female, but saw no bird of the kind. Farther eastward, I do not think they are now to be found. I shall describe the manners of this bird as observed in the countries where it is most abundant, and having resided for many years in Kentucky and Louisiana, may be understood as referring chiefly to them.

The Turkey is irregularly migratory, as well as irregularly gregarious. With reference to the first of these circumstances, I have to state, that whenever the *mast* [1] of one portion of the country happens greatly to exceed that of another, the Turkeys are insensibly led toward that spot, by gradually meeting in their haunts with more fruit the nearer they advance towards the place where it is most plentiful. In this manner flock follows after flock, until one district is entirely deserted, while another is, as it were, overflowed by them. But as these migrations are irregular, and extend over a vast expanse of country, it is necessary that I should describe the manner in which they take place.

About the beginning of October, when scarcely any of the seeds and fruits have yet fallen from the trees, these birds assemble in flocks, and gradually move towards the rich bottom lands of the Ohio and Mississippi. The males, or, as they are more commonly called, the *gobblers,* associate in parties of from ten to a hundred, and search for food apart from the females; while the latter are seen either advancing singly, each with its brood of young, then about two-thirds grown, or in connexion with other families, forming parties often amounting to seventy or eighty individuals, all intent on shunning the old cocks, which, even when the young birds have attained this size, will fight with, and often destroy them by repeated blows on the head. Old and young, however, all move in the same course, and on foot, unless their progress be interrupted by a river, or the hunter's dog force them to take wing. When they come upon a river, they betake themselves to the highest eminences, and there often remain a whole day, or sometimes two, as if for the purpose of consultation. During this time, the males are heard

---

[1] In America, the term *mast* is not confined to the fruit of the beech, but is used as a general name for all kinds of forest fruits, including even grapes and berries.

gobbling, calling, and making much ado, and are seen strutting about, as if to raise their courage to a pitch befitting the emergency. Even the females and young assume something of the same pompous demeanour, spread out their tails, and run round each other, *purring* loudly, and performing extravagant leaps. At length, when the weather appears settled, and all around is quiet, the whole party mounts to the tops of the highest trees, whence, at a signal, consisting of a single *cluck,* given by a leader, the flock takes flight for the opposite shore. The old and fat birds easily get over, even should the river be a mile in breadth; but the younger and less robust frequently fall into the water,—not to be drowned, however, as might be imagined. They bring their wings close to their body, spread out their tail as a support, stretch forward their neck, and, striking out their legs with great vigour, proceed rapidly towards the shore; on approaching which, should they find it too steep for landing, they cease their exertions for a few moments, float down the stream until they come to an accessible part, and by a violent effort generally extricate themselves from the water. It is remarkable, that immediately after thus crossing a large stream, they ramble about for some time, as if bewildered. In this state, they fall an easy prey to the hunter.

When the Turkeys arrive in parts where the mast is abundant, they separate into smaller flocks, composed of birds of all ages and both sexes, promiscuously mingled, and devour all before them. This happens about the middle of November. So gentle do they sometimes become after these long journeys, that they have been seen to approach the farmhouses, associate with the domestic fowls, and enter the stables and corncribs in quest of food. In this way, roaming about the forests, and feeding chiefly on mast, they pass the autumn and part of the winter.

As early as the middle of February, they begin to experience the impulse of propagation. The females separate, and fly from the males. The latter strenuously pursue, and begin to gobble or to utter the notes of exultation. The sexes roost apart, but at no great distance from each other. When a female utters a call-note, all the gobblers within hearing return the sound, rolling note after note with as much rapidity as if they intended to emit the last and the first together, not with spread tail, as when fluttering round the females on the ground, or practising on the branches of the trees on which they have roosted for the night, but much in the manner of the domestic turkey, when an unusual or unexpected noise elicits its singular hubbub. If the call of the female comes from the ground, all the males immediately fly towards the spot, and the moment they reach it, whether the hen be in sight or not, spread out and erect their tail, draw the head back on the shoulders, despress their wings with a quivering motion, and strut pompously about, emitting at the same time a succession of puffs from the lungs, and stopping now and then to listen and look. But whether they spy the female or not, they continue to puff and strut, moving with as much celerity as their ideas of ceremony seem to admit. While thus occupied, the males often encounter each other, in which case desperate battles take place, ending in bloodshed, and often in the loss of many lives, the weaker falling under the repeated blows inflicted upon their head by the stronger.

I have often been much diverted, while watching two males in fierce conflict, by seeing them move alternately backwards and forwards, as either had obtained a better hold, their wings drooping, their tails partly raised, their body-feathers ruffled, and their heads covered with blood. If, as they thus struggle, and gasp for breath, one of them should lose his hold, his chance is over, for the other, still holding fast, hits him violently with spurs and wings, and in a few minutes brings him to the ground. The moment he is dead, the conqueror treads him under foot, but, what is strange, not with hatred, but with all the motions which he employs in caressing the female.

When the male has discovered and made up to the female (whether such a combat has previously taken place or not), if she be more than one year old, she also struts and gobbles, turns round him as he continues strutting, suddenly opens her wings, throws herself towards him, as if to put a stop to his idle delay, lays herself down, and receives his dilatory caresses. If the cock meet a young hen, he alters his mode of procedure. He struts in a different manner, less pompously and more energetically, moves with rapidity, sometimes rises from the ground, taking a short flight around the hen, as is the manner of some Pigeons, the Red-breasted Thrush, and many other birds, and on alighting, runs with all his might, at the same time rubbing his tail and wings along the ground, for the space of perhaps ten yards. He then draws near the timorous female, allays her fears by purring, and when she at length assents, caresses her.

When a male and a female have thus come together, I believe the connexion continues for that season, although the former by no means confines his attentions to one female, as I have seen a cock caress several hens, when he happened to fall in with them in the same place, for the first time. After this the hens follow their favourite cock, roosting in his immediate neighbourhood, if not on the same tree, until they begin to lay, when they separate themselves, in order to save their eggs from the male, who would break them all, for the purpose of protracting his sexual enjoyments. The females then carefully avoid him, excepting during a short period each day. After this the males become clumsy and slovenly, if one may say so, cease to fight each other, give up gobbling or calling so frequently, and assume so careless a habit, that the hens are obliged to make all the advances themselves. They *yelp* loudly and almost continually for the cocks, run up to them, caress them, and employ various means to rekindle their expiring ardour.

Turkey-cocks when at roost sometimes strut and gobble, but I have more generally seen them spread out and raise their tail, and emit the pulmonic puff, lowering their tail and other feathers immediately after. During clear nights, or when there is moonshine, they perform this action at intervals of a few minutes, for hours together, without moving from the same spot, and indeed sometimes without rising on their legs, especially towards the end of the love-season. The males now become greatly emaciated, and cease to gobble, their *breast-sponge* becoming flat. They then separate from the hens, and one might suppose that they had entirely deserted their neighbourhood. At such seasons I have found them lying by the side of a log, in some retired part of the dense woods and cane thickets, and often permitting one to approach within a few feet. They are then unable to fly, but run swiftly, and to a great distance. A slow-turkey-hound has led me miles before I could flush the same bird. Chases of this kind I did not undertake for the purpose of killing the bird, it being then unfit for eating, and covered with ticks, but with the view of rendering myself acquainted with its habits. They thus retire to recover flesh and strength, by purging with particular species of grass, and using less exercise. As soon as their condition is improved, the cocks come together again, and recommence their rambles. Let us now return to the females.

About the middle of April, when the season is dry, the hens begin to look out for a place in which to deposit their eggs. This place requires to be as much as possible concealed from the eye of the Crow, as that bird often watches the Turkey when going to her nest, and, waiting in the neighbourhood until she has left it, removes and eats the eggs. The nest, which consists of a few withered leaves, is placed on the ground, in a hollow scooped out, by the side of a log, or in the fallen top of a dry leafy tree, under a thicket of sumach or briars, or a few feet within the edge of a cane-brake, but always in a dry place. The eggs, which are of a dull cream colour, sprinkled with red dots, sometimes amount to twenty, although the more usual number is from ten to fifteen. When depositing her eggs, the female always approaches the nest with extreme caution, scarcely ever taking the same course twice; and when about to leave them, covers them carefully with leaves, so that it is very difficult for a person who may have seen the bird to discover the nest. Indeed, few Turkeys' nests are found, unless the female has been suddenly started from them, or a cunning Lynx, Fox, or Crow has sucked the eggs and left their shells scattered about.

Turkey hens not unfrequently prefer islands for depositing their eggs and rearing their young, probably because such places are less frequented by hunters, and because the great masses of drifted timber which usually accumulate at their heads, may protect and save them in cases of great emergency. When I have found these birds in such situations, and with young, I have always observed that a single discharge of a gun made them run immediately to the pile of drifted wood, and conceal themselves in it. I have often walked over these masses, which are frequently from ten to twenty feet in height, in search of the game which I knew to be concealed in them.

When an enemy passes within sight of a female, while laying or sitting, she never moves, unless she knows that she has been discovered, but crouches lower until he has passed. I have frequently approached within five or six paces of a nest, of which I was previously aware, on assuming an air of carelessness, and whistling or talking to myself, the female remaining undisturbed; whereas if I went cautiously towards it, she would never suffer me to approach within twenty paces, but would run off, with her tail spread on one side, to a distance of twenty or thirty yards, when assuming a stately gait, she would walk about deliberately, uttering every now and then a cluck. They seldom abandon their nest, when it has been discovered by men; but, I believe, never go near it again, when a snake or other animal has sucked any of the eggs. If the eggs have been destroyed or carried off, the female soon yelps again for a male; but, in general, she rears only a single brood each eason. Several hens sometimes associate together, I believe for their mutual safety, deposit their eggs in the same nest, and rear their broods together. I once found three sitting on forty-two eggs. In such cases, the common nest is always watched by one of the females, so that no Crow, Raven, or perhaps even Pole-cat, dares approach it.

The mother will not leave her eggs, when near hatching, under any circumstances, while life remains. She will even allow an enclosure to be made around her, and thus suffer imprisonment, rather than abandon them. I once witnessed the hatching of a brood of Turkeys, which I watched for the purpose of securing them together with the parent. I concealed myself on the ground within a very few feet, and saw her raise herself half the length of her legs, look anxiously upon the eggs, cluck with a sound peculiar to the mother on such occasions, carefully remove each half-empty shell, and with her bill caress and dry the young birds, that already stood tottering and attempting to make their way out of the nest. Yes, I have seen this, and have left mother and young to better care than mine could have proved,—to the care of their Creator and mine. I have seen them all emerge from the shell, and, in a few moments after, tumble, roll, and push each other forward, with astonishing and inscrutable instinct.

Before leaving the nest with her young brood, the mother shakes herself in a violent manner, picks and adjusts the feathers about her belly, and assumes quite a different aspect. She alternately inclines her eyes obliquely upwards and sideways, stretching out her neck, to discover hawks or other enemies, spreads her wings a little as she walks, and softly clucks to keep her innocent offspring close to her. They move slowly along, and as the hatching generally takes place in the afternoon, they frequently return to the nest to spend the first night there. After this, they remove to some distance, keeping on the highest undulated grounds, the mother dreading rainy weather, which is extremely dangerous to the young, in this tender state, when they are only covered by a kind of soft hairy down, of surprising delicacy. In very rainy seasons, Turkeys are scarce, for if once completely wetted, the young seldom recover. To prevent the disastrous effects of rainy weather, the mother, like a skilful physician, plucks the buds of the spice-wood bush, and gives them to her young.

In about a fortnight, the young birds, which had previously rested on the ground, leave it and fly, at night, to some very large low branch, where they place themselves under the deeply curved wings of their kind and careful parent, dividing themselves for that purpose into two nearly equal parties. After this, they leave the woods during the day, and approach the natural glades or prairies, in search of strawberries, and subsequently of dewberries, blackberries and grasshoppers, thus obtaining abundant food, and enjoying the beneficial influence of the sun's rays. They roll themselves in deserted ants' nests, to clear their growing feathers of the loose scales, and prevent ticks and other vermin from attacking them, these insects being unable to bear the odour of the earth in which ants have been.

The young Turkeys now advance rapidly in growth, and in the month of August are able to secure themselves from unexpected attacks of Wolves, Foxes, Lynxes, and even Cougars, by rising quickly from the ground, by the help of their powerful legs, and reaching with ease the highest branches of the tallest trees. The young cocks shew the tuft on the breast about this time, and begin to gobble and strut, while the young hens purr and leap, in the manner which I have already described.

The old cocks have also assembled by this time, and it is probable that all the Turkeys now leave the extreme north-western districts, to remove to the Wabash, Illinois, Black River, and the neighbourhood of Lake Erie.

STUDY QUESTIONS

1.   Why does Audubon begin his ornithological biographies with the wild turkey?

2.   Does he limit his subject in any way?

3.   What sentence serves as the structural center of the essay, by dividing it
      into two parts? Where does each of these parts begin?
4.   Does Audubon reveal his own personality in this essay?
5.   How does he keep the reader aware of the precarious existence these
      game birds lead?
6.   What word do we now use instead of "moonshine"? What does moon-
      shine mean today—as a noun, as a verb?

Walter Van Tilburg Clark **HOOK**

Walter Van Tilburg Clark (1901–   ) is a highly regarded writer and teacher of creative writing, whose stories and novels about
the West have helped rescue Western fiction from the popularizers
of the Western "myth." His *The Ox-Bow Incident* (1940) is
considered a classic Western novel. Among his other well-known
works are *The City of Trembling Leaves* (1945), *The Track of the
Cat* (1949), and *The Watchful Gods and Other Stories* (1950).
He has been in great demand as a teacher of writers. He was
Writer in Residence at the University of Nevada, Visiting Lecturer
at the Universities of Iowa, Utah, Wyoming, California, Washington, Oregon, and Stanford University and Reed College. In 1945
he won the O'Henry Memorial Award for *The Wind and the Snow
of Winter*.

Hook, the hawks' child, was hatched in a dry spring among the
oaks, beside the seasonal river, and was struck from the nest early. In
the drouth his single-willed parents had to extend their hunting ground
by more than twice, for the ground creatures upon which they fed died
and dried by the hundreds. The range became too great for them to
wish to return and feed Hook, and when they had lost interest in each
other they drove Hook down into the sand and brush and went back to
solitary courses over the bleaching hills.

Unable to fly yet, Hook crept over the ground, challenging all
large movements with recoiled head, erected, rudimentary wings, and
the small rasp of his clattering beak. It was during this time of abysmal
ignorance and continual fear that his eyes took on the first quality of a
hawk, that of being wide, alert and challenging. He dwelt, because of his
helplessness, among the rattling brush which grew between the oaks
and the river. Even in his thickets and near the water, the white sun was

the dominant presence. Except in the dawn, when the land wind stirred, or in the late afternoon, when the sea wind became strong enough to penetrate the half-mile inland to this turn in the river, the sun was the major force, and everything was dry and motionless under it. The brush, small plants and trees alike husbanded the little moisture at their hearts; the moving creatures waited for dark, when sometimes the sea fog came over and made a fine, soundless rain which relieved them.

The two spacious sounds of his life environed Hook at this time. One was the great rustle of the slopes of yellowed wild wheat, with over it the chattering rustle of the leaves of the California oaks, already as harsh and individually tremulous as in autumn. The other was the distant whisper of the foaming edge of the Pacific, punctuated by the hollow shoring of the waves. But these Hook did not yet hear, for he was attuned by fear and hunger to the small, spasmodic rustlings of live things. Dry, shrunken, and nearly starved, and with his plumage delayed, he snatched at beetles, dragging in the sand to catch them. When swifter and stronger birds and animals did not reach them first, which was seldom, he ate the small, silver fish left in the mud by the failing river. He watched, with nearly chattering beak, the quick, thin lizards pause, very alert, and raise and lower themselves, but could not catch them because he had to raise his wings to move rapidly, which startled them.

Only one sight and sound not of his world of microscopic necessity was forced upon Hook. That was the flight of the big gulls from the beaches, which sometimes, in quealing play, came spinning back over the foothills and the river bed. For some inherited reason, the big, ship-bodied birds did not frighten Hook, but angered him. Small and chewed-looking, with his wide, already yellowing eyes glaring up at them, he would stand in an open place on the sand in the sun and spread his shaping wings and clatter his bill like shaken dice. Hook was furious about the swift, easy passage of gulls.

His first opportunity to leave off living like a ground owl came accidentally. He was standing in the late afternoon in the red light under the thicket, his eyes half-filmed with drowse and the stupefaction of starvation, when suddenly something beside him moved, and he struck, and killed a field mouse driven out of the wheat by thirst. It was a poor mouse, shriveled and lice ridden, but in striking, Hook had tasted blood, which raised nest memories and restored his nature. With started neck plumage and shining eyes, he tore and fed. When the mouse was devoured, Hook had entered hoarse adolescence. He began to seek with a conscious appetite, and to move more readily out of shelter. Impelled by the blood appetite, so glorious after his long preservation upon the flaky and bitter stuff of bugs, he ventured even into the wheat in the open sun beyond the oaks, and discovered the small trails and holes among the roots. With his belly often partially filled with flesh, he grew rapidly in strength and will. His eyes were taking on their final change, their yellow growing deeper and more opaque, their stare more constant, their challenge less desperate. Once during this transformation, he surprised a ground squirrel, and although he was ripped and wing-bitten and could not hold his prey, he was not dismayed by the conflict, but exalted. Even while the wing was still drooping and the pinions not grown back, he was excited by other ground squirrels and pursued them futilely, and was angered by their dusty escapes. He realized that his world was a great arena for killing, and felt the magnificence of it.

The two major events of Hook's young life occurred in the same day. A little after dawn he made the customary essay and succeeded in flight. A little before sunset, he made his first sustained flight of over two hundred yards, and at its termination struck and slew a great buck squirrel whose thrashing and terrified gnawing and squealing gave him a wild delight. When he had gorged on the strong meat, Hook stood upright, and in his eyes was the stare of the hawk, never flagging in intensity but never swelling beyond containment. After that the stare had only to grow more deeply challenging and more sternly controlled as his range and deadliness increased. There was no change in kind. Hook has mastered the first of the three hungers which are fused into the single, flaming will of a hawk, and he had experienced the second.

The third and consummating hunger did not awaken in Hook until the following spring, when the exultation of space had grown slow and steady in him, so that he swept freely with the wind over the miles of coastal foothills, circling, and ever in sight of the sea, and used without struggle the warm currents lifting from the slopes, and no longer desired to scream at the range of his vision, but intently sailed above his shadow swiftly climbing to meet him on the hillsides, sinking away and rippling across the brush-grown canyons.

That spring the rains were long, and Hook sat for hours, hunched and angry under their pelting, glaring into the fogs of the river valley, and killed only small, drenched things flooded up from their tunnels. But when the rains had dissipated, and there were sun and sea wind again, the game ran plentiful, the hills were thick and shining green, and the new river flooded about the boulders where battered turtles climbed up to shrink and sleep. Hook then was scorched by the third hunger. Ranging farther, often forgetting to kill and eat, he sailed for days with growing rage, and woke at night clattering on his dead tree limb, and struck and struck and struck at the porous wood of the trunk, tearing it away. After days, in the draft of a coastal canyon miles below his own hills, he came upon the acrid taint he did not know but had expected, and sailing down it, felt his neck plumes rise and his wings quiver so that he swerved unsteadily. He saw the unmated female perched upon the tall and jagged stump of a tree that had been shorn by storm, and he stooped, as if upon game. But she was older than he, and wary of the gripe of his importunity, and banked off screaming, and he screamed also at the intolerable delay.

At the head of the canyon, the screaming pursuit was crossed by another male with a great wing-spread, and the light golden in the fringe of his plumage. But his more skillful opening played him false against the ferocity of the twice-balked Hook. His rising maneuver for position was cut short by Hook's wild, upward swoop, and at the blow he raked desperately and tumbled off to the side. Dropping, Hook struck him again, struggled to clutch, but only raked and could not hold, and, diving, struck once more in passage, and then beat up, yelling triumph, and saw the crippled antagonist side-slip away, half-tumble once, as the ripped wing failed to balance, then steady and glide obliquely into the cover of brush on the canyon side. Beating hard and stationary in the wind above the bush that covered his competitor, Hook waited an instant, but when the bush was still, screamed again, and let himself go off with the current, reseeking, infuriated by the burn of his own wounds, the thin choke-thread of the acrid taint.

On a hilltop projection of stone two miles inland, he struck her down, gripping her rustling body with his talons, beating her wings down with his wings, belting her head when she whimpered or thrashed, and at last clutching her neck with his hook and, when her coy struggles had given way to stillness, succeeded.

In the early summer, Hook drove the three young ones from their nest, and went back to lone circling above his own range. He was complete.

II

Throughout that summer and the cool, growthless weather of the winter, when the gales blew in the river canyon and the ocean piled upon the shore, Hook was master of the sky and the hills of his range. His flight became a lovely and certain thing, so that he played with the treacherous currents of the air with a delicate ease surpassing that of the gulls. He could sail for hours, searching the blanched grasses below him with telescopic eyes, gaining height against the wind, descending in mile-long, gently declining swoops when he curved and rode back, and never beating either wing. At the swift passage of his shadow within their vision, gophers, ground squirrels and rabbits froze, or plunged gibbering into their tunnels beneath matted turf. Now, when he struck, he killed easily in one hard-knuckled blow. Occasionally, in sport, he soared up over the river and drove the heavy and weaponless gulls downstream again, until they would no longer venture inland.

There was nothing which Hook feared now, and his spirit was

wholly belligerent, swift and sharp, like his gaze. Only the mixed smells and incomprehensible activities of the people at the Japanese farmer's home, inland of the coastwise highway and south of the bridge across Hook's river, troubled him. The smells were strong, unsatisfactory and never clear, and the people, though they behaved foolishly, constantly running in and out of their built-up holes, were large, and appeared capable, with fearless eyes looking up at him, so that he instinctively swerved aside from them. He cruised over their yard, their gardens, and their bean fields, but he would not alight close to their buildings.

But this one area of doubt did not interfere with his life. He ignored it, save to look upon it curiously as he crossed, his afternoon shadow sliding in an instant over the chicken-and-crate-cluttered yard, up the side of the unpainted barn, and then out again smoothly, just faintly, liquidly rippling over the furrows and then over the stubble of the grazing slopes. When the season was dry, and the dead earth blew on the fields, he extended his range to satisfy his great hunger, and again narrowed it when the fields were once more alive with the minute movements he could not only see but anticipate.

Four times that year he was challenged by other hawks blowing up from behind the coastal hills to scud down his slopes, but two of these he slew in mid-air, and saw hurtle down to thump on the ground and lie still while he circled, and a third, whose wing he tore, he followed closely to earth and beat to death in the grass, making the crimson jet out from its breast and neck into the pale wheat. The fourth was a strong flier and experienced fighter, and theirs was a long, running battle, with brief, rising flurries of striking and screaming, from which down and plumage soared off.

Here, for the first time, Hook felt doubts, and at moments wanted to drop away from the scoring, burning talons and the twisted hammer strokes of the strong beak, drop away shrieking, and take cover and be still. In the end, when Hook, having outmaneuvered his enemy and come above him, wholly in control, and going with the wind, tilted and plunged for the death rap, the other, in desperation, threw over on his back and struck up. Talons locked, beaks raking, they dived earthward. The earth grew and spread under them amazingly, and they were not fifty feet above it when Hook, feeling himself turning toward the underside, tore free and beat up again on heavy, wrenched wings. The other, stroking swiftly, and so close to down that he lost wing plumes to a bush, righted himself and planed up, but flew on lumberingly between the hills and did not return. Hook screamed the triumph, and made a brief pretense of pursuit, but was glad to return, slow and victorious, to his dead tree.

In all these encounters Hook was injured, but experienced only the fighter's pride and exultation from the sting of wounds received in successful combat. And in each of them he learned new skill. Each time the wounds healed quickly, and left him a more dangerous bird.

In the next spring, when the rains and the night chants of the little frogs were past, the third hunger returned upon Hook with a new violence. In this quest, he came into the taint of a young hen. Others too were drawn by the unnerving perfume, but only one of them, the same with which Hook had fought his great battle, was a worthy competitor. This hunter drove off two, while two others, game but neophytes, were glad enough that Hook's impatience would not permit him to follow and kill. Then the battle between the two champions fled inland, and was a tactical marvel, but Hook lodged the neck-breaking blow, and struck again as they dropped past the treetops. The blood had already begun to pool on the gray, fallen foliage as Hook flapped up between branches, too spent to cry his victory. Yet his hunger would not let him rest until, late in the second day, he drove the female to ground among the laurels of a strange river canyon.

When the two fledglings of this second brood had been driven from the nest, and Hook had returned to his own range, he was not only complete, but supreme. He slept without concealment on his bare limb, and did not open his eyes when, in the night, the heavy-billed cranes coughed in the shallows below him.

III

The turning point of Hook's career came that autumn, when the brush in the canyons rustled dryly and the hills, mowed close by the cattle, smoked under the wind as if burning. One midafternoon, when the black clouds were torn on the rim of the sea and the surf flowered white and high on the rocks, raining in over the low cliffs, Hook rode the wind diagonally across the river mouth. His great eyes, focused for small things, stirring in the dust and leaves, overlooked so large and slow a movement as that of the Japanese farmer rising from the brush and lifting the two black eyes of his shotgun. Too late Hook saw and, startled, swerved, but wrongly. The surf muffled the reports, and nearly without sound, Hook felt the minute whips of the first shot, and the astounding, breath-taking blow of the second.

Beating his good wing, tasting the blood that quickly swelled into his beak, he tumbled off with the wind and struck into the thickets on the far side of the river mouth. The branches tore him. Wild with rage, he thrust up and clattered his beak, challenging, but when he had fallen over twice, he knew that the trailing wing would not carry, and then heard the boots of the hunter among the stones in the river bed and, seeing him loom at the edge of the bushes, crept back among the thickest brush and was still. When he saw the boots stand before him, he reared back, lifting his good wing and cocking his head for the serpent-like blow, his beak open but soundless, his great eyes hard and very shining. The boots passed on. The Japanese farmer, who believed that he had lost chickens, and who had cunningly observed Hook's flight for many afternoons, until he could plot it, did not greatly want a dead hawk.

When Hook could hear nothing but the surf and the wind in the thicket, he let the sickness and shock overcome him. The fine film of the inner lid dropped over his big eyes. His heart beat frantically, so that it made the plumage of his shot-aching breast throb. His own blood throt-tled his breathing. But these things were nothing compared to the lightning of pain in his left shoulder, where the shot had bunched, shattering the airy bones so the pinions trailed on the ground and could not be lifted. Yet, when a sparrow lit in the bush over him, Hook's eyes flew open again, hard and challenging, his good wing was lifted and his beak strained open. The startled sparrow darted piping out over the river.

Throughout that night, while the long clouds blew across the stars and the wind shook the bushes about him, and throughout the next day, while the clouds still blew and massed until there was no gleam of sunlight on the sand bar, Hook remained stationary, enduring his sick-ness. In the second evening, the rains began. First there was a long, running patter of drops upon the beach and over the dry trees and bushes. At dusk there came a heavier squall, which did not die entirely, but slacked off to a continual, spaced splashing of big drops, and then returned with the front of the storm. In long, misty curtains, gust by gust, the rain swept over the sea, beating down its heaving, and coursed up the beach. The little jets of dust ceased to rise about the drops in the fields, and the mud began to gleam. Among the boulders of the river bed, darkling pools grew slowly.

Still Hook stood behind his tree from the wind, only gentle drops reaching him, falling from the upper branches and then again from the brush. His eyes remained closed, and he could still taste his own blood in his mouth, though it had ceased to come up freshly. Out beyond him, he heard the storm changing. As rain conquered the sea, the heave of the surf became a hushed sound, often lost in the crying of the wind. Then gradually, as the night turned toward morning, the wind also was broken by the rain. The crying became fainter, the rain settled toward steadiness, and the creep of the waves could be heard again, quiet and regular upon the beach.

At dawn there was no wind and no sun, but everywhere the roaring of the vertical, relentless rain. Hook then crept among the rapid drippings of the bushes, dragging his torn sail, seeking better shelter. He stopped often and stood with the shutters of film drawn over his eyes. At midmorning he found a little cave under a ledge at the base of the sea cliff. Here, lost without branches and leaves about him, he settled to await improvement.

When, at midday of the third day, the rain stopped altogether, and the sky opened before a small, fresh wind, letting light through to glitter upon a tremulous sea, Hook was so weak that his good wing trailed also to prop him upright, and his open eyes were lusterless. But his wounds were hardened, and he felt the return of hunger. Beyond his shelter, he heard the gulls flying in great numbers and crying their joy at the cleared air. He could even hear, from the fringe of the river, the ecstatic and unstinted bubblings and chirpings of the small birds. The grassland, he felt, would be full of the stirring anew of the close-bound life, the undrowned insects clicking as they dried out, the snakes slithering down, heads half erect, into the grasses where the mice, gophers and ground squirrels ran and stopped and chewed and licked themselves smoother and drier.

With the aid of this hunger, and on the crutches of his wings, Hook came down to stand in the sun beside his cave, whence he could watch the beach. Before him, in ellipses on tilting planes, the gulls flew. The surf was rearing again, and beginning to shelve and hiss on the sand. Through the white foam-writing it left, the long-billed pipers twinkled in bevies, escaping each wave, then racing down after it to plunge their fine drills into the minute double holes where the sand crabs bubbled. In the third row of breakers two seals lifted sleek, streaming heads and barked, and over them, trailing his spider legs, a great crane flew south. Among the stones at the foot of the cliff, small red and green crabs made a little, continuous rattling and knocking. The cliff swallows glittered and twanged on aerial forays.

The afternoon began auspiciously for Hook also. One of the two gulls which came squabbling above him dropped a freshly caught fish to the sand. Quickly Hook was upon it. Gripping it, he raised his good wing and cocked his head with open beak at the many gulls which had circled and come down at once toward the fall of the fish. The gulls sheered off, cursing raucously. Left alone on the sand, Hook devoured the fish and, after resting in the sun, withdrew again to his shelter.

IV

In the succeeding days, between rains, he foraged on the beach. He learned to kill and crack the small green crabs. Along the edge of the river mouth, he found the drowned bodies of mice and squirrels and even sparrows. Twice he managed to drive feeding gulls from their catch, charging upon them with buffeting wing and clattering beak. He grew stronger slowly, but the shot sail continued to drag. Often, at the choking thought of soaring and striking and the good, hot-blood kill, he strove to take off, but only the one wing came up, winnowing with a hiss, and drove him over onto his side in the sand. After these futile trials, he would rage and clatter. But gradually he learned to believe that he could not fly, that his life must now be that of the discharged nestling again. Denied the joy of space, without which the joy of loneliness was lost, the joy of battle and killing, the blood lust, became his whole concentration. It was his hope, as he charged feeding gulls, that they would turn and offer battle, but they never did. The sandpipers, at his approach, fled peeping, or, like a quiver of arrows shot together, streamed out over the surf in a long curve. Once, pent beyond bearing, he disgraced himself by shrieking challenge at the businesslike heron which flew south every evening at the same time. The heron did not even turn his head, but flapped and glided on.

Hook's shame and anger became such that he stood awake at night. Hunger kept him awake also, for these little leavings of the gulls could not sustain his great body in its renewed violence. He became aware that the gulls slept at night in flocks on the sand, each with one leg tucked under him. He discovered also that the curlews and the pipers, often mingling, likewise slept, on the higher remnant of the bar. A sensation of evil delight filled him in the consideration of protracted striking among them.

There was only half of a sick moon in a sky of running but far-separated clouds on the night when he managed to stalk into the center of the sleeping gulls. This was light enough, but so great was his vengeful pleasure that there broke from him a shrill scream of challenge as he first struck. Without the power of flight behind it, the blow was not murderous, and this newly discovered impotence made Hook crazy, so that he screamed again and again as he struck and tore at the felled gull. He slew the one, but was twice knocked over by its heavy flounderings, and all the others rose above him, weaving and screaming, protesting in the thin moonlight. Wakened by their clamor, the wading birds also took wing, startled and plaintive. When the beach was quiet again, the flocks had settled elsewhere, beyond his pitiful range, and he was left alone beside the single kill. It was a disappointing victory. He fed with lowering spirit.

Thereafter, he stalked silently. At sunset he would watch where the gulls settled along the miles of beach, and after dark he would come like a sharp shadow among them, and drive with his hook on all sides of him, till the beatings of a poorly struck victim sent the flock up. Then he would turn vindictively upon the fallen and finish them. In his best night, he killed five from one flock. But he ate only a little from one, for the vigor resulting from occasional repletion strengthened only his ire, which became so great at such a time that food revolted him. It was not the joyous, swift, controlled hunting anger of a sane hawk, but something quite different, which made him dizzy if it continued too long, and left him unsatisfied with any kill.

Then one day, when he had very nearly struck a gull while driving it from a gasping yellowfin, the gull's wing rapped against him as it broke for its running start, and, the trailing wing failing to support him, he was knocked over. He flurried awkwardly in the sand to regain his feet, but his mastery of the beach was ended. Seeing him, in clear sunlight, struggling after the chance blow, the gulls returned about him in a flashing cloud, circling and pecking on the wing. Hook's plumage showed quick little jets of irregularity here and there. He reared back, clattering and erecting the good wing, spreading the great, rusty tail for balance. His eyes shone with a little of the old pleasure. But it died, for he could reach none of them. He was forced to turn and dance awkwardly on the sand, trying to clash bills with each tormentor. They banked up quealing and returned, weaving about him in concentric and overlapping circles. His scream was lost in their clamor, and he appeared merely to be hopping clumsily with his mouth open. Again he fell sideways. Before he could right himself, he was bowled over, and a second time, and lay on his side, twisting his neck to reach them and clappering in blind fury, and was struck three times by three successive gulls, shrieking their flock triumph.

Finally he managed to roll to his breast, and to crouch with his good wing spread wide and the other stretched nearly as far, so that he extended like a gigantic moth, only his snake head, with its now silent scimitar, erect. One great eye blazed under its level brow, but where the other had been was a shallow hole from which thin blook trickled to his russet gap.

In this crouch, by short stages, stopping repeatedly to turn and drive the gulls up, Hook dragged into the river canyon and under the stiff cover of the bitter-leafed laurel. There the gulls left him, soaring up with great clatter of their valor. Till nearly sunset Hook, broken spirited and enduring his hardening eye socket, heard them celebrating over the waves.

When his will was somewhat replenished, and his empty eye socket had stopped the twitching and vague aching which had forced him often to roll ignominiously to rub it in the dust, Hook ventured from the protective lacings of his thicket. He knew fear again, and the challenge of his remaining eye was once more strident, as in adolescence. He dared not return to the beaches, and with a new, weak hunger, the home hunger, enticing him, made his way by short hunting journeys back to the wild wheat slopes and the crisp oaks. There was in Hook an unwonted sensation now, that of the ever-neighboring possibility of death. This sensation was beginning, after his period as a mad bird on the beach, to solidify him into his last stage of life. When, during his slow homeward passage, the gulls wafted inland over him, watching the earth with curious, miserish eyes, he did not cower, but neither did he challenge, either by opened beak or by raised shoulder. He merely watched carefully, learning his first lessons in observing the world with one eye.

At first the familiar surroundings of the bend in the river and the tree with the dead limb to which he could not ascend, aggravated his humiliation, but in time, forced to live cunningly and half-starved, he lost much of his savage pride. At the first flight of a strange hawk over his realm, he was wild at his helplessness, and kept twisting his head like an owl, or spinning in the grass like a small and feathered dervish, to keep the hateful beauty of the wind-rider in sight. But in the succeeding weeks, as one after another coasted his beat, his resentment declined, and when one of the raiders, a haughty yearling, sighted his upstaring eye, and plunged and struck him dreadfully, and failed to kill him only because he dragged under a thicket in time, the second of his great hungers was gone. He had no longer the true lust to kill, no joy of battle, but only the poor desire to fill his belly.

Then truly he lived in the wheat and the brush like a ground owl, ridden with ground lice, dusty or muddy, ever half-starved, forced to sit for hours by small holes for petty and unsatisfying kills. Only once during the final months before his end did he make a kill where the breath of danger recalled his valor, and then the danger was such as a hawk with wings and eyes would scorn. Waiting beside a gopher hole, surrounded by the high, yellow grass, he saw the head emerge, and struck, and was amazed that there writhed in his clutch the neck and dusty coffin-skull of a rattlesnake. Holding his grip, Hook saw the great, thick body slither up after, the tip an erect, strident blur, and writhe on the dirt of the gopher's mound. The weight of the snake pushed Hook about, and once threw him down, and the rising and falling whine of the rattles made the moment terrible, but the vaulted mouth, gaping from the closeness of Hook's grip, so that the pale, envenomed sabers stood out free, could not reach him. When Hook replaced the grip of his beak with the grip of his talons, and was free to strike again and again at the base of the head, the struggle was over. Hook tore and fed on the fine, watery flesh, and left the tattered armor and the long, jointed bone for the marching ants.

When the heavy rains returned, he ate well during the period of the first escapes from flooded burrows, and then well enough, in a vulture's way, on the drowned creatures. But as the rains lingered, and the burrows hung full of water, and there were no insects in the grass and no small birds sleeping in the thickets, he was constantly hungry, and finally unbearably hungry. His sodden and ground-broken plumage stood out raggedly about him, so that he looked fat, even bloated, but underneath it his skin clung to his bones. Save for his great talons and clappers, and the rain in his down, he would have been like a handful of air. He often stood for a long time under some bush or ledge, heedless of the drip, his one eye filmed over, his mind neither asleep or awake, but between. The gurgle and swirl of the brimming river, and the sound of chunks of the bank cut away to splash and dissolve in the already muddy flood, became familiar to him, and yet a torment, as if that great, ceaselessly working power of water ridiculed his frailty, within which only the faintest spark of valor still glimmered. The last two nights before the rain ended, he huddled under the floor of the bridge on the coastal highway, and heard the palpitant thunder of motors swell and roar over him. The trucks shook the bridge so that Hook, even in his famished lassitude, would sometimes open his one great eye wide and startled.

V

After the rains, when things became full again, bursting with growth and sound, the trees swelling, the thickets full of song and chatter, the fields, turning green in the sun, alive with rustling passages, and the moonlit nights strained with the song of the peepers all up and down the river and in the pools in the fields, Hook had to bear the return of the one hunger left him. At times this made him so wild that he forgot himself and screamed challenge from the open ground. The fretfulness of it spoiled his hunting, which was not entirely a matter of patience. Once he was in despair, and lashed himself through the grass and thickets, trying to rise when that virgin scent drifted for a few moments above the current of his own river. Then, breathless, his beak agape, he saw the strong suitor ride swiftly down on the wind over him, and heard afar the screaming fuss of the harsh wooing in the alders. For that moment even the battle heart beat in him again. The rim of his good eye was scarlet, and a little bead of new blood stood in the socket of the other. With beak and talon, he ripped at a fallen log, and made loam and leaves fly from about it.

But the season of love passed over to the nesting season, and Hook's love hunger, unused, shriveled in him with the others, and there remained in him only one stern quality befitting a hawk, and that the negative one, the remnant, the will to endure. He resumed his patient, plotted hunting, now along a field of the Japanese farmer, but ever within reach of the river thickets.

Growing tough and dry again as the summer advanced, inured to the family of the farmer, whom he saw daily, stooping and scraping with sticks in the ugly, open rows of their fields, where no lovely grass rustled and no life stirred save the shameless gulls, which walked at the heels of the workers, gobbling the worms and grubs they turned up, Hook became nearly content with his shard of life. The only longing or resentment to pierce him was that which he suffered occasionally when forced to hide at the edge of the mile-long bean field from the wafted cruising and the restive, down-bent gaze of one of his own kind. For the rest, he was without flame, a snappish, dust-colored creature, fading into the grasses he trailed through, and suited to his petty ways.

At the end of that summer, for the second time in his four years, Hook underwent a drouth. The equinoctial period passed without a rain. The laurel and the rabbit-brush dropped dry leaves. The foliage of the oaks shriveled and curled. Even the night fogs in the river canyon failed. The farmer's red cattle on the hillside lowed constantly, and could not feed on the dusty stubble. Grass fires broke out along the highways, and ate fast in the wind, filling the hollows with the smell of smoke, and died in the dirt of the shorn hills. The river made no sound. Scum grew on its vestigial pools, and turtles died and stank among the rocks. The dust rode before the wind, and ascended and flowered to nothing between the hills, and every sunset was red with the dust in the air. The people in the farmer's house quarreled, and even struck one another. Birds were silent, and only the hawks flew much. The animals lay breathing hard for very long spells, and ran and crept jerkily. Their flanks were fallen in, and their eyes were red.

At first Hook gorged at the fringe of the grass fires on the multitudes of tiny things that came running and squeaking. But thereafter there were the blackened strips on the hills, and little more in the thin, crackling grass. He found mice and rats, gophers and ground-squirrels, and even rabbits, dead in the stubble and under the thickets, but so dry and fleshless that only a faint smell rose from them, even on the sunny days. He starved on them. By early December he had wearily stalked the length of the eastern foothills, hunting at night to escape the voracity of his own kind, resting often upon his wings. The queer trail of his short steps and great horned toes zigzagged in the dust and was erased by the wind at dawn. He was nearly dead, and could make no sound through the horn funnels of his clappers.

Then one night the dry wind brought him, with the familiar, lifeless dust, another familiar scent, troublesome, mingled and unclear. In his vision-dominated brain he remembered the swift circle of his flight a year past, crossing in one segment, his shadow beneath him, a yard cluttered with crates and chickens, a gray barn and then again the plowed land and the stubble. Traveling faster than he had for days, impatient of his shrunken sweep, Hook came down to the farm. In the dark wisps of cloud blown among the stars over him, but no moon, he stood outside the wire of the chicken run. The scent of fat and blooded birds reached him from the shelter, and also within the enclosure was water. At the breath of the water, Hook's gorge contracted, and his tongue quivered and clove in its groove of horn. But there was the wire. He stalked its perimeter and found no opening. He beat it with his good wing, and felt it cut but not give. He wrenched at it with his beak in many places, but could not tear it. Finally, in a fury which drove the thin blood through him, he leaped repeatedly against it, beating and clawing. He was thrown back from the last leap as from the first, but in it he had risen so high as to clutch with his beak at the top wire. While he lay on his breast on the ground, the significance of this came upon him.

Again he leapt, clawed up the wire, and, as he would have fallen, made even the dead wing bear a little. He grasped the top and tumbled within. There again he rested flat, searching the dark with quick-turning head. There was no sound or motion but the throb of his own body. First he drank at the chill metal trough hung for the chickens. The water was cold, and loosened his tongue and his tight throat, but it also made him drunk and dizzy, so that he had to rest again, his claws spread wide to brace him. Then he walked stiffly, to stalk down the scent. He trailed it up the runway. Then there was the stuffy, body-warm air, acrid with droppings, full of soft rustlings as his talons clicked on the board floor. The thick, white shapes showed faintly in the darkness. Hook struck quickly, driving a hen to the floor with one blow, its neck broken and stretched out stringily. He leaped the still pulsing body, and tore it. The rich, streaming blood was overpowering to his dried senses, his starved, leathery body. After a few swallows, the flesh choked him. In his rage, he struck down another hen. The urge to kill took him again, as in those nights on the beach. He could let nothing go. Balked of feeding, he was compelled to slaughter. Clattering, he struck again and again. The henhouse was suddenly filled with the squawking and helpless rushing and buffeting of the terrified, brainless fowls.

Hook reveled in mastery. Here was game big enough to offer weight against a strike, and yet unable to soar away from his blows. Turning in the midst of the turmoil, cannily, his fury caught at the perfect pitch, he struck unceasingly. When the hens finally discovered the outlet, and streamed into the yard, to run around the fence, beating and squawking, Hook followed them, scraping down the incline, clumsy and joyous. In the yard, the cock, a bird as large as he, and much heavier, found him out and gave valiant battle. In the dark, and both earthbound, there was little skill, but blow upon blow, and only chance parry. The still squawking hens pressed into one corner of the yard. While the duel went on, a dog, excited by the sustained scuffling, began to bark. He continued to bark, running back and forth along the fence on one side. A light flashed on in an uncurtained window of the farmhouse, and streamed whitely over the crates littering the ground.

Enthralled by his old battle joy, Hook knew only the burly cock before him. Now, in the farthest reach of the window light, they could see each other dimly. The Japanese farmer, with his gun and lantern, was already at the gate when the finish came. The great cock leapt to jab with his spurs and, toppling forward with extended neck as he fell, was struck and extinguished. Blood had loosened Hook's throat. Shrilly he cried his triumph. It was a thin and exhausted cry, but within him as good as when he shrilled in mid-air over the plummeting descent of a fine foe in his best spring.

The light from the lantern partially blinded Hook. He first turned and ran directly from it, into the corner where the hens were huddled. They fled apart before his charge. He essayed the fence, and on the second try, in his desperation, was out. But in the open dust, the dog was on him, circling, dashing in, snapping. The farmer, who at first had not fired because of the chickens, now did not fire because of the dog, and, when he saw that the hawk was unable to fly, relinquished the sport to the dog, holding the lantern up in order to see better. The light showed his own flat, broad, dark face as sunken also, the cheekbones very prominent, and showed the torn-off sleeves of his shirt and the holes in the knees of his overalls. His wife, in a stained wrapper, and barefooted, heavy black hair hanging around a young, passionless face, joined him hesitantly, but watched, fascinated and a little horrified. His son joined them too, encouraging the dog, but quickly grew silent. Courageous and cruel death, however it may afterward sicken the one who has watched it, is impossible to look away from.

In the circle of the light, Hook turned to keep the dog in front of him. His one eye gleamed with malevolence. The dog was an Airedale, and large. Each time he pounced, Hook stood ground, raising his good wing, the pinions newly torn by the fence, opening his beak soundlessly, and, at the closest approach, hissed furiously, and at once struck. Hit and ripped twice by the whetted horn, the dog recoiled more quickly from several subsequent jumps and, infuriated by his own cowardice, began to bark wildly. Hook maneuvered to watch him, keeping his head turned to avoid losing the foe on the blind side. When the dog paused, safely away, Hook watched him quietly, wing partially lowered, beak closed, but at the first move again lifted the wing and gaped. The dog whined, and the man spoke to him encouragingly. The awful sound of his voice made Hook for an instant twist his head to stare up at the immense figures behind the light. The dog again sallied, barking, and Hook's head spun back. His wing was bitten this time, and with a furious side-blow, he caught the dog's nose. The dog dropped him with a yelp, and then, smarting, came on more warily, as Hook propped himself up from the ground again between his wings. Hook's artificial strength was waning, but his heart still stood to the battle, sustained by a fear of such dimension as he had never known before, but only anticipated when the arrogant young hawk had driven him to cover. The dog, unable to find any point at which the merciless, unwinking eye was not watching him, the parted beak waiting, paused and whimpered again.

"Oh, kill the poor thing," the woman begged.

The man, though, encouraged the dog again, saying, "Sick him; sick him."

The dog rushed bodily. Unable to avoid him, Hook was bowled down, snapping and raking. He left long slashes, as from the blade of a knife, on the dog's flank, but before he could right himself and assume guard again, was caught by the good wing and dragged, clattering, and seeking to make a good stroke from his back. The man followed them to keep the light on them, and the boy went with him, wetting his lips with his tongue and keeping his fists closed tightly. The woman remained behind, but could not help watching the diminished conclusion.

In the little, palely shining arena, the dog repeated his successful maneuver three times, growling but not barking, and when Hook thrashed up from the third blow, both wings were trailing, and dark, shining streams crept on his black-fretted breast from the shoulders. The great eye flashed more furiously than it ever had in victorious battle, and the beak still gaped, but there was no more clatter. He faltered when turning to keep front; the broken wings played him false even as props. He could not rise to use his talons.

The man had tired of holding the lantern up, and put it down to rub his arm. In the low, horizontal light, the dog charged again, this time throwing the weight of his forepaws against Hook's shoulder, so that Hook was crushed as he struck. With his talons up, Hook raked at the dog's belly, but the dog conceived the finish, and furiously worried the feathered bulk. Hook's neck went limp, and between his gaping clappers came only a faint chittering, as from some small kill of his own in the grasses.

In this last conflict, however, there had been some minutes of the supreme fire of the hawk whose three hungers are perfectly fused in the one will; enough to burn off a year of shame.

Between the great sails the light body lay caved and perfectly still. The dog, smarting from his cuts, came to the master and was praised. The woman, joining them slowly, looked at the great wingspread, her husband raising the lantern that she might see it better.

"Oh, the brave bird," she said.

STUDY QUESTIONS

1. Audubon's "Wild Turkey" is an excellent piece of expository prose. Clark's "Hook" is a short story. Explain the difference in form.

2. Clark's story is divided into five sections. What major development of the plot occurs in each of these sections?

3.   How are Sections I and IV related?
4.   When does Clark provide the first suggestion of Hook's approaching confrontation with the gulls? With the Japanese farmer?
5.   In Section III, why does the farmer permit the hawk to live?
6.   How do the reactions of the farmer and his wife to Hook's battle with the dog differ?

HE WAS THERE

Joseph Wood Krutch BEFORE CORONADO

Joseph Wood Krutch (1893–   ) was born in Knoxville, Tennessee. He received his B.A. (1915) from the University of Tennessee and his M.A. (1916) and Ph.D. (1932) from Columbia University. He has taught English, journalism, and drama at Columbia; lectured at the New School for Social Research; served as drama critic for *The Nation;* and acted as president of the New York Drama Critics Circle. Krutch now lives in Tucson, Arizona, and is a trustee of the Arizona-Sonora Desert Museum. He has edited the works of William Congreve, Eugene O'Neill, Marcel Proust, and Thomas Gray; and written critical studies of Restoration comedy, and of Samuel Johnson, Edgar Allan Poe, and Henry David Thoreau. Other books include *The Modern Temper* (1929), *The Measure of Man* (1954), National Book Award winner, *The Desert Year* (1952), and *Grand Canyon* (1958).

According to an ancient and anonymous jocosity the bravest man who ever lived must have been the first to eat an oyster—alive.

A soberer judgment might want to make a case for that equally forgotten hero of paleolithic times who first domesticated fire. It must have been one of the first of his home-building achievements, but no wolf destined to turn into a dog and no buffalo destined to become a cow can possibly have seemed one-tenth so dangerous as devouring flame. Early man, like every other animal, must have long been accustomed to flee from it in abject terror. We shall never know what Prometheus first dared snatch a bit from some forest fire or some erupting volcano. But when he put it down in the middle of the domestic circle he must have said, "This I can tame and use."

Reprinted from *The American Scholar,* XXIV (Winter, 1954–55), by permission of the author.

Long before even his day, courage of some sort must have been a characteristic of living things and even the tamer of fire was not the first hero. Perhaps the first and greatest of all was whatever little blob of jelly—not yet either plant or animal but a little of both—first consented to take on the responsibility of being alive at all. And surely the second greatest was that plant or animal which first dared leave the water where, ever since the very dawn of creation, every other organism before it had been born and died. Men are talking now about journeys to the moon or to Mars, but neither is more unsuited to human life than the bare earth was to the first creatures who risked it.

For millions of years only the submerged areas of the earth had been habitable. It was in water that the first hypothetical one-celled creatures, too insubstantial to leave fossil remains, must have been generated. None ventured out of it during millions of years while stony skeletons were evolved and became the earliest sure evidence of life in some of the oldest rocks. In water also stayed all the wormlike and squidlike and shrimplike creatures which represented, in their day, the highest development of life. Meanwhile, during the major part of the earth's history, during considerably more than half the time since life began, all dry land was desert to a degree almost inconceivable—without soil of any kind, as bare as the moon, and subject to no changes except those produced by geological forces. Volcanoes flowed and mountains heaved. Rain falling on an earth without any plant cover to protect it washed cruel gullies as remorselessly as they are cut in the most un-qualified "bad lands" of today. Had any creature of that time been capable of thought, life in any medium other than water would have seemed as fantastic as life without an atmosphere would seem to us.

Then at some time, geologists say it was probably something like three hundred million years ago, the first living thing dared to expose itself temporarily to the deadly air. If it was an animal, as some think most probable, then it must have rushed back (or perhaps ducked back) before the gills through which it breathed could dry out. It could hardly have done much more during many thousands of years after the first bold venture, because it could not actually live beyond easy reach of water until its whole anatomy and physiology had undergone fundamen-tal changes. But patience is a quality which the universe seems never to have lacked (until man came along) and it was always the animal which broke most rashly with all previous tradition, which presently became the most highly developed and the most competent—as well as the least patient.

So far as I am concerned I see no reason to apologize for calling that animal a "hero" or for referring to his "courage." Such terms can have no real meaning except in connection with something which is alive and when we talk about "the suffering earth" or the "nobility" of a mountain range we are merely using a figure of speech. But it is hard to say just where reality begins or to decide just which animal or even which plant is still too simple to be capable of something genuinely analogous to daring and courage. If these virtues are real in man, then they are real because they began to be so as soon as there was anything in the universe which could defy law and habit by risking something which had never been done before.

Few of us are so committed to a merely mechanical behaviorism that we would refuse to call brave and adventurous the first human pioneers who came to live in the American West. So in their own way were the plants and animals who had preceded them there. And so, *a fortiori*, were those far back in time who first dared learn how to adapt themselves to that desert which all dry land then was. If daring to do what our intelligence recognizes as dangerous constitutes "courage," then the animal who similarly rejects the imperatives of its instinct is exhibiting a virtue at least analogous, and so, in some still dimmer fashion, is the simplest creature, animal or even vegetable, which refuses to obey its long established reflexes. The whole course of evolution is directed by just such courageous acts. It must have its countless unremembered heroes who created diversity by daring to do what no member of its species had ever done before.

Most scientists, I am well aware, would object strenuously to any such line of reasoning. But then many scientists are firmly convinced that in man himself there is also no such thing as either daring or courage as distinguished from a reflex, congenital or conditioned. And perhaps that conclusion is inevitable if you begin by denying their reality to all creatures "lower" than man. If every other animal is a machine then why shouldn't human beings be machines also. And if to speak of the "courage" of some very lowly creature is to indulge in exaggeration, it is at least an exaggeration opposite and corrective to a more usual one.

Is it possible, one may ask, to guess at the identity of the first great pioneer and radical who came to dry land? Or is it, like the song the Sirens sang, "beyond all conjecture?" Does he have a name and can we honor him by saying, "But for you and your enterprise I might still be a fish?" At least our own direct amphibious ancestors came to land only because that pioneer's descendants were there to be eaten!

Well, if the paleontologists are right—and their evidence seems pretty good—we can answer this question. As a matter of fact, I met only the day before yesterday one of the almost unchanged relatives of the first air-breathing creatures, and he did not seem especially proud. He crawled on eight legs out from under a board in my storeroom and I confess that, though I do not do such things lightly, I put my foot upon him. Before he was crushed into nothing he was about two inches long and pale straw in color. He carried two pinchers before him and over his back he carried a long tail with a sting at its end. He was, in short, one of the least popular of desert dwellers—a scorpion.

Finding out about one's ancestors, especially correlative ones, is often a risky business and perhaps most people would rather not know how much all of us are indebted to this rather unattractive creature. But so far as geologists can tell from the fossils they study and date, the first animal actually capable of breathing air was not only a member of the scorpion kind but amazingly like the one we step on when we find him.

To even the most uninstructed eye a scorpion fossilized during the Silurian or Devonian epoch—say something like three hundred million years ago—is unmistakably a scorpion. If one of them were to come to life again and crawl out of his stone sarcophagus into your desert patio, you would not be particularly surprised by his appearance unless you happened to be a biologist especially devoted to the study of that group of animals called arachnids to which the scorpion belongs. There are several species now common hereabout—some, like the victim of my brutality, only two inches long and some several times that length. A three hundred million year old specimen would look to the casual eye like merely a sort one had not happened to see before and not much more different from the familiar kinds than they are from one another.

In the highly improbable event that a living dinosaur should be found in some African or South American hiding place, it would create quite a stir in even the popular press and any big-game hunter would count it a high distinction to shoot one. Yet anyone who happens to live in one of the many parts of the earth where scorpions abound can have the privilege of stepping upon a creature who has been going about his business (such as it is) far longer than any dinosaur went about dinosaur business. As a matter of fact, scorpions put in their appearance more years before the first dinosaur than have slipped away since the last known dinosaur decided that he and his kind had had their day.

The horseshoe crab and the gingko tree are sometimes called "living fossils," and the epithet has more recently been applied to that strange fish known as Latimeria which was taken not many years ago off the coast of Africa in spite of the fact that it, as well as all its immediate relatives, was supposed to have become extinct a very long time ago. Yet no sort of fish is much older than the scorpion, and the horseshoe crab is not as nearly like any very ancient form as the scorpion in my storeroom is like his Silurian ancestor. He may not be much to look at, but the least we can do is to regard him in the spirit of the naturalist Sutherland when he contemplated the living members of a tribe somewhat less ancient than the scorpions: "If the test of nobility is antiquity of family, then the cockroach that hides behind the kitchen sink is the true aristocrat. He does not date back merely to the three brothers who came over in 1640 or to William the Conqueror. Wherever there have been great epoch-making movements of people he has been with them heart and soul. . . . Since ever a ship turned a foamy furrow in the sea he has been a passenger, not a paying one certainly but still a passenger. But man himself is but a creature of the last twenty minutes or so compared with the cockroach, for, from its crevice by the kitchen sink, it can point its antennae to the coal in the hod and say: 'When that was being made my family was already well established.' " Scorpions have never been as closely associated with man as the cockroach, but they may not consider that anything to be ashamed of and on the score of antiquity they have a right to snub the cockroaches as upstarts, relatively speaking at least.

It may seem odd that they have hung on so long while changing so little. It may seem even odder that they shall be found in deserts despite the fact that they are so similar to the scorpions which had recently left the water. But they do not insist upon its being dry and some species will even tolerate a certain amount of cold. Though there are none in New England or in the Great Lakes region, they are found in the Alps and on our continent as far north as southern Canada. On the whole, however, they prefer warm climates and they have been in the Southwest for a long, long time. Tracks almost precisely like those made by a living species have been found in the Coconino sandstone which was laid down in Permian times or not more than a million or a million and a half years after scorpions took the first drastic step out of the water.

Most people today underestimate the intelligence and awareness of most creatures other than man because recent official science has often encouraged them to do so. But the scorpion is probably even dumber than he looks. At first sight you would have no reason to suppose that his senses were much less keen or his awareness much less dim than those of any common insect. But they are. By comparison even a beetle, to say nothing of a bee, an ant or a fly, is a miracle of alertness and competence. The life which I extinguished when I stepped on my specimen was about as dim as we can imagine life to be. The scorpion's brain stopped growing not long after he left the water and braininess had not got very far by then.

Neither his habits nor his character are very engaging even as such things go. The young—miniature replicas of their parents—are born alive and like the young of the wolf spider they clamber about on their mother's back until they are old enough to take care of themselves. But maternal solicitude is probably a rather large term to use in connection with the mother's tolerance, and at least until mating times comes around, scorpions do not seem to do anything very interesting. They skulk under bits of wood or stone and they sometimes choose to hide in shoes incautiously left in their neighborhood. I have never seen a scorpion outside captivity do anything more interesting than to nibble rather languidly at the body of a moth who had come to my light.

In fact, watching scorpions closely even in captivity does not provide much excitement most of the time. If two or three are kept together one sometimes absentmindedly eats a companion but the cannibalism, which is usual, is probably nothing very deliberate. The poor things not only have a very rudimentaiy brain but also eyesight which is probably just keen enough to distinguish the dark corners where they hide from the bright light they avoid and too dim even to make them aware of movement. Probably they do not actually perceive anything they do not touch.

As one observer has put it, if you see two together then they are either making love or one of them is being eaten. Even anatomically the most interesting thing about scorpions is their curious way of breathing. Insects have, of course, no lungs. They have merely ramifying tubes open to the outside which permit the penetration of air into the body cavity. But scorpions, being even older than the insect tribe, have what are called book lungs—curious purselike organs which no insect possesses, though spiders, more nearly related to scorpions than to insects, often have both the insect's tubes or tracheae and the scorpion's book lungs. No doubt book lungs, which are a sort of air-breathing gills, were invented close to the water's edge.

So far as I know no detailed account of the mating habits of the Arizona species has ever been published, but in a creature which varies so little they are probably the same as those described in Henri Fabre's classic account of the kind which live in Provence and also, more recently, of a Philippine species. Male and female stand face to face with their tails raised and their stings touching. The male takes his partner by the claw and then backs away, leading her with him. This holding of hands in a sort of dance may last for more than an hour, after which the couple disappears under a stone or into some other recess, the male walking backward as he conducts his partner. This sounds almost romantic and it probably does involve a sort of courtship. But the holding of hands is also probably necessary because creatures which are deaf and almost blind can't afford to lose one another once happy accident has brought them together. And though human lovers have been known on occasion to call one another "good enough to eat," we are likely to be shocked when the female scorpion takes this extravagant metaphor literally, as she frequently does.

Even the scorpion's venom is said to be of some very ancient kind quite different from that of the serpent. And for once a creature commonly regarded as dangerous really is so to some slight extent. The largest kind are relatively innocuous and capable of giving, as I have been informed by a friend who knows from direct experience, nothing worse than a wasp sting. But two Arizona species, neither more than about two inches long, can be deadly to small children and may give even an adult several painful days in bed. Records kept at the Arizona State University over a period of thirty-six years ending in 1965 charge them with causing seventy-five fatalities during that time, or more than three times as many as rattlesnakes can be blamed for.[1] Naturalists get rather tired of insisting that few animals are dangerous at all and very few indeed anything like so dangerous as we like to imagine them, and it is almost a relief for them to be able to say: Scorpions really do sting, some species really are deadly to small children, and even adults should beware of them.

Even so, we tend to exaggerate their dangerousness both because we always do exaggerate such dangers and also perhaps because in the scorpion we recognize something terrifyingly ancient. Nevertheless, even the so-called deadly sort are deadly only to the very young or the very feeble and I myself have seen a healthy adult who had been stung by one ready to go back to his work after keeping fingers in ice water for an hour. By comparison with the automobile, they have very little effect upon the life expectancy of any inhabitant of the desert country. And though men have doubtless been killing them on sight at least since the earliest stone age, men must have found them impressive also, because Scorpio was put among the zodiacal constellations a very long time ago. And it is appropriate that this constellation, inconspicuous in the north, becomes very prominent in the summer sky above the desert.

So much, then, for this creature which, only a few pages back, I insisted upon endowing with "daring" and with "courage" because it ventured upon the land some three hundred millions of years ago. Judged even by the acuteness of its senses, much less by its intelligence, it belongs very low indeed in the hierarchy of life. What a long, long way it was from, say, the scorpion's eye—too primitive almost to deserve the name—to the eye of even so primitive an insect as the praying mantis. Yet the fact remains that between the scorpion and man himself the distance is not nearly so great as it is between the socrpion and anything which does not live at all. The difference between seeing, no matter how dimly, and not seeing at all is greater than the difference between the scorpion's vision and ours. It is easier to imagine how, given time enough, a scorpion could become a man than it is to imagine how sea water and mineral substances could have become a scorpion. Primitive as his eye is, it is indubitably an eye. Its owner can see with it—however dimly. And seeing itself is a process beyond comprehension. It involves

---

[1] These statistics have been updated by the editors with the permission of the author.

awareness of some sort. Perhaps the difference between the scorpion's courage and what is possible for us is no greater than that between his eyesight and ours. Yet who would refuse to use the word "seeing" to describe what even a scorpion can do? Why should we not assume that his courage and ours are no less essentially, though remotely, the same?

Granting all this it is, however, still possible to wonder why this once so adventurous creature became so soon a very paragon of conservatism. As the first air-breather he may very well have been the remote ancestor of all the insects who were to proceed from originality to originality until they became capable of achievements which even man cannot wholly grasp. But this prototype of the insect himself continues to crawl upon the desert and to poison human beings with his ancient venom millions of years after almost all the other creatures which were even his near contemporaries gave up their effort to survive in their original forms. Like the horseshoe crab and the gingko tree, he should have become extinct eons ago. But he has changed even less than they and become one of the most striking examples not of evolution but of a refusal to evolve. Some of the irrational distaste and fear which the sight of him inspires in most people is partly the result of their dim half-realization that he comes down from a past too remote not to suggest unimaginable horrors. He is a living reminder of "the dark and backward abysm of time" and, like the earliest myths of the human race, he suggests the monstrous beginnings of instinct and mind and emotion. He is altogether too much like some bad dream and we would rather not be reminded of it.

As to the mystery of why he is still here, we shall have to be content to put him down as a left-over without knowing precisely how he managed to achieve that humble status. A long time ago he wandered into the desert pretty much what he is now and found that he could survive there, partly no doubt because his demands are modest and he can satisfy them without exposing himself very much. He eats insects which are plentiful and he can do without water as well as without food for long periods. Like the members of certain very old human families he has little to be proud of except the achievements of his remote ancestors, and if he were capable of pride he might, like them, grow prouder just in proportion as he comes to be more and more remote in time from them and their virtues. Like such people, he also makes us wonder what became of all the greatness which was once in his race. Did the scorpion use up all the daring of his tribe in his one great exploit all those millions of years ago? Did he squander it all at once like the wits at the Mermaid Tavern, each of whom seemed resolved to:

Put his whole wit in one jest
And live a fool the rest of his dull life?

It is a pleasant fancy but one had better not put it into words when there are any paleontologists about. We honor the scorpion for his early achievement but it has to be admitted that he doesn't seem to have done much to be proud of in recent years.

STUDY QUESTIONS

1. Who was Coronado?
2. What is the reason for the two breaks in Krutch's text?
3. How does Krutch answer the objection to which he calls the reader's attention in the eighth paragraph?
4. What evidence does Krutch provide to dispel our fears of the scorpion's dangerousness?
5. In the last two paragraphs, Krutch suggests that he has been more fanciful than scientific. Are there any other paragraphs in which his fancy seems to get the best of him?
6. Despite Krutch's "pleasant fancy" and sometimes bantering tone, we never doubt the truthfulness of what he tells us about the scorpion. Why? How does his lucid, informal style help us to accept him as an authority on scorpions?

Isaac Asimov **THE HEAVENLY ZOO**

Isaac Asimov (1920–   ) was born in Petrovichi, Russia, and became a United States citizen in 1928. A biochemist, he received his B.S. (1939), M.A. (1941), and Ph.D. (1948) from Columbia University. His verbal skill earned him the American Chemical Society's James T. Grady Award for scientific writing. Asimov's books include *Pebble in the Sky* and *I, Robot* (1950), *The Intelligent Man's Guide to Science* (1960), *Words from Myths* (1961), *View from a Height* (1963), *A Short History of Biology* and *Quick and Easy Math* (1964), and *Of Time and Space and Other Things* (1965).

On July 20, 1963 there was a total eclipse of the Sun, visible in parts of Maine, but not quite visible in its total aspect from my house. In order to see the total eclipse I would have had to drive two hundred miles, take a chance on clouds, then drive back two hundred miles, braving the traffic congestion produced by thousands of other New Englanders with the same notion.

I decided not to (as it happened, clouds interfered with seeing, so it was just as well) and caught fugitive glimpses of an eclipse that was only 95 per cent total, from my backyard. However, the difference between a 95 per cent eclipse and a 100 per cent eclipse is the difference between a notion of water and an ocean of water, so I did not feel very overwhelmed by what I saw.

What makes a total eclipse so remarkable is the sheer astronomical accident that the Moon fits so snugly over the Sun. The Moon is just large enough to cover the Sun completely (at times) so that a temporary night falls and the stars spring out. And it is just small enough so that during the Sun's obscuration, the corona, especially the brighter parts near the body of the Sun, is completely visible.

The apparent size of the Sun and Moon depends upon both their actual size and their distance from us. The diameter of the Moon is 2160 miles while that of the Sun is 864,000 miles. The ratio of the diameter of the Sun to that of the Moon is 864,000/2160 or 400. In other words, if both were at the same distance from us, the Sun would appear to be 400 times as broad as the Moon.

However, the Sun is farther away from us than the Moon is, and therefore appears smaller for its size than the Moon does. At great distances, such as those which characterize the Moon and the Sun, doubling the distance halves the apparent diameter. Remembering that, consider that the average distance of the Moon from us is 238,000 miles while that of the Sun is 93,000,000 miles. The ratio of the distance of the Sun to that of the Moon is 93,000,000/238,000 or 390. The Sun's apparent diameter is cut down in proportion.

In other words, the two effects just about cancel. The Sun's greater distance makes up for its greater size and the result is that the Moon and the Sun *appear* to be equal in size. The apparent angular diameter of the Sun averages 32 minutes of arc, while that of the Moon averages 31 minutes of arc.[1]

These are average values because both Moon and Earth possess elliptical orbits. The Moon is closer to the Earth (and therefore appears larger) at some times than at others, while the Earth is closer to the Sun (which therefore appears larger) at some times than at others. This variation in apparent diameter is only 3 per cent for the Sun and about 5 per cent for the Moon, so that it goes unnoticed by the casual observer.

There is no astronomical reason why Moon and Sun should fit so well. It is the sheerest of coincidence, and only the Earth among all the

---

[1] One degree equals 60 minutes, so that both Sun and Moon are about half a degree in diameter.

planets is blessed in this fashion. Indeed, if it is true, as astronomers suspect, that the Moon's distance from the Earth is gradually increasing as a result of tidal friction, then this excellent fit even here on Earth is only true of our own geologic era. The Moon was too large for an ideal total eclipse in the far past and will be too small for any total eclipse at all in the far future.

Of course, there is a price to pay for this excellent fit. The fact that the Moon and Sun are roughly equal in apparent diameter means that the conical shadow of the Moon comes to a vanishing point near the Earth's surface. If the two bodies were exactly equal in apparent size the shadow would come to a pointed end exactly at the Earth's surface, and the eclipse would be total for only an instant of time. In other words, as the Moon covered the last sliver of Sun (and kept on moving, of course) the first sliver of Sun would begin to appear on the other side.

Under the most favorable conditions, when the Moon is as close as possible (and therefore as apparently large as possible) while the Sun is as far as possible (and therefore as apparently small as possible), the Moon's shadow comes to a point well below the Earth's surface and we pass through a measurable thickness of that shadow. In other words, after the unusually large Moon covers the last sliver of the unusually small Sun, it continues to move for a short interval of time before it ceases to overlap the Sun and allows the first sliver of it to appear at the other side. An eclipse, under the most favorable conditions, can be 7½ minutes long.

On the other hand, if the Moon is smaller than average in appearance, and the Sun larger, the Moon's shadow will fall short of the Earth's surface altogether. The small Moon will not completely cover the larger Sun, even when both are centered in the sky. Instead, a thin ring of Sun will appear all around the Moon. This is an "annular eclipse" (from a Latin word for "ring"). Since the Moon's apparent diameter averages somewhat less than the Sun's, annular eclipses are a bit more likely than total eclipses.

This situation scarcely allows astronomers (and ordinary beauty-loving mortals, too) to get a good look, since not only does a total eclipse of the Sun last for only a few minutes, but it can be seen only over that small portion of the Earth's surface which is intersected by the narrow shadow of the Moon.

To make matters worse, we don't even get as many eclipses as we might. An eclipse of the Sun occurs whenever the Moon gets between ourselves and the Sun. But that happens at every new Moon; in fact the Moon is "new" because it is between us and the Sun so that it is the opposite side (the one we don't see) that is sunlit, and we only get, at best, the sight of a very thin crescent sliver of light at one edge of the Moon. Well, since there are twelve new Moons each year (sometimes thirteen) we ought to see twelve eclipses of the Sun each year, and sometimes thirteen. No?

No! At most we see five eclipses of the Sun each year (all at widely separated portions of the Earth's surface, of course) and sometimes as few as two. What happens the rest of the time? Let's see.

The Earth's orbit about the Sun is all in one plane. That is, you can draw an absolutely flat sheet through the entire orbit. The Sun itself will be located in this plane as well. (This is no coincidence. The law of gravity makes it necessary.)

If we imagine this plane of the Earth's orbit carried out infinitely to the stars, we, standing on the Earth's surface, will see that plane cutting the celestial sphere into two equal halves. The line of intersection will form a "great circle" about the sky, and this line is called the "ecliptic."

Of course, it is an imaginary line and not visible to the eye. Nevertheless, it can be located if we use the Sun as a marker. Since the plane of the Earth's orbit passes through the Sun, we are sighting along the plane when we look at the Sun. The Sun's position in the sky always falls upon the line of the ecliptic. Therefore, in order to mark out the ecliptic against the starry background, we need only follow the apparent path of the Sun through the sky. (I am referring now not to the daily path from east to west, which is the reflection of Earth's rotation, but rather the path of the Sun from west to east against the starry background, which is the reflection of the Earth's revolution about the Sun.)

Of course, when the Sun is in the sky the stars are not visible, being blanked out by the scattered sunlight that turns the sky blue. How then can the position of the Sun among the stars be made out?

Well, since the Sun travels among the stars, the half of the sky which is invisible by day and the half which is visible by night shifts a bit from day to day and from night to night. By watching the night skies throughout the year the stars can be mapped throughout the entire circuit of the ecliptic. It then becomes possible to calculate the position of the Sun against the stars on each particular day, since there is always just one position that will account for the exact appearance of the night sky on any particular night.

If you prepare a celestial sphere—that is, a globe with the stars marked out upon it—you can draw an accurate great circle upon it representing the Sun's path. The time it takes the Sun to make one complete trip about the ecliptic (in appearance) is about 365¼ days, and it is this which defines the "year."

The Moon travels about the Earth in an ellipse and there is a plane that can be drawn to include its entire orbit, this plane passing through the Earth itself. When we look at the Moon we are sighting along this plane, and the Moon marks out the intersection of the plane with the starry background. The stars may be seen even when the Moon is in the sky, so that marking out the Moon's path (also a great circle) is far easier than marking out the Sun's. The time it takes the Moon to make one complete trip about its path, about 27⅓ days, defines the "sidereal month."

Now if the plane of the Moon's orbit about the Earth coincided with the plane of the Earth's orbit about the Sun, both Moon and Sun would mark out the same circular line against the stars. Imagine them starting from the same position in the sky. The Moon would make a complete circuit of the ecliptic in 28 days, then spend an additional day and a half catching up to the Sun, which had also been moving (though much more slowly) in the interval. Every 29½ days there would be a new Moon and an eclipse of the Sun.

Furthermore, once every 29½ days, there would be a full Moon, when the Moon was precisely on the side opposite to that of the Sun so that we would see its entire visible hemisphere lit by the Sun. But at that time the Moon should pass into the Earth's shadow and there would be a total eclipse of the Moon.

All this does not happen every 29½ days because the plane of the Moon's orbit about the Earth does *not* coincide with the plane of the Earth's orbit about the Sun. The two planes make an angle of 5° 8' (or 308 minutes of arc). The two great circles, if marked out on a celestial sphere, would be set off from each other at a slight slant. They would cross at two points, diametrically opposed, and would be separated by a maximum amount exactly halfway between the crossing point. (The crossing points are called "nodes," a Latin word meaning "knots.")

If you have trouble visualizing this, the best thing is to get a basketball and two rubber bands and try a few experiments. If you form a great circle of each rubber band (one that divides the globe into two equal halves) and make them non-coincident, you will see that they cross each other in the manner I have described.

At the points of maximum separation of the Moon's path from the ecliptic, the angular distance between them is 308 minutes of arc. This is a distance equal to roughly ten times the apparent diameter of either the Sun or the Moon. This means that if the Moon happens to overtake the Sun at a point of maximum separation, there will be enough space between them to fit in nine circles in a row, each the apparent size of Moon or Sun.

In most cases, then, the Moon, in overtaking the Sun, will pass above it or below it with plenty of room to spare, and there will be no eclipse.

Of course, if the Moon happens to overtake the Sun at a point near one of the two nodes, then the Moon does get into the way of the Sun and an eclipse takes place. This happens only, as I said, from two to five times a year. If the motions of the Sun and Moon are adequately analyzed mathematically, then it becomes easy to predict when such meetings will take place in the future, and when they have taken place in the past, and exactly from what parts of the Earth's surface the eclipse will be visible.

Thus, Herodotus tells us that the Ionian philosopher, Thales, predicted an eclipse that came just in time to stop a battle between the Lydians and the Medians. (With such a sign of divine displeasure, there was no use going on with the war.) The battle took place in Asia Minor sometime after 600 b.c., and astronomical calculations show that a total eclipse of the Sun was visible from Asia Minor on May 28, 585 b.c. This star-crossed battle, therefore, is the earliest event in history which can be dated to the exact day.

The ecliptic served early mankind another purpose besides acting as a site for eclipses. It was an eternal calendar, inscribed in the sky.

The earliest calendars were based on the circuits of the Moon, for as the Moon moves about the sky, it goes through very pronounced phase changes that even the most casual observer can't help but notice. The 29½ days it takes to go from new Moon to new Moon is the "synodic month."

The trouble with this system is that in the countries civilized enough to have a calendar, there are important periodic phenomena (the flooding of the Nile, for instance, or the coming of seasonal rains, or seasonal cold) that do not fit in well with the synodic month. There weren't a whole number of months from Nile flood to Nile flood. The average interval was somewhere between twelve and thirteen months.

In Egypt it came to be noticed that the average intervals between the floods coincided with one complete Sun-circuit (the year). The result was that calendars came to consist of years subdivided into months. In Babylonia and, by dint of copying, among the Greeks and Jews, the months were tied firmly to the Moon, so that the year was made up sometimes of 12 months and sometimes of 13 months in a complicated pattern that repeated itself every 19 years. This served to keep the years in line with the seasons and the months in line with the phases of the Moon. However, it meant that individual years were of different lengths.

The Egyptians and, by dint of copying, the Romans and ourselves, abandoned the Moon and made each year equal in length, and each with 12 slightly long months. The "calendar month" averaged 30½ days long in place of the 29½ days of the synodic month. This meant the months fell out of line with the phases of the Moon, but mankind survived that.

The progress of the Sun along the ecliptic marked off the calendar, and since the year (one complete circuit) was divided into 12 months it seemed natural to divide the ecliptic into 12 sections. The Sun would travel through one section in one month, through the section to the east of that the next month, through still another section the third month, and so on. After 12 months it would come back to the first section.

Each section of the ecliptic has its own pattern of stars, and to identify one section from another it is the most natural thing in the world to use those patterns. If one section has four stars in a roughly square configuration it might be called "the square"; another section might be the "V-shape," another the "large triangle," and so on.

Unfortunately, most people don't have my neat, geometrical way of thinking and they tend to see complex figures rather than simple, clean shapes. A group of stars arranged in a V might suggest the head and horns of a bull, for instance. The Babylonians worked up such imaginative patterns for each section of the ecliptic and the Greeks borrowed these, giving each a Greek name. The Romans borrowed the list next, giving them Latin names, and passing them on to us.

The following is the list, with each name in Latin and in English: 1) Aries, the Ram; 2) Taurus, the Bull; 3) Gemini, the Twins; 4) Cancer, the Crab; 5) Leo, the Lion; 6) Virgo, the Virgin; 7) Libra, the Scales; 8) Scorpio, the Scorpion; 9) Sagittarius, the Archer; 10) Capricornus, the Goat; 11) Aquarius, the Water-Carrier; 12) Pisces, the Fishes.

As you see, seven of the constellations represent animals. An eighth, Sagittarius, is usually drawn as a centaur, which may be considered an animal, I suppose. Then, if we remember that human beings are part of the animal kingdom, the only strictly nonanimal constellation is Libra. The Greeks consequently called this band of constellations *o zodiakos kyklos* or "the circle of little animals," and this has come down to us as the Zodiac.

In fact, in the sky as a whole, modern astronomers recognize 88 constellations. Of these 30 (most of them constellations of the southern skies, invented by moderns) represent inanimate objects. Of the remaining 58, mostly ancient, 36 represent mammals (including 14 human beings), 9 represent birds, 6 represent reptiles, 4 represent fish, and 3 represent arthropods. Quite a heavenly zoo!

Odd, though, considering that most of the constellations were invented by an agricultural society, that not one represents a member of the plant kingdom. Or can that be used to argue that the early stargazers were herdsmen and not farmers?

The line of the ecliptic is set at an angle of 23½° to the celestial equator since, as is usually stated, the Earth's axis is tipped 23½°.

At two points, then, the ecliptic crosses the celestial equator and those two crossing points are the "equinoxes" ("equal nights"). When the Sun is at those crossing points, it shines directly over the equator and days and nights are equal (twelve hours each) the world over. Hence, the name.

One of the equinoxes is reached when the Sun, in its path along the ecliptic, moves from the southern celestial hemisphere into the northern. It is rising higher in the sky (to us in the Northern Hemisphere) and spring is on its way. That, therefore, is the "vernal equinox," and it is on March 20.

On that day (at least in ancient Greek times) the Sun entered the constellation of Aries. Since the vernal equinox is a good time to begin the year for any agricultural society, it is customary to begin the list of the constellations of the Zodiac, as I did, with Aries.

The Sun stays about one month in each constellation, so it is in Aries from March 20 to April 19, in Taurus from April 20 to May 20, and so on (at least that was the lineup in Greek times).

As the Sun continues to move along the ecliptic after the vernal equinox, it moves farther and farther north of the celestial equator, rising higher and higher in our northern skies. Finally, halfway between the two equinoxes, on June 21, it reaches the point of maximum separation between ecliptic and celestial equator. Momentarily it "stands still" in its north-south motion, then "turns" and begins (it appears to us) to travel south again. This is the time of the "summer solstice," where "solstice" is from the Latin meaning "sun stand-still."

At that time the position of the Sun is a full $23\frac{1}{2}°$ north of the celestial equator and it is entering the constellation of Cancer. Consequently the line of $23\frac{1}{2}°$ north latitude on Earth, the line over which the Sun is shining on June 20, is the "Tropic of Cancer." ("Tropic" is from a Greek word meaning "to turn.")

On September 23, the Sun has reached the "autumnal equinox" as it enters the constellation of Libra. It then moves south of the celestial equator, reaching the point of maximum southerliness on December 21, when it enters the constellation of Capricorn. This is the "winter solstice," and the line of $23\frac{1}{2}°$ south latitude on the Earth is (you guessed it) the "Tropic of Capricorn."

Here is a complication! The Earth's axis "wobbles." If the line of the axis were extended to the celestial sphere, each pole would draw a slow circle, 47° in diameter, as it moved. The position of the celestial equator depends on the tilt of the axis and so the celestial equator moves bodily against the background of the stars from east to west in a direction parallel to the ecliptic. The position of the equinoxes (the intersection of the moving celestial equator with the unmoving ecliptic) travels westward to meet the Sun.

The equinox completes a circuit about the ecliptic in 25,760 years, which means that in 1 year the vernal equinox moves 360/25,760 or 0.014 degrees. The Sun, in making its west-to-east circuit, comes to the vernal equinox which is 0.014 degrees west of its position at the last crossing. The Sun must travel that additional 0.014 degrees to make a truly complete circuit with respect to the stars. It takes 20 minutes of motion to cover that additional 0.014 degrees. Because the equinox precedes itself and is reached 20 minutes ahead of schedule each year, this motion of the Earth's axis is called "the precession of the equinoxes."

Because of the precession of the equinoxes, the vernal equinox moves one full constellation of the Zodiac every 2150 years. In the time of the Pyramid builders, the Sun entered Taurus at the time of the vernal equinox. In the time of the Greeks, it entered Aries. In modern times, it enters Pisces. In A.D. 4000 it will enter Aquarius.

The complete circle made by the Sun with respect to the stars takes 365 days, 6 hours, 9 minutes, 10 seconds. This is the "sidereal year." The complete circle from equinox to equinox takes 20 minutes less; 365 days, 5 hours, 48 minutes, 45 seconds. This is the "tropical year," because it also measures the time required for the Sun to move from tropic to tropic and back again.

It is the tropical year and not the sidereal year that governs our seasons, so it is the tropical year we mean when we speak of *the* year.

The scholars of ancient times noted that the position of the Sun in the Zodiac had a profound effect on the Earth. Whenever it was in Leo, for instance, the Sun shone with a lion's strength and it was invariably hot; when it was in Aquarius, the water-carrier usually tipped his urn so that there was much snow. Furthermore, eclipses were clearly meant to indicate catastrophe, since catastrophe always followed eclipses. (Catastrophes also always followed lack of eclipses but no one paid attention to that.)

Naturally, scholars sought for other effects and found them in the movement of the five bright star-like objects, Mercury, Venus, Mars, Jupiter, and Saturn. These, like the Sun and Moon, moved against the starry background and all were therefore called "planetes" ("wanderers") by the Greeks. We call them "planets."

The five star-like planets circle the Sun as the Earth does and the planes of their orbits are tipped only slightly to that of the Earth. This means they seem to move in the ecliptic, as the Sun and Moon do, progressing through the constellations of the Zodiac.

Their motions, unlike those of the Sun and the Moon, are quite complicated. Because of the motion of the Earth, the tracks made by the star-like planets form loops now and then. This made it possible for the

Greeks to have five centuries of fun working out wrong theories to account for those motions.

Still, though the theories might be wrong, they sufficed to work out what the planetary positions were in the past and what they would be in the future. All one had to do was to decide what particular influence was exerted by a particular planet in a particular constellation of the Zodiac; note the positions of all the planets at the time of a person's birth; and everything was set. The decision as to the particular influences presents no problem. You make any decision you care to. The pseudo-science of astrology invents such influences without any visible difficulty. Every astrologer has his own set.

To astrologers, moreover, nothing has happened since the time of the Greeks. The period from March 20 to April 19 is still governed by the "sign of Aries," even though the Sun is in Pisces at that time nowadays, thanks to the precession of the equinoxes. For that reason it is now necessary to distinguish between the "signs of the Zodiac" and the "constellations of the Zodiac." The signs *now* are what the constellations *were* two thousand years ago. I've never heard that this bothered any astrologer in the world.

All this and more occurred to me some time ago when I was invited to be on a well-known television conversation show that was scheduled to deal with the subject of astrology. I was to represent science against the other three members of the panel, all of whom were professional astrologers.

For a moment I felt that I must accept, for surely it was my duty as a rationalist to strike a blow against folly and superstition. Then other thoughts occurred to me.

The three practitioners would undoubtedly be experts at their own particular line of gobbledygook and could easily speak a gallon of nonsense while I was struggling with a half pint of reason.

Furthermore, astrologers are adept at that line of argument that all pseudo-scientists consider "evidence." The line would be something like this, "People born under Leo are leaders of men, because the lion is the king of beasts, and the proof is that Napoleon was born under the sign of Leo."

Suppose, then, I were to say, "But one-twelfth of living human beings, amounting to 250,000,000 individuals, were born in Taurus. Have you, or has anybody, ever tried to determine whether the proportion of leaders among them is significantly greater than among non-Leos? And how would you test for leadership, objectively, anyway?"

Even if I managed to say all this, I would merely be stared at as a lunatic and, very likely, as a dangerous subversive. And the general public, which, in this year of 1964, ardently believes in astrology and supports more astrologers in affluence (I strongly suspect) than existed in all previous centuries combined, would arrange lynching parties.

So as I wavered between the desire to fight for the right, and the suspicion that the right would be massacred and sunk without a trace, I decided to turn to astrology for help. Surely, a bit of astrologic analysis would tell me what was in store for me in any such confrontation.

Since I was born on January 2, that placed me under the sign of Capricornus—the goat.

That did it! Politely, but very firmly, I refused to be on the program!

STUDY QUESTIONS

1. Why does Asimov call this essay "The Heavenly Zoo"?
2. Explain, in a few short sentences, why the moon "fits so snugly" over the sun.
3. How does a *sidereal month* differ from a *synodic month?* A *sidereal year* from a *tropical year?* What are the *equinoxes?* The *solstices?*
4. What differentiation does Asimov make between the *signs* of the Zodiac and the *constellations* of the Zodiac?
5. What does Asimov accomplish by his humorous conclusion?

WE AREN'T
Stephen Vincent Benét **SUPERSTITIOUS**

Stephen Vincent Benét (1898–1943) was born in Bethlehem, Pennsylvania, and was the younger brother of William Rose Benét. Among his classmates at Yale, where he received an M.A., were Archibald MacLeish, Philip Barry, and Thornton Wilder. *Heavens and Earth,* a book of poems, was published in 1920, but Benét achieved real fame with two short stories—"Johnny Pye and the Fool Killer" and "The Devil and Daniel Webster." With support from a Guggenheim Fellowship, he wrote *John Brown's Body* (1928), the distinctly American classic that won a Pulitzer Prize. Benét did propagandist work during World War II. His use of American history and folklore made him both a critical and popular success during his own lifetime, but his reputation has now diminished.

Usually, our little superstitious rituals and propitiations don't hurt our daily lives. Usually. And then, on occasion, a superstition—a belief— flares into crowd-madness and kills and kills again before it has run its course. As it did in Salem Village, in 1692.

That story is worth retelling, as a very typical example of what wild belief and crowd hysteria can do to an average community. For Salem Village, in 1691, was no different in any way, from any one of a dozen little New England hamlets. It didn't expect celebrity or notoriety and its citizens were the average people of their day and age. There was the main road and the parsonage and the meeting house, the block house, the Ingersoll house where travelers put up for the night, the eight or nine other houses that made up the village. Beyond, lay the outlying farms with their hard working farmers—a few miles away lay Salem Town itself—fifteen miles away, the overgrown village that was Boston. King Philip's War had been over for some fourteen years and the Colony recovering from the shock of it—there were still individual slayings by Indians but the real power of the Indian was very largely broken. Men might look forward, with hope, to peace and thriving for a time.

And, as for the men and women of Salem Village—they were tough and knotty stock, if you like, not widely lettered, not particularly tolerant, especially in religion—but no different from their neighbors at Andover and Topsfield or in Boston itself. There were sensible men and stupid men among them, model housewives and slatterns, trouble makers and more peaceable folk. The names were the Puritan names that we are accustomed to reverence—Mercy and Abigail and Deborah, Nathaniel and Samuel and John: They lived a life of hard work and long winters, drank rum on occasion, took their religion with that mixture of grimness and enthusiasm that marked the Puritan, and intended, under God's providence, to beat wilderness and Indian, and wax and increase in the land. They were a great deal more human, crotchety and colorful than the schoolbook pictures of dour-faced men in steeple-crowned hats would suggest. In fact, if you want to find out how human they were, you have only to read Judge Sewall's diary. He was one of the judges at the Salem witch trials—and heartily sorry for it, later. But his Pepysian account of his own unsuccessful courtship of Madam Winthrop, and how he brought her gloves and sweets, is in the purest vein of unconscious farce.

And yet, to this ordinary community in the early Spring of 1692, came a madness that was to shake all Massachusetts before its fever was burned out. We are wiser, now. We do not believe in witches. But if, say, three cases of Asiatic cholera were discovered in your own home-town, and certified as such by the local board of health—and if your local newspaper promptly ran a boxed warning to all citizens on the front page—you would have some faint idea of how the average Salem Villager felt, when the "afflicted children" denounced their first victims.

For witchcraft, to almost all the New Englanders of 1692, was as definite, diagnosable and dangerous an evil as bubonic plague. It had its symptoms, its prognosis and its appalling results. Belief in it was as firmly fixed in most people's minds as belief in the germ theory of disease is in ours. Cotton Mather was one of the most able and prom-ising young ministers of his day. But when, in 1688, in Boston, an eleven-year-old girl named Martha Goodwin accused an unhappy Irish Cath-olic laundress of bewitching her, Cotton Mather believed the eleven-year-old girl. In fact, he took the precocious brat into his own house, to study her symptoms and cure them by fasting and prayer, and wrote and published an elaborate, scientific account of his treatment of the case—which doubtless played its own part in preparing men's minds for the Salem madness.

True, there had been only some twenty witch trials in New Eng-land up to the Salem affair—compared to the hundreds and thousands of hangings, burnings, duckings, drownings, that had gone on in Europe and the British Isles during the last few centuries. But people believed in witches—why should they not? They were in the Bible—even the Bible itself said, "Thou shalt not suffer a witch to live." They were in every old wives' tale that was whispered about the winter fires. And, in 1692, they were in Salem Village.

Three years before, Salem Village had got a new minister—the Reverend Samuel Parris, ex-merchant in the West Indies. He seems to have been a self-willed, self-important man with a great sense of his own and the church's dignity, and, no sooner were he and his family well settled in the parsonage, than a dispute began as to whether the par-sonage property belonged to him or to the congregation. But there was nothing unusual about that—Salem Village was a rather troublesome parish and two, at least, of the three previous ministers had had salary and other difficulties with the good folk of Salem. The quarrel dragged on like the old boundary dispute between Salem and Topsfield, creating faction and hard feeling, a typically New England affair. But there were boundary disputes elsewhere and other congregations divided in mind about their ministers.

But the most important thing about Samuel Parris was neither his self-importance nor his attempt to get hold of the parsonage property. It was the fact that he brought with him to Salem Village, two West Indian servants—a man known as John Indian and a woman named Tituba. And when he bought those two or their services in the West Indies, he was buying a rope that was to hang nineteen men and women of New England—so odd are the links in the circumstantial chain.

Perhaps the nine-year-old Elizabeth Parris, the daughter of the parsonage, boasted to her new friends of the odd stories Tituba told and the queer things she could do. Perhaps Tituba herself let the report of her magic powers be spread about the village. She must have been as odd and imagination-stirring a figure as a parrot or a tame monkey in the small New England town. And the winters were long and white—and any diversion a godsend.

In any case, during the winter of 1691–92, a group of girls and women began to meet nightly at the parsonage, with Tituba and her fortune-telling as the chief attraction. Elizabeth Parris, at nine, was the youngest—then came Abigail Williams, eleven and Ann Putnam, twelve. The rest were older—Mercy Lewis, Mary Wolcott and Elizabeth Hubbard were seventeen, Elizabeth Booth and Susan Sheldon, eighteen, and Mary Warren and Sarah Churchill, twenty. Three were servants—Mercy Lewis had been employed by the Reverend George Burroughs, a previous minister of Salem Village, and now worked for the Putnams—Mary Warren was a maid at the John Procters', Sarah Churchill at the George Jacobs'. All, except for Elizabeth Parris, were adolescent or just leaving adolescence.

The elder women included a pair of gossipy, superstitious busybodies—Mrs. Pope and Mrs. Bibber—and young Ann Putnam's mother, Ann Putnam, Senior, who deserves a sentence to herself.

For the Putnams were a powerful family in the neighborhood and Ann Putnam, married at seventeen and now only thirty, is described as handsome, arrogant, temperamental and high-strung. She was also one of those people who can cherish a grudge and revenge it.

The circle met—the circle continued to meet—no doubt with the usual giggling, whispering and gossip. From mere fortune-telling it proceeded to other and more serious matters—table-rapping, perhaps, and a little West Indian voodoo—weird stories told by Tituba and weird things shown, while the wind blew outside and the big shadows flickered on the wall. Adolescent girls, credulous servants, superstitious old women—and the two enigmatic figures of Tituba, the West Indian, and Ann Putnam, Sr.

But soon the members of the circle began to show hysterical symptoms. They crawled under tables and chairs, they made strange sounds, they shook and trembled with nightmare fears. The thing became a village celebrity—and more. Something strange and out of nature was happening—who had ever seen normal young girls behave like these young girls? And no one—certainly not the Reverend Samuel Parris—even suggested that a mixed diet of fortune-telling, ghost stories and voodoo is hardly the thing for impressionable minds during a long New England winter. Hysteria was possession by an evil spirit; pathological lying, the Devil putting words into one's mouth. No one suggested that even Cotton Mather's remedy of fasting and prayer would be a good deal better for such cases than widespread publicity. Instead the Reverend Samuel became very busy. Grave ministers were called in to look at the afflicted children. A Dr. Gregg gave his opinion. It was almost too terrible to believe, and yet what else could be believed? Witchcraft!

Meanwhile, one may suppose, the "afflicted children," like most hysterical subjects, enjoyed the awed stares, the horrified looks, the respectful questions that greeted them, with girlish zest. They had been unimportant girls of a little hamlet—now they were, in every sense of the word, spot news. And any reporter knows what that does to certain kinds of people. They continued to writhe and demonstrate—and be the center of attention. There was only one catch about it. If they were really bewitched—somebody must be doing the bewitching—

On the 29th of February, 1692, in the midst of an appropriate storm of thunder-and-lightning, three women, Sarah Good, Sarah Osburn and Tituba, were arrested on the deadly charge of bewitching the children.

The next day, March 1, two Magistrates, Justice Hathorne and Justice Corwin, arrived with appropriate pomp and ceremony. The first hearing was held in the crowded meetinghouse of the Village—and all Salem swarmed to it, as crowds in our time have swarmed to other sleepy little villages, suddenly notorious.

The children—or the children and Tituba—had picked their first victims well. Sarah Good and Sarah Osburn were old women of no particular standing in the community. Sarah Good had been a beggar and a slattern—her husband testified, according to report and with a smugness that makes one long to kick him, that she "either was a witch or would be one very quickly," ending "I may say, with tears, that she is an enemy to all good." As for Sarah Osburn, she had married a redemptioner servant after the death of her former husband and probably lost caste in consequence. Also, she had been bedridden for some time and therefore not as regular in her church attendance as a good Christian should be.

We can imagine that meetinghouse—and the country crowd within it—on that chill March day. At one end was the majesty of the law—and the "afflicted children" where all might see them and observe. Dressed in their best, very likely, and with solicitous relatives near at hand. Do you see Mercy Lewis? Do you see Ann Putnam? And then the whole crowd turned to one vast, horrified eye. For there was the accused—the old woman—the witch!

The justices—grim Justice Hathorne in particular—had, evidently, arrived with their minds made up. For the first question addressed to Sarah Good was, bluntly:

"What evil spirit have you familiarity with?"

"None," said the piping old voice. But everybody in the village knew worthless Sarah Good. And the eye of the audience went from her to the deadly row of "afflicted children" and back again.

"Have you made no contracts with the devil?" proceeded the Justice.

"No."

The Justice went to the root of the matter at once.

"Why do you hurt these children?"

A rustle must have gone through the meetinghouse at that. Aye, that's it—the Justice speaks shrewdly—hark to the Justice! Aye, but look, too! Look at the children! Poor things, poor things!

"I do not hurt them. I scorn it," said Sarah Good, defiantly. But the Justice had her, now—he was not to be brushed aside.

"Who then do you employ to do it?"

"I employ nobody."

"What creature do you employ then?" For all witches had familiars.

"No creature, but I am falsely accused." But the sweat must have been on the old woman's palms by now.

The Justice considered. There was another point—minor but illuminating.

"Why did you go away muttering from Mr. Parris, his house?"

"I did not mutter but I thanked him for what he gave my child."

The Justice returned to the main charge, like any prosecuting attorney.

"Have you made no contract with the devil?"

"No."

It was time for Exhibit A. The Justice turned to the children. Was Sarah Good one of the persons who tormented them? Yes, yes!—and a horrified murmur running through the crowd. And then, before the awe-stricken eyes of all, they began to be tormented. They writhed, they grew stiff, they contorted, they were stricken moaning or speechless. Yet, when they were brought to Sarah Good and allowed to touch her, they grew quite quiet and calm. For, as everyone knew, a witch's physical body was like an electric conductor—it reabsorbed, on touch, the malefic force discharged by witchcraft into the bodies of the tormented. Everybody could see what happened—and everybody saw. When the meetinghouse was quiet, the Justice spoke again.

"Sarah Good, do you not see now what you have done? Why do you not tell us the truth? Why do you torment these poor children?"

And with these words, Sarah Good was already hanged. For all that she could say was, "I do not torment them." And yet everyone had seen her, with their own eyes.

The questions went on—she fumbled in her answers—muttered a bit of prayer. Why did she mutter? And didn't you see how hard it was for her to pronounce the name of God? Pressed and desperate, she finally said that if anyone tormented the children, it must be Sarah Osburn—she knew herself guiltless. The pitiful fable did not save her. To Boston Jail.

Sarah Osburn's examination followed the same course—the same prosecutor's first question—the same useless denial—the same epileptic feats of the "afflicted children"—the same end. It was also brought out that Sarah Osburn had said that "she was more like to be bewitched than to be a witch"—very dangerous that!—and that she had once had a nightmare about "a thing all black like an Indian that pinched her in the neck."

Then Tituba was examined and gave them their fill of marvels, prodigies and horrors.

The West Indian woman, a slave in a strange land, was fighting for her life and she did it shrewdly and desperately. She admitted, repentantly, that she had tormented the children. But she had been forced to do so. By whom? By Goody Good and Goody Osburn and two other witches whom she hadn't yet been able to recognize. Her voodoo knowledge aided her—she filled the open ears of Justices and crowd with tales of hairy familiars and black dogs, red cats and black cats and yellow birds, the phantasm of a woman with legs and wings. And everybody could see that she spoke the truth. For, when she was first brought in, the children were tormented at her presence, but as soon as she had confessed and turned King's evidence, she was tormented herself, and fearfully. To Boston Jail with her—but she had saved her neck.

The hearing was over—the men and women of Salem and its outlying farms went broodingly or excitedly back to their homes to discuss the fearful workings of God's providence. Here and there a common-sense voice murmured a doubt or two—Sarah Good and Sarah Osburn were no great losses to the community—but still, to convict two old women of heinous crime on the testimony of greensick girls and a West Indian slave! But, on the whole, the villagers of Salem felt relieved. The cause of the plague had been found—it would be stamped out and the afflicted children recover. The Justices, no doubt, congratulated themselves on their prompt and intelligent action. The "afflicted children" slept, after a tiring day—they were not quite so used to such performances as they were to become.

As for the accused women, they went to Boston Jail—to be chained there, while waiting trial and gallows. There is an item of, "To chains for Sarah Good and Sarah Osburn, 14 shillings," in the jailor's record. Only,

Sarah Osburn was not to go to the gallows—she died in jail instead, some five and a half weeks later, at a recorded expense to the Colony of one pound, three shillings and five-pence for her keep. And Tituba stayed snugly in prison till the madness collapsed—and was then sold by the Colony to defray the expenses of her imprisonment. One wonders who bought her and whether she ever got back to the West Indies. But, with that, her enigmatic figure disappears from the scene.

Meanwhile, on an outlying farm, Giles Corey, a turbulent, salty old fellow of 81, began to argue the case with his wife, Martha. He believed, fanatically, in the "afflicted children." She did not, and said so—even going so far as to say that the magistrates were blinded and she could open their eyes. It was one of those marital disputes that occur between strong-willed people. And it was to bring Martha Corey to the gallows and Giles Corey to an even stranger doom.

Yet now there was a lull, through which people whispered.

As for what went on in the minds of "the afflicted children," during that lull, we may not say. But this much is evident. They had seen and felt their power. The hearing had been the greatest and most exciting event of their narrow lives. And it was so easy to do—they grew more and more ingenious with each rehearsal. You twisted your body and groaned—and grown people were afraid.

Add to this, the three girl-servants, with the usual servants' grudges against present or former masters. Add to this, that high-strung, dominant woman, Ann Putnam, Sr., who could hold a grudge and remember it. Such a grudge as there might be against the Towne sisters, for instance—they were all married women of the highest standing, particularly Rebecca Nurse. But they'd taken the Topsfield side in that boundary dispute with Salem. So suppose—just suppose—that one of them were found out to be a witch? And hadn't Tituba deposed that there were other women, besides Good and Osburn, who made her torment the children?

On March 19, Martha Corey and Rebecca Nurse were arrested on the charge of witchcraft. On March 21, they were examined and committed. And, with that, the real reign of terror began.

For if Martha Corey, notably religious and Godfearing, and Rebecca Nurse, saintly and thoughtful, could be witches, no one in Salem or New England was safe from the charge. The examinations were brutally unfair—the "children" yet bolder and more daring. They would interrupt questions now to shout that "a black man" was whispering in the prisoner's ear—if the accused stood still, they were tormented, if she moved her hands, they suffered even greater agonies. Their self-confidence became monstrous—there was no trick too fantastic for them to try. When Deodat Lawson, a former minister of Salem and a well-educated and intelligent man, came to Ingersoll's on March 19, he first saw Mary Wolcott who "as she stood by the door was bitten, so that she cried out of her wrist, and, looking at it, we saw apparently the marks of teeth, both upper and lower set, on each side of her wrist." It would not have deceived a child—but Mary Wolcott was one of the "afflicted children" and her words and self-bitings were as gospel. He then went to the parsonage, where Abigail Williams, another afflicted child, put on a very effective vaudeville-act indeed, throwing firebrands around the house, crying "Whish, whish, whish!" and saying that she was being tormented by Rebecca Nurse who was trying to make her sign the Devil's book.

After that, there was, obviously, nothing for the Reverend Lawson to do but to preach a thunderous sermon on the horrors of witchcraft—interrupted by demonstrations and cries from "the afflicted"—and thus do his little bit toward driving the madness on. For by now, Salem Village, as a community, was no longer sane.

Let us get the rest of it over quickly. The Salem witches ceased to be Salem's affair—they became a matter affecting the whole colony. Sir William Phips, the new governor, appointed a special court of Oyer and Terminer to try the cases. And the hangings began.

On January 1, 1692, no one, except possibly the "Circle children" had heard of Salem witches. On June 10, Bridget Bishop was hanged. She had not been one of the first accused, but she was the first to suffer. She had been married three times, kept a roadhouse on the road to Beverley where people drank rum and played shovelboard, and dressed, distinctively for the period, in a "black cap and black hat and red paragon bodice broidered and looped with diverse colors." But those seem to have been her chief offences. When questioned, she said "I never saw the Devil in my life."

All through the summer, the accusations, the arrest, the trials came thick and fast till the jails were crowded. Nor were those now accused friendless old beldames like Sarah Good. They included Captain John Alden (son of Miles Standish's friend) who saved himself by breaking jail, and the wealthy and prominent Englishes who saved themselves by flight. The most disgraceful scenes occurred at the trial of the saintly Rebecca Nurse. Thirty-nine citizens of Salem were brave enough to sign a petition for her and the jury brought in a verdict of "not guilty." The mob in the sweating courtroom immediately began to cry out and the presiding judge as much as told the jury to reverse their verdict. They did so, to the mob's delight. Then the Governor pardoned her. And "certain gentlemen of Salem"—and perhaps the mob—persuaded him into reversing his pardon. She was hanged on Gallows Hill on July 19 with Sarah Good, Sarah Wilds, Elizabeth How and Susanna Martin.

Susanna Martin's only witchcraft seems to have been that she was an unusually tidy woman and had once walked a muddy road without getting her dress bedraggled. No, I am quoting from testimony, not inventing. As for Elizabeth How, a neighbor testified, "I have been acquainted with Goodwife How as a naybor for nine or ten years and I never saw any harm in her but found her just in her dealings and faithful to her promises . . . I never heard her revile any person but she always pitied them and said, 'I pray God forgive them now'," But the children cried, "I am stuck with a pin. I am pinched," when they saw her—and she hanged.

It took a little more to hang the Reverend George Burroughs. He had been Salem Village's second minister—then gone on to a parish in Maine. And the cloth had great sanctity. But Ann Putnam and Mercy Lewis managed to doom him between them—with the able assistance of the rest of the troupe. Mr. Burroughs was unfortunate enough to be a man of unusual physical strength—anyone who could lift a gun by putting four fingers in its barrel, must do so by magic arts. Also, he had been married three times. So when the ghosts of his first two wives, dressed in winding-sheets, appeared in a sort of magic-lantern show to Ann Putnam and cried out that Mr. Burroughs had murdered them—the cloth could not save him then. Perhaps one of the most pathetic documents connected with the trials is the later petition of his orphaned children. It begins, "We were left a parcel of small children, helpless—"

Here and there, in the records, gleams a flash of frantic common sense. Susanna Martin laughs when Ann Putnam and her daughter go into convulsions at her appearance. When asked why, she says, "Well I may, at such folly. I never hurt this woman or her child in my life." John Procter, the prosperous farmer who employed Mary Warren, said sensibly, before his arrest, "If these girls are left alone, we will all be devils and witches. They ought all to be sent to the whipping-post." He was right enough about it—but his servant helped hang him. White-haired old George Jacobs, leaning on his two sticks, cried out, "You tax me for a wizard, you might as well tax me for a buzzard!" Nevertheless, he hanged. A member of the Nurse family testifies, "Being in court this 29th June, 1692, I saw Goodwife Bibber pull pins out of her clothes and hold them between her fingers and clasp her hands around her knee and then she cried out and said Goodwife Nurse pinched her." But such depositions did not save Rebecca Nurse or her sister, Mary Easty.

Judge, jury and colony preferred to believe the writhings of the children, the stammerings of those whose sows had died inexplicably, the testimony of such as Bernard Peach who swore that Susanna Martin had flown in through his window, bent his body into the shape of a "whoope" and sat upon him for an hour and a half.

One hanging on June 10, five on July 19, five on August 19, eight on September 22, including Mary Easty and Martha Corey. And of these the Reverend Noyes remarked, with unction, "What a sad thing it is to see eight firebrands of hell hanging there!" But for stubborn Giles Corey a different fate was reserved.

The old man had begun by believing in the whole hocus-pocus. He had quarreled with his wife about it. He had seen her arrested as a witch, insulted by the magistrates, condemned to die. Two of his sons-in-law had testified against her—he himself had been closely questioned as to her actions and had made the deposition of a badgered and simple man. Yes, she prayed a good deal—sometimes he couldn't hear what she said—that sort of thing. The memory must have risen to haunt him when she was condemned. Now, he himself was in danger.

Well, he could die as his wife would. But there was the property— his goods, his prospering lands. By law, the goods and property of those convicted of witchcraft were confiscated by the State and the name attainted. With a curious, grim heroism, Giles Corey drew up a will leaving that property to the two sons-in-law who had not joined in the prevailing madness. And then at his trial, he said "I will not plead. If I deny, I am condemned already in courts where ghosts appear as witnesses and swear men's lives away."

A curious, grim heroism? It was so. For those who refused to plead either guilty or not guilty in such a suit were liable to the old English punishment called *peine forte et dure*. It consisted in heaping weights or stones upon the unhappy victim till he accepted a plea—or until his chest was crushed. And exactly that happened to old Giles Corey. They heaped the stones upon him until they killed him—and two days before his wife was hanged, he died. But his property went to the two loyal sons-in-law, without confiscation—and his name was not attainted. So died Giles Corey, New England to the bone.

And then, suddenly and fantastically as the madness had come, it was gone.

Not without other victims. At Andover, for instance, the wife of a citizen had fallen unaccountably ill. The first thought had been to call in two of the "afflicted children" as experts on witchcraft. As a result, something like fifty people were arrested and several hanged. But, after the hangings of September 22, the special court of Oyer and Terminer did not meet again—though the jails were crowded with accused and condemned.

The "afflicted children," at long last, had gone too far. They had accused the Governor's lady. They had accused Mrs. Hall, the wife of the minister at Beverley and a woman known throughout the colony for her virtues. And there comes a point when driven men and women revolt against blood and horror. It was that which ended Robespierre's terror—it was that which ended the terror of the "afflicted children." The thing had become a *reductio ad absurdum*. If it went on, logically, no one but the "afflicted children" and their protégées would be left alive.

So the madness died. In January, 1693, the Superior Court brought twenty-one to trial and condemned three. But no one was executed. In May, 1693, a proclamation emptied the jails.

So it ended. And Cotton Mather published *Wonders of the Invisible World* to prove it had all been true and Robert Calef, of Boston, promptly replied with *More Wonders of the Invisible World,* confuting and attacking Cotton Mather. And, in 1706, Ann Putnam made public confession that she had been deluded by the Devil in testifying as she had. She had testified in every case but one. And in 1711, the colony of Massachusetts paid 50 pounds to the heirs of George Burroughs, 21 pounds to the heirs of Giles Corey—578 pounds in all to the heirs of various victims. An expensive business for the colony, on the whole.

What happened to the survivors? Well, the Reverend Samuel Parris quit Salem Village to go into business in Boston and died at Sudbury in 1720. And Ann Putnam died in 1716 and from the stock of the Putnams sprang Israel Putnam, the Revolutionary hero. And from the stock of the "witches," the Nurses and the others, sprang excellent and distinguished people of service to State and nation. And hanging Judge Hathorne's descendant was Nathaniel Hawthorne. And Cotton Mather remained a brilliant minister, but his ambitions, on the whole, did not prosper as he thought they should. While as for the sanctimonious Dr. Noyes who spoke so unctuously of the "eight firebrands of hell," according to legend, he got his just deserts. For the legend goes that Sarah Good cursed him, saying, "I am no witch and because you say I am, God will give you blood to drink"—and he is supposed to have died of a hemorrhage of the throat. But Mercy Lewis and the rest of the "afflicted children" did not die so. They went on and lived their lives.

And I have not even spoken of the fifty-five who actually confessed to being witches—or the solemn examination of a five-year-old child for witchcraft—or of how two of the Carrier boys were hung up by the heels to make them testify against their mother—or of the time when Benjamin Hutchinson and Eleazer Putnam went stabbing with their rapiers at invisible cats and were solemnly assured they had slain three witches, equally invisible.

We have no reason to hold Salem up to obloquy. It was a town, like another, and a strange madness took hold of it. But it is no stranger thing to hang a man for witchcraft than to hang him for the shape of his nose or the color of his skin. We are not superstitious, no. Well, let us be a little sure we are not. For persecution follows superstition and intolerance as fire follows the fuse. And, once we light that fire, we cannot foresee where it will end or what it will consume—any more than they could in Salem, two hundred and forty-five years ago.

STUDY QUESTIONS

1. Why does Benét feel that this historical narrative has relevance in a twentieth-century society?
2. Why did the "afflicted" children pretend that they were bewitched?
3. What does Benét mean when he says that the children "had picked their victims well"?
4. What is a "familiar," as Benét uses the word?
5. How did Giles Cory triumph over his judges?
6. Does the last paragraph seem an integral part of the essay? Why?

THE NEW MEDICINE
Newsweek **AND ITS WEAPONS**

Call him Harry Wilson, a 46-year-old sales executive. He had just strolled out of a restaurant with his wife when he felt a sudden crushing pressure on his chest and slumped to the sidewalk, the victim of a heart attack.

A clot had formed in an artery of his heart, part of the heart muscle was no longer pumping blood, blood pressure had fallen and his skin was already cold. In a matter of minutes an ambulance was rushing him to the hospital—and the beginning of a month-long battle to save his life.

The oldest of human emotions would be exposed in that time: a man struck down in his prime, a wife alone, children wondering if they would ever see their father again. But these fears would be met by the newest creations of human ingenuity. There is, of course, no "right" time to have a coronary, but for Wilson and literally thousands of others who fall victim to heart attacks, liver disorders, kidney failures and other killer diseases, something extra is now working to sustain their lives today. Doctors and nurses bring not only their traditional skills and time-tested drugs to the battle but also an extraordinary array of life-saving mechanical and electronic aids that didn't exist a few years ago.

Some items represent fallout from military research, the space program and even the atomic bomb; still others are the products of new alliances between industrial giants and hospitals. Lockheed and the

Mayo Clinic, for example, are collaborating on a new computerized system of hospital care; North American Aviation is working on an emphysema belt that makes the breath of life easier for men and women suffering lung damage. In some modern operating rooms where the New Medicine is practiced, the technicians manning the machines and monitors often outnumber the doctors.

Alarm: In hospitals from Newport News, Va., to Mountain View, Calif., heart patients like Wilson are taken to coronary intensive-care units where electrodes similar to those used by the Gemini astronauts are placed on their chest and legs so that technicians can monitor their electrocardiogram, pulse and blood pressure around the clock. Three hours after Wilson was admitted, an alarm flashed on the central control desk—his heart had stopped beating. Within seconds, a nurse had wheeled a cart to the bedside. Called the Max (for Maximum Care), the cart was equipped with everything needed for cardiac resuscitation. Quickly a doctor placed two plunger-like electrodes on Wilson's chest and gave him a 100-watt shock that started his heart going again.

Sometimes coronaries are followed by a pulmonary embolism—a clot lodged in a blood vessel in the lung. As soon as he coughed blood—a telltale sign—Wilson was wheeled to the nuclear-medicine lab and given an injection of radioactive albumin particles. When the particles passed through the tiny capillaries in the lung, a scanner outside the chest picked up the radiation and printed out a picture of the lung in black dots. A wedge-shaped blank in the scan pinpointed the portion of the lung not receiving blood, confirming the doctors' diagnosis. Wilson was given anticoagulant drugs.

The physicians also checked for clots with a thermograph. This distant relative of the U.S. Army's sniperscope and of space satellite detectors measures the heat given off in the form of infra-red radiations by various parts of the body. Variations in the intensity of the infra-red appear as "hot" and "cold" spots on film. The area of a clot—with its seriously diminished blood supply—is cold, and shows up much darker than the normal areas on the thermograph.

Four weeks after the attack that struck him down, Wilson, 20 pounds lighter and the drug digitalis in his pocket, walked out of the hospital. But he wasn't beyond the ministrations of the New Medicine yet. The heart attack had damaged the nerve center—or pacemaker—that controls the regularity of the heartbeat; he could suffer from heart block culminating in heart failure. To prevent this, surgeons supplied him with an artificial pacemaker made possible by advances in miniaturized computer parts.

The pacemaker comes in several models. Wilson's is a 2½-inch plastic, battery-powered generator installed under the skin high on the chest. It is connected to the heart with a plastic-coated wire threaded through a vein under the collarbone and into the right pumping chamber, or ventricle. Over a three-year period, the generator releases minibursts of electricity to keep the heart beating at a steady rate. When the generator wears out, it can be easily replaced during a relatively simple chest operation. A two-speed model comes with a magnetized actuator shaped like a ball-point pen. "If the wearer wants to increase his heart rate in order to play a set of tennis or run to catch a train," explains James Nelson of GE's X-ray department in Milwaukee, "he simply passes the pen over the spot on his body where the battery is implanted to speed the impulse."

Innovations: Nothing, it seems, is so far out that it can't be applied in the New Medicine. A NASA metal alloy, originally used for bearings, is being tested for artificial hip and elbow joints. An accelerometer intended to measure the impact of micrometeorites against spacecraft has been converted into a means of measuring minute muscle tremors in diagnosing neurologic disease. And the lunar walker, developed for unmanned exploration of the moon's surface, has been adapted as a walking wheelchair to allow paraplegics to climb stairs by manipulating manual or chin-strap controls.

So much is happening in the field of biomedical engineering that a group of doctors and manufacturers recently formed the Association for Advancement of Medical Instrumentation as a clearinghouse for information. "The big firms are loaded with technicians who can help us solve our problems," says Harvard's Dr. John P. Merrill, a pioneer in the use of the artificial kidney and kidney transplants. Merrill visualizes the day when artificial kidneys and other hardware will be subjected to government tests by some sort of Federal Spare Parts Administration similar to the way medications are policed by the Food and Drug Administration.

The Federal government's involvement in the biomedical field is already large. In the fiscal year ending in June, expenditures for applied research are estimated at $832 million. And only last week, the U.S. Public Health Service awarded more than $2.5 million—the largest grant since passage of the 1946 Hill-Burton program for hospital construction—to the University of Southern California to develop an automated system for diagnosis, continuous monitoring and treatment of the critically ill.

But the New Medicine still leaves many old problems unsolved. Gadgetry and special-care units add to the already soaring costs of medical care. A heart-lung machine costs $15,000 and the average openheart operation may cost $3,000. A cobalt unit for deep cancer therapy can run as high as $95,000 and the charge for each treatment may be $15 or $20. The cost of the hardware is only part of the price the patient must pay, of course. For each new device, a technician with the skills to run it must be found—and medical technologists of all kinds are in short supply. And sometimes the shortage of skilled hands spells disaster. Just three months ago, three patients at Hennepin County General Hospital in Minneapolis died of salt and mineral depletion while being "run" on the hospital's artificial kidney machine because of an improper mixture of the solution used in the machine.

Personal Touch: Moreover, the huge radiotherapy units, glowing oscilloscopes and snake-like catheters characteristic of the New Medicine can have a frightening effect on patients. "You can put in all the machinery you want," says a doctor at the National Institutes of Health, "but the patient wants some attention from a person, not a machine."

Sometimes, too, physicians become bedazzled and overly dependent on the machine gadgetry of their surroundings. One NIH official recalls a brain surgeon who balked at proceeding with a relatively routine operation when an electrical defect occurred in one of the operating-room monitors. After his initial dismay, he was persuaded to go on without the monitor. "I think there is a tyranny of technology," says Dr. Irving S. Cooper of New York's St. Barnabas Hospital. "The machine is not the message."

Still, an estimate 12,000 persons are living useful lives today wearing implanted heart pacemakers. Hundreds have been saved by artificial heart valves made of metal and plastic. And rapidly, even these experimental methods of treatment are being supplanted by more ingenious techniques. Some of the newest weapons of the New Medicine:

Gas Endarterectomy

Heart attacks kill about 525,000 Americans annually. They occur because fatty deposits of atherosclerosis clog the coronary arteries feeding the heart muscle. Although surgeons have learned how to remove or clear obstructed blood vessels elsewhere in the body, few have successfully operated on the delicate coronaries. Recently, Doctors Philip Sawyer, Martin Kaplitt and Sol Sobel of the State University of New York Downstate Medical Center in Brooklyn have developed a way of clearing the coronaries with injections of carbon dioxide.

The procedure, called a gas endarterectomy, imitates the destructive pattern of the disease known as dissecting aneurysm. The surgeons insert a fine hypodermic needle attached to a carbon-dioxide cylinder into the wall of the artery. A few jets of the gas tear the lining away from the artery wall, at the same time loosening the fatty core of atherosclerosis. A small incision is then made in the artery and another burst of gas frees the deposit completely. Then the surgeons simply remove the core with forceps.

The Laser Knife

The laser started out as a possible death ray; its military uses are still untested, but its role as a tool of surgery is being demonstrated daily. Lasers produce bursts of light millions of times brighter than sunlight when electrical energy strikes a gas such as argon and makes it emit light which is amplified and reflected repeatedly. The result is light of one pure wave length instead of the usual jumble of waves from the whole spectrum. This "coherent" light can be focused in a narrow beam with enough heat to cut through diamonds and the precision to raise a blister on a single red blood cell.

To date, lasers have been used most successfully in medicine to repair small tears and defects in the retina, the lining at the back of the eye. Through a focusing scope, the ophthalmologist aims the laser at the defect and fires a brief burst of energy. The beam passes harmlessly through the lens of the eye, but it burns the layer of blood vessels behind the retina. This layer, called the choroid, oozes a thick substance that hardens, gluing the retina to the back of the eye. Hundreds of cases have been treated satisfactorily by laser at New York's Columbia-Presbyterian Medical Center.

Lasers have been used to destroy skin cancers. And since laser light tends to be absorbed more readily by dark tissue than by light tissue, lasers are being tried experimentally in the destruction of malignant melanoma, a darkly pigmented and usually lethal form of cancer. In some cases the beam has destroyed individual growths, usually on the skin, but no one has yet reported any complete cures. Some researchers fear the use of lasers in cancer surgery because the beams may splatter cancer cells from the tumor and hasten spread of the disease to other parts of the body.

Cryosurgery

The most promising of the new surgical methods is cryosurgery, destruction of tissue by freezing. The technique was pioneered by Dr. Irving Cooper, director of neurosurgery at St. Barnabas, to relieve the rigidity and uncontrollable tremors of Parkinson's disease by freezing a tiny cluster of nerve cells inside the brain. The patient is given a local anesthetic and a dime-size hole is cut in his skull. Guided by a series of Polaroid X-rays, Cooper inserts a probe the size of a crochet needle into the thalamus, about 2½ inches deep in the brain. He then circulates liquid nitrogen at temperatures ranging from—94 to—58 degrees Fahrenheit through the probe, controlling the temperature at the uninsulated tip by the rate of flow. The rest of the probe is vacuum-insulated,

Thermos-bottle fashion, to avoid damage to normal tissue as it rests in the brain.

A ball of frozen tissue gradually forms around the tip and, since the patient is conscious, Cooper can gauge the effect by observing his hand movements. The procedure is safe, because if the ice ball grows too large and the patient shows signs of paralysis, he has 30 seconds to raise the probe temperature and avert permanent damage.

Cryosurgery is being tested increasingly in other types of surgery. Cooper, for example, has frozen brain tumors that are too deep in the brain to be removed by conventional methods. After destruction by freezing, the dead tumor breaks down and is removed by the blood stream. "It looks very promising," Cooper notes, "but I don't want to shout about it yet." At Buffalo VA hospital, Dr. Andrew Gage has frozen bone tumors by wrapping a freezing coil around the bone shaft. The dead bone forms a structure around which new bone forms, Gage reports. Dr. Maurice J. Gonder, also of Buffalo VA, and his associate Dr. Ward A. Soanes have found the cryosurgical probe a good way to remove the prostate gland with relatively little pain and blood loss. And Dr. William G. Cahan of New York's Memorial Hospital has used cryosurgery to remove tonsils, to stop abnormal uterine bleeding (by destroying the lining of the uterus) and to control bleeding and relieve pain from large incurable tumors. Cryosurgery, Cahan notes, "bids well for becoming the most versatile modality in medicine."

Treatment Under Pressure

Hyperbaric oxygen chambers look like huge submarines moored improbably to hospital basement floors. The resemblance is apt; patients undergoing open-heart surgery in the chambers are given pure oxygen to breathe while the chamber pressure is raised to about three times normal atmospheric pressure. This saturates their blood and body tissues with up to fifteen times the normal concentration of oxygen—giving the surgeon more time to operate.

Chicago's Lutheran General Hospital has three chambers ranging in size from 23 feet to 41 feet long; one contains a fully equipped operating room, another, a six-bed intensive-care unit, and the third is used for research and isolation of patients with severe infections. Together they cost more than $1.1 million to install. In addition to heart surgery, hyperbaric therapy has proved its worth in the treatment of tetanus and gas gangrene, because the bacteria causing these diseases are killed by oxygen in heavy concentration.

Some researchers have found that hyperbaric oxygen treatments improve a stroke victim's chances of recovery by compensating for the impaired blood supply to the brain; the chambers have also averted the need for amputation in patients with injuries or atherosclerotic deposits that cut off circulation to the arms or legs. Finally, they are widely used in operations to repair heart defects in infants, whose circulatory systems are often too tiny to be hooked to the tubes of a heart-lung machine.

A novel variation of high-pressure therapy has been devised by Doctors W. James Gardner and John Storer of Cleveland's Huron Road Hospital. They adapted the principle of the flyer's G-suit to treat shock and abdominal bleeding. In shock, blood pressure drops, causing blood to drain from the brain and lungs to pool in the abdomen. When shock patients are placed in the inflatable plastic suit, the pressure forces blood back into the upper part of the body. The suit also can reduce internal hemorrhage by closing the bleeding vessels. Gardner and Storer have also developed a plastic G-splint that works on the same pressure principle. The inflated splint holds an injured arm or leg on a cushion of air and protects it from infection at the same time.

Super-Clean Care

Control of infection remains one of the biggest problems in U.S. hospitals, especially for patients with severe burns or cancer patients receiving drugs that suppress their ability to produce antibodies against disease. The space program's experience with "White Rooms" made dustfree by elaborate controls demonstrates what can be done to create a super-clean area. The medical version is the "life island," a transparent plastic canopy that completely engulfs the patient's bed. A filtered ventilating unit at the foot of the bed provides fresh air nearly 100 per cent free of bacteria and dust particles. Before being placed in the life island, the patient showers with hexachlorophene solution twice a day for three days and takes antibiotics to rid his body of bacteria.

Sterile Food: The patient's meals come from cans and are passed through an ultraviolet-treated portal on prewrapped, sterilized plates; even his razor and toothbrush are sterilized. Doctors and nurses tend the patient through plastic sleeves constructed in the canopy wall. At the National Institutes of Health in Bethesda, Md., an electronic stethoscope is being used to take readings of the patient's chest sounds from a distance. Among the life island's most promising uses: patients may be able to take higher doses of cancer-killing drugs without threat of infection.

NIH is now planning entire clean rooms built around the laminar-flow principle. Conceived initially for dust-free aerospace processes such as satellite assembly and checkout, laminar flow protects the patient with a curtain of air. In one laminar-flow room, air is filtered into the end where the patient's bed is located and is expelled at the other. Visitors entering at the exit end are, in effect, standing downstream and unable to contaminate the patient.

Ultrasonic Treatment

To relieve bronchial and lung congestion in infants with such disorders as pneumonia and cystic fibrosis, an inherited disease that clogs the lungs with mucus, physicians at Chicago's Children's Memorial Hospital have devised an ultrasonic nebulizer adapted by Dr. David Allen from a paint sprayer. A decongestant fog to break up the mucus is brewed in a container with a quartz crystal in the bottom. When the crystal is set in vibration at ultrasound frequencies, the water breaks up into fine particles that are then pumped into a plastic canopy over the child's bed. The size of the particles is controlled by changing the crystal frequency. Since the distance the mist will travel down into the baby's chest is determined by particle size—the smallest go farthest— physicians can aim treatment at any level—from the windpipe to the lungs. For most infections, a child spends all day in the fog tent for three or four days; Allen is convinced that the ultrasonic fog therapy shortens time in the hospital.

Atomic Attack

Radiation therapy and drugs are standard treatment for adult forms of leukemia, but both can damage normal tissue while combating the cancer. Researches have recently begun experiments with extracorporeal blood irradiators. The irradiator at the Brookhaven National Laboratory, Upton, N.Y., is a 5-foot-high steel dome containing a core of cobalt 60, a potent source of gamma rays. The leukemia patient is attached to the irradiator by means of plastic tubes permanently placed in an artery and a vein in the forearm; the tubes are joined together when not in use. During irradiation, in effect, all the patient's blood is shipped outside his body for treatment. As his blood flows into the device, the cancerous white cells are exposed to the radio-cobalt source, while his body is shielded by lead and steel shielding (the red cells are less vulnerable to radiation). Two patients are treated at a time, lying in beds on either side of the irradiation unit.

At Boston's Massachusetts General Hospital, Dr. Benjamin Barnes has tested a way of irradiating a 48-year-old leukemia patient's blood with an irradiator worn on the wrist. Plastic tubes in the blood vessels in his arm conduct blood through a plastic capsule that is about an inch long and contains a small cylinder of strontium 90. This radioactive isotope produces beta rays which pass no further than the walls of the capsule. During a month of treatment, Barnes reports, the patient's lymphocytes (the white cells involved in one form of leukemia) dropped from a count of 40,000 to 1,000. Treatment was stopped because the effect of further loss of lymphocytes might be dangerous. Barnes reports that his patient seems "substantially" improved after wrist-irradiator treatment.

Max Care

At least a third of the patients rushed to hospitals after heart attacks die despite the best medical care. Usually the cause of death is a disturbance in the electrical system that regulates the heartbeat; the ventricles, or pumping chambers, may fibrillate—flutter uncontrollably—and fail to pump blood properly. Or the heart may stop beating entirely. Coronary-care units rapidly being established in a growing number of hospitals are beginning to reduce the death toll from arrhythmias.

In a typical unit, the patient is monitored continuously by electro-cardiographs, blood-pressure and pulse recorders at his bed and at a central control console. At the first sign of serious abnormality in the heart rhythm, an alarm sounds at the control desk and at key stations throughout the hospital. While the patient is given oxygen, his heart-beat may be returned to normal by plunger-like electrodes that deliver a shock through the chest wall. In some units, "demand pacemakers" are attached to the patient's chest and back to restore automatically normal heart rate if it should slow down or speed up.

For hospitals that don't have separate coronary-care units, Dr. Joel J. Nobel of Philadelphia's Graduate Pain Research Foundation and biomedical engineer Richard M. Rauch designed the Max emergency cart. A rolling operating table, the cart is equipped with defibrillator, mechanical cardiac-massage pump, oxygen mask, EKG oscilloscope and blood-pressure recorder, drugs and surgical instruments.

Coronary intensive care, some experts believe, can cut heart-attack deaths in the U.S. by 50,000 a year. At Philadelphia's Presbyterian Medical Center, the survival rate of patients admitted after coronaries has increased by a third. But most cardiologists agree that the record could be even better if serious arrhythmias could be prevented from occurring in the first place. Of the 130 patients admitted to the coronary unit at Boston's Peter Bent Brigham Hospital during the first year of operation none has died from serious arrhythmias, mainly because the staff was trained to look for early-warning changes in the EKG and gave the patients drugs to prevent trouble.

Artificial Kidneys

The artificial kidney, the first mechanical substitute for a human organ, has been used since the 1940s to help patients with infections, shock or some types of high blood pressure get over the crisis of kidney failure. But in the last seven years, doctors have started using artificial kidneys to sustain the lives of patients afflicted with renal disease. The patients, wearing permanently attached plastic tubes in their arms or legs, report to the hospital once or twice a week for dialysis—having their blood cleansed of accumulated wastes.

The Washington VA hospital has one of the most modern kidney centers, capable of handling ten patients at a time. The fluid that removes poisons from the patient's blood is mixed automatically and delivered from a central storage tank to five bedside units, each serving two patients. The center can treat up to 25 patients a week.

Unfortunately, there are still not enough artificial kidneys to go around. Approximately 700 patients are receiving treatment in hospitals or in their homes, yet at least 5,000 Americans develop a form of renal disease each year that could be treated by chronic dialysis—if machines were available. One of the main reasons for the kidney gap is cost. Some kidneys cost $3,000; just changing coils costs $25 per treatment. For the hospital, staffing a kidney machine may cost $10,000 to $25,000 a year per patient, while the cost for a dialysis in special home units may range from $5,000 to $15,000. Recently, Dr. Willem Kolff, who developed the first artificial kidney more than two decades ago, has ingeniously fashioned a cheaper artificial kidney unit out of an old washing machine. The whole rig cost $350, and each dialysis costs $16.

Scanning the Body

The use of radioactive isotopes to trace diseases throughout the body was one of the most dramatic postwar developments in medical diagnosis. Radioactive iodine, one of the oldest diagnostic isotopes, travels to the thyroid gland; a radio-sensitive scanner records radiation from the isotope and prints a map of the gland. A light area on the map might be a cancer. Radioactive gold collects in the liver, acting as a way of detecting a malignancy or the scar tissue of cirrhosis. More sensitive scanners and isotopes that produce better pictures while exposing the patient to less radiation are rapidly becoming available.

One of the best scanners is the "gamma camera," developed at the University of California's Donner Lab. Gamma rays emitted from an isotope create faint flashes of light on a crystal that are then amplified by phototubes. A computer relays the flashes to a picture tube where they can be recorded on Polaroid film as a series of white dots, showing the distribution of the isotope in the patient's body. After administration of technetium, for example, a patient can be examined for a brain tumor in three minutes, as compared with up to one hour for older scanning equipment. The camera also can provide a rapid series of Polaroid shots to trace the flow of blood to reveal, for example, where a stroke has occluded the blood supply to the brain.

Ultrasound, working on the same principle as naval sonar, is another important diagnostic tool. Ultrasonic scanners emit sound waves, measure the time they take to echo from tissues inside the body and record the "contacts" on an oscilloscope. An ultrasonic probe attached to a tweezer device has been used to locate and remove a tiny metal fragment inside the eye. Sound waves can also locate brain tumors by showing that the midline membrane separating the two halves of the cerebrum has been squeezed to one side. And they can measure the size of a baby's head inside the womb, helping the obstetrician decide whether a Caesarean section is necessary without X-rays—a radiation hazard to mother or child.

A Spare Heart

The grand achievement in medical technology within the next few years will be the artificial heart. The National Heart Institute is spending $7 million this year to support artificial-heart research; some experts believe the goal could be reached by 1970. Just last year, Dr. Michael E. DeBakey of Houston's Baylor University College of Medicine and Dr. Adrian Kantrowitz of the State University of New York Downstate Medical Center in Brooklyn were able to implant partial replacements for the heart in critically ill patients.

Both devices are made of plastic and synthetic fabric. They are actually air-driven pumps to take over part of the work of the left ventricle—the heart's main pumping chamber. One of DeBakey's patients, a 37-year-old woman with rheumatic heart disease, recovered after a ten-day boost from the pump.

The DeBakey auxiliary heart, designed with the aid of Rice University engineers, is a plastic globe about the size of a grapefruit containing a double lining of plastic fabric. It is installed on the left side of the chest, the top half protruding above the ribs. The Kantrowitz auxiliary ventricle is a curved Dacron tube containing a flexible rubber lining and was designed by an Avco-Everett Research Laboratory team led by physicist Arthur Kantrowitz, the surgeon's brother. The device is placed entirely inside the chest.

Kantrowitz points out that the left ventricle is the first to fail in serious heart disease, and that a perfected ventricle booster would adequately serve 98 per cent of heart patients. As for a completely artificial heart, the Brooklyn surgeon says: "I want to leave that to the next generation."

Priority: The Cleveland Clinic's Willem Kolff has constructed several models intended to replace the heart—and they are startlingly like the real thing and have four chambers. The hearts are made of silicone or natural rubber, have a synthetic valve system and a right ventricle to pump blood to the lungs, as well as a left one to send blood to the body. Air-driven from outside the body, like the DeBakey and Kantrowitz ventricles, one of Kolff's hearts kept a calf alive for two days until blood clots formed.

Kolff must solve the clotting problem and perfect the valves that open and close the chambers before it is ready for use in people. Moreover, sensitive controls are needed for regulating blood flow in and out of the heart. With the aid of NASA's Lewis Research Center, Kolff and his colleagues are experimenting with a mechanical control system that would simulate the pumping pattern of the natural heart and help the artificial heart's four chambers work in harmony. "Naturally," says Kolff, "I believe that the artificial heart is the major priority for the immediate future."

What about the more distant future? The era of collaboration between doctor and engineer is just getting under way. Other parts of the body will be constructed. Researchers at Western Reserve and the Case Institute are working on computerized artificial arms. Researchers at Baylor are trying to devise synthetic skin to cover burns. And many technologists speak seriously of an artificial liver, stomach, intestine and pancreas, made of exotic plastics, metals and ingenuity. Indeed, miniaturized computers might even make possible a synthetic brain. "We cannot duplicate God's work," says one member of Kolff's team, "but we can come very close."

STUDY QUESTIONS

1. According to *Newsweek*, the newest weapons against illness and disease are the result of alliances between medicine and what two unlikely sources?

2. What old problems has the "New Medicine" left unsolved?

3. What does *Newsweek* predict will be medicine's "grand achievement"? Which artificial organ has already proven successful?

4. The *Newsweek* article is replete with technical jargon. Explain *cryosurgery, the life island, Max,* and *the laminar-flow principle.*

THE OBLIGATION
Rachel Carson TO ENDURE

Rachel Carson (1907–1964) was born in Springdale, Pennsyl-
vania and attended Pennsylvania College for Women and Johns
Hopkins University. She was awarded honorary doctorates by
Oberlin College, the Drexel Institute of Technology, and Smith
College. She received the George Westinghouse AAAS Science
Writing Award (1950), a Guggenheim Fellowship (1951), the
John Barroughs Medal (1952), and the Page-One Award (1952).
Her books include *Under the Sea Wind* (1941), *The Sea Around
Us* (1951), *The Edge of the Sea* (1956), and *Silent Spring*
(1962). *Silent Spring* became one of the most controversial books
of the past decade.

The history of life on earth has been a history of interaction
between living things and their surroundings. To a large extent, the
physical form and the habits of the earth's vegetation and its animal life
have been molded by the environment. Considering the whole span of
earthly time, the opposite effect, in which life actually modifies its
surroundings, has been relatively slight. Only within the moment of time
represented by the present century has one species—man—acquired significant power to alter the nature of his world.

During the past quarter century this power has not only increased
to one of disturbing magnitude but it has changed in character. The
most alarming of all man's assaults upon the environment is the contamination of air, earth, rivers, and sea with dangerous and even lethal
materials. This pollution is for the most part irrecoverable; the chain of
evil it initiates not only in the world that must support life but in living
tissues is for the most part irreversible. In this now universal contamination of the environment, chemicals are the sinister and little-
recognized partners of radiation in changing the very nature of the
world—the very nature of its life. Strontium 90, released through nuclear
explosions into the air, comes to earth in rain or drifts down as fallout,
lodges in soil, enters into the grass or corn or wheat grown there, and in
time takes up its abode in the bones of a human being, there to remain

until his death. Similarly, chemicals sprayed on croplands or forests or gardens lie long in soil, entering into living organisms, passing from one to another in a chain of poisoning and death. Or they pass mysteriously by underground streams until they emerge and, through the alchemy of air and sunlight, combine into new forms that kill vegetation, sicken cattle, and work unknown harm on those who drink from once pure wells. As Albert Schweitzer has said, "Man can hardly even recognize the devils of his own creation."

It took hundreds of millions of years to produce the life that now inhabits the earth—eons of time in which that developing and evolving and diversifying life reached a state of adjustment and balance with its surroundings. The environment, rigorously shaping and directing the life it supported, contained elements that were hostile as well as supporting. Certain rocks gave out dangerous radiation; even within the light of the sun, from which all life draws its energy, there were short-wave radiations with power to injure. Given time—time not in years but in millennia—life adjusts, and a balance has been reached. For time is the essential ingredient; but in the modern world there is no time.

The rapidity of change and the speed with which new situations are created follow the impetuous and heedless pace of man rather than the deliberate pace of nature. Radiation is no longer merely the background radiation of rocks, the bombardment of cosmic rays, the ultraviolet of the sun that have existed before there was any life on earth; radiation is now the unnatural creation of man's tampering with the atom. The chemicals to which life is asked to make its adjustment are no longer merely the calcium and silica and copper and all the rest of the minerals washed out of the rocks and carried in rivers to the sea; they are the synthetic creations of man's inventive mind, brewed in his laboratories, and having no counterparts in nature.

To adjust to these chemicals would require time on the scale that is nature's; it would require not merely the years of a man's life but the life of generations. And even this, were it by some miracle possible, would be futile, for the new chemicals come from our laboratories in an endless stream; almost five hundred annually find their way into actual use in the United States alone. The figure is staggering and its implications are not easily grasped—500 new chemicals to which the bodies of men and animals are required somehow to adapt each year, chemicals totally outside the limits of biologic experience.

Among them are many that are used in man's war against nature. Since the mid-1940's over 200 basic chemicals have been created for use in killing insects, weeds, rodents, and other organisms described in the modern vernacular as "pests"; and they are sold under several thousand different brand names.

These sprays, dusts, and aerosols are now applied almost universally to farms, gardens, forests, and homes—nonselective chemicals that have the power to kill every insect, the "good" and the "bad," to still the song of birds and the leaping of fish in the streams, to coat the leaves with a deadly film, and to linger on in soil—all this though the intended target may be only a few weeds or insects. Can anyone believe it is possible to lay down such a barrage of poisons on the surface of the earth without making it unfit for all life? They should not be called "insecticides," but "biocides."

The whole process of spraying seems caught up in an endless spiral. Since DDT was released for civilian use, a process of escalation has been going on in which ever more toxic materials must be found. This has happened because insects, in a triumphant vindication of Darwin's principle of the survival of the fittest, have evolved super races immune to the particular insecticide used, hence a deadlier one has always to be developed—and then a deadlier one than that. It has happened also because, for reasons to be described later, destructive insects often undergo a "flareback," or resurgence, after spraying, in numbers greater than before. Thus the chemical war is never won, and all life is caught in its violent crossfire.

Along with the possibility of the extinction of mankind by nuclear war, the central problem of our age has therefore become the contamination of man's total environment with such substances of incredible potential for harm—substances that accumulate in the tissues of plants and animals and even penetrate the germ cells to shatter or alter the very material of heredity upon which the shape of the future depends.

Some would-be architects of our future look toward a time when it will be possible to alter the human germ plasm by design. But we may easily be doing so now by inadvertence, for many chemicals, like radiation, bring about gene mutations. It is ironic to think that man might determine his own future by something so seemingly trivial as the choice of an insect spray.

All this has been risked—for what? Future historians may well be amazed by our distorted sense of proportion. How could intelligent beings seek to control a few unwanted species by a method that contaminated environment and brought the threat of disease and death even to their own kind? Yet this is precisely what we have done. We have done it, moreover, for reasons that collapse the moment we examine them. We are told that the enormous and expanding use of pesticides is necessary to maintain farm production. Yet is our real problem not one of *overproduction?* Our farms, despite measures to remove acreages from production and to pay farmers *not* to produce, have yielded such a staggering excess of crops that the American taxpayer in 1962 is paying out more than one billion dollars a year as the total carrying cost of the surplus-food storage program. And is the situation helped when one branch of the Agriculture Department tries to reduce production while another states, as it did in 1958, "It is believed generally that reduction of crop acreages under provisions of the Soil Bank will stimulate interest in use of chemicals to obtain maximum production on the land retained in crops."

All this is not to say there is no insect problem and no need of control. I am saying, rather, that control must be geared to realities, not to mythical situations, and that the methods employed must be such that they do not destroy us along with the insects.

The problem whose attempted solution has brought such a train of disaster in its wake is an accompaniment of our modern way of life. Long before the age of man, insects inhabited the earth—a group of extraordinarily varied and adaptable beings. Over the course of time since man's advent, a small percentage of the more than half a million species of insects have come into conflict with human welfare in two principal ways: as competitors for the food supply and as carriers of human disease.

Disease-carrying insects become important where human beings are crowded together, especially under conditions where sanitation is poor, as in time of natural disaster or war or in situations of extreme poverty and deprivation. Then control of some sort becomes necessary. It is a sobering fact, however, as we shall presently see, that the method of massive chemical control has had only limited success, and also threatens to worsen the very conditions it is intended to curb.

Under primitive agricultural conditions the farmer had few insect problems. These arose with the intensification of agriculture—the devotion of immense acreages to a single crop. Such a system set the stage for explosive increases in specific insect populations. Single-crop farming does not take advantage of the principles by which nature works; it is agriculture as an engineer might conceive it to be. Nature has introduced great variety into the landscape, but man has displayed a passion for simplifying it. Thus he undoes the built-in checks and balances by which nature holds the species within bounds. One important natural check is a limit on the amount of suitable habitat for each species. Obviously then, an insect that lives on wheat can build up its population to much higher levels on a farm devoted to wheat than on one in which wheat is intermingled with other crops to which the insect is not adapted.

The same thing happens in other situations. A generation or more ago, the towns of large areas of the United States lined their streets with the noble elm tree. Now the beauty they hopefully created is threatened with complete destruction as disease sweeps through the elms, carried by a beetle that would have only limited chance to build up large populations and to spread from tree to tree if the elms were only occasional trees in a richly diversified planting.

Another factor in the modern insect problem is one that must be viewed against a background of geologic and human history: the spreading of thousands of different kinds of organisms from their native homes to invade new territories. This worldwide migration has been studied and graphically described by the British ecologist Charles Elton in his recent book *The Ecology of Invasions.* During the Cretaceous Period, some hundred million years ago, flooding seas cut many land bridges between continents and living things found themselves confined in what Elton calls "colossal separate nature reserves." There, isolated from others of their kind, they developed many new species. When some of the land masses were joined again, about 15 million years ago, these species began to move out into new territories—a movement that is not only still in progress but is now receiving considerable assistance from man.

The importation of plants is the primary agent in the modern spread of species, for animals have almost invariably gone along with the plants, quarantine being a comparatively recent and not completely effective innovation. The United States Office of Plant Introduction alone has introduced almost 200,000 species and varieties of plants from all over the world. Nearly half of the 180 or so major insect enemies of plants in the United States are accidental imports from abroad, and most of them have come as hitchhikers on plants.

In new territory, out of reach of the restraining hand of the natural enemies that kept down its numbers in its native land, an invading plant or animal is able to become enormously abundant. Thus it is no accident that our most troublesome insects are introduced species.

These invasions, both the naturally occurring and those dependent on human assistance, are likely to continue indefinitely. Quarantine and massive chemical campaigns are only extremely expensive ways of buying time. We are faced, according to Dr. Elton, "with a life-and-death need not just to find new technological means of suppressing this plant or that animal"; instead we need the basic knowledge of animal populations and their relations to their surroundings that will "promote an even balance and damp down the explosive power of outbreaks and new invasions."

Much of the necessary knowledge is now available but we do not use it. We train ecologists in our universities and even employ them in our governmental agencies but we seldom take their advice. We allow the chemical death rain to fall as though there were no alternative, whereas in fact there are many, and our ingenuity could soon discover many more if given opportunity.

Have we fallen into a mesmerized state that makes us accept as inevitable that which is inferior or detrimental, as though having lost the will or the vision to demand that which is good? Such thinking, in the words of the ecologist Paul Shepard, "idealizes life with only its head out of water, inches above the limits of toleration of the corruption of its own environment . . . Why should we tolerate a diet of weak poisons, a home in insipid surroundings, a circle of acquaintances who are not quite our enemies, the noise of motors with just enough relief to prevent insanity? Who would want to live in a world which is just not quite fatal?"

Yet such a world is pressed upon us. The crusade to create a chemically sterile, insect-free world seems to have engendered a fanatic zeal on the part of many specialists and most of the so-called control agencies. On every hand there is evidence that those engaged in spraying operations exercise a ruthless power. "The regulatory entomologists . . . function as prosecutor, judge and jury, tax assessor and collector and sheriff to enforce their own orders," said Connecticut entomologist Neely Turner. The most flagrant abuses go unchecked in both state and federal agencies.

It is not my contention that chemical insecticides must never be used. I do contend that we have put poisonous and biologically potent chemicals indiscriminately into the hands of persons largely or wholly ignorant of their potentials for harm. We have subjected enormous numbers of people to contact with these poisons, without their consent and often without their knowledge. If the Bill of Rights contains no guarantee that a citizen shall be secure against lethal poisons distributed either by private individuals or by public officials, it is surely only because our forefathers, despite their considerable wisdom and foresight, could conceive of no such problem.

I contend, furthermore, that we have allowed these chemicals to be used with little or no advance investigation of their effect on soil, water, wildlife, and man himself. Future generations are unlikely to condone our lack of prudent concern for the integrity of the natural world that supports all life.

There is still very limited awareness of the nature of the threat. This is an era of specialists, each of whom sees his own problem and is unaware of or intolerant of the larger frame into which it fits. It is also an era dominated by industry, in which the right to make a dollar at whatever cost is seldom challenged. When the public protests, confronted with some obvious evidence of damaging results of pesticide applications, it is fed little tranquilizing pills of half truth. We urgently need an end to these false assurances, to the sugar coating of unpalatable facts. It is the public that is being asked to assume the risks that the insect controllers calculate. The public must decide whether it wishes to continue on the present road, and it can do so only when in full possession of the facts. In the words of Jean Rostand, "The obligation to endure gives us the right to know."

STUDY QUESTIONS

1. What does Rachel Carson feel is the central problem of our age?
2. According to Miss Carson, how has the history of man's relationship to his environment changed in the twentieth century?
3. How has the chemical contamination of man's environment upset the balance of nature?
4. In what way is man's experimenting with the atom "unnatural"?
5. How has Darwin's principle of the survival of the fittest escalated the production of toxic materials?
6. What two factors have increased the effectiveness of insect invasions?

USING A PLAGUE
Loren Eiseley   **TO FIGHT A PLAGUE**

Loren Eiseley (1907–   ) was born in Lincoln, Nebraska. He received his A.B. (1933) from the University of Nebraska, and his A.M. (1935) and Ph.D. (1937) from the University of Pennsylvania. He taught at the University of Kansas and Oberlin College before returning, in 1947, to the University of Pennsylvania where he is now University Professor in anthropology and the history of science and head of the Department of the History and Philosophy of Science. A Guggenheim fellow, he has published widely in both popular periodicals and learned journals. *Darwin's Century* was given the Phi Beta Kappa science award in 1959, and *The Firmament of Time* (1960) received the John Barroughs medal and the Lecomte de Nouy (Novy) award. His other books include *The Immense Journey* (1951) and *Francis Bacon and the Modern Temper* (1952).

A few days ago I stood amidst the marshes of a well-known wildlife refuge. As I studied a group of herons through my glasses, there floated

A review of *Silent Spring* by Rachel Carson. Reprinted by permission of the author. First published in *The Saturday Review*. Copyright © 1962.

by the margin of my vision the soapy, unsightly froth of a detergent discharged into the slough's backwaters from some source upstream. Here nature, at first glance, seemed green and uncontaminated. As I left, however, I could not help wondering how long it would be before seeping industrial wastes destroyed the water-life on which those birds subsisted—how long it would be before poisonous and vacant mudflats had replaced the chirping frogs and waving cattails I loved to visit. I thought also of a sparkling stream in the Middle West in which, as a small boy, I used to catch sunfish, but which today is a muddy, lifeless treacle filled with oil from a nearby pumping station. No living thing now haunts its polluted waters.

These two episodes out of my own experience are trifling, however, compared with that virulent facet of man's activities treated in Rachel Carson's latest book. It is a devastating, heavily documented, relentless attack upon human carelessness, greed, and irresponsibility—an irresponsibility that has let loose upon man and the countryside a flood of dangerous chemicals in a situation which, as Miss Carson states, is without parallel in medical history. "No one," she adds, "yet knows what the ultimate consequences may be."

Silent Spring is her account of those floods of insecticides and well-intentioned protective devices which have indiscriminately slaughtered our wildlife of both forest and stream. Such ill-considered activities break the necessary food chains of nature and destroy the livelihood of creatures not even directly affected by the pesticides. The water run-off from agricultural and forested areas carries to our major rivers and to the seas chemicals which may then impregnate the food we eat. We have no assurance that we are not introducing into nature heavy concentrates of non-natural substances whose effects are potentially as dangerous as those that came to light in the dramatic medical episode that shocked the public in recent weeks. I refer, of course, to the foetal monsters produced by the sleep drug Thalidomide. Imperfect though the present legal controls in the field of direct medical experiment may be, they are less inadequate than in the domain of agricultural chemistry, where aerial spraying is cascading a rain of poison over field and farmland.

D'Arcy Thompson, the great British biologist of the late nineteenth century, commented astutely in 1897 that the increasing tempo of human cultural evolution produces a kind of evolution of chance itself—an increasing dissonance and complexity of change beyond what one finds in the world before man came. Though this evolution of chance arises within the human domain, it does not long remain confined to it. Instead, the erratic and growingly unpredictable fantasies created in the human mind invade nature itself. Tremendous agricultural productivity is correlated with the insatiable demands of ever-growing populations.

Wastes in the air and wastes polluting the continental arteries increasingly disrupt the nature that we have taken for granted since the first
simple hunters wandered out of the snowy winter of the Ice Age and
learned to live in cities.

Man's sanitary engineering, in western civilization, never
amounted to much until the middle phase of the industrial revolution
and the discovery of the relation of bacteria to disease. Now it is
apparent that man must learn to handle more wisely the products of his
own aspiring chemistry. He is faced with the prospect of learning to be a
creative god in nature without, at the same time, destroying his surroundings and himself through thoughtless indifference to the old green
world out of which he has so recently emerged and to which (though he
forgets) he is as indissolubly bound in his own way as the herons that
stalked before my field glasses.

Essentially there are two ways of approaching the control of noxious insects: a natural and a chemical means. I am deliberately confining
my remarks here, not to the effect of man's accidental industrial wastes
upon his environment—a subject worthy of attention in itself—but to his
deliberate and largely post-World War II use of peculiar carbon compounds in crop dusting and other forms of insect control. DDT is an
excellent and spectacular example. With the passage of time the chemical industries have pressed more and more such substances upon the
receptive public. Extensive research has been carried on in this field,
frequently with results, at first glance, of an impressive character. That
there may be other results, less favorable when viewed over a longer
time span, is not always so well publicized.

The reason that Rachel Carson has chosen the more conservative
biological approach to the problem of insect control lies in the following
facts: Ill or uncontrolled spraying with deadly chemicals destroys beneficial as well as undesirable forms of life; furthermore, the poisonous
residues may and do find their way into human food. Secondly, because
insect generations are short and their numbers large, they rapidly become immune to the poisons that originally decimated them. By contrast, birds and the higher mammals, including man, cannot rapidly
develop this selective immunity. They are eventually threatened not
only by tougher and more formidable insect disease-carriers, but also by
progressively dangerous chemicals devised against the mounting numbers of insects that refuse to succumb but whose natural enemies—the
birds and fish—are being slaughtered in growing numbers by these same
chemicals. The normal balance of life is thus increasingly disrupted.
Man is whetting the cutting edge of natural selection, but its edge is
turned against himself and his allies in the animal world.

In case after case, Miss Carson succeeds in documenting her thesis
with complete adequacy. It is not pleasant to learn of the casual spray-

ing of the landscape with chemicals capable of mutagenic effects and regarded by some authorities as representing as great a menace as high levels of radiation. Nor is it reassuring to read that the hydrocarbons have an affinity for mammalian germ cells. At present there is no law on the statute books that requires manufacturers to demonstrate the genetic effects, as distinguished from the toxicity, of their concoctions. Nor is there any way of controlling what the average uninformed farmer may do with his insecticides. An equally ill-educated and impatient public wants its weeds, gnats, and mosquitoes eliminated in one fell blow. It is not sophisticated enough to trouble over the looming demise of our beautiful national bird, the bald eagle, nor to connect the return of many supposedly eliminated pests with the fact that the newer generation may be able to flourish in a sack of DDT and thus be twice as formidable.

The biological controls which Miss Carson favors, along with other informed biologists, are not just more careful and discreet use of pesticides, but also such clever natural manipulations as the release of sterilized screw worm flies, causing a greater reduction in the population of this parasite than any insecticide would have achieved. Successful experiments such as this depend upon precise knowledge of the life history of an organism. They strike directly at the heart of the problem. They do not leave poisonous residues or resistant life-strains, nor do they result in the mass killing that frequently destroys valuable food chains on which even man is in the long run dependent.

All of these facts Rachel Carson has set forth sensibly in the quiet, rational prose for which she is famous. If her present book does not possess the beauty of *The Sea Around Us*, it is because she has courageously chosen, at the height of her powers, to educate us upon a sad, an unpleasant, an unbeautiful topic, and one of our own making. *Silent Spring* should be read by every American who does not want it to be the epitaph of a world not very far beyond us in time.

STUDY QUESTIONS

1. What episodes from his own experience does Eiseley use in support of Miss Carson's thesis?
2. What two basic means of approaching the control of noxious insects are open to men?
3. According to Eiseley, what facts led Miss Carson to choose the more conservative of these two approaches?

William J. Darby   SILENCE, MISS CARSON

William J. Darby (1913–   ) was born in Galloway, Arkansas, and received his B.S. (1936) and M.D. (1937) from the University of Arkansas and his M.S. (1941) and Ph.D. (1942) from the University of Michigan. He is now head of the Department of Biochemistry and director of the Division of Nutrition, School of Medicine, at Vanderbilt University. He has served with the National Research Council and the World Health Organization. Darby is coauthor of *Nutrition and Diet in Health and Disease* and codiscoverer of vitamin M and the activity of pteroylglutamic acid in sprue.

Silent Spring starts with a bit of dramatic description of a situation which the author then acknowledges does not actually exist. It then orients the reader to its subject matter by stating that "only within . . . the present century has man . . . acquired significant power to alter the nature of his world." It identifies as irrecoverable and "for the most part irreversible" the effects of "this now universal contamination of the environment (in which) chemicals are the sinister and little recognized partners of radiation in changing the very nature of the world, the very nature of life itself." Man has, according to Miss Carson, now upset that ideal state of "adjustment and balance" of life on this planet through "synthetic creations of man's inventive mind, brewed in his laboratory, and having no counterpart in nature." These products, the reader is told, are "staggering in number," have "power to kill," have "incredible potential for harm," represent a "train of disaster," result in a "chemical death rain," and are being used with "little or no advance investigation of their effect on soil, water, wildlife, and man himself." She further warns the reader that all of these sinister chemicals will not only extinguish plant life, wild life, aquatic life, and man, but they will produce cancer, leukemia, sterility, and cellular mutations.

There are 297 pages devoted to reiteration of these views. There then follows a 55-page "list of principal sources" designed to impress the reader with the extent of the support for Miss Carson's views. This list uses an extender and is artificially colored and flavored. Its apparent bulk is made one third greater through devoting a line of type to identify each page on which a source bears, and by repeating in full the title of each source in relation to recurrent pages. Its bulk will appeal to those readers who are as uncritical as the author, or to those who find the flavor of her product to their taste. These consumers will include the organic gardeners, the antifluoride leaguers, the worshipers of "natural foods," those who cling to the philosophy of a vital principle, and pseudo-scientists and faddists.

The flavor of this product is indicated in part by the source list. She refers frequently to testimony given at 1950, 1951, and 1952 Congressional hearings, seldom to later years, and to the opinions of Morton S. Siskind and W. C. Hueper.

The author ignores the sound appraisals of such responsible, broadly knowledgeable scientists as the President of the National Academy of Sciences, the members of the President's Scientific Advisory Committee, the Presidents of the Rockefeller Foundation and Nutrition Foundation, the several committees of the National Academy of Sciences-National Research Council (including the Food and Nutrition Board, the Agricultural Board, the Food Protection Committee) who have long given thoughtful study to these questions, and the special advisory committees appointed by the governors of California and Wisconsin. The latter committees were chaired by two distinguished scientist-presidents of universities, Dr. Emil Mrak and the late Dr. Conrad A. Elvehjem.

All of these groups of scientists have recognized the essentiality of use of agricultural chemicals to produce the food required by the expanding world population and to sustain an acceptable standard of living and health. They have recognized the safety of proper use of agricultural chemicals and, indeed, the benefits to the consumer which accrue from their proper use in food and agricultural production.

Miss Carson's book adds no new factual material not already known to such serious scientists as those concerned with these developments, nor does it include information essential for the reader to interpret the knowledge. It does confuse the information and so mix it with her opinions that the uninitiated reader is unable to sort fact from fancy. In view of the mature, responsible attention which this whole subject receives from able, qualified scientific groups such as those identified in the foregoing (and whom Miss Carson chooses to ignore); in view of her scientific qualifications in contrast to those of our distinguished scientific leaders and statesmen, this book should be ignored.

Logically, it should be possible to terminate this review here. Unfortunately, however, this book will have wide circulation on one of the standard subscription lists. It is doubtful that many readers can bear to wade through its high-pitched sequences of anxieties. It is likely to be perused uncritically, to be regarded by the layman as authoritative (which it is not), and to arouse in him manifestations of anxieties and psychoneuroses exhibited by some of the subjects cited by the author in the chapter "The Human Price." Indeed, the author's efforts at appraising psychologic evidence concerning the effects of substances reveal a remarkable lack of competence as a psychiatrist, even as great a lack in the area of toxicology or even knowledge of existing regulatory controls. The obvious effect of all of this on the reader will be to aggravate unjustifiably his own neurotic anxiety.

Her thesis is revealed by the dedicatory quotations: "Man has lost the capacity to foresee and to forestall. He will end by destroying the earth." (Albert Schweitzer) "Our approach to nature is to beat it into submission. We would stand a better chance of survival if we accommodated ourselves to this planet and viewed it appreciatively instead of skeptically and dictatorially." (E. B. White)

Such a passive attitude as the latter coupled with such pessimistic (and to this reviewer, unacceptable) philosophy as the former, means the end of all human progress, reversion to a passive social state devoid of technology, scientific medicine, agriculture, sanitation, or education. It means disease, epidemics, starvation, misery, and suffering incomparable and intolerable to modern man. Indeed, social, educational, and scientific development is prefaced on the conviction that man's lot will be and is being improved by greater understanding of and thereby increased ability to control or mold those forces responsible for man's suffering, misery, and deprivation.

The author's motivation is not quite so evident, but the emotional call to write the book is revealed by her acknowledgment that "In a letter written in January 1958, Olga Owens Huckins told me of her own bitter experience of a small world made lifeless, and so brought my attention sharply back to a problem with which I had long been concerned. I then realized *I must write this book*" (italics are the reviewer's).

So impelled, Miss Carson has effectively used several literary devices to present her thesis and make it appear to be a widely held scientific one. She "name-drops" by quoting or referring to renowned scientists out of context. A statement divorced from its original meaning is then approximated to an opinion of the author or else to a question posed by her with an implied answer. The reader is led to conclude thereby that the authority mentioned is in accord with the author's position. Nobel prize winners are recognized as especially useful names for such a purpose.

Another device used is that of confusion of the reader with (to him) unintelligible scientific jargon or irrelevant discussions of cellular processes.

Miss Carson's failure to distinguish between the occupational and residue hazards is common to almost all popular writers on this subject. The occupational hazard associated with the manufacture and application of agricultural chemicals is similar to that of other work and can, should be, and is being reduced. That accidents have occurred is well known, but this is no more reason to ban useful chemicals than is the lamentable occurrence of preventable automobile or airplane accidents reason to ban these modern modes of transportation. Despite all of the implications of harm from residues on foods, Miss Carson has not produced one single example of injury resulting to man from these residues.

Miss Carson is infatuated with biologic control and the balance of nature. Despite her statement that the really effective control of insects is that applied by nature, one must observe that the very ineffectiveness of such control is the raison d'être of chemical pesticides.

She commits the scientifically indefensible fallacy of considering that any substance which in any quantity is toxic must per se be a poison. By such a definition almost everything—water, salt, sugar, amino acids, minerals, vitamins A or D, etc.—is a poison. She gives the reader a mistaken concept of tolerances. Tolerances are not ill-defined levels of maximum quantities which can be ingested without acute harm. They are minimum amounts of a substance which should exist when the chemical has been employed in good and proper beneficial practice. They are based on extensive use data and toxicologic testing in animals and frequently metabolic studies in man. They include a very wide margin of safety, usually being set at 100 times the *minimum* amount of the substance which induces any physiologic effect in the most sensitive of at least two species of animals for lifetime or two-to four-year periods.

The benefit of use of chemicals, charges Miss Carson, is for the producer. She ignores the requirement under the Miller bill that a chemical must be *effective,* which means benefit to the consumer. She fails to recognize that "the consumer" includes the producer, farmer, wholesaler, retailer, equipment manufacturer, their families, and even the scientists who evaluate the chemicals. The toxicologists in industry, in the Food and Drug Administration, in our universities and research institutes have, as consumers, equal stake in protecting the nation's health as does Miss Carson—and I believe, are better qualified to assume this protection.

Her ignorance or bias on some of the considerations throws doubt on her competence to judge policy. For example, she indicates that it is neither wise nor responsible to use pesticides in the control of insect-borne diseases. The July–August 1962 *World Health* (WHO publication) reports that a malaria eradication program in Mexico has since 1957 reduced the malaria area from 978,185 sq. km. with 18 million inhabitants to 224,500 sq. km. with 1.5 million inhabitants. "In most areas the simple technique of indoor spraying of houses proved effective . . ."; where bedbugs were resistant to DDT, an insecticide mixture was successfully used. "As a result of the campaign, the Mexican Government is expanding its agricultural programme, distributing land, and undertaking irrigation and hydroelectric schemes." It is most doubtful that Miss Carson really is ignorant of these and other facts which any objective appraisal of this subject demands. Instead, it seems that a call to write a book has completely outweighed any semblance of scientific objectivity.

The public may be misled by this book. If it stimulates the public to press for unwise and ill-conceived restrictions on the production, use, or development of new chemicals, it will be the consumer who suffers. If, on the other hand, it inspires some users to read and heed labels more carefully, it may aid in the large educational effort in which industry, government, colleges, and many other groups are engaged (despite Miss Carson's implication that they are not.)

The responsible scientist should read this book to understand the ignorance of those writing on the subject and the educational task which lies ahead.

STUDY QUESTIONS

1. What does Darby seek to accomplish by the numerous quotations in the first paragraph?
2. What objections does he raise to Miss Carson's bibliography?
3. What significance does Darby find in Miss Carson's reference to testimony given in 1950–1952 Congressional hearings? Is this significance explicit or implicit?
4. What effect does Darby feel *Silent Spring* will have on the layman?
5. How does Darby explain Miss Carson's having ignored the statistics he presents?

SCIENCE HAS SPOILED
Philip Wylie   **MY SUPPER**

Philip Wylie (1902–   ) was born in Beverly, Massachusetts. He was a student at Princeton from 1920 to 1923, and received an honorary Litt. D. from the University of Miami, Florida. Wylie has been on the *New Yorker* staff, written screenplays for Paramount and Metro-Goldwyn-Mayer, and contributed to *Redbook*, the *Saturday Evening Post, Reader's Digest,* and *Look*. He is the recipient of a Freedom Foundation medal (1953). His books include *Heavy Laden* (1928), *Gladiator* (1930), *Generation of Vipers* (1942), *An Essay in Morals* (1947), *The Answer* (1956), and *The Innocent Ambassadors* (1957). *Generation of Vipers* includes the famous discussion of "Moms."

I am a fan for Science. My education is scientific and I have, in one field, contributed a monograph to a scientific journal. Science, to my mind, is applied honesty, the one reliable means we have to find out truth. That is why, when error is committed in the name of Science, I feel the way a man would if his favorite uncle had taken to drink.

Over the years, I have come to feel that way about what science has done to food. I agree that America can set as good a table as any nation in the world. I agree that our food is nutritious and that the diet of most of us is well-balanced. What America eats is handsomely packaged; it is usually clean and pure; it is excellently preserved. The only trouble with it is this: year by year it grows less good to eat. It appeals increasingly to the eye. But who eats with his eyes? Almost everything used to taste better when I was a kid. For quite a long time I thought that observation was merely another index of advancing age. But some years ago I married a girl whose mother is an expert cook of the kind called "old-fashioned." This gifted woman's daughter (my wife) was taught her mother's venerable skills. The mother lives in the country and still plants an old-fashioned garden. She still buys dairy products from the neighbors and, in so far as possible, she uses the same materials her mother and grandmother did—to prepare meals that are superior. They are just as good, in this Year of Grace, as I recall them from my courtship. After eating for a while at the table of my mother-in-law, it is sad to go back to eating with my friends—even the alleged "good cooks" among them. And it is a gruesome experience to have meals at the best big-city restaurants.

Take cheese, for instance. Here and there, in big cities, small stores and delicatessens specialize in cheese. At such places, one can buy at least some of the first-rate cheeses that we used to eat—such as those we had with pie and in macaroni. The latter were sharp but not too sharp. They were a little crumbly. We called them American cheeses, or even rat cheese; actually, they were Cheddars. Long ago, this cheese began to be supplanted by a material called "cheese foods." Some cheese foods and "processed" cheese are fairly edible; but not one comes within miles of the old kinds—for flavor.

A grocer used to be very fussy about his cheese. Cheddar was made and sold by hundreds of little factories. Representatives of the factories had particular customers, and cheese was prepared by hand to suit the grocers, who knew precisely what their patrons wanted in rat cheese, pie cheese, American and other cheeses. Some liked them sharper; some liked them yellower; some liked anise seeds in cheese, or caraway.

What happened? Science—or what is called science—stepped in. The old-fashioned cheeses didn't ship well enough. They crumbled, became moldy, dried out. "Scientific" tests disclosed that a great majority of the people will buy a less-good-tasting cheese if that's all they can get. "Scientific marketing" then took effect. Its motto is "Give the people the least quality they'll stand for." In food, as in many other things, the "scientific marketers" regard quality as secondary so long as they can sell most persons anyhow; what they are after is "durability" or "shippability."

It is not possible to make the very best cheese in vast quantities at a low average cost. "Scientific sampling" got in its statistically nasty work. It was found that the largest number of people will buy something that is bland and rather tasteless. Those who prefer a product of a pronounced and individualistic flavor have a variety of preferences. Nobody is altogether pleased by bland foodstuff, in other words; but nobody is very violently put off. The result is that a "reason" has been found for turning out zillions of packages of something that will "do" for nearly all and isn't even imagined to be superlatively good by a single soul!

Economics entered. It is possible to turn out in quantity a bland, impersonal, practically imperishable substance more or less resembling, say, cheese—at lower cost than cheese. Chain groceries shut out the independent stores and "standardization" became a principal means of cutting costs.

Imitations also came into the cheese business. There are American duplications of most of the celebrated European cheeses, mass-produced and cheaper by far than the imports. They would cause European foodlovers to gag or guffaw—but generally the imitations are all that's available in the supermarkets. People buy them and eat them.

Perhaps you don't like cheese—so the fact that decent cheese is hardly ever served in America any more, or used in cooking, doesn't matter to you. Well, take bread. There has been (and still is) something of a hullabaloo about bread. In fact, in the last few years, a few big bakeries have taken to making a fairly good imitation of real bread. It costs much more than what is nowadays called bread, but it is edible. Most persons, however, now eat as "bread" a substance so full of chemicals and so barren of cereals that it approaches a synthetic.

Most bakers are interested mainly in how a loaf of bread looks. They are concerned with how little stuff they can put in it—to get how much money. They are deeply interested in using chemicals that will keep bread from molding, make it seem "fresh" for the longest possible time, and so render it marketable and shippable. They have been at this monkeyshine for a generation. Today a loaf of "bread" looks deceptively real; but it is made from heaven knows what and it resembles, as food, a solidified bubble bath. Some months ago I bought a loaf of the stuff and, experimentally, began pressing it together, like an accordion. With a little effort, I squeezed the whole loaf to a length of about one inch!

Yesterday, at the home of my mother-in-law, I ate with country-churned butter and home-canned wild strawberry jam several slices of actual bread, the same thing we used to have every day at home. People who have eaten actual bread will know what I mean. They will know that the material commonly called bread is not even related to real bread, except in name.

II

For years, I couldn't figure out what had happened to vegetables. I knew, of course, that most vegetables, to be enjoyed in their full deliciousness, must be picked fresh and cooked at once. I knew that vegetables cannot be overcooked and remain even edible, in the best sense. They cannot stand on the stove. That set of facts makes it impossible, of course, for any American restaurant—or, indeed, any city-dweller separated from supply by more than a few hours—to have decent fresh vegetables. The Parisians managed by getting their vegetables picked at dawn and rushed in farmers' carts to market, where no middleman or marketman delays produce on its way to the pot.

Our vegetables, however, come to us through a long chain of command. There are merchants of several sorts—wholesalers before the retailers, commission men, and so on—with the result that what were once edible products become, in transit, mere wilted leaves and withered tubers.

Homes and restaurants do what they can with this stuff—which my mother-in-law would discard on the spot. I have long thought that the famed blindfold test for cigarettes should be applied to city vegetables. For I am sure that if you puréed them and ate them blindfolded, you couldn't tell the beans from the peas, the turnips from the squash, the Brussels sprouts from the broccoli.

It is only lately that I have found how much science has had to do with this reduction of noble victuals to pottage. Here the science of genetics is involved. Agronomists and the like have taken to breeding all sorts of vegetables and fruits—changing their original nature. This sounds wonderful and often is insane. For the scientists have not as a rule taken any interest whatsoever in the taste of the things they've tampered with!

What they've done is to develop "improved" strains of things for every purpose but eating. They work out, say, peas that will ripen all at once. The farmer can then harvest his peas and thresh them and be done with them. It is extremely profitable because it is efficient. What matter if such peas taste like boiled paper wads?

Geneticists have gone crazy over such "opportunities." They've developed string beans that are straight instead of curved, and all one length. This makes them easier to pack in cans, even if, when eating them, you can't tell them from tender string. Ripening time and identity of size and shape are, nowadays, more important in carrots than the fact that they taste like carrots. Personally, I don't care if they hybridize onions till they are big as your head and come up through the snow; but, in doing so, they are producing onions that only vaguely and feebly remind you of onions. We are getting some varieties, in fact, that have less flavor than the water off last week's leeks. Yet, if people don't eat onions because they taste like onions, what in the name of Luther Burbank do they eat them for?

The women's magazines are about one third dedicated to clothes, one third to mild comment on sex, and the other third to recipes and pictures of handsome salads, desserts, and main courses. "Institutes" exist to experiment and tell housewives how to cook attractive meals and how to turn leftovers into works of art. The food thus pictured looks like famous paintings of still life. The only trouble is it's tasteless. It leaves appetite unquenched and merely serves to stave off famine.

I wonder if this blandness of our diet doesn't explain why so many of us are overweight and even dangerously so. When things had flavor, we knew what we were eating all the while—and it satisfied us. A teaspoonful of my mother-in-law's wild strawberry jam will not just provide a gastronome's ecstasy: it will entirely satisfy your jam desire. But, of the average tinned or glass-packed strawberry jam, you need half a cupful to get the idea of what you're eating. A slice of my mother-in-law's apple pie will satiate you far better than a whole bakery pie.

That thought is worthy of investigation—of genuine scientific investigation. It is merely a hypothesis, so far, and my own. But people—and their ancestors—have been eating according to flavor for upwards of a billion years. The need to satisfy the sense of taste may be innate and important. When food is merely a pretty cascade of viands, with the texture of boiled cardboard and the flavor of library paste, it may be the instinct of *genus homo* to go on eating in the unconscious hope of finally satisfying the ageless craving of the frustrated taste buds. In the days when good-tasting food was the rule in the American home, obesity wasn't such a national curse.

How can you feel you've eaten if you haven't tasted, and fully enjoyed tasting? Why (since science is ever so ready to answer the beck and call of mankind) don't people who want to reduce merely give up eating and get the nourishment they must have in measured doses shot into their arms at hospitals? One ready answer to that question suggests that my theory of overeating is sound: people like to taste! In eating, they try to satisfy that like.

The scientific war against deliciousness has been stepped up enormously in the last decade. Some infernal genius found a way to make biscuit batter keep. Housewives began to buy this premixed stuff. It saved work, of course. But any normally intelligent person can learn, in a short period, how to prepare superb baking powder biscuits. I can make better biscuits, myself, than can be made from patent batters. Yet soon after this fiasco became an American staple, it was discovered that a half-baked substitute for all sorts of breads, pastries, rolls, and the like could be mass-manufactured, frozen—and sold for polishing off in the home oven. None of these two-stage creations is as good as even a fair sample of the thing it imitates. A man of taste, who had eaten one of my wife's cinnamon buns, might use the pre-mixed sort to throw at starlings —but not to eat! Cake mixes, too, come ready-prepared—like cement and not much better-tasting compared with true cake.

It is, however, "deep-freezing" that has really rung down the curtain on American cookery. Nothing is improved by the process. I have yet to taste a deep-frozen victual that measures up, in flavor, to the fresh, unfrosted original. And most foods, cooked or uncooked, are destroyed in the deep freeze for all people of sense and sensibility. Vegetables with crisp and crackling texture emerge as mush, slippery and stringy as hair nets simmered in Vaseline. The essential oils that make peas peas—and cabbage cabbage—must undergo fission and fusion in freezers. Anyhow, they vanish. Some meats turn to leather. Others to wood pulp. Everything, pretty much, tastes like the mosses of tundra, dug up in midwinter. Even the appearance changes, oftentimes. Handsome comestibles you put down in the summer come out looking very much like the corpses of woolly mammoths recovered from the last Ice Age.

Of course, all this scientific "food handling" tends to save money. It certainly preserves food longer. It reduces work at home. But these facts, and especially the last, imply that the first purpose of living is to avoid work—at home, anyhow.

Without thinking, we are making an important confession about ourselves as a nation. We are abandoning quality—even, to some extent, the quality of people. The "best" is becoming too good for us. We are suckling ourselves on machine-made mediocrity. It is bad for our souls, our minds, and our digestion. It is the way our wiser and calmer forebears fed, not people, but hogs: as much as possible and as fast as possible, with no standard of quality.

The Germans say, "*Mann ist was er isst*—Man is what he eats." If this be true, the people of the U.S.A. are well on their way to becoming a faceless mob of mediocrities, of robots. And if we apply to other attributes the criteria we apply these days to appetite, that is what would happen! We would not want bright children any more; we'd merely want them to look bright—and get through school fast. We wouldn't be interested in beautiful women—just a good paint job. And we'd be opposed to the most precious quality of man: his individuality, his differentness from the mob.

There are some people—sociologists and psychologists among them—who say that is exactly what we Americans are doing, are becoming. Mass man, they say, is on the increase. Conformity, standardization, similarity—all on a cheap and vulgar level—are replacing the great American ideas of colorful liberty and dignified individualism. If this is so, the process may well begin, like most human behavior, in the home—in those homes where a good meal has been replaced by something-to-eat-in-a-hurry. By something not very good to eat, prepared by a mother without very much to do, for a family that doesn't feel it amounts to much anyhow.

I call, here, for rebellion.

STUDY QUESTIONS

1. How does Wylie define *science?*
2. Why does he put quotation marks around "scientific" tests, "scientific marketing," and "scientific sampling"?
3. To what does Wylie attribute the changes in cheese and bread? The "improvements" in vegetables? The deep-freezing of a variety of foods?
4. With what connotation does Wylie use "pottage"?
5. What hypothesis does Wylie advance to explain overweight Americans?

SECTION 4 | LANGUAGE

"The Soul of Wit"

POLITICS AND

George Orwell **THE ENGLISH LANGUAGE**

George Orwell (1903–1950) was the pen name of Eric Blair, who was born in Bengal, India. He graduated from Eton College, served with the Indian Imperial Police in Burma from 1922 to 1927, and then returned to England to begin his career as a writer. His works include *Burmese Days* (1934), *Homage to Catalonia* (1936), *Dickens, Dali and Others* (1946), and *Shooting an Elephant* (1950). However, his fame is primarily the result of *Animal Farm* (1946), a classic novel of social protest, and *1984* (1949), one of the most famous modern satires.

Most people who bother with the matter at all would admit that the English language is in a bad way, but it is generally assumed that we cannot by conscious action do anything about it. Our civilization is decadent and our language—so the argument runs—must inevitably share in the general collapse. It follows that any struggle against the abuse of language is a sentimental archaism, like preferring candles to electric light or hansom cabs to aeroplanes. Underneath this lies the half-conscious belief that language is a natural growth and not an instrument which we shape for our own purposes.

Now, it is clear that the decline of a language must ultimately have political and economic causes: it is not due simply to the bad influence of this or that individual writer. But an effect can become a cause, reinforcing the original cause and producing the same effect in an intensified form, and so on indefinitely. A man may take to drink because he feels himself to be a failure, and then fail all the more completely because he drinks. It is rather the same thing that is happening to the English language. It becomes ugly and inaccurate because our thoughts are foolish, but the slovenliness of our language makes it easier for us to have foolish thoughts. The point is that the process is reversible. Modern English, especially written English, is full of bad habits which spread by imitation and which can be avoided if one is willing to take the necessary trouble. If one gets rid of these habits one can think more clearly, and to think clearly is a necessary first step towards political regeneration: so that the fight against bad English is not frivolous and is not the exclusive concern of professional writers. I will come back to this presently, and I hope that by that time the meaning of what I have said here will have become clearer. Meanwhile, here are five specimens of the English language as it is now habitually written.

These five passages have not been picked out because they are especially bad—I could have quoted far worse if I had chosen—but because they illustrate various of the mental vices from which we now suffer. They are a little below the average, but are fairly representative samples. I number them so that I can refer back to them when necessary:

"(1) I am not, indeed, sure whether it is not true to say that the Milton who once seemed not unlike a seventeenth-century Shelley had not become, out of an experience ever more bitter in each year, more alien [*sic*] to the founder of that Jesuit sect which nothing could induce him to tolerate."

Professor Harold Laski
(Essay in *Freedom of Expression*).

"(2) Above all, we cannot play ducks and drakes with a native battery of idioms which prescribes such egregious collocations of vocables as the Basic *put up with* for *tolerate* or *put at a loss* for *bewilder*."

Professor Lancelot Hogben (*Interglossa*).

"(3) On the one side we have the free personality: by definition it is not neurotic, for it has neither conflict nor dream. Its desires, such as they are, are transparent, for they are just what institutional approval keeps in the forefront of consciousness; another institutional pattern would alter their number and intensity; there is little in them that is natural, irreducible, or culturally dangerous. But *on the other side*, the social bond itself is nothing but the mutual reflection of these self-secure integrities. Recall the definition of love. Is not this the very picture of a small academic? Where is there a place in this hall of mirrors for either personality or fraternity?"

Essay on psychology in *Politics* (New York).

"(4) All the 'best people' from the gentlemen's clubs, and all the frantic fascist captains, united in common hatred of Socialism and bestial horror of the rising tide of the mass revolutionary movement, have turned to acts of provocation, to foul incendiarism, to medieval legends of poisoned wells, to legalize their own destruction of proletarian organizations, and rouse the agitated petty-bourgeoisie to chauvinistic fervour on behalf of the fight against the revolutionary way out of the crisis."

Communist pamphlet.

"(5) If a new spirit *is* to be infused into this old country, there is one thorny and contentious reform which must be tackled, and that is the humanization and galvanization of the B.B.C. Timidity here will bespeak cancer and atrophy of the soul. The heart of Britain may be sound and of strong beat, for instance, but the British lion's roar at present is like that of Bottom in Shakespeare's *Midsummer Night's Dream*—as gentle as any sucking dove. A virile new Britain cannot continue indefinitely to be traduced in the eyes or rather ears, of the world by the effete languors of Langham Place, brazenly masquerading as 'standard English.' When the Voice of Britain is heard at nine o'clock, better far and infinitely less ludicrous to hear aitches honestly dropped than the present priggish, inflated, inhibited, school-ma'amish arch braying of blameless bashful mewing maidens!"

Letter in *Tribune*.

Each of these passages has faults of its own, but, quite apart from avoidable ugliness, two qualities are common to all of them. The first is staleness of imagery: the other is lack of precision. The writer either has a meaning and cannot express it, or he inadvertently says something else, or he is almost indifferent as to whether his words mean anything or not. This mixture of vagueness and sheer incompetence is the most marked characteristic of modern English prose, and especially of any kind of political writing. As soon as certain topics are raised, the concrete melts into the abstract and no one seems able to think of turns of speech that are not hackneyed: prose consists less and less of *words* chosen for the sake of their meaning, and more and more of *phrases* tacked together like the sections of a prefabricated hen-house. I list below, with notes and examples, various of the tricks by means of which the work of prose-construction is habitually dodged:

Dying Metaphors. A newly invented metaphor assists thought by evoking a visual image, while on the other hand a metaphor which is technically "dead" (e.g. *iron resolution*) has in effect reverted to being an ordinary word and can generally be used without loss of vividness. But in between these two classes there is a huge dump of worn-out metaphors which have lost all evocative power and are merely used because they save people the trouble of inventing phrases for themselves. Examples are: *Ring the changes on, take up the cudgels for, toe the line, ride roughshod over, stand shoulder to shoulder with, play into the hands of, no axe to grind, grist to the mill, fishing in troubled waters, on the order of the day, Achilles' heel, swan song, hotbed.* Many of these are used without knowledge of their meaning (what is a "rift," for instance?), and incompatible metaphors are frequently mixed, a sure sign that the writer is not interested in what he is saying. Some metaphors now current have been twisted out of their original meaning without those who use them even being aware of the fact. For example, *toe the line* is sometimes written *tow the line.* Another example is *the hammer and the anvil,* now always used with the implication that the anvil gets the worst of it. In real life it is always the anvil that breaks the hammer, never the other way about: a writer who stopped to think what he was saying would be aware of this, and would avoid perverting the original phrase.

Operators or *Verbal False Limbs.*   These save the trouble of picking out appropriate verbs and nouns, and at the same time pad each sentence with extra syllables which give it an appearance of symmetry. Characteristic phrases are: *render inoperative, militate against, make contact with, be subjected to, give rise to, give grounds for, have the effect of, play a leading part (role) in, make itself felt, take effect, exhibit a tendency to, serve the purpose of, etc., etc.* The keynote is the elimination of simple verbs. Instead of being a single word, such as *break, stop, spoil, mend, kill,* a verb becomes a *phrase,* made up of a noun or adjective tacked on to some general-purposes verb such as *prove, serve, form, play, render.* In addition, the passive voice is wherever possible used in preference to the active, and noun constructions are used instead of gerunds (*by examination of* instead of *by examining*). The range of verbs is further cut down by means of the *-ize* and *de-* formation, and the banal statements are given an appearance of profundity by means of the *not un-* formation. Simple conjunctions and prepositions are replaced by such phrases as *with respect to, having regard to, the fact that, by dint of, in view of, in the interests of, on the hypothesis that;* and the ends of sentences are saved from anticlimax by such resounding commonplaces as *greatly to be desired, cannot be left out of account, a development to be expected in the near future, deserving of serious consideration, brought to a satisfactory conclusion,* and so on and so forth.

Pretentious Diction.   Words like *phenomenon, element, individual* (as noun), *objective, categorical, effective, virtual, basic, primary, promote, constitute, exhibit, exploit, utilize, eliminate, liquidate,* are used to dress up simple statement and give an air of scientific impartiality to biased judgments. Adjectives like *epoch-making, epic, historic, unforgettable, triumphant, age-old, inevitable, inexorable, veritable,* are used to dignify the sordid processes of international politics, while writing that aims at glorifying war usually takes on an archaic colour, its characteristic words being: *realm, throne, chariot, mailed fist, trident, sword, shield, buckler, banner, jackboot, clarion.* Foreign words and expressions such as *cul de sac, ancien régime, deus ex machina, mutatis mutandis, status quo, gleichschaltung, weltanschauung,* are used to give an air of culture and elegance. Except for the useful abbreviations *i.e., e.g.,* and *etc.,* there is no real need for any of the hundreds of foreign phrases now current in English. Bad writers, and especially scientific, political and sociological writers, are nearly always haunted by the notion that Latin or Greek words are grander than Saxon ones, and unnecessary words like *expedite, ameliorate, predict, extraneous, deracinated, clandestine, subaqueous* and hundreds of others constantly gain ground from their Anglo-Saxon opposite numbers.[1] The jargon peculiar to Marxist writing (*hyena, hangman, cannibal, petty bourgeois, these gentry, lacquey, flunkey, mad dog, White Guard,* etc.) consists largely of words and phrases translated from Russian, German or French; but the normal way of coining a new word is to use a Latin or Greek root with the appropriate affix and, where necessary, the -ize formation. It is often easier to make up words of this kind (*deregionalize, impermissible, extramarital, nonfragmentatory* and so forth) than to think up the English words that will cover one's meaning. The result, in general, is an increase in slovenliness and vagueness.

Meaningless Words. In certain kinds of writing, particularly in art criticism and literary criticism, it is normal to come across long passages which are almost completely lacking in meaning.[2] Words like *romantic, plastic, values, human, dead, sentimental, natural, vitality,* as used in art criticism, are strictly meaningless in the sense that they not only do not point to any discoverable object, but are hardly ever expected to do so by the reader. When one critic writes, "The outstanding feature of Mr. X's work is its living quality," while another writes, "The immediately striking thing about Mr. X's work is its peculiar deadness,"

---

[1] An interesting illustration of this is the way in which the English flower names which were in use till very recently are being ousted by Greek ones, *snapdragon* becoming *antirrhinum, forget-me-not* becoming *myosotis,* etc. It is hard to see any practical reason for this change of fashion: it is probably due to an instinctive turning-away from the more homely word and a vague feeling that the Greek word is scientific.

[2] Example: "Comfort's catholicity of perception and image, strangely Whitmanesque in range, almost the exact opposite in aesthetic compulsion, continues to evoke that trembling atmospheric accumulative hinting at a cruel, an inexorably serene timelessness . . . Wrey Gardiner scores by aiming at simple bull's-eyes with precision. Only they are not so simple, and through this contented sadness runs more than the surface bitter-sweet of resignation." (*Poetry Quarterly.*)

the reader accepts this as a simple difference of opinion. If words like *black* and *white* were involved, instead of the jargon words *dead* and *living*, he would see at once that language was being used in an improper way. Many political words are similarly abused. The word *Fascism* has now no meaning except in so far as it signifies "something not desirable." The words *democracy, socialism, freedom, patriotic, realistic, justice*, have each of them several different meanings which cannot be reconciled with one another. In the case of a word like *democracy*, not only is there no agreed definition, but the attempt to make one is resisted from all sides. It is almost universally felt that when we call a country democratic we are praising it: consequently the defenders of every kind of régime claim that it is a democracy, and fear that they might have to stop using the word if it were tied down to any one meaning. Words of this kind are often used in a consciously dishonest way. That is, the person who uses them has his own private definition, but allows his hearer to think he means something quite different. Statements like *Marshal Pétain was a true patriot, The Soviet Press is the freest in the world, The Catholic Church is opposed to persecution*, are almost always made with intent to deceive. Other words used in variable meanings, in most cases more or less dishonestly, are: *class, totalitarian, science, progressive, reactionary, bourgeois, equality*.

Now that I have made this catalogue of swindles and perversions, let me give another example of the kind of writing that they lead to. This time it must of its nature be an imaginary one. I am going to translate a passage of good English into modern English of the worst sort. Here is a well-known verse from *Ecclesiastes:*

"I returned and saw under the sun, that the race is not to the swift, nor the battle to the strong, neither yet bread to the wise, nor yet riches to men of understanding, nor yet favour to men of skill; but time and chance happeneth to them all."

Here it is in modern English:

"Objective considerations of contemporary phenomena compels the conclusion that success or failure in competitive activities exhibits no tendency to be commensurate with innate capacity, but that a considerable element of the unpredictable must invariably be taken into account."

This is a parody, but not a very gross one. Exhibit (3), above, for instance, contains several patches of the same kind of English. It will be seen that I have not made a full translation. The beginning and ending of the sentence follow the original meaning fairly closely, but in the middle the concrete illustrations—race, battle, bread—dissolve into the vague phrase "success or failure in competitive activities." This had to be so, because no modern writer of the kind I am discussing—no one capable of using phrases like "objective consideration of contemporary phenomena"—would ever tabulate his thoughts in that precise and detailed way. The whole tendency of modern prose is away from concreteness. Now analyse these two sentences a little more closely. The first contains forty-nine words but only sixty syllables, and all its words are those of everyday life. The second contains thirty-eight words of ninety syllables: eighteen of its words are from Latin roots, and one from Greek. The first sentence contains six vivid images, and only one phrase ("time and chance") that could be called vague. The second contains not a single fresh, arresting phrase, and in spite of its ninety syllables it gives only a shortened version of the meaning contained in the first. Yet without a doubt it is the second kind of sentence that is gaining ground in modern English. I do not want to exaggerate. This kind of writing is not yet universal, and outcrops of simplicity will occur here and there in the worst-written page. Still, if you or I were told to write a few lines on the uncertainty of human fortunes, we should probably come much nearer to my imaginary sentence than to the one from *Ecclesiastes*.

As I have tried to show, modern writing at its worst does not consist in picking out words for the sake of their meaning and inventing images in order to make the meaning clearer. It consists in gumming together long strips of words which have already been set in order by someone else, and making the results presentable by sheer humbug. The attraction of this way of writing is that it is easy. It is easier—even quicker, once you have the habit—to say *In my opinion it is a not unjustifiable assumption that* than to say *I think*. If you use ready-made phrases, you not only don't have to hunt about for words; you also don't have to bother with the rhythms of your sentences, since these phrases are generally so arranged as to be more or less euphonious. When you are composing in a hurry—when you are dictating to a stenographer, for instance, or making a public speech—it is natural to fall into a pretentious, Latinized style. Tags like *a consideration which we should do well to bear in mind* or *a conclusion to which all of us would readily assent* will save many a sentence from coming down with a bump. By using stale metaphors, similes and idioms, you save much mental effort, at the cost of leaving your meaning vague, not only for your reader but for yourself. This is the significance of mixed metaphors. The sole aim of a metaphor is to call up a visual image. When these images clash—as in *The Fascist octopus has sung its swan song, the jackboot is thrown into the melting pot*—it can be taken as certain that the writer is not seeing a mental image of the objects he is naming; in other words he is not really thinking. Look again at the examples I gave at the beginning of this essay. Professor Laski (1) uses five negatives in fifty-three words. One of these is superfluous, making nonsense of the whole passage, and in addition there is the slip *alien* for akin, making further nonsense, and several avoidable pieces of clumsiness which increase the general vagueness. Professor Hogben (2) plays ducks and drakes with a battery which is able to write prescriptions, and, while disapproving of the everyday phrase *put up with*, is unwilling to look *egregious* up in the dictionary and see what it means. (3), if one takes an uncharitable attitude towards it, is simply meaningless: probably one could work out its intended meaning by reading the whole of the article in which it occurs. In (4), the writer knows more or less what he wants to say, but an accumulation of stale phrases chokes him like tea leaves blocking a sink. In (5), words and meaning have almost parted company. People who write in this manner usually have a general emotional meaning—they dislike one thing and want to express solidarity with another—but they are not interested in the detail of what they are saying. A scrupulous writer, in every sentence that he writes, will ask himself at least four questions, thus: What am I trying to say? What words will express it? What image or idiom will make it clearer? Is this image fresh enough to have an effect? And he will probably ask himself two more: Could I put it more shortly? Have I said anything that is avoidably ugly? But you are not obliged to go to all this trouble. You can shirk it by simply throwing your mind open and letting the ready-made phrases come crowding in. They will construct your sentences for you—even think your thoughts for you, to a certain extent—and at need they will perform the important service of partially concealing your meaning even from yourself. It is at this point that the special connection between politics and the debasement of language becomes clear.

In our time it is broadly true that political writing is bad writing. Where it is not true, it will generally be found that the writer is some kind of rebel, expressing his private opinions and not a "party line." Orthodoxy, of whatever colour, seems to demand a lifeless, imitative style. The political dialects to be found in pamphlets, leading articles, manifestos, White Papers and the speeches of under-secretaries do, of course, vary from party to party, but they are all alike in that one almost never finds in them a fresh, vivid, home-made turn of speech. When one watches some tired hack on the platform mechanically repeating the familiar phrases—*bestial atrocities, iron heel, bloodstained tyranny, free peoples of the world, stand shoulder to shoulder*—one often has a curious feeling that one is not watching a live humun being but some kind of dummy: a feeling which suddenly becomes stronger at moments when the light catches the speaker's spectacles and turns them into blank discs which seem to have no eyes behind them. And this is not altogether fanciful. A speaker who uses that kind of phraseology has gone some distance towards turning himself into a machine. The appropriate noises are coming out of his larynx, but his brain is not involved as it would be if he were choosing his words for himself. If the speech he is making is one that he is accustomed to make over and over again, he may be almost unconscious of what he is saying, as one is when one utters the responses in church. And this reduced state of consciousness, if not indispensable, is at any rate favourable to political conformity.

In our time, political speech and writing are largely the defence of the indefensible. Things like the continuance of British rule in India, the Russian purges and deportations, the dropping of the atom bombs on Japan, can indeed be defended, but only by arguments which are too brutal for most people to face, and which do not square with the professed aims of political parties. Thus political language has to consist largely of euphemism, question-begging and sheer cloudy vagueness. Defenceless villages are bombarded from the air, the inhabitants driven out into the countryside, the cattle machine-gunned, the huts set on fire with incendiary bullets: this is called *pacification*. Millions of peasants are robbed of their farms and sent trudging along the roads with no more than they can carry: this is called *transfer of population* or *rectification of frontiers*. People are imprisoned for years without trial, or shot in the back of the neck or sent to die of scurvy in Arctic lumber camps: this is called *elimination of unreliable elements*. Such phraseology is needed if one wants to name things without calling up mental pictures of them. Consider for instance some comfortable English professor defending Russian totalitarianism. He cannot say outright, "I believe in killing off your opponents when you can get good results by doing so." Probably, therefore, he will say something like this:

"While freely conceding that the Soviet régime exhibits certain features which the humanitarian may be inclined to deplore, we must, I think, agree that a certain curtailment of the right to political opposition is an unavoidable concomitant of transitional periods, and that the rigours which the Russian people have been called upon to undergo have been amply justified in the sphere of concrete achievement."

The inflated style is itself a kind of euphemism. A mass of Latin words falls upon the facts like soft snow, blurring the outlines and covering up all the details. The great enemy of clear language is insincerity. When there is a gap between one's real and one's declared aims, one turns as it were instinctively to long words and exhausted idioms, like a cuttlefish squirting out ink. In our age there is no such thing as "keeping out of politics." All issues are political issues, and politics itself is a mass of lies, evasions, folly, hatred and schizophrenia. When the general atmosphere is bad, language must suffer. I should expect to find—this is a guess which I have not sufficient knowledge to verify—that the German, Russian and Italian languages have all deteriorated in the last ten or fifteen years, as a result of dictatorship.

But if thought corrupts language, language can also corrupt thought. A bad usage can spread by tradition and imitation, even among people who should and do know better. The debased language that I have been discussing is in some ways very convenient. Phrases like *a not unjustifiable assumption, leaves much to be desired, would serve no good purpose, a consideration which we should do well to bear in mind,* are a continuous temptation, a packet of aspirins always at one's elbow. Look back through this essay, and for certain you will find that I have again and again committed the very faults I am protesting against. By this morning's post I have received a pamphlet dealing with conditions in Germany. The author tells me that he "felt impelled" to write it. I open it at random, and here is almost the first sentence that I see: "(The Allies) have an opportunity not only of achieving a radical transformation of Germany's social and political structure in such a way as to avoid a nationalistic reaction in Germany itself, but at the same time of laying the foundations of a co-operative and unified Europe." You see, he "feels impelled" to write—feels, presumably, that he has something new to say— and yet his words, like cavalry horses answering the bugle, group themselves automatically into the familiar dreary pattern. This invasion of one's mind by ready-made phrases (*lay the foundations, achieve a radical transformation*) can only be prevented if one is constantly on guard against them, and every such phrase anaesthetizes a portion of one's brain.

I said earlier that the decadence of our language is probably curable. Those who deny this would argue, if they produced an argument at all, that language merely reflects existing social conditions, and that we cannot influence its development by any direct tinkering with words and constructions. So far as the general tone or spirit of a language goes, this may be true, but it is not true in detail. Silly words and expressions have often disappeared, not through any evolutionary process but owing to the conscious action of a minority. Two recent examples were *explore every avenue* and *leave no stone unturned,* which were killed by the jeers of a few journalists. There is a long list of flyblown metaphors which could similarly be got rid of if enough people would interest themselves in the job; and it should also be possible to laugh the *not un-* formation out of existence,[3] to reduce the amount of Latin and Greek in the average sentence, to drive out foreign phrases and strayed scientific words, and, in general, to make pretentiousness unfashionable. But all these are minor points. The defence of the English language implies more than this, and perhaps it is best to start by saying what it does *not* imply.

To begin with it has nothing to do with archaism, with the salvaging of obsolete words and turns of speech, or with the setting up of a "standard English" which must never be departed from. On the con-

---

[3] One can cure oneself of the *not un-* formation by memorizing this sentence:
A not unblack dog was chasing a not unsmall rabbit across a not ungreen field.

trary, it is especially concerned with the scrapping of every word or idiom which has outworn its usefulness. It has nothing to do with correct grammar and syntax, which are of no importance so long as one makes one's meaning clear, or with the avoidance of Americanisms, or with having what is called a "good prose style." On the other hand it is not concerned with fake simplicity and the attempt to make written English colloquial. Nor does it even imply in every case preferring the Saxon word to the Latin one, though it does imply using the fewest and shortest words that will cover one's meaning. What is above all needed is to let the meaning choose the word, and not the other way about. In prose, the worst thing one can do with words is to surrender to them. When you think of a concrete object, you think wordlessly, and then, if you want to describe the thing you have been visualizing you probably hunt about till you find the exact words that seem to fit. When you think of something abstract you are more inclined to use words from the start, and unless you make a conscious effort to prevent it, the existing dialect will come rushing in and do the job for you, at the expense of blurring or even changing your meaning. Probably it is better to put off using words as long as possible and get one's meaning as clear as one can through pictures or sensations. Afterwards one can choose—not simply *accept*—the phrases that will best cover the meaning, and then switch round and decide what impression one's words are likely to make on another person. This last effort of the mind cuts out all stale or mixed images, all prefabricated phrases, needless repetitions, and humbug and vagueness generally. But one can often be in doubt about the effect of a word or a phrase, and one needs rules that one can rely on when instinct fails. I think the following rules will cover most cases:

(i) Never use a metaphor, simile or other figure of speech which you are used to seeing in print.

(ii) Never use a long word where a short one will do.

(iii) If it is possible to cut a word out, always cut it out.

(iv) Never use the passive where you can use the active.

(v) Never use a foreign phrase, a scientific word or a jargon word if you can think of an everyday English equivalent.

(vi) Break any of these rules sooner than say anything outright barbarous.

These rules sound elementary, and so they are, but they demand a deep change of attitude in anyone who has grown used to writing in the style now fashionable. One could keep all of them and still write bad English, but one could not write the kind of stuff that I quoted in those five specimens at the beginning of this article.

I have not here been considering the literary use of language, but merely language as an instrument for expressing and not for concealing or preventing thought. Stuart Chase and others have come near to claiming that all abstract words are meaningless, and have used this as a pretext for advocating a kind of political quietism. Since you don't know what Fascism is, how can you struggle against Fascism? One need not swallow such absurdities as this, but one ought to recognize that the present political chaos is connected with the decay of language, and that one can probably bring about some improvement by starting at the verbal end. If you simplify your English, you are freed from the worst follies of orthodoxy. You cannot speak any of the necessary dialects, and when you make a stupid remark its stupidity will be obvious, even to yourself. Political language—and with variations this is true of all political parties, from Conservatives to Anarchists—is designed to make lies sound truthful and murder respectable, and to give an appearance of solidity to pure wind. One cannot change this all in a moment, but one can at least change one's own habits, and from time to time one can even, if one jeers loudly enough, send some worn-out and useless phrase—some *jackboot, Achilles' heel, hotbed, melting pot, acid test, veritable inferno* or other lump of verbal refuse—into the dustbin where it belongs.

STUDY QUESTIONS

1. What do each of the five examples illustrate that Orwell finds objectionable?
2. What is a dying metaphor? Can you add examples to those Orwell gives?
3. According to Orwell, what is the connection between politics and the debasement of language?
4. In what ways does language corrupt thought, and thought corrupt language?
5. Compare MacDonald's view ("The Decline and Fall of English," p. 334) on the debasement of English with Orwell's.

William Hazlitt   ON FAMILIAR STYLE

William Hazlitt (1778–1830) was born in Kent, England. He first studied to become a Unitarian minister, then decided to become a painter. After studying painting for a time, he turned to writing for a career and became a leading critic and essayist of his day. His

From *Table Talk* (1821–1822).

range of critical interests included art, literature, nature, and the customs and manners of English life. Many of his essays are models of irony and sarcasm. His works include *Lectures on the English Poets* (1818), *Table Talk* (1821–1822), and *Notes on a Journey Through France and Italy* (1826).

It is not easy to write a familiar style. Many people mistake a familiar for a vulgar style, and suppose that to write without affectation is to write at random. On the contrary, there is nothing that requires more precision, and, if I may so say, purity of expression, than the style I am speaking of. It utterly rejects not only all unmeaning pomp, but all low, cant phrases, and loose, unconnected, *slipshod* allusions. It is not to take the first word that offers, but the best word in common use; it is not to throw words together in any combinations we please, but to follow and avail ourselves of the true idiom of the language. To write a genuine familiar or truly English style, is to write as any one would speak in common conversation, who had a thorough command and choice of words, or who could discourse with ease, force, and perspicuity, setting aside all pedantic and oratorical flourishes. Or to give another illustration, to write naturally is the same thing in regard to common conversation, as to read naturally is in regard to common speech. It does not follow that it is an easy thing to give the true accent and inflection to the words you utter, because you do not attempt to rise above the level of ordinary life and colloquial speaking. You do not assume indeed the solemnity of the pulpit, or the tone of stage-declamation: neither are you at liberty to gabble on at a venture, without emphasis or discretion, or to resort to vulgar dialect or clownish pronunciation. You must steer a middle course. You are tied down to a given and appropriate articulation, which is determined by the habitual associations between sense and sound, and which you can only hit by entering into the author's meaning, as you must find the proper words and style to express yourself by fixing your thoughts on the subject you have to write about. Any one may mouth out a passage with a theatrical cadence, or get upon stilts to tell his thoughts: but to write or speak with propriety and simplicity is a more difficult task. Thus it is easy to affect a pompous style, to use a word twice as big as the thing you want to express: it is not so easy to pitch upon the very word that exactly fits it. Out of eight or ten words equally common, equally intelligible, with nearly equal pretensions, it is a matter of some nicety and discrimination to pick out the very one, the preferableness of which is scarcely perceptible, but decisive. The reason why I object to Dr. Johnson's style is, that there is no discrimination, no variety in it. He uses none but "tall, opaque words," taken from the "first row of the rubric":—words with the greatest number of syllables, or Latin phrases with merely English terminations. If a fine style depended on this sort of arbitrary pretension, it would be fair to judge of an author's elegance by the measurement of his words, and the substitution of foreign circumlocutions (with no precise associations) for the mother-tongue. How simple it is to be dignified without ease, to be pompous without meaning! Surely, it is but a mechanical rule for avoiding what is low to be always pedantic and affected. It is clear you cannot use a vulgar English word, if you never use a common English word at all. A fine tact is shewn in adhering to those which are perfectly common, and yet never falling into any expressions which are debased by disgusting circumstances, or which owe their signification and point to technical or professional allusions. A truly natural or familiar style can never be quaint or vulgar, for this reason, that it is of universal force and applica-bility, and that quaintness and vulgarity arise out of the immediate connection of certain words with coarse and disagreeable, or with confined ideas. The last form what we understand by *cant* or *slang* phrases.—To give an example of what is not very clear in the general statement. I should say that the phrase *To cut with a knife,* or *To cut a piece of wood,* is perfectly free from vulgarity, because it is perfectly common: but to *cut an acquaintance* is not quite unexceptionable, be-cause it is not perfectly common or intelligible, and has hardly yet escaped out of the limits of slang phraseology. I should hardly therefore use the word in this sense without putting it in italics as a license of expression, to be received *cum grano salis.*[1] All provincial or bye-phrases come under the same mark of reprobation—all such as the writer transfers to the page from his fireside or a particular *coterie,* or that he invents for his own sole use and convenience. I conceive that words are like money, not the worse for being common, but that it is the stamp of custom alone that gives them circulation or value. I am fastidious in this respect, and would almost as soon coin the currency of the realm as counterfeit the King's English. I never invented or gave a new and unauthorized meaning to any word but one single one (the term *imper-sonal* applied to feelings) and that was in an abstruse metaphysical discussion to express a very difficult distinction. I have been (I know) loudly accused of revelling in vulgarisms and broken English. I cannot speak to that point: but so far I plead guilty to the determined use of acknowledged idioms and common elliptical expressions. I am not sure that the critics in question know the one from the other, that is, can distinguish any medium between formal pedantry and the most barba-rous solecism. As an author, I endeavour to employ plain words and popular modes of construction, as were I a chapman and dealer, I should common weights and measures.

The proper force of words lies not in the words themselves, but in their application. A word may be a fine-sounding word of an unusual

---

[1] With a grain of salt.

length, and very imposing from its learning and novelty, and yet in the connection in which it is introduced, may be quite pointless and irrelevant. It is not pomp or pretension, but the adaptation of the expression to the idea that clenches a writer's meaning:—as it is not the size or glossiness of the materials, but their being fitted each to its place, that gives strength to the arch; or as the pegs and nails are as necessary to the support of the building as the large timbers, and more so than the mere shewy, unsubstantial ornaments. I hate any thing that occupies more space than it is worth. I hate to see a load of band-boxes go along the street, and I hate to see a parcel of big words without any thing in them. A person who does not deliberately dispose of all his thoughts alike in cumbrous draperies and flimsy disguises, may strike out twenty varieties of familiar everyday language, each coming somewhat nearer to the feeling he wants to convey, and at last not hit upon that particular and only one, which may be said to be identical with the exact impression in his mind. This would seem to shew that Mr. Cobbett is hardly right in saying that the first word that occurs is always the best. It may be a very good one; and yet a better may present itself on reflection or from time to time. It should be suggested naturally, however, and spontaneously, from a fresh and lively conception of the subject. We seldom succeed by trying at improvement, or by merely substituting one word for another that we are not satisfied with, as we cannot recollect the name of a place or person by merely plaguing ourselves about it. We wander farther from the point by persisting in a wrong scent, but it starts up accidentally in the memory when we least expected it, by touching some link in the chain of previous association.

There are those who hoard up and make a cautious display of nothing but rich and rare phraseology;—ancient medals, obscure coins, and Spanish pieces of eight. They are very curious to inspect; but I myself would neither offer nor take them in the course of exchange. A sprinkling of archaisms is not amiss; but a tissue of obsolete expressions is more fit *for keep than wear*. I do not say I would not use any phrase that had been brought into fashion before the middle or the end of the last century; but I should be shy of using any that had not been employed by any approved author during the whole of that time. Words, like clothes, get old-fashioned, or mean and ridiculous, when they have been for some time laid aside. Mr. Lamb is the only imitator of old English style I can read with pleasure; and he is so thoroughly imbued with the spirit of his authors, that the idea of imitation is almost done away. There is an inward unction, a marrowy vein both in the thought and feeling, an intuition, deep and lively, of his subject, that carries off any quaintness or awkwardness arising from an antiquated style and dress. The matter is completely his own, though the manner is assumed. Perhaps his ideas are altogether so marked and individual, as to require

their point and pungency to be neutralised by the affectation of a
singular but traditional form of conveyance. Tricked out in the prevailing costume, they would probably seem more startling and out of the
way. The old English authors, Burton, Fuller, Coryate, Sir Thomas
Browne, are a kind of mediators between us and the more eccentric and
whimsical modern, reconciling us to his peculiarities. I do not, however,
know how far this is the case or not, till he condescends to write like one
of us. I must confess that what I like best of his papers under the
signature of Elia (still I do not presume, amidst such excellence, to
decide what is most excellent) is the account of *Mrs. Battle's Opinions
on Whist*, which is also the most free from obsolete allusions and turns of
expressions—

A well of native English undefiled.

To those acquainted with his admired prototypes, these *Essays* of the
ingenious and highly gifted author have the same sort of charm and
relish, that Erasmus's *Colloquies* or a fine piece of modern Latin have to
the classical scholar. Certainly, I do not know any borrowed pencil that
has more power or felicity of execution than the one of which I have
here been speaking.

It is as easy to write a gaudy style without ideas, as it is to spread a
pallet of shewy colours, or to smear in a flaunting transparency. "What do
you read?"—"Words, words, words."—"What is the matter?"—"*Nothing*,"
it might be answered. The florid style is the reverse of the familiar. The
last is employed as an unvarnished medium to convey ideas; the first is
resorted to as a spangled veil to conceal the want of them. When there is
nothing to be set down but words, it costs little to have them fine. Look
through the dictionary, and cull out a *florilegium*, rival the *tulipomania*.
Rouge high enough, and never mind the natural complexion. The vulgar, who are not in the secret, will admire the look of preternatural
health and vigour; and the fashionable, who regard only appearances,
will be delighted with the imposition. Keep to your sounding general-
ities, your tinkling phrases, and all will be well. Swell out an unmeaning
truism to a perfect tympany of style. A thought, a distinction is the rock
on which all this brittle cargo of verbiage splits at once. Such writers
have merely *verbal* imaginations, that retain nothing but words. Or their
puny thoughts have dragon-wings, all green and gold. They soar far
above the vulgar failing of the *Sermo humi obrepens* [2]—their most ordinary speech is never short of an hyperbole, splendid, imposing, vague,
incomprehensible, magniloquent, a cento of sounding common-places. If
some of us, whose "ambition is more lowly," pry a little too narrowly

---

[2] Plain style that creeps up unexpectedly.

into nooks and corners to pick up a number of "unconsidered trifles," they never once direct their eyes or lift their hands to seize on any but the most gorgeous, tarnished, thread-bare patch-work set of phrases, the left-off finery of poetic extravagance, transmitted down through successive generations of barren pretenders. If they criticise actors and actresses, a huddled phantasmagoria of feathers, spangles, floods of light, and oceans of sound float before their morbid sense, which they paint in the style of Ancient Pistol. Not a glimpse can you get of the merits or defects of the performers: they are hidden in a profusion of barbarous epithets and wilful rhodomontade. Our hypercritics are not thinking of these little fantoccini beings—

That strut and fret their hour upon the stage—

but of tall phantoms of words, abstractions, *genera* and *species,* sweeping clauses, periods that unite the Poles, forced alliterations, astounding antitheses—

And on their pens *Fustian* sits plumed.

If they describe kings and queens, it is an Eastern pageant. The Coronation at either House is nothing to it. We get at four repeated images—a curtain, a throne, a sceptre, and a foot-stool. These are with them the wardrobe of a lofty imagination; and they turn their servile strains to servile uses. Do we read a description of pictures? It is not a reflection of tones and hues which "nature's own sweet and cunning hand laid on," but piles of precious stones, rubies, pearls, emeralds, Golconda's mines, and all the blazonry of art. Such persons are in fact besotted with words, and their brains are turned with the glittering, but empty and sterile phantoms of things. Personifications, capital letter, seas of sunbeams, visions of glory, shining inscriptions, the figures of a transparency, Britannia with her shield, or Hope leaning on an anchor, make up their stock in trade. They may be considered as *hieroglyphical* writers. Images stand out in their minds isolated and important merely in themselves, without any ground-work of feeling—there is no context in their imaginations. Words affect them in the same way, by the mere sound, that is, by their possible, not by their actual application to the subject in hand. They are fascinated by first appearances, and have no sense of consequences. Nothing more is meant by them than meets the ear: they understand or feel nothing more than meets their eye. The web and texture of the universe, and of the heart of man, is a mystery to them: they have no faculty that strikes a chord in unison with it. They cannot get beyond the daubings of fancy, the varnish of sentiment. Objects are not linked to feelings, words to things, but images revolve in splendid mockery, words represent themselves in their strange rhapsodies. The categories of such a mind are pride and ignorance—pride in outside show, to which they sacrifice every thing, and ignorance of the true worth and hidden structure both of words and things. With a sovereign contempt for what is familiar and natural, they are the slaves of vulgar affection—of a routine of high-flown phrases. Scorning to imitate realities, they are unable to invent any thing, to strike out one original idea. They are not copyists of nature, it is true; but they are the poorest of all plagiarists, the plagiarists of words. All is far-fetched, dear-bought, artificial, oriental in subject and allusion: all is mechanical, conventional, vapid, formal, pedantic in style and execution. They startle and confound the understanding of the reader, by the remoteness and obscurity of their illustrations: they soothe the ear by the monotony of the same everlasting round of circuitous metaphors. They are the *mock-school* in poetry and prose. They flounder about between fustian in expression, and bathos in sentiment. They tantalise the fancy but never reach the head nor touch the heart. Their Temple of Fame is like a shadowy structure raised by Dulness to Vanity, or like Cowper's description of the Empress of Russia's palace of ice, as "worthless as in shew 'twas glittering"—

It smiled, and it was cold!

STUDY QUESTIONS

1. What is Hazlitt's definition of "familiar style"? Does it correspond to what is meant by familiar style today?
2. Would MacDonald ("The Decline and Fall of English," see p. 334) agree with Hazlitt's ideas on language? Explain.
3. To what extent does Hazlitt ascribe to the principle of usage in determining whether or not a word or expression is "free from vulgarity"?
4. What principal methods does Hazlitt use in defining familiar style?
5. Hazlitt says that it is easier to affect a pompous style than to write a familiar one. Do you agree? Explain.

THE NEW

James G. Thurber **VOCABULARIANISM**

James G. Thurber (1894–1961), humorist and satirist, was born in Columbus, Ohio. He was educated at Ohio State University,

then worked as a code clerk in the Department of State and as a
newspaper reporter, before joining the staff of *The New Yorker* in
1926. His many stories, fables, and essays earned him an outstanding reputation and a permanent place in American letters. He
is coauthor with E. B. White of *Is Sex Necessary?* (1929), and
the author of *The Owl in the Attic* (1931), *The Seal in the Bedroom* (1932), *My Life and Hard Times* (1933), *The Middle-
Aged Man on the Flying Trapeze* (1935), *Fables for Our Time*
(1940), *The Thurber Carnival* (1945), *The Thirteen Clocks*
(1950), and *Thurber Country* (1953).

A sensitive gentleman in one of Henry James's novels exclaims at
the end, triumphantly, "Then there we are!" not because he and his fair
companion have arrived at a solution of anything but because they have
come upon an embraceable impasse.

The expression Embraceable Impasse (I stress it with capitals
deliberately) might well become a part of the jargon of today's diplomacy, which so often seems content to settle for a phrase in place of a
way out. One such phrase, Calculated Risk, has been going great guns
among the politicians and statesmen. It was used repeatedly by an
adult guest on an American radio discussion panel made up of juveniles.
(I am glad and eager to announce that we have millions of teenagers in
America more interested in using their minds than in brandishing knives
or bicycle chains.) Finally one youth interrupted the adult to say "I
don't know what you mean by Calculated Risk." The grown-up was as
bewildered as if the youngster had said "I don't know whom you mean
by Harry Truman." This particular Calculated Risk was being applied to
the Russo-American plan of exchange students, and the adult guest
floundered a bit in trying to explain what he meant.

Now I have made some study of the smoke-screen phrases of the
political terminologists, and they have to be described rather than defined. Calculated Risk, then, goes like this: "We have every hope and
assurance that the plan will be successful, but if it doesn't work we knew
all the time it wouldn't, and said so."

There is, to be sure, a kind of menacing Alice in Wonderland
meaninglessness in a great deal of modern political phraseology. What
used to be called a tenable position could now often be called, quite
fittingly, a Tenniel position. To add to the unmeaningfulness of it all,
there is the continual confusing contribution of the abbreviationists. We
have in America a product called No-Cal, short for No Calories, and
another Decaf, meaning "coffee from which caffein has been removed."
Before long, I fear, Calculated Risk will become Cal-Ris, and then all the
other celebrated phrases will be abbreviated, for the sake of making
even less sense than before in front-page headlines. We shall have to
have a special glossary, perhaps, to help us figure out "Pea-Coex" and
"Ag-Reapp" and "Mass-Retal." I should think even the most backward

student of world affairs would understand "Sum-Con." Then the Marxist intellectuals will hit them with those old brickbats called Obscurantism and Obfuscationism. The meaning of these two words will be described, in my own forthcoming dictionary, like this: "You are seeking to distort our objectives by exposing them to the scrutiny of the unfairest of all bourgeois virtues, namely truth."

Somewhere in my proposed lexicon I shall have to wedge in what a lady said to me when I told her I was writing a short piece about the time, if any, of Man on earth. She said, with a distressed sigh, "So much has already been written about everything that you can't find out anything about it."

The brain of our species is, as we know, made up largely of potassium, phosphorus, propaganda, and politics, with the result that how not to understand what should be clearer is becoming easier and easier for all of us. Sanity, soundness, and sincerity, of which gleams and stains can still be found in the human brain under powerful microscopes, flourish only in a culture of clarification, which is now becoming harder and harder to detect with the naked eye. My dictionary, in attacking or circling about the terminology of the declarificationists, will contain such directives as this, for the bewildermentation of exchange students on all sides: "When you find that they are superior to us in any field, remember that their superiority is inferior to ours."

Let us mourn for a moment the death of Latin in American high schools. That ancient sword of Cicero, lyre of Catullus, and thunder of Virgil has become the pallid valet of the lawyer and the doctor, laying out their double-breasted polysyllabics, workaday clichés, and full-dress circumlocutions. "I had to let my secretary go," a doctor told me. "She could never remember the Latin for cod liver oil." In my day, Latin was taught in high schools to prepare the youthful mind for the endless war between meaning and gobbledegook. But it was a mental discipline, and discipline has become a bad word in America, for the idiotic reason that we identify it with regimentation, and hence damn it as Communistic. Recent surveys in my country indicate that Latin and certain other difficult subjects were eliminated from school curricula because they were simply too hard for Junior and his sister to understand, and interfered with the coziness of their security. An aroused America is now, I am glad to say, interested in the rehabilitation of our declining educational system. We have long had, in our colleges and universities, easy courses variously known as snap, soft, cinch, and pudd, which seems to be short for "pudding." I asked a pretty girl graduate of the University of Kansas if she had taken any pudd courses, and she said she had taken two. Common Insect Pests and Native Shrubs and Trees. "They were so dull I failed them both," she told me.

The tendency of tired American businessmen and statesmen to use slang and slogan will, I hope, disappear with the revival of true education. When our recent President used the word "gimmick" for "political device" he seemed to open the door for a flood of Hollywood shibboleth. I can only pray that Washington does not fall into the use of "switcheroo" and "twisterino."

My concern about the precarious state of the English language in the hands or on the tongues of politicians shows up in recurring nightmares. I dreamed one night I was at some kind of Sum-Con, and two famous lines, one English, the other American, became garbled slightly and unfortunately conjoined. They were Browning's "Beautiful Evelyn Hope is dead," and that proud boast of all New England inns, "George Washington slept here." They came out in my nightmare like this: "Beautiful Evelyn Hope is deaf. George Washington slapt her."

"Gentlemen, this means war," said a grave voice in my dream, and I woke up. It was hard to get back to sleep, and I thought many thoughts. I began worrying again about the death of Latin, and I said aloud, waking up my wife, "What does he know of English who only English knows?" The restoration of Latin in our schools is not going to save Man from himself, to be sure, but it would help in the coming struggle for a world regime of sense and sanity. *Hoc est*, at any rate, *in votis*.

STUDY QUESTIONS

1. Can you think of any current expressions you frequently hear that Thurber could have used to illustrate his point?
2. What does Thurber mean when he says, "In my day, Latin was taught in high schools to prepare the youthful mind for the endless war between meaning and gobbledegook"?
3. Compare Thurber's tone in this selection with MacDonald's in "The Decline and Fall of English," p. 334. What is the principal difference?
4. In what way is the personal anecdote at the conclusion of Thurber's essay appropriate to his thesis?

HELL AND ITS
H. L. Mencken **OUTSKIRTS**

Henry Louis Mencken (1880–1956), editor, critic, columnist, and scholar, was born in Baltimore, Maryland. For many years he was editor and columnist for the *Baltimore Sun*, and then later literary critic and editor of *Smart Set* magazine. He gained a reputation as a master of wit and invective. The American public, particularly the middle class, became his special target. He helped to found *The American Mercury,* a magazine devoted to satire and comment on American life, politics, and customs. He is well known among students of the English language for his scholarly *The American Language* (1919) and its two supplements. Titles of his other books are *The Philosophy of Friedrich Nietzsche* (1908), *In Defense of Women* (1918), *Prejudices* (in six series, 1919–1927), *Treatise on the Gods* (1930), *Treatise on Right and Wrong* (1934), and *A Mencken Chrestomathy* (1949).

> *It doesn't matter what they preach,*
> *Of high or low degree:*
> *The old Hell of the Bible*
> *Is Hell enough for me.*
>
> *'Twas preached by Paul and Peter;*
> *They spread it wide and free;*
> *'Twas Hell for old John Bunyan*
> *And it's Hell enough for me.*

The author of these elegiac strophes, Frank Lebby Stanton, has been moldering in the red clay of Georgia for a long, long while, but what he wrote went straight to the hearts of the American people, and there it still glows warmly. Hell remains the very essence not only of their dogmatic theology but also of their everyday invective. They employ it casually more than any other *Kulturvolk,* and perhaps more than all others put together. They have enriched it with a vast store of combinations, variations, licks, breaks, and riffs. They have made it roar and howl, and they have made it coo and twitter. It helps to lift them when supersonic waves of ecstasy rush through their lymphatic systems, and it soothes them when they roll in the barbed wire of despair. To find its match, you must go to the Buddhist *Om mani padma Hum,* meaning anything you please, or the Moslem *al-hamdu lil'lah,* meaning the same, or the ancient Mesopotamian Word from the Abyss, *Muazaga-gu-abzu.* Even so, *hell* is far ahead, for, compared to it, all these ejaculations have a pale and pansy cast, as does *hell* itself in nearly every other language; e.g., *enfer* in French, *infierno* in Spanish, *helvede* in Danish, *jigoku* in Japanese, and *Hölle* in German. So long ago as 1880, in the appendix on "The Awful German Language" to "A Tramp Abroad," Mark Twain derided *Hölle* as "chipper, frivolous and unimpressive" and marveled that anyone invited to go there could "rise to the dignity of feeling insulted." He had never heard, apparently, of the even more flaccid Finnish *manala,* which in These States would be the name of an infant food or perhaps of a female infant among the Bible-searchers of the Dust Bowl.

Hell is one of the most ancient and honorable terms in English, and etymologists in their dusty cells have traced it to the first half of the ninth century. It is thus appreciably older than either *home* or *mother* and nearly five centuries older than its great rival, *damn*. But it was not until Shakespeare's time that it began to appear in the numerous blistering phrases that now glorify it—e.g., *go to hell, to hell with, hell to pay, hell is loose, hellcat,* and so on—and even then it rose only to be knocked down, for Shakespeare's time also saw the beginnings of the Puritan murrain, and once the bluenoses were in power they put down all strong language with a brutal hand. At the Restoration, of course, it was reliberated, but only in a spavined state. The Cavaliers, male and female, were great swearers, but their oaths were nearly all cautious and cushioned. Such examples as *gadzooks, zounds, 'sdeath, 'sblood, by'r Lady, a plague on't, rat me, split my windpipe, marry,* and *burn me* are heard in America today, when they are heard at all, only among candidates in theology and Boy Scouts. The English, indeed, have never recovered from the blight of Puritanism, and their swearing strikes all other civilized peoples as puny. They are constantly working up a pother over such forms as *bloody,* which to the rest of the world are quite innocuous. *Good gracious,* which appeared in Oliver Goldsmith's "Good Natur'd Man" in 1768, seems to have been regarded in that day as pretty pungent, and *mercy,* which preceded it by some years, was frowned upon as blasphemous. "Our armies," says Uncle Toby in *Tristram Shandy,* "swore terribly in Flanders," but at home such virtuosity was rare, even among the military. In the wars of our own time, the swearing of the English has provoked the contempt of both their allies and their enemies. In both World War I and World War II, they depended mainly upon a couple of four-letter words that are obscene but not profane, and what they made of them showed little ingenuity or imagination. The American military borrowed these terms in a spirit probably more derisory than admiring, and dropped them the instant they were restored to Mom.

But as the brethren of the Motherland lost their Elizabethan talent for wicked words it was transferred to these shores. Even the Puritans of New England, once they settled down, took to cussing out one another in a violent manner, and thousands of them were sent to the stocks or whipping post for it by their baffled magistrates. The heroes of the Revolution not only swore in all the orthodox forms but also invented a new expletive, *tarnation,* which survived until the Mexican War. As Dr. Louise Pound has demonstrated with great learning, both *tarnation* and *darn* were derived from *eternal* and the former preceded the latter in refined use. George Washington himself cut loose with *hell* and *damn* whenever the imbecilities of his brass went too far. But it was the great movement into the West following the War of 1812 that really laid the foundations of American profanity and got *hell* firmly on its legs. Such striking forms as *to raise hell, to hell around, hell-bent for election, to be hell on, to play hell with, what the hell, heller, merry hell, hellish, hellcat, hell on wheels, hell and high water, from hell to breakfast, a hoot in hell, the hell of it, hell's a-poppin', the hell you say, hell with the lid off,* and *the hinges of hell* were then invented by the gallant fellows, many of them fugitives from Eastern sheriffs, who legged it across the great plains to die for humanity at the hands of Indians, buffalo, catamounts, rattlesnakes, bucking broncos, and vigilance committees. For nearly two generations nine-tenths of the new terms in America, whether profane or not, came from the region beyond Wheeling, West Virginia, and were commonly called Westernisms. It was not until after the Civil War that the newspaper wits of the East began to contribute to the store, and not until after World War I that concocting such things became the monopoly of Hollywood press agents, radio mountebanks, and Broadway columnists.

The great upsurge of *hell* that rose to a climax in the Mexican War era naturally upset the contemporary wowsers, and they busied themselves launching euphemistic surrogates. Some of these seem to have been imported from the British Isles, along with Dundreary whiskers, soda water, and bathing; for example, *by heck,* which originated there as a substitute for *by Hector,* itself a substitute for *by God,* but was already obsolete at home by the time it appeared in America. Here it not only flourished among the prissy in its prototypical form but also moved over into the domain of *hell* and gave birth to *a heck of a, to raise heck, to run like heck, colder than heck, to play heck with, to beat heck, what the heck,* and *go to heck.* Other deputies for *hell* were invented on American soil, notably *thunder* and *blazes. Go to thunder* in the sense of *go to hell* is traced by the "Dictionary of American English" to 1848 and marked an Americanism, and at about the same time *thunderation* began to be used for *damnation.* But soon *thunderation* was used in place of *hell,* as in *what the thunderation.* It is possible that German immigration helped to spread it in its various forms, for a favorite German expletive in those days was *Donnerwetter;* i.e., thundery weather. But this is only a guess, and, like all other learned men, I am suspicious of guessing.

After the Civil War there was another great upsurge of wowserism, culminating in the organization of the Comstock Society in 1873 [1] and of the Woman's Christian Temperance Union the year following. Neither organization devoted itself specifically to profanity, but the moral indignation that radiated from both of them soon began to afflict it, and

---

[1] Its legal name was The New York Society for the Suppression of Vice. In 1947 that name was changed to the Society to Maintain Public Decency. Old Anthony Comstock was snatched up to Heaven in 1915 and succeeded by John S. Sumner.

by 1880 it was being denounced violently in thousands of far-flung evangelical pulpits. In this work, the leader was the Reverend Sam Jones, who had been converted and ordained a Methodist clergyman in 1872. Sam roared against cussing as he roared against boozing, but the Devil fetched him by seducing him into using stronger and stronger language himself, and toward the end of his life I more than once heard him let go with objurgations that would have cheered a bouncer clearing out a Sailor's Bethel. Even the Catholics, who ordinarily never mistake the word for the deed, joined the crusade, and in 1882 they were reviving the Holy Name Society, which had been organized back in 1274 and then forgotten. This combined assault had some effect; indeed, it probably had much more effect than it has been given credit for. At all events, the lush profanity of the Civil War era began to shrink and pale, and such unearthly oaths as *Jesus Christ and John Jacob Astor, by the high heels of St. Patrick,* and *by the double-barreled jumping Jiminetty* began to vanish from the American repertory. *God damn* kept going downhill throughout my youth in the eighties and nineties, and by the time I came of age I seldom used it. Many new euphemisms took the places of the forthright oaths of an earlier day, and one of them, *hully gee,* quickly became so innocuous that when Edward W. Townsend introduced it into "Chimmie Fadden," in 1895, it fell almost as flat as the four-letter words with which the lady novelists now pepper their pages.

But *hell* and *damn* somehow survived this massacre—maybe because the new euphemisms left a man choking and gasping when the steam really rose in his gauges, or maybe because some amateur canon lawyer discovered that in their naked state, uncoupled to sacred names, they are not officially blasphemous. Whatever the reason, American profanity was saved, and to this day it revolves around them and recruits itself from their substance. *Damn* is plainly the feebler of the two, despite its crashing effect when used by a master. *Hell* is enormously more effective, if only because it is more protean. For one phrase embodying the former there are at least forty embodying the latter, and many of them are susceptible to elegant and ingenious permutations. It is impossible for *damn* to bust loose, or to freeze over; it is impossible to knock it out of anyone, or to give it to anyone, or to beat it, or to raise it, or to think of a snowball or a bat in it, or to link it to high water, or to be *damn*-bent for election, or to plunge from *damn*-to-breakfast, or to *damn* around, or to get the *damn* out of any place, or to pull its lid off, or to think of it as having hubs or hinges. There is no such thing as a *damn*-hound, a *damn*cat, a *damn*hole, or a *damn*ion. Nothing is as black as *damn,* as busy as *damn,* as hot (or cold) as *damn,* or as deep, crazy, dumb, clever, cockeyed, crooked, touchy, dead, drunk, nervous, dull, expensive, scared, funny, hungry, lonely, mad, mean, poor, real, rotten, rough, serious, sick, smart, or sore as *damn*. *Damn* is a simple verb and its only child is a simple adjective, but *hell* ranges over all the keys of the grammatical scale and enters into combinations as avidly as oxygen.

There was a time when men learned in the tongues turned trembling backs upon such terms, but in recent years they have shown a libido for studying them, and the result is a rising literature. One of the earliest of the new monographs upon the subject—and still one of the best—was published in *American Speech* in August, 1931, by Dr. L. W. Merryweather. Probing scientifically, he discovered a great deal about *hell* that no one had ever noticed before. It can be slung about, he found, through nearly all the parts of speech. It can be used to represent almost every shade of meaning from yes to no, so that *hell of a time* may mean both the seraphic felicity of a police sergeant in a brewery and the extreme discomfort of a felon in the electric chair. A thing may be either *hotter than hell* or *colder than hell*. A *hellcat* may be either a woman so violent that her husband jumps overboard or nothing worse than a college cheerleader. *What in hell* is a mere expression of friendly interest, but *who the hell says so* is a challenge to fight. Merryweather threw out the suggestion that the upsurge and proliferation of *hell* in the Old West may have been due to Mormon influence. The Saints, he said, were very pious fellows and avoided the vain use of sacred names, but they were also logicians and hence concluded that the use of terms of precisely opposite connotation might be allowable, and even praiseworthy. At all events, they began to swear *by hell* and to call ordinary Christians *hellions* and *sons of hell*, and these terms were quickly borrowed by the miners, trappers, highwaymen, and others who invaded their Zion, and out of them flowed some of the most esteemed terms in *hell* of today. Whether Merryweather was right here I do not presume to say, but in another of his conclusions he undoubtedly slipped, as even savants sometimes do. "Today," he said, "*hell* fills so large a place in the American vulgate that it will probably be worn out in a few years more, and will become obsolescent." We all know now that nothing of the sort has happened. *Hell*, in fact, is flourishing as never before. I have many hundreds of examples of its use in my archives, and new ones are being added almost every day.

A large number of swell ones were assembled into a monograph by another scholar, Dr. Bartlett Jere Whiting, published in *Harvard Studies and Notes in Philology and Literature*, Vol. XX, 1938. Whiting, a sequestered philologian interested chiefly in Old and Middle England, sought his material not in the market place but in books—mostly novels of the 1920–37 period. But even within this narrow and somewhat dephlogisticated field he found enough phrases based on *hell* to fill twenty-four pages of the austere journal in which he wrote. I have space for only a few examples: *holy hell, fifteen kinds of hell, to batter hell* into, assorted hell, the seven hinges of hell, thicker than fiddlers in hell, four naked bats out of hell, like a shot out of hell, the chance of a celluloid collar in hell, three hurrahs in hell, hell's own luck, hell up Sixth Street, hell on toast, from hell to Harvard, hell gone from nowhere, like a hangman from hell, hell's half acre, hell-for-leather, and what the red (or bloody) hell. Whiting duly noted hell of a business, hurry, jam, job, life, mess, place, note, row, time, and way but overlooked George Ade's hell of a Baptist. He added some euphemisms for hell—for example, billy-be-damned, billy-ho, and blazes—but he had to admit that these "makeshifts and conscience-easers," as he called them, were all pretty feeble.

Robert Southey, more than a century ago, investigated the names of the principal devils of Hell, and not only printed a list of them in one of his books but also suggested that some might be useful as cuss words; e.g., Lacahabarrutu, Buzache, Knockadawe, Baa, and Ju. There were, however, no takers for his suggestion and he got no further with the subject. In Harlem, according to Zora Neale Hurston, the dark geographers have discovered that there is a hotter Hell lying somewhat south of the familiar Christian resort, and have given it the name of Beluthahatchie. So far, not much has been learned about its amperage, sociology, or public improvements, but its temperature has been fixed tentatively somewhere between that of a blast furnace and that of the sun. These Afro-American explorers also believe that their spectroscopes have found three suburbs of Hell proper, by name Diddy-wah-diddy, Ginny Gall, and West Hell. Unhappily, not much is known about them, though several ghosts returned to earth report that Diddy-wah-diddy is a sort of Long Island, given over mainly to eating houses and night clubs, and that West Hell lies beyond the railroad tracks and is somewhat tacky.

STUDY QUESTIONS

1. According to Mencken, what is the early history of the word hell? What is the effect of his noting that it is older than either home or mother?

2. What evidence does he cite for the growth of the use of hell in this country?

3. Look up the meaning of the word wowser. What, according to Mencken, did the wowsers have to do with the history of the word hell in this country?

4. To Mencken, hell is much stronger and more effective than damn. How does he support his opinion? Do you agree?

5. Can you add any phrases based on hell to the list Mencken gives as collected by Dr. Whiting? What is the status of hell and phrases based on it today?

6.   Examine Mencken's diction. It has been called vigorous. Can you cite
     his use of particular words that justify this? How does he use certain
     words to make judgments?

THE DECLINE AND FALL

Dwight MacDonald   OF ENGLISH

Dwight MacDonald (1906–   ) was born in New York City. He
received his undergraduate degree from Yale University in 1928.
He became a critic, political commentator, and reviewer, and has
been a regular contributor to numerous magazines and journals.
He has been editor of *Fortune* magazine and *Partisan Review*. He
founded and edited the magazine *Politics*. Among his books are
Memoirs of a Revolutionist (1957), *Henry Wallace, the Man and
the Myth* (1948), and *Parodies: An Anthology from Chaucer to Beerbohm and After* (1960), which he edited.

Now that English has become the most widely used common language in the world, the great lingua franca of our time, it is ironical that
signs of disintegration are appearing in its chief home, the U.S.A. It is as
though Alexander the Great, encamped on the Indus, had received news
of an insurrection back in Macedon.

In *Words and Idioms* (1925) the late Logan Pearsall Smith wrote:

> More and more, too, this standard speech, and the respect for its
> usages, is being extended, and there is not the slightest danger at the
> present day that its authority or dominance will be questioned or disre-
> garded. The danger lies rather in the other direction—that in our scrupu-
> lous and almost superstitious respect for correct English we may forget
> that other and freer forms of spoken English have also their value. . . .
> The duty of [the educated classes] is, under normal conditions, one of
> conservatism, of opposition to the popular tendencies. But when the
> forces of conservatism become too strong, they may do well to relax their
> rigour and lean more to the democratic side.

Mr. Smith, an American living in England, was a connoisseur of
English whose *Trivia* is still readable because of its style. But he was a
bad prophet. In 1957 another authority, Sir Ernest Gowers, addressing
the English Association in London, felt obliged to strike rather a different note:

First published in *Life* International, © 1962 Time, Inc. Reprinted in *Against the
American Grain: Essays in Mass Culture*, by Dwight MacDonald (Random House).

Strange things are happening in the English language. The revolt against the old grammarians seems to be producing a school of thought who hold that grammar is obsolete and it does not matter how we write so long as we can make ourselves understood. It cannot be denied that if we had to choose between the two, it would be better to be ungrammatical than unintelligible. But we do not have to choose between the two. We can rid ourselves of those grammarians' fetishes which make it more difficult to be intelligible without throwing the baby away with the bath water.

The democratic ignoramus (who may have a Ph.D.) is now to be feared more than the authoritarian pedant. For the forces of tradition and conservation in the use of English have been weakened, and the forces of disintegration strengthened, to a degree which Logan Pearsall Smith could not have anticipated a mere thirty-five years ago.

It is not a question of the language changing. All languages change and often for the better—as the de-sexualization of English nouns and the de-inflection of English verbs and adjectives. I don't know which "grammarians' fetishes" Sir Ernest had in mind, but my own list would include: "It's me" (the man who says "It's I" is a prig); the split infinitive (often much neater, as "to thoroughly examine"); prepositions at the end of sentences (which H. W. Fowler in *Modern English Usage* sees as "an important element in the flexibility of the language"); the who-whom bother (I have my own opinion of the receptionist who says "Whom do you wish to see?"); and all the nonsense about "shall" v. "will" and "can" v. "may."

Such finicky "refinements," analogous to the extended little finger in drinking tea, have nothing to do with the problem of good English. What is to the point is that the language is being massacred, particularly by us Americans. When the comedian Phil Silvers says "I feel nauseous" when he means "nauseated," or the television commentator David Susskind speaks of "a peripatetic rush" when he means "precipitate," or the Consumers Commercial Corporation begins a sales letter: "As a good customer of ours, we want to be sure you know that . . . ," or models in ads request each other to "Scotch me lightly" or to "cigarette me" (not to mention "to host" and "to gift")—when these little contretemps occur, one shrugs and lights a Winston, which tastes good like a cigarette should. But then one reads the opening of a feature article in the respected New York *Herald Tribune:* "Bernard Goldfine's troubles keep multiplying. Aside from the prospect of spending more time in prison, his family already is fighting . . . over the estate." Or, in a recent issue of *Dissent,* a highbrow quarterly, such locutions as "Mr. Jadhav's angry retort to my remarks about Rommanohar Lohia and his Socialist party are regrettable. . . ." Or, in a *New York Times* review: "Oddly enough, of all the great plays that the great Eugene O'Neill wrote, only nine talking films (according to our reckoning) have been made of them."

The *Times* is especially disturbing because of its justified prestige as a newspaper. Its critical departments tirelessly chip away at the structure of English prose. The *Times Book Review,* the most influential critical organ in America as far as sales go, is a veritable lead mine of bad English. As, recently:

> Though random samplings disclose the daily Buchwald column to be considerably less of a gastronomic delight than his year-end ragouts, still . . . the pay-dirt to raw-ore ratio runs high, and his humor remains a green isle in the rising tide of dullness.

And the rot extends much higher than journalism. Those who should be the guardians of the language, namely the members of our learned professions, have developed a new vocabulary which is as barbarously specialized as the beatniks' lingo and which has had as disastrous an effect on English. "The concept of sociocultural levels is a heuristic means of analyzing developmental sequences and internal structures. The approach seeks hierarchies both of organization and of sequence—the autonomous nuclear family, extended families of various types superimposed upon the nuclear family, or a multicommunity state unifying hitherto independent settlements." So states a recent article in *Daedalus,* the official organ of the American Academy of Arts and Sciences, a prestigious review which any aspiring academic would be proud to be printed in. American universities are factories of bad prose. On a single page of the February 4, 1962, *New York Times Book Review* two college presidents masquerading as critics commit grammatical howlers that should not be forgiven a fifth-grader. "The worst effect of this composite approach," writes Dr. Edward D. Eddy Jr., president of Chatham College, "is to instill in the college graduate the notion that somehow he or she must be different than others because a degree was granted." Dr. Eddy's degree hasn't made him different "than" others. Dr. Francis H. Horn, president of the University of Rhode Island, swings into action lower down the same page: "An eminent mathematician with more than thirty years experience as teacher and administrator, his voice must be heard and his observations receive serious consideration. . . ." Now, class . . .

Even when the writer is professionally engaged in the study of English, the result, while grammatical, is often deplorable. Thus Professor Albert H. Marckwardt, a scholar of repute, can find no better words to end his recent work on *American English* than:

> It is our responsibility to realize whither the language is tending, and the duty of our schools and teachers to promulgate healthy linguistic attitudes. If this is done, we may be certain that some individuals can and will attain greatness in the use of the language, which in turn will

make of it a more flexible and sensitive medium for the rest of us. In this sense, a new era lies before all the English-speaking people.

Physician, heal thyself.

As for Dr. Marckwardt's coming "new era" to be promoted by "healthy linguistic attitudes," these concepts strike a chill into anyone who has been following what some of our learned men have been doing to English of late. The revisions of the King James Bible are a case in point, as is the third edition of the unabridged Merriam-Webster dictionary. This last, as I have noted earlier, is one of the many unfortunate effects of that new method of language study called Structural Linguistics.[1]

The origins of Structural Linguistics go back to the end of the last century when the Danish scholar Otto Jespersen put forward a theory that change in language is not only natural but good, and when the Oxford English Dictionary began publishing its thirteen volumes. Up to then the prevailing view of English was that it was a logical structure based on Latin and that any departure from the rules deduced from this assumption meant deterioration and vulgarization. The difficulty was that English, like all living languages, was in fact in a constant state of change, and that the changes were usually away from the grammarians' and purists' notions of what English really *was*. By the end of the nineteenth century, there seemed to be two languages: English as she was spoke and English as the grammarians insisted she should be spoke (and wrote)—a real language versus a Platonic archetype that was as mystical and hard to grasp as the Holy Ghost. The importance of the Oxford English Dictionary, which began to appear in 1884 and published its last volume in 1928, was that it followed the changes in the meaning of each word by giving examples of usage from the Anglo-Saxon period on. There was no doubt about it, the language had constantly changed.

Structural Linguistics is an American invention and its impact has been felt mostly in America. I am incompetent to judge its technical claims but my impression is that it is—scientifically—greatly superior to the approach of the old grammarians. The trouble is that, like some other scientific advances—one thinks of Freud—it has been applied to

---

[1] A distinction is sometimes made between Structural Linguistics and Descriptive Linguistics, the former term being used for the purely scientific methods developed by such scholars as Chomsky, Lees, and Harris, and the latter for the application of these methods to teaching and lexicography. It is useful (and fair) to distinguish the scholars from the vulgarizers, but this terminology is not common, so I have followed the usual practice and used Structural Linguistics to cover both the doctrine and its practical application.

areas which, because they involve qualitative judgments, simply cannot be reduced to the objective, quantitative terms of science. Such areas are the teaching of English and the making of dictionaries.

The basic principles of Structural Linguistics are defined as follows in *The English Language Arts,* a book published in 1952 by the Commission on the English Curriculum of the National Council of Teachers of English:

1. Language changes constantly.
2. Change is normal.
3. Spoken language is the language.
4. Correctness rests upon usage.
5. All usage is relative.

At first glance, these principles seem unexceptionable, indeed almost truisms. But a closer look reveals that the last three are half-truths, the most dangerous of formulations; half a truth is *not* better than no truth at all.

It may be natural for the Structural Linguists, who have devoted most of their attention to primitive languages, to assume that the "real" language is the spoken one and not the written one, but this has not always been true: many of the words coined from Latin and Greek in the Elizabethan period, words we still use, were introduced by scholars or poets in their writings. Today, what with far greater literacy and the proliferation of printed matter, the written word would seem to be even more important than in the past.

"Correctness rests upon usage" is more nearly true, but the Structural Linguists underestimate the influence of purists, grammarians and schoolmarms. It is true that Swift, an arch-conservative, objected to such eighteenth century neologisms as *mob, bully, sham, bubble* and *banter,* all of which have since become standard English. But he also objected, and successfully, to contractions like *disturb'd,* to *phiz* for *face, hyp* for *hypochondriac,* and *pozz* for *positive.* The purists have won at least two major victories: they have made the double negative, often used by Shakespeare and a perfectly legitimate means of emphasis, a stigma of illiteracy, and they have crusaded so effectively against *ain't* that, though Webster's Third alleges differently, it can't be used any more even as a contraction of *am not* without danger of cultural excommunication. One may deplore these victories, as I do, but we cannot deny they have taken place, as the Structural Linguists sometimes seem to do.

"All usage is relative" is either a truism (different classes and localities speak differently) or else misleading. "The contemporary linguist does not employ the terms 'good English' and 'bad English' except in a purely relative sense," *The English Language Arts* explains. "He recognizes the fact that language is governed by the situation in which it occurs." But this principle leads to an undemocratic freezing of status, since "irregardless" and "he knowed" are standard usage in certain circles, and those not the richest or best educated. So the Horatio Alger of today, bemused by teachers well grounded in Structural Linguistics, will keep on massacring the king's English because his fellow newsboys do ("language is governed by the situation in which it occurs") and the philanthropic merchant will be so appalled by Horatio's double negatives that he will not give him The Job. In their *Modern American Grammar and Usage* (1956), J. N. Hook and E. G. Mathews, writing in the orthodox canon, observe apropos of what they delicately call "substandard English"; "We must re-emphasize that this language is not wrong; it is merely not in harmony with the usages generally found in books . . . or heard in the conversations of those persons with a strong consciousness of language." They then give an example of substandard English: "Bein's he uz a'ready late, he done decide not to pay her no mind." If this is not wrong, it seems hardly worth the bother to teach English at all.

One of the far-out books in the canon is a 1960 paperback called *Linguistics and Your Language,* by Robert A. Hall, Jr., professor of linguistics at Cornell. Browsing through Professor Hall's book is an unsettling experience. "A dictionary or grammar is not as good an authority for your own speech as the way you yourself speak," he observes. Thus: "*Hisn, hern* and so forth are often heard from illiterate people, perhaps more often than from people who know how to read and write; but there is no necessary connection." (I do like "perhaps more often" and "no necessary connection.") Then Dr. Hall goes all the way: " 'Correct' spelling, that is, obedience to the rules of English spelling as grammarians and dictionary-makers set them up, has come to be a major shibboleth in our society. . . . Consequently, anyone who goes through our schooling system has to waste years of his life in acquiring a wasteful and, in the long run, damaging set of spelling habits, thus ultimately unfitting himself to understand the nature of language." English spelling is indeed maddeningly illogical, but we're stuck with it. For one thing, if spelling is to be "relativized" according to "the situation in which it occurs," it would be impossible to look up a word in the dictionary, which would be all right with Dr. Hall, who believes that the free, democratic and linguistically structured citizen should not bow to authority. Logically, Dr. Gove should agree with him, but in fact Dr. Gove edited Webster's Third. And logically, Dr. Hall should not submit to shibboleths of "correct" spelling imposed on us by authoritarian grammarians, but in fact he does; every word in his book is "correctly" spelled.

One of Dr. Hall's special fields is pidgin English and one gets the impression he thinks it just about as good as any other kind—after all, it *communicates,* doesn't it? Me writem big fella book along say teacher man no savvy more nobody other fella.

Dr. Hall is a member of the academic establishment, which brings up the question of how effectively Americans are being taught to use their language. Last year the National Council of Teachers of English published a disturbing report: *The National Interest and the Teaching of English.* Its main findings were: some four million U.S. school children have "reading disabilities"; 150,000 students failed college entrance tests in English in 1960; two-thirds of America's colleges have to provide remedial work in English. The same note was sounded in another recent report, by the Council for Basic Education. This report estimates that 35 per cent of all U.S. students are seriously retarded in reading. It blames mostly the "whole-word" or "look-say" method of reading instruction which has become standard in American public schools, by which the child is taught to recognize only whole words instead of to build up words by learning his alphabet and its sounds (the "phonic" system which was traditional until the 'thirties). The child learns not his ABC's but his AT-BAT-CAT's. This device enables the successful pupils to recognize 1,342 words by the end of the third grade. The report claims that the old-fashioned phonic method would produce twice as big a vocabulary by the end of the *first* grade.

There is also the comparison of Soviet and American school programs recently made by Dr. Arther S. Trace: *What Ivan Knows That Johnny Doesn't.* Dr. Trace confined himself to demonstrating the inferiority of our textbooks and curricula in reading, history, literature, foreign languages and geography—we already know how superior Soviet schools are in physics and mathematics. His findings about reading are to the point here. Ivan in the *first* grade uses a primer that has 2,000 words, which is just 500 more than Johnny gets in his *fourth*-grade readers. Ivan reads Tolstoy in the first grade; Johnny reads Mary Louise Friebele, whose works include A *Good, Big Fire, The Blue and Yellow Boats,* and A *Funny Sled.* By the fourth grade, Ivan is coping with a vocabulary of 10,000 words, which is more than five times as many as Johnny has learned in school (though, of course, he is at liberty to pick up as many extracurricular words as he likes; our educationists have not so far discovered a way to prevent children getting wised up outside the classroom, such as supplementing Mary Louise Friebele with a little Dickens read by flashlight under the bedclothes). This result is achieved, according to Dr. Trace, by another Rube Goldbergian device called "vocabulary control" which actually is designed to *reduce* the number of new words that a school child will encounter. The theory is that too many new words may have a traumatic effect.

As might be expected, the illiteracy of the young is even worse when it comes to writing. The University of Pittsburgh recently tested 450,000 high-school students and found that only one out of a hundred was able to produce a five-minute theme without faults in English. In my own slight experience teaching English—three months at Northwestern University several years ago—I was struck by the contrast between the fluency of my students when they spoke in class and the difficulty most of them had in producing a grammatical and correctly spelled composition. The only explanation I could think of was that they had learned to speak outside the classroom—and to write inside it.

The jeremiads of the National Council of Teachers of English seem to be written from the moon. They offer no criticism of the things outside observers think are responsible for student illiteracy: the "look-say" method of teaching reading, infantile textbooks, and "vocabulary control." For these are part of official doctrine and it would be unthinkable that the illiteracy the Council deplores might be caused by the educational techniques the Council approves. The Council has quite a lot to say about Structural Linguistics, and all favorable. If only, one gathers, more teachers were indoctrinated with this approach, what wonders would follow.

The English scholar I. A. Richards, who, with C. K. Ogden, wrote *The Meaning of Meaning* and later invented Basic English, delivered himself of some thoughts and emotions on this topic in 1955:

> There are vast areas of so-called "purely descriptive" linguistics which are a grim danger at present to the conduct of language, to education, to standards of intelligence. . . . The appeal to mere *usage* . . . is a case in point. Every useful feature of language was *not in use* once upon a time. Every degradation of language too starts somewhere. Behind usage is the question of efficiency. Inefficient language features are not OK, however widespread their use. Of course, to the linguistic botanist it is important to preserve all varieties until they have been collected and described. But that is not the point of view of the over-all study of language, its services and its powers. That over-all view is, I am insisting, inescapably NORMATIVE. It is concerned . . . with the maintenance and improvement of the use of language.

The word "normative," which implies there is a norm or standard, produces the same reactions in a Structural Linguist as "integration" does in a Southern White Supremacist. Dr. Richards instanced as an example of the degradation of English the growing interchangeability of *disinterested* and *uninterested*, which Webster's Third gives as synonyms. The Structural Linguist position on these words was explained in a recent article in *College Composition and Communication* by Dr. Robert J. Geist. Dr. Geist could see no reason for making a fuss: "I think it can safely be stated that a word means what a speaker intends it to mean and what a hearer interprets it to mean." That there might be some discrepancy between what a speaker intends and what a hearer interprets, and that language is efficient only insofar as it reduces this discrepancy—these truisms didn't occur to Dr. Geist at the moment of writing the foregoing sentence. But he seems to have vaguely sensed later on that something was wrong; at least he does add a parenthesis: "(I use *disinterested* to mean *impartial* only.)" Like other permissive linguists, he doesn't dare to practice what he preaches.

The whole matter of the development of English is more complicated than it is thought to be by either the old-school grammarians or the Structural Linguists. In the early period of the language, when it was in a state of chronic (and creative) flux, nobody bothered much about correctness. Even spelling was not taken seriously—our greatest writer spelled his name Shakespeare, Shakspere, or Shakspeare as the spirit moved him. It was not until 1721 that the first real dictionary appeared, when Nathaniel Bailey had the novel idea of trying to include *all* the words. Up to then, there had only been lists of "hard words." Such lists were welcomed because of the enormous accretion of new words, mostly invented from Greek or Latin roots, in the Elizabethan and Jacobean periods. Conservatives denounced these as "inkhorn terms"—i.e., used only in writing to show one's learning—and so many of them were. But most have survived. A contemporary rhetorician composed a parody "inkhorn" letter; while many have perished (*revolute, obtestate, fatigate, splendidious*), most are still current (*affability, ingenious, fertile, contemplate, clemency, verbosity*). By 1650, the language was settling down, the new words were largely accepted, and even spelling was beginning to be standardized. "Some people if they but spy a hard word are as much amazed as if they met with a hobgoblin," Edward Phillips wrote contemptuously in his *New World of Words* (1658).

But usage was not really fixed until the eighteenth century when the literate public expanded suddenly—between 1700 and 1800 the publication of new books quadrupled—because of the rise of the bourgeoisie and the beginning of the industrial revolution. The new-rich classes wanted to show they were cultured gentlemen and so offered a market for dictionaries and grammars, which played the same social role as the books of etiquette which first became popular then. (In Soviet Russia a similar sudden rise in literacy similarly connected with industrialization has produced similar effects—*kulturny* is a potent word there, applied to everything from diction to using a handkerchief to blow one's nose.) In the eighteenth century the literary atmosphere was favorable to the language's becoming standardized. The creative surge of 1550–1650 had ebbed and now, from Pope to Johnson, there followed an Augustan age of classic consolidation. Swift was an impassioned conservative who hoped to "fix the language." But he was not alone in fearing that, if change went on unchecked, in a few generations his own works "shall hardly be understood without an interpreter." He tried to revive Dryden's proposal for an English Academy—on the model of the French Academy founded by Cardinal Richelieu in the preceding century— which would have for its object, in the words of the French Academy's statute: "to give definite rules to our language, and to render it pure, eloquent and capable of treating the arts and sciences [and] to establish a certain usage of words." Nothing came of this project, despite impressive intellectual backing. Even Dr. Johnson, hardly a permissive type, opposed it in the preface to his dictionary (1755) as hostile to "the spirit of English liberty." Johnson also advanced a more pragmatic criticism: "Those who have been persuaded to think well of my design require that it should fix our language and put a stop to those alterations which time and chance have hitherto been suffered to make in it without opposition. With this consequence I will confess that I flattered myself for a while; but now begin to fear that I have indulged expectations which neither reason nor experience can justify." He pointed out that there is "no example of a nation that has preserved their words and phrases from mutability"—later purists must have shuddered at the confusion of plural and singular—and noted that "the French language has visibly changed under the inspection of the academy." The grammarians of the eighteenth and nineteenth centuries, lacking Johnson's common sense, objected to change per se because their model of a proper language, Latin, had not changed for 1,500 years. But it had not changed because it was a dead language for precisely that period; the Latin that continued to live, monks' Latin, changed until it became a patois related to Latin as pidgin English is related to English.

On the other hand, while no permanent deep freeze is possible in a language, the fact is that English has been to some extent "fixed" in the last two centuries. (Johnson's dictionary was an important factor in the fixing.) The forces that tended this way in the eighteenth century became much stronger in the nineteenth when there was more literacy, more social mobility, and more industrialization—there seems to be some relation between the requirements of a rationalized industrial society and the standardization of language. More and more people came into the cultural market place—ambitious workingmen who wanted to "better" themselves, *nouveaux riches* who wanted to be considered gentlemen. The upper classes hitherto had used English with the easy negligence of proprietors who can do as they like with their own, but now the rich were not so secure in their ownership. Now began the long dominance of the grammarians and the schoolmarms. The economic base was exposed by Bernard Shaw: "People know very well that certain sorts of speech cut off a person forever from getting more than three or four pounds a week all their life long—sorts of speech which make them entirely impossible to certain professions." The ambitious workingman who uses Webster's Third as a guide will be in for some rude shocks when he says "I ain't" to the personnel director.

Or he may not be. The personnel manager may say "ain't" to *him*. Perhaps the most ominous sign of the decay of English in the United States, the vanishing of the very notion of standards under the pressure of the vulgarians and the academicians, is the recent decision of the Sherwin Cody School of English to drop its traditional advertising punch line: "DO *you* MAKE THESE MISTAKES IN ENGLISH?" For forty years this has been a classic of correspondence-school advertising, on a par with "THEY LAUGHED WHEN I SAT DOWN AT THE PIANO." Now it is obsolete. "The key fact is," an executive of the school has explained, "people don't want to speak good English any more. The correspondence course used to be popular among people who wanted to advance themselves and speak better. Now no one cares about grammatical errors." And indeed the horrible examples that the school's ads used to cite—"Leave them lay," "Between you and I"—would be swallowed without a wink by any good Structural Linguist.

English is not just a convenient means of communicating, as the Structural Linguists seem to think. The language of a people, like its art and literature and music and architecture, is a record of its past that has much to say to the present. If this connection is broken, then a people gets into the condition of a psychotic who has lost contact with his past. Superseding the King James Version of the Bible with a translation in the modern idiom is like updating Shakespeare—"The problem of existence or nonexistence confronts us." Language is a specially important part of a people's past, or culture, because everybody is exposed to it and has to learn to use it. The evolution of words is a capsule history of the race, as one can verify by reading a few pages of the Oxford English Dictionary. There is always a struggle between tradition and novelty. If the society is too permissive, novelty has it too easy and the result is language that has lost contact with its past and that is, usually, ineffective as communication because it is vague and formless—in beatnik slang "man" and "like" have degenerated to mere interruptions, more stammer than grammar.

Language does indeed change, but there must be some brakes and it is the function of teachers, writers and lexicographers to apply them.[2]

---

[2] Everybody, including myself, now sneers at the "schoolmarms," and they do have some ghastly mistakes on their conscience. But at least they accepted

It is their job to make it tough for new words and usages to get into circulation so that the ones that survive will be the fittest. *Mob* made it despite Swift, but *pozz* didn't; the point is not that Swift was right or wrong but that he had a sense of the language, which he used as well as any writer has, and that he cared enough about it to raise the question. Today the best English is written and spoken in London—the contrast is painful between the letters-to-the-editor departments of the London *Times* and the *New York Times*—because there an educated class still values the tradition of the language. For English, like other languages, is an aesthetic as well as a practical means of communication. It is compounded of tradition and beauty and style and experience and not simply of what happens when two individuals meet in a barroom, or a classroom. "We must write for the people in the language of kings," Bertolt Brecht once said. Americans seem to be reversing his maxim.

STUDY QUESTIONS

1. MacDonald contends that the English language is being "massacred," and cites examples to support his contention. What does he find objectionable in each of the examples?
2. What are the shortcomings he finds in the structural linguistics approach to language study? How does he support his views?
3. What is MacDonald's position on the older, traditional approach to language?
4. How does he regard change in language?
5. According to MacDonald, what is the teacher's responsibility?
6. Would MacDonald be more inclined to agree with Follett's views ("Sabotage in Springfield," p. 355) or with Evans' ("But What's a Dictionary For?" p. 364)? Explain.

---

responsibility and at least they understood their pupils needed prescription as well as description. And the worst mistake they made, as my friend Dean Moody Prior, of Northwestern University, has recently pointed out to me, was to humbly transmit to their students the theories about language that were dominant in the scholarly circles of their day. I can see the linguists of the year 2,000 (who will by then have developed some vast new theory, perhaps based on the Jungian racial unconscious) sneering at the "schoolmarms" of the sixties with their myopic and dogmatic adherence to outworn notions, i.e., Structural Linguistics. And I can see the schoolmarms again taking the rap (*slang*) rather than the eminent scholars whose theories they accepted with a faith as incautious as it was touchingly modest. When does a teacher become a schoolmarm? When the Authorities he or she relies on are considered outdated by the new Authorities. Up to then, he or she is a member in good standing of the National Council of Teachers of English and a useful member of society.

PREFACE TO WEBSTER'S
THIRD NEW INTERNATIONAL
Philip B. Gove **DICTIONARY**

Philip B. Gove (1902–   ) is editor in chief of the controversial
Webster's Third New International Dictionary. He received his
A.B. from Dartmouth College, his A.M. from Harvard, and his
Ph.D. from Columbia. After teaching for several years at Rice
University and New York University, he joined the staff of the
Merriam-Webster Company. He has published widely in the
learned journals and is active in professional organizations; he is
the author of *The Imaginary Voyage of Prose Fiction* (1941).

WEBSTER'S THIRD NEW INTERNATIONAL DICTIONARY is a completely
new work, redesigned, restyled, and reset. Every line of it is new. This
latest unabridged Merriam-Webster is the eighth in a series which has
its beginning in Noah Webster's *American Dictionary of the English
Language,* 1828. On Webster's death in 1843 the unsold copies and
publishing rights of his dictionary were acquired by George and Charles
Merriam, who in 1847 brought out a revision edited by Noah Webster's
son-in-law, Professor Chauncey A. Goodrich of Yale College. The 1847
edition became the first Merriam-Webster unabridged dictionary.* G. &
C. Merriam Company now offers WEBSTER'S THIRD NEW INTERNATIONAL
DICTIONARY to the English-speaking world as a prime linguistic aid to
interpreting the culture and civilization of today, as the first edition
served the America of 1828.

   As the number of students in school and college jumps to ever-
increasing heights, the quantity of printed matter necessary to their
education increases too. Not only are more words used more often with

---

   * The successors in the Merriam-Webster series are *American Dictionary of the
English Language,* popularly known as the *Unabridged,* 1864, edited by Dr. Noah
Porter, president of Yale College; *Webster's International Dictionary,* 1890,
Noah Porter, editor in chief; *Webster's New International Dictionary,* 1909, Dr.
William Torrey Harris, U. S. Commissioner of Education, editor in chief, and
F. Sturges Allen, general editor; *Webster's New International Dictionary, Second
Edition,* 1934, Dr. William Allan Neilson, president of Smith College, editor in
chief, and Dr. Thomas A. Knott, general editor.

these increases; words must be used more economically and more efficiently both in school and out. More and more do people undertaking a new job, practicing a new hobby, or developing a new interest turn to how-to pamphlets, manuals, and books for both elementary instruction and advanced guidance. Where formerly they had time to learn by doing, they now need to begin by reading and understanding what has been recorded. A quick grasp of the meanings of words becomes necessary if one is to be successful. A dictionary opens the way to both formal learning and to the daily self-instruction that modern living requires. It is the key also to the daily newspaper and to a vast number of other periodicals that demand our attention. This edition has been prepared with a constant regard for the needs of the high school and college student, the technician, and the periodical reader, as well as of the scholar and professional. It undertakes to provide for the changes in public interest in all classes of words as manifested by what people want to read, discuss, and study. The dictionary more than ever is the indispensable instrument of understanding and progress.

G. & C. Merriam Company have produced this THIRD NEW INTERNATIONAL at a cost of over $3,500,000. The budgetary and technical planning underlying its production has been directed and coordinated since 1953 by the Company's president, Mr. Gordon J. Gallan. His activity, understanding, and cooperation have contributed indispensably to its editorial completion and have made possible the maintenance of a Merriam-Webster permanent office staff constituted according to need. This staff is in effect a faculty which specializes in different branches of knowledge much as a small college faculty does. Listed among the resident editors are a mathematician, a physicist, a chemist, a botanist, a biologist, a philosopher, a political scientist, a comparative religionist, a classicist, a historian, and a librarian as well as philologists, linguists, etymologists, and phoneticians whose specialty is the English language itself. Their academic affiliations and their degrees can be seen one by one in the "Merriam-Webster Editorial Staff" that follows this preface. Besides the office staff over two hundred other scholars and specialists have served as outside consultants in supplementary reviewing, revising, and submitting new definitions in subjects in which they are authorities. The range and experience of this special knowledge appear in the listing of their names alphabetically after the editorial staff.

In conformity with the principle that a definition, to be adequate, must be written only after an analysis of usage, the definitions in this edition are based chiefly on examples of usage collected since publication of the preceding edition. Members of the editorial staff began in 1936 a systematic reading of books, magazines, newspapers, pamphlets, catalogs, and learned journals. By the time of going to press the collection contained just under 4,500,000 such new examples of recorded usage, to be added to more than 1,665,000 citations already in the files for previous editions. Further, the citations in the indispensable many-volume *Oxford English Dictionary*, the new citations in Sir William Craigie's four-volume *Dictionary of American English* and Mitford M. Mathews' two-volume *Dictionary of Americanisms*, neither of which was available to the editors of the preceding edition, and the uncounted citations in dozens of concordances to the Bible and to works of English and American writers and in numerous books of quotations push the citation background for the definitions in this dictionary to over ten million. This figure does not include freely consulted text matter in the office library of reference books. Nor does it include thousands of text-books in the private and academic libraries of the editors and consultants, nor books consulted in the Springfield City Library whose librarians have generously given the editorial staff ready and frequent access to its large and valuable word-hoard.

While dictionaries of special subjects, glossaries, indexes, and checklists are collected and examined to verify the existence of special words, no word has been entered in this dictionary merely on the authority of another dictionary, special or general, and no definition in this dictionary has been derived from any other dictionary (except, of course, Merriam-Webster predecessors). Learned and industrial organizations have created numerous committees of nomenclature to collect, define, and standardize the terminology in their fields. Some of the staff editors serve as advisory members of such committees. Nevertheless prescriptive and canonical definitions have not been taken over nor have recommendations been followed unless confirmed by independent investigation of usage borne out by genuine citations.

The primary objective of precise, sharp defining has been met through development of a new dictionary style based upon completely analytical one-phrase definitions throughout the book. Since the head-word in a definition is intended to be modified only by structural elements restrictive in some degree and essential to each other, the use of commas either to separate or to group has been severely limited, chiefly to units in apposition or in series. The new defining pattern does not provide for a predication which conveys further expository comment. Instead of encyclopedic treatment at one place of a group of related terms, each term is defined at its own place in the alphabet. Every phrase in lowercase roman type following a heavy black colon and running to the next heavy colon or to a divisional number or letter is a complete definition of one sense of the word to which it is attached. Defining by synonym is carefully avoided by putting all unqualified or undifferentiated terms in small capital letters. Such a term in small capitals should not be considered a definition but a cross-reference to a definition of equivalent meaning that can be substituted for the small capitals.

A large number of verbal illustrations mostly from the mid-twentieth century has been woven into the defining pattern with a view to contributing considerably to the user's interest and understanding by showing a word used in context. The illustration is often a brief combination of words that has actually been used in writing and when this is so the illustration is attributed to its author or source. More than 14,000 different authors are quoted for their use of words or for the structural pattern of their words but not for their opinions or sentiments.

A number of other features are (1) the recognition and separate entry (with part-of-speech label) of verb-plus-adverb compounds (as *run down*) that function like one-word verbs in every way except for having a separable suffix, (2) the recognition (by using the label *n* for noun) that substantive open compounds (as *clothes moth*) belong in the same class as nouns written solid or hyphened, (3) the recognition (by using the label *often attrib*) of nouns that often function as adjectives but otherwise do not behave like the class of adjectives, (4) the indication (by inserting suffix-symbols, as -s or -es, -ed/-ing/-s or -es, -er/-est) of the inflectional forms of nouns, verbs, adjectives, and adverbs at which the forms are not written out in full, (5) the recognition (by beginning entries with a lowercase letter and by inserting either the label *cap, usu cap, often cap,* or *sometimes cap*) that words vary considerably in capitalization according to circumstances and environment, (6) the recognition (by not using at all the status label *colloquial*) that it is impossible to know whether a word out of context is colloquial or not, and (7) the incorporation of abbreviations alphabetically in the main vocabulary.

In continuation of Merriam-Webster policy the editors of this new edition have held steadfastly to the three cardinal virtues of dictionary making: accuracy, clearness, and comprehensiveness. Whenever these qualities are at odds with each other, accuracy is put first and foremost, for without accuracy there could be no appeal to WEBSTER'S THIRD NEW INTERNATIONAL as an authority. Accuracy in addition to requiring freedom from error and conformity to truth requires a dictionary to state meanings in which words are in fact used, not to give editorial opinion on what their meanings should be.

In the editorial striving for clearness the editors have tried to make the definitions as readable as possible. Even so, the terminology of many subjects contains words that can be adequately and clearly explained only to those who have passed through preliminary stages of initiation, just as a knowledge of algebra is prerequisite for trigonometry. A dictionary demands of its user much understanding and no one person can understand all of it. Therefore there is no limit to the possibilities for clarification. Somewhat paradoxically a user of the dictionary benefits in proportion to his effort and knowledge, and his contribution is an essential part of the process of understanding even though it may involve only a willingness to look up a few additional words.

Comprehensiveness requires maximum coverage with a minimum of compromise. The basic aim is nothing less than coverage of the current vocabulary of standard written and spoken English. At the same time the scientific and technical vocabulary has been considerably expanded to keep pace with progress especially in physical science (as in electronics, nuclear physics, statistics, and soil science), in technology (as in rocketry, communications, automation, and synthetics), in medicine, and in the experimental phases of natural science. Therefore space has been found not only for new terms but also for new uses of old terms, for English like other living languages is in a metabolic process of constant change. The changes affect not only word stock but meaning, syntax, morphology, and pronunciation.

The demands for space have made necessary a fresh judgment on the claims of many parts of the old vocabulary. This dictionary is the result of a highly selective process in which discarding material of insubstantial or evanescent quality has gone hand in hand with adding terms that have obtained a place in the language. It confines itself strictly to generic words and their functions, forms, sounds, and meanings as distinguished from proper names that are not generic. Selection is guided by usefulness, and usefulness is determined by the degree to which terms most likely to be looked for are included. Many obsolete and comparatively useless or obscure words have been omitted. These include in general words that had become obsolete before 1755 unless found in well-known major works of a few major writers.

In definitions of words of many meanings the earliest ascertainable meaning is given first. Meanings of later derivation are arranged in the order shown to be most probable by dated evidence and semantic development. This arrangement applies alike to all meanings whether standard, technical, scientific, historical, or obsolete. No definitions are grouped alphabetically by subject labels. In fact this edition uses very few subject labels. It depends upon the definition for incorporating necessary subject orientation.

The pronunciation editor is Mr. Edward Artin. This edition shows as far as possible the pronunciations prevailing in general cultivated conversational usage, both informal and formal, throughout the English-speaking world. It does not attempt to dictate what that usage should be. It shows a wide variety of acceptable pronunciations based on a large file of transcriptions made by attentive listening to actual educated speech in all fields and in all parts of the country—the speech of those expecting to be completely understood by their hearers. The facility with which such speech can be checked today by television, radio, and recordings has made it possible to show more representative and more realistic pronunciations than in the past.

To this end the Merriam-Webster pronunciation key has been revised. Many of the symbols of preceding editions have been retained, some with slight alteration, a few substitutions have been made, and some symbols that have outlived their usefulness have been dropped altogether. It is still fundamentally a diacritical key that makes use of many of the conventions of English spelling and is based on the principles that every distinct significant sound should have a distinct symbol to represent it and that no sound should be represented in more than one way. The elimination of symbols for all nonsignificant differences in sound makes it possible for transcriptions to convey to speakers in different parts of the English-speaking world sounds proper to their own speech. The new pronunciation alphabet is designed to represent clearly the standard speech of educated Americans.

It should be clearly understood that in striving to show realistic pronunciations definite limitations are fixed by the very nature of a dictionary. Each word must be isolated and considered apart from its place in connected spoken discourse. It is impracticable to show in a dictionary many kinds of variations—rising or falling pitch, syllabic emphasis or lack of emphasis, contraction or prolongation of sounds—to which the pronunciation of a word is susceptible under the influence of other words temporarily associated with it. Some of these variations are discussed under several headings in "Guide to Pronunciation," which contains also several paragraphs on the subject of correctness in pronunciation.

The etymologist for this edition is Dr. Charles R. Sleeth. In the etymologies the aim has been to retrace step by step the line of transmission by which the words have come down to modern English from the language in which they are first recorded. The present work adheres in this respect to the sound general principles governing the presentation of word histories in previous editions and indeed applies them with a consistency that has not previously been attained. With particular care it traces back to Middle English every word which is recorded in Middle English; also it carefully distinguishes the age of borrowings from French by giving the source language as Old French if the word came into English before 1300, as Middle French if it came into English between 1300 and 1600, and as French only if it came into English in the seventeenth century or later.

The etymologies fall into four general groups based on the origins of English words. Native words (as *hound*) that have been in the language as long as it has existed are traced back first through Middle English to Old English and then to Germanic languages other than English and to Indo-European languages other than Germanic. Old and well-established borrowings (as *chief, add,* and *dialect*) that have been in English since medieval or Renaissance times and come from languages, usually French, Latin, or often indirectly Greek, which belong, like English, to the Indo-European language family are traced back through their immediate source to their ultimate source in as much detail as native words. Many more recent borrowings (as *éclair, anile, hubris, sforzando, lariat, dachshund, smorgasbord, galore, muzhik,* and *karma*) are incorporated into the network of Indo-European etymology more thoroughly than in earlier dictionaries by going beyond the immediate source to either a list of cognates or a cross-reference to another entry. Borrowings (as *bushido, tepee, sheikh, sampan,* and *taboo*) from non-Indo-European languages are traced to the immediate source and analyzed into their parts if in the source language they are compounds or derivatives.

In the modern technical vocabulary of the sciences it is difficult if not impossible to adhere strictly to the principle of tracing step by step the line of transmission of a word, because such vocabulary has expanded rapidly in numerous fields and has been transmitted freely across language boundaries. Very few works of reference give full or systematic information about the language of origin of technical terms in any one field, and consequently it is impossible for the etymological staff of a general dictionary to garner and present such information about the technical terms of all fields. The present work attempts a new solution of this problem by introducing the label ISV (for International Scientific Vocabulary), for use in the etymology of such words when their language of origin is not positively ascertainable but they are known to be current in at least one language other than English. Examples of the use of ISV and further details about it are given in "Explanatory Notes," 7.6. Some ISV words (like *haploid*) have been created by taking a word with a rather general and simple meaning from one of the languages of antiquity, usually Latin or Greek, and conferring upon it a very specific and complicated meaning for the purposes of modern scientific discourse. More typically, however, ISV words are compounds or derivatives, made up of constituents that can be found entered in their own alphabetical position with their own ulterior etymology, again generally involving Latin or Greek. In either case an ISV etymology as given in the present work incorporates the word into the system of Indo-European etymology as well as if the immediate source language were known and stated. At the same time, use of ISV avoids the often untenable implication that the word in question was coined in English, and recognizes that the word as such is a product of the modern world and gets only its raw materials, so to speak, from antiquity.

The scheme of biological classification used has been concerted in consultation between Dr. Mairé Weir Kay, staff biologist, and specialists in the several divisions of taxonomy. It is planned to coordinate in the broadest way with current professional usage and specifically avoids undue reliance on any single school or system. The total taxonomic coverage is far more extensive than this characterization might imply and is designed to include and link with the preferred scheme both historically important though now disused terminology and the more important terms pertinent to divergent schools of professional thought (as in the question of whether the leguminous plants constitute one or several families).

Words that are believed to be trademarks have been investigated in the files of the United States Patent Office. No investigation has been made of common law trademark rights in any word since such investigation is impracticable. Those that have current registrations are shown with an initial capital and are also identified as trademarks. The inclusion of any word in this dictionary is not, however, an expression of the publishers' opinion on whether or not it is subject to proprietary rights. Indeed, no definition in this dictionary is to be regarded as affecting the validity of any trademark.

This dictionary has a vocabulary of over 450,000 words. It would have been easy to make the vocabulary larger although the book, in the format of the preceding edition, could hardly hold any more pages or be any thicker. By itself, the number of entries is, however, not of first importance. The number of words available is always far in excess of and for a one-volume dictionary many times the number that can possibly be included. To make all the changes mentioned only to come out with the same number of pages and the same number of vocabulary entries as in the preceding edition would allow little or no opportunity for new words and new senses. The compactness and legibility of Times Roman, a typeface new to Merriam-Webster dictionaries, have made possible more words to a line and more lines to a column than in the preceding edition, and a larger size page makes a better proportioned book.

The preparation of this edition has absorbed 757 editor-years. This figure does not include the time of typists, photocopiers, and clerical assistants or the time of over 200 consultants. The book appears, like its predecessor, after more than ten years of active full-time preparation. It is hardly necessary to observe that no one editor could harmonize all the diverse and disparate matter by reading and criticizing every line or even determine and keep firm control over editorial policy, nor could an editorial board of fixed membership. Instead the editor in chief has used his editors one by one and has delegated multiple responsibilities to them individually as occasion required. In this way members of the Merriam-Webster staff have been grouped and regrouped to form hundreds of task forces performing simultaneously thousands of missions. The editor can say with gratitude and relief that the accomplishment is not a one-man dictionary. "What individual," asks Noah Webster in his preface, "is competent to trace to their source, and define in all their various applications, popular, scientific, and technical, sixty or seventy thousand words!"

WEBSTER'S THIRD NEW INTERNATIONAL DICTIONARY is a collaborative effort. Without the cooperation of the scholarly, scientific, and technical world, the specialized guidance of our outside consultants, and the ingenuity of the compositors and printers, G. & C. Merriam Company and its permanent editorial staff could not have brought the work to its successful culmination. Those most deeply involved with overall responsibility deserve special mention here. Three associate editors, Mr. Artin, Dr. Kay, and Dr. Sleeth, have already been named in this preface. Among others who have shared large responsibilities are these associate editors: Miss Anne M. Driscoll, Dr. Philip H. Goepp, Mr. Hubert P. Kelsey, Dr. Howard G. Rhoads, and Dr. H. Bosley Woolf; two assistant editors, Miss Ervina E. Foss and Mrs. Laverne W. King; and the departmental secretary, Mrs. Christine M. Mullen.

It is now fairly clear that before the twentieth century is over every community of the world will have learned how to communicate with all the rest of humanity. In this process of intercommunication the English language has already become the most important language on earth. This new Merriam-Webster unabridged is the record of this language as it is written and spoken. It is offered with confidence that it will supply in full measure that information on the general language which is required for accurate, clear, and comprehensive understanding of the vocabulary of today's society.

Springfield, Mass.   PHILIP B. GOVE
June 1, 1961

STUDY QUESTIONS

1.   What is meant by the principle "that a definition, to be adequate, must be written only after an analysis of usage"?
2.   Why did the editors elect not to use the status label "colloquial"? See Follett ("Sabotage in Springfield," p. 355) and Evans ("But What's a Dictionary For?" p. 364) on this point.

3. According to the "Preface," what is the basic aim of *Webster's Third?*
4. What are the limitations to showing in a dictionary the realistic pronunciation of words?
5. What are the four general groups of the etymologies in *Webster's Third?*

SABOTAGE
Wilson Follett   IN SPRINGFIELD

Wilson Follett (1887–1963) was born in Ahleborough, Massachusetts. He received his A.B. from Harvard in 1909, and had a distinguished career as a writer, critic, and editor. He was a frequent contributor to such publications as *Harper's, Saturday Review, Virginia Quarterly,* and *Bookman.* He translated *Molière, the Man Seen Through the Plays,* by Ramon Fernandez, but he is perhaps best known to scholars of American literature as the editor of the twelve-volume works of Stephen Crane.

Of dictionaries, as of newspapers, it might be said that the bad ones are too bad to exist, the good ones too good not to be better. No dictionary of a living language is perfect or ever can be, if only because the time required for compilation, editing, and issuance is so great that shadows of obsolescence are falling on parts of any such work before it ever gets into the hands of a user. Preparation of *Webster's Third New International Dictionary of the English Language* began intensively in the Springfield establishment of G. & C. Merriam Company in 1936, but the century was nine months into its seventh decade before any outsider could have his first look at what had been accomplished. His first look is, of course, incompetent to acquaint him with the merits of the new work; these no one can fully discover without months or years of everyday use. On the other hand, it costs only minutes to find out that what will rank as the great event of American linguistic history in this decade, and perhaps in this quarter century, is in many crucial particulars a very great calamity.

Why should the probable and possible superiorities of the Third New International be so difficult to assess, the shortcomings so easy? Because the superiorities are special, departmental, and recondite, the shortcomings general and within the common grasp. The new dictionary comes to us with a claim of 100,000 new words or new definitions. These run almost overwhelmingly to scientific and technological terms or meanings that have come into existence since 1934, and especially to words classified as ISV (belonging to the international scientific vocabulary). No one person can possibly use or even comprehend all of them; the coverage in this domain, certainly impressive to the nonspecialist, may or may not command the admiration of specialists. It is said that historians of the graphic arts and of architecture were displeased with the 1934 Webster, both for its omissions and for some definitions of what it included in their fields. Its 1961 successor may have disarmed their reservations; only they can pronounce.

But all of us may without brashness form summary judgments about the treatment of what belongs to all of us—the standard, staple, traditional language of general reading and speaking, the ordinary vocabulary and idioms of novelist, essayist, letter writer, reporter, editorial writer, teacher, student, advertiser; in short, fundamental English. And it is precisely in this province that Webster III has thrust upon us a dismaying assortment of the questionable, the perverse, the unworthy, and the downright outrageous.

Furthermore, what was left out is as legitimate a grievance to the ordinary reader as anything that has been put in. Think—if you can—of an unabridged dictionary from which you cannot learn who Mark Twain was (though *mark twain* is entered as a leadsman's cry), or what were the names of the twelve apostles, or that the Virgin was Mary the mother of Jesus of Nazareth, or what and where the District of Columbia is!

The disappointment and the shock are intensified, of course, because of the unchallenged position earned by the really unabridged immediate predecessor of this strange work. *Webster's New International Dictionary*, Second Edition (1934), consummated under the editorship of William Allan Neilson, at once became the most important reference book in the world to American writers, editors, teachers, students, and general readers—everyone to whom American English was a matter of serious interest. What better could the next revision do than extend the Second Edition in the direction of itself, bring it up to date, and correct its scattering of oversights and errata?

The 1934 dictionary had been, heaven knows, no citadel of conservatism, no last bastion of puristical bigotry. But it had made shrewd reports on the status of individual words; it had taken its clear, beautifully written definitions from fit uses of an enormous vocabulary by judicious users; it had provided accurate, impartial accounts of the endless guerrilla war between grammarian and antigrammarian and so given every consultant the means to work out his own decisions. Who could wish the forthcoming revision any better fortune than a comparable success in applying the same standards to whatever new matter the new age imposed?

Instead, we have seen a century and a third of illustrious history largely jettisoned; we have seen a novel dictionary formula improvised, in great part out of snap judgments and the sort of theoretical improvement that in practice impairs; and we have seen the gates propped wide open in enthusiastic hospitality to miscellaneous confusions and corruptions. In fine, the anxiously awaited work that was to have crowned cisatlantic linguistic scholarship with a particular glory turns out to be a scandal and a disaster. Worse yet, it plumes itself on its faults and parades assiduously cultivated sins as virtues without precedent.

Examination cannot proceed far without revealing that Webster III, behind its front of passionless objectivity, is in truth a fighting document. And the enemy it is out to destroy is every obstinate vestige of linguistic punctilio, every surviving influence that makes for the upholding of standards, every criterion for distinguishing between better usages and worse. In other words, it has gone over bodily to the school that construes traditions as enslaving, the rudimentary principles of syntax as crippling, and taste as irrelevant. This revolution leaves it in the anomalous position of loudly glorifying its own ancestry—which is indeed glorious—while tacitly sabotaging the principles and ideals that brought the preceding Merriam-Webster to its unchallengeable pre-eminence. The Third New International is at once a resounding tribute of lip service to the Second and a wholesale repudiation of it—a sweeping act of apology, contrition, and reform.

The right-about-face is, of course, particularly evident in the vocabulary approved. Within a few days of publication the new dictionary was inevitably notorious for its unreserved acceptance as standard of *wise up, get hep* (it uses the second as a definition of the first), *ants in one's pants, one for the book; hugeous, nixie, passel, hepped up* (with *hepcat* and *hepster*), *anyplace, someplace,* and so forth. These and a swarm of their kind it admits to full canonical standing by the suppression of such qualifying status labels as *colloquial, slang, cant, facetious,* and *substandard.* The classification *colloquial* it abolishes outright: "it is impossible to know whether a word out of context is colloquial or not." Of *slang* it makes a chary occasional use despite a similar reservation: "No word is invariably slang, and many standard words can be given slang connotations or used so inappropriately as to become slang." *Cornball* is ranked as slang, *corny* is not.

The overall effect signifies a large-scale abrogation of one major responsibility of the lexicographer. He renounces it on the curious ground that helpful discriminations are so far beyond his professional competence that he is obliged to leave them to those who, professing no competence at all, have vainly turned to him for guidance. If some George Ade of the future, aspiring to execute a fable in slang, were to test his attempt by the status labels in Webster III, he would quickly discover with chagrin that he had expressed himself almost without exception in officially applauded English. With but slight exaggeration we can say that if an expression can be shown to have been used in print by some jaded reporter, some candidate for office or his speech writer, some potboiling minor novelist, it is well enough credentialed for the full blessing of the new lexicography.

This extreme tolerance of crude neologisms and of shabby diction generally, however, is but one comparatively trifling aspect of the campaign against punctilio. We begin to sound its deeper implications when we plunge into the definitions and the copious examples that illustrate and support them. Under the distributive pronoun *each* we find, side by side: "(each of them is to pay his own fine) (each of them are to pay their own fine)." Where could anyone look for a neater, more succinct way to outlaw the dusty dogma that a pronoun should always agree in number with its antecedent? Here is the same maneuver again under another distributive, *everybody:* "usu. referred to by the third person singular (everybody is bringing his own lunch) but sometimes by a plural personal pronoun (everybody had made up their minds). "Or try *whom* and *whomever:* "(a . . . recruit whom he hoped would prove to be a crack salesman) (people . . . whom you never thought would sympathize) . . . (I go out to talk to whomever it is) . . . (he attacked whomever disagreed with him)." It is, then, all right to put the subject of a finite verb in the accusative case—"esp. after a preposition or a verb of which it might mistakenly be considered the object."

Shall we look into what our dictionary does with a handful of the more common solecisms, such as a publisher might introduce into a cooked-up test for would-be copy editors? Begin with *center around* (or *about*). It seems obvious that expressions derived from Euclidean geometry should make Euclidean sense. A center is a point; it is what things are around, not what is around them; they center *in* or *on* or *at* the point. The Second Edition defined the Great White Way as "That part of Broadway . . . centering about Times Square"—patently an oversight. Is it the same oversight that produces, in the Third: "*heresy* . . . 3: a group or school of thought centering around a particular heresy"? We look up *center* itself, and, lo: "(a story to tell, centered around the political development of a great state) . . . (more scholarship than usual was centered around the main problems)," followed by several equivalent specimens.

Here is *due to.* First we come on irreproachable definitions, irreproachably illustrated, of *due* noun and *due* adjective, and we think we are out of the woods. Alas, they are followed by the manufacture of a

composite preposition, *due to,* got up solely to extenuate such abomina-
tions as "the event was canceled due to inclement weather." An adjective can modify a verb, then. And here is a glance at that peculiarly
incriminating redundancy of the slipshod writer, *equally as:* "equally
opposed to Communism as to Fascism." The intolerable *hardly than* or
scarcely than construction is in full favor: "hardly had the birds dropped
than she jumped into the water and retrieved them." The sequence
different than has the double approbation of editorial use and a citation:
conjunctive *unlike* means "in a manner that is different than," and a
passage under *different* reads "vastly different in size than it was twenty-
five years ago." Adjectival *unlike* and conjunctive *unlike* both get illustrations that implicitly commend the unanchored and grammarless
modifier: "so many fine men were outside the charmed circle that, unlike
most colleges, there was no disgrace in not being a club man"; "unlike in
the gasoline engine, fuel does not enter the cylinder with air on the
intake stroke."

This small scattering should not end without some notice of that
darling of the advanced libertarians, *like* as a conjunction, first in the
meaning of *as,* secondly (and more horribly) in that of *as if.* Now, it is
well known to the linguistic historian that *like* was so used for a long
time before and after Langland. But it is as well known that the language rather completely sloughed off this usage; that it has long been no
more than a regional colloquialism, a rarely seen aberration among
competent writers, or an artificially cultivated irritant among defiant
ones. The *Saturday Evening Post,* in which *like* for *as* is probably more
frequent than in any other painstakingly edited magazine, has seldom if
ever printed that construction except in reproducing the speech or
tracing the thoughts of characters to whom it might be considered
natural. The aguments for *like* have been merely defensive and permissive. Not for centuries has there been any real pressure of authority on a
writer to use *like* as a conjunction—until our Third New International
Dictionary decided to exert its leverage.

How it is exerted will appear in the following: "(impromptu programs where they ask questions much like I do on the air) . . . (looks
like they can raise better tobacco) (looks like he will get the job) (wore
his clothes like he was . . . afraid of getting dirt on them) (was like he'd
come back from a long trip) (acted like she felt sick) . . . (sounded like
the motor had stopped) . . . (the violin now sounds like an old masterpiece should) (did it like he told me to) . . . (wanted a doll like she saw
in the store window) . . . (anomalies like just had occurred)."

By the processes represented in the foregoing and countless others
for which there is no room here, the latest Webster whittles away at one
after another of the traditionary controls until there is little or nothing
left of them. The controls, to be sure, have often enough been over-

valued and overdone by pedants and purists, by martinets and bigots; but more often, and much more importantly, they have worked as aids toward dignified, workmanlike, and cogent uses of the wonderful language that is our inheritance. To erode and undermine them is to convert the language into a confusion of unchanneled, incalculable williwaws, a capricious wind blowing whithersoever it listeth. And that, if we are to judge by the total effect of the pages under scrutiny—2720 of them and nearly 8000 columns of vocabulary, all compact, set in Times roman—is exactly what is wanted by the patient and dedicated saboteurs in Springfield. They, if they keep their ears to the ground, will hear many echoes of the despairing cry already wrung from one editorial assitant on a distinguished magazine that still puts its faith in standards: "Why have a Dictionary at all if anything goes?"

The definitions are reinforced, it will have been conveyed, with copious citations from printed sources. These citations occupy a great fraction of the total space. They largely account for the reduction in the number of entries (from 600,000 to 450,000) and for the elimination of the Gazetteer, the Biographical Dictionary, and the condensed key to pronunciation and symbols that ran across the bottoms of facing pages—all very material deprivations. Some 14,000 authors, we are told, are represented in the illustrative quotations—"mostly from the mid-twentieth century."

Can some thousands of authors truly worth space in a dictionary ever be found in any one brief period? Such a concentration can hardly fail to be, for the purposes of a dictionary, egregiously overweighted with the contemporary and the transient. Any very short period, such as a generation, is a period of transition in the history of English, and any great mass of examples drawn primarily from it will be disproportionately focused on transitional and ephemeral elements. To say that recording English *as we find it today* is precisely the purpose of a new dictionary is not much of a retort. For the bulk of the language that we use has come down to us with but minor, glacially slow changes from time out of mind, and a worthy record of it must stand on a much broader base than the fashions of yesterday.

It is, then, a mercy that among the thousands of scraps from recent authors, many of them still producing, we can also find hundreds from Shakespeare, the English Bible, Fielding, Dickens, Hawthorne, Melville, Henry James, Mark Twain, and so on. But the great preponderance of latter-day prose, little of it worth repeating and a good deal of it hardly worth printing in the first place, is likely to curtail by years the useful life of the Third New International.

So much is by the way. When we come to the definitions proper we face something new, startling, and formidable in lexicography. The definitions, all of them conformed to a predetermined rhetorical pattern, may be products of a theory—Gestaltist, perhaps?—of how the receiving mind works. The pattern, in the editor's general preface, is described as follows: "The primary objective of precise, sharp defining has been met through development of a new dictionary style based upon completely analytical one-phrase definitions throughout the book. Since the head-word in a definition is intended to be modified only by structural elements restrictive in some degree and essential to each other, the use of commas either to separate or to group has been severely limited, chiefly to elements in apposition or in series. The new defining pattern does not provide for a predication which conveys further expository comment."

This doctrine of the strictly unitary definition is of course formulated and applied in the interest of a logical integrity and a simplification never before consistently attained by lexical definitions. What it produces, when applied with the rigor here insisted on, is in the first place some of the oddest prose ever concocted by pundits. A typical specimen, from the definition of the simplest possible term: "*rabbit punch* . . . : a short chopping blow delivered to the back of the neck or the base of the skull with the edge of the hand opposite the thumb that is illegal in boxing." When the idea, being not quite so simple, requires the one-phrase statement of several components, the definition usually turns out to be a great unmanageable and unpunctuated blob of words strung out beyond the retentive powers of most minds that would need the definition at all. Both theory and result will emerge clearly enough from a pair of specimens, the first dealing with a familiar everyday noun, the second with a mildly technical one:

> *groan* . . . 1: a deep usu. inarticulate and involuntary often strangled sound typically abruptly begun and ended and usu. indicative of pain or grief or tension or desire or sometimes disapproval or annoyance.

> *kymograph* . . . 1: a recording device including an electric motor or clockwork that drives a usu. slowly revolving drum which carries a roll of plain or smoked paper and also having an arrangement for tracing on the paper by means of a stylus a graphic record of motion or pressure (as of the organs of speech, blood pressure, or respiration) often in relation to particular intervals of time.

About these typical definitions as prose, there is much that any good reader might well say. What must be said is that the grim suppression of commas is a mere crotchet. It takes time to read such definitions anyway; commas in the right places would speed rather than slow the reading and would clarify rather than obscure the sense, so that the unitary effect—largely imaginary at best—would be more helped than hurt. In practice, the one-phrase design without further expository predication lacks all the asserted advantages over a competently written definition of the free conventional sort; it is merely much more difficult to write, often impossible to write well, and tougher to take in. Compare the corresponding definitions from the Second Edition:

> *groan* . . . A low, moaning sound; usually, a deep, mournful sound uttered in pain or great distress; sometimes, an expression of strong disapprobation; as, the remark was received with *groans*.

> *kymograph* . . . *a* An automatic apparatus consisting of a motor revolving a drum covered with smoked paper, on which curves of pressure, etc., may be traced.

Everyone professionally concerned with the details of printed English can be grateful to the new Webster for linking the parts of various expressions that have been either hyphenated compounds or separate words—*highlight, highbrow* and *lowbrow, overall, wisecrack, lowercase* and *uppercase*, and so on. Some of the unions now recognized were long overdue; many editors have already got them written into codes of house usage. But outside this small province the new work is a copy editor's despair, a propounder of endless riddles.

What, for example, are we to make of the common abbreviations *i.e.* and *e.g.?* The first is entered in the vocabulary as *ie* (no periods, no space), the second as *e g* (space, no periods). In the preliminary list, "Abbreviations Used in This Dictionary," both are given the customary periods. (Oddly, the list translates its *i.e.* into "that is," but merely expands *e.g.* into "exempli gratia.") Is one to follow the vocabulary or the list? What point has the seeming inconsistency?

And what about capitalization? All vocabulary entries are in lowercase except for such abbreviations as ARW (air raid warden), MAB (medical advisory board), and PX (post exchange). Words possibly inviting capitalization are followed by such injunctions as *cap, usu cap, sometimes not cap, usu cap 1st A, usu cap A&B.* (One of the small idiosyncrasies is that "usu.," the most frequent abbreviation, is given a period when roman, denied it when italic.) From *america*, adjective—all proper nouns are excluded—to *american yew* there are over 175 consecutive entries that require such injunctions; would it not have been simpler and more economical to capitalize the entries? A flat "*cap*," of course, means "always capitalized." But how often is "usually," and when is "sometimes"? We get dictionaries expressly that they may settle such problems for us. This dictionary seems to make a virtue of leaving them in flux, with the explanation that many matters are subjective and that the individual must decide them for himself—a curious abrogation of authority in a work extolled as "more useful and authoritative than any previous dictionary."

The rock-bottom practical truth is that the lexicographer cannot abrogate his authority if he wants to. He may think of himself as a detached scientist reporting the facts of language, declining to recommend use of anything or abstention from anything; but the myriad consultants of his work are not going to see him so. He helps create, not a book of fads and fancies and private opinions, but a Dictionary of the English Language. It comes to every reader under auspices that say, not "Take it or leave it," but rather something like this: "Here in 8000 columns is a definitive report of what a synod of the most trustworthy American experts consider the English language to be in the seventh decade of the twentieth century. This is your language; take it and use it. And if you use it in conformity with the principles and practices here exemplified, your use will be the most accurate attainable by any American of this era." The fact that the compilers disclaim authority and piously refrain from judgments is meaningless: the work itself, by virtue of its inclusions and exclusions, its mere existence, is a whole universe of judgments, received by millions as the Word from on high.

And there we have the reason why it is so important for the dictionary maker to keep his discriminations sharp, why it is so damaging if he lets them get out of working order. Suppose he enters a new definition for no better reason than that some careless, lazy, or uninformed scribbler has jumped to an absurd conclusion about what a word means or has been too harrassed to run down the word he really wanted. This new definition is going to persuade tens of thousands that, say, *cohort,* a word of multitude, means one associate or crony "(he and three alleged housebreaking cohorts were arraigned on attempted burglary charges)" or that the vogue word *ambivalence,* which denotes simultaneous love and hatred of someone or something, means "continual oscillation between one thing and its opposite (novels . . . vitiated by an ambivalence between satire and sentimentalism)." To what is the definer contributing if not to subversion and decay? To the swallower of the definition it never occurs that he can have drunk corruption from a well that he has every reason to trust as the ultimate in purity. Multiply him by the number of people simultaneously influenced, and the resulting figure by the years through which the influence continues, and a great deal of that product by the influences that will be disseminated through speech and writing and teaching, and you begin to apprehend the scope of the really enormous disaster that can and will be wrought by the lexicographer's abandonment of his responsibility.

STUDY QUESTIONS

1. What does Follett believe to be the responsibility of the lexicographer? Compare his view with that expressed in the "Preface" to *Webster's Third New International Dictionary.*

2.   What are his chief objections to *Webster's Third?*
3.   In what respects does he judge *Webster's New International Dictionary,*
      Second Edition (1934), to be a superior dictionary?
4.   What does Follett say about the citations that reinforce the definitions?
      Why does he feel that a great number of citations from contemporary
      prose will curtail the useful life of the dictionary?
5.   How would you describe Follett's tone in this review? What particular
      words and expressions reflect his tone?

BUT WHAT'S

Bergen Evans   **A DICTIONARY FOR?**

Bergen Evans (1902–   ) was born in Franklin, Ohio. He received his A.B. from Miami University (Ohio) and his A.M. and
Ph.D. from Harvard University. He was a Rhodes Scholar and
received his B.Litt. from Oxford University. He has taught at
Miami University, and is now professor of English at Northwestern
University. He is author of *The Natural History of Nonsense*
(1946) and *Comfortable Words* (1962) and is coauthor of *A
Dictionary of Contemporary American Usage* (1957). He is the
recipient of the George Foster Peabody Award for excellence in
radio and television broadcasting.

The storm of abuse in the popular press that greeted the appearance of *Webster's Third New International Dictionary* is a curious
phenomenon. Never has a scholarly work of this stature been attacked
with such unbridled fury and contempt. An article in the *Atlantic*
viewed it as a "disappointment," a "shock," a "calamity," "a scandal and
a disaster." *The New York Times,* in a special editorial, felt that the
work would "accelerate the deterioration" of the language and sternly
accused the editors of betraying a public trust. The *Journal* of the
American Bar Association saw the publication as "deplorable," "a
flagrant example of lexicographic irresponsibility," "a serious blow to the
cause of good English." *Life* called it "a non-word deluge," "monstrous," "abominable," and "a cause for dismay." They doubted that
"Lincoln could have modelled his Gettysburg Address" on it—a concept
of how things get written that throws very little light on Lincoln but a
great deal on *Life.*

What underlies all this sound and fury? Is the claim of the G. & C.

Reprinted with permission of the author. First published in *The Atlantic Monthly,* May
1962.

Merriam Company, probably the world's greatest dictionary maker, that the preparation of the work cost $3.5 million, that it required the efforts of three hundred scholars over a period of twenty-seven years, working on the largest collection of citations ever assembled in any language—is all this a fraud, a hoax?

So monstrous a discrepancy in evaluation requires us to examine basic principles. Just what's a dictionary for? What does it propose to do? What does the common reader go to a dictionary to find? What has the purchaser of a dictionary a right to expect for his money?

Before we look at basic principles, it is necessary to interpose two brief statements. The first of these is that a dictionary is concerned with words. Some have tables of weights and measures on the flyleaves. Some list historical events, and some, home remedies. And there's nothing wrong with their so doing. But the great increase in our vocabulary in the past three decades compels all dictionaries to make more efficient use of their space. And if something must be eliminated, it is sensible to throw out these extraneous things and stick to words.

Yet wild wails arose. The *Saturday Review* lamented that one can no longer find the goddess Astarte under a separate heading—though they point out that a genus of mollusks named after the goddess is included! They seemed to feel that out of sheer perversity the editors of the dictionary stooped to mollusks while ignoring goddesses and that, in some way, this typifies modern lexicography. Mr. Wilson Follett, folletizing (his mental processes demand some special designation) in the *Atlantic*, cried out in horror that one is not even able to learn from the Third International "that the Virgin was Mary the mother of Jesus!"

The second brief statement is that there has been even more progress in the making of dictionaries in the past thirty years than there has been in the making of automobiles. The difference, for example, between the much-touted Second International (1934) and the much-clouted Third International (1961) is not like the difference between yearly models but like the difference between the horse and buggy and the automobile. Between the appearance of these two editions a whole new science related to the making of dictionaries, the science of descriptive linguistics, has come into being.

Modern linguistics gets its charter from Leonard Bloomfield's *Language* (1933). Bloomfield, for thirteen years professor of Germanic philology at the University of Chicago and for nine years professor of linguistics at Yale, was one of those inseminating scholars who can't be relegated to any department and don't dream of accepting established categories and procedures just because they're established. He was as much an anthropologist as a linguist, and his concepts of language were shaped not by Strunk's *Elements of Style* but by his knowledge of Cree Indian dialects.

The broad general findings of the new science are:

1. All languages are systems of human conventions, not systems of natural laws. The first—and essential—step in the study of any language is observing and setting down precisely what happens when native speakers speak it.

2. Each language is unique in its pronunciation, grammar, and vocabulary. It cannot be described in terms of logic or of some theoretical, ideal language. It cannot be described in terms of any other language or even in terms of its own past.

3. All languages are dynamic rather than static, and hence a "rule" in any language can only be a statement of contemporary practice. Change is constant—and normal.

4. "Correctness" can rest only upon usage, for the simple reason that there is nothing else for it to rest on. And all usage is relative.

From these propositions it follows that a dictionary is good only insofar as it is a comprehensive and accurate description of current usage. And to be comprehensive it must include some indication of social and regional associations.

New dictionaries are needed because English has changed more in the past two generations than at any other time in its history. It has had to adapt to extraordinary cultural and technological changes, two world wars, unparalleled changes in transportation and communication, and unprecedented movements of populations.

More subtly, but pervasively, it has changed under the influence of mass education and the growth of democracy. As written English is used by increasing millions and for more reasons than ever before, the language has become more utilitarian and more informal. Every publication in America today includes pages that would appear, to the purist of forty years ago, unbuttoned gibberish. Not that they are; they simply show that you can't hold the language of one generation up as a model for the next.

It's not that you mustn't. You *can't*. For example, in the issue in which *Life* stated editorially that it would follow the Second International, there were over forty words, constructions, and meanings which are in the Third International but not in the Second. The issue of *The New York Times* which hailed the Second International as the authority to which it would adhere and the Third International as a scandal and a betrayal which it would reject used one hundred and fifty-three separate words, phrases, and constructions which are listed in the Third International but not in the Second and nineteen others which are condemned in the Second. Many of them are used many times, more than three hundred such uses in all. The Washington *Post*, in an editorial captioned "Keep Your Old Webster's," says, in the first sentence, "don't throw it away," and in the second, "hang on to it." But the old Webster's labels *don't* "colloquial" and doesn't include "hang on to," in this sense, at all.

In short, all of these publications are written in the language that the Third International describes, even the very editorials which scorn it. And this is no coincidence, because the Third International isn't setting up any new standards at all; it is simply describing what *Life*, the Washington *Post*, and *The New York Times* are doing. Much of the dictionary's material comes from these very publications, the *Times*, in particular, furnishing more of its illustrative quotations than any other newspaper.

And the papers have no choice. No journal or periodical could sell a single issue today if it restricted itself to the American language of twenty-eight years ago. It couldn't discuss half the things we are interested in, and its style would seem stiff and cumbrous. If the editorials were serious, the public—and the stockholders—have reason to be grateful that the writers on these publications are more literate than the editors.

And so back to our questions: what's a dictionary for, and how, in 1962, can it best do what it ought to do? The demands are simple. The common reader turns to a dictionary for information about the spelling, pronunciation, meaning, and proper use of words. He wants to know what is current and respectable. But he wants—and has a right to—the truth, the full truth. And the full truth about any language, and especially about American English today, is that there are many areas in which certainty is impossible and simplification is misleading.

Even in so settled a matter as spelling, a dictionary cannot always be absolute. *Theater* is correct, but so is *theatre*. And so are *traveled* and *travelled, plow* and *plough, catalog* and *catalogue,* and scores of other variants. The reader may want a single certainty. He may have taken an unyielding position in an argument, he may have wagered in support of his conviction and may demand that the dictionary "settle" the matter. But neither his vanity nor his purse is any concern of the dictionary's; it must record the facts. And the fact here is that there are many words in our language which may be spelled, with equal correctness, in either of two ways.

So with pronunciation. A citizen listening to his radio might notice that James B. Conant, Bernard Baruch, and Dwight D. Eisenhower pronounce *economics* as ECKuhnomiks, while A. Whitney Griswold, Adlai Stevenson, and Herbert Hoover pronounce it EEKuhnomiks. He turns to the dictionary to see which of the two pronunciations is "right" and finds that they are both acceptable.

Has he been betrayed? Has the dictionary abdicated its responsibility? Should it say that one *must* speak like the president of Harvard or like the president of Yale, like the thirty-first President of the United States or like the thirty-fourth? Surely it's none of its business to make a choice. Not because of the distinction of these particular speakers; lexicography, like God, is no respecter of persons. But because so widespread and conspicuous a use of two pronunciations among people of this elevation shows that there *are* two pronunciations. Their speaking establishes the fact which the dictionary must record.

Among the "enormities" with which *Life* taxes the Third International is its listing of "the common mispronunciation" *heighth*. That it is labeled a "dialectal variant" seems, somehow, to compound the felony. But one hears the word so pronounced, and if one professes to give a full account of American English in the 1960s, one has to take some cognizance of it. All people do not possess *Life's* intuitive perception that the word is so "monstrous" that even to list it as a dialect variation is to merit scorn. Among these, by the way, was John Milton, who, in one of the greatest passages in all literature, besought the Holy Spirit to raise him to the "highth" of his great argument. And even the *Oxford English Dictionary* is so benighted as to list it, in full boldface, right alongside of *Height* as a variant that has been in the language since at least 1290.

Now there are still, apparently, millions of Americans who retain, in this as in much else, some of the speech of Milton. This particular pronunciation seems to be receding, but the *American Dialect Dictionary* still records instances of it from almost every state on the Eastern seaboard and notes that it is heard from older people and "occasionally in educated speech," "common with good speakers," "general," "widespread."

Under these circumstances, what is a dictionary to do? Since millions speak the word this way, the pronunciation can't be ignored. Since it has been in use as long as we have any record of English and since it has been used by the greatest writers, it can't be described as substandard or slang. But it is heard now only in certain localities. That makes it a dialectal pronunciation, and an honest dictionary will list it as such. What else can it do? Should it do?

The average purchaser of a dictionary uses it most often, probably, to find out what a word "means." As a reader, he wants to know what an author intended to convey. As a speaker or writer, he wants to know what a word will convey to his auditors. And this, too, is complex, subtle, and forever changing.

An illustration is furnished by an editorial in the Washington *Post* (January 17, 1962). After a ringing appeal to those who "love truth and accuracy" and the usual bombinations about "abdication of authority" and "barbarism," the editorial charges the Third International with "pretentious and obscure verbosity" and specifically instances its definition of "so simple an object as a door."

The definition reads:

a movable piece of firm material or a structure supported usu. along one side and swinging on pivots or hinges, sliding along a groove, rolling up and down, revolving as one of four leaves, or folding like an accordion by means of which an opening may be closed or kept open for passage into or out of a building, room, or other covered enclosure or a car, airplane, elevator, or other vehicle.

Then follows a series of special meanings, each particularly defined and, where necessary, illustrated by a quotation.

Since, aside from roaring and admonishing the "gentlemen from Springfield" that "accuracy and brevity are virtues," the *Post's* editorial fails to explain what is wrong with the definition, we can only infer from "so simple" a thing that the writer takes the plain, downright, man-in-the-street attitude that a door is a door and any damn fool knows that.

But if so, he has walked into one of lexicography's biggest booby traps: the belief that the obvious is easy to define. Whereas the opposite is true. Anyone can give a fair description of the strange, the new, or the unique. It's the commonplace, the habitual, that challenges definition, for its very commonness compels us to define it in uncommon terms. Dr. Johnson was ridiculed on just this score when his dictionary appeared in 1755. For two hundred years his definition of a network as "any thing reticulated or decussated, at equal distances, with interstices between the intersections" has been good for a laugh. But in the merriment one thing is always overlooked: no one has yet come up with a better definition! Subsequent dictionaries defined it as a mesh and then defined a mesh as a network. That's simple, all right.

Anyone who attempts sincerely to state what the word *door* means in the United States of America today can't take refuge in a log cabin. There has been an enormous proliferation of closing and demarking devices and structures in the past twenty years, and anyone who tries to thread his way through the many meanings now included under *door* may have to sacrifice brevity to accuracy and even have to employ words that a limited vocabulary may find obscure.

Is the entrance to a tent a door, for instance? And what of the thing that seals the exit of an airplane? Is this a door? Or what of those sheets and jets of air that are now being used, in place of old-fashioned oak and hinges, to screen entrances and exits. Are they doors? And what of those accordion-like things that set off various sections of many modern apartments? The fine print in the lease takes it for granted that they are doors and that spaces demarked by them are rooms—and the rent is computed on the number of rooms.

Was I gypped by the landlord when he called the folding contraption that shuts off my kitchen a door? I go to the Second International,

which the editor of the *Post* urges me to use in preference to the Third
International. Here I find that a door is

> The movable frame or barrier of boards, or other material, usually
> turning on hinges or pivots or sliding, by which an entranceway into a
> house or apartment is closed and opened; also, a similar part of a piece of
> furniture, as in a cabinet or bookcase.

This is only forty-six words, but though it includes the cellar door, it
excludes the barn door and the accordion-like thing.

So I go on to the Third International. I see at once that the new
definition is longer. But I'm looking for accuracy, and if I must sacrifice
brevity to get it, then I must. And, sure enough, in the definition which
raised the *Post's* blood pressure, I find the words "folding like an accordion." The thing *is* a door, and my landlord is using the word in one of
its currently accepted meanings.

We don't turn to a work of reference merely for confirmation. We
all have words in our vocabularies which we have misunderstood, and to
come on the true meaning of one of these words is quite a shock. All our
complacency and self-esteem rise to oppose the discovery. But eventually we must accept the humiliation and laugh it off as best we can.

Some, often those who have set themselves up as authorities, stick
to their error and charge the dictionary with being in a conspiracy
against them. They are sure that their meaning is the only "right" one.
And when the dictionary doesn't bear them out they complain about
"permissive" attitudes instead of correcting their mistake.

The New York Times and the *Saturday Review* both regarded as
contemptibly "permissive" the fact that one meaning of one word was
illustrated by a quotation from Polly Adler. But a rudimentary knowledge of the development of any language would have told them that the
underworld has been a far more active force in shaping and enriching
speech than all the synods that have ever convened. Their attitude is
like that of the patriot who canceled his subscription to the *Dictionary of
American Biography* when he discovered that the very first volume
included Benedict Arnold!

The ultimate of "permissiveness," singled out by almost every
critic for special scorn, was the inclusion in the Third International of
finalize. It was this, more than any other one thing, that was given as the
reason for sticking to the good old Second International—that "peerless
authority on American English," as the *Times* called it. But if it was
such an authority, why didn't they look into it? They would have found
finalize if they had.

And why shouldn't it be there? It exists. It's been recorded for two
generations. Millions employ it every day. Two Presidents of the United
States—men of widely differing cultural backgrounds—have used it in

formal statements. And so has the Secreta y-General of the United Nations, a man of unusual linguistic attainment. It isn't permitting the word but omitting it that would break faith with the reader. Because it is exactly the sort of word we want information about.

To list it as substandard would be to imply that it is used solely by the ignorant and the illiterate. But this would be a misrepresentation: President Kennedy and U Thant are highly educated men, and both are articulate and literate. It isn't even a freak form. On the contrary, it is a classic example of a regular process of development in English, a process which has given us such thoroughly accepted words as *generalize, minimize, formalize,* and *verbalize.* Nor can it be dismissed on logical grounds or on the ground that it is a mere duplication of *complete.* It says something that *complete* doesn't say and says it in a way that is significant in the modern bureaucratic world: one usually *completes* something which he has initiated but *finalizes* the work of others.

One is free to dislike the word. I don't like it. But the editor of a dictionary has to examine the evidence for a word's existence and seek it in context to get, as clearly and closely as he can, the exact meaning that it conveys to those who use it. And if it is widely used by well-educated, literate, reputable people, he must list it as a standard word. He is not compiling a volume of his own prejudices.

An individual's use of his native tongue is the surest index to his position within his community. And those who turn to a dictionary expect from it some statement of the current status of a word or a grammatical construction. And it is with the failure to assume this function that modern lexicography has been most fiercely charged. The charge is based on a naïve assumption that simple labels can be attached in all instances. But they can't. Some words are standard in some constructions and not in others. There may be as many shades of status as of meaning, and modern lexicography instead of abdicating this function has fulfilled it to a degree utterly unknown to earlier dictionaries.

Consider the word *fetch,* meaning to "go get and bring to." Until recently a standard word of full dignity ("Fetch me, I pray thee, a little water in a vessel"—I Kings 17:10), it has become slightly tainted. Perhaps the command latent in it is resented as undemocratic. Or maybe its use in training dogs to retrieve has made some people feel that it is an undignified word to apply to human beings. But, whatever the reason, there is a growing uncertainy about its status, and hence it is the sort of word that conscientious people look up in a dictionary.

Will they find it labeled "good" or "bad"? Neither, of course, because either applied indiscriminately would be untrue. The Third International lists nineteen different meanings of the verb *to fetch.* Of these some are labeled "dialectal," some "chiefly dialectal," some "obsolete," one "chiefly Scottish," and two "not in formal use." The primary meaning—"to go after and bring back"—is not labeled and hence can be accepted as standard, accepted with the more assurance because the many shades of labeling show us that the word's status has been carefully considered.

On grammatical questions the Third International tries to be equally exact and thorough. Sometimes a construction is listed without comment, meaning that in the opinion of the editors it is unquestionably respectable. Sometimes a construction carries the comment "used by speakers and writers on all educational levels though disapproved by some grammarians." Or the comment may be "used in substandard speech and formerly also by reputable writers." Or "less often in standard than in substandard speech." Or simply "dial."

And this very accurate reporting is based on evidence which is presented for our examination. One may feel that the evidence is inadequate or that the evaluation of it is erroneous. But surely, in the face of classification so much more elaborate and careful than any known heretofore, one cannot fly into a rage and insist that the dictionary is "out to destroy . . . every vestige of linguistic punctilio . . . every criterion for distinguishing between better usages and worse."

Words, as we have said, are continually shifting their meanings and connotations and hence their status. A word which has dignity, say, in the vocabulary of an older person may go down in other people's estimation. Like *fetch*. The older speaker is not likely to be aware of this and will probably be inclined to ascribe the snickers of the young at his speech to that degeneration of manners which every generation has deplored in its juniors. But a word which is coming up in the scale—like *jazz*, say, or, more recently, *crap*—will strike his ear at once. We are much more aware of offenses given us than of those we give. And if he turns to a dictionary and finds the offending word listed as standard—or even listed, apparently—his response is likely to be an outburst of indignation.

But the dictionary can neither snicker nor fulminate. It records. It will offend many, no doubt, to find the expression *wise up*, meaning to inform or to become informed, listed in the Third International with no restricting label. To my aging ears it still sounds like slang. But the evidence—quotations from the *Kiplinger Washington Letter* and the *Wall Street Journal*—convinces me that it is I who am out of step, lagging behind. If such publications have taken to using *wise up* in serious contexts, with no punctuational indication of irregularity, then it is obviously respectable. And finding it so listed and supported, I can only say that it's nice to be informed and sigh to realize that I am becoming an old fogy. But, of course, I don't have to use it (and I'll be damned if I will! "Let them smile, as I do now, At the old forsaken bough Where I cling").

In part, the trouble is due to the fact that there is no standard for standard. Ideas of what is proper to use in serious, dignified speech and writing are changing—and with breathtaking rapidity. This is one of the major facts of contemporary American English. But it is no more the dictionary's business to oppose this process than to speed it up.

Even in our standard speech some words are more dignified and some more informal than others, and dictionaries have tried to guide us through these uncertainties by marking certain words and constructions as "colloquial," meaning "inappropriate in a formal situation." But this distinction, in the opinion of most scholars, has done more harm than good. It has created the notion that these particular words are inferior, when actually they might be the best possible words in an informal statement. And so—to the rage of many reviewers—the Third International has dropped this label. Not all labels, as angrily charged, but only this one out of a score. And the doing so may have been an error, but it certainly didn't constitute "betrayal" or "abandoning of all distinctions." It was intended to end a certain confusion.

In all the finer shades of meaning, of which the status of a word is only one, the user is on his own, whether he likes it or not. Despite *Life's* artless assumption about the Gettysburg Address, nothing worth writing is written *from* a dictionary. The dictionary, rather, comes along afterwards and describes what *has been* written.

Words in themselves are not dignified, or silly, or wise, or malicious. But they can be used in dignified, silly, wise, or malicious ways by dignified, silly, wise, or malicious people. *Egghead,* for example, is a perfectly legitimate word, as legitimate as *highbrow* or *long-haired.* But there is something very wrong and very undignified, by civilized standards, in a belligerent dislike for intelligence and education. *Yak* is an amusing word for persistent chatter. Anyone could say, "We were just yakking over a cup of coffee," with no harm to his dignity. But to call a Supreme Court decision *yakking* is to be vulgarly insulting and so, undignified. Again, there's nothing wrong with *confab* when it's appropriate. But when the work of a great research project, employing hundreds of distinguished scholars over several decades and involving the honor of one of the greatest publishing houses in the world, is described as *confabbing* (as *The New York Times* editorially described the preparation of the Third International), the use of this particular word asserts that the lexicographers had merely sat around and talked idly. And the statement becomes undignified—if not, indeed, slanderous.

The lack of dignity in such statements is not in the words, nor in the dictionaries that list them, but in the hostility that deliberately seeks this tone of expression. And in expressing itself the hostility frequently shows that those who are expressing it don't know how to use a dictionary. Most of the reviewers seem unable to read the Third International and unwilling to read the Second.

The *American Bar Association Journal*, for instance, in a typical outburst ("a deplorable abdication of responsibility"), picked out for special scorn the inclusion in the Third International of the word *irregardless*. "As far as the new Webster's is concerned," said the *Journal*, "this meaningless verbal bastard is just as legitimate as any other word in the dictionary." Thirty seconds spent in examining the book they were so roundly condemning would have shown them that in it *irregardless* is labeled "nonstand"—which means "nonstandard," which means "not conforming to the usage generally characteristic of educated native speakers of the language." Is that "just as legitimate as any other word in the dictionary"?

The most disturbing fact of all is that the editors of a dozen of the most influential publications in America today are under the impression that *authoritative* must mean *authoritarian*. Even the "permissive" Third International doesn't recognize this identification—editors' attitudes being not yet, fortunately, those of the American people. But the Fourth International may have to.

The new dictionary may have many faults. Nothing that tries to meet an ever-changing situation over a terrain as vast as contemporary English can hope to be free of them. And much in it is open to honest, and informed, disagreement. There can be linguistic objection to the eradication of proper names. The removal of guides to pronunciation from the foot of every page may not have been worth the valuable space it saved. The new method of defining words of many meanings has disadvantages as well as advantages. And of the half million or more definitions, hundreds, possibly thousands, may seem inadequate or imprecise. To some (of whom I am one) the omission of the label "colloquial" will seem meritorious; to others it will seem a loss.

But one thing is certain: anyone who solemnly announces in the year 1962 that he will be guided in matters of English usage by a dictionary published in 1934 is talking ignorant and pretentious nonsense.

STUDY QUESTIONS

1. What type of argument does Evans use to answer the critics of *Webster's Third?*

2. According to Evans, what is the responsibility of the lexicographer? Compare his view with Follett's ("Sabotage in Springfield").

3. The title of Evans' essay is a question. What is his answer to this question?

4. Compare Evans' views on the status symbol *colloquial* with Follett's views.

5. What general outline does Evans follow in this essay? Compare his tone with Follett's.

HOW SHALL
Max Beerbohm   **I WORD IT?**

Max Beerbohm (1872–1956), well-known critic and satirist, was
born in London. He received his A.B. degree from Merton College, Oxford. After gaining an early reputation for his satirical
essays in the famous *Yellow Book,* he succeeded George Bernard
Shaw as drama critic of the *Saturday Review.* In addition to
countless essays published in magazines, he wrote *The Happy
Hypocrite* (1897), *More* (1899), *Yet Again* (1907), *And Even
Now* (1920), *A Variety of Things* (1928), *Mainly on the Air*
(1946), and *Around Theatres* (1953). He was knighted in 1939.

It would seem that I am one of those travellers for whom the
railway bookstall does not cater. Whenever I start on a journey, I find
that my choice lies between well-printed books which I have no wish to
read, and well-written books which I could not read without permanent
injury to my eyesight. The keeper of the bookstall, seeing me gaze
vaguely along his shelves, suggests that I should take *Fen Country
Fanny* or else *The Track of Blood* and have done with it. Not wishing
to hurt his feelings, I refuse these works on the plea that I have read
them. Whereon he, divining despite me that I am a superior person, says
"Here is a nice little handy edition of More's *Utopia*" or "Carlyle's
French Revolution" and again I make some excuse. What pleasure
could I get from trying to cope with a masterpiece printed in diminutive
grey-ish type on a semi-transparent little grey-ish page? I relieve the
bookstall of nothing but a newspaper or two.

The other day, however, my eye and fancy were caught by a book
entitled *How Shall I Word It?* and sub-entitled *A Complete Letter
Writer for Men and Women.* I had never read one of these manuals,
but had often heard that there was a great and constant "demand" for
them. So I demanded this one. It is no great fun in itself. The writer is
no fool. He has evidently a natural talent for writing letters. His style is,
for the most part, discreet and easy. If you were a young man writing "to
Father of Girl he wishes to Marry" or "thanking Fiancée for Present" or

"reproaching Fiancée for being a Flirt," or if you were a mother "asking Governess her Qualifications" or "replying to Undesirable Invitation for her Child," or indeed if you were in any other one of the crises which this book is designed to alleviate, you might copy out and post the specially-provided letter without making yourself ridiculous in the eyes of its receiver—unless, of course, he or she also possessed a copy of the book. But—well, can you conceive any one copying out and posting one of these letters, or even taking it as the basis for composition? You cannot. That shows how little you know of your fellow-creatures. Not you nor I can plumb the abyss at the bottom of which such humility is possible. Nevertheless, as we know by that great and constant "demand," there the abyss is, and there multitudes are at the bottom of it. Let's peer down . . . No, all is darkness. But faintly, if we listen hard, is borne up to us a sound of the scratching of innumerable pens—pens whose wielders are all trying, as the author of this handbook urges them, to "be original, fresh, and interesting" by dint of more or less strict adherence to sample.

Giddily you draw back from the edge of the abyss. Come!—here is a thought to steady you. The mysterious great masses of helpless folk for whom *How Shall I Word It?* is written are sound at heart, delicate in feeling, anxious to please, most loth to wound. For it must be presumed that the author's style of letter-writing is informed as much by a desire to give his public what it needs, and will pay for, as by his own beautiful nature; and in the course of all the letters that he dictates you will find not one harsh word, not one ignoble thought or unkind insinuation. In all of them, though so many are for the use of persons placed in the most trying circumstances, and some of them are for persons writhing under a sense of intolerable injury, sweetness and light do ever reign. Even "yours truly, Jacob Langton," in his "letter to his Daughter's Mercenary Fiancé," mitigates the sternness of his tone by the remark that his "task is inexpressibly painful." And he, Mr. Langton, is the one writer who lets the post go out on his wrath. When Horace Masterton, of Thorpe Road, Putney, receives from Miss Jessica Weir, of Fir Villa, Blackheath, a letter "declaring her Change of Feelings," does he upbraid her? No; "it was honest and brave of you to write to me so straightforwardly and at the back of my mind I know you have done what is best. . . . I give you back your freedom only at your desire. God bless you, dear." Not less admirable is the behaviour, in similar case, of Cecil Grant (14, Glover Street, Streatham). Suddenly, as a bolt from the blue, comes a letter from Miss Louie Hawke (Elm View, Deerhurst), breaking off her betrothal to him. Haggard, he sits down to his desk; his pen traverses the notepaper—calling down curses on Louie and on all her sex? No; "one cannot say good-bye for ever without deep regret to days that have been so full of happiness. I must thank you sincerely for all your great kindness to me. . . . With every sincere wish for your future happiness," he bestows complete freedom on Miss Hawke. And do not imagine that in the matter of self-control and sympathy, of power to understand all and pardon all, the men are lagged behind by the women. Miss Leila Johnson (The Manse, Carlyle) has observed in Leonard Wace (Dover Street, Saltburn) a certain coldness of demeanour; yet "I do not blame you; it is probably your nature"; and Leila in her sweet forbearance is typical of all the other pained women in these pages: she is but one of a crowd of heroines.

Face to face with all this perfection, the not perfect reader begins to crave some little outburst of wrath, of hatred or malice, from one of these imaginary ladies and gentleman. He longs for—how shall he word it?—a glimpse of some bad motive, of some little lapse from dignity. Often, passing by a pillar-box, I have wished I could unlock it and carry away its contents, to be studied at my leisure. I have always thought such a haul would abound in things fascinating to a student of human nature. One night, not long ago, I took a waxen impression of the lock of the pillar-box nearest to my house, and had a key made. This implement I have as yet lacked either the courage or the opportunity to use. And now I think I shall throw it away. . . . No, I shan't. I refuse, after all, to draw my inference that the bulk of the British public writes always in the manner of this handbook. Even if they all have beautiful natures they must sometimes be sent slightly astray by inferior impulses, just as are you and I.

And, if err they must, surely it were well they should know how to do it correctly and forcibly. I suggest to our author that he should sprinkle his next edition with a few less righteous examples, thereby both purging his book of its monotony and somewhat justifying its subtitle. Like most people who are in the habit of writing things to be printed, I have not the knack of writing really good letters. But let me crudely indicate the sort of thing that our manual needs. . . .

LETTER FROM POOR MAN TO OBTAIN MONEY FROM RICH ONE.

[*The English law is particularly hard on what is called blackmail. It is therefore essential that the applicant should write nothing that might afterwards be twisted to incriminate him.*—ED.]

DEAR SIR,
      To-day, as I was turning out a drawer in my attic, I came across a letter which by a curious chance fell into my hands some years ago, and which, in the stress of grave pecuniary embarrassment, had escaped my memory. It is a letter written by yourself to a lady, and the date shows it to have been written shortly after your marriage. It is of a confidential nature, and might, I fear, if it fell into the wrong hands, be cruelly

misconstrued. I would wish you to have the satisfaction of destroying it in person. At first I thought of sending it on to you by post. But I know how happy you are in your domestic life; and probably your wife and you, in your perfect mutual trust, are in the habit of opening each other's letters. Therefore, to avoid risk, I would prefer to hand the document to you personally. I will not ask you to come to my attic, where I could not offer you such hospitality as is due to a man of your wealth and position. You will be so good as to meet me at 3.0 A.M. (sharp) to-morrow (Thursday) beside the tenth lamp-post to the left on the Surrey side of Waterloo Bridge; at which hour and place we shall not be disturbed.

I am, dear Sir,

Yours respectfully,

JAMES GRIDGE.

LETTER FROM YOUNG MAN REFUSING TO PAY HIS TAILOR'S BILL.

Mr. Eustace Davenant has received the half-servile, half-insolent screed which Mr. Yardley has addressed to him. Let Mr. Yardley cease from crawling on his knees and shaking his fist. Neither this posture nor this gesture can wring one bent farthing from the pockets of Mr. Davenant, who was a minor at the time when that series of ill-made suits was supplied to him and will hereafter, as in the past, shout (without prejudice) from the house-tops that of all the tailors in London Mr. Yardley is at once the most grasping and the least competent.

LETTER TO THANK AUTHOR FOR INSCRIBED COPY OF BOOK

DEAR MR. EMANUEL FLOWER,

It was kind of you to think of sending me a copy of your new book. It would have been kinder still to think again and abandon that project. I am a man of gentle instincts, and do not like to tell you that "A Flight into Arcady" (of which I have skimmed a few pages, thus wasting two or three minutes of my not altogether worthless time) is trash. On the other hand, I am determined that you shall not be able to go around boasting to your friends, if you have any, that this work was not condemned, derided, and dismissed by your sincere well-wisher, WREXFORD CRIPPS.

LETTER TO MEMBER OF PARLIAMENT UNSEATED AT GENERAL ELECTION

DEAR MR. POBSBY-BURFORD,

Though I am myself an ardent Tory, I cannot but rejoice in the crushing defeat you have just suffered in West Odgetown. There are moments when political conviction is overborne by personal sentiment; and this is one of them. Your loss of the seat that you held is the more striking by reason of the splendid manner in which the northern and eastern divisions of Odgetown have been wrested from the Liberal Party. The great bulk of the newspaper-reading public will be puzzled by your extinction in the midst of our party's triumph. But then, the great mass of the newspaper-reading public has not met you. I have. You will probably not remember me. You are the sort of man who would not remember anybody who might not be of some definite use to him. Such, at least, was one of the impressions you made on me when I met you last summer at a dinner given by our friends the Pelhams. Among the other things in you that struck me were the blatant pomposity of your manner, your appalling flow of cheap platitudes, and your hoggish lack of ideas. It is such men as you that lower the tone of public life. And I am sure that in writing to you thus I am but expressing what is felt, without distinction of party, by all who sat with you in the late Parliament.

The one person in whose behalf I regret your withdrawal into private life is your wife, whom I had the pleasure of taking in to the aforesaid dinner. It was evident to me that she was a woman whose spirit was well-nigh broken by her conjunction with you. Such remnants of cheerfulness as were in her I attributed to the Parliamentary duties which kept you out of her sight for so very many hours daily. I do not like to think of the fate to which the free and independent electors of West Odgetown have just condemned her. Only, remember this: chattel of yours though she is, and timid and humble, she despises you in her heart.

I am, dear Mr. Pobsby-Burford,
Yours very truly,
HAROLD THISTLAKE.

LETTER FROM YOUNG LADY IN ANSWER TO INVITATION FROM OLD SCHOOLMISTRESS.

MY DEAR MISS PRICE,

How awfully sweet of you to ask me to stay with you for a few days but how *can* you think I may have forgotten you for of course I think of you so very often and of the three ears I spent at your school because it is such a joy not to be there any longer and if one is at all down it bucks one up derectly to remember that *thats* all over atanyrate and that one has enough food to nurrish one and not that awful monottany of life and not the petty fogging daily tirrany you went in for and I can imagin no greater thrill and luxury in a way than to come and see the whole dismal grind still going on but without me being in it but this would be *rather* beastly of me wouldnt it so please dear Miss Price dont expect me and do excuse mistakes of English Composition and Spelling and etcetra in your affectionate old pupil,

EMILY THÉRÈSE LYNN-ROYSTON.

ps, I often rite to people telling them where I was edducated and highly reckomending you.

LETTER IN ACKNOWLEDGEMENT OF WEDDING PRESENT.

DEAR LADY AMBLESHAM,

Who gives quickly, says the old proverb, gives twice. For this reason I have purposely delayed writing to you, lest I should appear to thank you more than once for the small, cheap, hideous present you sent me on the occasion of my recent wedding. Were you a poor woman, that little bowl of ill-imitated Dresden china would convict you of tasteless-ness merely; were you a blind woman, of nothing but an odious parsi-mony. As you have normal eyesight and more than normal wealth, your gift to me proclaims you at once a Philistine and a miser (or rather did so proclaim you until, less than ten seconds after I had unpacked it from its wrappings of tissue paper, I took it to the open window and had the satisfaction of seeing it shattered to atoms on the pavement). But stay! I perceive a possible flaw in my argument. Perhaps you were guided in your choice by a definite wish to insult me. I am sure, on reflection, that this was so. *I shall not forget.*

Yours, etc.,
CYNTHIA BEAUMARSH.

PS. My husband asked me to tell you to warn Lord Amblesham to keep out of his way or to assume some disguise so complete that he will not be recognised by him and horsewhipped.

PPS. I am sending copies of this letter to the principal London and provincial newspapers.

LETTER FROM . . .

But enough! I never thought I should be so strong in this line. I had not foreseen such copiousness and fatal fluency. Never again will I tap these deep dark reservoirs in a character that had always seemed to me, on the whole, so amiable.

STUDY QUESTIONS

1. In the opening paragraph, what does Beerbohm indirectly tell us about himself?
2. What is Beerbohm's criticism of the models in the letter-writing manual? What does he see as the rhetorical strategy in these letters?
3. Examine each of the letters he writes and determine his rhetorical strategy.

BUCK FANSHAW'S

Mark Twain   **FUNERAL**

Mark Twain, pen name for Samuel Langhorne Clemens (1835–
1910), internationally known humorist and satirist, was born in
Florida, Missouri, and spent his boyhood in Hannibal, Missouri. In
his youth and early manhood he worked at a variety of occupa-
tions—journeyman printer, steamboat pilot, newspaper reporter,
prospector, free-lance writer, and lecturer. His experiences gave
him a lifetime of material for his writings. In his own time he
enjoyed an international reputation as a wit and social commentator. In his later years he became bitterly cynical, but to most
Americans he is remembered as the author of *Tom Sawyer* (1876)
and *The Adventures of Huckleberry Finn* (1884).

Somebody has said that in order to know a community, one must
observe the style of its funerals and know what manner of men they bury
with most ceremony. I cannot say which class we buried with most éclat
in our "flush times," the distinguished public benefactor or the distinguished rough—possibly the two chief grades or grand divisions of society honored their illustrious dead about equally; and hence, no doubt,
the philosopher I have quoted from would have needed to see two
representative funerals in Virginia before forming his estimate of the
people.

There was a grand time over Buck Fanshaw when he died. He was
a representative citizen. He had "killed his man"—not in his own quarrel,
it is true, but in defense of a stranger unfairly beset by numbers. He had
kept a sumptuous saloon. He had been the proprietor of a dashing
helpmeet whom he could have discarded without the formality of a
divorce. He had held a high position in the fire department and been a
very Warwick in politics. When he died there was great lamentation
throughout the town, but especially in the vast bottom-stratum of society.

On the inquest it was shown that Buck Fanshaw, in the delirium of
a wasting typhoid fever, had taken arsenic, shot himself through the
body, cut his throat, and jumped out of a four-story window and broken
his neck—and after due deliberation, the jury, sad and tearful, but with

Chapter VI in *Roughing It* by Mark Twain. Reprinted by permission of Harper & Row,
publishers.

intelligence unblinded by its sorrow, brought in a verdict of death "by the visitation of God." What could the world do without juries?

Prodigious preparations were made for the funeral. All the vehicles in town were hired, all the saloons put in mourning, all the municipal and fire-company flags hung at half-mast, and all the firemen ordered to muster in uniform and bring their machines duly draped in black. Now—let us remark in parentheses—as all the peoples of the earth had representative adventurers in the Silverland, and as each adventurer had brought the slang of his nation or his locality with him, the combination made the slang of Nevada the richest and the most infinitely varied and copious that had ever existed anywhere in the world, perhaps, except in the mines of California in the "early days." Slang was the language of Nevada. It was hard to preach a sermon without it, and be understood. Such phrases as "You bet!" "Oh, no, I reckon not!" "No Irish need apply," and a hundred others, became so common as to fall from the lips of a speaker unconsciously—and very often when they did not touch the subject under discussion and consequently failed to mean anything.

After Buck Fanshaw's inquest, a meeting of the short-haired brotherhood was held, for nothing can be done on the Pacific coast without a public meeting and an expression of sentiment. Regretful resolutions were passed and various committees appointed; among others, a committee of one was deputed to call on the minister, a fragile, gentle, spiritual new fledgling from an Eastern theological seminary, and as yet unacquainted with the ways of the mines. The committeeman, "Scotty" Briggs, made his visit; and in after days it was worth something to hear the minister tell about it. Scotty was a stalwart rough, whose customary suit, when on weighty official business, like committee work, was a fire-helmet, flaming red flannel shirt, patent-leather belt with spanner and revolver attached, coat hung over arm, and pants stuffed into boot-tops. He formed something of a contrast to the pale theological student. It is fair to say of Scotty, however, in passing, that he had a warm heart, and a strong love for his friends, and never entered into a quarrel when he could reasonably keep out of it. Indeed, it was commonly said that whenever one of Scotty's fights was investigated, it always turned out that it had originally been no affair of his, but that out of native good-heartedness he had dropped in of his own accord to help the man who was getting the worst of it. He and Buck Fanshaw were bosom friends, for years, and had often taken adventurous "pot-luck" together. On one occasion, they had thrown off their coats and taken the weaker side in a fight among strangers, and after gaining a hard-earned victory, turned and found that the men they were helping had deserted early, and not only that, but had stolen their coats and made off with them. But to return to Scotty's visit to the minister. He was on a sorrowful mission,

now, and his face was the picture of woe. Being admitted to the presence he sat down before the clergyman, placed his fire-hat on an unfinished manuscript sermon under the minister's nose, took from it a red
silk handkerchief, wiped his brow and heaved a sigh of dismal impres-
siveness, explanatory of his business. He choked, and even shed tears;
but with an effort he mastered his voice and said in lugubrious tones:

"Are you the duck that runs the gospel-mill next door?"

"Am I the—pardon me, I believe I do not understand?"

With another sigh and a half-sob, Scotty rejoined:

"Why you see we are in a bit of trouble, and the boys thought
maybe you would give us a lift, if we'd tackle you—that is, if I've got the
rights of it and you are the head clerk of the doxology-works next door."

"I am the shepherd in charge of the flock whose fold is next door."

"The which?"

"The spiritual adviser of the little company of believers whose
sanctuary adjoins these premises."

Scotty scratched his head, reflected a moment, and then said:

"You ruther hold over me, pard. I reckon I can't call that hand.
Ante and pass the buck."

"How? I beg pardon. What did I understand you to say?"

"Well, you've ruther got the bulge on me. Or maybe we've both
got the bulge, somehow. You don't smoke me and I don't smoke you.
You see, one of the boys has passed in his checks, and we want to give
him a good send-off, and so the thing I'm on now is to roust out
somebody to jerk a little chin-music for us and waltz him through
handsome."

"My friend, I seem to grow more and more bewildered. Your observations are wholly incomprehensible to me. Cannot you simplify them in
some way? At first I thought perhaps I understood you, but I grope now.
Would it not expedite matters if you restricted yourself to categorical
statements of fact unencumbered with obstructing accumulations of
metaphor and allegory?"

Another pause, and more reflection. Then, said Scotty:

"I'll have to pass, I judge."

"How?"

"You've raised me out, pard."

"I still fail to catch your meaning."

"Why, that last lead of yourn is too many for me—that's the idea. I
can't neither trump nor follow suit."

The clergyman sank back in his chair perplexed. Scotty leaned his
head on his hand and gave himself up to thought. Presently his face
came up, sorrowful but confident.

"I've got it now, so's you can savvy," he said. "What we want is a
gospel-sharp. See?"

"A what?"

"Gospel-sharp. Parson."

"Oh! Why did you not say so before? I am a clergyman—a parson."

"Now you talk! You see my blind and straddle it like a man. Put it there!"—extending a brawny paw, which closed over the minister's small hand and gave it a shake indicative of fraternal sympathy and fervent gratification.

"Now we're all right, pard. Let's start fresh. Don't you mind my snuffling a little—becuz we're in a power of trouble. You see, one of the boys has gone up the flume—"

"Gone where?"

"Up the flume—throwed up the sponge, you understand."

"Thrown up the sponge?"

"Yes—kicked the bucket—"

"Ah—has departed to that mysterious country from whose bourne no traveler returns."

"Return! I reckon not. Why, pard, he's *dead!*"

"Yes, I understand."

"Oh, you do? Well I thought maybe you might be getting tangled some more. Yes, you see he's dead again—"

"*Again!* Why, has he ever been dead before?"

"Dead before? No! Do you reckon a man has got as many lives as a cat? But you bet you he's awful dead now, poor old boy, and I wish I'd never seen this day. I don't want no better friend than Buck Fanshaw. I knowed him by the back; and when I know a man and like him, I freeze to him—you hear *me*. Take him all round, pard, there never was a bullier man in the mines. No man ever knowed Buck Fanshaw to go back on a friend. But it's all up, you know, it's all up. It ain't no use. They've scooped him."

"Scooped him?"

"Yes—death has. Well, well, well, we've got to give him up. Yes, indeed. It's a kind of a hard world, after all, *ain't* it? But pard, he was a rustler! You ought to seen him get started once. He was a bully boy with a glass eye! Just spit in his face and give him room according to his strength, and it was just beautiful to see him peel and go in. He was the worst son a thief that ever drawed breath. Pard, he was *on* it! He was on it bigger than an Injun!"

"On it? On what?"

"On the shoot. On the shoulder. On the fight, you understand. *He* didn't give a continental for *any*body. *Beg* your pardon, friend, for coming so near saying a cuss-word—but you see I'm on an awful strain, in this palaver, on account of having to cramp down and draw everything so mild. But we've got to give him up. There ain't any getting around that, I don't reckon. Now if we can get you to help plant him—"

"Preach the funeral discourse? Assist at the obsequies?"

"Obs'quies is good. Yes. That's it—that's our little game. We are going to get the thing up regardless, you know. He was always nifty himself, and so you bet you his funeral ain't going to be no slouch—solid-silver door-plate on his coffin, six plumes on the hearse, and a nigger on the box in a biled shirt and a plug hat—how's that for high? And we'll take care of *you*, pard. We'll fix you all right. There'll be a kerridge for you; and whatever you want, you just 'scape out and we'll 'tend to it. We've got a shebang fixed up for you to stand behind, in No. 1's house, and don't you be afraid. Just go in and toot your horn, if you don't sell a clam. Put Buck through as bully as you can, pard, for anybody that knowed him will tell you that he was one of the whitest men that was ever in the mines. You can't draw it too strong. He never could stand it to see things going wrong. He's done more to make this town quiet and peaceable than any man in it. I've seen him lick four Greasers in eleven minutes, myself. If a thing wanted regulating, *he* warn't a man to go browsing around after somebody to do it, but he would prance in and regulate it himself. He warn't a Catholic. Scasely. He was down on 'em. His word was, 'No Irish need apply!' But it didn't make no difference about that when it came down to what a man's rights was—and so, when some roughs jumped the Catholic boneyard and started in to stake out town lots in it he *went* for 'em! And he *cleaned* 'em, too! I was there, pard, and I seen it myself."

"That was very well indeed—at least the impulse was—whether the act was strictly defensible or not. Had deceased any religious convictions? That is to say, did he feel a dependence upon, or acknowledge allegiance to a higher power?"

More reflection.

"I reckon you've stumped me again, pard. Could you say it over once more, and say it slow?"

"Well, to simplify it somewhat, was he, or rather had he ever been connected with any organization sequestered from secular concerns and devoted to self-sacrifice in the interests of morality?"

"All down but nine—set 'em up on the other alley, pard."

"What did I understand you to say?"

"Why, you're most too many for me, you know. When you get in with your left I hunt grass every time. Every time you draw, you fill; but I don't seem to have any luck. Let's have a new deal."

"How? Begin again?"

"That's it."

"Very well. Was he a good man, and—"

"There—I see that; don't put up another chip till I look at my hand. A good man, says you? Pard, it ain't no name for it. He was the best man that ever—pard, you would have doted on that man. He could lam any

galoot of his inches in America. It was him that put down the riot last
election before it got a start; and everybody said he was the only man
that could have done it. He waltzed in with a spanner in one hand and a
trumpet in the other, and sent fourteen men home on a shutter in less
than three minutes. He had that riot all broke up and prevented nice
before anybody ever got a chance to strike a blow. He was always for
peace, and he would *have* peace—he could not stand disturbances. Pard,
he was a great loss to this town. It would please the boys if you could
chip in something like that and do him justice. Here once when the
Micks got to throwing stones through the Methodis' Sunday-school
windows, Buck Fanshaw, all of his own notion, shut up his saloon and
took a couple of six-shooters and mounted guard over the Sunday-
school. Says he, 'No Irish need apply!' And they didn't. He was the
bulliest man in the mountains, pard! He could run faster, jump higher,
hit harder, and hold more tanglefoot whisky without spilling it than any
man in seventeen counties. Put that in, pard—it'll please the boys more
than anything you could say. And you can say, pard, that he never shook
his mother."

"Never shook his mother?"

"That's it—any of the boys will tell you so."

"Well, but why *should* he shake her?"

"That's what *I* say—but some people does."

"Not people of any repute?"

"Well, some that averages pretty so-so."

"In my opinion the man that would offer personal violence to his
own mother, ought to—"

"Cheese it, pard; you've banked your ball clean outside the string.
What I was a drivin' at, was, that he never *throwed off* on his mother—
don't you see? No indeedy. He give her a house to live in, and town lots,
and plenty of money; and he looked after her and took care of her all the
time; and when she was down with the smallpox I'm d—d if he didn't set
up nights and nuss her himself! *Beg* your pardon for saying it, but it
hopped out too quick for yours truly. You've treated me like a gentleman, pard, and I ain't the man to hurt your feelings intentional. I think
you're white. I think you're a square man, pard. I like you, and I'll lick
any man that don't. I'll lick him till he can't tell himself from a last year's
corpse! Put it *there!*" [Another fraternal handshake—and exit.]

The obsequies were all that "the boys" could desire. Such a marvel
of funeral pomp had never been seen in Virginia. The plumed hearse,
the dirge-breathing brass-bands, the closed marts of business, the flags
drooping at half-mast, the long, plodding procession of uniformed secret
societies, military battalions and fire companies, draped engines, carriages of officials, and citizens in vehicles and on foot, attracted multitudes of spectators to the sidewalks, roofs, and windows; and for years

afterward, the degree of grandeur attained by any civic display in Virginia was determined by comparison with Buck Fanshaw's funeral.

Scotty Briggs, as a pall-bearer and a mourner, occupied a prominent place at the funeral, and when the sermon was finished and the last sentence of the prayer for the dead man's soul ascended, he responded, in a low voice, but with feeling:

"AMEN. No Irish need apply."

As the bulk of the response was without apparent relevancy, it was probably nothing more than a humble tribute to the memory of the friend that was gone; for, as Scotty had once said, it was "his word."

Scotty Briggs, in after days, achieved the distinction of becoming the only convert to religion that was ever gathered from the Virginia roughs; and it transpired that the man who had it in him to espouse the quarrel of the weak out of inborn nobility of spirit was no mean timber whereof to construct a Christian. The making him one did not warp his generosity or diminish his courage; on the contrary it gave intelligent direction to the one and a broader field to the other. If his Sunday-school class progressed faster than the other classes, was it matter for wonder? I think not. He talked to his pioneer small-fry in a language they understood! It was my large privilege, a month before he died, to hear him tell the beautiful story of Joseph and his brethren to his class "without looking at the book." I leave it to the reader to fancy what it was like, as it fell, riddled with slang, from the lips of that grave, earnest teacher, and was listened to by his little learners with a consuming interest that showed that they were as unconscious as he was that any violence was being done to the sacred proprieties!

STUDY QUESTIONS

1. In addition to Scotty's and the minister's language, we have the language of the author, who introduces the story and concludes it. Compare his manner of speech with that of the other two.
2. Make note of the many different expressions Scotty and the minister use for death and funeral. Can you add to these?
3. Some of Scotty's expressions are current today. What are some of them?

SECTION 5 | EDUCATION

"Unwillingly to School"

DON'T SEND JOHNNY

Hugh Kenner **TO COLLEGE**

Hugh Kenner (1923–   ) was born in Petersborough, Canada. He received his B.A. and M.A. from the University of Toronto and his Ph.D. from Yale University. He is professor of English at the University of California, Santa Barbara. Mr. Kenner has received fellowships from the American Council of Learned Societies and the Guggenheim Foundation. In 1950 he won the Porter Prize at Yale. He is an outstanding scholar and the author of numerous articles on contemporary literature. In addition to his studies on T. S. Eliot and Samuel Beckett, he is the author of *The Poetry of Ezra Pound, Wyndham Lewis,* and *Dublin's Joyce.*

Johnny goes by the official title of "student." Yet Johnny's is the face every professor would prefer to see anywhere but in his classroom, where it blocks with its dreary smile, or its stoical yawn, the educational process on which we are proud to spend annually billions of dollars. By his sheer inert numbers he is making the common pursuit of professors and students—real students—impossible.

No one, least of all his professor, wills Johnny an injustice. Even the dean of students, whose lot he renders abysmal, finds it impossible not to like him, though some miraculous multiplication of loafers and fish sends Johnnies in an endless column trooping past the dean's receptionist, to stammer out their tale of dragging grades and just not digging the stuff.

Johnnies by the thousand, by the hundred thousand, clutter up every college in the land, where they long ago acquired a numerical majority. If you have a teenager in your home, thinking of college, the chances are you have Johnny. On behalf of my 400,000 colleagues in the academic profession, I'd be grateful if you'd keep him home.

Though Johnny is by definition multitudinous and anonymous, bits of Johnnyism stick in every teacher's mind. I remember the set neon smile that greeted me class after class for three whole weeks from a front-row seat just next to the door. The smile's owner and operator—let's call her Jonnie—never said a word, never took a note, never turned a page in her copy of *Gulliver's Travels*. Then, the day after I assigned a paper, the smile was gone, and so was she, apparently for good.

A month later, having heard that I would welcome some explanation, Jonnie turned up in my office, smiling. No, she couldn't do papers at all, not at all. Then what, pray, had brought her to a university, where, as everyone knows, one does papers? Well, she had enrolled on the advice of her psychiatrist. He had said the College Experience would be good therapy. Unwilling to monkey with therapy, I referred her, smile and all, to the dean. I've forgotten what he decided. There are so many Johnnies and Jonnies.

And there is no end to what their mentors and counselors, not to say psychiatrists, expect a university to do. Teach Johnny to behave like a gentleman. Prevent his simultaneous presence with Jonnie in parked cars after 10 P.M. Help him (her) get to know girls (boys). Improve his work habits. Open his mind (he has nothing but prejudices). Shut his mouth (he does nothing but talk). Tighten his morals. Loosen his imagination. Spread beneath his slack chin the incredible banquet of Western Civilization. And discharge him fit to earn a better living, make a better marriage and digest (Lord help him) *The New York Times.*

The parents and mentors who expect all this expect it not of the college but of the College Experience, which is turning, accordingly, into the experience of living in a whole cityful of Johnnies. (I've just been told by a Sunday supplement that within 35 years many colleges with enrollments of 100,000 to 200,000 will have become cities in their own right.)

Johnny (Jonnie) expects none of the wonders of the College Experience, except *in re* girls (boys). Johnny is amiably devoid of expectations. One might say that he goes where he's shoved. One might affirm with more tact that he lends himself amiably to the College Experience, having no better plans. That is what marks him as Johnny, not as a student. A student has a vocation for study. But there's really nothing that Johnny comes to campus burning to learn about.

"Real education," wrote Ezra Pound 30 years ago, "must ultimately be limited to men who INSIST on knowing; the rest is mere sheepherding."

The mind that insists on knowing is (alas) not to be identified by tests, which explains why, despite the well-publicized vigilance of admissions officers, the number of campus Johnnies keeps rising. A mind that insists on knowing has begun to focus its energies by the time it has been in the world 16 years. By 17 or 18—the age of a college freshman—it has learned the taste of knowledge and the sensation of reaching for more. It may spell erratically, if it is served (like Yeats) by a deficient visual memory. It may calculate imperfectly, if it is (like Einstein) more at home with concepts than with operations. There may be strange gaps in its information, since a young mind cannot be everywhere at once.

But what it does not know it will encounter with pleasure. And it *must* learn, as a cat must eat. It may not yet know where its need for knowledge is meant to be satisfied. It may tack about, sails taut, without regard for curricular symmetry, changing majors perhaps more than once. But its tireless curiosity is unmistakable. In time, if all goes well, it will accept training, and the lifelong responsibilities of keeping itself trained.

But Johnny has no such appetite, no such momentum. When Johnny applies his brand-new ball-point to his first blue book, each sentence comes out smudged with his unmistakable pawprint. "Newspaper comics are good because they put a rosy glow on the grayish realities of the mind": There you have Johnny ingenuously expressing the state of *his* mind—a gray place which Pogo can occasionally animate, and a place of Good Things and Bad Things where Pogo is a Good Thing.

"The three main groups of people are the well-educated, semieducated and semiuneducated." There is all mankind characterized (a feat that taxed Aristotle), complete with a category for Johnny himself; he never forgets himself.

I am not inventing these examples. A colleague of mine gleaned a dozen like them in a single afternoon, from freshman themes at a university that accepts only the top one-eighth of the high-school crop. What they illustrate isn't primarily the "inability to express oneself," i.e., technical difficulties with the English language. What they illustrate is something deeper, probably irremediable; a happy willingness to emulate the motions of thought, since a teacher is standing there expecting such motions, along with a nearly total want of experience of what the process of thinking feels like.

"And this is why we should have no prejudice against Negroes and other lower races." That mind, we may say with some confidence, doesn't insist upon knowing. It doesn't know even its own most blatant contradictions. "To analyze this theory, it can be broken down into two parts: men and women." That's what men and women are, for the nonce—they are the parts of Johnny's theory. "The result is a ridiculous fiasco under which the roof falls in." It is indeed, and one does not know whether to marvel more at the oppressive weight of that fiasco, crashing through the roof like a half-ton bear, or at the innocent ease with which Johnny, supposing ideas to be weightless, pats them to and fro like bubbles.

But examples don't define a problem which by its very nature arises out of sheer multitudinousness. The amiable dumbbell has for decades been a part of campus folklore, like the absentminded professor. It is when you multiply him by a million that he grows ominous, swamping the campus as with creeping molasses. His uncle of 40 years ago, Joe College, had no more interest in learning than Johnny has, but none of Johnny's baleful power. With a certain talent for grotesque stylization, he conducted his entertaining ballet of raccoon coats, hip flasks, and whiffenpoofery, while the business of the academy, a considerably more modest business than today, went on.

What has created the Johnny problem isn't some freakish metamorphosis of Joe College into numberless protozoa, but rather the nearly universal conviction that everybody ought to spend four years at college if it can possibly be managed.

Johnny's parents, needless to say, believe this. His state legislator, despite the fantastic costs, tries to believe it, since his constituents seem to. The prospective employer believes it: let Johnny check "none" where the personnel blank inquires after "college record," and Johnny will be lucky to be issued a pick and shovel, let alone a sample kit. Even the college, caught in competitions for funds (which tend to hinge on enrollments, has come to believe it believes it.

Meanwhile B.A.'s grow so common that employers who once demanded them now demand M.A.'s, and the Master's requirement in some fields (not just the academic) has been upgraded to the Ph.D. In the years since Robert M. Hutchins sardonically proposed that we achieve our desires with less trouble by granting every American citizen a B.A. at birth, we have moved closer and closer to a utopia in which everyone receives it at 21, in return for doing classroom time. One already hears talk of attendance being compulsory through age 20. In California, where problems tend to surface before New England need worry about them, the state population rose 50 percent in one decade, and the college population 82 percent. It grows easy to foresee the day when 50 percent of the population of California (and, after a suitable time lag, of Massachusetts, of New York, of Illinois and, yes of Montana) will be employed at teaching the other 50 percent, perhaps changing ends at the half.

Clearly something has got to bust, and no one doubts what: the idea of a university. As an institution for (in Thomas Jefferson's words) "the instruction of those who will come after us," it's already being trampled out of recognizable existence by hordes of Johnnies.

The real student, struggling against suffocation of the soul, draws back, or beefs about how "the class" is holding things up, or starts feeling superior (and energy expended in nourishing a feeling of superiority is wholly lost). At worst, from being eager he turns merely "sensitive," and allows his zeal to be leached away. He is deprived, and can rightfully resent being deprived, of the kind of company he deserves to expect at a place where, often at considerable sacrifice, he has elected to invest four years of his life.

The professors suffer too. For one thing, they are coming off the production line too rapidly (though the harried trustees, looking wildly around at teaching machines and television hookups say "Not rapidly enough!"). Since there's no way of growing scholars at a pace keyed to the amoebalike increase of Johnnies, substitutes have begun to be manufactured. As real students are swamped by Johnnies, real professors must coexist with a swarm of Johnny-professors.

And like the real students, the real professors grow obsessed with futility, and unless they succeed, as some do, in isolating themselves with advanced students, fall victim to the real occupational hazard of the profession: an inability to believe that anybody can be taught anything. I once heard of a man who was so startled by the discovery of a real student that, lest she slip over his horizon, he divorced his wife and married her. I don't believe that story, but it's indicative; the professor who told it to me found it believable.

There's no doubt that as a nation we settle for only the side effects and the fringe benefits of what we invest in universities: the products of physics labs and research stations, and the economic advantages, to which our economy has been attuned ever since the G. I. Bill, of keeping several million young people off the labor market as long as possible. We are getting even this, though, at the price of a colossal wastage of time and spirit—the time and spirit of the real students on whose behalf the system is allegedly being run. If by the year 2000, as President Clark Kerr of California expects, educational institutions will be the largest single force in the economy, and if attendance to the age of 20 is compulsory, as Dr. Dwayne Orton of I.B.M. expects, why then the economy will in the lifetime of most of us have begun devoting its principal energies to the maintenance of huge concentration camps for keeping Johnnies by the multimillion agreeably idle.

So do we kick out Johnny? Alas, things will never be that simple again. Our social and economic system has come to depend on Johnny, B.A., in ways that can probably never be unstitched. Moreover, the College Experience probably *is* the most important event in the lives of most of the people who undergo it, even of the hundreds of thousands who learn very little. It is their time of access to the intellectual traffic patterns that define the quality of American life. A Kansan and a Georgian who have both been to college—merely been there—will have more to say to one another than a Vermonter who has and a Vermonter who hasn't. The College Experience is our folk ritual for inducting our adolescents into the 20th century. As part of our established religion, it must be treated as immune from curtailment.

Very well, then: the College Experience for Johnny, in his Johnny-classrooms. But let us, in the name of sanity, allow the real students to have *their* version of the College Experience. That means either separate-but-equal facilities, or (better, I think), some college equivalent of the two-track high schools that already exist.

One way of arranging a two-track college with minimum disruption is to permit only the real students to pursue majors. The University of Toronto has been doing that for more than half a century. Two decades ago I was one of a group of 40 freshman English majors there. In the sophomore year there were 20 of us, in the junior year 10; there the ruthless cutting stopped. But the missing 30 were not slung out of school. All but a few hopeless cases were "permitted," as the official formula had it, "to transfer to the pass course," which meant that, if they wanted to stay on at college, they abandoned the major and enrolled in "pass arts."

Pass arts was a three-year humanities mixture, leading to the degree of B.A. And it wasn't a ghetto for dropouts; many students enrolled in it to start with. Its degree satisfied employers, parents and the Ontario College of Education. It satisfied Johnny just fine. It gave the university all the advantages of bigness, as the quality of the library testified. It wasn't conducive to snobbery or segregation; every honor student took a couple of pass courses a year, in subjects peripheral to his major.

It was, in short, a two-track system, with the tracks parallel, and with means for switching laggards onto the slow track.

Everyone, we agree, should have access to all the education he can absorb. Everyone who can absorb education deserves, I would add, a chance to absorb it, free from the distracting tramp of the million-footed Johnny. As colleges now operate, the idea that everybody should be sent to them is nonsense. The only hope is to start operating them differently, detached from the dogma that Johnny is by birthright a student. He needs, in fact, explicit treatment as a nonstudent. There's no inherent reason why the nation's universities shouldn't make special curricular arrangements for several million nonstudents, any more than there's an inherent reason why one of the nation's universities shouldn't be the world's largest purveyor of white mice. (One of them is.)

STUDY QUESTIONS

1.   According to Kenner, what has created the Johnny problem?
2.   In what ways is Johnny different from the real student?
3.   Do you judge Kenner's proposal for the "Johnny problem" a practical solution? Would you be willing to take a "Johnny-curriculum"?
4.   Compare Kenner's proposal with Hutchins' proposal ("Colleges Are Obsolete").
5.   This essay originally appeared in a magazine designed for the general public. In what ways did Kenner direct his essay to this audience? Note the diction, sentence structure, organization, and general structure.

COLLEGES

Robert M. Hutchins ARE OBSOLETE

Robert M. Hutchins (1899–   ) was born in Brooklyn, New York. He received his education at Yale University, where he was named Dean of the Law School in 1928. Mr. Hutchins became well-known for his unconventional ideas about higher education. When he became chancellor of the University of Chicago in 1945, he instituted many changes in the curriculum and in educational procedures. In 1951 he became associate director of the Ford Foundation, and in 1954 he was selected as president of the Funds for the Republic. Mr. Hutchins is an outspoken but highly respected critic of higher education; his writings have appeared in numerous publications.

The aims, methods, and organization of the American college are open to such serious question that the college itself may not be long for this world.

Its condition is obscured by its reputation. A college degree is now regarded as the passport to "success." We are told by the United States Office of Education that male citizens who have finished four years of college or more will have a lifetime income of $360,604, whereas those who have merely completed high school will make only $224,417. For a total outlay that may be as little as $6,000, the college graduate gets back $136,187, an excellent return on a modest investment.

Reprinted with permission of the author. First published in *Saturday Evening Post*, September 1965.

Dr. Frank Bowles, when he was president of the College Entrance Examination Board, said, "The arguments for going to college that are now in use are basically economic. They are only occasionally intellectual, or even cultural. It is true that college catalogs all have a standard paragraph stating that the college aim is 'preparation of the whole man for life through establishment of social, cultural, or intellectual values,' but I would doubt seriously that anyone, including the man writing the statement, is prepared to state precisely how this is to be done."

I would doubt seriously whether Doctor Bowles or anyone else could state precisely how a college prepares a student to make money.

Suppose we found, as I am sure we would, that men who join country clubs early in life make more money than those social outcasts who never got by an admissions committee. We would not conclude that belonging to a country club was the passport to "success." We would say that membership was an effect and not a cause.

So it is with going to college. A young man who goes to college has already succeeded. He has succeeded in getting born into a "good home" and a relatively prosperous family, one that has both the means and the inclination to push him to the degree. The college does not establish his earning power. That is established before he enters.

In a period of declining employment, when an employer has more applicants than he has jobs, he will take the man, other things being equal, who has the most schooling. Why not? The graduate will come from a "better" home, he is likely to be more "civilized," and there is always the chance that he may have learned something. Hence, at the bottom of the Depression, you had to have a college degree in order to qualify as a floorwalker in a department store.

So today the colleges are a kind of personnel system for business. It is convenient for an employer to limit his choices to college graduates. But little pretense is made that college education is good preparation for business.

College education is not good preparation for business, except in the sense that it is, or ought to be, good preparation for life. If a man who has a trained mind is likely to do better in business than one who has an undeveloped mind, then a college graduate is, or ought to be, better prepared for business than one who is without as many educational advantages.

But this is simply saying that college education ought to make a man better at everything. It ought to make him a better art critic, a better citizen and a better husband, not because he has taken courses in how to be an art critic or in the problems of citizenship or—Heaven forbid!—in marriage, but because he is more intelligent.

The question, then, is: Do our colleges help their students become more intelligent?

The answer is, on the whole, no.

The best way to help young men and women become more intelligent is to put them into a vital intellectual community that is thinking together about important things.

The American college is not an intellectual community, and it cannot become one.

Its methods, organization and location in the educational system must defeat attempts to transform it into an intellectual community.

The method is the course, a quarter or a semester long, with course examinations and course credits. The organization is departmental, with departments composed of specialists. The place in the educational system is between the high school and the graduate school. All these practices and positions are untenable.

Americans shrink from judgments of quality and take refuge in judgments of quantity. We do not know whether a picture or a building or a college is good, but we do know how big it is and how much it cost. These quantitative judgments are easy because they are open to anybody who can count, and they are usually subject to instant verification.

Since we do not know what a good education is and will not take the trouble to find out, we educate by the numbers. College education is 120 semester hours. Going to college is doing time.

Since the 120 semester hours are taught by specialists, they can add up to comprehension only by accident. The student is never compelled to put together what the specialists have told him, because he is examined course by course by the teacher who taught the course. His IBM card must show he passed the requisite number of courses with the minimum numerical average, and that is all.

Teachers and students pursuing different specialties have a hard time forming an intellectual community. Without some common understanding and aim such a community would appear to be impossible. The variety of course offerings—there must be a great variety if all the specialists are to have a crack at the students and all the students' interests are to be represented—reflects and perpetuates the absence of common understanding. (The president of a small college in Missouri once boasted to me that it would take a student 25 years to go through all the courses his college offered.)

Hence some college presidents seriously argue that intercollegiate football is indispensable because it is the only way to "unite" the college.

There is no remedy for these disorders as long as the American college occupies its present place in the educational system.

A student ready to specialize should go to the place where the best specialists are—that is, to the university. The only hope I can see for the student who needs understanding and comprehension of himself, his society, and the world about him lies in the creation of a new home for the liberal education.

The late William C. De Vane, longtime dean of Yale College, stated (a little optimistically, I fear), "It is still possible to obtain a liberal education in the better small college today, perhaps, but the older, dedicated teachers are retiring and are replaced by inexperienced and narrowly trained young scholars and scientists, if replacements with any training can be found at all."

Dean De Vane continued: "Many forces are making for the deterioration of teaching in the colleges. . . .

"The chief force in this trend is the excessive emphasis and premium which is put upon research in all fields by the universities. What the university does today in the name of research, the college will try to do tomorrow in the name of prestige."

The spirit and practices of the university have already absorbed the last two years of most work in colleges. Some junior and senior programs are frankly "preprofessional." They are all highly specialized.

The high school is reaching into the college from the other end. In many colleges today up to 50 percent of the entering freshmen are admitted to advanced standing. This means that they have already taken some courses the college offers. If the high school can take over more and more of the first two years, and the university is taking over all of the last two, why should there be a college at all?

Life is learning. The man who stops learning is as good as dead. The essence of community is learning together. The political community arises when the citizens are learning together to govern themselves. The democratic political community arises when all the citizens are learning together to govern themselves. The democratic political community arises when all the people are citizens. The democratic vision is that all the people are engaged in argument about the good of the community and the methods of achieving it.

The education that prepares for such a life in such a community is liberal education. It supplies the intellectual techniques and the intellectual framework necessary to a life of learning and a life in the political dialogue. It frees a man from the prison-house of his class, race, time, place, background, family and even of his nation, for the purpose of understanding and taking part in the great task of becoming human and helping to form a world community.

Hence the most urgent challenge in American education today is to build a new home for liberal education.

Suppose we took the four years beginning with the junior year in high school and ending with the sophomore year in college and created an institution dedicated to liberal education. The teachers assembled should be chosen because they are willing to devote their lives to figuring out what liberal education is and helping students achieve it. Their common concern with this undertaking would lay the foundations of a vital intellectual community.

Since this would be the object, the teachers would be as concerned with learning as the students. They would be committed to lifelong learning even for themselves. Since they would believe that the most pressing educational job this country has is to reinvigorate liberal education, they might be willing to forgo temptations to win the Nobel prize or its equivalents and the prestige that comes from dealing only with "advanced" students in the upper reaches of research.

The students would come to share with them the desire for learning rather than the desire for "success." Prompted by the example of teachers still willing to learn, they might try it themselves.

Students might be examined at the end of four years, not to discover what percentage of what they had been told they could remember, but to find out whether they could think about the questions raised by the books they had read and the discussions in which they had taken part.

The American college today is confused about its own aims, and it confuses those of the high school and the university. The new institution I am proposing would clarify the whole educational system and give each unit a recognizable purpose by removing the principal source of confusion.

What would this new institution do for the country? It would give us enlightened citizens, and I can think of nothing we need more. We are at the beginning of an era of unprecedented change. The common response is fear and resentment. The natural consequence of fear and resentment is the desire to escape into some imaginary status quo ante, like the world of Sleeping Beauty.

The liberally educated man is not afraid of change, because he has knocked down the prison walls and is ready for a life of learning.

We may be on our way to a learning, instead of a working, society. Automation and cybernetics may relieve us of the necessity of labor. If they do, what are we going to do with ourselves?

One thing we might do is to learn—to learn how to be human and how to organize and operate a human society. For this we need liberal education. If liberal education is to flourish, it needs a new home.

STUDY QUESTIONS

1. Why, according to Hutchins, is the American college not an intellectual community?
2. What distinctions does Hutchins make between the college and the university?

3.   Do you agree with Hutchins that going to college is an effect and not a cause of success, that is, earning power?

4.   Compare Hutchins' proposal with Kenner's ("Don't Send Johnny to College"). Which do you believe is the more acceptable proposal?

5.   Describe the general structure of this essay. What part does argumentation play in the development of ideas?

6.   What is the effect of the numerous short paragraphs in the selection?

COLLEGE

John William Gardner   AND THE ALTERNATIVES

John William Gardner (1912–   ) was born in Los Angeles, California. After receiving his B.A. and M.A. from Stanford University and his Ph.D. from the University of California at Berkeley, he taught psychology at Connecticut College and at Mount Holyoke College. As an outspoken critic of U. S. education, he has worked to bring about reforms in procedure and curricula. Before he became Secretary of Health, Education, and Welfare in 1965, he was president of the Carnegie Corporation and the Carnegie Foundation for the Advancement of Teaching.

Who Should Go to College

All of the conflicting and confusing notions which Americans have concerning equality, excellence and the encouragement of talent may be observed with crystal clarity in the current discussions of "who should go to college." In the years ahead these discussions will become more heated. Pressure of enrollments will make it far harder to get into the better colleges, and there will be a lively debate over who has a "right" to a college education.

A good deal of this debate will center around issues of quality versus quantity in education. Douglas Bush eloquently enunciated one extreme position in the phrase, "Education for all is education for none." [1]

Arguments about quality in higher education tend to be heated and rather pointless. There are many reasons why such conversations become muddled, the foremost being that they so often degenerate into arguments over "elite" versus "mass" education. People who engage in

From *Excellence* by John W. Gardner. Copyright © 1961 by John W. Gardner. Reprinted by permission of Harper & Row, Publishers.

———
[1] Douglas Bush, "Education for All Is Education for None," *New York Times Magazine,* January 9, 1955, p. 13.

these arguments are like the two washerwomen Sydney Smith observed leaning out of their back windows and quarreling with each other across the alley: "They could never agree," Smith said, "because they were arguing from different premises."[2] In the case of arguments over "elite" versus "mass" education, I am convinced that both premises should be vacated, because behind the arguments is the assumption that a society must decide whether it wishes to educate a few people exceedingly well *or* to educate a great number of people rather badly.

This is an imaginary dilemma. It is possible to have excellence in education and at the same time to seek to educate everyone to the limit of his ability. A society such as ours has no choice but to seek the development of human potentialities at all levels. It takes more than an educated elite to run a complex, technological society. Every modern, industrialized society is learning that hard lesson.

The notion that so-called quality education and so-called mass education are mutually exclusive is woefully out of date. It would not have survived at all were there not a few remarkably archaic characters in our midst. We all know that some of the people calling most noisily for quality in education are those who were *never* reconciled to the widespread extension of educational opportunity. To such individuals there is something inherently vulgar about large numbers of people. At the other extreme are the fanatics who believe that the chief goal for higher education should be to get as many youngsters as possible—regardless of ability—into college classrooms. Such individuals regard quality as a concept smacking faintly of Louis XIV.

But neither extreme speaks for the American people, and neither expresses the true issues that pose themselves today. It would be fatal to allow ourselves to be tempted into an anachronistic debate. *We must seek excellence in a context of concern for all.* A democracy, no less than any other form of society, must foster excellence if it is to survive; and it should not allow the emotional scars of old battles to confuse it on this point.

Educating everyone up to the limit of his ability does not mean sending everyone to college. Part of any final answer to the college problem must be some revision of an altogether false emphasis which the American people are coming to place on college education. This false emphasis is the source of great difficulties for us. In Virginia they tell the story of the kindly Episcopal minister who was asked whether the Episcopal Church was the only path to salvation. The minister shook his head—a bit sadly, perhaps. "No, there are other paths," he said, and then added, "but no gentleman would choose them." Some of our attitudes toward college education verge dangerously on the same position.

---

[2] W. H. Auden (ed.), *Selected Writings of Sydney Smith,* Farrar, Straus & Giroux, Inc., 1956, p. xiv.

There are some people who seem to favor almost limitless expansion of college attendance. One hears the phrase "everyone has a right to go to college." It is easy to dispose of this position in its extreme form. There are some youngsters whose mental deficiency is so severe that they cannot enter the first grade. There are a number of youngsters out of every hundred whose mental limitations make it impossible for them to get as far as junior high school. There are many more who can progress through high school only if they are placed in special programs which take into account their academic limitations. These "slow learners" could not complete high school if they were required to enroll in a college-preparatory curriculum.

It is true that some who fall in this group would not be there if it were not for social and economic handicaps. But for most of them, there is no convincing evidence that social handicaps are a major factor in their academic limitations. Children with severe or moderate intellectual limitations appear not infrequently in families which are able to give them every advantage, and in which the possibilities of treatment have been exhaustively explored. Such children can be helped by intelligent attention, but the hope that any major change can be accomplished in their academic limitations is usually doomed to disappointment.

With each higher grade an increasing number of youngsters find it difficult or impossible to keep up with the work. Some drop out. Some transfer to vocational or industrial arts programs. A great many never complete high school.

Presumably, college students should only be drawn from the group which is able to get through high school. So the question becomes: "Should all high school graduates go to college?" The answer most frequently heard is that "all should go to college who are qualified for it"—but what do we mean by *qualified?* Probably less than 1 per cent of the college-age population is qualified to attend the California Institute of Technology. There are other colleges where 10, 20, 40 or 60 per cent of the college-age population is qualified to attend.

It would be possible to create institutions with standards so low that 90 per cent of the college-age population could qualify. In order to do so it would be necessary only to water down the curriculum and provide simpler subjects. Pushed to its extreme, the logic of this position would lead us to the establishment of institutions at about the intellectual level of summer camps. We could then include almost all of the population in these make-believe colleges.

Let us pursue this depressing thought. If it were certain that almost all of the eighteen- to twenty-two-year-old population could benefit greatly by full-time attendance at "colleges" of this sort, no one could reasonably object. But one must look with extreme skepticism upon the notion that all high school graduates can profit by continued formal schooling. There is no question that they can profit by continued *education*. But the character of this education will vary from one youngster to the next. Some will profit by continued book learning; others by some kind of vocational training; still others by learning on the job. Others may require other kinds of growth experiences.

Because college has gained extraordinary prestige, we are tempted to assume that the only useful learning and growth comes from attending such an institution, listening to professors talk from platforms, and reproducing required information on occasions called examinations. This is an extremely constricting notion. Even in the case of intellectually gifted individuals, it is a mistake to assume that the only kind of learning they can accomplish is in school. Many gifted individuals might be better off if they could be exposed to alternative growth experiences.

In the case of the youngster who is not very talented academically, forced continuance of education may simply prolong a situation in which he is doomed to failure. Many a youngster of low ability has been kept on pointlessly in a school which taught him no vocation, exposed him to continuous failure and then sent him out into the world with a record which convinced employers that he must forever afterward be limited to unskilled or semi-skilled work. This is not a sensible way to conserve human resources.

Properly understood, the college or university is the instrument of *one kind of further education of those whose capacities fit them for that kind of education.* It should not be regarded as the sole means of establishing one's human worth. It should not be seen as the unique key to happiness, self-respect and inner confidence.

We have all done our bit to foster these misconceptions. And the root of the difficulty is our bad habit of assuming that the only meaningful life is the "successful" life, defining success in terms of high personal attainment in the world's eyes. Today attendance at college has become virtually a prerequisite of high attainment in the world's eyes, so that it becomes, in the false value framework we have created, the only passport to a meaningful life. No wonder our colleges are crowded.

The crowding in our colleges is less regrettable than the confusion in our values. *Human dignity and worth should be assessed only in terms of those qualities of mind and spirit that are within the reach of every human being.*

This is not to say that we should not value achievement. We should value it exceedingly. It is simply to say that achievement should not be confused with human worth. Our recognition of the dignity and worth of the individual is based upon moral imperatives and should be of universal application. In other words, everyone has a "right" to that recognition. Being a college graduate involves qualities of mind which can never be universally possessed. Everyone does not have a right to be a college graduate, any more than everyone has a right to run a four-minute mile.

What we are really seeking is what James Conant had in mind when he said that the American people are concerned not only for equality of opportunity but for equality of respect. Every human being wishes to be respected regardless of his ability, and in moral terms we are bound to grant him that right. The more we allow the impression to get abroad that only the college man or woman is worthy of respect in our society, the more we contribute to a fatal confusion which works to the injury of all concerned. If we make the confusing assumption that college is the sole cradle of human dignity, need we be surprised that every citizen demands to be rocked in that cradle?

The Need for Institutional Diversity

But a scaling down of our emphasis on college education is only part of the answer. Another important part of the answer must be a greatly increased emphasis upon individual differences, upon many kinds of talent, upon the immensely varied ways in which individual potentialities may be realized.

If we develop such an indomitable concern for individual differences, we will learn to laugh at the assumption that a college education is the only avenue to human dignity and social worth. We would educate some youngsters by sending them on to college. We would educate others in other ways. We would develop an enormous variety of patterns to fit the enormous variety of individuals. And no pattern would be regarded as socially superior or involving greater human dignity than any other pattern.

But the plain fact is that college education is firmly associated in the public mind with personal advancement, upward social mobility, market value and self-esteem. And if enough of the American people believe that one must attend college in order to be accorded respect and confidence, then the very unanimity of opinion makes the generalization true.

It is particularly true, unfortunately, in the crude categories of the employment file. A cynical friend of mine said recently, "Everyone has two personalities these days—the one under his hat and the one in his employment file. The latter is the most important—and it is made up of primitive categories. Have you held too many jobs? (Never mind why.) Did you go to a good college? (Never mind if you were the campus beachcomber.) Does your job record show a steady rise in responsibilities? (Never mind if you played politics every inch of the way.)"

If we are to do justice to individual differences, if we are to provide suitable education for each of the young men and women who crowd into our colleges and universities, then we must cultivate diversity in our higher educational system to correspond to the diversity of the clientele. There is no other way to handle within one system the enormously disparate human capacities, levels of preparedness and motivations which flow into our colleges and universities.

But we cannot hope to create or to maintain such diversity unless we honor the various aspects of that diversity. Each of the different kinds of institutions has a significant part to play in creating the total pattern, and each should be allowed to play its role with honor and recognition.

We do not want all institutions to be alike. We want institutions to develop their individualities and to keep those individualities. None must be ashamed of its distinctive features so long as it is doing something that contributes importantly to the total pattern, and so long as it is striving for excellence in performance. The highly selective, small liberal arts college should not be afraid to remain small. The large urban institution should not be ashamed that it is large. The technical institute should not be apologetic about being a technical institute. Each institution should pride itself on the role that it has chosen to play and on the special contribution which it brings to the total pattern of American higher education.

Such diversity is the only possible answer to the fact of individual differences in ability and aspirations. And furthermore, it is the only means of achieving *quality* within a framework of quantity. For we must not forget the primacy of our concern for excellence. We must have diversity, but we must also expect that every institution which makes up that diversity will be striving, in its own way, for excellence. This may require a new way of thinking about excellence in higher education—a conception that would be applicable in terms of the objectives of the institution. As things now stand, the word *excellence* is all too often reserved for the dozen or two dozen institutions which stand at the very zenith of our higher education in terms of faculty distinction, selectivity of students and difficulty of curriculum. In these terms it is simply impossible to speak of a junior college, for example, as excellent. Yet sensible men can easily conceive of excellence in a junior college.

The traditionalist might say, "Of course! Let Princeton create a junior college and one would have an institution of unquestionable excellence!" That may be correct, but it may also lead us down precisely the wrong path. If Princeton Junior College were excellent, it might not be excellent in the most important way that a community college can be excellent. It might simply be a truncated version of Princeton. A comparably meaningless result would be achieved if General Motors tried to add to its line of low-priced cars by marketing the front half of a Cadillac.

We shall have to be more flexible than that in our conception of excellence. We must develop a point of view that permits each kind of institution to achieve excellence *in terms of its own objectives*.

In higher education as in everything else there is no excellent performance without high morale. No morale, no excellence! And in a great many of our colleges and universities the most stubborn enemy of high morale has been a kind of hopelessness on the part of both administration and faculty—hopelessness about ever achieving distinction as an institution. Not only are such attitudes a corrosive influence on morale, they make it virtually certain that the institution will never achieve even that kind of excellence which is within its reach. For there *is* a kind of excellence within the reach of every institution.

In short, we reject the notion that excellence is something that can only be experienced in the most rarified strata of higher education. It may be experienced at every level and in every serious kind of higher education. And not only may it be experienced everywhere, but we must *demand* it everywhere. We must ask for excellence in every form which higher education takes. We should not ask it lightly or amiably or good naturedly; we should demand it vigorously and insistently. We should assert that a stubborn striving for excellence is the price of admission to reputable educational circles, and that those institutions not characterized by this striving are the slatterns of higher education.

We must make the same challenging demands of students. We must never make the insolent and degrading assumption that young people unfitted for the most demanding fields of intellectual endeavor are incapable of rigorous attention to *some sort of standards*. It is an appalling error to assume—as some of our institutions seem to have assumed—that young men and women incapable of the highest standards of intellectual excellence are incapable of any standards whatsoever, and can properly be subjected to shoddy, slovenly and trashy educational fare. College should be a demanding as well as an enriching experience—demanding for the brilliant youngster at a high level of expectation and for the less brilliant at a more modest level.

It is no sin to let average as well as brilliant youngsters into college. It *is* a sin to let any substantial portion of them—average or brilliant—drift through college without effort, without growth and without a goal. That is the real scandal in many of our institutions.

Though we must make enormous concessions to individual differences in aptitude, we may properly expect that every form of education be such as to stretch the individual to the utmost of his potentialities. And we must expect each student to strive for excellence in terms of the kind of excellence that is within his reach. Here again we must recognize that there may be excellence or shoddiness in every line of human endeavor. We must learn to honor excellence (indeed to *demand* it) in every socially accepted human activity, however humble the activity, and to scorn shoddiness, however exalted the activity. As I said in another connection: "An excellent plumber is infinitely more admirable than an incompetent philosopher. The society which scorns excellence in plumbing because plumbing is a humble activity and tolerates shoddiness in philosophy because it is an exalted activity will have neither good plumbing nor good philosophy. Neither its pipes nor its theories will hold water."

Opportunities Other Than College

Not long ago the mother of two teen-age boys came to me for advice. "Roger made a fine record in high school," she explained, "and when he was a senior we had exciting discussions of all the colleges he was interested in. Now Bobby comes along with terrible grades, and when the question of his future arises a silence descends on the dinner table. It breaks my heart!"

I knew something about Bobby's scholastic limitations, which were notable, and I asked warily what I might do to help.

"The high school principal says that with his record no college will take him," she said, "and that if one did take him he wouldn't last. I can't reconcile myself to that!"

"Have you discussed any possibilities other than college?" I asked.

She shook her head. "His father says he can get him a job driving a delivery truck. But I think he just says that to jar Bobby."

It took some time for me to explain all that I thought was deplorable in her attitude and that of her husband. Parents of academically limited children should not act as though any outcome other than college is a fate worse than death. By doing so they rule out of discussion a world of significant possibilities; and the failure to think constructively about those possibilities is a disfavor to the young person.

The great prestige which college education has achieved in our society leads us to assume—quite incorrectly—that it is the only form of continued learning after high school. The assumption is that the young person either goes to college and continues to learn, or goes to work and stops learning. Most parents, deans, counselors—indeed the young people themselves—have given little or no thought to the many ways of learning and growing which do not involve college. The result is that the path to college appears to be the only exciting possibility, the only path to self-development. No wonder many who lack the qualifications for college insist on having a try at it.

The young person who does not go on to college should look forward to just as active a period of growth and learning in the post-high school years as does the college youngster.

The nature of this continued learning will depend on the young person's interests and capacities. The bright youngster who has stayed out of college for financial reasons will require a different kind of program from that of the youngster who stayed out for lack of ability.

The majority of young people—at least, of boys—who terminate their education short of college do so because they lack academic ability. Most have had unrewarding experiences in the classroom and have a negative attitude toward anything labeled "learning" or "education." Even if they are not bitter about their school experiences, they are likely to feel that, having tried that path and failed, their salvation lies elsewhere. *What they must recognize is that there are many kinds of further learning outside formal high school and college programs. The fact that they have not succeeded in high school simply means that they must continue their learning in other kinds of situations.*

The opportunities for further education of boys and girls who leave the formal educational system are numerous and varied.

Training programs within industrial corporations have expanded enormously and constitute a respectable proportion of all education today. Apprenticeship systems are not as universal as they used to be in the skilled crafts or trades, but they are still in operation in every major industry, and offer wide opportunities for the ambitious youngster. (He must be warned, however, that in some of the older crafts and trades entry is jealously guarded; indeed in some it is held within family lines as a hereditary right.)

A few labor unions have impressive educational programs. The International Ladies Garment Workers Union, for example, conducts European tours, sponsors lecture series and offers a wide variety of courses.

Various branches of government offer jobs to high school graduates which involve an opportunity to learn while working. The Armed Services offer training in a great many occupational specialties.

Night classes in the public schools are breaking all attendance records; and more than one quarter of present attendance is in trade courses for semi-skilled or unskilled workers. These courses offer a surprising range of interesting opportunities for the young person who wishes to test his aptitudes and to develop various skills.

There also exist, in the amazingly variegated pattern of American education, many special schools—art schools, music schools, nursing schools and the like—which should be considered by the young person not going on to college. The boy who wishes to become an X-ray technician and the girl who wishes to be a practical nurse, for example, will find a great many schools throughout the country at which they may receive training.

Correspondence study offers the most flexible opportunities for study beyond high school, but the young people who do not go on to college usually have little enthusiasm for paper-and-pencil work, and that is what correspondence study amounts to. For those who can overcome this handicap, there is an open door to almost any conceivable subject. One can study accountancy or blueprint reading, creative writing or diesel mechanics, watch repairing or dressmaking, fingerprinting or foreign languages, music or petroleum technology. Almost the only limits are one's own interest and ability.

Educational opportunities on radio and television continue to expand. In certain parts of the country the high school graduate can study a considerable range of subjects through this medium—e.g., salesmanship, typing, composition, reading improvement and foreign languages.

Finally, jobs themselves are a form of education. Today most young people have a wide choice of jobs. They should look at the array of jobs available not simply from the standpoint of money and convenience but from the standpoint of their own further growth. If the young man is willing to think hard about his own abilities and interests, and then to look at available jobs as opportunities for self-development, he can look forward to years of learning and growth at least as rewarding as anything a college student might experience.

The possibilities reviewed here are by no means exhaustive, but they suggest the diverse paths open to the noncollege student. Some youngsters will want to get as far away as possible from "book learning" and some will not. Some will want vocational education and others may wish to continue their general education. Some will shun anything labeled a "school" or "course." But all should somehow continue learning.

In order to help young people in this direction, the following steps are essential:

1. We must make available to young people far more information than they now have on post-high school opportunities other than college.

2. Parents, teachers and high school counselors must recognize that if the youngster who is not going to college is to continue his growth and learning he must receive as much sagacious help and counsel as a college-bound student.

3. We must do what we can to alter the negative attitude toward education held by many youngsters who fail to go on to college. They must understand that they have been exposed to only one kind of learning experience and that the failures and frustrations encountered in school are not necessarily predictive of failure in every other kind of learning.

4. We must enable the young person to understand that his stature

as an individual and his value as a member of society depend upon continued learning—not just for four years or a decade, but throughout life.

STUDY QUESTIONS

1. Although Mr. Gardner does not define excellence in this selection, what does he apparently mean by it?
2. The author observes that "achievement should not be confused with human worth." Explain.
3. Compare Gardner's views on the college experience with Kenner's ("Don't Send Johnny to College") and Hutchins' ("Colleges Are Obsolete").
4. What is Gardner's solution to the problem created by the conflict of quality education and mass education?
5. What kind of supporting evidence does the author use with his generalizations?
6. Describe the general outline Gardner follows in this selection. Compare his prose style with that used by Kenner.

Harold Taylor   QUALITY AND EQUALITY

Harold Taylor (1914–   ) was born in Toronto, Canada. He received his B.A. from the University of Toronto and his Ph.D. from the University of London. He has a distinguished record as an educator, and was president of Sarah Lawrence College from 1945 to 1959. He is the author of *On Education and Freedom* (1954), *Reluctant Rebel, Secret Diary of Robert Patrick,* and *Art and the Intellect* (1960).

"The schools are the golden avenue of opportunity for able youngsters, but by the same token they are the arena in which less able youngsters discover their limitations." John Gardner's book has to do with this plain fact. He wishes to make it plainer, to have the country face up to it and to have educators deal with it wisely.

The way to deal with it is not to assume that in school the able and

(A review of *Excellence* by John W. Gardner.) Reprinted with the permission of *Saturday Review* and the author.

the less able are two different species of human being, separated by inherent qualities that screen out those who can contribute to their society and those who can't. Nor is ability to be measured by whether or not a boy or girl is admitted to a well-known college.

"Properly understood," says Mr. Gardner, "college or university is merely the instrument of one kind of further education for those whose interests and capacities fit them for that kind of further education. It should not be regarded as the sole means of establishing one's human worth. It should not be seen as the unique key to happiness, self-respect, and inner confidence."

There are varieties of talent, of motivation, of aptitude, of achievement, of excellence, and it is up to the social system and its educational instruments to make the most of each of the varieties. Otherwise we will build, on the basis of a false educational philosophy, a society that betrays its democratic values by constructing a stratified order. In such an order it will be assumed that those who go to college are those who should run the society, and that the rest are to be considered, and therefore may come to consider themselves, inferiors who work at whatever they can.

Following this path, we quickly reach a point at which no one takes pride in his work because he thinks it is beneath him, and standards of excellence in every part of life are abandoned in favor of a grudging, niggling effort to get as much as possible for doing as little as possible.

The cure for this is not to abandon the ideal of equality, or to deplore and ignore the attitude of those who have little opportunity for social advancement. It is to invent new forms of education that can deal with the entire range of individual talent and ability, to assure that each has an honorable place in his society.

This is a problem that is not confined to the United States and its educational system. It is also at the center of the Soviet effort to blend together vocational training in the factories and on the farms with high school education. It shows itself in the riots of Indian students against their universities—institutions that are ill-adapted to educating the younger generation for productive careers in jobs that need doing.

Once you announce a creed of equality, forces are set in motion which can explode into violence or dissipate into lethargy unless an educational system is put into effect which actually provides a variety of opportunities for a variety of talents.

Mr. Gardner's book has the virtue of going directly to questions that are in the minds of educators, parents, teachers, and students in the schools and colleges and dealing with them sympathetically on the basis of his personal knowledge of the American system as it works. He puts the educational problems in their proper setting, that is, as the outcome of certain social, political, and economic conditions and ideas, and as the result of conflicting aims held by Americans.

We are proud to have thrown off the weight of hereditary privilege, says Mr. Gardner, and we admire both the successful man and the system that makes success a matter of individual performance rather than of birth. At the same time we create new problems for the man whose talent is not of a kind that does well in an intensely competitive society, yet whose abilities must have their own chance to find expression.

In guarding against the excesses of a competitive order where performance "may foster an atmosphere of raw striving" we become overprotective of those who are left behind in the competition, and we fall into sentimental postures in the way we treat children. We become hypocritical and refuse to deal honestly with differences in ability. The conflict between the sentiment of compassion and the reality of human capacity becomes direct when "it proves impossible to enable each to fill his potentialities without treating each differently."

In the matter of tests for ability and achievement, for example, it is crucial that a fair means be established for sorting out the more able from the less able. But intelligence testing cannot account for differences in background, and there is more to intelligence than the ability to pass intelligence tests.

Mr. Gardner suggests that we use testing devices with discretion, as a form of diagnosis as much as a criterion of judgment. We must hold to the doctrine of multiple chances by which the individual is given a variety of means and occasions to prove his worth through the whole of his education and through the whole of his life.

This means an enlightened approach to the welfare of the individual, not only through formal education but also through all the other institutions of a democratic society, from slum clearance projects and social welfare programs to hospitals, adoption services, business institutions, adult education, the church, and the home.

Some 1,873,000 boys and girls are graduating from high school this year: 880,000 will not go to college; 900,000 others have already dropped out of high school. Mr. Gardner is concerned about this cross-section of American youth. They are in the majority and will continue to be.

In the overemphasis on college preparation, academic grades, and competitive selection, too little attention has been paid to the educational needs of this majority, both before and after they take jobs and marry. Leadership, and standards of performance, Mr. Gardner points out, must come, not merely from what used to be called the educated classes, but from every segment of the entire society. That is, of course, if the society is to grow in strength and remain democratic. In his Carnegie Corporation presidential report of 1960, Mr. Gardner analyzes the problem, suggests solutions, and calls for action.

The present book provides an intellectual basis for such action on many fronts. It also provides a balanced, informed, and positive statement of democratic belief by a man who, in temperament, experience, and performance, has shown himself to be a gifted educator.

J. Edward Dirks   NEO-KNIGHTHOOD

J. Edward Dirks (1919–   ) was born in Iowa. He received a B.A. from the University of Dubuque and Yale University and his Ph.D. from Columbia. An ordained minister of the United Presbyterian Church, he has a distinguished record as a teacher of religious education. He has taught at Columbia University, Lake Forest College, and Yale Divinity School. He has been director of the commission on higher education for the National Council of Churches and was the founder and editor of *Christian Scholarly*. He is author of the book *The Critical Theology of Theodore Parker* (1947).

This is a book dedicated to the proposition that excellence in all its forms and in all situations is attainable, even when it must be encouraged in a society which advocates the ideal of equality. In the realm of higher education as well as in the context of discussions concerning the image and prestige of America, the professed fear of a pervasive mediocrity, a lowering of standards of performance, and a persistent (sometimes a built-in) slovenliness reinforces the yearning for an elite and the domination of a group which rises to leadership. The author assumes that the demands of excellence and equality stand in this kind of conflict and internal contradiction, and that democracy has to overcome its equalitarian idealism if it is to be realistic about the need for excellence. This is the puzzle, then: how the very heart of democratic dogma can be

(A review of *Excellence* by John W. Gardner.) Copyright 1961, Christian Century Foundation. Reprinted by permission from the May 17, 1961 issue of *The Christian Century*.

maintained if at the same time Americans want to "let the best man win," identify, encourage and train their talented youth, and motivate toward leadership persons imbued with the idea of excellence.

The book calls the nation to commit itself anew to the goal of being a democratic society—the kind of democratic society which insists on excellence, in which free men are capable of performing at the level of high standards, and which reckons with the tragedy of a lost or obscured national purpose. "The long-run challenge," says the author, president of Carnegie Corp. and of the Carnegie Foundation for the Advancement of Teaching, "is nothing less than a challenge to our sense of purpose, our vitality and our creativity as a people." And "if we fail to meet this challenge, the stratagems of the moment will not save us." Striving toward meaningful goals, pursuing excellence through devoted action, producing men and women of intelligence, imagination and courage, are among the challenges set forth in Mr. Gardner's essay. But, one may ask, just how is this to be done? What is to be expected of American people? The answer is straightforward: "If you believe in a free society, be worthy of a free society. Every good man strengthens society."

Despite the ringing appeals for "toning up" the nation, despite the author's own passion for excellence and his sense of the nation's passion for it, one reads the book with the feeling that something muscular, rigorous and disciplined is missing. The interpretation of the term "excellence" is vague; excellence remains an illusory ideal, demanding devotion, dedication and commitment to "the virtues of our society." To *pursue* and to *excel*—words with virtually identical meanings—can be encouraged when a clear goal is somewhere in sight, or when we know realistically enough what must certainly be avoided in our running! But the phrase "the highest standards of performance" is ambiguous as a referent and of little help amid all the other relativities of our society.

Nearly ten years ago Reinhold Niebuhr wrote a book which reflected on "the ironic element in the American situation." A part of this element was identified by him with the "extravagant emphasis in our culture upon the value and dignity of the individual and upon individual liberty as the final value of life" (*The Irony of American History,* p. 7). The ironic contradiction into which Niebuhr suggested we are placed is to be found in the fact that our culture does not really value the individual as much as it pretends, and that if justice is to be maintained and our survival assured, individual liberty cannot—contrary to our ideology—be unqualifiedly made the end of. life. This is the necessary critique upon this book on excellence. But the structure of illusion built from our virtues has still not been clearly exposed, even in the state of threat through which we are passing. Our religious virtues and our national virtues tend to merge in this illusion; hence the religious roots of excellence are viewed as synonymous with the democratic roots of excellence.

However questionable may be the prescriptive sections of the book, it contains a valid analysis of the present situation in American culture—its "who cares?" attitudes, its wastefulness and consumer-consciousness, its persistent tendency to dismiss the importance of excellence in education, its lack of clarity regarding the social context which stimulates the pursuit of excellence. The flabbiness of our society is made visible; the dilemma of our democracy is acutely stated. Once we have passed through the prophetic and critical material, however, we need to permit our realism to continue into our pursuit of the ideal goals. If we lose it and lapse into a sentimental idealism, our espousal of the ideals of democracy will become absurd—as absurd as was Don Quixote's imitation of the ideals of medieval knight errantry. We cannot finally laugh at the betrayals of high performance (as we might at the illusions of the bogus knight), but with a profounder insight we can laugh at the contemporary anxiety which broods along over national goals and excellence (that is, at the bogus character of knighthood itself).

However great is the importance of our society's survival, the term "ironic" surely must be applied to our situation. The Christian prefers it because irony derives from the confidence that we can know the true God only where we have some awareness of the contradiction between his divine purposes and our human purposes, or even our highest aspirations. And the insights derived from such a recognition are nothing less than prerequisites for saving our civilization.

STUDY QUESTIONS

1. Compare and contrast Taylor's and Dirks' opinion of John W. Gardner's book *Excellence*. What does each single out for praise, and what does each point to as a fault or shortcoming?

2. What is the general form each reviewer follows? Do they differ in degree or kind?

3. Do they reveal any personal prejudices that may color their appraisal of the book? Who appears to be the more objective?

4. On the basis of the experience you had with *Excellence* (you read "College and the Alternatives"), which reviewer appears to be more accurate in his appraisal? Is he necessarily the more convincing of the two?

A SHORT HISTORY

Richard W. Armour   **OF HIGHER EDUCATION**

Richard W. Armour (1906–   ) was born in San Pedro, California. He received his A.B. from Pomona College and his A.M. and Ph.D. from Harvard University. He has taught at the University of Texas, Northwestern University, Scripps College, and Claremont Graduate School. At present he is Balch Lecturer in English literature at Scripps. Although Mr. Armour is known to the academic world as a scholar, the general public knows him as the author of many delightfully witty books. Among these are *It All Started with Columbus* (1953), *It All Started with Europa* (1955), *It All Started with Eve* (1956), *Twisted Tales from Shakespeare* (1957), *The Classics Reclassified* (1960), and *Through Darkest Adolescence* (1963).

Prehistoric Times

Little is known about higher education during the Stone Age, which is perhaps just as well.

Because of a weakness in the liberal arts, the B.A. was not offered, and there was only the B.S., or Bachelor of Stones. Laboratory facilities were meager, owing to lack of government contracts and support from private industry, but the stars were readily available on clear nights for those interested in astronomy.

Prehistoric students, being before history, failed to comprehend the fundamentals of the subject, such as its being divided into Ancient, Medieval, and Modern.

There were no college boards.

Nor were there any fraternities. The only clubs on the campus were those carried by the students.

Alumni organizations were in their infancy, where some of them have remained. The Alumni Secretary occupied a small cave, left behind when the Director of Development moved to a larger one. While waiting for contributions to come in, he idly doodled on the wall, completely unaware that art critics would someday mistake his drawings of certain members of the board of trustees for dinosaurs and saber-toothed tigers.

The Alumni Quarterly came out every quarter of a century, and was as eagerly awaited as it is today.

The Classical Period

In ancient Athens everyone knew Greek, and in ancient Rome everyone knew Latin, even small children—which those who have taken Elementary Greek or Elementary Latin will find hard to believe. Universities wishing to teach a language which had little practical use but was good for mental discipline could have offered English if they had thought of it.

Buildings were all in the classical style, and what looked like genuine marble was genuine marble.

The professors of the Peripatetic School kept moving from town to town, closely followed by students and creditors. Sometimes lectures were held in the Groves of Academe, where students could munch apples and occasionally cast an anxious eye at birds in the branches overhead.

Under the Caesars, taxation became so burdensome that Romans in the upper brackets found they might as well give money to their Alma Mater instead of letting the State have it. Thus it was that crowds often gathered along the Appian Way to applaud a spirited chariot race between the chairman of the funds drive and the tax collector, each trying to get to a good prospect first.

The word "donor" comes from the Latin *donare*, to give, and is not to be confused with *dunare*, to dun, though it frequently is.

When a prominent alumnus was thrown to the lions, customary procedure in the alumni office was to observe a moment of silence. Then the secretary, wrapping his toga a little more tightly around him, solemnly declared, "Well, we might as well take him off the cultivation list."

The Middle Ages

In the period known as the Dark Ages, or nighthood, higher education survived only because of illuminated manuscripts, which were discovered during a routine burning of a library. It is interesting to recontruct a typical classroom scene: a group of dedicated students clustered around a glowing piece of parchment, listening to a lecture in Advanced Monasticism, a ten-year course. If some found it hard to concentrate, it was because they were dreaming about quitting before exams and going off on a crusade.

Some left even sooner, before the end of the lecture, having spied a beautiful damsel being pursued by a dragon who had designs on her. The dragon was probably an art student who was out of drawing paper. Damsels, who were invariably in distress, wrought havoc on a young man's grade-point average.

Members of the faculty were better off than previously, because they wore suits of armor. Fully accoutered, and with their visors down, they could summon up enough courage to go into the President's office and ask for a promotion even though they had not published a thing.

At this time the alumni council became more aggressive in its fund drives, using such persuasive devices as the thumbscrew, the knout, the rack, and the wheel. A wealthy alumnus would usually donate generously if a sufficient number of alumni could cross his moat and storm his castle walls. A few could be counted on to survive the rain of stones, arrows, and molten lead. Such a group of alumni, known as "the committee," was customarily conducted to the castle by a troubadour, who led in the singing of the Alma Mater Song the while.

The Renaissance

During the Renaissance, universities sprang up all over Europe. You could go to bed at night, with not a university around, and the next morning there would be two universities right down the street, each with a faculty, student body, campanile, and need for additional endowment.

The first universities were in Italy, where Dante was required reading. Boccaccio was not required but was read anyhow, and in the original Italian, so much being lost in translation. Other institutions soon followed, such as Heidelberg, where a popular elective was Duelling 103a, b, usually taken concurrently with Elementary First Aid. In England there was Oxford, where, by curious coincidence, all of the young instructors were named Don. There was also Cambridge.

The important thing about the Renaissance, which was a time of awakening (even in the classroom), was education of the Whole Man. Previously such vital parts as the elbows and ear lobes had been neglected. The graduate of a university was supposed, above all, to be a Gentleman. This meant that he should know such things as archery, falconry, and fencing (subjects now largely relegated to Physical Education and given only one-half credit per semester), as well as, in the senior year, how to use a knife and fork.

During the Renaissance, the works of Homer, Virgil, and other classical writers were rediscovered, much to the annoyance of students.

Alumni officials concentrated their efforts on securing a patron:

someone rich like Lorenzo de' Medici, someone clever like Machiavelli, or (if they wished to get rid of a troublesome member of the administration) someone really useful like Lucrezia Borgia.

Colonial America

The first universities in America were founded by the Puritans. This explains the strict regulations about Late Hours, Compulsory Chapel, and No Liquor on the Campus which still exist at many institutions.

Some crafts were taught, but witchcraft was an extra-curricular activity. Witch-burning, on the other hand, was the seventeenth-century equivalent of hanging a football coach in effigy at the end of a bad season. Though deplored, it was passed off by the authorities as attributable to "youthful exuberance."

Harvard set the example for naming colleges after donors. William and Mary, though making a good try, failed to start a trend for using first names. It was more successful, however, in starting Phi Beta Kappa, a fraternity which permitted no rough stuff in its initiations. At first the Phi Beta Kappa key was worn on the key ring, but the practice went out with the discovery of the watch chain and vest.

During the Colonial Period, alumni officials limited their fundraising activities to alumni who were securely fastened, hands and legs, in the stocks. In this position they were completely helpless and gave generously, or could be frisked.

Revolutionary America

Higher education came to a virtual standstill during the Revolution—every able-bodied male having enlisted for the duration. Since the ROTC had not yet been established, college men were forced to have other qualifications for a commission, such as money.

General George Washington was given an honorary degree by Harvard, and this helped see him through the difficult winter at Valley Forge. Since he gave no commencement address, it is assumed that he made a substantial contribution to the building fund. Then again, mindful of the reputation he had gained through Parson Weems's cherry tree story, he may have established a chair in Ethics.

Unlike the situation during World War I, when colleges and universities abandoned the teaching of German in order to humiliate the Kaiser, the Colonists waged the Revolutionary War successfully without prohibiting the teaching of English. They did, however, force students to substitute such good old American words as "suspenders" for "braces," and themes were marked down when the spelling "tyre" was used for "tire."

The alumni publication, variously called the Alumni Bulletin, the Alumni Quarterly, and the Alumni Newsletter, was probably invented at this time by Benjamin Franklin, who invented almost everything else, including bifocals and kites. The first such publication was *Poor Alumnus' Almanac*, full of such homely sayings as "Early to bed and early to rise makes a man healthy, wealthy, and wise enough to write his Alma Mater into his will."

Contemporary America

In the nineteenth century, denominational colleges were founded in all parts of the country, especially Ohio. In the smaller of these colleges, money was mostly given in small denominations. A few colleges were not named after John Wesley.

State universities came into being at about the same time, and were tax supported. Every taxpayer was therefore a donor, but without getting his name on a building or being invited to dinner by the President. The taxpayer, in short, was in the same class as the Anonymous Giver, but not because he asked that his name be withheld. It was some of his salary that was withheld.

About the middle of the nineteenth century, women were admitted to college. This was done (1) to relieve men of having to take women's parts in dramatic productions, some women's parts being hard for men to supply, (2) to provide cheer leaders with shapelier legs and therefore more to cheer about, and (3) to recruit members for the Women's Glee Club. It was not realized, when they were admitted, that women would get most of the high marks, especially from professors who graded on curves.

In the twentieth century, important strides were made, such as the distinction which developed between education and Education. Teachers came to be trained in what were at first called Normal Schools. With the detection of certain abnormalities, the name was changed to Teachers Colleges.

John Dewey introduced Progressive Education, whereby students quickly knew more than their teachers and told them so. Robert Hutchins turned the University of Chicago upside down, thereby necessitating a new building program. At St. John's College everyone studied the Great Books, which were more economical because they did not come out each year in a revised edition. Educational television gave college professors an excuse for owning a television set, which they had previously maintained would destroy the reading habit. This made it possible for them to watch Westerns and old movies without losing status.

Of recent years, an increasing number of students spend their junior year abroad. This enables them to get a glimpse of professors who are away on Fulbrights or Guggenheims.

Student government has grown apace, students now not only governing themselves but giving valuable suggestions, in the form of ultimatums, to the President and Dean. In wide use is the Honor System, which makes the professor leave the room during an examination because he is not to be trusted.

Along with these improvements in education has come a subtle change in the American alumnus. No longer interested only in the record of his college's football team, he is likely to appear at his class reunion full of such penetrating questions as "Why is the tuition higher than it was in 1934?" "Is it true that 85 per cent of the faculty are Communists?" and "How can I get my son (or daughter) in?"

Alumni magazines have kept pace with such advances. The writing has improved, thanks to schools of journalism, until there is excitement and suspense even in the obituary column. Expression has reached such a high point of originality that a request for funds may appear, at first reading, to be a gift offer.

All in all, higher education has reached these heights of attainment:

Despite their questionable contribution to earning a living, the liberal arts are accepted as an excellent means of keeping young people off the streets for four years.

Young people, in turn, are continuing their studies longer and longer, having discovered this an excellent means of keeping out of the Army.

Faculty members, publishing more voluminously than ever, are making an important contribution to the national economy, especially to the pulp and paper industry.

The government is helping students with scholarships and professors with research grants, thereby enabling more and more students to go to college, where more and more professors are too busy with research grants to teach them.

Having surveyed the history of higher education from the Stone Age to the present, let us now make a careful analysis, or Study in Depth, of college today.

STUDY QUESTIONS

1.   In his humorous account of higher education, Armour makes a number of criticisms about college and college life. What are some of these?
2.   Note the number of instances in which he makes a play on words. What are other sources of humor in this selection?
3.   Does Armour's tone suggest how seriously we are to take his criticisms?

Graham Greene THE LOST CHILDHOOD

Graham Greene (1904–   ) was born in Berkhamstead, England, and educated at Balliol College, Oxford. He holds an honorary Litt.D. from Cambridge University. Although a well-known
playwright, essayist, and short-story writer, he is most famous for
his novels and "entertainments." These include *Babbling April*
(1925), *It's a Battlefield* (1934), *A Gun for Sale* (1926), *Brighton
Rock* (1938), *The Power and the Glory* (1940), *The Ministry of
Fear* (1943), *The Heart of the Matter* (1948), *The Thi d Man*
(1950), *The End of the Affair* (1951), *Twenty-one Stories* (1954),
The Quiet American (1955), *Our Man in Havana* (1958), *A
Burnt-out Case* (1961), and *The Comedians* (1966). His latest
volume of short stories was published in 1967.

Perhaps it is only in childhood that books have any deep influence
on our lives. In later life we admire, we are entertained, we may modify
some views we already hold, but we are more likely to find in books
merely a confirmation of what is in our minds already: as in a love affair
it is our own features that we see reflected flatteringly back.

But in childhood all books are books of divination, telling us about
the future, and like the fortune teller who sees a long journey in the
cards or death by water they influence the future. I suppose that is why
books excited us so much. What do we ever get nowadays from reading
to equal the excitement and the revelation in those first fourteen years?
Of course I should be interested to hear that a new novel by Mr. E. M.
Forster was going to appear this spring, but I could never compare that
mild expectation of civilized pleasure with the missed heartbeat, the
appalled glee I felt when I found on a library shelf a novel by Rider
Haggard, Percy Westerman, Captain Brereton or Stanley Weyman which
I had not read before. No, it is in those early years that I would look for
the crisis, the moment when life took a new slant in its journey towards
death.

I remember distinctly the suddenness with which a key turned in a
lock and I found I could read—not just the sentences in a reading book
with the syllables coupled like railway carriages, but a real book. It was
paper-covered with the picture of a boy, bound and gagged, dangling at

the end of a rope inside a well with the water rising above his waist—an adventure of Dixon Brett, detective. All a long summer holiday I kept my secret, as I believed: I did not want anybody to know that I could read. I suppose I half consciously realized even then that this was the dangerous moment. I was safe so long as I could not read—the wheels had not begun to turn, but now the future stood around on bookshelves everywhere waiting for the child to choose—the life of a chartered accountant perhaps, a colonial civil servant, a planter in China, a steady job in a bank, happiness and misery, eventually one particular form of death, for surely we choose our death much as we choose our job. It grows out of our acts and our evasions, out of our fears and out of our moments of courage. I suppose my mother must have discovered my secret, for on the journey home I was presented for the train with another real book, a copy of Ballantyne's *Coral Island* with only a single picture to look at, a coloured frontispiece. But I would admit nothing. All the long journey I stared at the one picture and never opened the book.

But there on the shelves at home (so many shelves for we were a large family) the books waited—one book in particular, but before I reach that one down let me take a few others at random from the shelf. Each was a crystal in which the child dreamed that he saw life moving. Here in a cover stamped dramatically in several colours was Captain Gilson's *The Pirate Aeroplane*. I must have read that book six times at least—the story of a lost civilization in the Sahara and of a villainous Yankee pirate with an aeroplane like a box kite and bombs the size of tennis balls who held the golden city to ransom. It was saved by the hero, a young subaltern who crept up to the pirate camp to put the aeroplane out of action. He was captured and watched his enemies dig his grave. He was to be shot at dawn, and to pass the time and keep his mind from uncomfortable thoughts the amiable Yankee pirate played cards with him—the mild nursery game of Kuhn Kan. The memory of that nocturnal game on the edge of life haunted me for years, until I set it to rest at last in one of my own novels with a game of poker played in remotely similar circumstances.

And here is *Sophy of Kravonia* by Anthony Hope—the story of a kitchen-maid who became a queen. One of the first films I ever saw, about 1911, was made from that book, and I can hear still the rumble of the Queen's guns crossing the high Kravonian pass beaten hollowly out on a single piano. Then there was Stanley Weyman's *The Story of Francis Cludde*, and above all other books at that time of my life *King Solomon's Mines*.

This book did not perhaps provide the crisis, but it certainly influenced the future. If it had not been for that romantic tale of Allan Quatermain, Sir Henry Curtis, Captain Good, and, above all, the ancient witch Gagool, would I at nineteen have studied the appointments list of the Colonial Office and very nearly picked on the Nigerian Navy for a career? And later, when surely I ought to have known better, the odd African fixation remained. In 1935 I found myself sick with fever on a camp bed in a Liberian native's hut with a candle going out in an empty whisky bottle and a rat moving in the shadows. Wasn't it the incurable fascination of Gagool with her bare yellow skull, the wrinkled scalp that moved and contracted like the hood of a cobra, that led me to work all through 1942 in a little stuffy office in Freetown, Sierra Leone? There is not much in common between the land of the Kukuanas, behind the desert and the mountain range of Sheba's Breast, and a tin-roofed house on a bit of swamp where the vultures moved like domestic turkeys and the pi-dogs kept me awake on moonlight nights with their wailing, and the white women yellowed by atebrin drove by to the club; but the two belonged at any rate to the same continent, and, however distantly, to the same region of the imagination—the region of uncertainty, of not knowing the way about. Once I came a little nearer to Gagool and her witch-hunters, one night in Zigita on the Liberian side of the French Guinea border, when my servants sat in their shuttered hut with their hands over their eyes and someone beat a drum and a whole town stayed behind closed doors while the big bush devil—whom it would mean blindness to see—moved between the huts.

But *King Solomon's Mines* could not finally satisfy. It was not the right answer. The key did not quite fit. Gagool I could recognize—didn't she wait for me in dreams every night in the passage by the linen cupboard, near the nursery door? and she continues to wait, when the mind is sick or tired, though now she is dressed in the theological garments of Despair and speaks in Spenser's accents:

> The longer life, I wote the greater sin,
> The greater sin, the greater punishment.

Yes, Gagool has remained a permanent part of the imagination, but Quatermain and Curtis—weren't they, even when I was only ten years old, a little too good to be true? They were men of such unyielding integrity (they would only admit to a fault in order to show how it might be overcome) that the wavering personality of a child could not rest for long against those monumental shoulders. A child, after all, knows most of the game—it is only an attitude to it that he lacks. He is quite well aware of cowardice, shame, deception, disappointment. Sir Henry Curtis perched upon a rock bleeding from a dozen wounds but fighting on with the remnant of the Greys against the hordes of Twala was too heroic. These men were like Platonic ideas: they were not life as one had already begun to know it.

But when—perhaps I was fourteen by that time—I took Miss Marjorie Bowen's *The Viper of Milan* from the library shelf, the future for better or worse really struck. From that moment I began to write. All the other possible futures slid away: the potential civil servant, the don, the clerk had to look for other incarnations. Imitation after imitation of Miss Bowen's magnificent novel went into exercise books—stories of sixteenth-century Italy or twelfth-century England marked with enormous brutality and a despairing romanticism. It was as if I had been supplied once and for all with a subject.

Why? On the surface *The Viper of Milan* is only the story of a war between Gian Galeazzo Visconti, Duke of Milan, and Mastino della Scala, Duke of Verona, told with zest and cunning and an amazing pictorial sense. Why did it creep in and colour and explain the terrible living world of the stone stairs and the never quiet dormitory? It was no good in that real world to dream that one would ever be a Sir Henry Curtis, but della Scala who at last turned from an honesty that never paid and betrayed his friends and died dishonoured and a failure even at treachery—it was easier for a child to escape behind his mask. As for Visconti, with his beauty, his patience and his genius for evil, I had watched him pass by many a time in his black Sunday suit smelling of mothballs. His name was Carter. He exercised terror from a distance like a snowcloud over the young fields. Goodness has only once found a perfect incarnation in a human body and never will again, but evil can always find a home there. Human nature is not black and white but black and grey. I read all that in *The Viper of Milan* and I looked round and I saw that it was so.

There was another theme I found there. At the end of *The Viper of Milan*—you will remember if you have once read it—comes the great scene of complete success—della Scala is dead, Ferrara, Verona, Novara, Mantua have all fallen, the messengers pour in with news of fresh victories, the whole world outside is cracking up, and Visconti sits and jokes in the wine light. I was not on the classical side or I would have discovered, I suppose, in Greek literature instead of in Miss Bowen's novel the sense of doom that lies over success—the feeling that the pendulum is about to swing. That too made sense; one looked around and saw the doomed everywhere—the champion runner who one day would sag over the tape; the head of the school who would atone, poor devil, during forty dreary undistinguished years; the scholar . . . and when success began to touch oneself too, however mildly, one could only pray that failure would not be held off for too long.

One had lived for fourteen years in a wild jungle country without a map, but now the paths had been traced and naturally one had to follow them. But I think it was Miss Bowen's apparent zest that made me want to write. One could not read her without believing that to write was to live and to enjoy, and before one had discovered one's mistake it was too late—the first book one does enjoy. Anyway she had given me my pattern—religion might later explain it to me in other terms, but the pattern was already there—perfect evil walking the world where perfect good can never walk again, and only the pendulum ensures that after all in the end justice is done. Man is never satisfied, and often I have wished that my hand had not moved further than *King Solomon's Mines,* and that the future I had taken down from the nursery shelf had been a district office in Sierra Leone and twelve tours of malarial duty and a finishing dose of blackwater fever when the danger of retirement approached. What is the good of wishing? The books are always there, the moment of crisis waits, and now our children in their turn are taking down the future and opening the pages. In his poem "Germinal" A.E. wrote:

> In ancient shadows and twilights
> Where childhood had strayed,
> The world's great sorrows were born
> And its heroes were made.
> In the lost boyhood of Judas
> Christ was betrayed.

STUDY QUESTIONS

1. Greene says that when he took Miss Marjorie Bowen's *The Vipers of Milan* from the library shelf, "The future for better or worse really struck." What does he mean by this?
2. When Greene first discovered that he could read, why did he want to keep it a secret?
3. How would you describe Greene's attitude toward his subject? What establishes the tone of this selection?
4. In what way is the stanza that concludes the selection related to Greene's thesis?
5. Has any book you read in your childhood had a lasting effect on you?

Francis Bacon OF STUDIES

Francis Bacon (1561–1626), English statesman, scholar, and writer, is best known today for his pithy essays, that are models for their concise expression and symmetry. Among his many works are

From the *Essayes or Councils, Civill and Morall* (London, 1625), No. 50. The text has been somewhat modernized.

Advancement of Learning (1605) and *Essays or Counsels, Civil and Moral* (1597). In 1618 he became Lord High Chancellor of England, under James I.

Studies serve for delight, for ornament, and for ability. Their chief use for delight is in privateness and retiring; for ornament, is in discourse; and for ability, is in the judgment and disposition of business; for expert men can execute, and perhaps judge of particulars, one by one; but the general counsels, and the plots and marshaling of affairs come best from those that are learned. To spend too much time in studies is sloth; to use them too much for ornament is affection; to make judgment wholly by their rules is the humor of a scholar. They perfect nature, and are perfected by experience; for natural abilities are like natural plants, that need pruning by study; and studies themselves do give forth directions too much at large, except they be bounded in by experience. Crafty men contemn studies, simple men admire them, and wise men use them; for they teach not their own use; but that is a wisdom without them and above them, won by observation. Read not to contradict and confute, nor to believe and take for granted, nor to find talk and discourse, but to weigh and consider. Some books are to be tasted, others to be swallowed, and some few to be chewed and digested; that is, some books are to be read only in parts; others to be read but not curiously, and some few to be read wholly, and with diligence and attention. Some books also may be read by deputy, and extracts made of them by others; but that would be only in the less important arguments and the meaner sort of books; else distilled books are, like common distilled waters, flashy things. Reading maketh a full man; conference a ready man; and writing an exact man. And, therefore, if a man write little, he had need have a great memory; if he confer little, he had need have a present wit; and if he read little, he had need have much cunning, to seem to know that he doth not. Histories make men wise; poets, witty; the mathematics, subtle; natural philosophy, deep; moral, grave; logic and rhetoric, able to contend: *Abeunt studia in mores!* [1] Nay, there is no stand or impediment in the wit but may be wrought out by fit studies; like as diseases of the body may have appropriate exercises. Bowling is good for the stone and reins, shooting for the lungs and breast, gentle walking for the stomach, riding for the head, and the like. So if a man's wit be wandering, let him study the mathematics; for in demonstrations, if his wit be called away never so little, he must begin again. If his wit be not apt to distinguish or find differences, let him study the schoolmen; for they are *cymini sectores!* [2] If he be not apt to beat over matters, and to call up one thing to prove and illustrate another, let him study the lawyers' cases. So every defect of the mind may have a special receipt.

---

[1] Studies form manners.

[2] Hair splitters.

STUDY QUESTIONS

1. In the sentence "Read not to contradict and confute, nor to believe and take for granted," what does Bacon mean?
2. Is the advice Bacon gives about learning valid today?
3. Both Bacon and Greene write about the importance of books. From reading their essays, do you believe they would agree with each other's views on books?
4. Describe Bacon's style. What are the most obvious characteristics of his sentence structure?

ON UNIVERSITY
William Makepeace Thackeray   **SNOBS**

William Makepeace Thackeray (1811–1863), one of the greatest English novelists of the nineteenth century, was born in Calcutta, India. He is best known for his satires of the snobbishness of the upper classes. *Vanity Fair* (1848) was the first of a number of novels that gained him a lasting reputation. Others include *Pendennis* (1850), *Henry Esmond* (1852), and *The Newcomes* (1855). He was also editor of the famous *Cornhill Magazine*.

I should like to fill several volumes with accounts of various University Snobs; so fond are my reminiscences of them, and so numerous are they. I should like to speak, above all, of the wives and daughters of some of the Professor-Snobs: their amusements, habits, jealousies; their innocent artifices to entrap young men; their picnics, concerts, and evening parties. I wonder what has become of Emily Blades, daughter of Blades, the Professor of the Mandingo language? I remember her shoulders to this day, as she sat in the midst of a crowd of about seventy young gentlemen, from Corpus and Catherine Hall, entertaining them with ogles and French songs on the guitar. Are you married, fair Emily of the shoulders? What beautiful ringlets those were that used to dribble over them!—what a waist!—what a killing sea-green shot-silk gown!—what a cameo, the size of a muffin! There were thirty-six young men of the University in love at one time with Emily Blades: and no words are

Reprinted from *Book of Snobs* (1848). Originally appeared in *Punch*, 1846–1847.

sufficient to describe the pity, the sorrow, the deep deep commiseration—the rage, fury, and uncharitableness, in other words—with which the Miss Trumps (daughters of Trumps, the Professor of Phlebotomy) regarded her, because she *didn't* squint, and because she *wasn't* marked with the small-pox.

As for the young University Snobs, I am getting too old, now, to speak of such very familiarly. My recollections of them lie in the far far past—almost as far back as Pelham's time.

We *then* used to consider Snobs raw-looking lads, who never missed chapel; who wore highlows and no straps; who walked two hours on the Trumpington road every day of their lives; who carried off the college scholarships, and who overrated themselves in hall. We were premature in pronouncing our verdict of youthful Snobbishness. The man without straps fulfilled his destiny and duty. He eased his old governor, the curate in Westmoreland, or helped his sisters to set up the Ladies' School. He wrote a "Dictionary," or a "Treatise on Conic Sections," as his nature and genius prompted. He got a fellowship: and then took to himself a wife, and a living. He presides over a parish now, and thinks it rather a dashing thing to belong to the "Oxford and Cambridge Club"; and his parishioners love him, and snore under his sermons. No, no, *he* is not a Snob. It is not straps that make the gentleman, or highlows that unmake him, be they ever so thick. My son, it is you who are the Snob if you lightly despise a man for doing his duty, and refuse to shake an honest man's hand because it wears a Berlin glove.

We then used to consider it not the least vulgar for a parcel of lads who had been whipped three months previous, and were not allowed more than three glasses of port at home, to sit down to pineapples and ices at each other's rooms, and fuddle themselves with champagne and claret.

One looks back to what was called a "wine-party" with a sort of wonder. Thirty lads round a table covered with bad sweetmeats, drinking bad wines, telling bad stories, singing bad songs over and over again. Milk punch—smoking—ghastly headache—frightful spectacle of dessert-table next morning, and smell of tobacco—your guardian, the clergyman, dropping in, in the midst of this—expecting to find you deep in Algebra, and discovering the gyp administering soda-water.

There were young men who despised the lads who indulged in the coarse hospitalities of wine-parties, who prided themselves in giving *recherché* little French dinners. Both wine-party-givers and dinner-givers were Snobs.

There were what used to be called "dressy" Snobs:—Jimmy, who might be seen at five o'clock elaborately rigged out, with a camellia in his buttonhole, glazed boots, and fresh kid-gloves twice a day;—Jessamy, who was conspicuous for his "jewellery,"—a young donkey, glittering all

over with chains, rings, and shirt-studs;—Jacky, who rode every day
solemnly on the Blenheim Road, in pumps and white silk stockings, with
his hair curled,—all three of whom flattered themselves they gave laws to
the University about dress—all three most odious varieties of Snobs.

Sporting Snobs of course there were, and are always—those happy
beings in whom Nature has implanted a love of slang; who loitered
about the horsekeeper's stables, and drove the London coaches—a stage
in and out—and might be seen swaggering through the courts in pink of
early mornings, and indulged in dice and blind-hookey at nights, and
never missed a race or a boxing-match; and rode flat-races, and kept bull-
terriers. Worse Snobs even than these were poor miserable wretches
who did not like hunting at all, and could not afford it, and were in
mortal fear at a two-foot ditch; but who hunted because Glenlivat and
Cinqbars hunted. The Billiard Snob and the Boating Snob were varieties
of these, and are to be found elsewhere than in universities.

Then there were Philosophical Snobs, who used to ape statesmen
at the spouting-clubs, and who believed as a fact that Government
always had an eye on the University for the selection of orators for the
House of Commons. There were audacious young free-thinkers, who
adored nobody or nothing, except perhaps Robespierre and the Koran,
and panted for the day when the pale name of priest should shrink and
dwindle away before the indignation of an enlightened world.

But the worst of all University Snobs are those unfortunates who
go to rack and ruin from their desire to ape their betters. Smith becomes
acquainted with great people at college, and is ashamed of his father the
tradesman. Jones has fine acquaintances, and lives after their fashion like
a gay free-hearted fellow as he is, and ruins his father, and robs his
sister's portion, and cripples his younger brother's outset in life, for the
pleasure of entertaining my lord, and riding by the side of Sir John. And
though it may be very good fun for Robinson to fuddle himself at home
as he does at College, and to be brought home by the policeman he has
just been trying to knock down—think what fun it is for the poor old soul
his mother!—the half-pay captain's widow, who has been pinching herself
all her life long, in order that that jolly young fellow might have a
University education.

STUDY QUESTIONS

1. Do you recognize any of the types of snobs Thackeray describes?
2. What does Thackeray regard as the worst type of snob? Why?
3. In the brief description Thackeray gives of his college experiences, do
    you find that it compares with college life today? Explain.
4. What students did Thackeray once think were snobs? Why did he
    change his mind?

PROFESSIONAL BRAWN
Russell Kirk **IN COLLEGE**

Russell Kirk (1918–   ), distinguished teacher, author, and columnist, is an authority on politics and political science. He has received degrees from Michigan State University, Duke University, and St. Andrews University, Scotland. He writes a syndicated daily newspaper column "To the Point" that is carried by over one hundred daily newspapers. He has received fellowships from the Guggenheim Foundation and the American Council of Learned Societies. Among his many publications are *Randolph of Roanoke* (1951), *The Conservative Mind* (1953), *Academic Freedom* (1955), *The American Cause* (1967), *Confessions of a Bohemian Tory* (1963), and *Fulminations of a Nocturnal Bookman* (1965).

Some years ago, a gentleman with whom I often disagree—Professor Henry Steele Commager—made a most sound observation. "There is no more reason for the young men of Harvard to furnish football entertainment to the public," he wrote, "than there is for the young ladies of Vassar to furnish night-club entertainment."

But some college presidents think otherwise. Last September, Dr. Norman Topping, president of the University of Southern California, made public his alarm at the encroachment of professional football upon the preserves of university football. Why, there might even occur—horrid to think—curtailment of major athletic events at eminent universities and colleges, should attendance at the college games continue to diminish because of the competition of the frankly professional teams. This melancholy outburst was provoked by the scheduling of professional matches at the Los Angeles Sports Arena, pushing USC out of the better dates. What shocking commercialism!

Tottering Hegemony

College baseball, for one reason or another, always has yielded pride of place to the professionals. But college football, and its younger partner basketball, have aspired to domination over the paid teams; for years, indeed, they exercised such a hegemony. Yet it seems to have

By permission of *National Review*, 150 East 35th Street, New York, New York 10016.

entered the mind of the public that fully professional teams are better, as sheer amusement, than the quasi-professional squads of the colleges. So the public's filthy lucre has been passing to the full-timers.

Though some universities would institute academic majors in tore-adorship and matadorship if it weren't for the Humane Society, I find myself unable to shed tears in company with President Topping. Indeed, the compulsory abandoning of quasi-commercial athletics under university and college sponsorship would be a considerable blow in the cause of the higher learning in America.

Whenever I write this sort of thing, aggrieved coaches protest to me that I must be against a sound mind in a sound body. But on the contrary, I find our average college man distressingly flabby, in part because he drives his sports car even if he is only proceeding to the corner drug store. Boxing, wrestling, and fencing I particularly endorse; and of course football, basketball, and baseball are all to the good—if they really have any place for the average collegian.

Our trouble is that the average collegian could no more play on a major college team than he could be appointed Librarian of Congress. Since the present object of college athletics is to bring a dubious fame to the institution, attract paying crowds, and please what a friend of mine call "the ersatz alumni," the famous college squads are recruited from brawny high-school quasi-professionals whom scouts draw in with promises of lavish athletic scholarships. The proportion of thugs among these gentry grows, and the proportion of dullards always has been tremendous.

President Topping, as quoted in a press dispatch, endeavors to argue that these are bright lads. "You've all seen and met great athletes who also are excellent students. It has been proven that sports and athletics are not mutually exclusive."

Um hum. Probably there have been some sensitive souls enlisted in the French Foreign Legion, too. I have known some football players who could do more than read and write, and even one who received a Rhodes Scholarship. But such achieved some intellectual elevation in spite of their innumerable hours spent in training not because of them. Probably the majority of football players graduate from college—when they do graduate—only because their professors have truckled down to the pressure from the coaches.

Where Waterloo Was Won

No national educational apparatus emphasizes field sports more than the British, from what we should call the lower grades up through the university. But theirs is genuine athleticism. At the English and Scottish universities, "athletic scholarships" would be regarded as the Mark of the Beast; and competition for the public's s.d., against the professional rugger and soccer teams, would provoke the appointment of a Royal Commission, fury in Parliament, and even the indignation of the penny press. British university students play for the fun of it, and probably would be annoyed if anyone came to see them except class-mates and a few locals. Any student who wants to play on a university team, and can master the fundamentals of the sport, has his chance: he doesn't have to be a gorilla. Though the British universities spend next to nothing on "athletic programs," the typical British student is in better condition than the American because he is not simply a spectator.

These strictures apply with equal force to our high schools. A reader who was once a Marine training instructor at Parris Island, and who is all for muscular vigor, writes to me in dispraise of the commer-cialized athleticism of Indiana high schools. "I personally heard the Richmond coach, during a speech to a group of businessmen, threaten—in all seriousness—that if the attendance at his football games did not increase, he was going to make arrangements to play his games in Dayton, where he knew he could draw a decent crowd."

When professional competition threatens the ascendant college sports of beer-drinking and necking, then I'll tremble for the survival of the Academy: but not when USC can't fill the Sports Arena.

STUDY QUESTIONS

1. What is Kirk's tone in this essay? Note particular words and expressions that establish his tone.

2. In the section "Tottering Hegemony," Kirk makes some serious charges against football, players, and coaches. What rhetorical method does he use to make these charges?

3. What purpose does the paragraph serve that describes the athletic programs in British colleges and universities?

4. Do you agree with Kirk in his appraisal of college football? What evidence could you cite to refute him?

ACADEMIC FREEDOM
Sidney Hook AND STUDENT RIOTS

Sidney Hook (1902–   ), philosopher and educator, was born in New York. At The City College of New York, where he received

his B.S., he won the Ward Medal for Logic. He received his M.A.
and Ph.D. from Columbia University. Currently he is chairman of
the philosophy department at Washington Square College, New
York University. He has been an active member of the Commission on Cultural Freedom and the Conference on Methods and
Philosophies, and he has been a recipient of a Guggenheim fellowship.

Americans are accustomed to reading about universities as storm
centers of political disturbance in Latin and Asiatic countries. In a
country like the United States, however, most criticism of student bodies
in the past has been directed against their political apathy. The fact,
therefore, that a building was seized by students at the Berkeley campus
of the University of California, bringing all administrative activities to a
halt, that a strike was declared, paralyzing teaching, and that the governor of the most populous state in the union, after the arrest of some 800
students, felt it necessary to appeal for problems to be solved "by
evolution not revolution," should give not only educators but all reflective citizens pause. It has focused attention upon a question of considerable complexity—the rights, and the responsibilities, of students.

Since so much of the controversy and agitation swirls around the
slogans of freedom, the first question to be asked is: Do students enjoy
the right of academic freedom? This depends on what is meant by
academic freedom. Perhaps the best short definition was offered by
Arthur O. Lovejoy, founder, together with John Dewey, of the American
Association of University Professors.

"Academic freedom," he wrote, "is the freedom of the teacher or
research worker in higher institutions of learning to investigate and
discuss the problems of his science and to express his conclusions,
whether through publications or the instruction of students, without
interference from political or ecclesiastical authority, or from the administrative officials of the institution in which he is employed, unless his
methods are found by qualified bodies of his own profession to be clearly
incompetent or contrary to professional ethics."

A number of interesting implications may be drawn from this
definition. First, academic freedom exists primarily for "teachers"—in the
most comprehensive sense of that term. Strictly speaking, it makes no
sense to talk of "academic freedom" for students. Students have a right
to freedom to learn. The best guarantee of freedom to learn is academic
freedom for those who teach them. Where teachers are deprived of
academic freedom, students are *ipso facto* deprived of the freedom to
learn.

The converse, however, is not true. It is simply false both in logic
and in fact to assert that freedom to teach and freedom to learn are
indivisible. Many things may interfere with the student's freedom to

learn—poverty, racial discrimination, inadequate transportation—which have no direct relevance to academic freedom. The latter may flourish in institutions to which students are unjustly denied the opportunity to enter. The movement to abolish poverty, discrimination and other social evils in order to give students access to education and to effective freedom to learn flows from their *moral* rights as persons and from their *civil* rights as citizens. They are not corollaries of academic freedom. To deny this would make the university responsible for the entire state of society and its reform.

Second, academic freedom is not a civil right like freedom of speech. A teacher who is dropped or refused a post on grounds of incompetence, because, say, he indoctrinates his students with the belief that the earth is flat, or that the Elders of Zion are engaged in a conspiracy to destroy America, or that Communists are twentieth-century Jeffersonian democrats, is not being deprived of freedom of speech. He can still proclaim his discovery from the house tops. As a citizen he can talk nonsense without let or hindrance. But in order to talk "nonsense" in the academy with impunity—and strange things *can* be heard within it!—a teacher must win the right to do so by certification from his peers that he is competent and by having acquired tenure. What may sound like nonsense to the plain citizen may be the birth of a revolutionary discovery.

The same consideration applies to the student.

There is no direct connection between the student's freedom to learn and his freedom of speech. The controlling consideration must be his freedom to learn. If restrictions are placed on freedom of speech— aside from those which exist on the freedom of *all* citizens—they must be justified by the educational needs of the student and reasonable institutional provisions for its expression. It is one thing to set up a miniature Hyde Park on some corner of the campus and encourage students to use it; it is another to allow them to call a mass meeting on Prexy's lawn at dawn.

Third, responsibility for the certification of a teacher's competence, and for interpreting and applying the rules of tenure, must ultimately lie in the hands of the faculty. The faculty should also set the educational standards which students are required to measure up to. Students may be free to learn but sometimes they don't learn enough. Students too, therefore, must earn the right to continue as students. Higher education is not a civil right like the right to a fair trial or other Bill of Rights freedoms that do not have to be earned.

Fourth, an important aspect of the faculty's responsibility for the entire educational enterprise is ultimate control over the classrooms, meeting halls and other educational facilities of the campus and over the conditions of their use. This has a bearing, as we shall see, on some crucial questions.

The extent to which these principles are applied is affected by the fact that legal authority in American higher institutions of learning is vested either in boards of regents or in corporate boards of laymen. While there is no practicable way of reversing this historical trend, immense progress has been made in winning over those with legal authority to the acceptance of enlightened principles of academic freedom which in effect entrust educational policy to the faculties. This has been a gradual and sometimes painful development, but today academic freedom is in a more flourishing state than ever before in its history. It is only when one remembers how many and onerous were the religious, political and social restrictions upon the teacher's freedom in the past that one can grasp the remarkable progress that has been made.

What is true of the teacher's academic freedom is also true of the student's freedom to learn. My own lifetime spans a period from relative tyranny in the classroom to open inquiry. During my freshman year in college, I gave two reports in a class in political science. In the first, I defended Charles A. Beard's approach to the Constitution—to the manifest disapproval of the teacher. In the second, I argued that Calhoun's logic was superior to Webster's in their famous debates. This was too much for the instructor who ejected me from the class with the indignant observation: "When you aren't preaching sedition you are preaching secession!" That could hardly happen today. Although conditions are not uniform, almost everywhere the climate of opinion and practice is healthier than it used to be.

The issues that agitate campuses today are more likely to arise from the behavior of students than from actions of the faculty. Of these, some stem from rules governing the students' personal and social behavior, and some from efforts to regulate their extracurricular political activities both on and off campus.

Confusion, and sometimes needless controversy, arise from a failure to distinguish between the area of conduct in which students may justifiably exercise their rights as individual citizens and that which is related to the specific function of the college and to the business which presumably brings the student to school. To indicate the relevance of this distinction, let us examine some of the concrete issues that have provoked controversy in recent years.

The first concerns the personal morality of students. Unfortunately, personal morality for many people refers exclusively to sexual behavior, but, properly understood, it embraces every form of individual conduct whose consequences have some bearing on the welfare of others. On the assumption that in institutions of higher learning we are not dealing with children, standards of personal deportment should initially be left to the students themselves. In the interests of safety, however, it is necessary to establish rules and regulations governing the use of cars, liquor, smoking and visits to dormitories, but, wherever possible, these rules should be administered by the students themselves. Anything students can properly do for themselves as adults should be left to them. To student self-government, broad-based and representative, can be entrusted many of the functions incidental to organized student life in the college community—although the faculty cannot forgo exercising some oversight as a kind of appeals body to see that fair play is done.

Should students be permitted to organize political groups on campus or invite speakers of extremist political views to address them? This kind of problem has occasioned far more bitter controversy than problems of purely personal behavior. And failure to define the issue properly has prevented the right kind of questions from being asked and the relevant considerations brought to bear.

A student request which may have considerable *educational* validity may be wrongfully denied because it is mistakenly put forward as a political demand. This is particularly true with respect to who should be allowed to speak on a university campus. This has nothing to do with questions of free speech or academic freedom. Political speakers can reach students in many ways. If the faculties do not permit the use of college facilities to individuals outside of the academic community, they are not denying the civil right of freedom of speech to speakers, who can easily address students off-campus, or the civil right of freedom to listen to students, who can attend their meetings off-campus. This is a false issue.

The genuine issue is the *educational* one. It is on educational, not political, grounds that a valid case can be made for permitting recognized student organizations to invite speakers of their choice to the campus to discuss any topic, no matter how controversial. The educational process cannot and should not be confined merely to the classroom. Students should be encouraged to pursue their educational interests on their own initiative, and contemporary issues which convulse society are legitimate subjects of inquiry.

Faculties and administrations often suffer from educational timidity. They are unduly fearful when a speaker of extremist views is invited to the campus. If a college is doing its job properly, it doesn't require Fascists or Communists to instruct its students about Fascism or Communism. But so long as students want to hear such speakers—often to see them in the flesh and to find out how they tick mentally—there can be no reasonable educational objection to their appearance—particularly if it is made clear that such speakers do not represent the views of the student body or faculty.

If students and faculty cannot cope with the "arguments" of the

Lincoln Rockwells and Gus Halls, then the college is failing badly in its educational task. In an open and honest forum, the cause of freedom and democracy can triumph over all challengers. And as for the vaunted "public image" (horrid phrase!) of the college, the prolonged controversy and newspaper publicity attendant upon banning a speaker is usually far more damaging than the one-day sensation provided by his appearance. For one thing seems assured by experience. A prolonged controversy over an invitation to an extremist almost always guarantees him an overflow audience when he does finally appear.

In the rare cases in which the need for control of student activities does arise, failure on the part of the faculty to draw the line means that it has abdicated from its educational responsibilities. For example, students, sometimes unfortunately abetted by junior faculty personnel, will occasionally try to break up meetings of speakers with whom they disagree. A self-respecting faculty cannot tolerate such activities. Similarly, if outside groups send professional organizers onto the campuses of large metropolitan universities to recruit students or to provoke incidents with the administration or faculties, they should be barred from access.

Then, too, small groups of students, zealots in some cause, will occasionally violate the rules of fair discussion and honest advocacy. I could fill a volume describing stratagems of this kind I have observed over a lifetime. A few students, for example, will organize a "Free Speech Forum" or something else with a libertarian flavor. Their first speaker will be Lincoln Rockwell or someone of his kidney. Thereafter, featured as "a reply" to Fascism, will come a succession of Communist speakers, sometimes paid from general student or school funds. The "educational" point of the forum is to build up Communism in its various disguises as the only real answer to Fascism.

Complaints about the absence of liberal speakers are met with the statement that liberals have been invited but refused to come. The evidence? A carbon copy of a letter to a liberal figure 2,000 miles or more distant, the original of which he may never have received. Where representatives of the student body are unable to prevent dishonest practices of this kind, the faculty is justified in stepping in.

The same general principles should govern student publications. On educational grounds, students should be encouraged to publish their own newspapers, periodicals and pamphlets, exchanging ideas, commenting on great issues, testing and challenging their teachers' views. But it would be ridiculous to say that this freedom is absolute and exempts them from restraints against slander and libel. Particularly obnoxious is the circulation of anonymous literature on campus defaming members of the student body or faculty.

Only those who believe it is possible to be liberal without being intelligent will affirm that the content of speech is always privileged irrespective of its effects.

The very fact that speech can be used not only for advocacy—which is permissible—but for incitement, defamation and slander—which is not— shows how absurd it is to hold that speech should never be restricted. There should be no prior censorship, of course, unless there is convincing evidence that a speaker plans to incite to violence. We do not have to wait for a mob actually to move to lynch someone before we stop the agitator inciting it.

The irony of the situation is that students in our mass institutions of learning suffer today far more from the failure of faculties to attend to the students' individual educational needs than from alleged suppressions of their freedom of speech. The students' freedom to learn is frustrated by crowding, inferior staffing and by the indifference of many faculties to the best methods of classroom teaching. Colleges still operate on the absurd assumption that anyone who knows anything can teach it properly. It is an open scandal that the worst teaching in the American system of education takes place at the college level.

In some universities, large introductory courses where skillful teaching is of critical importance in arousing student interest are turned over to young, inexperienced graduate assistants at the outset of their careers who stumble along by trial and error and groping imitation of the models of teaching they vaguely remember. No wonder they sometimes play up to students, joining them in their vague resentments against the educational establishment in a kind of compensatory camaraderie. Some observers believe that unless conditions change the real revolt on campus will some day be directed against the shoddy educational treatment to which students have been subjected. As the numbers of students grow the situation deteriorates.

A sense of proportion, a pinch of humor and a draft of common sense are wonderful specifics against friction, but they vanish when either students or faculty resort to ultimatums. Both sides have a mutual interest in keeping the educational enterprise going. When problems and difficulties arise they must be routed through recognized channels of petition, complaint and protest. The officially elected representatives of the student body should meet periodically with representatives of the faculty which, when grave issues are at stake, should sit as a committee of the whole.

Attempts by any group, even when it feels it has a legitimate grievance, to short-circuit official channels, to appeal over the heads of the representative student body for mass demonstrations or strikes, to threaten force and violence or to resort to so-called passive resistance should be condemned by both students and faculty. Such tactics are not only destructive of the atmosphere in which teaching and learning can take place, they prejudice the chances for reaching mutually satisfactory settlements.

The student "Free Speech Movement" at the University of California had every right to press for modification of university rules governing campus and off-campus activities. What was shocking, however, was its deliberate boycott and by-passing of the Associated Students, the elected representative organization of the student body. It neither used all the existing channels of protest nor sought to avail itself of the remedies open to it.

Even more shocking was the demagogic and odious comparison drawn by some students between the situation at the University, which, despite its restrictions, is still far more liberal than most, and the situation in Mississippi. And worst of all was the resort to tactics of mass civil disobedience which could only be justified in extreme situations in behalf of basic principles of freedom. Except in such situations, changes in the laws of a democratic community must be urged by practices within the law.

Almost as shocking as the action of the students in seizing University property was the failure of the faculty at Berkeley to condemn the action. Indeed, by failing to couple its call for an amnesty for students with a sharp rebuke for their actions, the faculty seemed to condone indirectly the students' behavior. Apparently those who wanted to be heroes were to be spared the consequences of their heroism.

The administration of the University also seems at fault in not anticipating developments on campus. Signs of student unrest and dissatisfaction were apparent many months ago. The faculty, therefore, should have been brought into the picture much earlier and entrusted with the formulation of rules of conduct, in consultation with official representatives of the student body, and with their subsequent enforcement.

The really disquieting aspect of the situation at the University of California, however, was the extremism of the student leaders, the lengths to which they were willing to go—at one point, bloodshed and possible loss of life seemed imminent—and the contemptuous and disingenuous account they gave of their behavior. One of them described their activities as "controversial measures to begin a dialogue." Student concern with the content and method of their education is sure to grow and should be encouraged. But if they are going to lie down, seize buildings and call strikes whenever their demands are not granted by faculty and administration, it bodes ill for the future.

Even before the events at Berkeley, I read literature distributed by a strong student group at the University of California calling for "the total elimination of course, grade and unit system of undergraduate learning" and urging other proposals—not all of them as silly. But what was definitely not silly or funny in the light of what has happened was the injunction to students to resort ultimately to "civil disobedience" to get their way! It is a safe bet to anyone who knows the psychology of students that once they get away with the tactic of civil disobedience in protesting a minor rule, their demands—and their conduct—will grow wilder and more unreasonable.

No service is done to students by flattering them or by giving them the impression they can acquire an education in any other way than by hard intellectual discipline—by accepting the logic of ideas and events. They cannot be encouraged too much to broaden their intellectual interests, and they certainly must not be discouraged from giving expression to their generous enthusiasms for civil rights, for human welfare, for peace with freedom. But good works off campus cannot be a substitute for good work on campus. Ultimately, the good causes our society always needs have a better chance of triumphing if their servitors equip themselves with the best education our colleges and universities can give them.

STUDY QUESTIONS

1. According to Hook, are there any restrictions on the students' right to learn? If so, what are they?

2. What should be the criteria for allowing student organizations to invite speakers to the campus? What possible problems could arise from using this criteria?

3. In his criticism of the Free Speech Movement at the University of California, what does Hook say about the faculty and the administration?

4. How is it that the students' freedom to learn depends on the academic freedom of the faculty but the converse is not true?

5. In Hook's view, why is it unreasonable to give students unrestricted freedom of speech?

ANOTHER PLANE
IN ANOTHER SPHERE:
Jeremy Larner **THE COLLEGE DRUG SCENE**

Jeremy Larner (1937–   ) was born in Olean, New York. He completed his undergraduate work at Brandeis University and attended the Graduate College of the University of California at Berkeley. He teaches at New York State University at Stony Brook, Long Island. His writings have appeared in the *Atlantic, Holiday, Nation,* and *Dissent.* He is coauthor of *The Addict in the Street.* His novel *Drive, He Said* won the Delta Award in 1965.

> Why do we try drugs? We really feel like we're limited so much. And we want to do so much. And we're always told we should try things and grow. It's part of the liberal arts education. It seems hypocritical of older people to tell us not to try certain things. We feel we can take care of ourselves.

While there are no significant statistics—any more than there are on virginity, and for the same reasons—drug-taking is becoming increasingly popular on American campuses. A variety of drugs can now be easily obtained at any college which draws its students from metropolitan areas—which means that the problem is most acute at the biggest and best universities and at some of the most prestigious small colleges. Marijuana is generally the drug of choice: a young man from an Eastern college claims, "I have yet to see a college party anywhere in the last two years where at least one-third of the kids have not been turned on."

The local marijuana connection is usually a fellow classmate. But if a student wants other drugs, or if he uses marijuana in large quantities, he need not seek further than the circle of hangers-on who live in the university community without attending college. In brief, availability is such that nearly every contemporary student must make up his mind whether or not he wants to try drugs—because he will certainly have the chance.

For most students, marijuana is something to be tried once or twice, to see what it's like. Those who consider themselves hip will smoke reefers "socially," in the same spirit in which executives drink martinis. Of these social smokers, a few will get to the point where they are turning on every day; and it is these few who will also try other drugs—for example, amphetamine "pep pills" in quantities that can cause psychotic distortions, berserk outbreaks, and even cerebral hemorrhage. Heroin, barbiturates, and other "hard narcotics" are also available for the self-destructive; but as a rule the hip thing is to take drugs for "exploration" rather than escape.

When drug use first comes to light on a given campus, college officials tend to protect the school's reputation by expelling the culprits and even by turning them over to the police. Experienced administrators, however, are learning to make a distinction between trying drugs and selling them, and in the former case are more likely to use probation or a psychiatric referral as a means of correction. The fact that drugs are illegal does not in itself serve as a deterrent. Students of all generations have traditionally sought out forbidden activities as a valuable part of their college education. Thus choosing one's drug, or no drugs, is regarded as a personal decision, like choosing friends, books, or clothes, to be made on personal grounds quite apart from the opinions or threats of authorities.

The modern student will accept responsibility for the effects his actions have on others, but beyond that he sees all arbitrary limits as impositions of the status quo. Personal responsibility, to him, implies the freedom to take risks that involve only himself and his development. He feels that if parents and school officials really believe in that "free inquiry" which is supposedly the ideal of a liberal education, they must respect his right to conduct his own quest by his own rules.

The drugs most talked about in terms of questing are the powerfully mind-disturbing hallucinogens (peyote, mescaline, psilocybin, LSD). Most of the daily pot-smokers will sooner or later try the hallucinogens. Other students are also curious to try them, partly for "kicks," partly because they feel challenged, and partly because they are attracted by claims of mystic and psychological revelation. The most extravagant of these claims emanate from grown-up enthusiasts who are devoting their careers to popularizing the hallucinogens.

For many young Americans, college represents four years of free experiment between the restrictions of the parental family and the responsibilities of the marital family. The student is aware that every choice he makes—both occupationally and personally—may have a telling effect on the adult he will become. He is under pressure to "find himself"—and quickly.

Like other Americans, the college student may look for his "self" in the products he consumes. Universities that are organized like supermarkets will only encourage such unsatisfying searches. Students, moreover, are susceptible to an existentialist strain of the disease called "conspicuous consumption." Rerouting the pursuit of the material, they seek to consume pure experience. They hope that by choosing the right activities they can create an external confirmation of the power and beauty they would like to feel within.

Drugs, as we shall see, are products that supply the illusion of choice while they simultaneously minister to the anxieties that choosing creates. The increasing use of drugs may be seen as a reflection of an unconscious belief in the commercials that pound home the connection between a judicious drug choice and the relief of any mental or physical "symptom." Such assumptions are not easily overcome by a generation that is, after all, the first whose members are lifelong TV viewers, bombarded from infancy by suggestions of false needs.

Marijuana

> To us a muggle wasn't any more dangerous or habit-forming than those other great American vices, the five-cent Coke and the ice-cream cone, only it gave you more kicks for your money.
>
> Us vipers began to know that we had a gang of things in common: we ate like starved cannibals who finally latch on to a missionary, and we laughed a whole lot and lazed around in an easygoing way, and we all decided that the muta had some aphrodisiac qualities too. . . . All the puffed-up strutting little people we saw around, jogging their self-important way along so chesty and chumpy, plotting and scheming and getting more wrinkled and jumpy all the time, made us all howl. . . . We were on another plane in another sphere compared to the musicians who were bottle babies, always hitting the jug and then coming up brawling after they got loaded. We liked things to be easy and relaxed, mellow and mild, not loud or loutish, and the scowling chin-out tension of the lushhounds with their false courage didn't appeal to us.

This classic description—from *Really the Blues* (1946) by Mezz Mezzrow and Bernard Wolfe—will serve to convey the general relaxation of the marijuana high and the good fellowship which prevails in the society of satisfied vipers. The *LaGuardia Report*—published in 1944 and still the standard scientific text on the subject—confirms that marijuana is non-addicting. The *Report* warns that marijuana taken in excess may produce anxiety as well as pleasant feelings, and that psychotic episodes are not unheard-of when the batch is strong and the smoker sensitive. The pleasurable response to pot is to some extent learned, and an experienced smoker will not continue once he has obtained the desired sensations. To quote the *Report:* "The description of the 'tea-pad parties' brings out clearly the convivial effect . . . and the absence of any rough or antagonistic behavior."

Obviously college administrators could not sanction pot, even if it were legal, any more than they sanction drinking. But students are contemptuous of the usual line about marijuana leading to heroin addiction. Since heroin is a depressant, its effects are entirely different from those described above, and are sought after by a different kind of person, one who is characteristically dissatisfied with marijuana. Commentators may fasten on the fact that heroin addicts "began" with pot, but it is just as accurate to say that they "began" with liquor. For most heroin addicts have at one time tried liquor as well as pot—and rejected both.

Since pot is outlawed, however, sooner or later a pot-smoker will come in contact with a connection who has other drugs for sale. This, to many students, represents the crucial difference between alcohol and marijuana. One drug is surrounded by accepted rituals, while consumption of the other is ipso facto connected with lawbreaking. Many feel that if marijuana were legalized, society would develop appropriate and enjoyable attitudes toward it. They feel that the comparison with alcohol is all in marijuana's favor. The White House Conference on Narcotic and Drug Abuse referred to alcohol as "the outstanding addictive drug in the United States." The country's five million alcoholics suffer from cirrhosis, nervous diseases, and even brain damage. Nicotine, too, has addictive properties, and cigarettes made from tobacco can cause lung cancer; whereas the *LaGuardia Report* tells us that "those who have been smoking marijuana for a period of years showed no mental or physical deterioration which may be attributed to the drug."

The upshot of misinformed fulminations about marijuana is that students in the know feel a certain superiority. They're entitled to smile when subjected to the liquor industry's 200-million-dollar annual barrage of advertising designed to link alcoholic intake with happiness, youth, and social power. They feel their product is better, cheaper, and less dangerous. And once they've tried pot and discovered that official warnings are based more on panic than fact, they are in a position to discredit apprehensions about any drug whatever.

The Hallucinogens

The hallucinogens—of which the laboratory synthetic LSD is by far the most powerful—produce a stunning impact on the mind. Distortions of time and space, intense color phenomena, and delusions of death and grandeur are commonly experienced. All sorts of thoughts, feelings, memories, fears, dreams, and images are released, often with an overlay of euphoria. Some psychiatrists see the hallucinogens as potentially useful in the treatment of various mental disorders, though most regard the experimental work in this field to date as inconclusive. Psychoanalysts have for years rejected techniques of artificial release—such as hypnotism and "truth serums"—on the grounds that psychoanalysis is not identical with the mere unearthing of material.

LSD cultists feel that under the effect of a hallucinogen, the mind activates inborn knowledge long "repressed" by civilization, knowledge which reveals the mystic "oneness" of the universe. The individual personality is supposedly dissolved in "The Void," where space and time vanish and all is impersonal "ecstasy." This experience, along with the emergence of "repressed" psychic material, is supposed to help the individual gain a transcendent perspective with which to reorient himself to the "illusory" world of earthbound humanity.

It is claimed that the regular use of LSD increases individual development and lovingness toward others, and that therefore the drug should be freely available. An LSD millennium is seen as inevitable, bringing with it the dissolution of human conflict and the recognition of the cult leaders as prophets of a scientific, philosophic, and historical "breakthrough."

Most psychiatrists, however, are wary of dangerous reactions to the hallucinogens. There are many verified reports of students in whom a hallucinatory drug touched off a latent psychosis so severe that hospitalization was required. Prolonged psychotic states, depression, recurring hallucinations, and suicide attempts (some successful) have resulted from the use of LSD—in some cases months after the drug was taken. As for the effects of LSD on the personality, medical investigators have noted the following: 1) dissociation and detachment, 2) personal insensitivity, superiority, 3) religious and philosophical solipsism, 4) impulsivity, poor judgment.

These observations, to be sure, depend on the observer's point of view. One of the chief concerns of the dedicated drug-taker is precisely to repudiate the values, judgments, and most basic perceptions of the persons he believes to represent a monolithic and repressive authority. He does his best to perceive school officials, scientists, teachers, psychiatrists, and indeed anyone who does not appreciate "the drug experience," as an organized "Establishment" conspiring to suppress individual "freedom."

The Dedicated Drug-User

It is now possible for a disaffected youngster to assume a highly developed role as drug-user. He usually begins with the perfection of a "cool" manner. The world is "too much"; his coolness announces that the cool one is invulnerable to involvement. He has taken the cure well in advance of the disease. To put it in consumer terms: desire is a weakness, because it expresses unfulfilled need. The cool one has found and taken the products that he needs.

To blow one's cool, then, is to reveal—to oneself as well as others—an inner lack. To maintain one's cool is to signify, "I've had it." The double meaning is intentional; for the cool one claims no great worldly future. He knows that his gestures are stylized; his pride is the masterly knowledge that in this world of appearances, style is all that matters.

Unlike others whom he sees as self-deluded, the cool one suits his actions to his ideas. He has found a philosophy simple enough to live by (almost). In this sense, he alone has achieved the academic ideal.

There is, after all, a twisted idealism involved in submitting oneself to drug experiments. Erik Erikson, in "The Problem of Ego Identity," tells us that some young people respond to environmental pressures by trying to create a "negative identity." According to Erikson, "many a late adolescent, if faced with continuing diffusion, would rather *be nobody or somebody bad, or indeed, dead—and this totally, and by free choice—than be not-quite somebody.*" (Italics his.) Drugs, in these terms, provide the idealist with a chance to control his own destiny and to go all the way. There is a distorted testing mechanism at work here; Erikson speaks of "a radical search for the rock bottom . . . a deliberate search"—as if the searcher could master a sense of unworthiness by seeking out and inflicting upon himself certain selected dangers. Drugs are like Russian roulette: if you survive, you must have something going for you. It shouldn't surpise us that one of the most common, popular, and easily induced drug delusions is the fantasy of rebirth.

If one is to be reborn, one needs replacements for the mortal, fallible parents and family whose existence dictates unendurable limitations. Says Erikson, "Young people often indicate in rather pathetic ways a feeling that only a merging with a 'leader' could save them. . . . the late adolescent wants to be an apprentice or a disciple, a follower, sex mate, or patient." The contemporary campus is replete with drug-givers who will gladly initiate the yearningly incomplete student into all of the above roles. The novice is then equipped with drug priests for parents and fellow acolytes for siblings. The members of the drug family are connected not by birth and mortality, but by destiny and salvation. They reinforce their new improved personalities with ceremonial rituals, an in-group language, and—above all—the taking of the sacrament.

Before long the initiate drug-taker is in turn initiating others. Their desire directed toward him helps to confirm him in his role of "holder" and to convince him that he is indeed in possession of something worthwhile. It is to his advantage that expectation and suggestibility play a tremendous role in an individual's reaction to drugs. He himself is no longer surprised by the sensations produced by powerful drugs; he has learned to enjoy them and to interpret them in accordance with his own desires. Therefore he can guide the initiate who is panicky under his first dose of, say, a hallucinogen, can calm him with lofty wisdom, and help him explain his experience in the language of the drug ideology.

As the drug-taker becomes drug-giver, he cultivates a transcendent personality. He views the world with the secret superiority of one who has access to something better. All of you are playing a game, he says in his every gesture, but you could be saved if you'd follow me. Reality for him is no longer the uncertainty of the ordinary world but the heightened visions he experiences when high. Should his would-be disciples reject their own visions as drug-induced delusions, he informs them that they are tied up in "ego games." For him, the only criteria for interpreting drug phenomena are the phenomena themselves.

The transcendent personality is particularly useful for a student supported by his parents or a technician performing a job he despises. Ordinarily such a situation would raise a crisis of identity centered around the problem of achieving independence and self-respect. But for the true holder, serving his drug postpones the questions, Who am I? and What can I do?

Further, those dedicated to drugs have avoided the ambiguities of democratic face-to-face personal relations. Clinging to an in-group solidarity, they divide the world into sages and fools, saints and devils, holders and seekers. Richard Blum, in his book *The Utopiates*, speculates that drug proselytizers are particularly afraid of seeking and being denied. So they reverse the process, becoming tempters and rejecters. For this writer, the essential point is that both seekers and tempters are still caught up in the infantile drama of power-testing. Unable to bear a grown-up world without absolute power, they have invented that power—and invested it both in drugs and in the parental figures who oppose drugs.

Getting Hung Up

"David" is a brilliant student at an excellent college, well aware of the advantages he's had, and aware also that much is expected of him. Here, David tells of a recent experience which caused him to give up drugs entirely:

> At the beginning of this year, I felt really low, I got completely bored with school, and I felt the teachers weren't giving me anything. I had been involved with a girl, but it ended at the end of the summer. And that was one of the things that really depressed me, you know, that I couldn't find anybody. Sex became a real drive, but since none of the chicks meant anything to me, sex itself became meaningless. I just didn't know what to do with myself. So I started smoking pot every day—to the point where I was high every minute.
>
> Grass had become a crutch all of a sudden. I turned on before I went to class, before dinner, before skiing. I felt that everything could be better. It wasn't just music and girls; it was everything.
>
> But after a few months, I got so I was tired all the time, my mouth was dry. I wasn't doing anything but getting high, and I couldn't get high anymore. I'd been dependent on getting high, and I wanted something to change. There had to be something that would *shake* me. No people were shaking me, no ideas were shaking me, and no course was

shaking me. And no experiences were shaking me, so I said, what can shake me? LSD, maybe. So I thought I'd try LSD, to see if it shakes me into something new.

At this point David contacted a disturbed young friend who had been taking drugs heavily since he was fourteen. When David arrived, his friend had taken four times what is considered a heavy dose of LSD and had been hallucinating for five days. He gave David a black market sugar cube and told him it contained a heavy dose of LSD. After swallowing the cube, David found out that it held *twice* a heavy dose. "I think he was so far out of it he knew he wasn't coming back, and he wanted to take me with him."

> So I took the cube. For a while it was nice, I'd lie down on the bed, hear some music, the music would sound nice, I'd see pretty colors dancing on the wall. But the fact that new and completely different, if not contradictory, ideas kept popping up in my mind, gradually began to depress me. I kept thinking I had the Answer to Life. I'd jump into one thing, then I'd say No, that's wrong; then another thing, then No, that's wrong . . . and finally I saw that the answers were just as illusory as the colors I saw on the wall.
> And when I started to feel my mind flipping out of my body, I thought, Jesus Christ, I don't care how simple the pleasures would be, I'd rather be *back there*. I'd rather be in a boring state than where I am now, because I cannot live this way, I don't want to be like this. I'll commit suicide if necessary. I thought that this was going to go on continually, and I just couldn't cope with it.

Though inside himself David felt desperately hysterical, his outer manner was so remote that he couldn't convince the college doctor he needed help. Finally, after three days of hallucinations, David found a doctor who administered an antidote.

The LSD experience caused David to reconsider his way of using marijuana:

> I realized afterwards that, as a result of smoking grass, the things that had been important to me were not only no longer important, I was incapable of doing them. I couldn't write, I couldn't think. I couldn't carry on normal relations with people. I saw how much time I'd been wasting. I mean, I sort of knew it all along. But when I took the LSD, I just had three days of intense fear and running around and nervous energy, and when I was brought back to earth, I said, God, your whole last few years have been like this! You haven't been doing anything; you've just been running around—and heading in toward a dead end. I hadn't been developing at all; I was just completely stagnant.

After telling his story, David gets into an argument with his roommate about a mutual friend who was once a brilliant musician but who now does nothing but stay high on pot all day long. David's roommate refers him to a long list of first-rate jazz musicians who are well-known vipers. David is forced to admit that the problem resides not in the marijuana itself but in the immaturity of his friend, who is "a weak, dependent person needing a crutch." The roommate presses further: isn't their musician friend just as well off staying high all day as he would be playing the piano? As long as he feels good, does it make any difference how he gets that way? David replies with some warmth:

> No, my friend does *not* feel good—he could be happier with music than with pot. Because music never ceases to move and develop. Pot, instead of broadening and deepening, just becomes less than it was at the beginning. You could say the same about any drug: it's a dead end.

The Mystique of "The Creative Experience"

Thousands of students would passionately object to David's separation of drugs and art. They would insist that drugs are indispensable for the understanding and creation of modern poetry, painting, music, fiction, and sculpture.

For reasons of social dislocation which the campus only mirrors, masses of the most confused, aimless, and sensitive young people are drawn to the arts and humanities. A common theme in the humanities is reverence for art—a reverence crudely reinforced by a society which has discovered the commodity value of culture. The student finds "great" art painstakingly analyzed by teachers who are masters of academic method. If he is not satisfied with mere learning, the student may be tempted to transcend the analysis and identify with the projected image of the artist. Art raises the possibility that one is possessed of a nonintellectual, unmeasurable, mysterious *something* that defies all academic categories. Under the circumstances, it is natural for the artistic student to be overly impressed with the notion that art is inspired by irrational mental states—even to the point where he regards insanity as a divine visitation.

For the would-be artist, drugs are a magic product advertising the separation of art from talent, time, judgment, and work. One turns on, and one has Visions. One digs music and painting with drug-heightened attention, and one has Revelations. If one tries to paint or write under the influence of drugs, the results are invariably disorganized and disappointing. Still, one has somehow been "creative." All that is necessary to call oneself an artist is to replace palpable creation with the notion of "the creative experience."

The trouble with "the creative experience" is that anyone can have it. But for those who cannot produce art itself, the drug ideology offers membership in an artistic consumer elite.

I recently met a young engineer who feels greater rapport with his girl when both are high. Every night they turn on while watching a TV movie and "really dig it." The engineer feels that everyone should smoke pot. "When I go out in the world looking for friends, the first question I ask myself is, do they smoke? Because if they don't they look at me like I'm a drug addict."

The engineer insists that he turns on not for escape but for "insight—to learn things about myself." As an example of his insight, he states that "ordinarily I have a masochistic streak: I let people get away with saying things they shouldn't. But when I'm high, I know what to answer."

The engineer's girl friend is an art student who claims she paints better when high. "I can paint and take in everything going on in the room at the same time." She enjoys the fact that so many of her friends use drugs. "You feel you're privileged—you're part of an artists' community."

College drug use reaches a peak at big city art schools. It's worth noting that at the art colleges young people in training to become fashion illustrators and advertising directors are exposed to a highly pretentious milieu. They make contact with future artists—and form an alliance between art and advertising which has proved effective in bringing visual art, more than any other, into the consumer market place. To be hip in the art world, one must now consume the newest thing in art in the same way one consumes drugs—for the latest sensation. Like "creative experience," the fabrication of "pop" art is within reach of anyone. And art fashions, like drug fashions, offer their consumers the justification of an in-group ideology.

The American Dream

Ever since the discovery of the New World and the Frontier, Americans have been looking for an absolute truth. This truth is thought to be natural and good, yet often it is to be attained through technical developments. Our politicians reflect these assumptions whenever they resort to the apocalyptic view of history, in which the United States is to play a divinely ordained dramatic role in directing the "progress" of the rest of the world.

D. H. Lawrence once described Americans as "Some insisting on the plumbing, and some on saving the world: these being the two great American specialties." The LSD missionaries are out to do both at the same time—to save the world by tinkering with the internal plumbing. As in the drug ads, the idea is happiness and fulfillment through the ingestion of a synthesized additive. If drug evangelists combine proselytism with claims of mystic serenity, it's not because of any profound "paradox," but because they are, at bottom, American innocents.

Another American tradition—which can be encountered in any decent course in American literature—is the myth of the New Self. The myth is that a powerful experience can purge a hero of his past and release innate powers which have been hitherto suppressed by an unnatural society. The desire is to rid oneself entirely of fear and guilt. For the American student, drugs are the latest platform from which the New Self may be announced. The young user may rejoice in a mode of being which seems utterly to bypass his everyday problems in coming to terms with the world. He can occupy, for a while, "another plane in another sphere"—where everything depends upon himself and what he puts into his mouth.

Newness, by its nature, is temporary. Before long there may be a letdown, an impingement of the dreary "old" self who has survived somehow after all—then a need, as David puts it, for something to "shake" one. That something, for the modern student, is closer than the campus drugstore. It will be ready for him as often as he has to have it.

Eventually he may wonder why. Speaking of "insight"—as young "heads" are so prone to do—the deepest insight one could gain from drugs would be to discover, not one's essential greatness, but the reason one needed to take drugs in the first place. This knowledge comes from life rather than manufactured chemicals. As a matter of fact, there is a tendency for collegiate drug-users, such as David, to reach a peak and then abruptly leave the drug scene. But until an individual can understand his drug need in terms of his own psychology, drug use for him will continue to be one of those symptoms that perpetuates its causes.

STUDY QUESTIONS

1. What is the rhetorical effect of the way Larner begins and ends his essay?
2. Would you describe Larner's prose voice as one that speaks with authority? How is the authority established and maintained?
3. Do you believe he is correct in his account of why students try drugs?
4. The author observes that most psychiatrists are wary of dangerous reactions to the hallucinogens. What are some of these reactions?
5. What are popular views about the connection between the use of drugs and the understanding of poetry, music, and painting? What are Larner's opinions on this?

THE NEW

Paul Goodman ARISTOCRATS

Paul Goodman (1911–   ) was born in New York City. He received his B.A. from The City College of New York and his Ph.D. from the University of Chicago. An expert in city planning and the many problems inherent in urban growth, he has lectured at the Massachusetts Institute of Technology, the University of Pennsylvania, Western Reserve University, Columbia University, and the University of California. He has taught at the University of Chicago, New York University, and Black Mountain University. He is currently a practicing psychotherapist affiliated with the New York Institute for Gestalt Therapy. A regular contributor to journals and magazines, Mr. Goodman has also written a number of books. His early works include *Stop Light* (1942), a volume of poetry; and two novels, *The Grand Piano* (1942) and *State of Nature* (1945). He is coauthor with his brother of *Communitas* (1947, a work on city planning) and is author of *Gestalt Therapy* (1951). His recent books are *Structure of Literature* (1954) and *Growing Up Absurd* (1960). The latter has proved to be extremely popular, with recent sales exceeding 1000 copies a week.

Predictions about the future of America during the next generation are likely to be in one of two sharply contrasting moods. On the one hand, the orthodox liberals foresee a Great Society in which all will live in suburban comfort or the equivalent; given a Head Start and Job Training, Negroes will go to college like everyone else, will be splendidly employed and live in integrated neighborhoods; billboards will be 200 yards off new highways, and the arts will flourish in many Lincoln Centers. On the other hand, gloomy social critics, and orthodox conservatives, see that we are headed straight for 1984, when everyone's life will be regimented from the cradle to the grave by the dictator in Washington; administrative double talk and Newspeak will be the only language; Negroes will be kept at bay by the police (according to the social critics) or will be the pampered shock troops of demagogs (according to the conservatives); we will all be serial numbers; civil liberties and independent enterprise will be no more.

Yet these predictions have much in common. They assume the continuation of the same trends and attitudes that are now in full sway. There will be increasing centralization in decision making, increasing mass education as we now know it, a stepped-up rate of technical growth and a growing Gross National Product, and more use of a technological style—of "planning" or "social engineering," depending on one's bias—with heavy use of computers. These same premises are seen by some as enriching and great, and by others as menacing and empty.

Oddly, however, both kinds of prediction describe the play and leave out Hamlet; namely, the next generation itself, the young people who are going to be the heirs to all this greatness or the slaves of this social engineering. I have not seen a single forecast that takes into account that present high school and college students will be of some importance in shaping society 20 years from now. Commencement speakers are eager to pass on the torch and they seem to be sure that there are ready hands to receive it. Yet the evidence is that students are not at all happy with the present trends and attitudes, whether the prediction is gloomy *or* rosy. For instance, in 1956, surveys showed that college students admired and wanted to work in big corporations, but last year (at Harvard) more seniors opted for the Peace Corps than for careers in business. Allow me a small personal example: My book *Growing Up Absurd* sells 1000 copies a week, of which the majority, my publisher guesses, are bought by high school students. This gives one pause; I wouldn't have thought they could read the words. Maybe they can't, but they get the message, that the conditions of our society are too inhuman to grow up in. For collegians that message is dated; they take it for granted.

I do not intend to predict what the future might look like if we take young people into account. I don't know (although I give plenty of advice, which they disregard). What I want to show, however, is that point by point, with remarkable precision, articulate students—and an indeterminate number of others—*live, feel and think in direct opposition to the premises on which both the rosy and the gloomy predictions are based*. It is so in their community life, their ethics and their politics. If only because of sheer numbers, the temper of young people must make a difference for the future. And it is whistling in the dark to think that their opposition is a "generational revolt" that will be absorbed as they grow older and wiser, for it is endemic in our system of things. If the planners continue to treat this temper as if it did not exist, the result will be still deeper alienation and worse ultimate disruption. My experience in Washington, as a Fellow of the Institute of Policy Studies, is that social and educational planners have about as much information of what happens on college campuses as the State Department has about Vietnam.

Community: About 50 percent of all Americans are now under 26. Of the college-age group, nearly 40 percent go to college—there are 6,000,000 in 2000 institutions. Of the present collegians, it is estimated that five percent are in some activity of the radical youth movement, usually "left" but sometimes "right." This does not seem a big proportion, but it has increased at least tenfold in the last decade, and it and the number of its alumni will certainly increase even more rapidly in the next years. We are thus speaking of several million people.

More important, they are the leaders. Radical collegians are not only middle class but they are also disproportionately the best academically and from the most prestigious schools. Unlike Negro youth, who are now causing such turmoil, collegians are a major economic force, looming large among the indispensable inheritors of the dominant power in society. And although—or perhaps because—they do not share a common ideology but rather a common sentiment and style, in showdown situations like the troubles in Berkeley, they have shown a remarkable solidarity and a common detestation for the liberal center, crossing even the apparent chasm between extreme right and extreme left.

A chief reason for their solidarity and their increase in numbers is mass higher education itself. For most, going to college has little academic value—indeed, one of their shared sentiments is resistance to being academically processed for the goals of the "system." In my opinion, about 15 percent, instead of 40 percent, ought to be in colleges; the rest, including most of the bright, would be better educated in other environments. Nevertheless, *the major colleges and universities are, in fact, many hundreds of physical and social communities of young people, with populations of a few thousand to 25,000, sharing a subculture, propagandizing one another and learning to distrust anybody over 30. Such collections of youth are a phenomenon unique in history.*

Consider some details from San Francisco State College, where I was hired as a teacher by the Associated Students last spring. With 15,000 students, the Associated Students collect $300,000 annually in dues, more than half of which is free and clear and which they use for untraditional purposes. These purposes include organizing a tenants' league, helping delinquents in a reformatory, running a tutorial program for Negro and Mexican children (with 300 collegian tutors), sponsoring a weekly television program on KQED, running an "experimental college" with offbeat courses, and hiring their own professors. They apply on their own for institutional grants from the Ford Foundation and the Poverty Program. In the fall of 1966, the experimental college registered 1600 students!

Or consider the college press, with its fairly captive audience of a couple of million, many of them daily. In a few cases, e.g., Harvard and Columbia, publication has gone off campus and is not under the tutelage of "faculty advisors." Increasingly, college papers subscribe to news services and print (and edit) national and international news; and they also use syndicated material, like Art Buchwald, Jules Feiffer, Russell Baker. Occasionally, the college paper is the chief daily of its town (e.g., the Cornell *Sun*). More important, there is a national student press service that could be a powerfully effective liaison for mobilizing opinion on common issues. Last winter I wrote a fortnightly column on student matters for a tiny college in Vermont, which the enterprising editor at once syndicated to 50 other college papers. On this model there could spring up a system of direct support, and control, of students' "own" authors, just as, of course, they now indirectly support them through magazines whose main circulation is collegiate.

Nor are these young people properly called "youth." The exigencies of the American system have kept them in tutelage, doing lessons, till 23 and 24 years of age, years past when young industrial workers used to walk union picket lines or when farmers carried angry pitchforks, or young men are now drafted into the Army. Thus, another cause of their shared resentment is the foolish attempt to arrest their maturation and regulate their social, sexual and political activity.

More than other middle-class generations, these young live a good deal by "interpersonal relations" and they are unusually careless, in their friendships, about status or getting ahead. I do not mean that they are especially affectionate or compassionate—they are averagely so—but they have been soaked in modern psychology, group therapy, sensitivity training; and as a style they go in for direct confrontation and sometimes brutal frankness. Add to this the lack of embarrassment due to animally uninhibited childhood, for their parents, by and large, were permissive about thumbsucking, toilet training, masturbation, informal dress, etc. They are the post-Freudian generation in this country—their parents were analyzed from 1920 to 1940. The effect of all this psychology—for example, long sessions of mutual analysis or jabber about LSD trips—can be tiresome, at least to me; but it is fatal to suburban squeamishness, race and moral prejudice, and to keeping up appearances. Still another cause of resentment at the colleges is the impersonality and distance of the teachers and the big classes that make dialog impossible. Students are avid for dialog. Sometimes this looks like clamoring for "attention," as our statesmen say about the demonstrators, but it is really insisting on being taken seriously as troubled human beings.

Middle-class privacy also tends to vanish. An innovation of the Beats was the community use of one another's pads, and this spirit of sharing has persisted in off-campus university communities, which are very different from paternalistic dormitories or fraternity row. In big cities there are rapidly growing bohemian student neighborhoods, usually— if only for the cheaper rent—located in racially mixed sections. Such neighborhoods, with their own coffeehouses and headquarters for student political clubs, cannot be controlled by campus administration. In the famous insurrection of Berkeley, Telegraph Avenue could easily rally 3000 students, ex-students, wives and pals. (The response of the University of California administration has been, characteristically, to try to root up the student neighborhood with Federally financed urban renewal.)

Inevitably, sexual activity and taking drugs loom overlarge in the public picture: for, whereas unkempt hair, odd company and radical politics may be disapproved, sex and drugs rouse middle-class anxiety, a more animal reaction. The statistics seem to show, however, that quantitatively there are not many more sexual goings on than since the Twenties. The difference is that the climate has finally become more honest and unhypocritical. Sexuality is affirmed as a part of life rather than as the Saturday religion of fraternity gang bangs covered by being drunk. Since there is more community altogether, sex tends to revert to the normalcy of back rural areas, with the beautiful difference of middle-class prudence and contraceptives. (Probably, since there is less moralism, there are more homosexual acts, though not, of course, any increase of homosexuality as a trait of character.) In the more earnest meaning of sex, love and marriage, however, the radical young still seem averagely messed up, no better than their parents. There is no remarkable surge of joy or poetry—the chief progress of the sexual revolution, so far, has been the freer treatment of small children that I mentioned above. The conditions of American society do not encourage manly responsibility and moral courage in men, and we simply do not know how to use the tenderness and motherliness of women. The present disposition of the radical young is to treat males and females alike; in my observation, this means that the women become camp followers, the opposite of the suburban situation in which they are tyrannical dolls. I don't know the answer.

Certainly the slogan "Make love, not war"—carried mainly by the girls—is political wisdom, if only because it costs less in taxes.

The community meaning of the widespread use of hallucinogenic drugs is ambiguous. (Few students use addictives; again, they are prudent.) I have heard students hotly defend the drugs as a means of spiritual and political freedom, or hotly condemn them as a quietist opiate of the people, or indifferently dismiss them as a matter of taste. I am myself not a hippie and I am unwilling to judge. It seems clear that the more they take pot, the less they get drunk, but I don't know if this is an advantage or a disadvantage. (I don't get drunk, either.) Certainly there is a difference between the quiet socializing of marijuana and the alcoholic socializing of the fraternities, suburbs and Washington. Also, being illegal and hard to procure, the drugs create conspiracy and a chasm between those who do and those who don't. As usual, the drug laws, like other moral laws, fail to eradicate the vice they intend to eradicate, but they produce disastrous secondary effects.

The LSD cult, especially, must be understood as part of a wave of religiosity in young persons that has included Zen, Christian and Jewish existentialism, a kind of psychoanalytic yoga, and the magic of the Book of Changes. On the campus, a young Protestant chaplain—or even a Catholic—is often the center of radical activity, which may include a forum for psychedelic theory as well as peace and Negro rights. Certainly the calculating rationalism of modern times is losing its self-evidence; and it is not the end of the world to flip. Personally, I don't like it when people flip, it is eerie; I like people to be in touch, and I think the heads are mistaken when they think they are communicating. Also, in our overtechnological society, I am intensely suspicious of Dr. Tim Leary's formula to "turn on, tune in and drop out" by chemical means. Yet by and large, the public repression in this field is grossly disproportionate to the occasional damage that has been proved; and frankly, the burden of proof is the other way: If we do not want young people to live in harmless dreams, we have to provide something better than the settled arithmetical delusions of Mr. McNamara, not to speak of Herman Kahn, author of *On Thermonuclear War.*

The shagginess and chosen poverty of student communities have nuances that might be immensely important for the future. We must remember that these are the young of the affluent society, used to a high standard of living and confident that, if and when they want, they can fit in and make good money. Having suffered little pressure of insecurity, they have little psychological need to climb; just as, coming from respectable homes, they feel no disgrace about sitting a few nights in jail. By confidence they are aristocrats—en masse. This, too, is unique in history. At the same time, the affluent standard of living that they have experienced at home is pretty synthetic and much of it useless and phony; whereas their chosen poverty is not degraded but decent, natural and in many ways more comfortable than their parents' standard, especially if they can always corral obvious goodies such as hi-fi equipment and motorcycles. Typically, they tour Europe on nothing, sleeping under bridges; but if they get really hungry, they can drop in at American Express to pick up their mail. Most of the major satisfactions of life—sex, paperback books, guitars, roaming, conversation, games and activist politics—in fact, cost little.

Thus, this is the first generation in America selective of its standard of living. If this attitude became general, it would be disastrous for the expanding Gross National Product. And there is obvious policy and defiance in their poverty and shagginess. They have been influenced by the voluntary poverty of the beat movement, which signified withdrawal from the trap of the affluent economy. Finally, by acquaintance they experience the harsher tone of the involuntary poverty of the Negroes and Spanish Americans whose neighborhoods they visit and with whom they are friends.

In a recent speech, Robert Hutchins pointed out that business can no longer recruit the bright young. He explained this by the fact that the universities are rich and can offer competitive rewards. But I do not think this is the essence, for we have seen that at Harvard, business cannot compete even with the Peace Corps. The essence is that the old drive to make a *lot* of money has lost its magnetism. Yet this does not seem to mean settling for security, for the young are increasingly risky. The magnet is a way of life that has meaning. This is a luxury of an aristocratic community.

Ethics: The chief (conscious) drive of the radical young is their morality. As Michael Harrington, author of *The Other America,* has put it, "They drive you crazy with their morality," since for it they disregard prudence and politics, and they mercilessly condemn day-to-day casuistry as if it were all utterly phony. When politically minded student leaders, like the Students for a Democratic Society, try to engage in "tactics" and "the art of the possible," they may temporarily gain in numbers, but they swiftly lose influence and begin to disintegrate. Yet indignation or a point of honor will rally the young in droves.

Partly, the drive to morality is the natural ingenuousness of youth, freed of the role playing and status seeking of our society. As aristocrats, not driven by material or ulterior motives, they will budge for ideals or not at all. Partly their absolutism is a disgusted reaction to cynicism and the prevalent adult conviction that "Nothing can be done. You can't fight city hall. Modern life is too complex." But mostly, I think, it is the self-righteousness of an intelligent and innocent new generation in a world where my own generation has been patently stupid and incompetent. They have been brought up on a literature of devastating criticism that has gone unanswered because there is no answer.

The right comparison to them is the youth of the Reformation, of *Sturm und Drang,* and of Russia of the Seventies and Eighties, who were brought up on their own dissenting theologians, *philosophes* and intelligentsia. Let us remember that those students did, indeed, ultimately lead revolutions.

The philosophical words are "authenticity" and "commitment," from the existentialist vocabulary. And it cannot be denied that our dominant society is unusually inauthentic. Newspeak and double talk are the lingua franca of administrators, politicians, advertisers and the mass media. These official people are not even lying; rather, there is an unbridgeable chasm between the statements made "on the record" for systemic reasons or the image of the corporation, and what is intended and actually performed. I have seen mature graduate students crack up in giggles of anxiety listening to the Secretary of State expound our foreign policy; when I questioned them afterward, some said that he was like a mechanical man, others that he was demented. And most campus blowups have been finally caused by administrators' animal inability to speak plain. The students have faithfully observed due process and manfully stated their case, but the administrators simply cannot talk like human beings. At this point it suddenly becomes clear that they are confronting not a few radical dissenters but a solid mass of the young, maybe a majority.

Two things seem to solidify dissent: administrative double talk and the singling out of "ringleaders" for exemplary punishment. These make young people feel that they are not being taken seriously, and they are not.

In principle, "authenticity" is proved by "commitment." You must not merely talk but organize, collect money, burn your draft card, go South and be shot at, go to jail. And the young eagerly commit themselves. However, a lasting commitment is hard to achieve. There are a certain number of causes that are pretty authentic and warrant engaging in: Give Negroes the vote, desegregate a hotel or a bus, commute Chessman's sentence to the gas chamber, abolish grading and get the CIA out of the university, abolish HUAC, get out of Vietnam, legalize marijuana and homosexuality, unionize the grapepickers. But it is rarely the case that any particular authentic cause can really occupy the thought and energy of more than a few for more than a while. Students cool off and hop from issue to issue, then some become angry at the backsliders; others foolishly try to prove that civil liberties, for instance, are not so "important" as Negro civil rights, for instance, or that university reform is not so "important" as stopping the bombing of Hanoi. Others, disillusioned, sink into despair of human nature. And committed causes distressingly vanish from view at the June vacation, when the community disperses.

Shrewder psychologists among the young advocate getting involved only in what you "enjoy" and gravitate to—e.g., don't tutor unless you like kids—but this is a weak motive compared with indignation or justice.

The bother is that, except with a few political or religious personalities, the students' commitments do not spring from their own vocations and life ambitions; and they are not related in a coherent program for the reconstruction of society. This is not the fault of the students. Most of the present young have unusually little sense of vocation; perhaps 16 continuous years of doing lessons by compulsion has not been a good way to find one's identity. And there *is* no acceptable program of reconstruction—nobody has spelled it out—only vague criteria. Pathetically, much "definite commitment" is a self-deceptive way of filling the void of sense of vocation and utopian politics. Negroes, who are perforce really committed to their emancipation, notice this and say that their white allies are spiritually exploiting them.

It is a difficult period of history for the young to find vocation and identity. Most of the abiding human vocations and professions, arts and sciences, seem to them, and are (to a degree) corrupt or corrupted: law, business, the physical sciences, social work—these constitute the hated System. And higher education, both curriculum and professors, which ought to be helping them find themselves, also seems bought out by the System. Students know that something is wrong in their schooling and they agitate for university reform; but since they do not know what world they want to make, they do not know what to demand to be taught.

Politics: It is not the task of age 18 to 25 to devise a coherent program of social reconstruction; for instance, to rethink our uses of technology, our methods of management, our city planning and international relations. They rightly accuse us of not providing them a program to work for. A small minority—I think increasing—turns to Marxism, as in the Thirties; but the Marxist theorists have also not thought of anything new and relevant to overripe societies. Most radical students, in my observation, listen to Marxist ideological speeches with polite lack of interest—"they are empty, man, empty"—and they are appalled by Marxist political bullying. On the other hand, they are disgusted with official anticommunism. By an inevitable backlash, since they think all American official speech is double talk, they disbelieve that Communist states are worse than our own.

What the American young do know, being themselves pushed around, itemized and processed, is that they have a right to a say in what affects them. They believe in democracy, which they have to call "participatory democracy," to distinguish it from double-talk democracy. Poignantly, in their ignorance of American history, they do not recognize that they are Congregationalists, town-meeting democrats, Jeffersonians, populists. But they know they want the opportunity to be responsible, to initiate and decide, instead of being mere personnel. Returning from their term overseas, the first thousand of the Peace Corps unanimously agreed that exercising responsibility and initiative had been the most worthwhile part of their experience, and they complained that back home they did not have the opportunity.

The primary area for seeking democracy would be, one would imagine, the universities, for that is where the students are and are coerced. And the radical students, who, we have seen, are among the best academically, have campaigned for *Lernfreiheit*—freedom from grading, excessive examination, compulsory attendance at lectures and prescribed subjects—and also for the ancient privilege of a say in designing the curriculum and evaluating the teachers. But unfortunately, as we have also seen, the majority of students do not care about higher education as such and are willing to put up with it as it is. They are in college for a variety of extrinsic reasons, from earning the degree as a union card to evading the draft. There is no mass base for university reform.

So instead of working in their own bailiwick, activist students have mainly sought participatory democracy for poor people, organizing rent strikes, opposing bureaucratic welfare procedures, and so forth. But there is an inherent dilemma in this. Negroes claim, perhaps correctly, that middle-class whites cannot understand their problems; if Negroes are going to run their own show, they have to dispense with white helpers. The present policy of the Student Nonviolent Coordinating Committee is that Negroes must solve their own peculiar problems, which are the only ones they care about and know anything about, and let their young white friends attend to changing the majority society. There is something in this. Certainly one would have expected Northern students to get their heads broken in the cafeteria at Tulane or the University of Mississippi, where they could talk with their peers face to face, as well as on the streets of country towns. And white Southern liberals have desperately needed more support than they have gotten.

But pushed too far, the rift with the middle-class students consigns poor people to a second-class humanity. The young Negroes cannot do without the universities, for there, finally, is where the showdown, the reconstruction of society, will be—although that showdown is not yet. Consider: Some pressing problems are universal; the poor must care about them, e.g., the atom bomb. Many pressing problems are grossly misconceived if looked at at short range from a poor man's point of view; only a broad human point of view can save Negroes from agitating for exactly the wrong things, as they have agitated for educational parks, when what is needed in schooling is a small human scale. Also, there is something spurious in Negro separatism, for a poor minority in a highly technological society will not engineer the housing and manufacture the cars that they intend to use. Finally, in fact, the Negroes are, perhaps unfortunately, much more American than Negro. Especially in the North, they are suckers for the whole American package, though it makes even less sense for them than for anybody else. The Negro subculture that is talked up has about the same value as the adolescent subculture; it has vitality and it does not add up to humanity.

As in other periods of moral change, only the young aristocrats and the intellectuals can *afford* to be disillusioned and profoundly radical.

And in a high technology, only the students will be able to construct a program.

In their own action organizations, the young are almost fanatically opposed to top-down direction. In several remarkable cases, e.g., Tom Hayden, Bob Moses, Mario Savio, gifted and charismatic leaders have stepped down because their influence had become too strong. By disposition, without benefit of history, they are reinventing anarchist federation and a kind of Rosa Luxemburgian belief in spontaneous insurrection from below. In imitating Gandhian nonviolence, they do not like to submit to rigid discipline, but each one wants to make his own moral decision about getting his head broken. If the Army really gets around to drafting them, it will have its hands full.

All this, in my opinion, probably makes them immune to take-over by centralists like the Marxists. When Trotskyites, for instance, infiltrate an organization and try to control it, the rest go home and activity ceases. When left to their own improvisation, however, the students seem surprisingly able to mount quite massive efforts, using elaborate techniques of communication and expert sociology. By such means they will never get power. But, indeed, they do not want power, they want meaning.

Parallel Institutions: The operative idea in participatory democracy is decentralizing, to multiply the number who are responsible, initiate and decide. In principle, there are two opposite ways of decentralizing: either by dividing overcentralized organizations where it can be shown that decentral organization is more efficient in economic, social and human costs, or at least not too inefficient; or by creating new small enterprises to fill needs that big organizations neglect or only pretend to fulfill.

Obviously, the first of these, to cut the present structures down to human size, is not in the power of the young. But it happens that it does require a vast amount of empirical research and academic analysis to find if, where and how decentralizing is feasible; and in current American academic style, there is no such research and analysis. So on 150 campuses, I have urged students to work on such problems. They seem fascinated, but I do not know if they are coming across. (To say it wryly, there is a fine organization called Students for a Democratic Society, but it is not enough evident that they are scholars for a democratic society.)

The other way of decentralizing, by creating parallel enterprises, better suits the student zeal for direct action, and they have applied it with energy and inventiveness. They have set up a dozen little "free universities" that I know about—probably there are many others—in or next to established institutions, to teach in a more personal way and to deal with contemporary subjects that are not yet standard curriculum, e.g., Castro's Cuba, Psychedelic Experience, Sensitivity Training, Thea-

ter of Participation. Some of these courses are action sociology, like
organizing labor or community development. In poor neighborhoods,
students have established a couple of radio stations, to broadcast local
news and propaganda and to give poor people a chance to talk into a
microphone. They have set up parallel community projects to combat
the welfare bureaucracy and channelize needs and grievances. In the
South, they have helped form "freedom" political machines, since the
established machines are lily white. They have offered to organize international service projects as an alternative to serving in the Army. (I have
not heard of any feasible attempts at productive cooperatives or planned
urban communities of their own, and students do not seem at all interested in rural reconstruction, though they should be.)

Regarded coldly, such parallel projects are pitifully insignificant
and doomed to pass away like so many little magazines. And, in fact, at
present, the most intense discussions among student radicals, causing
deep rifts, are on this theme. Some, following older thinkers like Michael
Harrington and Bayard Rustin (director of a civil rights and poverty
research institute) want to engage in "coalition politics," to become
effective by combining with the labor unions and leftish liberals in the
Democratic Party, to get control of some of the Federal money and to
campaign for A. Philip Randolph's (president of the Brotherhood of
Sleeping Car Porters) 185-billion-dollar budget to eliminate poverty.
This involves, of course, soft-pedaling protests for peace, community
action and university reform. Recent history, however, has certainly not
favored this point of view. Federal money is drying up and radical
coalition people who go to work for the Government get fired; nor is it
evident that, if it were spent for liberal social engineering, Randolph's
budget would make a better world—even if the money were voted.

Others, for example one wing of SDS, say that the use of participatory democracy and parallel institutions is not for themselves but to
consolidate people into a political party; it is not to provide models for
the reconstruction of society but, as a kind of initiation rite, to get into
the big game of numbers and power. This seems to me to give up on the
authenticity, meaning and beautiful spontaneous motivation that have, so
far, been the real power of the radical young and the source of what
influence they have had. And it presupposes that the young know where
they want to go as a party, rather than in what direction they *are* going
as a movement. But they don't know; they (and we) will have to find out
by conflict.

In my opinion, it is better to regard the parallel institutions as a
remarkable revival of a classical American movement, populism, that
seemed to have been dead. It is now reviving on the streets and among
citizens who storm city hall because they feel they have been pushed
around; in such a movement, the young are natural leaders. The princi-

ple of populism, as in 1880, is to get out from under the thumb of the barons and do it yourself. And perhaps the important step is the first one, to prove that self-help is possible at all. There may be hope of bringing to life many of our routinized institutions if we surround them with humanly meaningful enterprises. The most telling criticism of an overgrown institution is a simpler one that works better.

This was John Dewey's vision of the young 60 years ago: He thought of an industrial society continually and democratically renewed by its next generation, freely educated and learning by doing. Progressive education, free-spirited but practical, was a typical populist conception. And it is useful to regard the student movement as progressive education at the college and graduate-school level; for at this level, learning by doing begins to be indistinguishable from vocation, profession and politics. It is the opposite of the mandarin establishment that now rules the country, and of the social engineering that is now called education. Maybe this time around, the populist movement will succeed and change what we mean by vocation, profession and politics.

So, describing radical students—and I do not know how many others—we have noticed their solidarity based on community rather than ideology, their style of direct and frank confrontation, their democratic inclusiveness and aristocratic carelessness of status, caste or getting ahead, their selectivity of the affluent standard of living, their effort to be authentic and committed to their causes rather than merely belonging, their determination to have a say and their refusal to be processed as standard items, their extreme distrust of top-down direction, their disposition to anarchist organization and direct action, their disillusion with the system of institutions, and their belief that they can carry on major social functions in improvised parallel enterprises.

Some of these traits, in my opinion, are natural to all unspoiled young people. All of them are certainly in contradiction to the dominant organization of American society. By and large, this is as yet the disposition of a minority, but it is the only articulate disposition that has emerged; and it has continually emerged for the past ten years. It is a response not merely to "issues," such as civil rights or Vietnam, but to deeply rooted defects in our present system, and it will have an influence in the future. It will make for a more decent society than the Great Society and it may well save us from 1984.

STUDY QUESTIONS

1. Goodman notes that some of the traits of the new aristocrats are natural to all unspoiled young people. To what traits does he refer? Do you agree with him?

2.   What are the characteristics of the new aristocrats? Why do they prefer
      poverty?
3.   What is the attitude of the new aristocrats toward college?
4.   What does Goodman mean by interpersonal relationships? What rhe-
      torical method does he use to explain these relationships?
5.   According to Goodman, what in our society has helped create the new
      aristocracy?
6.   This essay originally appeared in *Playboy*. In what ways is this written
      for the *Playboy* audience?

Mark Schorer   **TO THE WIND**

Mark Schorer (1908–   ) was born in Sauk City, Wisconsin. He
received his A.B. and Ph.D. from the University of Wisconsin,
and his A.M. from Harvard University. He has taught in the
English departments at Dartmouth College, Harvard University,
and at present is Professor of English at the University of California at Berkeley. He is the author of many scholarly articles and a
number of books, both fiction and nonfiction. Some of his books
include *A House Too Old* (1935), *The Hermit Place* (1941), *The
State of Mind* (1947), *William Blake: The Politics of Vision*
(1946), *The Story* (1950), *The Wars of Love* (1954), *Sinclair
Lewis: An American Life* (1961). He has been a Fulbright
Scholar and a Guggenheim Fellow.

At twenty-three, with a particular kind of education and experience, I did not know that the struggle with guilt is endless, and when I
found myself embroiled in agonies of rationalization, the drama was
short and factitious. If there is no other guilt, there is always the failure
of imagination, which, among men, perhaps only Christ eluded.

At twenty-three, without any of the reasons one may legitimately
have at fifty, I felt that childhood was the best time in life, and with
empty, griefless eyes, I would look nostalgically back on my childhood as
I imagined it. Only then, I thought, were you really free, without
burdens; and thinking so, I would lapse into a reverie in which the
world wavered into unreality and I found myself vividly reliving some
trivial episode of my youth. Then I would feel that I was not merely
remembering the past as something remote and vague, but actually

living it, living through it as fully as the child had lived himself. Mistaking sentiment for sensuousness, I thought that I went through the past like a boy across a meadow in the sun, feeling the grass under the bare soles of his feet, the moist earth, the warm sun on his head, and in his heart the unknown song that we pretend a child forever sings.

I was remembering such a meadow when Jared Smith came to my office for the third time. A creek ran through the meadow, winding and turning, clear water running between steep banks of black earth, with shallow places where you could build a dam. I remembered a day when I followed this creek to its mouth at the river, wandering all of an afternoon along its banks in the long grass of the meadow, the earth moist and the sun warm.

Then Smith came in again, looking more grave than before. I didn't take him seriously. Too much of this sort of thing went on all of the time, and you came to expect it. Only most students were less persistent than Smith. This was the third time he had come about it, and I had grown increasingly impatient with him, so that now his state of near-hysteria did not move me. And if it had, there would still have been the fact that I could do nothing about it. His grades showed a certain average and I had turned that in for him; now the semester was over and the matter closed. Smith thought that if he could only make me see how important the thing was to him it would be easy enough for me to call someone up and say, "I've made an error. Jared Smith should have had a B instead of a C."

For the third time I tried to show him that this was impossible and I went over all his grades again, and all he kept saying was, "I see that, sir; I'm sure a C is exactly what I earned; but don't *you* see—"

Then he launched out into the whole tale again: he was a swimmer and he had given up swimming in order to put more time on his work; he broke with his fraternity in the middle of the term because it took up too much of the time that he wanted to give to his studies; he had sacrificed everything to studying and he had done well in everything except my course, but the C I gave him was enough to keep him out of the honorary society which was the only evidence he would ever have for his achievement.

"In high school they always thought I was stupid and I wanted to show them; I've *got* to have the grade because I've *got* to show them. You see, sir, they always thought I didn't have a brain at all, and now I've got to, I've *simply got to*—"

For the first time I began to see what an intense person he was, and at another time it might have surprised me, for I had come to think of him as a rather stolid youth. But now I was frankly bored. You read fifty or a hundred freshmen themes every week for nine months in the year and you soon find yourself without much interest in any one of your students; and you don't pay much attention to any individual's writing unless the student comes to you and takes it up with you himself. Smith had never asked for a conference, or even for any kind of casual assistance. Now I had gone over the whole matter three times and had tried each time to keep my patience, told him that I did think he was a high B student but that his writing simply didn't show it, that since the middle of the term it had been down to C and less almost consistently. Each time I said, "If you'd come to me before, we could have gone over your themes and perhaps straightened out your difficulty, but it's too late now to do anything about it except get the B next term. If you like, I'll see to it that you get another instructor, that is, if you think you'd do better with someone else—"

Against this he protested. "I know you've been fair with me, sir, but that isn't the point. The point is that you won't see now how important it is that I get a B. It means more than anything ever has, I've simply got to get it—"

I said again that he overemphasized grades, but that even if I agreed that making the honorary society was so important, I couldn't help him.

Finally he seemed to get the point. He looked at me steadily and then suddenly all the tenseness went from his body and he slumped down in the chair by my desk. He sat there for some minutes, completely dejected, staring at the floor, and at last got up and said, "All right. I'm sorry I bothered you. Thank you," and went out.

I haven't described him at all or tried to put down much about him beyond the facts of that last interview, because after he went out of my office that day, I never saw him again. And from this point on, the story is not Smith's but mine.

Late in the next afternoon a boy whom I had never seen before came rushing into my office. "You know Jared Smith?" he cried, and I, knowing somehow at once what had happened, feeling everything inside me contract in a spasm of faintness, said, "Yes, of course. Why?"

The boy stood with his mouth open, panting. "Sit down," I said.

At last it came. "His mother sent me. He committed suicide this afternoon. It's going to be in the papers—your name too. She asked me to say that the story didn't come from her and that she doesn't hold you responsible in any way."

I took hold of the edge of my desk and forced myself to say what seemed to be the most important thing at that moment, "Of course, I can't feel responsible."

A look of pain crossed the boy's blond face. He was quite young and very distressed. He said, "It's awful. It's too awful to think about!"

"Lord, yes!" I said. "You knew him well?"

He nodded.

"How did he do it?"

"Gas. There wasn't anyone at home. His mother was down-town at the movies. She came home and found him on the kitchen floor."

"Lord!"

I walked over to the window, looked down at the campus, and thought of the boy's body stretched out dead on a kitchen floor and gas still hissing from the stove. I felt myself struggling against something, I didn't know what or why, and wanted to turn round and tell his friend that I wasn't to blame, that nothing in the whole business could touch me. I did turn round, but I spoke quietly. "I'm terribly sorry. The whole thing is dreadful and please tell his mother that I can't say how sorry I am. But of course I'm *not* responsible. Any teacher is likely to have this sort of thing happen. Sometimes you can't possibly tell which students are hypersensitive, which hysterical—"

The look in the boy's face made me see that I was trying to defend myself (and before he spoke I asked myself, "Against what?"), and then he said, "He wasn't hysterical. I think you might have seen that he was sensitive." Scorn came into his eyes before he added, "But no one thinks you're to blame," and turned away from me.

Yet, when he looked back, his face was only sorrowful, his eyes bleached with loss, and when he got up to leave he offered me his hand. I thought for a second that I was going to lose my hold on the situation. Some gagged voice inside me was trying to protest that I didn't deserve this and that I couldn't be blamed. I thought that in the next moment I should be blubbering out that protest, and yet, when I took the boy's hand something else made me cold, almost rude. I said, "Thanks for coming. It was good of Mrs. Smith to send you. I don't mind the papers' running the story, because of course no one would blame me. Tell his mother how sorry I am. If she'd care to see me, I'd like very much to call." We looked at each other. His eyes were cold again, chilled by my voice.

"Good-bye," he said, and fled out as he had come, half-stumbling.

When you are young, I would keep thinking, remembering, you are free. I would think in the next three days (at night especially, and always remembering), when you are young you don't have to face such things, and that is the best time. Waking in the night suddenly, feeling the presence of that boy in the room, in the shadows, somewhere in the hiding dark, I would remember such an incident as this:

I am quite young—six or seven—and after supper one evening (it is summer; in the marshes along the river the frogs are setting up their monotonous croaking, soothing, comforting, a steady sound in the night

*that stabilizes the dark and makes it a friend) I leave the family assem-
bled at table and go into a little-used parlor. I must be very tired—from a
day of running in the bright, protecting sun—for I lie down on a sofa in
the dark of the parlor (and this I seem never to have done before), and
in the sleep that follows I hear voices and confusion and I have the
feeling that there are many people somewhere near; but the voices are
like the comforting croaking of the frogs, and I do not wake for a time,
until abruptly I am snatched out of sleep and I find myself in my father's
arms, and then in my mother's (and she is weeping with relief) and I see
the faces of my brother and sister, looking at me with something like
awe. Then slowly I awake, I see more people in the room, and I know
that outside the house half the town is assembled. Then, from a mixed
report from the whole family (breathless, broken, excited, relieved, all of
it mingled with weeping and laughing, with kisses and quick embraces)
I gather that I have been lost, that the whole town has been aroused,
that for the two hours I have been asleep in the little-used parlor, where
no one thought to look beyond a desperate glance into the dark, the
search has been going on. Then all of us go out on the front porch and I
am shown and the whole thing delights me. My mother still weeps
beside me, remembering her fright in the midst of her happiness and
gratitude.*

This was no new memory, suddenly recollected. It was part of a
childhood that I lived with constantly, always there, always somehow
adequate, where the memory of lying in a sun-bright meadow with the
steady drone of bees in clover in my ears was enough to soften any blow.
And so now again in those three days, those three nights especially, I
found myself going back, not searching and yet remembering. In bed,
with the ghost of that boy somewhere in the room, powerful against me,
I remembered this:

*Another summer day, late in the afternoon, and I am walking with
an aunt to the cemetery a mile out of the village. On the way we pass
a field of buckwheat, and my aunt stops in the path for a moment. "Buckwheat," she says, her arm lifted, and moves on, the flower-filled basket
on her arm swinging a little as she walks, bumping now and again
against her hip. At the cemetery we attend to the graves of relatives,
snipping grass with the shears from the basket, pulling up weeds, arranging flowers under white headstones pink in the low summer sun,
and when we start back to the village it is almost dusk. The air is very
quiet now and cooler, the dust of the day settled. Once more we pass the
buckwheat field and now, with a start, both of us smell in the air an
incredible sweetness. We stop again and breathe the perfume of the
buckwheat, stand still for perhaps five minutes—and then move on toward the village, marked in the dusk by a dozen yellow-lighted windows, friendly, home.*

But now, in the three dark nights, these memories were not strong. In the struggle that went on between the part of my brain that brought them up and the part that knew the boy was in the room, a thin ghost, pale, unhappy, accusing, the memories lost, until, on the third night, I found myself abruptly awake, sitting erect in my bed, perspiring, a scream that must have been mine echoing in my ears. In my fright I knew that I was helpless, that there was no escape from it, nothing with which to fight against it. Then my fear (and what was I fearing?) ebbed away, and I lay down again in the darkness and thought that now the boy was buried and that on the next day I would call on his mother. I would return the packet of his themes—the themes I had not dared to read again for fear that now I should see in them a whole cycle of hysteria that I had missed before, perhaps from careless reading—and then I would be done with the whole thing.

I fell asleep again. And next morning my childhood seemed far away. Now I remembered winter nights before the fire and the quiet sound of my father's voice reading aloud, but I *remembered* them only, as one remembers an image or a picture, not as something one is actually in. I remembered a pool where you fished for small perch, and a path leading up over a birch-covered hill and down to a strip of sandy beach by the river. But in these memories there was the threat of the end of something.

It was afternoon and time to go to the mother. Twice I had taken the rubber band from the packet of themes, twice brought myself to the point of reading them, but now, having decided, I stood by my desk and snapped the band firmly on the papers. I thought that if I read them and found nothing there—I remembered a theme called "War" (Jared Smith had been a pacifist) and another called "My Religious Views"—then I should be free and certain. But if I did find something there, some growing hysteria, some increasing despair (what *had* he said in the theme called "My Religious Views"?) then I might never be free. And I decided that I would rather be uncertain and slowly forget than know, and perhaps never be able to forget.

The mother let me into the apartment herself. She was a large woman, heavy and strong-looking, standing before me in the dark hall a great hulk of strength. I told her who I was and she said, "Oh-h-h," with a kind of long sigh, and then, "Please come in."

The room was all shadows and the windows were full of the gray beginning of the winter evening. The woman pulled a chair out of a corner and said, "Please sit down." Then she lit a lamp so that the light fell on me, and she stood over me, looking down, and said finally, "I didn't think of you as such a young man. I thought of you as somehow older. From Jared's accounts I thought that you'd been teaching for a long time. He felt at the end that you were treating him perfunctorily, as if every student were just another student and not a human being to you—any longer. But that could be true of the very young as well as of the older, couldn't it?"

She smiled and sat down across from me, her eyes quizzical and interested. It was almost as if I had come to have tea with her, as if in a moment we would begin to talk about literature. Her composure as she sat there made me feel my weakness.

I said, "Try to understand. We meet perhaps a hundred students a week, and we read a hundred themes, and it's difficult to do much with them individually. Especially if they don't come to you. He never did. I hardly knew him."

She leaned forward, concerned and apologetic. "Oh, I do understand that—quite! I didn't mean—"

"No, of course not. It was good of you to send the other boy to tell me. It would have been a blow if I'd just read about it in the papers or heard about it suddenly without some warning."

"Yes," she said. "I knew that."

"I've brought his themes. I thought you'd like to keep them. I can't tell you how upset I am about this."

"But, child," she said, smiling again. "I know you're not to blame. I know you couldn't have done anything about that grade. I told Jared so—"

"It isn't the grade," I said. "It's not having known him. It's not having seen in him the possibilities of the kind of hysteria that must have been behind his act. I should have seen that—if it was there. I certainly didn't. And now I don't know if it was there or not. I haven't had the courage to read his themes again, fearing that it might be. . . . Here they are." I leaned forward and gave them to her. She put them in her lap and folded her hands over them. I could see how calm she was by the steady rise and fall of her bosom, by the quiet hands in her lap.

Outside it had begun to snow very lightly. Through the window and the thin veil of snow I could see across a gray field to a bare tree standing beside a wooden fence, its empty branches reaching up into the dreary sky. I felt myself wavering away from the room and the woman across from me, to another tree in another place, an elm heavily laden with leaves, with great strong branches, with white clouds and a blue sky above it, and high in the tree somewhere, a platform with a boy lying on his stomach, reading, lost in the pages of a book, in the fabulous blue of the sky, in the almost mythical intricacies of branch and green, green leaf.

But the woman's voice wove itself into the myth (for now I knew that it was a myth, a dream of bliss that had never been, that could certainly never be again) and drew me from the imagined tree to the real tree and the dreary landscape outside, to the shadowy room, and to her hands, symbols of her quiet. She was saying, ". . . and of course, you must not let this disturb you, it might have happened to anyone. It was the merest chance that it happened to you. I hope that you will be able to see it that way. . . ."

"Yes, it might have happened to anyone else. But someone else might have seen what I failed to see, might have thought of Jared Smith as a person who was living too, who was alive, not just a hand that wrote themes, but a human being, with desires and a life to live. . . ."

(*The green of the tree, the fabulous strength of its branches, and the lost boy lost in the legend!*)

. . . with a home to go to and a childhood to remember, with burdens to bear (he bore them!) and a manhood to come to (he came to it!) . . . for if Jared Smith had ever had a childhood, he had put it behind him. He knew that it was no dream that he would meet in the hissing gas; he knew that in breathing in those fumes he was not losing himself in an impossible bliss but was taking on his burden and coming into his manhood.

The quiet voice again, ". . . always unstable, really, highly-strung, neurotic, I suppose, taking his disappointments terribly hard . . . no sense of proportion at all. . . . It was something I always feared. . . ."

Outside, the barren tree was lost in the winter evening. I got up. "I must go. It's late."

The mother rose with me. She put the packet of themes on a table and walked into the hall with me. I struggled into my coat. Then she put out her hand. "Thank you for coming."

I took her hand. It was cold. I said, "You're wonderful. Your composure—"

I felt her hand tighten in mine. She struggled to speak, and then, in a sudden, fearful sob, her voice was drowned in grief. Her whole body shook in a spasm of weeping as she sat abruptly on a little bench in the hall, weeping violently, sobs torn from her body with a fearful violence. She clamped her hands together between her knees and, swaying back and forth on the bench, spoke between her sobs, "Oh-h-h," (the long sigh tragic now) "I loved him, I loved him . . . you don't know, you don't *know* . . . there have been terrible moments . . . *you don't know!*"

The weeping of a frail, small woman I could have borne. But the racking violence of the grief in this woman, large and strong, as she sat rocking back and forth in the gloom, was more than I could bear. For a moment I had an impulse to share her grief, in the same violent sobbing to relieve myself in exhausting tears. But the second impulse was to flee, to leave her behind, to avoid the confession that tears from me would mean.

I opened the door and went out. In the street I ran through the snow and kept my head up, so that the wind could strike my face.

I ran blindly through the streets in no direction at all, and ran until my feet dragged, and yet would not stop. I pressed my eyes shut against the wind and went stumbling through drifts of snow that the sharpening wind was piling across the sidewalks. It was cold and the wind was biting, but I did not feel it. At last I came to a church, and saw it towering up into the sky, blacker than the night. I stood looking up at its great doorway and its steeple, and without thought I climbed its steps and sat down in the wide stone doorway, out of the wind. I had never been in the church, but out of some remote time I remembered nuns moving quietly across an altar, lighting tall candles, suffusing the white, glistening altar with a luminous warmth, giving to the stone images of pedestaled saints a soft, deceptive life. I had never knelt in a church, but now I thought that if I went in and knelt on a rail worn into grooves with many kneelings, if I could bury my head in my arms and empty my ears of the sound of weeping, I should find a penitent's peace. Then I began to say, "I am not to blame, God, I am *not*, I am *not* . . ." but no such peace came, and I wondered what I should do with this blame which was not mine but which I could not lose.

I thought of the confessional inside, at one side of the altar. If I could go in there and confess, and be forgiven, then I should be free again. *Confess! Confess!* something cried, some voice from the lost years, from the fabulous tree, from the fires on winter nights, some voice that came like the wind, sweeping across the sunny meadows, rippling the water of a child's dammed creek, *Confess!*

If I could confess, pour out my sins, empty myself of this pain . . . if I could!

Confess! Confess! the voice whistled, blowing through the branches of the unknown, the mythical tree, driving great billows of white cloud over a dream-blue sky.

But what? Confess what?

The voice answered (sadly now, soughing through the branches), *Confess . . . confess . . .*

But what? what?

Then, like an echo, weakly, from afar: *Confess* . . .

Yes, yes, but *what?*

And then the voice did not answer (*Oh, now the branches of the tree are bare and still, no longer the voice like the wind in the marvelous tree!*) and the silence tore me from that dream. I sat in the doorway, straining forward to hear an answer. But there was none and, suddenly ashamed and sobered, I leaned back against the door.

Something was ending. The desire to confess was but imagining that tree with its wonderful foliage that had never been. But the tree was dead, its branches bare, and all the lost years were dead, and the voice from the years was dead with them.

Then something had ended.

I went down the steps. The wind, sharper now than ever, came with a blast up the street, sweeping the snow before it. I stood in the empty street and let it blow at me and through me, blow the ashes of the years away into the dark sky.

Then I started back through the cold night, shivering, and re-solved to go back to the woman's house. Something had ended, and I could go back to her and say that the blame was mine and that I took it, that, like her son, I had found a place to lay the burden.

The wind blew strong, scattering the years across the sky.

I went back. But nothing ends. We do not grow this way, in moments. And these moments, when self-righteousness hardens, are really the most treacherous of all. Then we exchange one naïveté for another, one dream for another dream. I had achieved the new shutters of a half-apprehended experience, the blinkers of an unreal moral cour-age.

Yet how was I to know, then, that the years as I imagined them scattering across the sky were as unreal as Shelley's dead and gaudy leaves of good?

STUDY QUESTIONS

1. Why did the author elect to tell the story in the first person instead of the third person? What is to be gained in this story by the first per-son point of view?
2. What kind of boy was Jared? What are the sources in the story that give us information about Jared?
3. Was the young instructor justified in his actions in regard to Jared?
4. What feeling does the author expect the reader to have toward the young instructor? How is this indicated in the story?
5. What function do the flashback memories of the young instructor have in the story?
6. In the last two paragraphs, what does the young instructor tell us he has learned from the experience?

SECTION 6 | POPULAR CULTURE

"The Winter of Our Discontent"

HOW CULTURALLY
ACTIVE ARE
Elmo Roper **AMERICANS?**

Elmo Roper (1900–   ) was born in Hebron, Nebraska. He attended the University of Minnesota and the University of Edinburgh, and holds four honorary degrees. His distinguished record during World War II included service with the Office of Facts and Figures and the Office of Strategic Services. From 1935 to 1950 he was research director for the Fortune Survey of Public Service. The famed marketing consultant has taught at Columbia and serves as editor-at-large for the *Saturday Review*. His books include *You and Your Leaders* (1958).

In an era when culture is being promoted with all the enthusiasm once reserved for breakfast cereal and we are being reminded daily that ignorance is obsolete, how "cultural" are Americans? Where does learning rank in our range of interests?

The answers to some questions recently asked of a cross-section of adult Americans shed some light on our intellectual and cultural involvement. To begin with, respondents were offered a list of subjects and asked to name those in which they had "a good deal of interest." The results appear below:

Religion	49%
Sports	47
Music	46
Politics and government	40
International affairs	37
Cooking	36
Home decoration	35
History	22
Science	20
Literature	19
Art	13
No opinion	7

Reprinted from *Saturday Review*, XLIX, May 14, 1966 by permission of the author.

Clearly, the egghead still has a long way to go before he replaces the baseball player as a national hero. Religion, sports, and music command the broadest appeal and top the list of interests. Politics and international affairs, interests that for various people have varying degrees of intellectual content, barely edge out the frankly down-to-earth concerns of home and kitchen. And at the very bottom lie the clearly intellectual and cultural subjects (with the exception of music, which may or may not reflect as deep a cultural interest), each mentioned by less than a quarter of the people interviewed: history by 22 percent, science by 20 percent, literature 19 percent, with art trailing off at 13 percent.

The next question inquired how often people read books that they felt would "advance their knowledge or education in some way." Twenty-two percent replied "frequently," 29 percent said they did so "occasionally," and 46 percent said "rarely" or "never." Another question found that 35 percent had less than twenty-five books in the home, and another 35 percent between twenty-five and 100, with only 27 percent owning more than 100 books (3 percent didn't know). Other questions also were asked about newspaper and magazine reading, and educational achievement.

Who, then, are the culturally and intellectually involved? Needless to say, the various indices do not all work in the same direction. While the heavy book *readers* are apt to be found among the young (20–34), the heaviest book *ownership* comes at a later age (35–55). Interest in international affairs goes up with age; interest in science is higher with youth. Among the intellectually involved, traditional sex differences in interests are very much in evidence, with women leaning toward such subjects as art and literature, men toward science and politics.

But perhaps the most interesting difference is that women, particularly college-educated women, have *more* interests than men. On the list of interests, seven items were singled out as subjects of a "good deal of interest" by 50 percent or more of college women. Among college men, only three items elicited that degree of interest. Also, the low point of intellectual interest for college women is science, which nevertheless is called interesting by 24 percent. The cultural "low" of college men is art, which at 18 percent is comparable with their interest in the female realm of home decorating (16 percent) and cooking (10 percent).

To get a rough measure of the general level of cultural and intellectual activity in the population, a scale was developed on which each respondent was given a score. Respondents were given one point each for such activities as regular reading of two or more newspapers or "fairly regular" reading of any leading news magazine or magazines with intellectual content such as *Harper's*, the *New Yorker*, or *Saturday Review;* one point each for expressing a "good deal of interest" in politics and government, international affairs, art, history, science or literature; five points each for "frequent" reading of books to advance knowledge or having more than 100 books in the home; two points for attending college; five points for graduating; and five points for taking academic, business or professional courses since graduating from college—with a maximum possible score of thirty-five points.

Using this measure of what might be loosely described as the "level of cultural activity," respondents fell into four main groups. Fifty-one percent received scores of from zero to three, and might be described as the "culturally inert." Another 26 percent received scores of from four to nine, and might therefore be considered "fairly inactive" culturally. Thirteen percent received scores of from ten to fifteen, and might be described as "fairly active." Only 10 percent received scores over fifteen (out of a possible thirty-five), thereby gaining the description of "culturally active"—the term is relative!

What is the relationship between cultural activity and formal education? If you're culturally active, does it mean you've been to college? And if you've been to college, are you thereby culturally active?

The answer to the first question is, by and large, yes. Only 1 percent of grade school people and only 4 percent of the high school educated fell into the culturally active category, whereas 26 percent of those who had had some college and 62 percent of people with college degrees received culturally active scores (abetted, of course, by the credit given for college in their scores).

But the answer to the second question is another thing. Before everyone who's been to college starts resting on his cultural laurels, thinking of the great gap that separates him from the lowly people who make up the rest of the population, let him take a look at the ranking of interests by those with college backgrounds:

Has a good deal of interest in:

International affairs	60%
Politics and government	59
Music	56
Sports	53
Religion	49
Literature	39
History	37
Science	36
Home decoration	36
Cooking	31
Art	26

Political and international events replace religion, sports and music as the prime interests of the college educated. But pure cultural and intellectual interests still cluster, along with cooking and home décor, at the bottom of the list. Asked how often they read edifying books, 44 percent of college educated people answered "frequently"—which means that a majority read to learn infrequently after they leave the academic groves. Asked about book ownership (an easier test than book reading, and the books could be about anything), nearly one quarter (23 percent) of the college educated had less than fifty books in their homes, and just slightly over half (56 percent) owned more than 100 books.

All in all, it must be said that intellectual and cultural activity is still distinctly a minority taste. A college education is no guarantee of developed cultural or intellectual interests, although it certainly makes such interests more probable. In our national rush to get more and more people to college, it should perhaps be kept in mind that half the people who have gotten there show only minor intellectual after-effects. Regarding the other half who can be described as culturally and intellectually involved, the most important question is one that can not be answered by a survey. It is the depth and quality of that involvement.

Some years ago I wrote, "There is an urgent need—in fact a national survival need—for invigorating intellectual life, for upgrading the general regard for intellectual excellence. The United States must experience an intellectual renaissance or it will experience defeat. The time cannot be far off—if indeed it is not already here—when the *strength* of a nation, measured in terms of any kind of world competition, will depend less on the number of its bombs than on the number of its learned men."

The statement is equally valid today. Unquestionably, there have been changes in recent years in our attitude toward the intellectual life. But the changes have not gone far enough. There is no upsurge of intellectual interest in the young—except in the field of science. And too many people who consider themselves educated have really just gone through the motions. The question that should most concern our educators is not how far they can spread learning but how deep it goes.

STUDY QUESTIONS

1. Which of the subjects in Roper's list does he consider "cultural"? Are there any subjects you would add to the list?
2. Why does Roper make a distinction between book *owners* and book *readers*? Account for the fact that the heavy book readers are between the ages of 20 and 24.
3. Roper lists three magazines "with intellectual content": *Harper's*, the *New Yorker*, and *Saturday Review*. In your campus library, locate a copy of each of these magazines and decide whether or not you agree with him.

4.   Does Roper in any way suggest that his rating scale is not an accurate measure of what it is supposed to measure?

5.   What conclusions does Roper draw from his survey? Can you suggest other conclusions?

Frank Lloyd Wright   TALIESIN

Frank Lloyd Wright (1869–1959) was born at Richmond Center, Wisconsin. He has been called "the greatest of all architects" as a result of the nearly 500 structures he designed and saw completed between 1890 and 1959. He was educated by serving as chief assistant to famed Chicago architect, Louis H. Sullivan. Founder of the "Prairie School" of architecture, he was first successful in Europe, particularly in Germany, where his works were published in 1910. For six years he lived in Tokyo, the site of one of his most famous structures—The Imperial Hotel. Among his other works are New York's Guggenheim Museum and the Johnson and Son administration building and tower. His books include *Modern Architecture* (1931), *An Autobiography* and *The Disappearing City* (1932), *Architecture and Modern Life* (1937), *An Organic Architecture* (1939), *A Testament* (1957), and *The Natural House* (1959).

Taliesin was the name of a Welsh poet, a druid-bard who sang to Wales the glories of fine art. Many legends cling to that beloved reverend name in Wales.

Richard Hovey's charming masque, "Taliesin," had just made me acquainted with his image of the historic bard. Since all my relatives had Welsh names for their places, why not Taliesin for mine? . . . Literally the Welsh word means "shining brow."

This hill on which Taliesin now stands as "brow" was one of my favorite places when as a boy looking for pasque flowers I went there in March sun while snow still streaked the hillsides. When you are on the low hill-crown you are out in mid-air as though swinging in a plane, the Valley and two others dropping away from you leaving the tree-tops standing below all about you. And "Romeo and Juliet" still stood in plain view over to the southeast. The Hillside Home School was just over the ridge.

As a boy I had learned to know the ground-plan of the region in every line and feature. For me now its elevation is the modeling of the hills, the weaving and the fabric that clings to them, the look of it all in tender green or covered with snow or in full glow of summer that bursts into the glorious blaze of autumn. I still feel myself as much a part of it as the trees and birds and bees are, and the red barns. Or as the animals are, for that matter.

When family-life in Oak Park that spring of 1909 conspired against the freedom to which I had come to feel every soul was entitled, I had no choice, would I keep my self-respect, but go out a voluntary exile into the uncharted and unknown. Deprived of legal protection, I got my back against the wall in this way. I meant to live if I could an unconventional life. I turned to this hill in the Valley as my Grandfather before me had turned to America—as a hope and haven. But I was forgetful, for the time being, of Grandfather's Isaiah. His smiting and punishment.

And architecture by now was quite mine. It had come to me by actual experience and meant something out of this ground we call America. Architecture was something in league with the stones of the field, in sympathy with "the flower that fadeth and the grass that withereth." It had something of the prayerful consideration for the lilies of the field that was my gentle grandmother's: something natural to the great change that was America herself.

It was unthinkable to me, at least unbearable, that any house should be put *on* that beloved hill.

I knew well that no house should ever be *on* a hill or *on* anything. It should be *of* the hill. Belonging to it. Hill and house should live together each the happier for the other. That was the way everything found round about was naturally managed except when man did something. When he added his mite he became imitative and ugly. Why? Was there no natural house? I felt I had proved there was. Now I wanted a *natural* house to live in myself. I scanned the hills of the region where the rock came cropping out in strata to suggest buildings. How quiet and strong the rock-ledge masses looked with the dark red cedars and white birches, there, above the green slopes. They were all part of the countenance of southern Wisconsin.

I wished to be part of my beloved southern Wisconsin, too. I did not want to put my small part of it out of countenance. Architecture, after all, I have learned—or before all, I should say—is no less a weaving and a fabric than the trees are. And as anyone might see, a beech tree is a beech tree. It isn't trying to be an oak. Nor is a pine trying to be a birch, although each makes the other more beautiful when seen together.

The world had had appropriate buildings before—why not appropriate buildings now, more so than ever before? There must be some kind of house that would belong to that hill, as trees and the ledges of rock did; as Grandfather and Mother had belonged to it in their sense of it all.

There must be a natural house, not natural as caves and log-cabins were natural, but native in spirit and the making, having itself all that architecture had meant whenever it was alive in times past. Nothing at all I had ever seen would do. This country had changed all that old building into something inappropriate. Grandfather and Grandmother were something splendid in themselves that I couldn't imagine living in any period-houses I had ever seen or the ugly ones around there. Yes, there was a house that hill might marry and live happily with ever after. I fully intended to find it. I even saw for myself what it might be like. And I began to build it as the brow of that hill.

It was still a very young faith that undertook to build that house. It was the same faith, though, that plants twigs for orchards, vineslips for vineyards, and small whips to become beneficent shade trees. And it planted them all about!

I saw the hill-crown back of the house as one mass of apple trees in bloom, perfume drifting down the Valley, later the boughs bending to the ground with red and white and yellow spheres that make the apple tree no less beautiful than the orange tree. I saw plum trees, fragrant drifts of snow-white in the spring, loaded in August with blue and red and yellow plums, scattering them over the ground at a shake of the hand. I saw the rows on rows of berry bushes, necklaces of pink and green gooseberries hanging to the under side of the green branches. I saw thickly pendent clusters of rubies like tassels in the dark leaves of the currant bushes. I remembered the rich odor of black currants and looked forward to them in quantity.

Black cherries? White cherries? Those too.

There were to be strawberry beds, white, scarlet and green over the covering of clean wheat-straw.

And I saw abundant asparagus in rows and a stretch of great sumptuous rhubarb that would always be enough. I saw the vineyard now on the south slope of the hill, opulent vines loaded with purple, green and yellow grapes. Boys and girls coming in with baskets filled to overflowing to set about the rooms, like flowers. Melons lying thick in the trailing green on the hill slope. Bees humming over all, storing up honey in the white rows of hives beside the chicken yard.

And the herd that I would have! The gentle Holsteins and a monarch of a bull—a sleek glittering decoration of the fields and meadows as they moved about, grazing. The sheep grazing too on the upland slopes and hills, the plaintive bleat of little white lambs in spring.

Those grunting sows to turn all waste into solid gold.

I saw the spirited, well-schooled horses, black horses and chestnut mares with glossy coats and splendid strides, being saddled and led to the mounting-block for rides about the place and along the country lanes I loved—the best of companionship alongside. I saw sturdy teams ploughing in the fields. There would be the changing colors of the slopes, from seeding time to harvest. I saw the scarlet comb of the rooster and his hundreds of hens—their white eggs and the ducks upon the pond. Geese, too, and swans floating upon the water in the shadow of the trees.

I looked forward to peacocks Javanese and white on the low roofs of the buildings or calling from the walls of the courts. And from the vegetable gardens I walked into a deep cavern in the hill—modern equivalent of the rootcellar of my grandfather. I saw its wide sand floor planted with celery, piled high with squash and turnips, potatoes, carrots, onions, parsnips. Cabbages wrapped in paper and hanging from the roof. Apples, pears and grapes stored in wooden crates walled the cellar from floor to roof. And cream! All the cream the boy had been denied. Thick—so lifting it in a spoon it would float like an egg on the fragrant morning cup of coffee or ride on the scarlet strawberries.

Yes, Taliesin should be a garden and a farm behind a real work-shop and a good home.

I saw it all, and planted it all and laid the foundation of the herd, flocks, stable and fowl as I laid the foundation of the house.

All these items of livelihood came back—improved from boyhood.

And so began a "shining brow" for the hill, the hill rising unbroken above it to crown the exuberance of life in all these rural riches.

There was a stone quarry on another hill a mile away, where the yellow sand-limestone uncovered lay in strata like outcropping ledges in the façades of the hills. The look of it was what I wanted for such masses as would rise from these native slopes. The teams of neighboring farmers soon began hauling the stone over to the hill, doubling the teams to get it to the top. Long cords of this native stone, five hundred or more from first to last, got up there ready to hand, as Father Larson, the old Norse stone mason working in the quarry beyond, blasted and quarried it out in great flakes. The slabs of stone went down for pavements of terraces and courts. Stone was sent along the slopes into great walls. Stone stepped up like ledges on to the hill and flung long arms in any direction that brought the house to the ground. The ground! My Grandfather's ground. It was lovingly felt as intimate in all this.

Finally it was not so easy to tell where pavements and walls left off and ground began. Especially on the hill-crown, which became a low-walled garden above the surrounding courts, reached by stone steps walled into the slopes. A clump of fine oaks that grew on the hilltop stood untouched on one side above the court. A great curved stone-walled seat enclosed the space just beneath them, and stone pavement stepped down to a spring or fountain that welled up into a pool at the center of the circle. Each court had its fountain and the winding stream below had a great dam. A thick stone wall was thrown across it, to make a pond at the very foot of the hill and raise the water in the valley to within sight from Taliesin. The water below the falls thus made was sent by hydraulic ram up to a big stone reservoir built into the higher hill, just behind and above the hilltop garden, to come down again into the fountains and go on down to the vegetable gardens on the slopes below the house.

Taliesin, of course, was to be an architect's workshop, a dwelling as well, for young workers who would come to assist. And it was a farm cottage for the farm help. Around a rear court were to be farm buildings, for Taliesin was to be a complete living unit genuine in point of comfort and beauty, yes, from pig to proprietor. The place was to be self-sustaining if not self-sufficient, and with its domain of two hundred acres was to be shelter, food, clothes and even entertainment within itself. It had to be its own light-plant, fuelyard, transportation and water system.

Taliesin was to be recreation ground for my children and their children perhaps for many generations more. This modest human programme in terms of rural Wisconsin arranged itself around the hilltop in a series of four varied courts leading one into the other, the courts all together forming a sort of drive along the hillside flanked by low buildings on one side and by flower gardens against the stone walls that retained the hill-crown on the other.

The hill-crown was thus saved and the buildings became a brow for the hill itself. The strata of fundamental stone-work kept reaching around and on into the four courts, and made them. Then stone, stratified, went into the lower house walls and up from the ground itself into the broad chimneys. This native stone prepared the way for the lighter plastered construction of the upper wood-walls. Taliesin was to be an abstract combination of stone and wood as they naturally met in the aspect of the hills around about. And the lines of the hills were the lines of the roofs, the slopes of the hills their slopes, the plastered surfaces of the light wood-walls, set back into shade beneath broad eaves, were like the flat stretches of sand in the river below and the same in color, for that is where the material that covered them came from.

The finished wood outside was the color of gray tree-trunks in violet light.

The shingles of the roof surfaces were left to weather silver-gray like the tree branches spreading below them.

The chimneys of the great stone fireplaces rose heavily through all, wherever there was a gathering place within, and there were many such places. They showed great rock-faces over deep openings inside.

Outside they were strong, quiet, rectangular rock-masses bespeaking strength and comfort within.

Country masons laid all the stone with the stone-quarry for a pattern and the architect for a teacher. The masons learned to lay the walls in the long, thin, flat ledges natural to the quarry, natural edges out. As often as they laid a stone they would stand back to judge the effect. They were soon as interested as sculptors fashioning a statue; one might imagine they were as they stepped back, head cocked one side, to get the general effect. Having arrived at some conclusion they would step forward and shove the stone more to their liking, seeming never to tire of this discrimination. Many of them were artistic for the first time, and liked it. There were many masons from first to last, all good. Perhaps old Dad Signola, in his youth a Czech, was the best of them until Philip Volk came. Philip worked away five years at the place as it grew from year to year—for it will never be finished. And with not much inharmonious discrepancy, one may see each mason's individuality in his work at Taliesin to this day. I frequently recall the man as I see his work.

At that time, to get this mass of material to the hilltop meant organizing man and horse-power. Trucks came along years later. Main strength and awkwardness, directed by commanding intelligence, got the better of the law of gravitation by the ton as sand, stone, gravel and timber went up into appointed places. Ben Davis was commander of these forces at this time. Ben was a creative cusser. He had to be. To listen to Ben back of all this movement was to take off your hat to a virtuoso. Men have cussed between every word, but Ben split the words and artistically worked in an oath between every syllable. One day Ben with five of his men was moving a big rock that suddenly got away from its edge and fell over flat, catching Ben's big toe. I shuddered for that rock as, hobbling slowly back and forth around it, Ben hissed and glared at it, threatening, eyeing and cussing it. He rose to such heights, plunged to such depths of vengeance as I had never suspected, even in Ben. No Marseillaise nor any damnation in the mouth of a Mosaic prophet ever exceeded Ben at this high spot in his career as a cusser. William Blake says exuberance is beauty. It would be profane perhaps to say that Ben at this moment was sublime. But he was.

And in Spring Green (the names in the region are mostly simple like Black Earth, Blue Mounds, Cross Plains, Lone Rock, Silver Creek) I found a carpenter. William Weston was a natural carpenter. He was a carpenter such as architects like to stand and watch work. I never saw him make a false or unnecessary movement. His hammer, extra light with a handle fashioned by himself, flashed to the right spot every time like the rapier of an expert swordsman. He with his nimble intelligence and swift sure hand was a gift to any architect. That William stayed with and by Taliesin through trials and tribulations the better part of fourteen years. America turns up a good mechanic around in country places every so often. Billy was one of them.

Winter came. A bitter one. The roof was on, plastering done, windows in, men working now inside. Evenings the men grouped around the open fire-places, throwing cord-wood into them to keep warm as the cold wind came up through the floor boards. All came to work from surrounding towns and had to be fed and bedded down on the place somewhere during the week. Saturday nights they went home with money for the week's work in pocket, or its equivalent in groceries and fixings from the village. Their reactions were picturesque. There was Johnnie Vaughn who was, I guess, a genius. I got him because he had gone into some kind of concrete business with another Irishman for a partner, and failed. Johnnie said, "We didn't fail sooner because we didn't have more business." I overheard this lank genius, he was looking after the carpenters, nagging Billy Little, who had been foreman of several jobs in the city for me. Said Johnnie, "I built this place off a shingle." "Huh," said Billy, "that ain't nothin'. I built them places in Oak Park right off 'd the air." No one ever got even a little over the rat-like perspicacity of that little Billy Little.

Workmen never have enough drawings or explanations no matter how many they get—but this is the sort of slander an architect needs to hear occasionally.

The workmen took the work as a sort of adventure. It was adventure. In every realm. Especially in the financial realm. I kept working all the while to make the money come. It did. And we kept on inside with plenty of clean soft wood that could be left alone pretty much in plain surfaces. The stone, too, strong and protective inside, spoke for itself in certain piers and walls.

Inside floors, like the outside floors, were stone-paved or if not were laid with wide, dark-streaked cypress boards. The plaster in the walls was mixed with raw sienna in the box, went onto the walls natural, drying out tawny gold. Outside, the plastered walls were the same but grayer with cement. But in the *constitution* of the whole, in the way the walls rose from the plan and spaces were roofed over, was the chief interest of the whole house. The whole was supremely natural. The rooms went up into the roof, tent-like, and were ribanded overhead with marking-strips of waxed, soft wood. The house was set so sun came through the openings into every room sometime during the day. Walls opened everywhere to views as the windows swung out above the tree-tops, the tops of red, white and black oaks and wild cherry trees festooned with wild grape-vines. In spring, the perfume of the blossoms came full through the windows, the birds singing there the while, from sunrise to sunset—all but the several white months of winter.

I wanted a home where icicles by invitation might beautify the eaves. So there were no gutters. And when the snow piled deep on the roofs and lay drifted in the courts, icicles came to hang staccato from the eaves. Prismatic crystal pendants sometimes six feet long, glittered between the landscape and the eyes inside. Taliesin in winter was a frosted palace roofed and walled with snow, hung with iridescent fringes, the plate-glass of the windows shone bright and warm through it all as the light of the huge fire-places lit them from the firesides within, and streams of wood-smoke from a dozen such places went straight up toward the stars.

The furnishings inside were simple and temperate. Thin tan-colored flax rugs covered the floors, later abandoned for the severer simplicity of the stone pavements and wide boards. Doors and windows were hung with modest, brown checkered fabrics. The furniture was home-made of the same wood as the trim, and mostly fitted into the trim. I got a compliment on this from old Dan Davis, a rich and "savin'" Welsh neighbor who saw we had made it ourselves. "Gosh-dang it, Frank," he said. "Ye're savin' too, ain't ye?" Although Mother Williams, another neighbor, who came to work for me, said "Savin'? He's nothin' of the sort. He could 'ave got it most as cheap ready-made from that Sears and Roebuck . . . I know."

A house of the North. The whole was low, wide and snug, a broad shelter seeking fellowship with its surroundings. A house that could open to the breezes of summer and become like an open camp if need be. With spring came music on the roofs, for there were few dead roof-spaces overhead, and the broad eaves so sheltered the windows that they were safely left open to the sweeping, soft air of the rain. Taliesin was grateful for care. Took what grooming it got with gratitude and repaid it all with interest.

Taliesin's order was such that when all was clean and in place its countenance beamed, wore a happy smile of well-being and welcome for all.

It was intensely human, I believe.

Although, thanks to "bigger and better publicity" among those who besieged it Saturdays and Sundays from near and far, came several characteristic ladies whose unusual enterprise got them as far as the upper half of the Dutch door, standing open to the living room. They couldn't see me. I was lying on a long walled-seat just inside. They poked in their heads and looked about with Oh's and Ah's. A pause. In the nasal twang of the more aggressive one, "I wonder . . . I wonder, now, if I'd like living in a regular home?"

The studio, lit by a bank of tall windows to the north, really was a group of four studies, one large, three small. And in their midst stood a stone fire-proof vault for treasures. The plans, private papers, and such money as there was, took chances anywhere outside it. But the Taliesin library of Genroku embroidery and antique colored wood-block prints all stayed safely inside. As work and sojourn overseas continued, Chinese pottery and sculpture and Momoyama screens overflowed into the rooms where, in a few years, every single object used for decorative accent became an "antique" of rare quality.

If the eye rested on some ornament it could be sure of worthy entertainment. Hovering over these messengers to Taliesin from other civilizations and thousands of years ago, must have been spirits of peace and good-will? Their figures seemed to shed fraternal sense of kinship from their places in the stone or from the broad ledges where they rested.

Yes. It all actually happened as I have described it. It is all there now.

But the story of Taliesin, after all, is old: old as the human spirit. These ancient figures were traces of that spirit, left behind in the human procession as Time went on its way. They now came forward to rest and feel at home, that's all. So it seemed as you looked at them. But they were only the story within the story: ancient comment on the New.

The New lived for itself for their sake, as long ago they had lived, for its sake.

The storms of the north broke over the low-sweeping roofs that now sheltered a life in which hope purposefully lived at earnest work. The lightning in this region, always so crushing and severe, crashed (Isaiah) and Taliesin smiled. Taliesin was minding its own business, living up to its own obligations and to the past it could well understand. But the New, failing to recognize it as its own, still pursued and besieged, traduced and insulted it. Taliesin raged, wanted to talk back— and smiled. Taliesin was a "story" and therefore it and all in it had to run the gauntlet. But steadily it made its way through storm and stress, enduring all threats and slanderous curiosity for more than three years, and smiled—always. No one entering and feeling the repose of its spirit could ever believe in the storm of publicity that kept breaking outside because a kindred spirit—a woman—had taken refuge there for life.

STUDY QUESTIONS

1. Where did Taliesin get its name? Was it an appropriate name for Wright's new school?

2. Explain what Wright means by the statement that a house should not be *on* a hill, but *of* a hill. Point out details in Wright's description of Taliesin which indicate that his architects' workshop was indeed *of* the hill.

3.   Did Wright permit his workmen to be "creative" as they labored on
      Taliesin?
4.   What storms does Wright discuss in his last paragraph?
5.   Is there a rhetorical principle behind Wright's use of sentence fragments
      and one-sentence paragraphs?

Ashley Montagu   FRANK LLOYD WRIGHT

Ashley Montagu (1905–   ) was born in England and became a
United States citizen in 1940. An anthropologist and social biolo-
gist, he was educated at the Universities of London and Florence
and received his Ph.D. from Columbia in 1937. He has taught at
New York University, Rutgers, and The New School for Social
Research. Since 1930 he has served as a legal expert on scientific
problems related to race, and in 1949 he helped draft the
UNESCO statement on race. Among his books are *Coming into
Being among Australian Aborigines* (1937), *Man's Most Dangerous
Myth: The Fallacy of Race* (1942), *The Natural Superiority of
Women* (1953), *Life before Birth* (1964), and *The Idea of Race*
(1965).

The life of Frank Lloyd Wright as an architect could well serve as
the point of departure for a discussion of what is both right and what is
wrong with Americans. I do not say "with American judgment" or
"American critical taste," for much more is involved than that. Wright,
like the land of which he was a product, was full of promises, potential
talents which by their very prodigality endangered their possessor. Talents require discipline, and the greater the talents, the greater the
discipline required. What is talent? It is involvement. But involvement
is not enough. What is necessary for substantive achievement is disciplined involvement, the devotion to the critical and systematic, the
skillful organization of one's potentialities. Essentially this means the
sharpening of one's wits on the whetstone of all the best that has been
said, written, and done in the field of one's major interest. Genius can
afford to take shortcuts. Frank Lloyd Wright not only considered himself to be a genius, but also imperiously demanded of others that they be
in fealty bound to his own valuation of himself—a valuation to which
most Americans readily acceded. Americans like their geniuses to be

Reprinted by permission of G. P. Putnam's Sons from *The American Way of Life* by
Ashley Montagu; © 1967 by Ashley Montagu.

flamboyant, especially when they are homespun, as Frank Lloyd Wright
was, the "Prairie Genius," a gross national product, if ever there was
one.

But Frank Lloyd Wright was no genius. What was he then?

He was a huckster who had somehow blundered into architecture,
a vainglorious man of overweening arrogance, effrontery, hardness, and
insensitivity; a snake-oil salesman who talked convincingly of organic
architecture but who, when it came to putting the talk into practice,
committed the most atrocious blunders. I suppose the supreme early
example of Wright's idea of organic form is the Tree House in a Chicago
suburb. Here Wright built the house around the tree. I forget whether
the tree stands in the hall or in the living room—it doesn't matter which.
What does matter is that the house is a monument of ugliness and at the
same time a monument to the gullibility of mankind and the imprac-
ticability of a plausible theory.

Nevertheless, Americans went on taking Wright at his own valuation for more than two generations. Was not Wright a genius, the
greatest of American architects? Was he not always unconscionably late,
and with never so much as an apology? Were not his houses the most
talked about in America?

One of the most endearing qualities of Americans is their willingness to try almost everything. Those who could afford the luxury were
willing to try the conjurations of Wright and pay for the experiment he
called a house. The houses were not entirely wanting in magical qualities, but they were for the most part unlivable. The overhanging eaves
shut out the light, making the bleak interiors even more dingy than they
already were, a dinginess which was further emphasized by Wright's
penchant for the darkest woods, with which the rooms were frequently
paneled. As Henry Hope Reed, Jr., recently wrote, "Many of his houses,
even in sunny Pasadena, are so dark that you need a miner's lamp to find
your way about them. And, alas, the houses designed for 'the prairie' are
always to be found in second-class suburbs where 'the far-reaching
vistas' consist of views of the neighbors."

Wright built houses for cave dwellers, troglodytes, it would almost
seem as a practical joke practiced by the High Priest of Ugliness and
Contempt for Humanity.

Being a short man, Wright designed his rooms with very low
ceilings. This barbarity was made to appear as a very great innovation.
It was Wright "lowering the room on the American household." What in
fact "the Isadora Duncan of American architecture" was actually doing
was to play an egomaniacal joke on the American public. He would
show them what organic architecture was, and if he were unable to add
a cubit to his own stature, he would bring them down to his own
dimensions. And so he produced elaborate versions of the cave and

perpetrated what can be described only as the abysmal errors. "Organic architecture," forsooth!

The last of Wright's organic follies is among the worst of all his uglinesses, the Guggenheim Museum in New York. This has been appropriately dubbed a huge spiral of contempt for its contents. As anyone who has visited the museum knows, it is scarcely possible to hang a picture properly on its leaning walls, and what is worse, it is hardly possible to view a picture comfortably. It was Wright's final testament to his contempt for humanity.

The tragedy of Wright was that he was denied the discipline his fellow Americans might have given him through their criticism of his work, a criticism which might have prevented the development of that corrosive arrogance and self-blindness which made Frank Lloyd Wright the colossal failure he was.

STUDY QUESTIONS

1. If Montagu's thesis is stated in his first sentence, does his essay demonstrate the validity of that thesis?
2. How does Montagu define *talent*? What does he mean by *involvement*?
3. In what way is Wright a "flamboyant" personality?
4. Montagu's criticism of Wright is severe. Is this criticism aimed at Wright himself or at Wright's work? What evidence does Montagu provide for his judgment of the Tree House? What other evidence could he have provided?
5. Who does Montagu blame for Wright's "colossal failure" as an architect?

WHICH THEATER
Edward Albee **IS THE ABSURD ONE?**

Edward Albee (1928–   ) was born in Washington, D.C. He attended the Lawrenceville School, Valley Forge Military Academy, Choate School, and Trinity College, Hartford, Connecticut. Thorton Wilder has called him "the only great playwright we've had in America." His plays include *The Zoo Story* and *The Death of Bessie Smith* (1961), *Who's Afraid of Virginia Woolf?* (1962),

The Ballad of the Sad Cafe (1963), *Tiny Alice* (1964), and *A Delicate Balance* (1966). *Who's Afraid of Virginia Woolf?* won the New York Drama Critics Award, the American National Theater and Academy Award, the Foreign Press Association Award, five Tony's and three Outer Circle Critics awards. The Pulitzer Prize denied *Virginia Woolf* went to *A Delicate Balance*.

A theatre person of my acquaintance—a man whose judgment must be respected, though more for the infallibility of his intuition than for his reasoning—remarked just the other week, "The Theatre of the Absurd has had it; it's on its way out; it's through."

Now this, on the surface of it, seems to be a pretty funny attitude to be taking toward a theatre movement which has, only in the past couple of years, been impressing itself on the American public consciousness. Or is it? Must we judge that a theatre of such plays as Samuel Beckett's "Krapp's Last Tape," Jean Genet's "The Balcony" (both long, long runners off-Broadway) and Eugene Ionesco's "Rhinoceros"—which, albeit in a hoked-up production, had a substantial season *on* Broadway—has been judged by the theatre public and found wanting?

And shall we have to assume that The Theatre of the Absurd Repertory Company, currently playing at New York's off-Broadway Cherry Lane Theatre—presenting works by Beckett, Ionesco, Genet, Arrabal, Jack Richardson, Kenneth Koch and myself—being the first such collective representation of the movement in the United States, is also a kind of farewell to the movement? For that matter, just what *is* The Theatre of the Absurd?

Well, let me come at it obliquely. When I was told, about a year ago, that I was considered a member in good standing of The Theatre of the Absurd I was deeply offended. I was deeply offended because I had never heard the term before and I immediately assumed that it applied to the theatre uptown—Broadway.

What (I was reasoning to myself) could be more absurd than a theatre in which the esthetic criterion is something like this: A "good" play is one which makes money; a "bad" play (in the sense of "Naughty! Naughty!" I guess) is one which does not; a theatre in which performers have plays rewritten to correspond to the public relations image of themselves; a theatre in which playwrights are encouraged (what a funny word!) to think of themselves as little cogs in a great big wheel; a theatre in which imitation has given way to imitation of imitation; a theatre in which London "hits" are, willy-nilly, in a kind of reverse of chauvinism, greeted in a manner not unlike a colony's obeisance to the Crown; a theatre in which real estate owners and theatre party managements predetermine the success of unknown quantities; a theatre in which everybody scratches and bites for billing as though it meant access to the last bomb shelter on earth; a theatre in which, in a given season, there was not a single performance of a play by Beckett, Brecht, Chekhov, Genet, Ibsen, O'Casey, Pirandello, Shaw, Strindberg—or Shakespeare? What, indeed, I thought, could be more absurd than that? (My conclusions . . . obviously.)

For it emerged that The Theatre of the Absurd, aside from being the title of an excellent book by Martin Esslin on what is loosely called the avant-garde theatre, was a somewhat less than fortunate catch-all phrase to describe the philosophical attitudes and theatre methods of a number of Europe's finest and most adventurous playwrights and their followers.

I was less offended, but still a little dubious. Simply: I don't like labels; they can be facile and can lead to nonthink on the part of the public. And unless it is understood that the playwrights of The Theatre of the Absurd represent a group only in the sense that they seem to be doing something of the same thing in vaguely similar ways at approximately the same time—unless this is understood, then the labeling itself will be more absurd than the label.

Playwrights, by nature, are grouchy, withdrawn, envious, greedy, suspicious and, in general, quite nice people—and the majority of them wouldn't be caught dead in a colloquy remotely resembling the following:

> IONESCO: (*At a Left Bank cafe table, spying Beckett and Genet strolling past in animated conversation*) Hey! Sam! Jean!
> GENET: Hey, it's Eugene! Sam, it's Eugene!
> BECKETT: Well, I'll be damned. Hi there, Eugene boy.
> IONESCO: Sit down, kids.
> GENET: Sure thing.
> IONESCO: (*Rubbing his hands together*) Well, what's new in The Theatre of the Absurd?
> BECKETT: Oh, less than a lot of people think. (*They all laugh.*)

Etc. No. Not very likely. Get a playwright alone sometime, get a few drinks in him, and maybe he'll be persuaded to sound off about his "intention" and the like—and hate himself for it the next day. But put a group of playwrights together in a room, and the conversation—if there is any—will, more likely than not, concern itself with sex, restaurants and the movies.

Very briefly, then—and reluctantly, because I am a playwright and would much rather talk about sex, restaurants and the movies—and stumblingly, because I do not pretend to understand it entirely, I will try to define The Theatre of the Absurd. As I get it, The Theatre of the

Absurd is an absorption-in-art of certain existentialist and post-existentialist philosophical concepts having to do, in the main, with man's attempts to make sense for himself out of his senseless position in a world which makes no sense—which makes no sense because the moral, religious, political and social structures man has erected to "illusion" himself have collapsed.

Albert Camus put it this way: "A world that can be explained by reasoning, however faulty, is a familiar world. But in a universe that is suddenly deprived of illusions and of light, man feels a stranger. His is an irremediable exile, because he is deprived of memories of a lost homeland as much as he lacks the hope of a promised land to come. This divorce between man and his life, the actor and his setting, truly constitutes the feeling of Absurdity."

And Eugene Ionesco says this: "Absurd is that which is devoid of purpose. . . . Cut off from his religious, metaphysical, and transcendental roots, man is lost; all his actions become senseless, absurd, useless."

And to sum up the movement, Martin Esslin writes, in his book *The Theatre of the Absurd:* "Ultimately, a phenomenon like The Theatre of the Absurd does not reflect despair or a return to dark irrational forces but expresses modern man's endeavor to come to terms with the world in which he lives. It attempts to make him face up to the human condition as it really is, to free him from illusions that are bound to cause constant maladjustment and disappointment . . . For the dignity of man lies in his ability to face reality in all its senselessness; to accept it freely, without fear, without illusions—and to laugh at it."

Amen.

(And while we're on the subject of Amen, one wearies of the complaint that The Theatre of the Absurd playwrights alone are having at God these days. The notion that God is dead, indifferent, or insane—a notion blasphemous, premature, or academic depending on your persuasion—while surely a tenet of some of the playwrights under discussion, is, it seems to me, of a piece with Mr. Tennessee Williams' description of the Deity, in "The Night of the Iguana," as "a senile delinquent.")

So much for the attempt to define terms. Now, what of this theatre? What of this theatre in which, for example, a legless old couple live out their lives in twin ashcans, surfacing occasionally for food or conversation (Samuel Beckett's "Endgame"); in which a man is seduced, and rather easily, by a girl with three well-formed and functioning noses (Eugene Ionesco's "Jack, or The Submission"); in which, on the same stage, one group of Negro actors is playing at pretending to be white, and another group of Negro actors is playing at pretending to be Negro (Jean Genet's "The Blacks")?

What of this theatre? Is it, as it has been accused of being, obscure, sordid, destructive, anti-theatre, perverse and absurd (in the sense of foolish)? Or is it merely, as I have so often heard it put, that, "This sort of stuff is too depressing, too . . . too mixed-up; I go to the theatre to relax and have a good time."

I would submit that it is this latter attitude—that the theatre is a place to relax and have a good time—in conflict with the purpose of The Theatre of the Absurd—which is to make a man face up to the human condition as it really is—that has produced all the brouhaha and the dissent. I would submit that The Theatre of the Absurd, in the sense that it is truly the contemporary theatre, facing as it does man's condition as it is, is the Realistic theatre of our time; and that the supposed Realistic theatre—the term used here to mean most of what is done on Broadway—in the sense that it panders to the public need for self-congratulation and reassurance and presents a false picture of ourselves to ourselves is, with an occasional very lovely exception, really and truly The Theatre of the Absurd.

And I would submit further that the health of a nation, a society, can be determined by the art it demands. We have insisted of television and our movies that they not have anything to do with anything, that they be our never-never land; and if we demand this same function of our live theatre, what will be left of the visual-auditory arts—save the dance (in which nobody talks) and music (to which nobody listens)?

It has been my fortune, the past two or three years, to travel around a good deal, in pursuit of my career—Berlin, London, Buenos Aires, for example; and I have discovered a couple of interesting things. I have discovered that audiences in these and other major cities demand of their commercial theatre—and get—a season of plays in which the froth and junk are the exception and not the rule. To take a case: in Berlin, in 1959, Adamov, Genet, Beckett and Brecht (naturally) were playing the big houses; this past fall, Beckett again, Genet again, Pinter twice, etc. To take another case: in Buenos Aires there are over a hundred experimental theatres.

These plays cannot be put on in Berlin over the head of a protesting or an indifferent audience; these experimental theatres cannot exist in Buenos Aires without subscription. In the end—and it must always come down to this, no matter what other failings a theatre may have—in the end a public will get what it deserves, and no better.

I have also discovered, in my wanderings, that young people throng to what is new and fresh in the theatre. Happily, this holds true in the United States as well. At the various colleges I have gone to to speak I have found an eager, friendly and knowledgeable audience, an audience which is as dismayed by the Broadway scene as any proselytizer for the avant-garde. I have found among young people in audience which is not so preconditioned by pap as to have cut off half of its responses. (It is interesting to note, by the way, that if an off-Broadway play has a substantial run, its audiences will begin young and grow older; as the run goes on, cloth coats give way to furs, walkers and subway riders to taxi-takers. Exactly the opposite is true on Broadway.)

The young, of course, are always questioning values, knocking the status quo about, considering shibboleths to see if they are pronounceable. In time, it is to be regretted, most of them—the kids—will settle down to their own version of the easy, the standard; but in the meanwhile . . . in the meanwhile they are a wonderful, alert, alive, accepting audience.

And I would go so far as to say that it is the responsibility of everyone who pretends any interest at all in the theatre to get up off their six-ninety seats and find out what the theatre is *really* about. For it is a lazy public which produces a slothful and irresponsible theatre.

Now, I would suspect that my theatre-friend with the infallible intuition is probably right when he suggests that The Theatre of the Absurd (or the avant-garde theatre, or whatever you want to call it) as it now stands is on its way out. Or at least is undergoing change. All living organisms undergo constant change. And while it is certain that the nature of this theatre will remain constant, its forms, its methods—its devices, if you will—most necessarily will undergo mutation.

This theatre has no intention of running downhill; and the younger playwrights will make use of the immediate past and mould it to their own needs. (Harold Pinter, for example, could not have written "The Caretaker" had Samuel Beckett not existed, but Pinter is, nonetheless, moving in his own direction.) And it is my guess that the theatre in the United States will always hew more closely to the post-Ibsen/Chekhov tradition than does the theatre in France, let us say. It is our nature as a country, a society. But we will experiment, and we will expect your attention.

For just as it is true that our response to color and form was forever altered once the impressionist painters put their minds to canvas, it is just as true that the playwrights of The Theatre of the Absurd have forever altered our response to the theatre.

And one more point: The avant-garde theatre is fun; it is free-swinging, bold, iconoclastic and often wildly, wildly funny. If you will approach it with childlike innocence—putting your standard responses aside, for they do not apply—if you will approach it on its own terms, I think you will be in for a liberating surprise. I think you may no longer be content with plays that you can't remember halfway down the block. You will not only be doing yourself some good, but you will be having a great time, to boot. And even though it occurs to me that such a fine combination must be sinful, I still recommend it.

STUDY QUESTIONS

1. What does Albee find absurd about the Broadway theater? What word would Albee prefer as a description of his plays?
2. Does Albee answer *Time*'s charge (see "The Anatomy of *Angst*") that the artist is one of the major contributors to the anxiety of contemporary man?
3. Why does Albee prefer a *young* audience? How would Albee have an audience approach a play?
4. Albee feels that it is the nature of American society to make use of the immediate past and to mould that past to its own needs. Can you provide any examples from contemporary life, aside from the drama, which support this statement?
5. Explain *avant-garde, free-swinging, bold,* and *iconoclastic* as they apply to contemporary drama.

EDWARD ALBEE:
RED HERRINGS
Alfred Chester   **AND WHITE WHALES**

Alfred Chester (1928–   ) was born in Brooklyn. He attended New York University and in 1951 went to Paris for nine years. He has been a Guggenheim Fellow, and has had his short stories published with the O'Henry Prize stories and the *Best American Short Stories*. A novel, *Jamie Is My Heart's Desire,* was published in 1958 and a book of short stories, *Behold Goliath,* in 1964.

It is a truth universally acknowledged that no self-respecting piece of writing, if it wishes to be taken seriously, dare appear in public nowadays without three or four levels of meaning. The convention is part of our heritage from what in ancient times was called New Criticism and it has become the most expedient way a writer has of handing in his artistic credentials. Literature thus becomes a kind of graveyard to which the reader goes to dig up all the cadavers that have been carefully buried and labeled by the writers. And with the discovery of each new corpse, the reader cries, "Eureka!" or "Aha!" as if he never expected to find it there; the writer is held in higher esteem, and the work is recognized to be of merit. At both ends of the graveyard, it is a diverting and respectable pastime—like making up and figuring out the *Times* crossword puzzle. When all the graves have been plundered, and all the bodies sniffed and prodded, we have "the meaning" of the work.

There are any number of variations on graveyard technique, the most awesome being the one which invites the reader to do not only the exhuming, but the planting and labeling as well. We are told to supply our own meaning—"you read into it whatever you want to read into it"—and the instructions are conveyed to us by leaving out some key factor in the work: a motive, a quality of character, an object, anything whose absence functions as an absence rather than, as Mersault's lack of motive does in Camus's *The Stranger,* as a presence. J. D. Salinger, in the days when his fictions made him the Sweetheart of Sigma Chi, used the absence-as-absence technique in a sickeningly disingenuous story of enormous polish called "A Perfect Day for Bananafish." Seymour Glass (I feel as though I'm name-dropping) shoots himself for no apparent reason, but any old reason would obviously do, and we are asked to supply not the reason for the suicide but the meaning of the work. To the credit of his conscience as a man and an artist Salinger is evidently spending his literary life in atonement for that sinful story, though only with "Seymour—An Introduction" has he come to observe, or acknowledge, the rigorous difference between atonement and justification.

Now, these necrophilistinisms, while they may provide us with pre-packaged ideas, do not provide us with meaning. They may indirectly suggest the meaning of the culture that encourages them or of the person who employs them—but since the meaning of a work of art comes through the blood and nerves of the artist, we can't know the meaning except through our own blood and nerves, through our feelings. Mind comes lagging along afterward with thick lenses on, correcting themes, organizing logic, justifying diction and contradiction, and so on. To examine literature "in depth," as it is called, is to examine it at its most superficial and external. The vision and feelings of a writer are not to be found in his acquiescence to the fashion of graveyards; when the fashion changes, the graveyard will be locked (except to scholars with library passes), but the work will still exist. And its meaning will be where it always was. And except when the works are openly symbolistic or allegorical, if something in a piece of writing smells fishily symbolic or allegorical, it doesn't matter whether you uncover a red herring or a white whale, you will have uncovered nothing—you will have obscured. Melville's passion is not to be known by attributing an abstraction to Moby Dick. Kafka's anguish is not to be felt by substituting another word for castle.

The much celebrated one- and two-act talent of Edward Albee has at last come to Broadway-sized fruition and is packing them in at the Billy Rose Theater. It is a considerable talent. Albee has a sense of character and drama that isn't ordinary. He can put two people on the stage and make them immediately lifelike: they respond to each other at once, which is exciting, especially since the response is usually revulsion. He handles demotic and clichéd speech in such a way that it seems fresh. He has a sense of humor which, though it is practically always exerted at the expense of his characters, can often make you laugh out loud. And best of all, he isn't afraid of corny theatricalism—in this of course he has the blessings and the precedent of contemporary French playwrights— and possesses an energy that never seems to flag. *Who's Afraid of Virginia Woolf?* has all of Albee's virtues in over-abundance, and so it is a very entertaining play, witty, absorbing, even morbidly fascinating, and sincere in that peculiarly American use of the word—that is, when the feelings in the work refer us directly back to the author rather than to his characters. Naturally, Albee is there with his literary credentials, and in a huge way; in fact, one might say that he purveys to Broadway the largest graveyard ever, not excepting Tennessee Williams. But, to his credit, Albee keeps *Virginia Woolf* so diverting that up until the end of the second act you hardly notice the smell.

Since I want to go into this play in some detail, and since there may be readers who haven't managed or wanted to get past the jammed lobby or outrageous prices at the Billy Rose, a summary of the action may be helpful. *Virginia Woolf* gives us four almost unrelievedly nasty people who for something like three-and-a-half hours, our time and theirs, take part in a drunken orgy of back-biting, bitchery, humiliation, verbal castration, exposure, and physical mauling. Among them are the following weaknesses, crimes, and sins, imputed or established, sometimes duplicated or even quadruplicated: deceit, treachery, impotence, alcoholism, abortion, incest, patricide, matricide, attempted uxoricide, phantom filicide, and others more trivial like adultery and pederasty (this last is suggested by Martha and George who refer to their son several times as "the little bugger"). The major crimes or sins, or whatever one calls them nowadays, belong mainly to the older couple—and more specifically to the husband—who are George, a history professor, and his wife Martha, daughter of the college president. Aside from their violent battles, they are notable for making frequent provocative remarks about their twenty-one year old son who is away from home. The impression given the audience is that there is something about the boy they want to hide, and that they are as mean and merciless to him as they are to each other. The younger couple, guilty of relatively puny and typically modern offenses, are Nick, an ambitious biology professor (who is a naturalistic reminiscence of the young man in *The American Dream*, and Albee doesn't like him any better) with a smug, belligerent manner, and Honey, a simpering alcoholic; they are more or less indifferent to each other, and they have no children—a fact about which much is made. You can, perhaps, already make out the design of the play, and even though there is no vital interaction or fusion between the couples (except as Nick is used by Martha to hurt George), there is enough contrast and parallel to hang an evening on.

As a result of Martha's continual exposure of George's failures, the humiliation she causes him, and her final adultery with Nick, George revenges himself by inventing a telegram which purports to bear the message that "the little bugger" is dead. The invention takes place at the end of the second act (called *"Walpurgisnacht"*) but isn't sprung upon Martha until the end of the third. What happens then is better told after taking a look at Albee's method. One good way of doing this, since it leads us through the play, is to trace the gradual revelation about the sexuality of Honey and Nick.

The first important item comes in Act One when George questions Nick as to whether he and Honey have children. Nick says no, not yet, and then, further on, we hear:

> GEORGE: But you are going to have kids . . .
> NICK (*Hedging*): Yes . . . certainly. We . . . want to wait . . . a little . . . until we're settled.

Not odd really, but odd. And about five minutes later, we have the following:

> HONEY: Oh, it's late. . . . We should be getting home.
> GEORGE (*Nastily, but he is so preoccupied he hardly notices his own tone*): For what? You keeping the baby sitter up, or something?
> NICK (*Almost a warning*): I told you we didn't have children.
> GEORGE: Mm? (*Realizing*) Oh, I'm sorry. I wasn't even listening . . . or thinking . . . whichever one applies.
> NICK (*Softly, to Honey*): We'll go in a little while.

Now we smell a set-up. George is preoccupied because his wife, Martha, has mentioned the little bugger—in spite of George's warnings—and also because she is changing her clothes. If Nick speaks warningly, he has already proved so belligerent that we cannot distinguish one more hostility; and when he says to Honey that they will soon go, he is merely replying to her statement. It is all so neat and crafty, we almost overlook the fact that they are talking about children again, but when we do realize it, the deviousness of the writing raises the subject to prominence. Suspense enters, very subtly, very cleverly.

Things become more obvious in the second act, in dialogue between George and Nick, while Honey is off stage sick-drunk with Martha attending her.

> GEORGE: Your wife throws up a lot, eh?
> NICK: I didn't say that . . . I said she gets sick quite easily.
> GEORGE: Oh. I thought by sick you meant . . .
> NICK: Well, it's true . . . She . . . does throw up a lot. Once she starts . . . there's practically no stopping her . . . I mean, she'll go right on . . . for hours. Not all the time, but . . . regularly.
> GEORGE: You can tell time by her, hunh?
> NICK: Just about.
> GEORGE: Drink?
> NICK: Sure. . . . I married her because she was pregnant.
> GEORGE: (*Pause*) Oh? (*Pause*) But you said you didn't have any children . . . When I asked you, you said . . .
> NICK: She wasn't . . . really. It was a hysterical pregnancy. She blew up, and then she went down.
> GEORGE: And while she was up, you married her.

"Throws up" and "regularly" and "tell time by her"—what George has in mind is clear, or anyway clear enough, though the references are still veiled. Then Nick does something which is preposterously out of character, given what we know of him and his relationship to George: he tells about his marriage. The strangeness and suddenness of this confession make us hark back to the set-up in Act One, and we accept the unlikely because it explains what has gone before. Now, his confession is: "I married her because she was pregnant," and not: "because I *thought* she was pregnant." However, a moment later Nick admits to having married Honey because she was rich and suggests that he did not sleep with her before they married. Now the complications really abound, a new "depth" is achieved, and another character has been made to reveal himself as a cad of the first water; in this case Nick, through all these present betrayals of Honey and past betrayals of his own feelings.

Matters come to a head through George's treachery, but nothing is clarified. Having been humiliated and exposed by Martha and having been humiliated also by Nick who flirts openly with Martha (Honey is too drunk to notice), George tells an animal story in which he makes it clear to Honey that Nick has told him of her pregnancy. Honey realizes that Nick has betrayed her, and though she becomes hysterical, she too gives away no vital information. So if we come out enlightened in any way, it is with the knowledge that everyone on stage, except poor Honey, who will have her turn later, is if possible fouler than we thought.

And this brings us to the climactic dialogue, or *monologue à deux*, at the end of Act Two. Martha and Nick are off in the kitchen making—it would be silly to call it love—preparing, then, additional torments for George as well as a possible step up the ladder of success for Nick (Martha's father being head of the college). George, on stage alone, is joined by Honey, who has until then been sleeping it off. She enters, stupefied. This stupor, which at first looks like a clumsy technical device justifiable only on the grounds that the playwright is determined to make even egoless, stupid, terrified Honey an active as well as passive perpetrator of horror, is really part of Albee's plot to get us, willy nilly, into a position where we will have rather more than one foot in the graveyard.

Here is the relevant speech made by Honey in her stupor: "No! . . . I don't want any . . . I don't want them . . . Go 'way . . . (*Begins to cry*) I don't want any . . . any . . . children . . . I . . . don't . . . want . . . any . . . children. I'm afraid! I don't want to be hurt . . . Please!" Ah, at last, Honey Macbeth is going to spill the beans. In fact, it seems, she has already spilled them, for what follows is:

GEORGE (*Nodding his head . . . speaks with compassion*): I should have known.
HONEY (*Snapping awake from her reverie*): What! What?

And we cry with her, what, what?

GEORGE: I should have known . . . the whole business . . . the headaches . . . the whining . . . the . . .
HONEY (*Terrified*): What are you talking about?

Yes, George, what are you talking about? Hangover? Frustration? Frigidity?

GEORGE (*Ugly again*): Does he know that? Does that . . . stud you're married to know about that, hunh?

More confusion. More suspense. And more and more when Honey suddenly reacts not only to what George says but to George himself.

HONEY: About what? Stay away from me!

Does she want George because of what he's discovered and is she therefore projecting her heat upon him? In any case, George assures her that his intentions are not sexual, and he adds ". . . How do you do it? . . . How do you make your secret little murders studboy doesn't know about, hunh? Pills? Pills? You got a secret supply of pills? Or what? Apple jelly? Will power?"

So the truth is out at last. But what truth? We are being dumped into the graveyard. "Murder" (even when qualified by "little") is a

loaded word here: its violence is intended mainly to remind us that
George has not denied killing his mother and father and has, before our
eyes, attempted to strangle his wife. For we realize that, after all, Honey
has said nothing, and George's mind has said all. But if Honey is by
turns conveniently stupefied and conveniently silent, she is also conveniently frightened. Somehow George has hit home. And so has Albee—
he has impugned Honey and further impugned George by showing his
cruelty to her. We begin to realize that the "truth" about Nick and
Honey's reproductory dilemma will never be revealed as an objective
fact—and things galore start happening in the graveyard. *Rashomon*
looms up, Ionesco gets to work, Pirandello pirouettes upon a tombstone.
The inscriptions are tantalizing insofar as they are a little blurred.
Excitement. *Of course,* my dear, the *truth* is that we cannot *know* the
truth! All the red herrings, since they're meant as red herrings, are
magically turned into big white whales.

If there are any further doubts that the play has been relegated to
the graveyard, they are allayed at the beginning of Act III, when Nick is
revealed by Martha to be impotent, and since he doesn't deny it—"You
should try me some time when we haven't been drinking for ten hours,
and maybe . . ."—and since there is no evidence beyond the confusion
I've indicated, his impotence becomes dramatic reality. Looking back
upon everything, we can come up with gorgeous variations and conjec-
tures. Yet, it all seems so trivial; and the more Albee imposes his
method, the more trivial it seems. His design—scheme perhaps would be
a better word—is so labored, so crafty, so unfree, and the satisfaction it
gives us is the satisfaction of noticing an intricate shelf-arrangement at
the supermarket. Look at the climactic scene once more, the scene
between Honey and George. Shortly after the dialogue I've reported,
George gets the idea for the telegram, and this perfects the climax. It
links up both couples and their respective reproductive organs, and
completes the balance. We have one pair, Martha and Nick, in the act of
creation (off-stage, to be sure) and the other pair in the act of destruction. And what irony there is when you reflect that Nick turns out to be
impotent and that Martha is probably past menopause. Yet the total
effect is, finally, that it is all contrivance and that if the contrivance
functions at all in the play, it functions to conceal the fact that the
author is really out to do one thing: get his characters. And this impression becomes stronger during the last ten minutes.
For then! Oh, then! Symbols crashing, all styles mashing, allegories
splashing—*Enter the Playwright, in the guise of gravedigger.*

As Albee did in his first play, *The Zoo Story,* so does he in *Virginia
Woolf,* but on a much more lavish scale—and why not? This is Broadway.

He introduces a new, and apparently vital, element just moments before the show ends. It is a surprise, but no ordinary surprise ending, with the usual little thrill and the usual little shadow cast upon the author's integrity. It is, in its way, a surprise beginning, for it informs us that it has been on stage the whole time only we haven't known about it, and it makes extraordinary retroactive claims for having been chief motive, main symbol, and primal blueprint. In *The Zoo Story*, it isn't until the suicide-murder is effected that it goes back to become Jerry's aim throughout the play. And in *Virginia Woolf*, it is not until George tells Martha their son is dead that we discover there is no son and never was one, that "the little bugger" is an invention, and that the couple are barren and have been play-acting at having a son for the last twenty-one years and/or three acts and/or three-and-a-half hours.

Albee prepares for it, first of all, by calling attention to the play itself, to the fact that it is *Théâtre*, and that it is all absurd and ridiculous anyway, just like the French playwrights say, so let's make fun of it for a minute.

> GEORGE (*Appearing in the doorway, the snapdragons covering his face; speaks in a hideously cracked falsetto*): Flores; flores para los muertos. Flores.

These flowers are, I don't have to tell you, that bunch of forget-me-not red herrings that passed behind the scrim in *A Streetcar Named Desire*. Later, still calling attention to the play by the use of ritualism, Albee calls attention to the Church by the use of prayer. Martha and George go trancing and prancing, she into rhetoric, he into Latin: "*Libera me, Domine, de morte aeterna, in die illa tremenda. . . .*" And then we have the surprise itself. And we are nose-deep in The Play, Absurdity, Truth, Illusion and Reality, Faith and Science, the Past and the Present, the Emptiness of Human Life, and all the other carrion of fashionable intellect. I know it isn't cricket to ask, but what is the relationship between the surprise and the body of the play? What is different if we know the "truth" at the beginning or at the end?

The imaginary son, when revealed to be imaginary, has two seemingly equally important heads: one of them says that his parents are barren and the other one says they have created an illusion to sustain themselves with. Now, while the little bugger may be imaginary, he is neither the product nor the means of self-deception, for Martha and George are perfectly conscious of the fact that their son is a fiction.

> GEORGE: You know the rules, Martha! For Christ's sake, you know the rules! . . . You broke our rule, baby. You mentioned him . . . you mentioned him to someone else.

In other words, they know he isn't real—or why would they want to hide his existence? They know he is an illusion, and I can't, whether Albee wants me to or not, accept that human beings may be sustained by illusions they know to be such. What might possibly sustain them is the anguish, the lovely anguish, that comes when a man pretends to believe in what he wishes were true but knows is not. And this, directly more than indirectly, is an acknowledgment of reality, a facing of reality. So if the little bugger has two heads, the second does nothing but talk of the first, and the first says: sterility.

Sterility is our enlightenment, Albee's surprise. And in looking back upon the play, we find that the difference is all in ourselves. We feel something we didn't feel when the play was in the cruel fertile land: compassion. Every time the little bugger is mentioned, we hear "barrenness" instead. And Martha and George become less horrible. Anyway their blackness is less black, somewhat grayer. But our compassion comes only through our rewriting of the play—and evidently Albee did not want this or he would have done it himself. What he allows us, in fact, after the surprise, is pity, and the feeling of pity is always a kind of judgment. Our feelings tell us the truth. The playwright has walked out on stage with bench and gavel, full of self-righteousness, and has passed sentence on his characters: "Martha and George, for abominable behavior, for immoral actions, for being wicked parents and evil people, I hereby sentence you to sterility by retroaction." They become sterile by decree, not by virtue of dramatic reality. And no sooner do we feel this than we are aware that he has been imposing punishments on these people from the beginning—the chiefest of them being the length of time they must appear before us naked, deceitful, gruesome. It is only then, after the completion of their tortuous punishment, that the spectator is permitted some pity. And Martha and George go hobbling off alone, barren. No wonder the play is successful on Broadway; it provides the audience with a guided tour away from, and safely back at last into, the most repugnant kind of puritanical priggishness. The morality of *Virginia Woolf* is one which conceives that folly, desperation, frustration, hate, are not themselves their greatest penalties—as virtue is said to be its own reward—but must be judged and punished from above, beyond, without.

With our new knowledge, we look back upon Honey and Nick, and what do we see? The same unlovable pair. But now perhaps we see something we noticed earlier in a clearer light. In literature, as in life, unlovable people often get that way because they are unloved. And Mr. Albee does not love Honey and Nick; he hates them, maybe even more than he hates the other couple. He has pursued them through the play, tirelessly, relentlessly, whispering and shouting dark accusations, and although he has imposed upon them the same sentence given to Martha and George, he has done it so deviously that they can never come to Edward Albee's kind of grace—pity from the audience.

An excellent theme for the graduate student: the artist as judge. And it might prove interesting as a sociological phenomenon: "In the mid-20th century, writers, conscious of the moral breakdown . . . etc., etc." To all the other judges, the artist is now added. He too joins the world of loveless, wisdomless, truthless people who despise rather than comprehend. It is certainly a tempting thing to do in the face of the horror that surrounds us—to say: world, you are so awful and disgusting, I will not understand you. But who except saints and artists ever tried to understand mankind? Everyone else always tried to improve it—or own it or destroy it. Well, perhaps mankind cannot be improved, only made more comfortable. Or, perhaps after all it can. But no one was ever made better by judgment and hate, and it seems a bit silly for a writer deliberately to limit himself to the useless, even for the pleasure of sticking his tongue out at the world. It only means the world has finally won, that stupidity and lies have triumphed. And then, of course, the only proper place to look for art, as well as meaning, is in the graveyard.

STUDY QUESTIONS

1. What does Chester, or any critic, mean by *levels of meaning?*
2. How effective is Chester's metaphor of the graveyard? Is he consistent in his use of it? Is it the unifying idea of his review?
3. According to Chester, what are Albee's strong points as a dramatist?
4. Chester says he will provide a "helpful summary" of the play's action. What is a *summary,* and does Chester indeed summarize *Virginia Woolf?* To whom is his summary helpful?
5. Explain the title of Chester's review. Is it connected to the graveyard image? Where does it occur in the review itself?
6. According to Chester, how does Albee punish George and Martha?

HERE WE GO ROUND

Richard Gilman   **THE ALBEE BUSH**

Richard Gilman (1925–   ) was born in New York. He attended the University of Wisconsin (B.A., 1947), The New School for

Reprinted by permission of Richard Gilman, c/o Lynn Nesbit, Marvin Josephson Associates, Inc. Copyright © 1962 by Richard Gilman. From *Commonweal*, LXXVII (November 9, 1962).

Social Research, and the Sorbonne. From 1943 to 1946 he served with the U.S. Marines in the South Pacific. After seven years as a freelance writer, he became associate editor of *Jubilee Magazine*, then associate editor and drama critic for *The Commonweal*. He currently holds the same position at *Newsweek*. He has taught at Columbia, Stanford, and Yale. His work has appeared in *Bookweek*, *Horizon*, *American Heritage*, *Commentary*, *New Republic*, *Dissent*, *Tulane Drama Review*, and *The New York Times Book Review*.

Because *Who's Afraid of the Big Bad Wolf?* is copyrighted, the title of Edward Albee's first full-length play is sung by its characters to the tune of *Here We Go Round the Mulberry Bush*, thereby establishing a pattern for the evening's procedures and the public discussion that this unsettling work has provoked. Nearly everything is a substitution or an imposture: a folk melody when Mr. Albee would clearly have preferred a tinny contemporary one; an enormous three-act play whose conception rattles around in the space; experiment clothed in conventional attire so as to be allowed to live; on our part, the acceptance, as an imaginative breakthrough, of the play's intentions instead of its accomplishment, or its out-of-hand rejection on grounds having more to do with decorum than esthetics.

I accuse Albee of nothing. He is not a confidence-man, and if some people have given him theirs it is because there is nowhere else to put it. He is the American stage's young master *faute de mieux*. He makes us feel alive and of our time, he will not let us get away with our habitual evasions and behavior. He is in fact a transcriber of those evasions and that behavior, everything he has written, culminating in *Who's Afraid of Virginia Woolf?* being less a construction of new vision than a series of split-level suburban houses in which we can see ourselves the way the neighbors only speculate. He makes Lillian Hellman seem like the recording secretary of a garden club.

But he also makes a playwright like Ionesco, from whom he used to borrow certain materials, appear more than ever a model of fulness, unity, zest and staying-power. For *Virginia Woolf*, though the most interesting play of the season, a work of many compelling virtues, high seriousness and enormous verbal éclat, is an exemplary failure, a fascinating demonstration of the difficulties American playwrights face in trying to cope with all our sundered realities: the split between commerce and art, between tradition and the single voice, between surface and substance and between those aspects of the imagination we identify as form and content.

Hebbel wrote that content presents the task and form the solution. From the moment the curtain goes up on *Virginia Woolf* and we hear Albee's central characters—a history professor at a New England college and his wife, the daughter of the school's president—tell one another that

"You make me puke," and "I'm six years younger than you, always have been and always will be," and "If you existed, I'd divorce you," we are aware that there is going to be a struggle on a more consuming level than that of personal antagonism. For the ferocity of Albee's domestic scene, the feral quality of his naturalism, isn't going to be satisfied with a conventional theatrical destiny—there is going to be a mighty conflict between a dramatic task and its elusive solution.

The evening grows more and more violent. The love-hate relationship of the couple fills the stage with wounds, glancing blows, destructions of confidence and of attitudinal clichés, revulsions, weaponless and unbearable intimidations, bitter exaltations and hopeless embraces. The wife despises the husband for his lack of *cojones,* his inability to step into her father's shoes; he is revolted by her promiscuity and her intolerable sexual pressure. Another couple arrives, a young All-American biology instructor and his inane, ethereal wife, and they begin to function as audience for and participants in the marital horror story.

There is nothing "absurd," about this play. Albee has largely abandoned the specific parodic elements and dragooned whimsy of *The Sand Box* and *The American Dream* and the obliquities of *The Zoo Story* and has, if anything, returned to *The Death of Bessie Smith* for savage inspiration and neurotic prototypes. But he has advanced from that problem play. Here the action is more inward and the rhetoric, apart from a few speeches of improbable and high-pitched lamentation, is straightforward, cocky, brutal, knowing and tremendously *au courant* . . . and very funny.

When the wife, played robustly—too robustly, perhaps—by Uta Hagen, stretches out in a chair after an abortive off-stage dalliance with the visiting biologist and huskily announces "I'm the earth mother . . . and you're all flops," we are with Mr. Albee at his insider's best. And when the husband, whom Arthur Hill enacts crisply, but without much force, remarks that "I've been to college like everybody else," we receive confirmation about one source of Albee's appeal. He is the poet of post-Freudian, post-Riesmanian, post-intellectual, wised-up and not-to-be-had, experiential and disenchanted United States of America 1962 Man.

But poets, of course, want to sing, discover new lands of the imagination, be healers. That is Albee's self-imposed "task," and it is his downfall. The pressure in him towards the transcendence of naturalism and psychological notation had previously resulted in the painfully co-erced denouement of *The Zoo Story* and the descent into incoherence of *The American Dream.* In *Virginia Woolf* the failure is on a larger scale. He has driven into the body of his scrupulously observed *Walpurgis-nacht* (the title of Act II; Act I is called *Fun and Games,* Act III *The Exorcism*) a shaft of fantasy designed to point up our sad psychic aridity and fix the relationship between reality and illusion. Its effect is to break the back of the play.

We had been led to believe that the couple have a son in college, much of their mutual recrimination having concerned his upbringing and present attitude towards them. In Act III we learn—as a *coup de théâtre*—that he is imaginary; unable to have children, they had invented him, keeping him a secret and using his legendary existence as the major bond uniting them in their enmity and need. But when the wife mentions him to the visitors, she breaks their pact and the husband decides to kill him off, announcing his death in an accident and thereby ending the reign of illusion. The play ends with the wife sorrowfully accepting the necessity to live without myths, while whispering that she remains "afraid of Virginia Woolf," afraid, presumably, of life, art and truth.

There is something doubly wrong with this. Structurally, it leaves the play in division from itself, the psychological realism separated by a gulf from the metaphysical data, just as in *The American Dream* the parody and fantasy lay gasping out of each other's reach. But more than this there is the question of vision, of dramatic truth and rightness, of the proper means to an end, in short, of a "task" and its solution. What Albee has done is to smuggle in an element alien to his physical procedure, asking it to carry the burden of revelation he cannot distill from his mere observation of behavior. He wants to say something profound about the human condition, and he ends, like O'Neill in *The Iceman Cometh*, offering a cliché about illusions.

The sharpest psychological observation will no longer communicate the kind of truth we need and that Albee, with acute but limited sensibility, keeps trying for. As so many developments in art have demonstrated, the psyche is only one element among others and needs to be *located*, tested against other realities, and not simply described. Naturalism gives us nothing but our reflections. However painful, bold and accurate they are, as in *Virginia Woolf*, they are not enough, we are not changed by them, as we are not ultimately changed by this play. The paradox is that human reality can best be apprehended today by indirection, by "inhuman" methods, which means a step beyond the literal, the behavioral, the natural. Our condition is extreme; old measures won't work, but neither will new half-measures, half-dramas such as Albee continues to produce.

STUDY QUESTIONS

1. According to Gilman, what is Albee's strongest point?
2. Gilman too uses the word *level*. What does he mean by it?

3.   Gilman concludes that *Virginia Woolf* is not "absurd." Are Gilman's reasons the same as those for which Albee rejects the label of "absurd"?
4.   What does Gilman mean by "post-Freudian, post-Riesmanian, post-intellectual, wised-up and not-to-be-had, experiential and disenchanted" man?
5.   Do Chester and Gilman find the same theme in *Virginia Woolf*?

WHO'S AFRAID
Ray Irwin   **OF VIRGINIA WOOLF, HUNH?**

Ray Irwin was born in Canada. He received his B.A. and Ph.D. from the University of Minnesota and his M.A. from Cornell University. Currently, he is Professor of Speech at Syracuse University. Formerly a professional actor and director, Irwin saw three of his one-act plays produced off-Broadway at the Sheridan Square Playhouse. His fiction and critical essays have appeared in the *Atlantic Monthly, Show,* the *New Yorker, Esquire, Parents' Magazine, College English,* and the *AAUP Journal.*

If *Who's Afraid of Virginia Woolf?* turns out to be as important a contribution to American dramaturgy as some critics think it might ("Mr. Albee can . . . be placed high among the important dramatists of the contemporary world theatre"—New York *Post;* "towers over the common run of contemporary plays"—*The New York Times;* "is a brilliantly original work of art"—*Newsweek*), the close-textual-analysis people will be picking at it before long, and also perhaps picking *on* it.

I am one of those people myself, and what I am reporting here is a little pilot study I have made of a recurring word I found in *Who's Afraid of Virginia Woolf?* that, so far as I have been able to learn, has not appeared in a play before. The word is "hunh." Probably I would not have noticed it had it turned up only occasionally, but I kept seeing it again and again (it is used a total of fifty-five times), and before I finished reading the play I suspected that this, like the sickness imagery in *Hamlet,* the blood imagery in *Macbeth,* and the light-flashes imagery in *Romeo and Juliet,* was not just fortuitous. Mr. Albee clearly had something special in mind.

What we call the "area breakdown" of "hunh" is this: it is used eighteen times in the first act, twenty-five times in the second, and twelve times in the third. George says it the most—twenty-seven times; Martha is next with twenty-six; and Nick is last with only two. Honey does not say it at all. I was able to find no meaningful patterns in the distribution of the word, but this does not mean they are not there. Later scholarship will perhaps reveal some.

Two explanations of the word's presence can easily be ruled out. First, it is not a typesetter's error, as are so many peculiarities of the first folio. This, one can be sure of, because the word is consistently spelled throughout. And, second, it is not Mr. Albee's private spelling of "huh." There are several "huh's" in the play, along with some "unh hunh's," an "ummmmmmmm," some "unh's," a "yaaahhhh," and a "nyyyy-aaaahhhhh."

Having thus established that "hunh" is in the play on purpose, I tried next to find it in the dictionary. Uh-unh. Even Webster III, containing, as it does, just about anything, has not sanctioned "hunh." "Huh" is there, though—origin unknown.

I then sought to learn how the word is supposed to be pronounced. I asked a lot of people, but there was not enough agreement among them to make the results statistically significant. I might, of course, have gone to the play and learned how the actors pronounced it, but that would have been an inordinate expenditure of time and money just for the sake of checking on one word, and an unauthorized one at that. Besides, if I know actors, they probably pronounce "hunh" any way they feel like it. I have never heard two Hamlets pronounce "foh" the same way, and the phonetics of "foh" are more self-evident than those of "hunh."

Actually, though, it does not matter a great deal precisely how Mr. Albee wants his word pronounced, for the approximate pronunciation is obvious enough from the spelling. The presence of the n means that "hunh" must be partly nasalized, and the final h directs the speaker to extend the word, making it longer than either "hun" or "huh." I know of only one person who used to use "hunh," or something very close to it, habitually. He was a boyhood friend, a dreamy kid who let his mouth hang open and who had trouble focusing on things that were said to him. When his mother would say, "Max, where did you put the scissors I saw you playing with?" he would answer, "Hunh?" and she would slap him.

Assuming, then, that Mr. Albee intends "hunh" to be pronounced with the mouth and the velum relaxed so as to produce a sort of primitive, nasal grunt, let us turn finally to the questions of why he uses the word and what, if anything, it symbolizes. I think he uses the word because it fits in very well with the diction of much of the rest of the play. People who say things like "You make me puke!"; "Look, sweet-heart, I can drink you under any goddamn table you want"; "Yeah . . . sure. Get over there!"; "Look, muckmouth . . . cut that out!"; "CAN . . . IT . . . MISTER!"; and "Then get your butt out of that chair and bring the little dip back in here" (unfortunately, the best examples cannot as yet be quoted in family magazines) probably say "hunh" quite a lot.

I am at the disadvantage of moving almost entirely in academic circles where locutions like those made by Mr. Albee's characters are never heard. I did, though, hear some of this sort of language when I was in Army boot camp, and it was often supplemented by a variety of animal-like sounds, especially if the speaker was a slack-jawed fellow to whom thinking and speaking came hard. And I do not doubt that a certain number of these sounds could be best represented orthographic-ally by "hunh."

I have some ideas on the symbolism of "hunh," too. I believe that in putting it into the throats of his characters, Mr. Albee is suggesting, although he may not know it, that language is coming full circle. In grunts it began, and to grunts it is returning. Nor is this the only full circle gesture that "hunh" symbolizes. Manners, he seems to be saying, are getting back to "hunh." Family life will soon be mostly "hunh," and perhaps also "ugh." Scholarship, ambition, loyalty, honesty, tact, virility, at least heterosexual virility, willpower—all are sinking to the level of "hunh."

Since textual analyses of this sort are traditionally descriptive rather than normative, I feel no obligation to marshal evidence that Mr. Albee doesn't know what the hell he's talking about. Besides, as I have said, I have led a life sheltered, for the most part, by the groves of academe, in which speech and situations and people such as those invented by Mr. Albee do not exist.

STUDY QUESTIONS

1. How does Irwin's approach to *Virginia Woolf* differ from that of Chester and Gilman? Is he more objective?
2. Irwin's anecdote about his dreamy friend is humorous. Does it advance his argument?
3. Under what disadvantage does Irwin claim he labors? Is he serious? How do you know?
4. Is Irwin's review *descriptive* or *normative?*
5. Which of the three reviews would be the most helpful to a potential theatergoer or moviegoer? Why?

DISNEY

John Mason Brown   **AND THE DANE**

John Mason Brown (1900–   ), critic, author, and lecturer, was
born in Louisville, Kentucky. He took his B.A. at Harvard in 1923
and an L.H.D. at Williams in 1941; his honorary degrees include
D.Litt.'s from the University of Montana (1942), Clark University
(1947), the University of Louisville (1948), Hofstra University
(1954), and Long Island University (1963). He has taught at the
University of Montana, Yale, Harvard, and Middleburg College, and
has been drama critic for *Theater Arts Monthly*, the *New York
Evening Post*, the *New York World-Telegram*, and the *Saturday
Review*. He edited *The Portable Woollcott* (1946), and *The Portable
Charles Lamb* (1949), and is the author of *The Modern Theater in
Revolt* (1929), *Two on the Aisle* (1938), *Many a Watchful Night*
(1944), *Seeing Things* (1946), and *Dramatic's Personal* (1963).

Of course, I wanted him to like it. I can't deny this. If I did, I
would lie in my paternal teeth. Every parent knows the same hopes, the
same fears when *that* afternoon at last comes around.

For both of us, this Saturday matinee was an adventure. For him,
because it was the first time he had ever seen *Hamlet;* for me, because I
was seeing it with him. And *Hamlet* shared with a boy of nine is *Hamlet*
rediscovered.

He had seen other plays. *The Rose and the Ring*, for example, as
done, and charmingly done, by the children of King-Coit School. This
had been his initiation. In it he had found nothing to doubt, everything
to believe, and suspense almost unbearable. But that had been at least
five years back, when both he and the world were younger.

Since then he had seen *It Happens on Ice*. He had laughed at the
clowns, marveled at the spectacle, and in a voice filled with dread asked
at the conclusion of each number, "Is it all over now?" He had also seen
Oklahoma! He had come to it, Victrola-prepared, knowing all its songs.
"Neat" was the word for *Oklahoma!*

But Maurice Evans in the GI *Hamlet*—this was something else. He

Reprinted in *Seeing Things* from *Saturday Review*, March 30, 1946. Reprinted
here by permission of the author.

did not know its song. My fingers were crossed. As I say, I hoped he would like it. You never know; you can never tell.

No form of cruelty is more cruel than exposing the young, when still too young, to books and plays ill-fated enough to have become classics. It is a murderous error; the kind of sulphurous mistake of more than paving-stone size, for which only good intentions can be responsible. The fact that both the living and the dead are equally defenseless against such foul play is the measure of its meanness.

To make a chore out of what should be a pleasure, to put the curse of obligation on what was meant to be absorbing, is to kill in the child the willingness to be pleased, and in the classic the ability to please. Masterpieces are masterpieces not because such grim conspirators as parents or teachers have told us that they are good. They are masterpieces because they tell us so themselves.

Yet they cannot be expected to speak for themselves until we are ready to hear them. Not to coin a phrase, there's the rub. For that happy conjunction of the man and the moment is as necessary for a book and its reader as Matthew Arnold knew it to be for the emergence of greatness in this world. When that moment will tick itself off, no one can foretell. It depends entirely upon the book and the individual.

Fortunately *Hamlet* can be approached on various levels. The difficulties of its language may pass unnoticed. Its inner anguishes may not be comprehended. Still it tells a story—and such a story. To the modern, no less than to the Elizabethan, its action remains the first of its excitements. The Ph.D.s move in only when the playgoers have moved out.

Quite naturally, one would expect a child to be more interested in what happens in the play than in what happens within the Prince's mind. But nowadays a boy comes to *Hamlet*—oh, perish the word!—"conditioned" in ways productive of unforeseeable results.

These war years, for example. They have accustomed him and his friends to every known weapon of mechanized destruction. After frequent newsreel exposures to, and hourly imitations of, the crash of buzz bombs, the drone of airplane motors, the rumble of tanks, the rat-tat-tat of machine guns, the swish of rockets, and the roar of navy guns, would a world seem unbearably tame in which death is brought about by mere poison or the quiet click of foils?

Then the comic books, those appalling polychrome termites which eat their way into every home, no matter how well guarded; into every weekly allowance, no matter how small; and into every budding mind, no matter how eager. They cannot be kept out. No doubt, in fairness they should not be. The young ought not to be exiled from an experience, common to their generation, which will one day prove a group memory. But what chance would Mary Arden's boy have against Blondie, or Superman? Was the Phantom the best homework for Shakespeare? Or Gandy and Sourpuss the proper preparation for Rosencrantz and Guildenstern? I must admit I wondered, more and more as that Saturday approached, with ever-increasing alarm.

And what about Disney, the greatest Walt the world has known since Whitman? In toy form in the nursery. In color in the comics. In books beyond counting. Above all, in the movies. Disney everywhere, Disney delectable because destructive. His creatures asking for no pity; creating pleasure by pain, living only to sock and, having socked or been socked, socking again. Could the Dane hope to compete with Donald Duck, Pluto, Monstro, the Big Bad Wolf, the Three Little Pigs, Dopey, and most particularly the redoubtable Mickey? Again I wondered. And hoped. And had my doubts.

How to unroll the red carpet for *Hamlet* was another question. I meant to prepare his mind for what he was to see without putting upon it the stigma of homework. I mentioned the play at breakfast for a week, naming it with as much excitement as if its title were synonymous with a fishing expedition, or a visit to the Hayden Planetarium, the Museum of Natural History, Schrafft's, or the Fleet.

Like many another apprehensive parent, I even fell back on the Lambs. Not for long—for only two pages, to be exact. I found my own eyes glazed as swiftly as his when I read that interminable first paragraph which begins, "Gertrude, Queen of Denmark, becoming a widow by the sudden death of King Hamlet, in less than two months after his death married his brother Claudius, which was noted by all people at the time for a strange act of indiscretion, or unfeelingness, or worse," etc. and etc.

Before I knew it, Saturday was upon us.

We lunched first. Not at home. At a restaurant. At Giovanni's, in feast-day style worthy of the event. While he sipped a preliminary Coke downstairs and I an old-fashioned, I tried in simpler language than the Lambs' to explain what he would see. It took more explanation than I had thought it would. I noticed that his eyes brightened whenever the Ghost was mentioned. Or whenever, in my narration, a cadaver bit the dust.

"Why don't they use pistols?" he asked while I was outlining the duel scene with its multiple jobs for the court mortician. It was only when I had described the poison foil, the poisoned wine, and the fury of the duel that he appeared to forgive Shakespeare for not having anticipated the age of the machine.

When he demanded, "They won't really be dead, will they?" I knew he was interested. For him, make-believe and reality were still blissfully, terrifyingly one—at least up to an uncertain point.

Traffic held us up so that we were a minute or so late in getting to the theatre. Hence we missed the first scene on the parapet. But a friendly Negro doorman did his bit for Shakespeare that afternoon.

"Yessuh," the doorman said to him, "the Ghost is walkin' now. It's too dark to go in there. You gotta wait. But never you fear—he'll walk again."

While we were waiting for the first scene to be over, I assured him for the tenth time that the Ghost was not real, and tried to tell him how the illusion of his disappearance would be achieved.

The auditorium was dark when, with other stragglers, we pushed our way in. After we reached our seats, I could hardly persuade him to take off his coat and muffler. His eyes were glued on the stage. I was pleased to see how, even for the young, *Hamlet* sweeps forward on its own feet without having to rely on footnotes.

He listened to every word. He was never bored. He sat far back in his seat, relaxed only during soliloquies. Whenever there was a threat of action, he pushed forward. Whenever the Ghost appeared, he stood up. Once, when an offstage cannon sounded in the darkness, he came close to turning a somersault into the lap of the woman who was sitting beyond him.

"Holy smokes, what's that?" he cried.

The intermission almost broke his heart. When I suggested that he go out with me while I had a cigarette, he was at first unwilling to leave. His was that nicest of nice fears. He was afraid they might start without waiting for the audience.

On the sidewalk we encountered the doorman for the second time. "Did you see the Ghost?" He beamed. "Well, you'll see him again. He ain't done walkin'."

On the way back to our seats came, "Is Mr. Maurice Evans married?"

"No," I replied, "I don't think so."

"Why doesn't he marry Ophelia?" he suggested. "She's a mighty pretty girl."

He was standing bolt upright during the whole of the play-within-the-play scene. The death of Polonius grieved him. "He's such a funny, nice old man; he made me laugh." But he started laughing again when Hamlet reached behind the curtains for Polonius's body, to say, "I'll lug the guts into the neighboring room."

He jumped as if dynamited at that moment when Laertes and his followers were storming the castle. And I almost had to hold him to prevent his crawling over the seat in front of him during the duel.

After Hamlet's body had been carried by the four captains up the stairs and the curtain had fallen, he stayed—taped to his seat—applauding. He applauded, and applauded, and applauded.

"How'd you like it?" I asked in the taxi, homeward bound.

"Gee, it was swell! I liked it better than *Oklahoma!*" Then a pause. "I liked it better than Donald Duck." Another pause—a long, reflective one. "'A little more than kin, and less than kind.'—Gee! That's pretty, isn't it?"

STUDY QUESTIONS

1. Why did Brown feel it so important that his son like *Hamlet?*
2. What does Brown say about the too-early introduction of the young to the classics? Do you agree? Who is responsible for this "foul" play?
3. What aspects of contemporary life condition the uninitiated theatergoer?
4. Explain what Brown means when he calls Disney "delectable but destructive."
5. Why did *Hamlet* appeal to the young eyes of Brown's son?
6. What was the ultimate proof that the boy had enjoyed the play?

THE DEATH

Diana Trilling   OF MARILYN MONROE

Diana Trilling (1905–   ) was born in New York City. She received her B.A. from Radcliffe in 1925. She was the fiction critic for *Nation* from 1942 to 1949 and columnist for *The New Leader* from 1957 to 1959. Mrs. Trilling's work has been published in the *Partisan Review, Harper's, Harper's Bazaar, Vogue, The Reporter, Look, The New York Times Magazine,* and *Esquire.* She edited both *The Portable D. H. Lawrence* (1947) and Lawrence's letters (1958), and published *Claremont Essays* in 1964. She is married to Lionel Trilling.

On a Sunday morning in August 1962, Marilyn Monroe, aged thirty-six, was found dead in the bedroom of her home in Los Angeles, her hand on the telephone as if she had just received or, far more likely, been about to make a call. On the night table next to her bed stood a formidable array of medicines, among them a bottle that had held twenty-five Nembutal pills, now empty. Two weeks later a team of psychiatrists, appointed by the state in conformity with California law, brought in its report on the background and circumstances of her death, declaring it a suicide. There had of course never been any suggestion of foul play. The death was clearly self-inflicted, a climax of extended mental suffering. In fact, it was soon revealed that on Saturday evening Marilyn Monroe had made an emergency call to the psychoanalyst who had been treating her for her acute sleeplessness, her anxieties and depression, and that he had paid her a visit. But the formal psychiatric verdict had to do with the highly technical question of whether the overdose of barbiturates was purposeful or accidental: had Marilyn Monroe *intended* to kill herself when she took the twenty-five sleeping pills? The jury of experts now ruled it was purposeful: she had wanted to die.

It is an opinion, or at least a formulation, that can bear, I believe, a certain amount of modification. Obviously, I'm not proposing that Marilyn Monroe's death was accidental in the sense that she took so large a dose of pills with no knowledge of their lethal properties. But I think it would be more precise to call this kind of death incidental rather than purposeful—incidental to the desire to escape the pain of living. I am not a psychiatrist and I never knew Marilyn Monroe, but it seems to me that a person can want to be released from consciousness without seeking actual death; that someone can want to stop living without wishing to die. And this is my feeling about Marilyn Monroe, that even when she had spoken of "wanting to die" she really meant that she wanted to end her suffering, not her life. She wanted to destroy consciousness rather than herself. Then, having taken the pills, she realized she might never return from the sleep she craved so passionately and reached for the phone for help.

But this is of course only speculation, and more appropriately engaged in by the medical profession than by the layman. For the rest of us, the motives surrounding Marilyn Monroe's suicide fade in importance before the all-encompassing reality of the act itself: Marilyn Monroe terminated her life. While the medical experts pondered the delicate difference between accident and suicide, the public recognized that the inevitable had at last occurred: Marilyn Monroe had killed herself. Shocked and grieved as everyone was, no one was at all surprised that she had died by her own hand, because for some years now the world had been prepared for just some such tragic outcome to one of the extraordinary careers of our time.

The potentiality of suicide or, at any rate, the threat of extreme mental breakdown had been, after all, conveyed to us by virtually every news story about Marilyn Monroe of recent years. I don't mean that it had been spelled out that she would one day take her life or otherwise go off the deep psychic end. But no one seemed able to write about her without reassuring us that despite her instability and the graveness of her emotional problems, she was still vital and eager, still, however precariously, a going concern. Marilyn Monroe was an earnest, ambitious actress, determined to improve her skill; Marilyn Monroe had failed in several marriages but she was still in pursuit of fulfillment in love; Marilyn Monroe had several times miscarried but she still looked forward to having children; Marilyn Monroe was seriously engaged in psychoanalysis; Marilyn Monroe's figure was better than ever; she was learning to be prompter; she was coping, or was struggling to cope, with whatever it was that had intervened in the making of her last picture—so, on the well-worn track, ran all the news stories. Even what may have been her last interview to appear in print (by the time it came out, she was already dead) sounded the same dominant chord of hopefulness, telling us of a Marilyn Monroe full of confidence that she would improve her acting and find her roles, and that between the two therapies, hard work and psychoanalysis, she would achieve the peace of mind that had for so long eluded her.

Where there is this much need for optimism, surely there is great peril, and the public got the message. But what is striking is the fact that throughout this period of her mounting difficulties, with which we were made so familiar, the popular image remained intact. Whatever we were told of her weak hold on life, we retained our image of Marilyn Monroe as the very embodiment of life energy. I think my response to her death was the common one: it came to me with the impact of a personal deprivation but I also felt it as I might a catastrophe in history or in nature; there was less in life, there was less of life, because she had ceased to exist. In her loss life itself had been injured.

In my own instance, it happens that she was already an established star before I knew her as anything except the latest pin-up girl. There is always this shield of irony some of us raise between ourselves and any object of popular adulation, and I had made my dull point of snubbing her pictures. Then one evening I chanced on a television trailer for *Bus Stop*, and there she was. I'm not even sure I knew whom I was seeing on the screen, but a light had gone on in the room. Where everything had been gray there was all at once an illumination, a glow of something beyond the ordinarily human. It was a remarkable moment, of a kind I don't recall having had with any other actress, and it has its place with certain rare, cherished experiences of art such as my youthful remembrance of Pavlova, the most perfect of performing artists, whose control of her body was like a radiance, or even the quite recent experience of seeing some photographs of Nijinsky in motion. Marilyn Monroe was in motion, too, which is important, since no still picture could quite catch her electric quality; in posed pictures the redundancy of flesh was what first imposed itself, dimming one's perception of its peculiar aliveness, of the translucence that infused body with spirit. In a moment's flash of light, the ironies with which I had resisted this sex idol, this object of an undifferentiating public taste, dropped from me never to be restored.

But mine was a minority problem; the world had long since recognized Marilyn Monroe's unique gift of physical being and responded to it as any such gift of life demands. From the start of her public career it had acknowledged the genius of biology or chemistry or whatever it was that set this young woman apart from the general kind. And once it had admitted her magic, nothing it was to learn of her "morbidity" could weigh against the conviction that she was alive in a way not granted the rest of us, or, more accurately, that she communicated such a charge of vitality as altered our imagination of life, which is of course the whole job and wonder of art.

Since her death it has occurred to me that perhaps the reason we were able to keep these two aspects in which we knew Marilyn Monroe—her life affirmation and her impulse to death—in such discreet balance was that they never presented themselves to us as mutually exclusive but, on the contrary, as two intimately related, even expectable, facets of her extraordinary endowment. It is as if the world that loved Marilyn Monroe understood that her superabundant biology had necessarily to provoke its own restraint, that this is the cruel law by which nature, or at least nature within civilization, punishes those of us who ask too much of life or bring too much to life. We are told that when one of the senses is defective, nature frequently provides a compensation in another of the senses; the blind often hear better than the seeing, or have a sharper sense of touch. What we are not told but perhaps understand nonetheless is the working of nature's system of negative compensation—the price we pay for gift, the revenge that life seems so regularly to take upon distinction. Certainly our awareness of the more, the plus, in Marilyn Monroe prepared us for some sort of minus. The fact that this young woman whose biological gift was so out of the ordinary was in mental pain seemed to balance the ledger. And one can speculate that had we not known of her emotional suffering, we would have been prepared for some other awful fate for her—an airplane disaster, maybe, or a deforming illness. So superstition may be thought of as an accurate reading of the harder rules of life.

And yet it is difficult to suppose the gods could be all that jealous. Had Marilyn Monroe not been enough punished in childhood to ensure her against further misfortune? Once this poor forlorn girl had been so magically brought into her own, the most superstitious of us had the right to ask happiness for her ever after. It was impossible to think of Marilyn Monroe except as Cinderella. The strange power of her physical being seemed best explained and justified by the extreme circumstances of her early life—the illegitimate birth, the mad mother, the orphanage and near-mad foster homes, the rape by one of her early guardians. If there was no good fairy in Marilyn Monroe's life and no Prince Charming, unless Hollywood, this didn't rob her story of its fairy-book miraculousness; it merely assimilated to the old tale our newer legend of the self-made hero or heroine. Grace Kelly had had her good Philadelphia family to pave her path and validate her right to a crown. But Marilyn Monroe reigned only by virtue of her beauty and her determination to be raised out of the squalor and darkness, and to shine in the full, the fullest, light. It is scarcely a surprise that the brighter her radiance, the more we listened for the stroke of midnight that would put a limit on such transcendence.

But it was not only the distance Marilyn Monroe had traveled from her unhappy beginnings that represented for us a challenge of reality, to be punished by reality. If her gift is to be regarded not as that of the stage or screen, which I think it primarily was not, but as the gift of biology, she was among those who are greatly touched with power; she was of the true company of artists. And her talent was so out of the range of the usual that we were bound to feel of it that it was not to be contained in society as we know it; therefore it proposed its own dissolution. Like any great artistic gift, Marilyn Monroe's power of biology was explosive, a primitive and savage force. It had, therefore and inevitably, to be a danger both to herself and to the world in which it did its work. All art is fierce in the measure that it matters, finally, and in its savagery it chooses either to push against society, against the restrictions that hedge it in, or against the artist himself. And no doubt it is the incapacity of most human beings to sustain this inordinate pressure that accounts for the fact that the artist is an exception in any civilized population. To mediate between the assault upon oneself and upon society, to keep alive in the battle and come out more or less intact, is a giant undertaking in which the native endowment of what we call talent is probably but a small element.

Among the very few weapons available to the artist in this monstrous struggle, naïveté can be the most useful. But it is not at all my impression that Marilyn Monroe was a naïve person. I think she was innocent, which is very different. To be naïve is to be simple or stupid on the basis of experience, and Marilyn Monroe was far from stupid; no one who was stupid could have been so quick to turn her wit against herself, or to manage the ruefulness with which she habitually replied to awkward questioning. To be innocent is to suffer one's experience without being able to learn self-protection from it; as if will-lessly, innocence is at the mercy of experience, unable to mobilize counterforces to fortune.

Of Ernest Hemingway, for example, I feel much as I do of Marilyn Monroe, that he was unable to marshal any adequate defense against the painful events of his childhood, and this despite his famous toughness and the courage he could call upon in war, in hunting, in all the dangerous enterprises that seduced him. He was an innocent man, not a naïve man, though not always intelligent. Marilyn Monroe offers us a similar paradox. Even while she symbolized an extreme of experience, of sexual knowingness, she took each new circumstance of life, as it came to her or as she sought it, like a newborn babe. And yet this was what made her luminous—her innocence. The glow was not rubbed off her by her experience of the ugliness of life because finally, in some vital depth, she had been untouched by it.

From the psychiatrist's point of view, too much innocence, a radical disproportion between what has happened to a person and what he has absorbed from his experience, is a symptom, and alarming. It can indicate a rude break in his connection with himself, and if he is in treatment, it suggests a difficult cure, since, in emotional logic, he will probably be as impervious to the therapy as to the events through which he has passed, and yet without any mitigation of suffering. In the creative spheres, an excess of innocence unquestionably exercises an enormous fascination on us; it produces the purity of expression which leads us to say of an artistic creation or performance that it is "out of this world." But the psychiatric judgment has to pick its way on tiptoe between the gift and the pathology. What constitutes a person's art may eventually spell his emotional undoing.

I can suppose of Marilyn Monroe that she was peculiarly elusive to the psychiatrists or analysts who tried to help her, that emotionally speaking she presented herself to them as a kind of blank page on which nothing had been written, failing to make the connection between herself and them even as she pleaded for it. And yet disconnection was at the heart of her gift, it defined her charm for the world, much as Hemingway's dissociation from his own experience was determinative of his gift.

For several decades, scores of writers have tried to imitate Hemingway's style: the flexibility and purity of his prose, the bright, cogent distance he was able to put between himself and the object under examination. But none has succeeded. And I believe this is because his prose was, among many other things, a direct report of the unbridgeable distance between external reality and his emotions. Just so, Marilyn Monroe was inimitable. Hollywood, Broadway, the night clubs: they all regularly produce their quota of sex queens, but the public takes them and leaves them, or doesn't really take them; the world is not enslaved as it was by Marilyn Monroe because none but Marilyn Monroe could suggest such a purity of sexual delight. The boldness with which she could parade herself and yet never be gross, her sexual flamboyance and bravado which yet breathed an air of mystery and even reticence, her voice which carried such ripe overtones of erotic excitement and yet was the voice of a shy child—these complications were integral to her gift. And they described a young woman trapped in some never-never land of unawareness.

What I imply here, of course, is a considerable factitiousness in Marilyn Monroe as a sexual figure. Certainly the two or three men I've known who met her in "real life" were agreed on her lack of direct sexual impact; she was sweet and beautiful and lovely, yes, but somehow not at all the arousing woman they had expected. The nature of true sexuality is most difficult to define, so much of what we find sexually compelling has its source in phantasies that have little to do with the primary sexual instinct. Especially in the case of a movie star we enter a realm where dream and biology make their easiest merger. The art of acting is the art of *performing as if,* and the success of this feat of suggestion depends upon the degree to which it speaks to some phantasy of the onlookers.

Marilyn Monroe spoke to our dreams as much as to our animal nature, but in a most unusual way. For what she appealed to was our determination to be rid of phantasy and to get down to the rock-bottom actuality. She gratified our wish to confront our erotic desires without romance, without diversion. And working within a civilization like ours, in which sexuality is so surrounded with restraints and fears and prohibitions, she perhaps came as close as possible to giving us the real thing. But she didn't give us the real thing; she merely acted as if she were giving it to us. She glamorized sexuality to the point at which it lost its terrors for us; and maybe it was this veil that she raised to sexual reality that permitted women, no less than men, to respond to her so generously. Instinctively, I think, women understood that this seemingly most sexual of female creatures was no threat to them.

The myth of Marilyn Monroe was thus even more of a myth than we realized, for this girl who was supposed to release us from our dreams into sexual actuality was in all probability not actual even to herself. Least of all could she have been sexually actual to herself and at the same time such a marvelous public performer of sex, such a conscious artist of sex. And we can conjecture that it was this deep alienation from her own feelings, including her sexual feeling, that enabled her to sustain the disorder of her early years even as long and as well as she did, and to speak of her awful childhood so simply and publicly. For most of us, the smallest "shame" in our past must be kept locked from others. We prefer that the least menacing of skeletons remain in the closet lest our current image of ourselves be violated by its emergence into the open. But Marilyn Monroe had no need for such reserves. She told the public the most gruesome facts of her personal history, for all the world as if we on the outside were worthy of such confidences—except that in some odd, generous response to her innocence, we exceeded ourselves in her instance and didn't take the advantage of her that we might have. Judged from the point of view of what we require of the artist, that he have the will and fearlessness to rise above the conventions which bind those of us with less gift, Marilyn Monroe's candor about her early life was something to be celebrated. But from another point of view her frankness was a warning that the normal barriers of self-protection were down or nonexistent, leaving her grievously exposed to the winds of circumstance.

And indeed the very word "exposed" is a key word in the pattern of her life. She was an actress and she exposed her person and her personality to the public gaze. She was an exposed human being who told the truth about herself too readily, too publicly. And more than most actresses, she exposed her body, with but inadequate understanding of what this involved. We recall, for instance, the awkward little scandal about her having once posed naked for a calendar and the bewildered poise, the really untoward innocence and failure of comprehension, with which she met the dismay of her studio, as if to say, "But that was me yesterday when I needed money. That isn't me today; today I have money." Just as today and yesterday were discontinuous with each other, she was discontinuous with herself, held together, one feels, only and all too temporarily by her success.

And this success was perhaps more intimately connected with her awareness of her physical appeal than we always understood. It may well have been the fact that she was so much and so admiringly in the public eye that gave Marilyn Monroe the largest part of her sense of a personal identity. Not long before her death, we now discover, she had herself photographed in the nude, carefully editing the many pictures as if to be certain she left the best possible record for posterity. The photographs leave, however, a record only of wasted beauty, at least of the famous body—while Marilyn Monroe's face is lovely as ever, apparently unscarred by her intense suffering, her body looked ravaged and ill, already drained of life. Recently the pictures have been published in an expensive magazine devoted to erotica. If their high price, prohibitive to the general buyer, could be interpreted as a precaution against their being too easily available to a sensation-seeking audience, the restraint was not really necessary. At the last, the nude Marilyn Monroe could excite no decent viewer to anything but the gentlest pity, and much fear.

But even before this ultimate moment the public success had been threatened. The great career was already failing. There had not been a Marilyn Monroe movie for a long time, and the last film she had worked on had had to be halted because she was unable to appear. And there was no private life to fall back upon, not even the formal structure of one: no marriage, no family, apparently not even friends. One had come, indeed, to think of her as the loneliest of people, so that it was not without bitterness that, on her death, one discovered that it was not only oneself who had wished to help her but many other strangers, especially women to whose protectiveness her extreme vulnerability spoke so directly. But we were the friends of whom she knew nothing, and among the people she knew it would seem that real relationships were out of reach across the desert emptiness that barricades whoever is out of touch with his feelings. One thinks of her that last evening of her life, alone and distraught, groping for human comfort and finding nothing but those endless bottles of medicine, and one confronts a pathos worse than tragedy.

Certainly it strains justice as well as imagination that the world's most glamorous woman should have been alone, with no date, on a Saturday night—for it was, in fact, a Saturday night when she killed herself. On other nights but Saturday, we are allowed our own company. Saturday night is when all American boys and girls must prove themselves sexually. This is when we must be "out," out in the world where we can be seen among the sexually chosen. Yet the American girl who symbolized sexual success for all of us spent her last Saturday night alone in despair. Every man in the country would have wanted to date Marilyn Monroe, or so he would say, but no man who knew her did.

Or, contemplating her loneliness, we think of her funeral, which, contrived to give her the peace and privacy that had so strenuously eluded her throughout her life, yet by its very restraint and limited attendance reminded us of the limitations of her actual connection with the world. Joe DiMaggio, who had been her husband for a few brief months earlier in her career, was the chief mourner. It was DiMaggio to whom, she had told us, it was impossible to be married because he had no conversation; at meals, instead of talking to her, he read the papers or looked at television. The more recent husband, *with* conversation, was not present, no doubt for his own inviolable reasons, but it was saddening. I do not know what, if anything, was read at the service, but I'd like to think it was of an elevated and literary kind, such as might be read at the funeral of a person of the first intellectual rank.

For of the cruelties directed at this young woman even by the public that loved her, it seems to me that the most biting, and unworthy of the supposedly enlightened people who were particularly guilty of it, was the mockery of her wish to be educated, or thought educated. Granting our right to be a bit confused when our sex idol protests a taste for Dostoevsky, surely the source of our discomfort must yet be located in our suspicions of Dostoevsky's worth for us and in our own sexual unease rather than in Marilyn Monroe. For what our mockery signifies is our disbelief that anyone who has enough sexuality needs to read Do-

stoevsky. The notion that someone with Marilyn Monroe's sexual advantages could have wanted anything except to make love robbed us of a
prized illusion, that enough sexual possibility is enough everything.

I doubt that sex was enough anything for Marilyn Monroe, except
the means for advancing herself in the world. One of the touching
revelations of her early life was her description of how she discovered
that somehow she was sexually different from other girls her age: the
boys all whistled at her and crowded to her like bears to honey, so she
came to realize that she must have something special about her, which
she could use to rise above her poor circumstances. Her sexual awareness, that is, came to her from outside herself. It would be my guess that
it remained outside her always, leaving a great emptiness, where a true
sexuality would have supplied her with a sense of herself as a person
with connection and content.

This void she tried to fill in every way available, with worldly
goods, with fame and public attention and marriage, and also in ways
that turned out to be unavailable, like children and domesticity—nothing
could be more moving than the eagerness with which she seized upon a
Jewish mother-in-law, even upon Jewish ceremonials and cooking, as if
in the home life of her last husband's people she would find the secret of
emotional plenitude. She also tried to fill her emptiness with books and
learning. How mean-spirited can we be, to have denied her whatever
might have added to her confidence that she was really a solid person
and not just an uninhabited body?

And that she had the intellectual capacity for education there can
be no question, had it but been matched with emotional capacity. No
one without a sharp native intelligence could have spoofed herself as
gracefully as she did or parried reporters with such finesse. If we are to
judge by her interviews, she was as singularly lacking in the endemic off-
stage dullness of actors and actresses, the trained courtesy and charm
that is only another boring statement of their self-love, as she was
deficient in the established defenses of her profession: one recalls no
instance of even implied jealousy of her colleagues or of censure of
others—directors, script-writers, husbands—for her own failures. Her generosity of spirit, indeed, was part of the shine that was on her. But
unfortunately it spared everyone but herself; she had never studied self-
justification. To herself she was not kind. She made fun of herself and of
all that she had to go on in life: her biology. Certainly this added to her
lovableness but it cut from under her the little ground that she could
call her own. When she exhibited her sexual abundance with that wonderful, gay exaggeration of hers, or looked wide-eyed upon the havoc
she wrought, it was her way of saying, "Don't be afraid. I don't take
myself seriously so you don't have to take me seriously either." Her
talent for comedy, in other words, was a public beneficence but a

personal depredation, for, far more than most people, she precisely needed the assurance that she weighed in the scheme of human life, that she had substance and reality, that she had all the qualifications that make for a person we take seriously. Herself a supplicant, she gave us comfort. Herself a beggar, she distributed alms.

At her death, several writers of good will who undertook to deal with the tragedy of her suicide blamed it on Hollywood. In the industry that had made millions from her and in the methods by which Hollywood had exploited her, they found the explanation of her failed life; they wrote about her as the sacrificial lamb on the altar of American vulgarity and greed. I share their disgust with Hollywood and I honor their need to isolate Marilyn Monroe from the nastiness that fed on her, but I find it impossible to believe that this girl would have been an iota better off were Hollywood to have been other than what we all know it to be, a madness in our culture.

The self-destructiveness that Marilyn Monroe carried within her had not been put there by the "system," however overbearing in its ugliness. Just as her sweetness was her own, and immune to the influences of Hollywood, her terrors were also her own. They were not implanted in her, though undoubtedly they were increased, by the grandiosity of being a star. Neither for better nor worse, I feel, was she essentially falsified or distorted by her public role, though she must often have suffered cruelly from the inescapability of the public glare. In fact, it would be my conjecture that had she never gone into the movies and become rich and world-famous, her troubled spirit would long since have had its way with her. She would have been equally undone, and sooner, and with none of the many alleviations and compensations that she must have known in these years of success.

This doesn't mean that I don't think she was a "victim." But she was not primarily a victim of Hollywood commercialism, or exploitation, or of the inhumanity of the press. She was not even primarily a victim of the narcissistic inflation that so regularly attends the grim business of being a great screen personality. Primarily she was a victim of her gift, a biological victim, a victim of life itself. It is one of the excesses of contemporary thought that we like to blame our very faulty culture for tragedies that are inherent in human existence—at least, inherent in human existence in civilization. I think Marilyn Monroe was a tragedy of civilization, but this is something quite else again from, and even more poignant than, being a specifically American tragedy.

STUDY QUESTIONS

1.   How can a person want to stop living without wishing to die?

2.   Mrs. Trilling feels that the world had been prepared for the tragic

outcome of Marilyn Monroe's career. How fully does she discuss that preparation?

3. Marilyn Monroe, when alive, was seemingly amused by the fact that she had become a symbol. What kind of a symbol does Mrs. Trilling make of her?

4. Mrs. Trilling discusses a number of paradoxes in Marilyn Monroe's life. How can paradox help us to understand as complicated a person as Marilyn Monroe?

5. How many different meanings does Mrs. Trilling assign to *exposed?*

6. Mrs. Trilling dismisses the claim that Hollywood was responsible for Marilyn Monroe's death. But she does criticize both Hollywood and the viewing public for their treatment of the star. What is the basis for her criticism?

THE CONQUEST
Marya Mannes **OF TRIGGER MORTIS**

Marya Mannes (1904–   ) was born in New York City. She holds an honorary L.H.D. from Hood College (Maryland). From 1942 to 1945 she was an intelligence analyst for the United States government. Her television appearances, university lecture tours, and numerous periodical articles have made her a familiar figure to the American public. She has published *Message from a Stranger*, a novel (1948), *More in Anger* (1958), *Subverse*, satiric verse (1959), *The New York I Know* (1961), and *But Will It Sell?* (1964).

The ruling was passed in 1970, over the total opposition of the TV and radio networks and after ten years of controversy, six investigations, 483 juvenile murders, and the complete reorganization of the Federal Communications Commission. What finally pushed it through was the discovery of *trigger mortis* in a number of American children born in widely separated areas. In this malformation the index finger is permanently hooked, forcing partial contraction of the whole hand in the position required for grasping a revolver. "The gun," said a distinguished anthropologist, "has become an extension of the American arm."

This mutation had been suspected some time before by others, who had found it worthy of note that in 1959, for instance, American toy manufacturers had sold more than $60 million worth of guns and revolvers and that on any given day on television between one and ten o'clock there were more than fifteen programs devoted to violence, and that in each of these programs a gun was fired at least once and usually several times. The only difference between the programs was that in some the shooting was done out of doors and often from horses and that in others it was done in hotel rooms, bars, or apartments. The first category was called Western and was considered a wholesome fight between good men and bad men in healthy country; the second was called Crime and Detective and was considered salubrious in its repeated implication that "crime does not pay," although the women and the interiors shown were usually expensive and the criminal's life, though short, a rich one.

Although this wholesale preoccupation with killing by gun coincided for many years with the highest rate of juvenile crime ever known in this country, and with open access to firearms for all who desired them, television and radio violence was considered by most experts of minimal importance as a contributory cause of youthful killing. Psychiatrists, social workers, program directors, advertisers, and sponsors had a handy set of arguments to prove their point. These (with translation appended) were the most popular:

Delinquency is a complex problem. No single factor is responsible. (Don't let's stick our necks out. Don't let's act. Don't let's lose money.)

It's all a matter of the home. (Blame the parents. Blame the neighborhood. Blame poverty.)

Crime and adventure programs are a necessary outlet for natural childhood aggressions. (Keep the little bastards quiet while Mummy fixes supper.)

We don't really know what influences children. (Let's wait till they kill somebody.)

Only disturbed or abnormal children are affected by what they see on programs. (And they are a minority. Let their psychiatrists worry about them.)

Everybody was very pleased with these conclusions, particularly the broadcasters, who could continue presenting thirty shootings a day secure in those sections of their old printed Code, which stated: ". . . such subjects as violence and sex shall be presented without undue emphasis and only as required by plot development or character delineation"; and "Television shall exercise care in . . . avoiding material which is excessively violent or would create morbid suspense, or other undesirable reactions in children." These same officials continued also to exercise care in not letting their own children look at the programs of violence which they broadcast.

So for years, and in spite of sporadic cries of alarm and protest from parents and a number of plain citizens, there were always enough experts to assure the public that crime and violence had nothing to do with crime and violence, and that gunplay was entertainment. Psychiatrists continued to say things like this about young killers: "The hostility, festering perhaps from the time he had been trained to the toilet, screamed for release," and educational groups came out periodically with reports on delinquency in which a suggested solution would be "to orient norm-violating individuals in the population towards a law-abiding lower-class way of life."

Dialogues like the following were frequent in Congressional investigations. This one occurred in a hearing of the Senate sub-committee on Juvenile Delinquency in 1954:

> SENATOR: "In your opinion, what is the effect of these Western movies on children?"
> EXPERT: "No one knows anything about it."
> SENATOR: "Well, of course, you know that little children 6, 7, 8 years old now have belts with guns. Do you think that is due to the fact that they are seeing these Western movies and seeing all this shooting?"
> EXPERT: "Oh, undoubtedly."

In the early 1950s, psychiatrist Fredric Wertham, from whose *The Circle of Guilt* the above was quoted, began a relentless campaign against what he called, in another book, *The Seduction of the Innocent*. Concentrating at first on horror and crime comics, the doctor moved inevitably into other fields of mass communication and provided impressive evidence along the way that although their gigantic dosage of violence could not be the sole factor in child criminality, it could certainly be considered a major one.

In attacking the slogan "It's all up to the home," he wrote: "Of course the home has a lot to do with it. But it is wrong to accuse the home as a cause in the usual abstract way, for the home is inseparable from other social circumstances to which it is itself vulnerable. . . . A hundred years ago the home could guard the children's safety; but with the new technological advances, the modern parent cannot possibly carry this responsibility. We need traffic regulations, school buses, school zones, and police to protect children from irresponsible drivers. Who will guard the child today from irresponsible adults who sell him incentives, blueprints, and weapons for delinquency?"

Wertham also countered the familiar claim that youthful violence was a result of wars by stating that it was not backed up by any scientific, concrete study and that neither the Second World War nor the Korean War explained the phenomenon: ". . . after the First World War the type of brutal violence currently committed on a large scale by the youngest children was almost unknown."

But Wertham was dismissed by many of his colleagues and much of the public as a man obsessed; too aggressively and intemperately committed to one cause—the rape of children's minds by mass communications—to be seriously considered. And the broadcasters and crime-comic publishers, first needled and exasperated by him, soon were able to view him with calm detachment as a crackpot. Thirty murders a day continued on the screen.

Then, early in 1959, the Nuffield Foundation in England put out a thick book called *Television and the Child,* by Hilde T. Himmelweit, A. N. Oppenheim, and Pamela Vince. For four years they examined thousands of children in five cities and of every class and background, and to this they joined a survey of American programming and viewing. They did not confine themselves to programming specifically for children, since it had long been obvious in England, as it was here, that children usually watched adult programs in preference. In more than four hundred pages of meticulous research, scientific detachment, and careful reasoning, they came to certain conclusions—the basis for a weight of further evidence that led, ten years later, to government intervention into broadcasting practices. Here are a few of their findings about the twenty percent of programs seen by children in their peak viewing hours that are devoted to aggression and violence:

"At the center of preoccupation with violence is the gun. Everyone has a gun ready for immediate use—even the barbers and storekeepers, who are not cowboys. People in Westerns take guns for granted. . . . Finally, while guns are used mostly for killing, they are also let off for fun. Nevertheless, guns spell power, they make people listen, and force them to do what is wanted.

"It is said that these programmes have two main desirable effects: they teach the lesson that crime does not pay; and they provide a harmless outlet through fantasy for the child's hostile feelings. We shall take issue with both statements. . . . The lesson as taught in these programmes is entirely negative (it is best not to offend against the law). . . . To present such a one-sided view, repeated week after week, is contrary to the recognized educational principle that a moral lesson, to be effective, must teach what should be done as well as what should not be done.

"More serious is the fact that . . . the child may equally well learn other, less desirable lessons from these programmes; that to shoot, bully, and cheat is allowed, provided one is on the right side of the law; and that relationships among people are built not on loyalty and affection but on fear and domination. . . ."

As for being a "harmless outlet for aggressive feelings," the authors—quoting the testimony of Dr. Eleanor E. Maccoby of Harvard that this discharge in fantasy alters nothing in the child's real life and so has no lasting values—write that when aggressive feelings exist, "They are not as a rule discharged on viewing crime and violence." "We cite three sets of data . . . [which] show that aggressive feelings are just as likely to be aroused as to be lessened through viewing these programmes—indeed, this seems more often to be the case." And, quoting Dr. Maccoby again, ". . . the very children who are presumably using the movie as an outlet for their aggressive feelings are the ones who carry away the aggressive content in their memories, for how long we do not know."

Miss Himmelweit and her colleagues sum up as follows: "It is suggested that crime and violence programmes increase tension and anxiety, increase maladjustment and delinquent behaviour, teach children techniques of crime, blunt their sensitivity to suffering and, related to this, suggest to them that conflict is best solved by aggression.

"Our findings and those of Maccoby suggest, then, that these programmes do not initiate aggressive, maladjusted, or delinquent behaviour, but may aid its expression. They may not affect a stable child, but they may evoke a response in the 5–10 percent of all children who are disturbed or at least emotionally labile, 'a group to be reckoned with by all the responsible people in the field of mass communications.'"

"We find . . . ," says the Nuffield Report, closing this chapter, "evidence that [these programs] may retard children's awareness of the serious consequences of violence in real life and may teach a greater acceptance of aggression as the normal, manly solution of conflict. . . . Just as a nation improves public hygiene when the evidence *suggests*, *without necessarily proving it* [my italics], that harm may otherwise result, so, we think, there is need of remedial action here."

The Nuffield Report authors had obviously fallen into the error of blaming the industry instead of the child. For in most "acceptable" studies of television and its influence, wrote Wertham, "the assumption seems to be that when anything goes wrong the child must be morbid but the entertainment normal. Why not assume . . . that our children are normal, that they like adventure and imagination, that they can be stimulated to excitement, but that maybe something is wrong with what they are looking at? Why assume that they need death and destruction . . . ?"

Voices, voices, voices. "Beefs," "squawks," the broadcasters called these surges of protest year after year. And they would point with pride to the one children's program out of ten that was educational, the one out of twenty that had no shooting.

But their biggest defense became, in the end, their undoing. They had assured themselves that by removing the physical effects of violence, the violence was stripped of its harm. They showed no blood, no close-ups of agony, no open wounds, no last convulsions of a riddled body. Men were shot, they clapped their hands to their stomachs and either fell forwards or backwards as the camera panned away and returned to the gun. And while the broadcasters felt this a noble concession to the sensibilities of young viewers ("Brutality or physical agony," says the NBC Code, "is not presented in detail nor indicated by offensive sound or visual effects"), they were in actuality presenting, day after day, two great immoralities: that shooting is clean—and easy. To pull a trigger requires neither strength nor skill nor courage: it is the bullet that kills. And to kill with a gun is quick and painless. Hero or criminal, both were cowards who answered questions by pulling triggers. This was the daily lesson for sixty million children for twenty years.

Until, of course, the people finally rose. Some cool legal heads first managed to draft legislation banning the sale of pornographic and sensational printed material without in any way curbing individual liberty or preventing the sale of *Lady Chatterley's Lover* or Aristophanes. And then came the famous FCC ruling Bylaw A 41-632. In effect, this gave the FCC, by then reorganized into a body of able and dedicated communications experts who functioned in areas of human values as well as in electronics, the power to revoke the license of any broadcaster showing fictionalized killing, whether by gun or knife or bludgeon, without also displaying the natural consequences to the person killed. The bill as originally drawn was a forthright ban on all fictionalized killing except by direct bodily means, without weapons: killing had to involve strength, skill, and direct physical involvement. But after long wrangling, the later version was adopted as being less tainted by censorship and more practicable. For if a program showing a killing had to show a head blown to bits at close range, or blood gushing from mouth and nose, or a jagged stomach wound—all natural results of shooting—the sponsor would not sell many goods. It was therefore far easier to cut out guns entirely.

Far easier, that is, for everyone but the writers. After the law was put into effect, there was mass unemployment among the television writers in Hollywood and New York. They had relied so long on their collaborator, the gun, that they were incapable of writing a plot without it. As Wertham quoted an experienced TV crime writer: "You have to work backwards. You're given a violent situation and you have to work within that framework." Start with the murder and then fit in the people. And suddenly the poor writers had to think up situations where people and ideas provided the excitement instead of a Colt 45. It was a period of anguish none of them will forget.

But for every ten writers who became alcoholics or joined insurance firms, one began to tap resources he had never used and to write well and truly for the first time. And after a hiatus of incredible sterility, when frantic producers threw in anything innocuous, however old and poor, to fill up the time formerly used by crime plays and Westerns, television slowly began to get better and better, more inventive both in the uses of realism and fantasy.

A new generation of American children grew up with no appetite for guns and no illusions about the fun of painless killing. Instead they learned judo or, through compulsory strenuous exercises then conducted daily by their schools, became a race of confident acrobats, able to show their prowess in feats of skill, daring, and endurance without knifing, stomping, or shooting anyone.

Disarmament—at least of the young—was finally a fact.

STUDY QUESTIONS

1. Define *trigger mortis*. What is *rigor mortis?*
2. What arguments were used to counteract the charge that television had contributed to the rising juvenile crime rate? How effective are Miss Mannes' parenthetical remarks in answering these arguments?
3. Why was Frederic Wertham's campaign dismissed by his colleagues and the public?
4. In self-defense, what modifications did the networks make?
5. In general, what is the tone of Miss Mannes' essay? Is it sarcastic? Satirical? Is the essay humorous?

Gore Vidal   TARZAN REVISITED

Gore Vidal (1925–   ) was born in West Point, New York. He attended Phillips Exeter Academy. He is equally famous for his novels, short stories, plays, and essays. Among Vidal's novels are *Williwaw* (1946), *In a Yellow Wood* (1947), *The City and the Pillar* (1948), *The Season of Comfort* (1949), *A Search for the King* and *Dark Green, Bright Red* (1950), *The Judgment of Paris* (1952), *Messiah* (1954), *Julian* (1964), and *Washington, D.C.* (1967). *A Thirsty Evil*, his collection of short stories, was published in 1956. His plays include *Visit to a Small Planet* (1957), *The Best Man* (1960), and *Romulus* (1962). His essays were published in 1962 as *Rocking the Boat*. Vidal has also written plays for screen and television. He was a Democratic-Liberal candidate for Congress in 1960.

First published in *Esquire* Magazine, December 1963. Reprinted by permission of the author.

There are so many things the people who take polls never get around to asking. Fascinated as we all are to know what our countrymen think of great issues (approving, disapproving, "don't-knowing," with that same shrewd intelligence which made a primeval wilderness bloom with Howard Johnson signs), the pollsters never get around to asking the sort of interesting personal questions our new-Athenians might be able to answer knowledgeably. For instance, how many adults have an adventure serial running in their heads? How many consciously daydream, turning on a story in which the dreamer ceases to be an employee of IBM and becomes a handsome demigod moving through splendid palaces, saving maidens from monsters (or monsters from maidens: this is a jaded time). Most children tell themselves stories in which they figure as powerful figures, enjoying the pleasures not only of the adult world as they conceive it but of a world of wonders unlike dull reality. Although this sort of Mittyesque daydreaming is supposed to cease in maturity, I suggest that more adults than we suspect are bemusedly wandering about with a full Technicolor extravaganza going on in their heads. Clad in tights, rapier in hand, the daydreamers drive their Jaguars at fantastic speeds through a glittering world of adoring love objects, mingling anachronistic historic worlds with science fiction. "Captain, the time-warp's been closed! We are now trapped in a parallel world, inhabited entirely by women, with three breasts." Though from what we can gather about these imaginary worlds, they tend to be more Adlerian than Freudian: The motor drive is the desire not for sex (other briefer fantasies take care of that) but for power, for the ability to dominate one's environment through physical strength. I state all this with perfect authority because I have just finished rereading several books by the master of American daydreamers, Edgar Rice Burroughs, whose works today, as anyone who goes into a drugstore or looks at a newsstand can see, have suddenly returned to great popularity.

When I was growing up, I read all twenty-three *Tarzan* books, as well as the ten *Mars* books. My own inner storytelling mechanism was vivid. At any one time, I had at least three serials going as well as a number of old faithful reruns. I used Burroughs as a source of raw material. When he went to the center of the earth à la Jules Verne (much too fancy a writer for one's taste), I immediately worked up a thirteen-part series, with myself as lead, and various friends as guest stars. Sometimes I used the master's material, but more often I adapted it freely to suit myself. One's daydreams tended to be Tarzanish prepuberty (physical strength and freedom) and Martian post-puberty (exotic worlds and subtle *combinaziones* to be worked out). After adolescence, if one's life is sufficiently interesting, the desire to tell oneself stories diminishes. My last serial ran into sponsor trouble when I was in the Second World War and was never renewed.

Until recently I assumed that most people were like myself: day-dreaming ceases when the real world becomes interesting and reason-ably manageable. Now I am not so certain. Pondering the life and success of Burroughs leads one to believe that a good many people find their lives so unsatisfactory that they go right on year after year telling themselves stories in which they are able to dominate their environment in a way that is not possible in this overorganized society.

"Most of the stories I wrote were the stories I told myself just before I went to sleep," said Edgar Rice Burroughs, describing his own work. He is a fascinating figure to contemplate, an archetype American dreamer. Born 1875, in Chicago, he was a drifter until he was thirty-six. Briefly, he served in the U.S. Cavalry; then he was a gold miner in Oregon, a cowboy in Idaho, a railroad policeman in Salt Lake City; he attempted several businesses that failed. He was perfectly in the old-American grain: The man who could take on almost any job, who liked to keep moving, who tried to get rich quick, but could never pull it off. And while he was drifting through the unsatisfactory real world, he consoled himself with an inner world where he was strong and hand-some, adored by beautiful women and worshiped by exotic races. Bur-roughs might have gone to his death, an unknown daydreamer, if he had not started reading pulp fiction. He needed raw material for his own inner serials and once he had used up his favorite source, Rider Hag-gard, he turned to the magazines. He was appalled at how poor the stories were. They did not compare with his own imaginings. He was like a lover of pornography who, unable to find works which excite him, turns to writing them. Burroughs promptly wrote a serial about Mars and sold it to *Munsey's*. His fellow daydreamers recognized a master. In 1914 he published his first book, *Tarzan of the Apes* (Rousseau's noble savage reborn in Africa), and history was made. To date the Tarzan books have sold over twenty-five million copies in fifty-six languages. There is hardly an American male of my generation who has not at one time or another tried to master the victory cry of the great ape as it once bellowed forth from the androgynous chest of Johnny Weismuller, while a thousand arms and legs were broken by attempts to swing from tree to tree in the backyards of the republic. Between 1914 and his death in 1950, Burroughs, the squire of Tarzana, California (a prophet honored by his own land), produced over sixty books, while enjoying the unique status of being the first American writer to be a corporation. Burroughs is said to have been a pleasant, unpretentious man who liked to ride and play golf. Not one to disturb his own unconscious with reality, he never set foot in Africa.

With a sense of recapturing childhood, I have just reread several Tarzan books. It is fascinating to see how much one recalls after a quarter century. At times the sense of *déjà vu* is overpowering. It is equally interesting to discover that one's memories of *Tarzan of the Apes* are mostly action scenes. The plot had slipped one's mind. It is a lot of plot, too. The beginning is worthy of Conrad. "I had this story from one who had no business to tell it to me, or to any other. I may credit the seductive influence of an old vintage upon the narrator for the beginning of it, and my own skeptical incredulity during the days that followed for the balance of the strange tale." It is 1888. The young Lord and Lady Greystoke are involved in a ship mutiny ("there was in the whole atmosphere of the craft that undefinable something which presages disaster"). They are put ashore on the west coast of Africa. They build a tree house. Here Burroughs is at his best. He tells you the size of the logs, the way to hang a door when you have no hinges, the problems of roofing. All his books are filled with interesting details on how things are made. The Greystokes have a child. They die. The "man-child" is taken up by Kala, a Great Ape, who brings him up as a member of her tribe of apes. Burroughs is a rather vague anthropologist. His apes have a language. They are carnivorous. They can, he suspects, mate with human beings. Tarzan grows up as an ape; he kills his first lion (with a full nelson); he teaches himself to read and write English by studying some books found in the cabin. The method he used, sad to say, is the currently fashionable "look-see." Though he can read and write, he cannot speak any language except that of the apes. He gets on well with the animal kingdom, with Tantor the elephant, Ska the vulture, Numa the lion (Kipling has added his grist to the Burroughs dream mill). Then white people arrive: Professor Archimedes Q. Porter and his daughter Jane. Also, a Frenchman named D'Arnot who teaches Tarzan to speak French, which is confusing. By coincidence, Jane's suitor is the current Lord Greystoke, who thinks the Greystoke baby is dead. Tarzan saves Jane from an ape. Then he puts on clothes and goes to Paris where he drinks absinthe. Next stop, America. In Wisconsin, he saves Jane Porter from a forest fire; then he nobly gives her up to Lord Greystoke, not revealing the fact that *he* is the real Lord Greystoke. Fortunately in the next volume, *The Return of Tarzan,* he marries Jane and they live happily ever after in Africa, raising a son John, who in turn grows up and has a son. Yet even as a grandfather, Tarzan continues to have adventures with people a foot high, with descendants of Atlantis, with the heirs of a Roman legion who think that Rome is still a success. All through these stories one gets the sense that one is daydreaming, too. Episode follows episode with no particular urgency. Tarzan is always knocked on the head and taken captive; he always escapes; there is always a beautiful princess or high priestess who loves him and assists him; there is always a loyal friend who fights beside him, very much in the Queequeg tradition which Leslie Fielder assures us is the urning in the fuel supply of the American psyche. But no matter how difficult the adventure, Tarzan, clad only in a loincloth with no weapon save a knife (the style is contagious), wins against all odds and returns to his shadowy wife.

These books are clearly for men. I have yet to meet a woman who found Tarzan interesting: no identification, as they say in series-land.

Stylistically, Burroughs is—how shall I put it?—uneven. He has moments of ornate pomp, when the darkness is "Cimmerian"; of redundancy, "she was hideous and ugly"; of extraordinary dialogue: "Name of a name," shrieked Rokoff. "Pig, but you shall die for this!" Or Lady Greystoke to Lord G.: "Duty is duty, my husband, and no amount of sophistries may change it. I would be a poor wife for an English lord were I to be responsible for his shirking a plain duty." Or the grandchild: "Muvver," he cried "Dackie doe? Dackie doe?" "Let him come along," urged Tarzan. "Dare!" exclaimed the boy turning triumphantly upon the governess, "Dackie do doe yalk!" Burroughs' use of coincidence is shameless even for a pulp writer. In one book he has three sets of characters shipwrecked at exactly the same point on the shore of Africa. Even Burroughs finds this a bit much. "Could it be possible [muses Tarzan] that fate had thrown him up at the very threshold of his own beloved jungle?" It was possible, of course; anything can happen in a daydream.

Though Burroughs is innocent of literature and cannot reproduce human speech, he does have a gift very few writers of any kind possess: he can describe action vividly. I give away no trade secrets when I say that this is as difficult for a Tolstoi as it is for a Burroughs (even William). Because it is so hard, the craftier contemporary novelists usually prefer to tell their stories in the first person, which is simply writing dialogue. In character, as it were, the writer settles for an impression of what happened rather than creating the sense of a happening. Tarzan *in action* is excellent.

There is something basic in the appeal of the 1914 Tarzan which makes me think that he can still hold his own as a daydream figure, despite the sophisticated challenge of his two contemporary competitors, Ian Fleming and Mickey Spillane. For most adults, Tarzan (and John Carter of Mars) can hardly compete with the conspicuous consumer consumption of James Bond or the sickly violence of Mike Hammer, but for children and adolescents, the old appeal continues. All of us need the idea of a world alternative to this one. From Plato's Republic to Opar to Bond-land, at every level, the human imagination has tried to imagine something better for itself than the existing society. Man left Eden when we got up off all fours, endowing most of his descendants with nostalgia as well as chronic backache. In its naïve way, the Tarzan legend returns us to that Eden where, free of clothes and the inhibitions of an oppressive society, a man can achieve in reverie his continuing need, which is, as William Faulkner put it in his high Confederate style, to prevail as well as endure. The current fascination with L.S.D. and non-addictive drugs—not to mention alcoholism—is all part of a general sense of frustration and boredom. The individual's desire to dominate his environment is not a desirable trait in a society which every day grows more and more confining. Since there are few legitimate releases for the average man, he must take to daydreaming. James Bond, Mike Hammer and Tarzan are all dream-selves, and the aim of each is to establish personal primacy in a world which in reality diminishes the individual. Among adults, increasing popularity of these lively inferior fictions strikes me as a most significant (and unbearably sad) phenomenon.

STUDY QUESTIONS

1. According to Vidal, what is the difference between an Adlerian and a Freudian imaginary world? Which of these worlds does Tarzan inhabit?
2. Which scenes in the Tarzan books does Vidal find most memorable? Why?
3. Why are men more interested in the Tarzan books than are women? Need one identify with a character in a literary work in order to find that work memorable?
4. What are Burroughs' faults as a novelist? Why, then, is Vidal so kind to him?
5. Is there any similarity between Tarzan and James Bond?
6. Of what does Vidal feel Tarzan is a symbol?

THE PHONOGRAPH:
THE TOY THAT SHRANK
Marshall McLuhan # THE NATIONAL CHEST

Marshall McLuhan (1911–   ) was born in Edmonton, Alberta. He received a B.A. (1933) and an M.A. (1934) from the University of Manitoba; and a B.A. (1936), an M.A. (1939), and a Ph.D. (1942) from Cambridge University. He has taught in the United States and Canada, and is currently at the Centre for Culture and

From *Understanding Media: The Extensions of Man* by Marshall McLuhan. Copyright © 1964 by Marshall McLuhan. Used by permission of McGraw-Hill Book Company.

Technology at the University of Toronto. A fellow of the Royal Society, McLuhan has written *The Mechanical Bride* (1951), *The Gutenberg Galaxy* (1962), *Understanding Media, The Extensions of Man* (1964), and *The Medium is the Massage* (1967).

The phonograph, which owes its origin to the electrical telegraph and the telephone, had not manifested its basically electric form and function until the tape recorder released it from its mechanical trappings. That the world of sound is essentially a unified field of instant relationships lends it a near resemblance to the world of electromagnetic waves. This fact brought the phonograph and radio into early association.

Just how obliquely the phonograph was at first received is indicated in the observation of John Philip Sousa, the brass-band director and composer. He commented: "With the phonograph vocal exercises will be out of vogue! Then what of the national throat? Will it not weaken? What of the national chest? Will it not shrink?"

One fact Sousa had grasped: The phonograph is an extension and amplification of the voice that may well have diminished individual vocal activity, much as the car has reduced pedestrian activity.

Like the radio that it still provides with program content, the phonograph is a hot medium. Without it, the twentieth century as the era of tango, ragtime, and jazz would have had a different rhythm. But the phonograph was involved in many misconceptions, as one of its early names—gramophone—implies. It was conceived as a form of auditory writing (*gramma*-letters). It was also called "graphophone," with the needle in the role of pen. The idea of it as a "talking machine" was especially popular. Edison was delayed in his approach to the solution of its problems by considering it at first as a "telephone repeater"; that is, a storehouse of data from the telephone, enabling the telephone to "provide invaluable records, instead of being the recipient of momentary and fleeting communication." These words of Edison, published in the *North American Review* of June, 1878, illustrate how the then recent telephone invention already had the power to color thinking in other fields. So, the record player had to be seen as a kind of phonetic record of telephone conversation. Hence, the names "phonograph" and "gramophone."

Behind the immediate popularity of the phonograph was the entire electric implosion that gave such new stress and importance to actual speech rhythms in music, poetry, and dance alike. Yet the phonograph was a machine merely. It did not at first use an electric motor or circuit. But in providing a mechanical extension of the human voice and the new ragtime melodies, the phonograph was propelled into a central place by some of the major currents of the age. The fact of acceptance of a new phrase, or a speech form, or a dance rhythm is already direct evidence of some actual development to which it is significantly related. Take, for example, the shift of English into an interrogative mood, since the arrival of "How about that?" Nothing could induce people to begin suddenly to use such a phrase over and over, unless there were some new stress, rhythm, or nuance in interpersonal relations that gave it relevance.

It was while handling paper tape, impressed by Morse Code dots and dashes, that Edison noticed the sound given off when the tape moved at high speed resembled "human talk heard indistinctly." It then occurred to him that indented tape could record a telephone message. Edison became aware of the limits of lineality and the sterility of specialism as soon as he entered the electric field. "Look," he said, "it's like this. I start here with the intention of reaching here in an experiment, say, to increase the speed of the Atlantic cable; but when I've arrived part way in my straight line, I meet with a phenomenon, and it leads me off in another direction and develops into a phonograph." Nothing could more dramatically express the turning point from mechanical explosion to electrical implosion. Edison's own career embodied that very change in our world, and he himself was often caught in the confusion between the two forms of procedure.

It was just at the end of the nineteenth century that the psychologist Lipps revealed by a kind of electric audiograph that the single clang of a bell was an intensive manifold containing all possible symphonies. It was somewhat on the same lines that Edison approached his problems. Practical experience had taught him that embryonically all problems contained all answers when one could discover a means of rendering them explicit. In his own case, his determination to give the phonograph, like the telephone, a direct practical use in business procedures led to his neglect of the instrument as a means of entertainment. Failure to foresee the phonograph as a means of entertainment was really a failure to grasp the meaning of the electric revolution in general. In our time we are reconciled to the phonograph as a toy and a solace; but press, radio, and TV have also acquired the same dimension of entertainment. Meantime, entertainment pushed to an extreme becomes the main form of business and politics. Electric media, because of their total "field" character, tend to eliminate the fragmented specialties of form and function that we have long accepted as the heritage of alphabet, printing, and mechanization. The brief and compressed history of the phonograph includes all phases of the written, the printed, and the mechanized word. It was the advent of the electric tape recorder that only a few years ago released the phonograph from its temporary involvement in mechanical culture. Tape and the l.p. record suddenly made the phonograph a means of access to all the music and speech of the world.

Before turning to the l.p. and tape-recording revolution, we should

note that the earlier period of mechanical recording and sound reproduction had one large factor in common with the silent picture. The
early phonograph produced a brisk and raucous experience not unlike
that of a Mack Sennett movie. But the undercurrent of mechanical music
is strangely sad. It was the genius of Charles Chaplin to have captured
for film this sagging quality of a deep blues, and to have overlaid it with
jaunty jive and bounce. The poets and painters and musicians of the
later nineteenth century all insist on a sort of metaphysical melancholy
as latent in the great industrial world of the metropolis. The Pierrot
figure is as crucial in the poetry of Laforgue as it is in the art of Picasso
or the music of Satie. Is not the mechanical at its best a remarkable
approximation to the organic? And is not a great industrial civilization
able to produce anything in abundance for everybody? The answer is
"Yes." But Chaplin and the Pierrot poets and painters and musicians
pushed this logic all the way to reach the image of Cyrano de Bergerac,
who was the greatest lover of all, but who was never permitted the
return of his love. This weird image of Cyrano, the unloved and unlovable lover, was caught up in the phonograph cult of the blues. Perhaps it
is misleading to try to derive the origin of the blues from Negro folk
music; however, Constant Lambert, English conductor-composer, in his
Music Ho!, provides an account of the blues that preceded the jazz of the
post-World War I. He concludes that the great flowering of jazz in the
twenties was a popular response to the highbrow richness and orchestral
subtlety of the Debussy-Delius period. Jazz would seem to be an effective bridge between highbrow and lowbrow music, much as Chaplin
made a similar bridge for pictorial art. Literary people eagerly accepted
these bridges, and Joyce got Chaplin into *Ulysses* as Bloom, just as Eliot
got jazz into the rhythms of his early poems.

Chaplin's clown-Cyrano is as much a part of a deep melancholy as
Laforgue's or Satie's Pierrot art. Is it not inherent in the very triumph of
the mechanical and its omission of the human? Could the mechanical
reach a higher level than the talking machine with its mime of voice and
dance? Do not T. S. Eliot's famous lines about the typist of the jazz age
capture the entire pathos of the age of Chaplin and the ragtime blues?

> When lovely woman stoops to folly and
> Paces about her room again, alone,
> She smoothes her hair with automatic hand,
> And puts a record on the gramophone.[1]

Read as a Chaplin-like comedy, Eliot's Prufrock makes ready sense.
Prufrock is the complete Pierrot, the little puppet of the mechanical
civilization that was about to do a flip into its electric phase.

It would be difficult to exaggerate the importance of complex

---

[1] From "The Waste Land" by T. S. Eliot in *Collected Poems* 1909–1962, New
York: Harcour), Brace & World, Inc., 1963.

mechanical forms such as film and phonograph as the prelude to the automation of human song and dance. As this automation of human voice and gesture had approached perfection, so the human work force approached automation. Now in the electric age the assembly line with its human hands disappears, and electric automation brings about a withdrawal of the work force from industry. Instead of being automated themselves—fragmented in task and function—as had been the tendency under mechanization, men in the electric age move increasingly to involvement in diverse jobs simultaneously, and to the work of learning, and to the programming of computers.

This revolutionary logic inherent in the electric age was made fairly clear in the early electric forms of telegraph and telephone that inspired the "talking machine." These new forms that did so much to recover the vocal, auditory, and mimetic world that had been repressed by the printed word, also inspired the strange new rhythms of "the jazz age," the various forms of syncopation and symbolist discontinuity that, like relativity and quantum physics, heralded the end of the Gutenberg era with its smooth, uniform lines of type and organization.

The word "jazz" comes from the French *jaser*, to chatter. Jazz is, indeed, a form of dialogue among instrumentalists and dancers alike. Thus it seemed to make an abrupt break with the homogeneous and repetitive rhythms of the smooth waltz. In the age of Napoleon and Lord Byron, when the waltz was a new form, it was greeted as a barbaric fulfillment of the Rousseauistic dream of the noble savage. Grotesque as this idea now appears, it is really a most valuable clue to the dawning mechanical age. The impersonal choral-dancing of the older, courtly pattern was abandoned when the waltzers held each other in a personal embrace. The waltz is precise, mechanical, and military, as its history manifests. For a waltz to yield its full meaning, there must be military dress. "There was a sound of revelry by night" was how Lord Byron referred to the waltzing before Waterloo. To the eighteenth century and to the age of Napoleon, the citizen armies seemed to be an individualistic release from the feudal framework of courtly hierarchies. Hence the association of waltz with noble savage, meaning no more than freedom from status and hierarchic deference. The waltzers were all uniform and equal, having free movement in any part of the hall. That this was the Romantic idea of the life of the noble savage now seems odd, but the Romantics knew as little about real savages as they did about assembly lines.

In our own century the arrival of jazz and ragtime was also heralded as the invasion of the bottom-wagging native. The indignant tended to appeal from jazz to the beauty of the mechanical and repetitive waltz that had once been greeted as pure native dancing. If jazz is considered as a break with mechanism in the direction of the discontinuous, the participant, the spontaneous and improvisational, it can also be seen as a return to a sort of oral poetry in which performance is both creation and composition. It is a truism among jazz performers that recorded jazz is "as stale as yesterday's newspaper." Jazz is alive, like conversation; and like conversation it depends upon a repertory of available themes. But performance is composition. Such performance insures maximal participation among players and dancers alike. Put in this way, it becomes obvious at once that jazz belongs in that family of mosaic structures that reappeared in the Western world with the wire services. It belongs with symbolism in poetry, and with the many allied forms in painting and in music.

The bond between the phonograph and song and dance is no less deep than its earlier relation to telegraph and telephone. With the first printing of musical scores in the sixteenth century, words and music drifted apart. The separate virtuosity of voice and instruments became the basis of the great musical developments of the eighteenth and nineteenth centuries. The same kind of fragmentation and specialism in the arts and sciences made possible mammoth results in industry and in military enterprise, and in massive cooperative enterprises such as the newspaper and the symphony orchestra.

Certainly the phonograph as a product of industrial, assembly-line organization and distribution showed little of the electric qualities that had inspired its growth in the mind of Edison. There were prophets who could foresee the great day when the phonograph would aid medicine by providing a medical means of discrimination between "the sob of hysteria and the sigh of melancholia . . . the ring of whooping cough and the hack of the consumptive. It will be an expert in insanity, distinguishing between the laugh of the maniac and drivel of the idiot. . . . It will accomplish this feat in the anteroom, while the physician is busying himself with his last patient." In practice, however, the phonograph stayed with the voices of the Signori Foghornis, the basso-tenores, robusto-profundos.

Recording facilities did not presume to touch anything so subtle as an orchestra until after the First War. Long before this, one enthusiast looked to the record to rival the photograph album and to hasten the happy day when "future generations will be able to condense within the space of twenty minutes a tone-picture of a single lifetime: five minutes of a child's prattle, five of the boy's exultations, five of the man's reflections, and five from the feeble utterances of the deathbed." James Joyce, somewhat later, did better. He made *Finnegans Wake* a tone poem that condensed in a single sentence all the prattlings, exultations, observations, and remorse of the entire human race. He could not have conceived this work in any other age than the one that produced the phonograph and the radio.

It was radio that finally injected a full electric charge into the world of the phonograph. The radio receiver of 1924 was already superior in sound quality, and soon began to depress the phonograph and record business. Eventually, radio restored the record business by extending popular taste in the direction of the classics.

The real break came after the Second War with the availability of the tape recorder. This meant the end of the incision recording and its attendant surface noise. In 1949 the era of electric hi-fi was another rescuer of the phonograph business. The hi-fi quest for "realistic sound" soon merged with the TV image as part of the recovery of tactile experience. For the sensation of having the performing instruments "right in the room with you" is a striving toward the union of the audile and tactile in a finesse of fiddles that is in large degree the sculptural experience. To be in the presence of performing musicians is to experience their touch and handling of instruments as tactile and kinetic, not just as resonant. So it can be said that hi-fi is not any quest for abstract effects of sound in separation from the other senses. With hi-fi, the phonograph meets the TV tactile challenge.

Stereo sound, a further development, is "all-around" or "wrap-around" sound. Previously sound had emanated from a single point in accordance with the bias of visual culture with its fixed point of view. The hi-fi changeover was really for music what cubism had been for painting, and what symbolism had been for literature; namely, the acceptance of multiple facets and planes in a single experience. Another way to put it is to say that stereo is sound in depth, as TV is the visual in depth.

Perhaps it is not very contradictory that when a medium becomes a means of depth experience the old categories of "classical" and "popular" or of "highbrow" and "lowbrow" no longer obtain. Watching a blue-baby heart operation on TV is an experience that will fit none of the categories. When l.p. and hi-fi and stereo arrived, a depth approach to musical experience also came in. Everybody lost his inhibitions about "highbrow," and the serious people lost their qualms about popular music and culture. Anything that is approached in depth acquires as much interest as the greatest matters. Because "depth" means "in interrelation," not "in isolation." Depth means insight, not point of view; and insight is a kind of mental involvement in process that makes the content of the item seem quite secondary. Consciousness itself is an inclusive process not at all dependent on content. Consciousness does not postulate consciousness of anything in particular.

With regard to jazz, l.p. brought many changes, such as the cult of "real cool drool," because the greatly increased length of a single side of a disk meant that the jazz band could really have a long and casual chat among its instruments. The repertory of the 1920s was revived and given new depth and complexity by this new means. But the tape recorder in combination with l.p. revolutionized the repertory of classical music. Just as tape meant the new study of spoken rather than written languages, so it brought in the entire musical culture of many centuries and countries. Where before there had been a narrow selection from periods and composers, the tape recorder, combined with l.p., gave a full musical spectrum that made the sixteenth century as available as the nineteenth, and Chinese folk song as accessible as the Hungarian.

A brief summary of technological events relating to the phonograph might go this way:

The telegraph translated writing into sound, a fact directly related to the origin of both the telephone and phonograph. With the telegraph, the only walls left are the vernacular walls that the photograph and movie and wirephoto overleap so easily. The electrification of writing was almost as big a step into the nonvisual and auditory space as the later steps soon taken by telephone, radio, and TV.

The telephone: speech without walls.

The phonograph: music hall without walls.

The photograph: museum without walls.

The electric light: space without walls.

The movie, radio, and TV: classroom without walls.

Man the food-gatherer reappears incongruously as information-gatherer. In this role, electronic man is no less a nomad than his paleolithic ancestors.

STUDY QUESTIONS

1. How did Edison fail to grasp the full potential of the phonograph?
2. What contribution did Charlie Chaplin make to the history of the phonograph?
3. McLuhan finds the waltz and jazz similar in at least one respect. Is the similarity meaningful?
4. Define *walls* as McLuhan uses the word at the end of his essay.
5. Comment on McLuhan's tendency to begin sentences and paragraphs with *it*.

Eudora Welty POWERHOUSE

Eudora Welty (1909–   ) was born in Jackson, Mississippi, where she now lives. She attended Mississippi State College for Women, the University of Wisconsin, and Columbia. Her first short stories were published in the 1930s in *The Southern Review;* her considerable skill resulted in Katherine Anne Porter writing the introduction to *A Curtain of Green* (1941). Miss Welty's other books include *The Robber Bridegroom* (1942), and *The Ponder Heart* (1954). She is a member of the National Institute of Arts and Letters and an honorary consultant in American letters of the Library of Congress.

Powerhouse is playing! He's here on tour, from the city—Powerhouse and His Keyboard—Powerhouse and His Tasmanians—all the things he calls himself! There's no one in the world like him. You can't tell what he is. He looks Asiatic, monkey, Babylonian, Peruvian, fanatic, devil. He has pale gray eyes, heavy lids, maybe horny like a lizard's, but big glowing eyes when they're open. He has feet size twelve, stomping both together on either side of the pedals. He's not coal black—beverage-colored; looks like a preacher when his mouth is shut, but then it opens—vast and obscene. And his mouth is going every minute, like a monkey's when it looks for fleas. Improvising, coming upon a very light and childish melody, *smooch*—he loves it with his mouth. Is it possible that he could be this! When you have him there performing for you, that's what you feel. You know people on a stage—and people of a darker race—so likely to be marvelous, frightening.

This is a white dance. Powerhouse is not a show-off like the Harlem boys—not drunk, not crazy, I think. He's in a trance; he's a person of joy, a fanatic. He listens as much as he performs—a look of hideous, powerful rapture on his face. Big arched eyebrows that never stop traveling. When he plays, he beats down piano and seat and wears them away. He is in motion every moment—what could be more obscene? There he is with his great head, big fat stomach, little round piston legs, and long yellow-sectioned strong fingers, at rest about the size of bananas. Of course you know how he sounds—you've heard him on records; but still you need to see him. He's going all the time, like skating around the skating rink or rowing a boat. It makes everybody crowd around, here in this shadowless steel-trussed hall with the rose-like posters of Nelson Eddy and the testimonial for the mind-reading horse in handwriting magnified five hundred times.

Powerhouse is so monstrous he sends everybody into oblivion. When any group, any performers, come to town, don't people always come out and hover near, leaning inward about them, to learn what it is? What is it? Listen. Remember how it was with the acrobats. Watch them carefully; hear the least word, especially what they say to one another, in another language; don't let them escape you—it's the only time for hallucination, the last time. They can't stay. They'll be somewhere else this time tomorrow.

Powerhouse has as much as possible done by signals. Everybody, laughing as if to hide a weakness, will sooner or later hand him up a written request. Powerhouse reads each one, studying with a secret face: that is the face which looks like a mask, anybody's; there is a moment when he makes a decision. Then a light slides under his eyelids and he says, "Ninety-two!" or some combination of figures—never a name. Before a number the band is all frantic, misbehaving, pushing, like children in a schoolroom, and he is the teacher getting silence. His hands over the keys, he says sternly, "You-all ready? You-all ready to do some serious walking?"—waits—then, STAMP. Quiet. STAMP, for the second time. This is absolute. Then a set of rhythmic kicks against the floor to communicate the tempo. Then, "Oh Lord," say the distended eyes from beyond the boundary of the trumpets; "Hello and good-bye"—and they are all down the first note like a waterfall.

This note marks the end of any known discipline. Powerhouse seems to abandon them all; he himself seems lost—down in the song—yelling up like somebody in a whirlpool—not guiding them, hailing them only. But he knows, really. He cries out, but he must know exactly. "Mercy! . . . What I say! . . . Yeah!" and then drifting, listening,—"Where that skin-beater?" (wanting drums),—and starting up and pouring it out in the greatest delight and brutality. On the sweet pieces, such a leer for everybody! He looks down so benevolently upon all the faces and whispers the lyrics, and if you could hear him at this moment on "Marie, the Dawn Is Breaking"! He's going up the keyboard with a few fingers in some very derogatory triplet routine; he gets higher and higher, and then he looks over the end of the piano, as if over a cliff. But not in a show-off way: the song makes him do it.

He loves the way they all play, too—all those next to him. The far section of the band is all studious—wearing glasses, every one; they don't count. Only those playing around Powerhouse are the real ones. He has a bass fiddler from Vicksburg, black as pitch, named Valentine, who plays with his eyes shut and talking to himself, very young. Powerhouse has to keep encouraging him: "Go on, go on, give it up, bring it on out there!" When you heard him like that on records, did you know he was really pleading?

He calls Valentine out to take a solo.

"What you going to play?" Powerhouse looks out kindly from behind the piano; he opens his mouth and shows his tongue, listening.

Valentine looks down, drawing against his instrument, and says without a lip movement, "Honeysuckle Rose."

He has a clarinet player named Little Brother, and loves to listen to anything he does. He'll smile and say, "Beautiful!" Little Brother takes a step forward when he plays and stands at the very front, with the whites of his eyes like fishes swimming. Once when he played a low note Powerhouse muttered in dirty praise, "He went clear downstairs to get that one!"

After a long time, he holds up the number of fingers to tell the band how many choruses still to go—usually five. He keeps his directions down to signals.

It's a bad night outside. It's a white dance, and nobody dances, except a few straggling jitterbugs and two elderly couples; everybody just stands around the band and watches Powerhouse. Sometimes they steal glances at one another. Of course, you know how it is with *them*— they would play the same way, giving all they've got, for an audience of one. . . . When somebody, no matter who, gives everything, it makes people feel ashamed for him.

II

Late at night, they play the one waltz they will ever consent to play. By request, "Pagan Love Song." Powerhouse's head rolls and sinks like a weight between his waving shoulders. He groans and his fingers drag into the keys heavily, holding on to the notes, retrieving. It is a sad song.

"You know what happened to me?" says Powerhouse.

Valentine hums a response, dreaming at the bass.

"I got a telegram my wife is dead," says Powerhouse, with wandering fingers.

"Uh-huh?"

His mouth gathers and forms a barbarous O, while his fingers walk up straight, unwillingly, three octaves.

"Gipsy? Why, how come her to die? Didn't you just phone her up in the night last night long distance?"

"Telegram say—here the words: 'Your wife is dead.' " He puts four-four over the three-four.

"Not but four words?" This is the drummer, an unpopular boy named Scoot, a disbelieving maniac.

Powerhouse is shaking his vast cheeks. "What the hell was she trying to do? What was she up to?"

"What name has it got signed, if you got a telegram?" Scoot is spitting away with those wire brushes.

Little Brother, the clarinet player, who cannot now speak, glares and tilts back.

"Uranus Knockwood is the name signed." Powerhouse lifts his eyes open. "Ever heard of him?" A bubble shoots out on his lip, like a plate on a counter.

Valentine is beating slowly on with his palm and scratching the strings with his long blue nails. He is fond of a waltz; Powerhouse interrupts him.

"I don't know him. Don't know who he is." Valentine shakes his head with the closed eyes, like an old mop.

"Say it again."

"Uranus Knockwood."

"That ain't Lenox Avenue."

"It ain't Broadway."

"Ain't ever seen it wrote out in any print, even for horse-racing."

"Hell, that's on a star, boy, ain't it?" Crash of the cymbals.

"What the hell was she up to?" Powerhouse shudders. "Tell me, tell me, tell me." He makes triplets, and begins a new chorus. He holds three fingers up.

"You say you got a telegram." This is Valentine, patient and sleepy, beginning again.

Powerhouse is elaborate. "Yas, the time I go out—go way downstairs along a long *corridor* to where they puts us. Coming back, steps out and hands me a telegram: 'Your wife is dead.'"

"Gipsy?" The drummer is like a spider over his drums.

"Aaaaaa!" shouts Powerhouse, flinging out both powerful arms for three whole beats to flex his muscles, then kneading a dough of bass notes. His eyes glitter. He plays the piano like a drum sometimes—why not?

"Gipsy? Such a dancer?"

"Why you don't hear it straight from your agent? Why it ain't come from headquarters? What you been doing, getting telegrams in the *corridor*, signed nobody?"

They all laugh. End of that chorus.

"What time is it?" Powerhouse calls. "What the hell place is this? Where is my watch and chain?"

"I hang it on you," whimpers Valentine. "It still there."

There it rides on Powerhouse's great stomach, down where he can never see it.

"Sure did hear some clock striking twelve while ago. Must be *midnight*."

"It going to be intermission," Powerhouse declares, lifting up his finger with the signet ring.

He draws the chorus to an end. He pulls a big Northern hotel towel out of the deep pocket in his vast, special-cut tux pants and pushes his forehead into it.

"If she went and killed herself !" he says with a hidden face. "If she up and jumped out that window!" He gets to his feet, turning vaguely, wearing the towel on his head.

"Ha, ha!"

"Sheik, sheik!"

"She wouldn't do that." Little Brother sets down his clarinet like a precious vase, and speaks. He still looks like an East Indian queen, implacable, divine, and full of snakes. "You ain't going to expect people doing what they says over long distance."

"Come on!" roars Powerhouse. He is already at the back door; he has pulled it wide open, and with a wild, gathered-up face is smelling the terrible night.

III

Powerhouse, Valentine, Scoot, and Little Brother step outside into the drenching rain.

"Well, they emptying buckets," says Powerhouse in a mollified voice. On the street he holds his hands out and turns up the blanched palms like sieves.

A hundred dark, ragged, silent, delighted Negroes have come around from under the eaves of the hall, and follow wherever they go.

"Watch out, Little Brother, don't shrink," says Powerhouse. "You just the right size now—clarinet don't suck you in. You got a dry throat, Little Brother, you in the desert?" He reaches into the pocket and pulls out a paper of mints. "Now hold 'em in your mouth—don't chew 'em. I don't carry around nothing without limit."

"Go in that joint and have beer," says Scoot, who walks ahead.

"Beer? Beer? You know what beer is? What do they say is beer? What's beer? Where I been?"

"Down yonder where it say World Cafe, that do?" They are across the tracks now.

Valentine patters over and holds open a screen door warped like a seashell, bitter in the wet, and they walk in, stained darker with the rain and leaving footprints. Inside, sheltered dry smells stand like screens around a table covered with a red-checkered cloth, in the centre of which flies hang onto an obelisk-shaped ketchup bottle. The midnight walls are checkered again with admonishing "Not Responsible" signs and black-figured smoky calendars. It is a waiting, silent, limp room. There is a burnt-out-looking nickelodeon, and right beside it a long-necked wall instrument labeled "Business Phone, Don't Keep Talking." Circled phone numbers are written up everywhere. There is a worn-out peacock feather hanging by a thread to an old, thin, pink, exposed light bulb, where it slowly turns around and around, whoever breathes.

A waitress watches.

"Come here, living statue, and get all this big order of beer we fixing to give."

"Never seen you before anywhere." The waitress moves and comes forward and slowly shows little gold leaves and tendrils over her teeth. She shoves up her shoulders and breasts. "How I going to know who you might be—robbers? Coming in out of the black night right at midnight, setting down so big at my table!"

"Boogers," says Powerhouse, his eyes opening lazily as in a cave.

The girl screams delicately with pleasure. Oh Lord, she likes talk and scares.

"Where you going to find enough beer to put out on this-here table?"

She runs to the kitchen with bent elbows and sliding steps.

"Here's a million nickels," says Powerhouse, pulling his hand out of his pocket and sprinkling coins out, all but the last one, which he makes vanish like a magician.

Valentine and Scoot take the money over to the nickelodeon, which is beginning to look as battered as a slot machine, and read all the names of the records out loud.

"Whose 'Tuxedo Junction'?" asks Powerhouse.

"You know whose."

"Nickelodeon, I request you please to play 'Empty Bed Blues' and let Bessie Smith sing."

Silence: they hold it, like a measure.

"Bring me all those nickels on back here," says Powerhouse. "*Look* at that! What you tell me the name of this place?"

"White dance, week night, raining—Alligator, Mississippi—long ways from home."

"Uh-huh."

"Sent for You Yesterday and Here You Come Today" plays.

The waitress, setting the tray of beer down on a back table, comes up taut and apprehensive as a hen. "Says in the kitchen, back there putting their eyes to little hole peeping out, that you is Mr. Powerhouse. . . . They knows from a picture they seen."

"They seeing right tonight—that is him," says Little Brother.

"You him?"

"That is him in the flesh," says Scoot.

"Does you wish to touch him?" asks Valentine. "Because he don't bite."

"You passing through?"

"Now you got everything right."

She waits like a drop, hands languishing together in front.

"Babe, ain't you going to bring the beer?"

She brings it, and goes behind the cash register and smiles, turning different ways. The little fillet of gold in her mouth is gleaming.

"The Mississippi River's here," she says once.

Now all the watching Negroes press in gently and bright-eyed through the door, as many as can get in. One is a little boy in a straw sombrero which has been coated with aluminum paint all over. Powerhouse, Valentine, Scoot, and Little Brother drink beer, and their eyelids come together like curtains. The wall and the rain and the humble beautiful waitress waiting on them and the other Negroes watching enclose them.

"Listen!" whispers Powerhouse, looking into the ketchup bottle and very slowly spreading his performer's hands over the damp wrinkling cloth with the red squares. "How it is. My wife gets missing me. Gipsy. She goes to the window. She looks out and sees you know what. Street. Sign saying 'Hotel.' People walking. Somebody looks up. Old man. She looks down, out the window. Well? . . . Sssst! Plooey! What she do? Jump out and bust her brains all over the world."

He opens his eyes.

"That's it," agrees Valentine. "You gets a telegram."

"Sure she misses you," Little Brother adds.

"Now, it's nighttime." How softly he tells them! "Sure. It's the nighttime. She say, 'What do I hear? Footsteps walking up the hall? That him?' Footsteps go on off. It's not me. I'm in Alligator, Mississippi; she's crazy. Shaking all over. Listens till her ears and all grow out like old music-box horns, but still she can't hear a thing. She says, 'All right! I'll jump out the window then.' Got on her nightgown. I know that nightgown, and she thinking there. Says, 'Ho hum, all right,' and jumps out the window. Is she mad at me! Is she crazy! She don't leave *nothing* behind her!"

"Ya! Ha!"

"Brains and insides everywhere—Lord, Lord."

All the watching Negroes stir in their delight, and to their higher delight he says affectionately, "Listen! Rats in here."

"That must be the way, Boss."

"Only, naw, Powerhouse, that ain't true. That sound too *bad*."

"Does? I even know who finds her," cries Powerhouse. "That no-good pussy-footed crooning creeper, that creeper that follow around after me, coming up like weeds behind me, following around after me everything I do and messing around on the trail I leave. Bets my numbers, sings my songs, gets close to my agent like a betsy-bug—when I going out he just coming in. I got him now! I got him spotted!"

"Know who he is?"

"Why, it's that old Uranus Knockwood!"

"Ya! Ha!"

"Yeah, and he coming now, he going to find Gipsy. There he is, coming around that corner, and Gipsy kadoodling down—oh-oh! Watch out! Sssst-flooey! See, there she is in her little old nightgown, and her insides and brains all scattered round."

A sigh fills the room.

"Hush about her brains. Hush about her insides."

"Ya! Ha! You talking about her brains and insides—old Uranus Knockwood," says Powerhouse, "look down and say, 'Lord!' He say, 'Look here what I'm walking in!'"

They all burst into halloos of laughter. Powerhouse's face looks like a big hot iron stove.

"Why, he picks her up and carries her off!" he says.

"Ya! Ha!"

"Carries her *back* around the corner . . ."

"Oh, Powerhouse!"

"You know him."

"Uranus Knockwood!"

"Yeahhh!"

"He take our wives when we gone!"

"He come in when we goes out!"

"Uh-huh!"

"He go out when we comes in!"

"Yeahhh!"

"He standing behind the door!"

"Old Uranus Knockwood!"

"You know him."

"Middle-size man."

"Wears a hat."

"That's him."

Everybody in the room moans with reassurance. The little boy in the fine silver hat opens a paper and divides out a jelly roll among his followers.

And out of the breathless ring somebody moves forward like a slave, leading a great logy Negro with bursting eyes, and says, "This-here is Sugar-Stick Thompson, that dove down to the bottom of July Creek and pulled up all those drownded white people fall out of a boat. Last summer—pulled up fourteen."

"Hello," says Powerhouse, turning and looking around at them all with his great daring face until they nearly suffocate.

Sugar-Stick, their instrument, cannot speak; he can only look back at the others.

"Can't even swim. Done it by holding his breath," says the fellow with the hero.

Powerhouse looks at him seekingly.

"I his half-brother," the fellow puts in.

They step back.

"Gipsy say," Powerhouse rumbles gently again, looking at *them*, " 'What is the use? I'm gonna jump out so far—so far—*Ssssst—*' "

"Don't, Boss, don't do it again," says Little Brother.

"It's awful," says the waitress. "I hates that Mr. Knockwoods. All that the truth?"

"Want to see the telegram I got from him?" Powerhouse's hand goes to the vast pocket.

"Now wait, now wait, Boss." They all watch him.

"It must be the real truth," says the waitress, sucking in her lower lip, her luminous eyes turning sadly, seeking the windows.

"No, Babe, it ain't the truth." His eyebrows fly up and he begins to whisper to her out of his vast oven mouth. His hand stays in his pocket. "Truth is something worse—I ain't said what, yet. It's something hasn't come to me, but I ain't saying it won't. And when it does, then want me to tell you?" He sniffs all at once, his eyes come open and turn up, almost too far. He is dreamily smiling.

"Don't, Boss. Don't, Powerhouse!"

"Yeahhh!"

"Oh!" The waitress screams.

"Go on, git out of here!" bellows Powerhouse, taking his hand out of his pocket and clapping after her red dress.

The ring of watchers breaks and falls away.

"*Look* at that! Intermission is up," says Powerhouse.

He folds money under a glass, and after they go out Valentine leans back in and drops a nickel in the nickelodeon behind them, and it lights up and begins to play, and the feather dangles still. That was going to be a Hawaiian piece.

"Take a telegram!" Powerhouse shouts suddenly up into the rain. "Take a answer.—Now what was that name?"

They get a little tired.

"Uranus Knockwood."

"You ought to know."

"Yas? Spell it to me."

They spell it all the ways it could be spelled. It puts them in a wonderful humor.

"Here's the answer. Here it is right here. 'What in the hell you talking about? Don't make any difference: I gotcha.' Name signed: Powerhouse."

"That going reach him, Powerhouse?" Valentine speaks in a maternal voice.

"Yas, yas."

All hushing, following him up the dark street at a distance, like old rained-on black ghosts, the Negroes are afraid they will die laughing.

Powerhouse throws back his vast head into the steaming rain, and a look of hopeful desire seems to blow somehow like a vapor from his own dilated nostrils over his face and bring a mist to his eyes.

"Reach him and come out the other side."

"That's it, Powerhouse, that's it. You got him now."

Powerhouse lets out a long sigh.

"But ain't you going back there to call up Gipsy long distance, the way you did last night in that other place? I seen a telephone. . . . Just to see if she there at home?"

There is a measure of silence. That is one crazy drummer that's going to get his neck broken some day.

"No," growls Powerhouse. "No! How many thousand times tonight I got to say *No?*"

He holds up his arm in the rain, like someone swearing.

"You sure-enough unroll your voice some night, it about reach up yonder to her," says Little Brother, dismayed.

They go on up the street, shaking the rain off and on them like birds.

IV

Back in the dance hall they play "San" (99). The jitterbugs stiffen and start up like windmills stationed over the floor, and in their orbits (one circle, another, a long stretch and a zigzag) dance the elderly couples with old smoothness, undisturbed and stately.

When Powerhouse first came back from intermission (probably full of beer, everyone said) he got the band tuned up again not by striking the piano keys for the pitch: he just opened his mouth and gave falsetto howls—in A, D, and so on. They tuned by him. Then he took hold of the piano, like seeing it for the first time, and tested it for strength, hit it down in the bass, played an octave with his elbow, and opened it and examined its interior, and leaned on it with all his might. He played it for a few minutes with terrific force and got it under his power—then struck into something fragile and smiled. You couldn't remember any of the things he said—just inspired remarks that came out of his mouth like smoke.

They've requested "Somebody Loves Me," and he's already done twelve or fourteen choruses, piling them up nobody knows how, and it will be a wonder if he ever gets through. Now and then he calls and shouts, "Somebody loves me! Somebody loves me—I wonder who!" His mouth gets to be nothing but a volcano when he gets to the end.

"Somebody loves me—I wonder who!

"Maybe—" He uses all his right hand on a trill.

"Maybe—" He pulls back his spread fingers and looks out upon the place where he is. A vast, impersonal, and yet furious grimace transfigures his wet face.

"—Maybe it's you!"

STUDY QUESTIONS

1.   Why does Miss Welty use the present tense? How would the past tense change the effect of her story?

2.   Miss Welty is careful to tell the reader exactly what numbers Powerhouse and his band play. Is there any significance in these particular songs insofar as they contribute to the development of the plot?

3.   Is Uranus Knockwood real? What is humorous about, "Brains and insides everywhere—Lord, Lord."?

4.   What is the reason for Powerhouse's "furious grimace"?

5.   Of what kind of corruption is Powerhouse an example?

THE MARVELOUS

Tom Wolfe   MOUTH

Tom Wolfe (1931–   ) was born in Richmond, Virginia. He received his B.A. from Washington and Lee (1951) and his Ph.D. from Yale (1957). He has been a reporter for the *Springfield* (Mass.) *Union,* the *Washington Post,* and the *New York Herald Tribune.* His essays have been published in 1965 under the title of *The Kandy-Kolored Tangerine-Flake Streamline Baby.* Wolfe is as talented an artist as he is a writer; his drawings have been exhibited in a one-man show.

First published in *Esquire* Magazine. Reprinted with permission of Farrar, Straus & Giroux, Inc. from *The Kandy-Kolored Tangerine-Flake Streamline Baby* by Tom Wolfe. Copyright © 1963 by Thomas Wolfe.

One thing that stuck in my mind, for some reason, was the way that Cassius Clay and his brother, Rudy, and their high-school pal, Tuddie King, and Frankie Tucker, the singer who was opening in Brooklyn, and Cassius' pride of "foxes," Sophia Burton, Dottie, Frenchie, Barbara and the others, and Richie Pittman and "Lou" Little, the football player, and everybody else up there in Cassius' suite on the forty-second floor of the Americana Hotel kept telling time by looking out the panorama window and down at the clock on top of the Paramount Building on Times Square. Everybody had a watch. Cassius, for example, is practically a watch fancier. But, every time, somebody would look out the panorama window, across the City Lights scene you get from up high in the Americana and down to the lit-up clock on that whacky Twenties-modern polyhedron on top of the Paramount Building.

One minute Cassius would be out in the middle of the floor re-enacting his "High Noon" encounter with Sonny Liston in a Las Vegas casino. He has a whole act about it, beginning with a pantomime of him shoving open the swinging doors and standing there bowlegged, like a beer delivery man. Then he plays the part of the crowd falling back and whispering, "It's Cassius Clay, Cassius Clay, Cassius Clay, Cassius Clay." Then he plays the part of an effete Las Vegas hipster at the bar with his back turned, suddenly freezing in mid-drink, as the hush falls over the joint, and sliding his eyes around to see the duel. Then he plays the part of Cassius Clay stalking across the floor with his finger pointed at Sonny Liston and saying, "You big ugly bear," "You big ugly bear," about eighteen times, "I ain't gonna fight you on no September thirtieth, I'm gonna fight you right now. Right here. You too ugly to run loose, you big ugly bear. You so ugly, when you cry, the tears run down the back of your head. You so ugly, you have to sneak up on the mirror so it won't run off the wall," and so on, up to the point where Liston says, "Come over here and sit on my knee, little boy, and I'll give you your orange juice," and where Cassius pulls back his right and three guys hold him back and keep him from throwing it at Liston, "And I'm hollering, 'Lemme go,' and I'm telling them out the side of my mouth, 'You better *not* lemme go.'" All this time Frankie Tucker, the singer, is contorted across one of the Americana's neo-Louis XIV chairs, breaking up and exclaiming, "That's my man!"

The next minute Cassius is fooling around with Rudy's phonograph-and-speaker set and having some fun with the foxes. The foxes are seated around the room at ornamental intervals, all ya-ya length silk sheaths, long legs and slithery knees. Cassius takes one of Rudy's cool jazz records or an Aretha Franklin or something like that off the phonograph and puts on one of the 45-r.p.m. rock-and-roll records that the singers keep sending to him at the hotel.

"Those are Rudy's records, I don't *dig* that mess. I'm just a boy from Louisville"—he turns his eyes up at the foxes—"I dig rock and roll. Isn't that right?"

All the girls are hip, and therefore cool jazz fans currently, so most of them think the whole thing over for a few seconds before saying, "That's right."

Cassius puts a 45-r.p.m. on and says, "This old boy's an alley singer, nobody ever heard of him, he sings about beans and bread and all that old mess."

Cassius starts laughing at that and looking out over the city lights, out the panorama window. The girls aren't sure whether he is laughing with or at the alley singer.

Cassius scans the foxes and says, "This is *my* crowd. They don't dig that other mess, either."

The girls don't say anything.

"Is that your kinda music? I know it's *hers*," he says, looking at Francine, who is sitting pretty still. "She's about to fall over."

And maybe at this point somebody says, "What time is it?" And Rudy or somebody looks out the panorama window to the clock on the Paramount Building and says, "Ten minutes to ten."

Cassius had just come from the Columbia Records studio, across from the hotel at Seventh Avenue and 52nd, where he was making an album, *I Am the Greatest,* a long pastiche of poems and skits composed wholly in terms of his impending fight with Sonny Liston. The incessant rehearsing of his lines for two weeks, most of them lines he had sprung at random at press conferences and so forth over a period of a year and a half, had made Cassius aware, as probably nothing else, of the showman's role he was filling. And made him tempted by it.

After cutting up a little for Frankie Tucker and the foxes and everybody—showing them how he could *act*, really—he went over to one side of the living room and sat in a gangster-modern swivel chair and propped his feet up on the panorama-window ledge and talked a while. Everybody else was talking away in the background. Somebody had put the cool jazz back on and some husky girl with one of those augmented-sevenths voices was singing "Moon Over Miami."

"What's that club Leslie Uggams was at?" Cassius asked.

"The Metropole."

"The Metropole, that's right. That's one of the big ones out there, ain't it?"

His designation of the Metropole Café as "a big one" is an interesting thing in itself, but the key phrase is "out there." To Cassius, New York and the hot spots and the cool life are out there beyond his and Rudy's and Tuddie's suite at the Americana and beyond his frame of reference. Cassius does not come to New York as the hip celebrity, although it would be easy enough, but as a phenomenon. He treats Broadway as though these were still the days when the choirboys at Lindy's would spot a man in a white Palm Beach-brand suit heading up from 49th Street and say, "Here comes Winchell," or "Here comes Hellinger," or even the way Carl Van Vechten's Scarlet Creeper treated 125th Street in the days of the evening promenade. Cassius likes to get out amongst them.

About 10:15 P.M. he motioned to Sophia and started leaving the suite. All five girls got up and followed. The procession was spectacular even for Seventh Avenue on a crowded night with the chocolate-drink stands open. Cassius, six feet three, two hundred pounds, was wearing a black-and-white-checked jacket, white tab-collared shirt and black tie, light gray Continental trousers, black pointed-toe Italian shoes, and walking with a very cocky walk. The girls were walking one or two steps behind, all five of them, dressed in slayingly high couture. There were high heels and garden-party hats. Down at the corner, at 52nd Street, right at the foot of the hotel, Cassius stopped, looked all around and began loosening up his shoulders, the way prizefighters do. This, I found out, is Cassius' signal, an unconscious signal, that he is now available for crowd collecting. He got none on that corner, but halfway down to 51st Street people started saying, "That's Cassius Clay, Cassius Clay, Cassius Clay, Cassius Clay," the way he had mimicked it back in the hotel. Cassius might have gotten his crowd at 51st Street—he was looking cocky and the girls were right behind him in a phalanx, looking gorgeous—but he headed on across the street, when the light changed, over to where two fellows he knew were standing a quarter of the way down the block.

"Here he comes. Whatta you say, champ?"

"Right, man. Hey," said Cassius, referring the girls to the taller and older of the two men, "I want you all to meet one of the greatest singers in New York." A pause there. "What is your name, man, I meet so many people here."

"Hi, Pinocchio," said one of the foxes, and the man smiled.

"Pinocchio," said Cassius. Then he said, "You see all these queens are with me?" He made a sweeping motion with his hand. The girls were around him on the sidewalk. "All these foxes."

"That's sump'n else, man."

Cassius could have gotten his crowd easily on the sidewalk outside the Metropole. When it's warm, there is always a mob out there looking in through the front doorway at the band strung out along the bandstand, which is really more of a shelf. If there is a rock-and-roll band, there will always be some Jersey teen-agers outside twisting their ilia to it. That night there was more of a Dixieland or jump band on, although Lionel Hampton was to come on later, and Cassius entered, by coincidence, while an old tune called "High Society" was playing. All the foxes filed in, a step or so behind. The Metropole Café has not seen many better entrances. Cassius looked gloriously bored.

The Metropole is probably the perfect place for a folk hero to show up at in New York. It is kind of a crossroads, or ideal type, of all the hot spots and live joints in the country. I can tell you two things about it that will help you understand what the Metropole is like, if you have never been there. First, the color motif is submarine green and Prussian blue, all reflected in huge wall-to-wall mirrors. If the stand-up beer crowd gets so thick you can't see over them to the bandstand, you can always watch through the mirrors. Second, the place attracts high-livers of a sort that was there that night. I particularly remember one young guy, standing there at the bar in the submarine-green and Prussian-blue light with sunglasses on. He had on a roll-collar shirt, a silvery tie, a pale-gray suit of the Continental cut and pointed black shoes. He had a king-size cigarette pasted on his lower lip, and when the band played "The Saints," he broke into a terribly "in" and hip grin, which brought the cigarette up horizontal. He clapped his hands and hammered his right heel in time to the drums and kept his eyes on the trumpet player the whole time. The thing is, kids don't even do that at Williams College anymore, but they do it at the Metropole.

This same kid came over to ask Cassius for his autograph at one point. He thought "The Saints" was hip, but he must not have thought autograph-hunting was very hip. He wanted an autograph, however. He handed Cassius a piece of paper for his autograph and said, "It's not for me, it's for a buddy of mine, he wants it." This did not score heavily with Cassius.

"Where's your pen?" he said.

"I don't have a pen," the kid said. "It's for a friend of mine."

"You ain't got no pen, man," said Cassius.

About a minute later the kid came back with a pen, and Cassius signed the piece of paper, and the kid said, "Thank you, Cassius, you're a gentleman." He said it very seriously. "It's for a buddy of mine. You're a real gentleman."

That was the tone of things that night in the Metropole. Everything was just a little off, the way Cassius saw it.

From the moment he walked into the doorway of the Metropole, people were trying to prod him into the act.

"You *really* think you can beat Sonny Liston, man?"

"Liston must fall in eight."

"You *really* mean that?"

"If he gives me any jive, he goes in five," Cassius said, but in a terribly matter-of-fact, recitative voice, all the while walking on ahead, with the foxes moseying in behind him, also gloriously bored.

His presence spread over the Metropole immediately. As I said, it is the perfect place for folk heroes, for there is no one in there who is not willing to be impressed. The management, a lot of guys in tuxedos with the kind of Hollywood black ties that tuck under the collars and are adorned with little pearl stickpins and such devices—the management was rushing up. A guy at the bar, well-dressed, came up behind Cassius and touched him lightly at about the level of the sixth rib and went back to the bar and told his girl, "That's Cassius Clay. I just touched him, no kidding."

They sat all the foxes down in a booth at about the middle of the Metropole Café and gave Cassius a chair by himself right next to them. Lionel Hampton came up with the huge smile he has and shook Cassius' hand and made a fuss over him without any jive about when Liston must fall. Cassius liked that. But then the crowd came around for autographs, and they wanted him to go into his act. It was a hell of a noisy place.

But the crowd at the Metropole hit several wrong notes. One was hit by a white man about fifty-five, obviously a Southerner from the way he talked, who came up to Clay from behind—people were gaggled around from all sides—and stuck the blank side of a Pennsylvania Railroad receipt, the kind you get when you buy your ticket on the train, in his face and said in a voice you could mulch the hollyhocks with:

"Here you are, boy, put your name right there."

It was more or less the same voice Mississippians use on a hot day when the colored messenger boy has come into the living room and is standing around nervously. "Go ahead, boy, sit down. Sit in that seat right there."

Cassius took the Pennsylvania Railroad receipt without looking up at the man, and held it for about ten seconds, just staring at it.

Then he said in a slightly accusing voice, "Where's your pen?"

"I don't have a pen, boy. Some of these people around here got a pen. Just put your name right there."

Cassius still didn't look up. He just said, "Man, there's one thing you gotta learn. You don't *ever* come around and ask a man for an autograph if you ain't got no pen."

The man retreated and more people pressed in.

Cassius treats the fact of color—but not race—casually. Sometimes, when he is into his act, he will look at somebody and say, "You know, man, you lucky, you seen me here in living color." One time, I remember, a CBS news crew was filming an interview with him in the Columbia Records Studio A, at 799 Seventh Avenue, when the cameraman said to the interviewer, who was moving in on Cassius with the microphone: "Hey, Jack, you're throwing too much shadow on Cassius. He's dark enough already."

All the white intellectuals in the room cringed. Cassius just laughed. In point of fact, he is not very dark at all.

But he does not go for any of the old presumptions, such as, "Put your name right there, boy."

Another wrong note was hit when a middle-aged couple came up. They were white. The woman struck you as a kind of Arkansas Blanche Dubois. They looked like they wanted autographs at first. They did in a way. They were both loaded. She had an incredible drunk smile that spread out soft and gooey like a can of Sherwin-Williams paint covering the world. She handed Cassius a piece of paper and a pencil and wanted him to write down both his name *and* her name. He had just about done that when she put her hand out very slowly to caress his cheek.

"Can I touch you?" she said. "I just want to touch you."

Cassius pulled his head back.

"Naw," he said. "My girl friends might get jealous."

He didn't call them foxes to her. He said it in a nice way. After she left, though, he let her have it. It was the only time I ever heard him say anything contemptuously of anyone.

"Can I *touch* you, can I *touch* you," he said. He could mimic her white Southern accent in a fairly devastating way.

"Naw, you can't touch me," he said, just as if he were answering her face to face. "Nobody can touch me."

As a matter of fact, Cassius is good at mimicking a variety of white Southern accents. He doesn't do it often, but when he does it, it has an extra wallop because he has a pronounced Negro accent of his own, which he makes no attempt to polish. He only turns it on heavier from time to time for comic effect. Once I heard him mimic both himself, a Louisville Negro, and newspapermen, Louisville whites, in one act.

I had asked him if the cocky act he was putting on all over the country, and in England for that matter, surprised the people who knew him back home. What I was getting at was whether he had been a cocky kid in Louisville back in the days before anybody ever heard of him. He changed the direction slightly.

"They believe anything you tell 'em about me back in Louisville. Newspapermen used to come around and I'd give 'em predictions and they'd say, 'What is this boy doing?'

"I had a fight with Lamar Clark, I believe it was, and I said [*Clay mimicking Clay, heavy, high-flown, bombastic Negro accent*]: 'Lamar will fall in two.' I knocked him out in two, and they said [*Clay mimicking drawling Kentucky Southern accent*]: 'Suht'n'ly dee-ud.' " (Certainly did.)

"I said, 'Miteff will fall in six.'

"They said, 'Suht'n'ly dee-ud.'

"I said, 'Warren will fall in four.'

"They said, 'Suht'n'ly dee-ud.' "

Clay had a lot better look on his face when people came by to admire what he had become rather than the funny act he puts on.

One young Negro, sharp-looking, as they say, in Continental clothes with a wonderful pair of Latin-American sunglasses, the kind that are narrow like the mask the Phantom wears in the comic strip, came by and didn't ask Cassius when Liston would fall. He shot an admiring, knowing look at the foxes, and said, "Who are all these girls, man?"

"Oh, they just the foxes," said Cassius.

"Man, I like your choice of foxes, I'm telling you," the kid said. This tickled Cassius and he leaned over and told it to Sophia.

The kid, meantime, went around to the other side of the booth. He had a glorified version of how Cassius was living. He believed Cassius as he leaned over to the girls when the waiter came around and said, "You get anything you want. I own this place. I own all of New York." (Sophia gave him a derisive laugh for that.)

The kid leaned over to one of the girls and said: "Are you all his personal property?"

"What are you talking about, boy. What do you mean, his *personal property?*"

"You know, *his*," said the kid. He was getting embarrassed, but he still had traces of a knowing look salivating around the edges.

"Why do we have to be his personal property?"

"Well, like, I mean, you know," said the kid. His mouth had disintegrated completely into an embarrassed grin by now, but his eyes were still darting around, as if to say, "Why don't they level with me. I'm a hip guy."

Cassius also liked it when a Negro he had met a couple of nights before, an older guy, came around and didn't ask when Liston would fall.

"I saw a crowd on the sidewalk out there, and I might have *known* you'd be inside," he told Cassius. "What's going on?"

"Oh, I'm just sitting here with the foxes," said Cassius.

"You sure are," the fellow said.

A young white kid with a crew cut said, "Are you afraid of Liston?"

Cassius said mechanically, "That big ugly bear? If I was worried, I'd be out training and I'm out partying."

Cassius had a tall, pink drink. It was nothing but Hawaiian Punch, right out of the can.

"How you gonna beat him?"

"I'll beat that bear in eight rounds. I'm strong and I'm beautiful and I'll beat that bear in eight rounds."

"You promise?" said the kid. He said it very seriously and shook Cassius' hand, as though he were getting ready to go outside and drop off a couple of grand with his Weehawken bookmaker. He apparently squeezed pretty hard. This fellow being a fighter and all, a guy ought to shake hands like a man with him.

Cassius pulled his hand away suddenly and wrung it. "Don't ever squeeze a fighter's hand, man. That hand's worth about three hundred thousand dollars," he said, making a fist. "You don't have to shake hands, you doing good just to lay eyes on me."

The kid edged off with his buddy and he was saying, "He said, 'Don't ever squeeze a fighter's hand.'"

By now Cassius was looking slightly worse than gloriously bored. "If they don't stop worrying me," he said, "I'm gonna get up and walk out of here."

Sophia leaned over and told me, "He doesn't mean that. He loves it."

Of all the girls, Sophia seemed to be closest to him. She found him amusing. She liked him.

"You know, he's really a normal boy," she told me. She threw her head to one side as if to dismiss Cassius' big front. "Oh, he's got a big mouth. But aside from that, he's a real normal boy."

The foxes were beginning to stare a little morosely into their Gin Fizzes and Brandy Alexanders and Sidecars, and even the stream of autograph seekers was slowing down. It was damned crowded and you could hardly hear yourself talk. Every now and then the drummer would go into one of those crazy sky-rocketing solos suitable for the Metropole, and the trumpet player would take the microphone and say, "That's what Cassius Clay is going to do to Sonny Liston's head!" and Cassius would holler, "Right!" but it was heavy weather. By this time Richie Pittman had dropped in, and Cassius motioned to him. They got up and went out "for some air." At the doorway there was a crowd on the sidewalk looking in at the bandstand, as always. They made a fuss over Cassius, but he just loosened his shoulders a little and made a few wisecracks. He and Richie started walking up toward the Americana.

It was after midnight, and at the foot of the hotel, where this paseo-style sidewalk pans out almost like a patio, there was a crowd gathered around. Cassius didn't miss that. They were watching three street musicians, colored boys, one with a makeshift bass—a washtub turned upside down with a cord coming up out of the bottom, forming a single string; a drum—a large tin-can bottom with spoons as sticks; and one guy dancing. They were playing "Pennies from Heaven," a pretty good number for three guys getting ready to pass the hat. Cassius just walked up to the edge of the crowd and stood there. One person noticed him, then another, and pretty soon the old "That's Cassius Clay, Cassius Clay,

Cassius Clay" business started. Cassius' spirits were rising. "Pennies from Heaven" stopped, and the three colored boys looked a little non-plussed for a moment. The show was being stolen. Somebody had said something about "Sonny Liston," only this time Cassius had the 150-watt eyes turned on, and he was saying, "The only thing I'm worried about is, I don't want Sonny Liston trying to crash *my* victory party the way I crashed his. I'm gonna tell him right before the fight starts so he won't forget it, 'Sonny,' I'm gonna tell him, 'Sonny Liston, I don't want you trying to crash my victory party tonight, you hear that? I want you to hear that now, 'cause you ain't gonna be *able* to hear anything eight rounds from now.' And if he gives me any jive when I tell him that, if he gives me any jive, he must fall in five."

A soldier, a crank-sided kid who looked like he must have gone through the battered-child syndrome at about age four, came up to take the role of Cassius' chief debater. Cassius likes that when he faces a street crowd. He'll hold a press conference for anybody, even a soldier on leave on Seventh Avenue.

"Where you gonna go after Sonny Liston whips you?" the kid said. "I got some travel folders right here."

"Boy," said Cassius, "you talk about traveling. I want you to go to that fight, 'cause you gonna see the launching of a human satellite. Sonny Liston."

The crowd was laughing and carrying on.

"I got some travel folders," the kid said. "You better look 'em over. I can get you a mask, too."

"You gonna bet against me?" said Cassius.

"Every cent I can get my hands on," said the kid.

"Man," said Cassius, "you better save your money, 'cause there's gonna be a total eclipse of the Sonny."

Cassius was standing there looking like a million dollars, and Richie was standing by, sort of riding shotgun. By this time, the crowd was so big, it was spilling off the sidewalk into 52nd Street. All sorts of incredible people were moving up close, including sclerotic old men with big-lunch ties who edged in with jag-legged walks. A cop was out in the street going crazy, trying to prod everybody back on the sidewalk. A squad car drove up, and the cop on the street put on a real tough tone, "All right, goddamn it," he said to an old sclerotic creeper with a big-lunch tie, "get up on the sidewalk."

Cassius looked around at me as if to say, "See, man? That's only what I predicted"—which is to say, "When I walk down the street, the crowds, they have to call the police."

The autograph business had started now, and people were pushing in with paper and pens, but Cassius wheeled around toward the three colored boys, the musicians, and said, "Autographs are one dollar tonight. Everyone puts one dollar in there" (the musicians had a corduroy-ribbed box out in front of the tub) "gets the autograph of Cassius Clay, the world's strongest fighter, the world's most beautiful fighter, the onliest fighter who predicts when they will fall."

The colored boys took the cue and started up with "Pennies from Heaven" again. The kid who danced was doing the merengue by himself. The kid on the bass was flailing away like a madman. All the while Cassius was orating on the corner.

"Come on, man, don't put no fifty cents in there, get that old dollar bill outa there. Think at all you're getting free here, the music's so fine and here you got Cassius Clay right here in front of you in living color, the next heavyweight champion of the world, the man who's gon' put old man Liston in orbit."

The dollar bills started piling up in the box, and the solo merengue kid was dervishing around wilder still, and Cassius wouldn't let up.

"Yeah, they down there right now getting that Medicare ready for that old man, and if I hit him in the mouth he's gonna need Denticare. That poor ol' man, he's so ugly, his wife drives him to the gym every morning 'fore the sun comes up, so nobody'll have to look at him 'round home. Come on, man, put yo' money in that box, people pay good money to hear this—"

The bass man was pounding away, and Cassius turned to me and said, behind his hand, "Man, you know one thing? If I get whipped, they gonna run me outa the country. You know that?"

Then he threw his head back and his arms out, as if he were falling backward. "Can you see me flat out on my back like this?"

The colored kids were playing "Pennies from Heaven," and Cassius Clay had his head thrown back and his arms out, laughing, and looking straight up at the top of the Americana Hotel.

STUDY QUESTIONS

1. Why does Wolfe begin so abruptly?
2. Wolfe begins three consecutive paragraphs with "Cassius" and a verb in the present tense. What does he accomplish by this rhetorical parallelism?
3. Is there any evidence that Clay does not take himself seriously, that he is amused by his public image? Can you tell Wolfe's attitude toward Clay?
4. Sophie says Clay has a *big* mouth; Wolfe calls it *marvelous*. What does each mean?
5. What is the point of Wolfe's final paragraph?

NOTES

Susan Sontag ON CAMP

Susan Sontag (1933–   ) was born in New York City, spent her childhood in Tucson, Arizona, and attended high school in Los Angeles. She was educated at the University of Chicago and Harvard University. Her first novel, *The Benefactor,* appeared in 1963 and her second, *Death Kit,* in 1967. She has published short stories in *Harper's Bazaar, Harper's,* and *The Partisan Review;* and essays in *The New York Review of Books, Commentary,* and *The Nation. Against Interpretation,* (1966), a collection of her critical writings, included the reprinting of her now famous essay on "camp." Miss Sontag was the recipient of a Rockefeller Foundation Grant (1964), a Merrill Foundation Grant (1965), and a Guggenheim Fellowship (1966–1967).

Many things in the world have not been named; and many things, even if they have been named, have never been described. One of these is the sensibility—unmistakably modern, a variant of sophistication but hardly identical with it—that goes by the cult name of "Camp."

A sensibility (as distinct from an idea) is one of the hardest things to talk about; but there are special reasons why Camp, in particular, has never been discussed. It is not a natural mode of sensibility, if there be any such. Indeed the essence of Camp is its love of the unnatural: of artifice and exaggeration. And Camp is esoteric—something of a private code, a badge of identity even, among small urban cliques. Apart from a lazy two-page sketch in Christopher Isherwood's novel *The World in the Evening* (1954), it has hardly broken into print. To talk about Camp is therefore to betray it. If the betrayal can be defended, it will be for the edification it provides, or the dignity of the conflict it resolves. For myself, I plead the goal of self-edification, and the goad of a sharp conflict in my own sensibility. I am strongly drawn to Camp, and almost as strongly offended by it. That is why I want to talk about it, and why I can. For no one who wholeheartedly shares in a given sensibility can analyze it; he can only, whatever his intention, exhibit it. To name a sensibility, to draw its contours and to recount its history, requires a deep sympathy modified by revulsion.

Though I am speaking about sensibility only—and about a sensibility that, among other things, converts the serious into the frivolous—these are grave matters. Most people think of sensibility or taste as the realm of purely subjective preferences, those mysterious attractions, mainly sensual, that have not been brought under the sovereignty of reason. They *allow* that considerations of taste play a part in their reactions to people and to works of art. But this attitude is naïve. And even worse. To patronize the faculty of taste is to patronize oneself. For taste governs every free—as opposed to rote—human response. Nothing is more decisive. There is taste in people, visual taste, taste in emotion—and there is taste in acts, taste in morality. Intelligence, as well, is really a kind of taste: taste in ideas. (One of the facts to be reckoned with is that taste tends to develop very unevenly. It's rare that the same person has good visual taste *and* good taste in people *and* taste in ideas.)

Taste has no system and no proofs. But there is something like a logic of taste: the consistent sensibility which underlies and gives rise to a certain taste. A sensibility is almost, but not quite, ineffable. Any sensibility which can be crammed into the mold of a system, or handled with the rough tools of proof, is no longer a sensibility at all. It has hardened into an idea. . . .

To snare a sensibility in words, especially one that is alive and powerful,[1] one must be tentative and nimble. The form of jottings, rather than an essay (with its claim to a linear, consecutive argument), seemed more appropriate for getting down something of this particular fugitive sensibility. It's embarrassing to be solemn and treatise-like about Camp. One runs the risk of having, oneself, produced a very inferior piece of Camp.

These notes are for Oscar Wilde.

"One should either be a work of art, or wear a work of art."
                        —*Phrases & Philosophies for the Use of the Young*

1. To start very generally: Camp is a certain mode of aestheticism. It is *one* way of seeing the world as an aesthetic phenomenon. That way, the way of Camp, is not in terms of beauty, but in terms of the degree of artifice, of stylization.

2. To emphasize style is to slight content, or to introduce an attitude which is neutral with respect to content. It goes without saying

---

[1] The sensibility of an era is not only its most decisive, but also its most perishable, aspect. One may capture the ideas (intellectual history) and the behavior (social history) of an epoch without ever touching upon the sensibility or taste which informed those ideas, that behavior. Rare are those historical studies—like Huizinga on the late Middle Ages, Febvre on 16th-century France—which do tell us something about the sensibility of the period.

that the Camp sensibility is disengaged, depoliticized—or at least apolitical.

3. Not only is there a Camp vision, a Camp way of looking at things. Camp is as well a quality discoverable in objects and the behavior of persons. There are "campy" movies, clothes, furniture, popular songs, novels, people, buildings. . . . This distinction is important. True, the Camp eye has the power to transform experience. But not everything can be seen as Camp. It's not *all* in the eye of the beholder.

4. Random examples of items which are part of the canon of Camp:

Zuleika Dobson
Tiffany lamps
Scopitone films
The Brown Derby restaurant on Sunset Boulevard in LA
The Enquirer, headlines and stories
Aubrey Beardsley drawings
Swan Lake
Bellini's operas
Visconti's direction of *Salome* and *'Tis Pity She's a Whore*
certain turn-of-the-century picture postcards
Schoedsack's *King Kong*
the Cuban pop singer La Lupe
Lynn Ward's novel in woodcuts, *God's Man*
the old Flash Gordon comics
women's clothes of the twenties (feather boàs, fringed and beaded dresses, etc.)
the novels of Ronald Firbank and Ivy Compton-Burnett
stag movies seen without lust

5. Camp taste has an affinity for certain arts rather than others. Clothes, furniture, all the elements of visual décor, for instance, make up a large part of Camp. For Camp art is often decorative art, emphasizing texture, sensuous surface, and style at the expense of content. Concert music, though, because it is contentless, is rarely Camp. It offers no opportunity, say, for a contrast between silly or extravagant content and rich form. . . . Sometimes whole art forms become saturated with Camp. Classical ballet, opera, movies have seemed so for a long time. In the last two years, popular music (post rock-'n'-roll, what the French call *yé yé*) has been annexed. And movie criticism (like lists of "The 10 Best Bad Movies I Have Seen") is probably the greatest popularizer of Camp taste today, because most people still go to the movies in a high-spirited and unpretentious way.

6. There is a sense in which it is correct to say: "It's too good to be Camp." Or "too important," not marginal enough. (More on this

later.) Thus, the personality and many of the works of Jean Cocteau are Camp, but not those of André Gide; the operas of Richard Strauss, but not those of Wagner; concoctions of Tin Pan Alley and Liverpool, but not jazz. Many examples of Camp are things which, from a "serious" point of view, are either bad art or kitsch. Not all, though. Not only is Camp not necessarily bad art, but some art which can be approached as Camp (example: the major films of Louis Feuillade) merits the most serious admiration and study.

"The more we study Art, the less we care for Nature."

—The Decay of Lying

7. All Camp objects, and persons, contain a large element of artifice. Nothing in nature can be campy. . . . Rural Camp is still man-made, and most campy objects are urban. (Yet, they often have a serenity—or a naïveté—which is the equivalent of pastoral. A great deal of Camp suggests Empson's phrase, "urban pastoral.")

8. Camp is a vision of the world in terms of style—but a particular kind of style. It is the love of the exaggerated, the "off," of things-being-what-they-are-not. The best example is in Art Nouveau, the most typical and fully developed Camp style. Art Nouveau objects, typically, convert one thing into something else: the lighting fixtures in the form of flowering plants, the living room which is really a grotto. A remarkable example: the Paris Métro entrances designed by Hector Guimard in the late 1890s in the shape of cast-iron orchid stalks.

9. As a taste in persons, Camp responds particularly to the markedly attenuated and to the strongly exaggerated. The androgyne is certainly one of the great images of Camp sensibility. Examples: the swooning, slim, sinuous figures of pre-Raphaelite painting and poetry; the thin, flowing, sexless bodies in Art Nouveau prints and posters, presented in relief on lamps and ashtrays; the haunting androgynous vacancy behind the perfect beauty of Greta Garbo. Here, Camp taste draws on a mostly unacknowledged truth of taste: the most refined form of sexual attractiveness (as well as the most refined form of sexual pleasure) consists in going against the grain of one's sex. What is most beautiful in virile men is something feminine; what is most beautiful in feminine women is something masculine. . . . Allied to the Camp taste for the androgynous is something that seems quite different but isn't: a relish for the exaggeration of sexual characteristics and personality mannerisms. For obvious reasons, the best examples that can be cited are movie stars. The corny flamboyant femaleness of Jayne Mansfield, Gina Lollobrigida, Jane Russell, Virginia Mayo; the exaggerated he-man-ness of Steve Reeves, Victor Mature. The great stylists of temperament and

mannerism, like Bette Davis, Barbara Stanwyck, Tallulah Bankhead, Edwige Feuillière.

10. Camp sees everything in quotation marks. It's not a lamp, but a "lamp"; not a woman, but a "woman." To perceive Camp in objects and persons is to understand Being-as-Playing-a-Role. It is the farthest extension, in sensibility, of the metaphor of life as theater.

11. Camp is the triumph of the epicene style. (The convertibility of "man" and "woman," "person" and "thing.") But all style, that is, artifice, is, ultimately, epicene. Life is not stylish. Neither is nature.

12. The question isn't, "Why travesty, impersonation, theatricality?" The question is, rather, "When does travesty, impersonation, theatricality acquire the special flavor of Camp?" Why is the atmosphere of Shakespeare's comedies (*As You Like It*, etc.) not epicene, while that of *Der Rosenkavalier* is?

13. The dividing line seems to fall in the 18th century; there the origins of Camp taste are to be found (Gothic novels, Chinoiserie, caricature, artificial ruins, and so forth.) But the relation to nature was quite different then. In the 18th century, people of taste either patronized nature (Strawberry Hill) or attempted to remake it into something artificial (Versailles). They also indefatigably patronized the past. Today's Camp taste effaces nature, or else contradicts it outright. And the relation of Camp taste to the past is extremely sentimental.

14. A pocket history of Camp might, of course, begin farther back—with the mannerist artists like Pontormo, Rosso, and Caravaggio, or the extraordinarily theatrical painting of Georges de La Tour, or Euphuism (Lyly, etc.) in literature. Still, the soundest starting point seems to be the late 17th and early 18th century, because of that period's extraordinary feeling for artifice, for surface, for symmetry; its taste for the picturesque and the thrilling, its elegant conventions for representing instant feeling and the total presence of character—the epigram and the rhymed couplet (in words), the flourish (in gesture and in music). The late 17th and early 18th century is the great period of Camp: Pope, Congreve, Walpole, etc., but not Swift; *les précieux* in France; the rococo churches of Munich; Pergolesi. Somewhat later: much of Mozart. But in the 19th century, what had been distributed throughout all of high culture now becomes a special taste; it takes on overtones of the acute, the esoteric, the perverse. Confining the story to England alone, we see Camp continuing wanly through 19th-century aestheticism (Burne-Jones, Pater, Ruskin, Tennyson), emerging full-blown with the Art Nouveau movement in the visual and decorative arts, and finding its conscious ideologists in such "wits" as Wilde and Firbank.

15. Of course, to say all these things are Camp is not to argue they

are simply that. A full analysis of Art Nouveau, for instance, would scarcely equate it with Camp. But such an analysis cannot ignore what in Art Nouveau allows it to be experienced as Camp. Art Nouveau is full of "content," even of a political-moral sort; it was a revolutionary movement in the arts, spurred on by a utopian vision (somewhere between William Morris and the Bauhaus group) of an organic politics and taste. Yet there is also a feature of the Art Nouveau objects which suggests a disengaged, unserious, "aesthete's" vision. This tells us something important about Art Nouveau—and about what the lens of Camp, which blocks out content, is.

16. Thus, the Camp sensibility is one that is alive to a double sense in which some things can be taken. But this is not the familiar split-level construction of a literal meaning, on the one hand, and a symbolic meaning, on the other. It is the difference, rather, between the thing as meaning something, anything, and the thing as pure artifice.

17. This comes out clearly in the vulgar use of the word Camp as a verb, "to camp," something that people do. To camp is a mode of seduction—one which employs flamboyant mannerisms susceptible of a double interpretation; gestures full of duplicity, with a witty meaning for cognoscenti and another, more impersonal, for outsiders. Equally and by extension, when the word becomes a noun, when a person or a thing is "a camp," a duplicity is involved. Behind the "straight" public sense in which something can be taken, one has found a private zany experience of the thing.

"To be natural is such a very difficult pose to keep up."
                                                    —An Ideal Husband

18. One must distinguish between naïve and deliberate Camp. Pure Camp is always naïve. Camp which knows itself to be Camp ("camping") is usually less satisfying.

19. The pure examples of Camp are unintentional; they are dead serious. The Art Nouveau craftsman who makes a lamp with a snake coiled around it is not kidding, nor is he trying to be charming. He is saying, in all earnestness: Voilà! the Orient! Genuine Camp—for instance, the numbers devised for the Warner Brothers musicals of the early thirties (42nd Street; The Golddiggers of 1933; . . . of 1935; . . . of 1937; etc.) by Busby Berkeley—does not mean to be funny. Camping—say, the plays of Noel Coward—does. It seems unlikely that much of the traditional opera repertoire could be such satisfying Camp if the melodramatic absurdities of most opera plots had not been taken seriously by their composers. One doesn't need to know the artist's private intentions. The work tells all. (Compare a typical 19th-century opera with

Samuel Barber's *Vanessa*, a piece of manufactured, calculated Camp, and the difference is clear.)

20. Probably, intending to be campy is always harmful. The perfection of *Trouble in Paradise* and *The Maltese Falcon*, among the greatest Camp movies ever made, comes from the effortless smooth way in which tone is maintained. This is not so with such famous would-be Camp films of the fifties as *All About Eve* and *Beat the Devil*. These more recent movies have their fine moments, but the first is so slick and the second so hysterical; they want so badly to be campy that they're continually losing the beat. . . . Perhaps, though, it is not so much a question of the unintended effect versus the conscious intention, as of the delicate relation between parody and self-parody in Camp. The films of Hitchcock are a showcase for this problem. When self-parody lacks ebullience but instead reveals (even sporadically) a contempt for one's themes and one's materials—as in *To Catch a Thief, Rear Window, North by Northwest*—the results are forced and heavy-handed, rarely Camp. Successful Camp—a movie like Carné's *Drôle de Drame;* the film performances of Mae West and Edward Everett Horton; portions of the Goon Show—even when it reveals self-parody, reeks of self-love.

21. So, again, Camp rests on innocence. That means Camp discloses innocence, but also, when it can, corrupts it. Objects, being objects, don't change when they are singled out by the Camp vision. Persons, however, respond to their audiences. Persons begin "camping": Mae West, Bea Lillie, La Lupe, Tallulah Bankhead in *Lifeboat*, Bette Davis in *All About Eve*. (Persons can even be induced to camp without their knowing it. Consider the way Fellini got Anita Ekberg to parody herself in *La Dolce. Vita*.)

22. Considered a little less strictly, Camp is either completely naïve or else wholly conscious (when one plays at being campy). An example of the latter: Wilde's epigrams themselves.

"It's absurd to divide people into good and bad. People are either charming or tedious."

—Lady Windemere's Fan

23. In naïve, or pure, Camp, the essential element is seriousness, a seriousness that fails. Of course, not all seriousness that fails can be redeemed as Camp. Only that which has the proper mixture of the exaggerated, the fantastic, the passionate, and the naïve.

24. When something is just bad (rather than Camp), it's often because it is too mediocre in its ambition. The artist hasn't attempted to do anything really outlandish. ("It's too much," "It's too fantastic," "It's not to be believed," are standard phrases of Camp enthusiasm.)

25. The hallmark of Camp is the spirit of extravagance. Camp is a woman walking around in a dress made of three million feathers. Camp is the paintings of Carlo Crivelli, with their real jewels and *trompe-l'oeil* insects and cracks in the masonry. Camp is the outrageous aestheticism of Sternberg's six American movies with Dietrich, all six, but especially the last, *The Devil Is a Woman*. . . . In Camp there is often something *démesuré* in the quality of the ambition, not only in the style of the work itself. Gaudí's lurid and beautiful buildings in Barcelona are Camp not only because of their style but because they reveal—most notably in the Cathedral of the Sagrada Familia—the ambition on the part of one man to do what it takes a generation, a whole culture to accomplish.

26. Camp is art that proposes itself seriously, but cannot be taken altogether seriously because it is "too much." *Titus Andronicus* and *Strange Interlude* are almost Camp, or could be played as Camp. The public manner and rhetoric of de Gaulle, often, are pure Camp.

27. A work can come close to Camp, but not make it, because it succeeds. Eisenstein's films are seldom Camp because, despite all exaggeration, they do succeed (dramatically) without surplus. If they were a little more "off," they could be great Camp—particularly *Ivan the Terrible I & II*. The same for Blake's drawings and paintings, weird and mannered as they are. They aren't Camp; though Art Nouveau, influenced by Blake, is.

What is extravagant in an inconsistent or an unpassionate way is not Camp. Neither can anything be Camp that does not seem to spring from an irrepressible, a virtually uncontrolled sensibility. Without passion, one gets pseudo-Camp—what is merely decorative, safe, in a word, chic. On the barren edge of Camp lie a number of attractive things: the sleek fantasies of Dali, the haute couture preciosity of Albicocco's *The Girl with the Golden Eyes*. But the two things—Camp and preciosity—must not be confused.

28. Again, Camp is the attempt to do something extraordinary. But extraordinary in the sense, often, of being special, glamorous. (The curved line, the extravagant gesture.) Not extraordinary merely in the sense of effort. Ripley's Believe-It-Or-Not items are rarely campy. These items, either natural oddities (the two-headed rooster, the eggplant in the shape of a cross) or else the products of immense labor (the man who walked from here to China on his hands, the woman who engraved the New Testament on the head of a pin), lack the visual reward—the glamour, the theatricality—that marks off certain extravagances as Camp.

29. The reason a movie like *On the Beach*, books like *Winesburg, Ohio* and *For Whom the Bell Tolls* are bad to the point of being laughable, but not bad to the point of being enjoyable, is that they are too dogged and pretentious. They lack fantasy. There is Camp in such bad movies as *The Prodigal* and *Samson and Delilah*, the series of

Italian color spectacles featuring the super-hero Maciste, numerous Japanese science fiction films (*Rodan, The Mysterians, The H-Man*) because, in their relative unpretentiousness and vulgarity, they are more extreme and irresponsible in their fantasy—and therefore touching and quite enjoyable.

30. Of course, the canon of Camp can change. Time has a great deal to do with it. Time may enhance what seems simply dogged or lacking in fantasy now because we are too close to it, because it resembles too closely our own everyday fantasies, the fantastic nature of which we don't perceive. We are better able to enjoy a fantasy as fantasy when it is not our own.

31. This is why so many of the objects prized by Camp taste are old-fashioned, out-of-date, *démodé*. It's not a love of the old as such. It's simply that the process of aging or deterioration provides the necessary detachment—or arouses a necessary sympathy. When the theme is important, and contemporary, the failure of a work of art may make us indignant. Time can change that. Time liberates the work of art from moral relevance, delivering it over to the Camp sensibility. . . . Another effect: time contrasts the sphere of banality. (Banality is, strictly speaking, always a category of the contemporary.) What was banal can, with the passage of time, become fantastic. Many people who listen with delight to the style of Rudy Vallee revived by the English pop group, The Temperance Seven, would have been driven up the wall by Rudy Vallee in his heyday.

Thus, things are campy, not when they become old—but when we become less involved in them, and can enjoy, instead of be frustrated by, the failure of the attempt. But the effect of time is unpredictable. Maybe Method Acting (James Dean, Rod Steiger, Warren Beatty) will seem as Camp some day as Ruby Keeler's does now—or as Sarah Bernhardt's does, in the films she made at the end of her career. And maybe not.

32. Camp is the glorification of "character." The statement is of no importance—except, of course, to the person (Loie Fuller, Gaudí, Cecil B. De Mille, Crivelli, de Gaulle, etc.) who makes it. What the Camp eye appreciates is the unity, the force of the person. In every move the aging Martha Graham makes she's being Martha Graham, etc., etc. . . . This is clear in the case of the great serious idol of Camp taste, Greta Garbo. Garbo's incompetence (at the least, lack of depth) as an *actress* enhances her beauty. She's always herself.

33. What Camp taste responds to is "instant character" (this is, of course, very 18th century); and, conversely, what it is not stirred by is the sense of the development of character. Character is understood as a state of continual incandescence—a person being one, very intense thing. This attitude toward character is a key element of the theatricalization of experience embodied in the Camp sensibility. And it helps account for

the fact that opera and ballet are experienced as such rich treasures of Camp, for neither of these forms can easily do justice to the complexity of human nature. Wherever there is development of character, Camp is reduced. Among operas, for example, *La Traviata* (which has some small development of character) is less campy than *Il Trovatore* (which has none).

"Life is too important a thing ever to talk seriously about it."

          —*Vera, or The Nihilists*

34. Camp taste turns its back on the good-bad axis of ordinary aesthetic judgment. Camp doesn't reverse things. It doesn't argue that the good is bad, or the bad is good. What it does is to offer for art (and life) a different—a supplementary—set of standards.

35. Ordinarily we value a work of art because of the seriousness and dignity of what it achieves. We value it because it succeeds—in being what it is and, presumably, in fulfilling the intention that lies behind it. We assume a proper, that is to say, straightforward relation between intention and performance. By such standards, we appraise *The Iliad*, Aristophanes' plays, The Art of the Fugue, *Middlemarch*, the paintings of Rembrandt, Chartres, the poetry of Donne, *The Divine Comedy*, Beethoven's quartets, and—among people—Socrates, Jesus, St. Francis, Napoleon, Savonarola. In short, the pantheon of high culture: truth, beauty, and seriousness.

36. But there are other creative sensibilities besides the seriousness (both tragic and comic) of high culture and of the high style of evaluating people. And one cheats oneself, as a human being, if one has *respect* only for the style of high culture, whatever else one may do or feel on the sly.

For instance, there is the kind of seriousness whose trademark is anguish, cruelty, derangement. Here we do accept a disparity between intention and result. I am speaking, obviously, of a style of personal existence as well as of a style in art; but the examples had best come from art. Think of Bosch, Sade, Rimbaud, Jarry, Kafka, Artaud, think of most of the important works of art of the 20th century, that is, art whose goal is not that of creating harmonies but of overstraining the medium and introducing more and more violent, and unresolvable, subject-matter. This sensibility also insists on the principle that an *oeuvre* in the old sense (again, in art, but also in life) is not possible. Only "fragments" are possible. . . . Clearly, different standards apply here than to traditional high culture. Something is good not because it is achieved, but because another kind of truth about the human situation, another experience of what it is to be human—in short, another valid sensibility—is being revealed.

And third among the great creative sensibilities is Camp: the sensibility of failed seriousness, of the theatricalization of experience. Camp refuses both the harmonies of traditional seriousness, and the risks of fully identifying with extreme states of feeling.

37. The first sensibility, that of high culture, is basically moralistic. The second sensibility, that of extreme states of feeling, represented in much contemporary "avant-garde" art, gains power by a tension between moral and aesthetic passion. The third, Camp, is wholly aesthetic.

38. Camp is the consistently aesthetic experience of the world. It incarnates a victory of "style" over "content," "aesthetics" over "morality," of irony over tragedy.

39. Camp and tragedy are antitheses. There is seriousness in Camp (seriousness in the degree of the artist's involvement) and, often, pathos. The excruciating is also one of the tonalities of Camp; it is the quality of excruciation in much of Henry James (for instance, *The Europeans, The Awkward Age, The Wings of the Dove*) that is responsible for the large element of Camp in his writings. But there is never, never tragedy.

40. Style is everything. Genet's ideas, for instance, are very Camp. Genet's statement that "the only criterion of an act is its elegance" [2] is virtually interchangeable, as a statement, with Wilde's "in matters of great importance, the vital element is not sincerity, but style." But what counts, finally, is the style in which ideas are held. The ideas about morality and politics in, say, *Lady Windemere's Fan* and in *Major Barbara* are Camp, but not just because of the nature of the ideas themselves. It is those ideas, held in a special playful way. The Camp ideas in *Our Lady of the Flowers* are maintained too grimly, and the writing itself is too successfully elevated and serious, for Genet's books to be Camp.

41. The whole point of Camp is to dethrone the serious. Camp is playful, anti-serious. More precisely, Camp involves a new, more complex relation to "the serious." One can be serious about the frivolous, frivolous about the serious.

42. One is drawn to Camp when one realizes that "sincerity" is not enough. Sincerity can be simple philistinism, intellectual narrowness.

43. The traditional means for going beyond straight seriousness—irony, satire—seem feeble today, inadequate to the culturally oversaturated medium in which contemporary sensibility is schooled. Camp introduces a new standard: artifice as an ideal, theatricality.

44. Camp proposes a comic vision of the world. But not a bitter or polemical comedy. If tragedy is an experience of hyperinvolvement, comedy is an experience of underinvolvement, of detachment.

---

[2] Sartre's gloss on this in *Saint Genet* is: "Elegance is the quality of conduct which transforms the greatest amount of being into appearing."

"I adore simple pleasures, they are the last refuge of the complex."

—A Woman of No Importance

45. Detachment is the prerogative of an elite; and as the dandy is the 19th century's surrogate for the aristocrat in matters of culture, so Camp is the modern dandyism. Camp is the answer to the problem: how to be a dandy in the age of mass culture.

46. The dandy was overbred. His posture was disdain, or else *ennui*. He sought rare sensations, undefiled by mass appreciation. (Models: *Des Esseintes* in Huysmans' *À Rebours, Marius the Epicurean*, Valéry's *Monsieur Teste*.) He was dedicated to "good taste."

The connoisseur of Camp has found more ingenious pleasures. Not in Latin poetry and rare wines and velvet jackets, but in the coarsest, commonest pleasures, in the arts of the masses. Mere use does not defile the objects of his pleasure, since he learns to possess them in a rare way. Camp—Dandyism in the age of mass culture—makes no distinction between the unique object and the mass-produced object. Camp taste transcends the nausea of the replica.

47. Wilde himself is a transitional figure. The man who, when he first came to London, sported a velvet beret, lace shirts, velveteen knee-breeches and black silk stockings, could never depart too far in his life from the pleasures of the old-style dandy; this conservatism is reflected in *The Picture of Dorian Gray*. But many of his attitudes suggest something more modern. It was Wilde who formulated an important element of the Camp sensibility—the equivalence of all objects—when he announced his intention of "living up" to his blue-and-white china, or declared that a doorknob could be as admirable as a painting. When he proclaimed the importance of the necktie, the boutonniere, the chair, Wilde was anticipating the democratic *esprit* of Camp.

48. The old-style dandy hated vulgarity. The new-style dandy, the lover of Camp, appreciates vulgarity. Where the dandy would be continually offended or bored, the connoisseur of Camp is continually amused, delighted. The dandy held a perfumed handkerchief to his nostrils and was liable to swoon; the connoisseur of Camp sniffs the stink and prides himself on his strong nerves.

49. It is a feat, of course. A feat goaded on, in the last analysis, by the threat of boredom. The relation between boredom and Camp taste cannot be overestimated. Camp taste is by its nature possible only in affluent societies, in societies or circles capable of experiencing the psychopathology of affluence.

"What is abnormal in Life stands in normal relations to Art. It is the only thing in Life that stands in normal relations to Art."

—A Few Maxims for the Instruction of the Over-Educated

50. Aristocracy is a position vis-à-vis culture (as well as vis-à-vis power), and the history of Camp taste is part of the history of snob taste. But since no authentic aristocrats in the old sense exist today to sponsor special tastes, who is the bearer of this taste? Answer: an improvised self-elected class, mainly homosexuals, who constitute themselves as aristocrats of taste.

51. The peculiar relation between Camp taste and homosexuality has to be explained. While it's not true that Camp taste *is* homosexual taste, there is no doubt a peculiar affinity and overlap. Not all liberals are Jews, but Jews have shown a peculiar affinity for liberal and reformist causes. So, not all homosexuals have Camp taste. But homosexuals, by and large, constitute the vanguard—and the most articulate audience—of Camp. (The analogy is not frivolously chosen. Jews and homosexuals are the outstanding creative minorities in contemporary urban culture. Creative, that is, in the truest sense: they are creators of sensibilities. The two pioneering forces of modern sensibility are Jewish moral seriousness and homosexual aestheticism and irony.)

52. The reason for the flourishing of the aristocratic posture among homosexuals also seems to parallel the Jewish case. For every sensibility is self-serving to the group that promotes it. Jewish liberalism is a gesture of self-legitimization. So is Camp taste, which definitely has something propagandistic about it. Needless to say, the propaganda operates in exactly the opposite direction. The Jews pinned their hopes for integrating into modern society on promoting the moral sense. Homosexuals have pinned their integration into society on promoting the aesthetic sense. Camp is a solvent of morality. It neutralizes moral indignation, sponsors playfulness.

53. Nevertheless, even though homosexuals have been its vanguard, Camp taste is much more than homosexual taste. Obviously, its metaphor of life as theater is peculiarly suited as a justification and projection of a certain aspect of the situation of homosexuals. (The Camp insistence on not being "serious," on playing, also connects with the homosexual's desire to remain youthful.) Yet one feels that if homosexuals hadn't more or less invented Camp, someone else would. For the aristocratic posture with relation to culture cannot die, though it may persist only in increasingly arbitrary and ingenious ways. Camp is (to repeat) the relation to style in a time in which the adoption of style—as such—has become altogether questionable. (In the modern era, each new style, unless frankly anachronistic, has come on the scene as an anti-style.)

"One must have a heart of stone to read the death of Little Nell without laughing."

—In conversation

54. The experiences of Camp are based on the great discovery that the sensibility of high culture has no monopoly upon refinement. Camp asserts that good taste is not simply good taste; that there exists, indeed, a good taste of bad taste. (Genet talks about this in *Our Lady of the Flowers*.) The discovery of the good taste of bad taste can be very liberating. The man who insists on high and serious pleasures is depriving himself of pleasure; he continually restricts what he can enjoy; in the constant exercise of his good taste he will eventually price himself out of the market, so to speak. Here Camp taste supervenes upon good taste as a daring and witty hedonism. It makes the man of good taste cheerful, where before he ran the risk of being chronically frustrated. It is good for the digestion.

55. Camp taste is, above all, a mode of enjoyment, of appreciation—not judgment. Camp is generous. It wants to enjoy. It only seems like malice, cynicism. (Or, if it is cynicism, it's not a ruthless but a sweet cynicism.) Camp taste doesn't propose that it is in bad taste to be serious; it doesn't sneer at someone who succeeds in being seriously dramatic. What it does is to find the success in certain passionate failures.

56. Camp taste is a kind of love, love for human nature. It relishes, rather than judges, the little triumphs and awkward intensities of "character." . . . Camp taste identifies with what it is enjoying. People who share this sensibility are not laughing at the thing they label as "a camp," they're enjoying it. Camp is a *tender* feeling.

(Here, one may compare Camp with much of Pop Art, which—when it is not just Camp—embodies an attitude that is related, but still very different. Pop Art is more flat and more dry, more serious, more detached, ultimately nihilistic.)

57. Camp taste nourishes itself on the love that has gone into certain objects and personal styles. The absence of this love is the reason why such kitsch items as *Peyton Place* (the book) and the Tishman Building aren't Camp.

58. The ultimate Camp statement: it's good *because* it's awful. . . . Of course, one can't always say that. Only under certain conditions, those which I've tried to sketch in these notes.

STUDY QUESTIONS

1. Define *camp* in twenty-five words or less.
2. Add to Miss Sontag's list of "campy" movies.
3. What does Miss Sontag mean when she says camp taste is *enjoyment*, not *judgment?* Does she herself *judge* any of the camp items in her essay?
4. Some social critics feel that the interest in *camp* reveals the decadence of American society. Is this view a tenable one?
5. Why does Miss Sontag number certain paragraphs and not others?

INDEX OF
AUTHORS AND TITLES

INDEX OF AUTHORS AND TITLES *

---

* Titles are italicized.